MEMORY WALK

IN THE LIGHT

MEMORY WALK IN THE LIGHT

~ . ~

MY CHRISTIAN YOGA LIFE
AS *A Course in Miracles*

Donald James Giacobbe

Miracle Yoga Services

Published by Miracle Yoga Services
— miracleyoga@gmail.com —
Cottonwood, Arizona

Printed in the United States of America

BISAC Subject Codes and Headings:

BIO502000   Biography and Autobiography: New Age

OCC027510   Body, Mind, and Spirit: Spirituality—Course in Miracles

OCC010000   Body, Mind, and Spirit: Meditation

Library of Congress Control Number: 2009912994

Giacobbe, Donald James
Memory Walk in the Light: My Christian Yoga Life as *A Course in Miracles*

ISBN 978-0-9843790-0-2

CONTENTS

DEDICATION

This autobiography is dedicated to my father, Salvatore Giacobbe, who taught me how to live a disciplined life, and to my mother, Elizabeth, who was my mentor in learning how to serve and love.

ACKNOWLEDGMENTS

I am grateful for the steadfast support, suggestions, and encouragement of my sister Lillian Blackburn and my friend Stuart Dean. I appreciate the editorial assistance of Amy Lyn Speech and Paul Smith. My thanks go to Jerry Paul, Paul Varelas, Deborah Lorensen, Nancy Bonfield, and Jayneen Muetzel for serving as proof readers. James Gregory was kind enough to take the photographs of me on the front cover, back cover, opposite the title page, and in Chapters 24, 27, and 51.

PREFACE

In 1939 the movie *Gone with the Wind* grabbed all the headlines, with Rhett Butler saying in the end, "Frankly, my dear, I don't give a damn," and Scarlett O'Hara vowing to get back her lost love. Yet flying under the radar there was another movie that was also about losing and getting back what is most dear to us. Today who hasn't seen the classic *The Wizard of Oz*? You know the story line. Dorothy was separated from her beloved home and spent the rest of her adventure seeking to get back. The Tin Man wanted to get back his missing heart. The Lion wanted to get back his courage. The Scarecrow wanted to get back his lost mind. Everyone got what they wanted. In the end Dorothy woke up from her unconscious delirium and discovered that she had never really left her home except in her imagination.

What does *The Wizard of Oz* have to do with this autobiography? My life has been very much like the adventure of Dorothy and her friends. I callously lost my heart and got it back. I embarrassingly lost my courage and got it back. Yes, I even lost my mind and got that back, too. And like Dorothy, I lost my Home and in an unexpected instant woke up and discovered that I had never left. Dorothy's story is really your story as well as my own because you, too, are seeking what is dearest to you.

Toward the end of her journey Dorothy was told by the good Witch of the North that she had the power to go home hidden within herself all along. To reach her goal Dorothy was instructed to remind herself of her heart's desire by repeating three times the famous line, "There's no place like home." Knowing and focusing on what you hold most dear, as Dorothy did, will help you to find it. So what do you hold most dear? Is it not love? Naturally you want to give and receive love from those who are closest to you. But, of course, you want more—you want the Divine Embrace, whether you consciously realize it or not. You may think that you have lost that Love, but can you really lose what is eternally yours?

When Dorothy was asked what she had learned, she said, "…if I ever go looking for my heart's desire again, I won't look any further than my own backyard. Because if it isn't there, I never really lost it to begin with!" Everything you really need in order to find your heart's desire is already within you and with the help of your friends—and everyone is your friend—you will find what is most dear to you within yourself. I hope that reading about my journey of loss and renewal will remind you that Divine Love is within you now—waiting for you to find It and share It with your brothers and sisters. There really is no place like your true Home within.

GRAPHICS NOTE

≈ ◦ ≈

Because I have an interest and background in art, visual imagery has played a prominent role in my life. Consequently, as you read about my life, the graphics in this autobiography will help you to visually see my life through my eyes. Interspersed throughout the text there are 131 black and white graphics displayed on 120 pages in the form of photographs, paintings, drawings, and diagrams. Miniature color versions of some of these graphics can be seen on the back cover to give you a better idea of what these images actually look like in color. The cover all by itself provides a thumbnail summary of my life. The front cover symbolizes my spiritual destiny in the Light, just as it is the spiritual destination of all of God's children. The images on the back cover collectively represent the "marriage of the East and West," which has been an ongoing theme of my life as a Christian seeker open to Eastern methods of spiritual growth. The paintings on the left side of the back cover represent spiritual awakening to one's true nature so prominent in Eastern philosophies. The painting of Jesus on the right side symbolizes forgiveness, which is a central message of Western spirituality and of *A Course in Miracles*. The two other paintings on the right side show images that represent specific memories of my past that required me to learn forgiveness. The painting on the bottom and in the middle of the back cover is called *Path to the Light* and is a visual representation of my overall spiritual journey. The symbolism behind all of these paintings will be elaborated upon in the text as I share various events unfolding in my life.

INTRODUCTION

~ • ~

When I was deciding on the title of this autobiography, I gave strong consideration to *Autobiography of a Christian Yogi* because of the book, *Autobiography of a Yogi*. When I read this life story of the Hindu guru, Yogananda, I appreciated learning about seekers living lives devoted to awakening to God and was inspired by examples of the divine manifested in this world. I was drawn to Eastern philosophy, which encourages inner spiritual seeking, yet I was also firmly rooted in my Western culture with its focus on maintaining outer loving relationships. I was centered in Christ, Who I did not feel was limited to the West. Rather, I felt that Jesus, having fully manifested His Christ nature, had embodied the best of the East through His own enlightenment in His resurrection and the best of the West in His emphasis on forgiveness and loving relationships. However, at that time there was a lack of available literature bridging the gap between the East and West. In this autobiography I have included the information that I would like to have had forty years ago when I was first consciously embarking on my spiritual path with one foot extending to the East and the other foot solidly planted in the West.

The blending of Eastern and Western spirituality is illustrated by the image on page 11, which can be seen in color on the back cover. In this image the sun symbolizes the transcendental spiritual awakening described in the East as enlightenment, satori, or samadhi. The clasped hands represent joining with others to form holy and loving relationships based on manifesting forgiveness, which is the hallmark of the West. In addition, the two arms reaching out to each other stand for the Eastern and Western sides of the world coming together. This cross-cultural spiritual influence will be elaborated upon in this book, especially in Chapter 43, "The Marriage of the East and West."

In writing this book the key question for me has been, "What would be most helpful for you, the reader, in terms of inspiring you to pursue spiritual growth?" I could have taken the direction of some inspirational life stories to create a one-sided picture of a spiritually guided life and to minimize personal shortcomings and dark shadows. However, I have taken the opposite direction by presenting an unvarnished version of my spiritual search, which includes unusual and uplifting spiritual experiences right alongside the numerous embarrassing warts of my life.

I hope that you are entertained by reading about my struggles and experiences in walking the spiritual path, yet providing entertainment is not my goal. I want you to know that you can walk a similar path in which you can overcome your own perceived shortcomings and have your own spiritual experiences. Fortunately there are specific techniques, which can be practiced by anyone to grow spiritually. For example, meditation and yoga practices are described later in this book. Some of the appendices provide easy-to-follow instructions and illustrations for beginners who want to learn how to practice Christian meditation or who want to establish a brief daily routine of doing very simple exercises and yoga postures.

There are many paths that can be taken. However, I can only present for your consideration the means that I myself have used for spiritual growth. I am grateful for my experience of the Roman Catholic faith that first nourished me in my childhood and then later sustained me in my early adult life. From that starting foundation, I will share with you my spiritual evolution, which has resulted in my current blending of the East and West with Christ remaining in the center of my life. But there was a ten-year period starting at age fourteen when I left behind my focus on Christ. That time period began with sowing the wild oats of youth and ended with a serious exploration of Zen Buddhism, which ironically brought me back to Christ. In my former practice of Zen meditation my goal was the elusive spiritual "gold medal" of enlightenment. I thought that one transcendent peak experience would answer every question of life. But what do Olympic athletes discover after their one-time experience of finally winning the gold medal? They usually discover that the real challenge in everyone's life is to find peace of mind and thus fulfillment in each moment of everyday life, where no medals are awarded or needed.

How can this peace of mind be obtained? Peace of mind is acquired through a refinement of one's own mind through a combination of human effort and divine grace. First must come the realization that one's current thought system is egocentric and inadequate to bring peace to the mind. This awareness leads to the decision to implement spiritual practices and to find a new and better thought system that represents a reversal of the ego-driven thinking of this world. In my own search I have been attracted to a combination of Christian and yoga spiritual practices, including daily meditation, body postures, and breathing practices, which could be called *Christian yoga*. Such tangible spiritual practices are necessary to calm and purify the mind as a preparation for the direct experience of the divine beyond the conceptual thinking of the mind. On the other hand, within the realm of concepts I still felt the necessity to find a thought system that could be the philosophical foundation for my practice of Christian yoga and could guide my mind in the activities of daily living.

Along the way in my growth there wasn't a clear, ready-made East/West thought system that I could simply adopt and use as a basis for my practice of Christian yoga. Consequently I had to formulate my own "buffet style" philosophy by picking up ideas here and there from Eastern and Western sources. The development of my philosophical thought system involved studying a variety of different Christian and Eastern philosophies and also reading books by writers attempting to synthesize different philosophies. For example, I familiarized myself with the writings of Aldous Huxley and Huston Smith on the "perennial philosophy," which seeks to identify the universal principles of truth underlying all religions. In addition, I relied on information from Edgar Cayce, who was both a psychic and a Christian open to Eastern influences. Then after this study I pieced together my own Christian/Eastern philosophy to form a basis for seeking the divine and living in the world of form.

Although I was very happy with my patchwork East/West philosophy, I encountered several friends who had adopted the thought system of *A Course in Miracles*. For many years I was exposed to this new thought system and resisted any involvement with it. However, as events turned out I have not only accepted *A Course in Miracles*, but now feel guided to share this teaching with others. This autobiography's subtitle is "My Christian Yoga Life as *A Course in Miracles*," and this has a dual meaning. One meaning is that my life itself has been a course in miracles, revealing God's immanent presence in the world and His transcendence beyond the world. The other meaning is that this autobiography is presented here as a way for you to learn about the principles of *A Course in Miracles* in the context of my attempts to manifest these principles in the course of my everyday living.

What is *A Course in Miracles*? It is a course in mind training set forth in three books for personal study and application, now usually combined into one volume. The *Text* presents the philosophical thought system that is the basis for this course of study. The *Workbook for Students* is a one-year course of daily practices to provide practical application of the thought system. The *Manual for Teachers* is for those who have learned the Course principles and would like to share their learning with others. The Course is not a religion and not associated with a church, but many Course students do come together for local study groups.

The Course integrates the ideas of Eastern philosophy into a Western context that can be applied by Christians of any denomination or even by followers of Christ who are not affiliated with any church. However, in addition to being inclusive of Eastern philosophy, the Course also offers a profound understanding of psychology from a spiritual perspective. This unique synthesis of Eastern and Western philosophy with psychology has attracted many spiritual seekers and from its inception in the seventies has had an amazing growth with no initial advertising.

Whatever personal growth benefit you gain from this autobiography will be due to your degree of *openness*. It takes a certain degree of openness for a Westerner and/or follower of Christ to consider the true inner value of yoga beyond the obvious physical health benefits. An even greater degree of openness is necessary to be willing to examine carefully the principles of *A Course in Miracles*. These principles can be very challenging for anyone accustomed to traditional Christian thinking. For many seekers the Course is presented in such an intellectual manner that it is hard to understand and seems difficult to apply to daily life. I hope that describing the Course as it relates to my life experiences will demonstrate the practical application of the Course principles.

Just as the Course was gradually introduced into my life, its principles are slowly brought into this autobiography with greater emphasis toward the end. If you have no previous experience studying the Course, this life story can be a good introduction. If you have some familiarity with the Course, yet have been confused by it, this autobiography may provide some clarity. If you already consider yourself to be a Course student, this life story can reinforce your current understanding and can provide insights into how to apply Course principles. If you are a Course student who considers the Course all by itself to be your entire spiritual path, you will find examples of forgiveness and relationships that may inspire you in your own spiritual practice of forgiveness. I respect those purely Course students who have dedicated their lives to mostly or exclusively focusing on forgiveness. However, I have spent my life giving equal weight to making inner contact with spirit and allowing that inner connection to be expressed outwardly, for example through loving relationships, because I want to embody and teach a balance of the East and West. The cornerstone of the Course is forgiveness, and the central message of yoga is opening to the divine presence. As an instructor of Christian yoga based on Course principles, I feel it is my mission to teach and be an example of both practicing forgiveness *and* opening to the experience of spirit.

The final goal of all spiritual seeking is to transcend the world of form and wake up in the heavenly Arms of God. Nevertheless, living a useful and meaningful life along the way is equally important—not only as a preparation for ultimate transcendence, but also as a manifestation of the divine presence in the here and now. The goal of Christian yoga is to simply live in Christ on a daily basis. What Christian yoga has to offer is an emphasis on finding our divine life in Christ within, with the aid of specific yoga disciplines, and then expressing our divine life outwardly. Christian yoga can lead to becoming what might be called a "spirit vessel"—a seeker who has an intimate experiential contact with the divine within and allows that divine spirit to flow outwardly into the lives of others.

The term *Christian yoga* can be applied to the practice of any seekers who combine following Christ with yoga disciplines, but in recent years I have adopted the term *Miracle Yoga* to describe the specific path of Christian yoga I have chosen, which combines Christ, yoga, and the Course. Hopefully this autobiography will foster a deeper appreciation and understanding of how to live in Christ through yoga and how to apply the spiritual principles of the Course in order to bring blessings into the lives of others.

The title of this autobiography, "Memory Walk in the Light," emphasizes my life as a concrete journey of forgiveness leading toward an abstract destination. My journey is different than yours, but in the end you and I will discover the same transcendental Light. This Light is the abstract destination to which I have devoted my life.

Many years ago a total stranger walked up to me and invited me to go on what he called a "memory walk" with him. I accepted his invitation, and since then my life has never been the same. Now I am inviting you to take a "memory walk" with me. This autobiography is a journey into the darkness of the past with the goal of arriving at the light of the present moment. My story bears witness to the truth that with the Love of God all things are possible. Quite naturally God's Love leads to forgiveness, which has shown me that, "The holiest of all the spots on earth is where an ancient hatred has become a present love."[1]

Just as I am convinced that God's Love goes with me on my journey, I am equally certain His Love abides with you on your journey. Who knows? Perhaps His Love has guided you to pick up this book and will inspire you to read it. If so, I hope you will be as blessed in taking this memory walk as I have been blessed in having the opportunity, through God's grace, to make it available to you. As we walk together through the memories of my life, I trust that you will absorb from my experiences whatever would be most helpful to assist you in your own unique, yet universal journey to the Light.

---

1. T-26.IX.6:1, p. 562 (p. 522). For those not familiar with references to *A Course in Miracles*, T-26 is the chapter number of the Text, IX means the ninth section of the chapter, the 6 is the sixth paragraph of that section, and the 1 means the first sentence in that paragraph. The page numbers in parenthesis (p. 522) are for the first edition of the Course. The page numbers not in parenthesis, such as 562, are for the second and third editions, in paperback or hard cover, of *A Course in Miracles*, Copyright © 1975, 1985, 1992, 2008 by the Foundation for Inner Peace, Inc., P.O. Box 598, Mill Valley, CA 94942- 0598. The ideas related to the Course in this autobiography represent my own interpretation and understanding.

AUTHOR'S NOTE

≈ ◦ ≈

Long ago, before I became consciously interested in the spiritual path, I was asked two questions as part of a simple psychological game. The first question was, "If you could be any animal, what animal would you be?" After I answered, I was asked the second question, which was, "What is your second choice of being an animal?" Before continuing to read, you may want to stop and play this game yourself in order to come up with your own first and second choice animals.

My first choice was a turtle, and my second choice was a dove. Then the person who asked me the questions told me that supposedly the first choice is how I appear to the world—my mask. The second choice is the inner me. A turtle has a hard shell and pulls his legs and arms in to defend himself from the world, which sounds suspiciously like how my ego operates. So if there is any merit to this game, then the defensiveness of my ego is the mask that I put out there for the whole world to see. I imagine that mask shows my best side, making me appear to be admirable and protecting me. However, it only puts a good outer face on what is actually a withdrawal into darkness, and doesn't have the positive effects I seek.

The *good* news is that there's a dove in me that can soar to the heavens. Unfortunately, at the time of this game, the inner dove was so well hidden that even I did not know it was there. Naturally I was all too aware of the turtle and the world of darkness in which the turtle seemed to live. This story is about my discovery of the dove and learning how to let the dove fly out of the darkness and into the light.

On the other hand, this is also the story of the turtle, who is slow to learn how to navigate in the world of appearances. I was certainly all turtle in my college years, and you will see in the first chapter that at that stage of my life, I was even given the nickname of "Turtle." I had not told my fraternity brothers about this simple game; they chose the name because they could see for themselves the turtle in me.

The opening chapter consists of a discussion by my fraternity brothers about me as Turtle. This particular conversation never in fact took place. However, the *events* described in this conversation really did happen and were actually juicy topics for fraternity gossip at the time. A word of caution: This specific conversation among fraternity brothers is crude and may be offensive to some readers. Such crudeness was a part of my life then, but, with minor exceptions, does not recur after the first chapter. The writing of this fabricated conversation spared me from having to write in the first person about circumstances that embarrass me now, and which are therefore easier to write about through the eyes, ears, and voices of others.

I shared the initial draft of this first chapter with a friend who was turned off by it. Wanting to be helpful, he suggested that, instead of a whole chapter, all I needed was one sentence stating that in my college years I was preoccupied with seeking sexual gratification. Here is how I responded:

> Thank you for letting me know you were offended by the content of the first chapter. I have recently received guidance to take out the most sexually explicit parts of this chapter. Also, I have sanitized the conversation in this chapter, in spite of the fact that some readers may conclude, "That's not how college students would talk."
>
> But I have not taken your advice to eliminate the entire chapter and replace it with one sentence acknowledging college indiscretions. Removing the chapter would not be sufficiently self-revealing to let the reader know I am serious about honestly sharing my life as a whole. I want to write a book in which readers can identify with my struggles. That means I must speak candidly about those struggles and lead the reader along the path I have taken to transcend the need for sexual gratification. Thus I cannot gloss over the challenge of sexuality, since this is a necessary part of life that each of us must come to grips with. Sex is one of the central aspects of establishing a sense of identity. Just as there are nude people in the concentration camp scenes of the movie *Schindler's List*, sexuality and occasional profanities are integral parts of this book for the sake of realism, not sensationalism. These limited references to sexuality need to be understood in the context of my seeking to explore and understand the meaning of life, and for this reason must be included. I hope to show the reader how I started out by being immersed in sexuality and evolved into becoming a celibate monk in the world, as I am now and have been for most of my life.

Some of the conversations, such as the dialogue in the first chapter, are entirely fictional, while other conversations are partially fictional because I couldn't remember the exact words spoken. But even if a seemingly outrageous event is being described, for instance, I am bearing witness to that event just as it happened. Also, in many cases names have been changed to protect the privacy of some of the people in my life. Otherwise events have been accurately recorded to the best of my ability—with the understanding that my experience of these events is entirely subjective. I make no claim to have a perfect memory, and my perceptions are subject to unintentional mistakes and distortions. Yet my intention throughout has been to faithfully record my life story with complete truthfulness.

One of the purposes of an autobiography is to provide the opportunity for the reader to come into the author's world to temporarily see life through his eyes. Thank you for your openness and willingness to come into my world to take this memory walk with me as we look at my memories together. The first four chapters in particular present a variety of different slices of my life. At the time these events happened, they appeared to be unrelated occurrences that did not fit together in any meaningful way. Consequently, these events will appear as disconnected to you as they did to me. Then later, you will see—as I eventually saw—these puzzle pieces of my life coming together and making sense. The solving of this puzzle revealed the unfolding of God's Plan for me as I walked and continue to walk a path that involves the "joining of the East and West" (illustrated on the opposite page and shown in color on the back cover).

I have attempted to write a primarily spiritual autobiography, but have also included some events that are important or meaningful to my life, though not directly uplifting or spiritual. Because I have aspired to write a spiritual autobiography in no way means that I have written a book that is egoless. As I proceeded to write about past events that involved ego investment, I could not prevent old unresolved feelings from being rekindled. Since the memories of those events were experienced through the lens of my ego, I found I could not write about them in a purely objective manner. As you read some of my life experiences you will possibly see my ego seeping through the pages, in spite of my best efforts to allow the Holy Spirit to speak through my words. As an author and as a person I do not have to be perfect, nor can I be. My hope is to bring my ego out of hiding so that at least I am not in denial about it and you, as the reader, are not in denial about it either. Nevertheless, I have discovered that struggling against my ego in the vain attempt to eradicate it only makes it stronger. I have learned to accept the ego intrusions in my writing as well as in my life and offer them to the Holy Spirit for healing. Perhaps it is helpful for you to know that my *memory walk in the light* means I am making my way out of darkness, but haven't gotten all the way out yet.

Finally, let me say also that the outward events of my life are not really important in themselves. They serve only as a means of uncovering who it is that is experiencing them. At this point in my life I am learning to shift the focus of my identity from the turtle to the dove. I am growing toward greater acceptance of the turtle, yet still realizing that the turtle is only a temporary illusion. I know I am really only the dove. Perhaps you too have your own outer shell of a turtle and inner wings of a dove. If this is the case, hopefully you will also discover that in spite of appearances, you are not really the turtle. You are the dove.

JOINING OF THE EAST AND WEST

HIGH SCHOOL CLASS OF 1963

1

TURTLE

≈ • ≈

Coming from a conservative New England town in Connecticut, I grew up in a mellow and innocent America where we ate homemade apple pie and laughed watching *I Love Lucy*. In my first semester of college I sat in my art history class waiting for my instructor to appear on the closed-circuit television monitor, fully expecting his typically dry academic presentation. Instead, he came on the screen with tears in his eyes and his voice trembling, announcing, "President Kennedy has been shot!" That was the day when America lost its innocence.

As disturbing as that event was, it did not jolt me into pondering, "What is the meaning of life?" My freshman year passed by without me ever asking, "Christ, where is the peace that surpasses understanding? God, where is Your Love?" In my sophomore year as the spring of 1965 began, the first combat troops were ordered to Vietnam. However, the national attention was riveted on disturbing television images of Alabama state troopers and local police using billy clubs and tear gas on over 600 nonviolent civil rights marchers in Selma. After this display of violence, called "Bloody Sunday," America watched as Dr. Martin Luther King, Jr. led his march that started in Selma and culminated with 25,000 peaceful protesters arriving at the State Capitol Building in Montgomery. In regard to public opinion, the 54-mile nonviolent pilgrimage was a sobering turning point in the civil rights movement in which the dark underbelly of American society was brought to the light for all to see.

Some college students from the North went to the South to be a part of that crusade for freedom—but I was not among them. That kind of altruism and social conscience was far beyond my narrow, self-absorbed vision. I was seeing the world through the voracious eyes of a twenty-year-old who wanted to gulp down every tantalizing sensation the world had to offer, without being able to digest any of it. With the encouragement of my older brother Rick, I was able to get into his fraternity, Omega Kappa Delta. It was generally considered to be the best fraternity with a lot of jocks and an *Animal House* mentality. As Turtle, I fit right in—all too well for my own good. The Beatles were singing the number one song, "Eight Days a Week," as my fraternity brothers held court in the cafeteria. You might think there would be a lot of "f' this and "f" that going on, but that wasn't the case. Then again, if the truth be told, my revisionist memory may have purged all the vulgarity out of my fraternity brothers' words since Rick and I never got into the habit of cursing ourselves. A few threats from our parents to wash out our mouths with soap were all it took to convince us as children to speak without swearing. On this particular day I wasn't there with my fraternity brothers, but I was the topic of their discussion.

"Hey, did you guys hear that Turtle made the dean's list?" Gordon asked as he sat down with the other fraternity brothers at their cafeteria table.

"No way! He got the name Turtle because he's so slow to wake up in the morning. In fact, sometimes he doesn't even get out of his bed until noon, so how the hell did he get on the dean's list?" Terry asked.

"Last semester he arranged his schedule so he had all his classes on Tuesdays and Thursdays, and he did his late sleeping and nightly partying on the other five days. But he didn't tell me he made the dean's list," said Frank, his roommate and best friend.

"He says he doesn't have to study too much because he's a very good listener, but it's more than that," Richie offered. "I was in a math class with him, and the teacher gave the class a homework problem involving angles of isosceles triangles. The next day the teacher asked who had solved the problem, and nobody raised their hand except for Turtle. The teacher asked him to come up to the blackboard and explain his answer. So Turtle went up and said he had ten solutions to the problem, which he handed over to the teacher, and then he proceeded to explain one of them on the blackboard. He explained the problem was difficult to solve in the decimal system, so he translated all the numbers into some different numbering system that he invented. He showed how easy the problem was to understand and resolve in this new numbering system. Then after solving the problem in his new system, he translated the numbers back to the decimal system to prove that the problem was resolved in both systems.

"I could understand his solution as he explained it, but for the life of me I couldn't understand how he could come up with that kind of solution. Everybody was stunned and especially the teacher. After class the teacher came over to Turtle and tried to encourage him to become a math major. Turtle told him he had already made plans to become an art major. Because they don't have an art major here at Central Connecticut, Turtle told him that for his junior and senior years he will have to transfer to Southern Connecticut so he can major in art."

"Turtle is already majoring in *fine art*—the fine art of debauchery and getting an A plus," added wisecracking Tony.

"I don't think I've ever seen him sober at any of our parties. At least he saves money on liquor since he's such a 'Two Beer Benny,'" Alex offered.

"What's a 'Two Beer Benny'?" the new brother, John, asked, as Alex knew he would.

"It means if you give him two beers he is in another world and might do anything. Then the next day you have to tell him what he did the night before because he doesn't even remember."

Sal, who was a huge lineman on the football team, interjected, "That's true. One time I had to carry him up the spiral staircase to his bedroom. The next day he couldn't even remember that he was throwing up on me as I was carrying him."

"Sal, he was probably throwing up on you because you were carrying him upside down," Tony sarcastically suggested.

"Come on, be nice to me or I'll carry you around upside down and see how you like it."

Tony successfully sidestepped Sal's response and redirected everyone's attention by pointing down the hall, "Here comes, Rick."

"Hi, Rick, we're sharing stories about your brother," Morgan explained and continued, "What I remember is the time at a party when Turtle left his date and came to my table. I said to him, 'I missed the last fraternity meeting, but I was told that even though you were nominated as the fraternity chaplain, you turned down the position.'

"Turtle said, 'Yeah, I said I didn't qualify due to excessive grossness.'

"I asked, 'Do you think you are the grossest fraternity brother?'

"'No,' he said, 'that distinction goes to Brad and Larry. As seniors they have more experience, but I would take third place. However, we are just outwardly gross, so our grossness shows. There is such a thing as *secret inner grossness*. How about you? Are you gross?'

"'I'm conservative.'

"'Well, Mr. Conservative Morgan, I can see the inner you. You are a secret seeker of grossness. I'll give you a test. This guy, Boris, had a blind date with Carla. He was told that she was very beautiful, but unpredictable. When Boris picked up Carla for the date, he was pleasantly surprised to find out for himself that Carla really was beautiful. He handed her a bouquet of flowers, and she said, "You pig."'

"'Boris took her out to dinner, and after eating, Boris asked, "Are you satisfied?"'

"'Carla responded, "You pig."'

"'Boris decided to bring her home, and sitting in the car he kissed her. "You pig," Carla told him. Carla got out of the car, and Boris thought she would walk away, but instead she waved for him to follow her into the house. When they were inside, Carla said, "I am going to slip into something more comfortable. I'll be right back." She left and came back in a negligee. Boris said, "You look exquisite." Carla responded, "You pig." But then she took Boris by the hand and led him to the bedroom, and she reclined on the bed.'"

Morgan paused for a long time, and Jackson asked impatiently, "Come on. So what happened next?"

"YOU PIG!" Morgan emphatically asserted to Jackson with a smile. "OK, it's a silly joke, but Turtle caught me in the same way I just now caught you, Jackson. He said to me, 'You pig,' and then he added while laughing, 'I told you that you were a secret seeker of grossness.' He couldn't stop laughing, which made us laugh with him. Then all of a sudden while he was still laughing hysterically, Turtle let out a ghastly penetrating shriek. Turtle looked as surprised as we did at where this loud shriek had come from, and for a few seconds he even looked a little embarrassed.

"After this he got up from his chair and stumbled his way to another table. The next day I asked if he could remember what had happened at the party, and he couldn't remember anything I just described. All he could remember is that he was getting drunk and left the party and he was lying down on a wooden table outside the party hall. He was going to go to sleep, but then said he had a sudden strong fear that he was in danger on that table, so he popped back up and went back to the party. He didn't remember anything after that."

"How about you, Rick? You must have some stories to tell about Turtle from growing up with him," Frank asked.

"I have an idea why Turtle had that feeling of danger when on that table. He may have been reliving a childhood experience that happened when he was so young that he couldn't tell you what happened. He was sitting in a rocking chair, and he put some pillows underneath himself to prop himself up. He was rocking so vigorously that he fell over backwards and his head landed on the radiator causing a gash in his head. Our parents cleared the wooden dining room table and laid him out there. The doctor rushed to the house and stitched up his head on that table. So maybe that experience of falling over and lying on the table was triggered in his mind, making him feel like he was in danger when he was on the table at the party."

Morgan confirmed, "He did say the danger feeling had something to do with falling, but he also said it felt like someone wanted to get him. He knew it sounded irrational, yet that was what he felt."

"He was right about someone wanting to get him, because the pledges were always out to get him. He even got the Big 'P' Award from last year," Rick said. The award was an engraved plaque that would go to the one brother who was voted the most liked and most disliked by the pledges.

The capital letter "P" had a dual meaning standing for "pal" and for another word that begins with a "p"—a slang word that means a difficult, hard-headed person, the opposite of a pal.

John spoke up, "Our pledge class this year would have given Turtle the Big 'P' Award again this year too, but they wanted to give it to someone who hadn't gotten it before. One time in the cafeteria I brought an orange soda to one of the brothers who had requested it, so then Turtle told me to get him 'a grape.' When I came back with a grape soda, he said, 'I didn't ask for a grape soda. I asked for a grape. Don't you know what the difference is between a grape and a grape soda? Go get me a grape.' Then after I came back with the grape, he gave me his pack of cigarettes and told me I had to carry them with me all the time in case he needed one. He was really serious when he talked to us.

"But then one day he took me aside and told me to do whatever any brother said, but to know that it's all a joke. He told me why he gave me his cigarettes. He had given his cigarettes to George, but George knew it was all a joke, so he would smoke some of Turtle's cigarettes. He gave me the pack because I would be so serious that I wouldn't dare smoke his cigarettes. And he was right, but he told me not to be so serious and to enjoy the pledge period as a joy ride. So he really deserved the Big 'P' Award because he was the best and worst brother all rolled into one. He was our number one kidnapping target, and we did kidnap him—even though we heard he was kidnapped last year also."

"Yeah, and you kidnapped me too," Frank stated in feigned indignation.

"We didn't really want you, because you were always nice to the pledges, but as his roommate you were available, and we couldn't find anyone else."

"At least the pledges last year didn't take me," Frank continued. "Let me tell you the full kidnapping story from last year. I was Turtle's roommate last year too, and I was working on the floor of our room on a color wheel for my art class. I was finishing up a complicated watercolor wheel with sixteen pieces that I had worked on for several days. Turtle kept on saying that he was feeling that the pledges were going to come and kidnap him that night. He had driven the pledges pretty hard to do nonsense tasks, but the idea of someone coming to get him that very day sounded a little like paranoia to me. But sure enough the pledges did show up in our room. So what did Turtle do? He bent down and picked up a giant pail of water he had placed there moments before, just for this occasion. He drenched the pledges with the water and tried to exit out a side door that swung into the kitchen. Turtle couldn't see that Brad, the pledge who's on the basketball team, was coming that way. When Turtle pushed the door to get out, the door slid over Brad's foot and injured his right toe so he couldn't play on the team for a few weeks. Of course, Turtle was grabbed and taken to a waiting car, while I was really upset because my watercolor wheel was totally destroyed by Turtle's pail of water!

"They left Turtle with two pledges while they went on the prowl for another brother. Turtle was in the back seat of the car with Tim sitting right next to him and Dean sitting in the front seat. Then Turtle suddenly jumped out the window and almost got away, but Tim grabbed one foot before it could clear the window. Dean leaped outside the car and grabbed Turtle while he was dangling upside down outside the car. The two pledges managed to get him back in the car by force and this time rolled up the windows.

"After a while of stewing in the back seat, Turtle decided to think his way out. He told Tim and Dean that they were breaking one of the sacred rules of the fraternity, which is that no pledge can kidnap a brother on his birthday. The gullible pledges foolishly accepted Turtle's totally fabricated rule, but they demanded proof that it really was in fact his birthday. Turtle pulled out his wallet and showed his driver's license with the date April 6, which by the way he hadn't even told *me* about. The pledges were dumbfounded and reluctantly agreed to let him go. Turtle strolled off and turned the corner out of their sight and then started running. Unfortunately for him the other pledges saw him escaping and ran him down until he locked himself in one of the brothers' cars. But the pledges came back with the car key, and this time the birthday story didn't work. Turtle and another brother, Steve, were carted off to the woods miles away, and then let out.

"Turtle was standing outside the car, and the pledges were about to leave. Then he bent his head into the car and said he wanted to say one thing before being left. But instead of saying anything more, he suddenly grabbed the keys out of the ignition and threw them deep into the woods, where he knew they couldn't be found in the dark. Turtle jumped up and down celebrating, because he thought he had turned the tables on the pledges so they would be just as stranded as he was. However, fortunately for the pledges, there was an extra key in the glove compartment, so they drove off knowing they had just dodged a bullet.

"Within ten minutes Turtle and Steve made their way to an electric company power station in the woods near there. An all-night attendant let them into the station to make a telephone call, and Turtle called me. At first I told him, 'I don't know if I have the time to help you out right now. I have to work on redoing my art project. *Somebody* threw water all over my color wheel and ruined it.' After he apologized, I agreed to drive out and pick Steve and him up. But what I remember about this experience is that Turtle was so hyped up about being kidnapped and so vigorous in his attempts to thwart the kidnapping. When I picked him up, his head was bleeding from his attempted escape from the car. It was like a life or death situation for him. For once he forgot, like he told John, 'It's all a joke.'"

"I've seen the serious side of Turtle recently too," Richie stated. "Did you guys know that Turtle is a hypnotist?"

"I don't believe it. Turtle doesn't put people to sleep—he's the one who sleeps all day," Tony said with a smile.

"It's true. I saw him put someone to sleep."

"Sure, he fed one of his dates a fifth of vodka and knocked her out," Tony suggested.

Richie responded, "Actually it was a date, but not *his* date. It was my girl friend, Janine. Turtle told me he was a hypnotist. So I challenged him to hypnotize me. According to Janine, who was with me, he did hypnotize me. However, even though I lost consciousness when he did it, I still didn't want to believe I had been hypnotized. Then Janine volunteered to be hypnotized. I took Turtle aside, and I asked him to give her a post-hypnotic suggestion to draw a picture of me, but to make the drawing actually look like a monkey. I watched Turtle hypnotize her with a solemn monotone voice, and he gave her the suggestion. After he woke her up, he asked her to make a pencil drawing of me. I sat motionless to serve as a model, and she kept taking looks at me as she drew.

"When she was finished, she proudly showed me the picture. I started laughing hysterically because it was a picture of a monkey. What surprised me was that Turtle was very serious, and he warned me to stop laughing. Turtle noticed that Janine was getting upset because I was laughing at her 'wonderful' art work, which she was convinced looked exactly like me, even though it was obviously a picture of a hairy monkey. But I couldn't stop laughing, and Janine really got upset because she felt I was insulting her artistic effort. Before things got out of hand, Turtle interceded and said he wanted to hypnotize Janine for a second time, and she agreed. He hypnotized her again and gave her a post-hypnotic suggestion to forget the previous suggestion and to forget her experience of making the drawing and being displeased with her boy friend. When she woke up, she had forgotten everything and felt refreshed. I got the impression that Turtle took his hypnotism role very seriously," Richie concluded.

"It seems to me also that Turtle is taking a serious turn recently. For example, he just gave up his cashier scam," said Gordon, who seemed to always know the latest news.

Right on cue, John asked, "What's this cashier scam?"

Pointing to the cafeteria cashier, Gordon explained, "Do you see that cashier, Gloria? Well, Turtle has been dating her."

"She doesn't look too foxy to me," assessed Morgan.

"Well, of course, she's not a model. She's a cashier, but as Turtle put it, 'It's not the beauty; it's the *booty* that's important.' So what Turtle would do is, he would fill his cafeteria tray with food and give Gloria a dollar. Then she would give him back four quarters."

"Did you hear what Vinny did?" Tony asked, and without waiting for a reply he continued, "Vinny followed Turtle in the food line, and when it was his turn to pay, he pointed to Turtle, who was walking away, and he told Gloria, 'I'm with him,' and he smiled and walked off."

"Yeah, I heard about that. Actually Turtle told me Gloria was upset about Vinny doing that, but that's not why Turtle is no longer going out with Gloria," Gordon explained. "Turtle told me he took Gloria to Brad and Larry's off-campus apartment. This is how he described their conversation after he drove her home:

"Gloria said, 'Your friends, Brad and Larry, were crude fellows, but at least you are good to me.' Turtle told me that Brad and Larry had been throwing Gloria's pocketbook back and forth to each other, making Gloria chase after it rather futilely. Plus Gloria made a quick exit when Brad and Larry began to sing and dance around the room while taking off their clothes. Turtle could have just agreed with Gloria that those guys are crude, but he hadn't been drinking, and so he decided not to lie to her, which he could have easily done. He told her, 'I knew what to expect when I took you to meet Brad and Larry. I am totally responsible for what happened tonight.'

"Gloria still wanted to take Turtle off the hook, so she said, 'But at least you're telling me the truth now, and I appreciate your honesty.'

"She was ready to forgive, but he wouldn't let that happen. He told her, 'Fraternity guys like me are just out for a good time, but you really need to find someone who wants to settle down. You deserve to find someone else who really loves you, and you will find that person.' Turtle said he wasn't just trying to get rid of her. It was just that he really felt she was a kind person, and she deserved to find someone to love her. So this is the serious side of Turtle."

Frank agreed, "I've also noticed Turtle is a little more subdued recently. Maybe it's because this is his last semester here before moving on to Southern next year."

"By the way, where is Turtle?" Tony asked. "He's usually here in the cafeteria hanging out this time of day."

Gordon clarified, "When I was coming over here, I noticed Turtle going into the theater building. But I don't know why he would be going there since he has no drama classes."

2

WHY?

≈ ∘ ≈

In the theater building there were the two black Tom McCann shoes dangling in mid air. There were two white socks, khaki pants, a black belt, Fruit of the Loom underpants and undershirt, and a white shirt—all hanging in mid air. I know I was wearing that outfit, not because I have such a good memory, but because that's what I liked to wear every day back then. Also there was a pair of glasses looking down at the hard metal theater seats below—seats that promised to kill or cripple my body if given the opportunity to do so. So there I was, hanging from the balcony. I wasn't identifying with my fraternity role as the cool Turtle; I was merely a frightened body holding on for dear life to two wooden spindles among the many that held up the balcony railing. That's the railing that prevented people from falling from the balcony—the railing that I climbed over to put myself into this precarious position. Why was I hanging there? At that moment I really did not know. At this point all I knew was that I needed to survive first and ask questions later. I lifted my leg up and planted it so that one foot was holding me up along with my two hands. Then with these three points of support I was able to inch my hands upward one at a time until I could pull myself back over the railing to safety.

I sat in a balcony seat much relieved and wondered why, why, why? I had absolutely zero intention to commit suicide, so that was not the reason at all. I felt I did this to show myself something—but what? I closed my eyes to hopefully let the answer come to my mind. What came to mind was a series of images from high school. The first image was seeing myself in the office of the assistant principal, Mr. Wilson. He was telling me, "Brian told me that you called him a 'fucking asshole,' and that is what started the fight between you and him." I was shocked by Brian's false accusation, yet perhaps even more stunned by hearing those two words pass the lips of the always proper Mr. Wilson.

"No! I never said that," I protested with indignation since cursing was something I rarely did. "What happened is that I was walking down the hall in between classes, and I stepped on Jared's foot accidentally. I said, 'I'm sorry. It was an accident.' But he must have thought it was intentional because he said, 'I'll meet you after school and beat you up for this.' I said, 'OK, I'll see you then.'

"Later in the day I saw Brian in the hall, but I thought he was Jared, his twin brother. I said, 'Are you going to show up after school for our fight?' He answered, 'So you want to fight! Why wait until after school?' Then Brian grabbed me. I grabbed him back and threw him down on the ground with me on top of him. Before anything else could happen some teachers pulled us apart, and that was all that happened."

Mr. Wilson looked at me skeptically, and said, "So you never swore at him."

"That's right."

Mr. Wilson got up and let Brian into the room and said, "I want you two to shake hands and make up."

Brian extended his hand, but I looked at Mr. Wilson and said, "I'll shake his hand as soon as he admits that I never swore at him." Brian took back his hand and didn't say anything.

Because Mr. Wilson could see I wasn't going to shake Brian's hand, he threatened, "If this happens again, I won't care whose fault it is. You will both be expelled. I'll see you both for detention after school."

The scene in my mind then switched to Mrs. Hackbarth's ancient history class, in which she was verbally quizzing us on the names of her favorite ancient history characters. "Let's start with Greece. Who fought bravely in wars, but ironically died of a fever?"

Someone answered, "Alexander the Great."

"OK. That was too easy. Let's see if you know my personal favorite Greek personality. Who was the scoundrel who repeatedly got into and out of more trouble than any other Greek?"

I spoke up, "Alcibiades," which I remembered because she had spoken about him in the past with noticeable admiration for his radical political and even sexual exploits. Her glowing description of him surprised me because Mrs. Hackbarth was one of the most conservative and stern teachers I had.

"Let's switch to Egypt. Who put all the gods of Egypt out of business by having everyone worship one God?"

"Akhenaten," another student offered.

"That was an easy one also. Here is my favorite woman. Who was the first important woman in recorded history?"

One of the girls in the class said, "It was the woman Egyptian pharaoh, but I can't pronounce her name. It's something like, 'Hepsepset.'"

"Close enough. It's pronounced Hatshepsut." I guessed Mrs. Hackbarth didn't consider the Biblical Eve to be part of recorded history.

I felt my mind had wandered too far away from answering the question of why I was hanging off of the balcony. However, four relevant works of art from my high school art class then came to mind. Along with these four images I envisioned my art teacher, Mr. Collier. What I remember most about him is that he noticed how much I tended to say, "I'm sorry," even when such a statement was uncalled for. His message to me was to do the best I could, and then I would have no reason to apologize. He helped me rid myself of habitually saying "I'm sorry," and his encouragement increased my self-confidence. In my imagination at this time, Mr. Collier was having a conversation with me that never happened, but maybe should have, to draw out the meaning of my art work. He asked me, "Why does this man's head have two spider eyes?"

In my ink drawing the round part of the spider's body was the colored part of the eye, and the legs of the spider's body were made to look like the eyelashes. I replied, "The spiders show the man is afraid of something. Maybe he is afraid of spiders themselves or what spiders symbolize."

Mr. Collier inquired, "And what do you think spiders symbolize to you?"

"To me they symbolize death, or perhaps the fear of death."

Then the scene switched to a print from a woodcut, which showed the front view of a boy's head. Mr. Collier asked, "What can you tell me about this picture?"

"It's obviously a boy in great pain," I said.

Immediately another woodcut came to mind showing the side view silhouette of a body sitting in darkness and bent forward over the legs with the head lowered. "How about this person? What's happening with him?" the imaginary Mr. Collier inquired.

"It could be a man's body, but it is probably the body of the boy in the previous picture. He is very depressed and in great pain, yet I don't know why. This is a picture of fear also, like the other pictures."

Finally my drawing of a barren tree appeared. The perspective was from the base of the tree looking up. There was only one giant branch on the tree, but there was a noticeable break in this branch, giving the impression that it could break and fall at any time. Most important of all, there was just one leaf already falling from the tree—twisting and turning as it fell through the air. The question came from Mr. Collier, "What does this represent?"

"It's an ending of some sort because this is the last leaf to fall, and it looks like the last branch is about to fall also. It looks like the tree is dying, and it's on its last legs. Maybe all four of these pictures are about death."

In my mind I began to put together a collage of death images that included these four pictures. Then came the image of Rob, my high school friend, who died in a car accident. Next was the mental picture of Craig, a fraternity brother, who also died in an accident. He had jacked up his car and was doing repairs underneath it, but the jack slipped, and the full weight of the car fell on him. Then along came the indelible memory of President Kennedy's death two years earlier.

In addition, I thought of life-threatening experiences like my brother Rick's car accident. He was driving down a steep hill in my hometown of Meriden, Connecticut, along with four high school buddies when the brakes totally gave out. At the bottom of the hill there was a house. Rick managed to elude the house itself and steered the car down the driveway adjacent to the house. The car slowed to a crawl as it approached some bushes, and everyone was relieved. But suddenly the bushes parted, and the car plummeted over the edge of an 80-foot railroad embankment. The *Meriden Record Journal* reported the car's fall: "Plunging off the edge, it flipped four or five times in mid-air to land right-side up facing in an easterly direction, according to the police report." The car rolled over repeatedly and was totally destroyed. One of Rick's friends suffered a minor injury, yet it was a miracle that Rick and his friends escaped with their lives. After this brush with death, Rick took high school studies seriously for the first time and as a result became academically successful, enabling him to go to college.

Next I pondered my own confrontation with death. During the previous summer I had gone on a date with a gloriously beautiful girl named Danielle. My parents had a small summer cottage at the beach, which didn't mean they were wealthy; it meant they had two mortgages. My youthful life in the house on 12 South View Street in Meriden was reserved and conservative like the rest of New England, so I wasn't much of a social butterfly there. But my days at 41 Dolphin Avenue in Westbrook were golden times, as bright as the summer sun. In the early years I could spend all day in the sun with friends, swimming, boating, fishing, clamming, playing, and enjoying outdoor games, as well as indoor games on rainy days.

In my teenage years during the summer, I was a tireless sun worshiper, mining the beaches for dates. During the evenings, to save effort, time, and money, I usually just took dates down to the sand dunes to "watch the submarine races." However, the date with Danielle was a special occasion. I had just gotten my driver's license, and for the first time I was able to convince my brother to let me borrow his car. Rick's last words were, "Be careful." It was a long drive to Danielle's house, but I was just happy to be driving Rick's ancient yet reliable 1951 Ford.

I had met Danielle once before, at a beach party; however I really didn't know her very well. When I picked her up, I was surprised she lived in such an elegant home. On the date she wanted to go to a jazz concert, which was expensive beyond my means. I told her I didn't like jazz music and suggested we go to the movies to see *Ocean's Eleven* with Frank Sinatra and the Rat Pack. After the movie I took her to a local seafood place, and we had onion rings. But it seemed to me she was sucking on a lemon all night. The only time she seemed to perk up was when she told me with an air of certainty that she was going to get married and have two children, a boy named Shawn and a girl named Susan. I wasn't sure if she would let her husband have any say in this, but I was sure that I wasn't in the running to be her husband in either her mind or mine. The fact that she was so stunningly attractive began to lose its luster when I first got the clear impression she was looking down on me. That happened right at the start of the date, when she looked disdainfully at the worn paint job on the old 1951 Ford that I was so proud to be driving.

As I drove up the steep twisting hill to take Danielle home, I decided to put this experience on the top of my list of all-time worst dates and was glad it would soon be over. I pulled into her driveway and waited in silence for her to get out and end this nightmare. However, she didn't move, and finally she announced demandingly, "I'm waiting for you to open my door."

"What? Do you have a broken arm?" I retorted, uncovering the hostility that had been brewing all night underneath a veneer of politeness. She, of course, got out and slammed the door behind her. I thought I would feel relieved, but instead I felt only steaming anger as I drove off. A light rain had started to fall as I proceeded down the steep hill. I was driving at the correct speed for ideal conditions, although not safely for wet roads. The car started to skid, and I made the mistake of coming down too hard on the brakes, which made the skid worse. Anger changed to fear as I lost control of the car. There was only a guard rail on the left side to prevent the car from plunging headlong over a cliff, and there was a threatening wall of rock on the other side.

I desperately held onto the wheel of the car, thinking my life depended upon it. I don't remember saying a specific prayer, but I did feel I was calling out for help at some level beyond myself. Then as a response to my calling out, I did something that totally surprised me even as I did it. I spontaneously took my hands completely off the steering wheel and my foot off the brakes. I can't explain logically why I let go, but it was a way of acknowledging the obvious—my life at that instant was no longer in my hands.

The car was spinning like a top, and I was just along for the ride—with life and death hanging in the balance. Suddenly the spinning came to an abrupt and jarring stop. The car slowly moved straight ahead through some bushes and into a vertical wall of rock. It was going so slowly when it hit the rock wall that the collision was only slightly jarring, and there was only a little damage to the front of the car, causing a leak in the radiator. After a moment to gather my senses, I backed the car up onto the road and drove home. When I got home and got out, I noticed that the left side of the rear metal bumper had been bent entirely backwards. That end of the bumper must have caught the guard rail and stopped the car from its uncontrollably wild spinning, thus saving my life. But what had possessed me to let go of the steering wheel at the precise instant that would allow that piece of metal to be in just the right position to save my life? It felt like something beyond me had given me the impulse to let go. As immature as I was then, I knew that I owed my life to divine intervention and not merely to a small piece of metal.

The last image that came to my mind was seeing myself standing on the stage of my high school auditorium, which served as a theater very much like the one I was sitting in but without the balcony. I was reciting the following words:

> To-morrow, and to-morrow, and to-morrow,
> Creeps in this petty pace from day to day
> To the last syllable of recorded time,
> And all our yesterdays have lighted fools
> The way to dusty death. Out, out, brief candle!
> Life's but a walking shadow, a poor player
> That struts and frets his hour upon the stage
> And then is heard no more: it is a tale
> Told by an idiot, full of sound and fury,
> Signifying nothing.[1]

I wasn't in a high school presentation of *Macbeth*. I was participating in the verbal portion of a senior-year essay contest. My English teacher told our class, "Please don't write an essay about world peace." The other English teachers could not have given the same instructions, because an essay on world peace won the contest. My essay was about a high school student who had to recite Macbeth's soliloquy about death, but forgot the words on stage. The essay was actually a first person soliloquy in which the student evaluated his intelligence in light of his poor recitation. In the end he affirmed, with seeming conviction, "That doesn't mean I am stupid." But he then paused uncertainly and asked, "Or does it?"

When I was on stage reciting my essay, I could afford to play the part of someone questioning his intelligence precisely because I was very secure about my own. However, my essay never really attempted to address the disquieting meaning of Macbeth's soliloquy. In the theater at college, looking back on my recitation of the essay, his pondering seemed particularly pertinent. Shakespeare often spoke of life in this world as a stage in which we are but players, and I felt that Turtle, the part I had been playing at college, was just acting with no substance. Playing the role of Turtle my life was "a walking shadow, a poor player that struts and frets his hour upon the stage." Normally people are dissatisfied because they don't get what they want, but I, as Turtle, got everything I wanted, and I still was not satisfied. I was playing out a part that superficially appeared to get applause, but in fact was "signifying nothing."

It occurred to me that I had to put myself in harm's way by hanging from the balcony in order to face "dusty death" and confront myself with the meaninglessness of my life. Sitting in the theater I felt I had identified the problem. However, I did not come to Macbeth's pessimistic conclusion that life is a showy exercise in futility with death as the final scene. I felt there was an answer to my problem of the meaninglessness of life and the finality of death, even though I could not come up with the solution at that time.

When I transferred from Central Connecticut to Southern Connecticut State College[2], I left the fraternity scene and likewise left behind the attention-getting Turtle persona. Yet dropping a high-profile role in a fraternity and picking up a new, low-profile role did not bring meaning to my life. Although meaningful questions had been raised, I did not accept the responsibility to seek out the answers that would bring purposefulness to my life. A new college, new friends, new sexual partners, and a new focus on art—all served as handy diversions from embarking on such a serious quest. My many distractions hid my dislike for the changing masks that I made and wore as my identity. I did not know there were deeper levels to my identity that were hidden from my conscious mind.

---

1. *Macbeth*, Act V, scene v.
2. In the 60s these were both called "colleges," but now have become Central Connecticut State University and Southern Connecticut State University.

3

RETURN TO
MY ROOTS

≈ • ≈

Two years after hanging over the balcony I graduated from college in the class of 1967. In the next two years I went to New York, found love, lost love, and experimented with drugs and Eastern philosophy. During all that time I had no clue why the meaninglessness of life had encompassed me four years earlier. Finally in 1969 after returning to my hometown of Meriden, Connecticut, I realized that the meaninglessness was due to leaving God out of my life.

God had been important to me as a child, but all that changed with the arrival of puberty in my teenage years. When hormones were running wildly through my body, I felt an inner conflict between my sexual desires and my spiritual side. I asked for guidance from the Holy Spirit. My Catholic faith taught me that the Holy Spirit is part of the Trinity, along with God the Father and the Son. I believed the Holy Spirit could provide divine help and understanding, either spontaneously or through prayer. However, I could not receive clear guidance so I finally told God, "You gave me these impulses. I can't give you my heart now, but when you take away these impulses, I will return to you." I made this prayer with tears because it felt like I was giving up my relationship with God, which had nourished me previously. After this decision to turn away from God, my adolescent practice of my Catholic faith became a façade. On Sundays my parents went to the early morning Mass, and I told them I was going to the later Mass. On the way to church I would stop to purchase *Sporting News Magazine* and spend an hour reading it in the church parking lot. When I saw people streaming out of church, that was my cue to go home. Eventually I stopped even pretending to go to church.

In 1969 back in my parents' home at age twenty-four, I felt that my prayer as an adolescent was answered, in that my preoccupation with sexual impulses was no longer the problem that it had been in the past. Since I felt God had done His part in answering my prayer, I kept my promise to come back to Him. I felt I was starting my life over with a whole

FIRST HOLY COMMUNION — MAY 1953

IF GOD HAD A FACE

new orientation. Previously I had been almost exclusively focused on myself. My new focus was on Christ as the center of my life. I began reading a book called *The Imitation of Christ*.[1] What stood out in my mind was its emphasis on the Biblical idea that "All is vanity."[2] I had lived only a short time, but even in my early twenties I could already see the vanity of the world. More importantly I could see my own personal vanity as a stumbling block. I was encouraged to follow the advice in the title to imitate the example of Jesus Christ.

My new orientation was actually a return to the roots of my spiritual upbringing as a Roman Catholic. I was surprised at how quickly I was able to rekindle that same feeling of innocence and freedom I had experienced as a thirteen-year-old at my confirmation. Our bishop came to my confirmation, and he dipped his fingers in olive oil and made the sign of the cross on my forehead, making me a soldier of Christ. I kissed his ring, feeling he represented Christ to me. The origins of my spiritual reawakening actually went back to five years earlier when I had my first confession followed by my First Holy Communion as a chubby eight-year-old in 1953 (shown on page 29). In the Mass I said the words, "Lord, I am not worthy to receive you, but only say the word, and I shall be healed." There was that sacred moment when the priest placed the host in my mouth and I ate the body of Christ for the first time. In preparation for this moment I had completed my Sunday school studies. I can even remember the first page of my catechism book that summed up my faith with the words, "The purpose of life is to know, love, and serve God and to love my brothers and sisters, treating them as I would like to be treated." I still subscribe to that purpose today and am grateful for the spiritual foundation that was laid in those formative years. However, in my later adult years I found some Catholic dogma to be limiting, and so I needed a different form of spirituality that would better express my desire to blend the East and West. Nevertheless, as a twenty-four-year old I had already traveled a rocky road in my life, and I needed the stability that a return to my childhood faith provided. Most of all, in my new orientation as a young adult Roman Catholic, I remember feeling the same cleanness of heart that I had experienced after my first confessions to the priest in my childhood.

I did my best to be aware of God's love in my prayer life and to become more loving in my daily life. I also focused on wanting to do God's Will, because I believe "God is love"[3] and so doing His Will means expressing love. However, I still had some fear of God, which was reflected in a painting that I made of Him, called *If God had a Face*. Of course, God does not have a human form, but my picture depicted a close-up of His face that displayed His awesomeness rather than His love.

JESUS ON THE CROSS

I also made a painting titled *Jesus on the Cross*. Unlike most crucifixion paintings, it was a close-up that showed his torso from the waist up and only part of his arms, with the border of the picture cutting off the arms above the elbows. During this time, I cut my finger and thought how concerned I was about it, and how inconsequential my cut was, compared to the suffering of Jesus. I put blood from my finger over the red mark of the sword wound in the side of Jesus in the painting. I also read many books about saints and martyrs. These were my heroes, and I thought how wonderful it would be to die for God, although the prospect scared the hell out of me. I was resolved to live for God, though I was not sure how that would evolve.

I enjoyed reading about the miracles of Mother Mary, and wondered why there seemed to be so few miracles happening in everyday life. I said the rosary three times a day and went to Mass every morning at 6:30 AM. In addition to the rosary, I felt guided to repeat the Name of Jesus in coordination with my breathing as a meditation practice. Specifically, I repeated the first syllable, "Je," with the inhalation and the second syllable, "sus," with the exhalation. I had never heard of anyone doing this particular Christian prayer technique, until I visited an abbey for a retreat. The abbot told me this type of prayer is a common practice, although it has many variations. Subsequently I read a book entitled *The Way of a Pilgrim*, which described a Russian seeker who had many adventures while praying. His prayer was the Name of Jesus in combination with a few other words, which he repeated as an unceasing prayer throughout all the activities of daily living. I was inspired by the following quotation:

> Many so-called enlightened people regard this frequent offering of one and the same prayer as useless and even trifling, calling it a mechanical and thoughtless occupation of simple people. But unfortunately they do not know the secret which is revealed as a result of this mechanical exercise; they do not know how this frequent service of the lips imperceptibly becomes a genuine appeal of the heart, sinks down into the inward life, becomes a delight, becomes, as it were, natural to the soul, bringing it light and nourishment and leading it on to union with God.[4]

I read both the Old and the New Testament all the way through three times, but still felt inadequate about my knowledge of the Bible, so I decided to take a college-level course at a seminary in West Hartford. I asked the teacher of the course, Father Max, if he would provide me with spiritual counseling, which he did for several months. His monastic order had a missionary calling in Chile, and I said, "I think I should go to Chile to serve God in your order."

Father Max asked, "Why do you say that?"

"I have made a lot of mistakes in my life. I want to do something to make up for my past and serve God."

"I noticed you did not say you 'want' to go to Chile. You said you think you 'should' go to Chile. Joining our order is not a vocation that is motivated by obligation to pay for the past. It is an expression of love coming from the heart. Do you understand what I am saying?"

"Yes, and I can't really say my heart is lovingly drawn to going to Chile."

"I don't want to discourage you from serving God. But God is Love, and you don't have to go somewhere else to serve Him. You can serve Him wherever you are and whatever you are doing. St. Augustine said, 'Love and do as you will.' I would suggest you find ways to open your heart and then let your service be an expression of an open heart." That was very good advice, which I sought to follow.

Turning to the field of social service, I obtained a job in Meriden working with mentally retarded young adults, whom I found to be very open-hearted, which in turn helped me to open my own heart. I was the manager of a program called the Independent Living Unit that encouraged clients to learn interpersonal skills as well as self-reliance. This is a standard kind of program today, but was considered a new approach in the 70s.

Of all my clients, I remember Alfred the best. When he came into the program, he looked like a frightened deer, having never been away from his family. He quickly acquired independent living skills, and his self-confidence soared. His socialization skills also improved dramatically, and eventually I was able to get him a job at a car wash. I helped Alfred open a bank account in his own name for him to save the money he made from his job. When his mother found out that Alfred could hold down a job, she immediately took him out of the program and closed his bank account. She already had control of his social security checks, but by taking him out of the program she could also keep his income from his job for herself and give him a very small allowance. It was easy to see that she was interested in her own financial gain rather than the personal benefits Alfred had acquired through living independently. Since Alfred wanted to go back to living with his mother, there was nothing I could do other than exercise non-attachment.

In spite of the success of the Independent Living Unit, the administrators decided to open the program to emotionally disturbed adolescents. I told my supervisors that it was inappropriate to combine emotionally disturbed adolescents with mentally retarded clients because these two populations had very different needs. My immediate supervisor fully agreed with me, but the supervisors above her disregarded our objections to having mixed populations. One day I found a mentally retarded client, Harold, crying. When I asked him why he was upset, he said, "Derek told me I am a dummy."

"He shouldn't have said that, Harold, because that is not true. You are making a lot of progress and have learned a lot of things since living here. You can do your own laundry now. Isn't that right?"

"Yes," Harold said as he wiped his tears aside.

"You have your own bank book and are learning how to handle your own money, aren't you?"

"Yes."

"So you can see, you are really learning a lot. Derek doesn't even have a job, and you do. I will talk to Derek because he is mistaken."

I found Derek in the pool room, where he was shooting pool alone. "Harold told me you called him a dummy."

"He is a dummy, isn't he?" Derek said flippantly.

"No, he is slow learner. I am trying to build up his self-worth so he can live up to his potential. It would be better if you didn't call him a dummy or any other derogatory term. Do you understand what I am telling you?"

Derek said emphatically, "No, I don't have to listen to anything you say." Then he abruptly turned his back to me to shoot pool.

A rage came over me, and I grabbed him from behind and pulled him to the ground even though he had a bigger body than I had. I did not punch or hit him. I restrained him so he was immobilized. Immediately I came to my senses and told him I would let him go. He got up and hollered at me, "If you ever do that to me again, I will hurt you bad!"

"I am sorry. I totally lost my head. I just can't have you hurt our mentally retarded clients, but what I did was wrong. I apologize. I won't touch you again," I said and walked away.

The next day my supervisor, Mary Johnson, confronted me. "Derek told me you attacked him from behind. Did you?"

"Yes, I did, just as he told you. I also apologized. I know I could be fired for this. I totally lost control of my emotions. This never happened before in my life, and it will never happen again." Mary realized I was trying to stand up for our mentally retarded clients and acknowledged that the emotionally disturbed clients should not be in this program at all. Mary Johnson had been in the hospital giving birth to her son at the same time my mother was in the hospital giving birth to me, so she had a real fondness for me. She forgave me and did not elevate the incident to her supervisor. I was off the hook, yet still felt terrible about what happened.

I did not tell Mary what had happened the previous night. When I was on my way home from work right after my altercation with Derek, I stopped to pick up two hitchhikers. One fellow plopped down on the front seat, and the other tumbled into the back. With a backward glance I noticed that they had brought beer into the back seat and that they were both drunk. I told them that if they wanted a ride they would have to leave the beer behind. They balked, and I could tell from their abrasive tone of voice that this could escalate into a physical confrontation if I forced the issue. I was driving on Main Street, which was well lighted, but they wanted me to go down a dark side street. I told them I would only drive along Main Street in the direction I was already going, toward the center of town.

Then without any warning the hitchhiker in the back seat forcefully struck the right side of my head with a beer can in his hand. I immediately slammed on the brakes and instantly jumped over the front seat and into the back of the car. I wrapped my left arm around his neck so he couldn't move and started to pummel him with my right fist. I punched his face several times before his partner in the front seat could get out of the car and open the back door to try to help his friend. The partner standing outside the car grabbed my feet and was trying to pull me off of his friend, whom I was still soundly thrashing. I told my battered opponent to tell his partner to stop pulling my feet or I would break his nose. Also I promised him that if his friend stopped trying to pull me out of the car, I would let them both go without further incident. He yelled for his partner to stop grabbing my feet, and his partner complied. I released my dazed opponent so he could get out of the car, and I got back in the driver's seat and drove off. I was already upset with myself for having gotten into an altercation with Derek earlier, and this fight added to my disappointment in myself. The excuse that I was defending myself in the car fight gave me no consolation because I felt I was not living up to my ideal of imitating Christ and expressing love.

I stayed working at this job for several more months; however, the two populations created an atmosphere that was not ideal for the growth of these clients. Finally I resigned in protest because the vision and ideals of the program had been compromised by the poor choices of those in authority. I learned many lessons while at this job, but still felt ashamed by my behavior in fighting with Derek. Although Mary Johnson had forgiven me, I couldn't seem to forgive myself. Instead of following Father Max's advice to open my heart, I had ended up doing just the opposite. In spite of my failure, I still felt committed to my high spiritual ideal of following in the footsteps of Jesus. I prayed for self-acceptance of my shortcomings and encouragement to improve.

Nevertheless, I was seeing shortcomings not only in myself, but in the dogma of my Roman Catholic religion, which I questioned. I could accept that God is love, but was disturbed by the contradiction of seeing a world of evil, suffering, and death. How could a God of love make such a world?

Why were my clients born with the handicap of mental retardation, and why were some individuals born with other kinds of handicaps? Even more disconcerting was the idea that a God of love could allow hell to exist, where souls are tortured and permanently cut off from God. If hell really existed, I would have to conclude that God must have conditional love, rather than perfect unconditional love. Yet I wanted to believe that God had perfect love, that God would never change, and God would never allow anyone to go to hell. When I had talked with Father Max and other priests about my concerns, I was told I needed to rely on faith and accept that there were mysteries in life that I could not comprehend. My dissatisfaction with this answer to inconsistencies led me to actively seek answers outside the framework of Roman Catholic dogma, but I had no intention of abandoning my focus on Christ.

At the time of my return to my Roman Catholic religion, I had rejected my former Eastern viewpoints. However, with my seeking to answer difficult theological questions, I again opened myself to looking at Eastern philosophy. I heard that a Christian monk was going to give a lecture at a yoga center in Hartford, and I went to hear him speak. His name was Brother David Steindl-Rast, and he was very knowledgeable about both Eastern and Western philosophy and spiritual practices.

He began his talk by asking the audience to give him all their questions. Then he explained that instead of answering these questions individually, he would attempt to remember them and give a talk that would collectively address the issues that these questions raised. When he completed his lecture, everyone was satisfied that the questions had indeed been remembered and answered. One of the questions was, "What do you think about interpreting the Bible literally?"

Brother David addressed this by saying, "Let's say you read a book in which a man professes his love by saying to a woman, 'I give you my heart.' Do you immediately get an image of him placing his bloody heart on a plate and giving it to her? Of course not. So we can get in trouble if we take everything literally. We need to be open to the Holy Spirit to hear what the words are really saying."

He had been asked about the Trinity and my memory of his answer was, "Think of a mother seeing her baby son from a distance and sending her love to him. The child looks up and sees his mother with love in her eyes and reaches his arms toward her. The mother responds to his love by picking him up. The child smiles broadly in gratitude for her love. The mother sees his smile and embraces the child lovingly. This is an example of the Trinity. God the Father creates the Son as an expression of His love. The Son in gratitude returns love back to the Father. They both embrace in a song of gratitude. The love and gratitude that exist between the Father and the Son is the Holy Spirit." I liked his emphasis on love throughout his lecture and felt that to truly follow Christ I would have to learn how to become more of an example of love, as Jesus was.

Following the lecture Brother David was asked, "Do you practice yoga yourself?" He said, "I don't do yoga postures. But I have found yoga breathing practices to be helpful for my spiritual life." I was inspired by his whole lecture and was particularly encouraged to hear that he found some Eastern practices helpful. This helped me to feel that I too could find a blending of the East and West in my own life. Remaining centered in Christ I continued to go to daily Mass at church, but added yoga practices to my spiritual life. Although there were yoga classes held at the Integral Yoga Center in Hartford, I preferred to do my disciplines at home because I felt the consistency of a daily routine would help me to internalize my practice.

1.Thomas A Kempis, *The Imitation of Christ*, (New York: E. P. Dutton; London: J. M. Dent [1941] 1960). Chapter 1 describes the vanities of the world.

2. Eccles. 1:2, *The Holy Bible, Revised Standard Version*, (New York: Thomas Nelson and Sons, 1952.), p. 694. All Old Testament quotes hereafter are taken from this version of the Bible and will be referenced only by chapter and verse.

3. First Letter of John 4:8 and 16, *The New Testament*, the Confraternity of Christian Doctrine edition, (Paterson, NJ: St. Anthony Guild Press, 1941), p. 682-683. The symbol "CCD" will be used in subsequent endnotes to indicate that the referenced quotations come from this edition of the Bible and will be referenced only by chapter and verse.

4. *The Way of a Pilgrim and The Pilgrim Continues His Way*, translated from the Russian by R.M. French. (New York: Seabury Press, 1972) p. 203. Originally published by the Seabury Press; rights owned by Winston Press, Inc., Minneapolis, MN.

4

CASTLE CRAIG AND CHILDHOOD MEMORIES

~ • ~

Climbing over the railing of the balcony at the college theater forced me to look at issues I didn't normally consider. After that experience in 1965 as Turtle pondering the reminders of death and the meaninglessness of my life, I did what most people do with unpleasant thoughts: I submerged them again into the subconscious mind so I could continue to function in everyday living. I felt that after my return to Christ in 1969, I had found the meaningfulness that I had sought by hanging from the balcony. But I was surprised to discover that whatever motivated me to do that had not been resolved.

I don't remember the exact year, but my discovery came in the early 70s at the time of an eclipse when I was living with my parents in Meriden. Just before the eclipse I intuitively felt I needed to drive to Castle Craig on top of a mountain in Hubbard Park.[1] Castle Craig doesn't fit the image of what most people would call a "castle" because it is just a cylindrical stone structure made as a replica of an old Norman tower. Normally, Castle Craig presented a majestic panoramic view since it is the highest point within fifty miles of the coast from Maine to Florida. But on this day the sky was cloudy and windy, making for poor visibility of the eclipse. I climbed the steps to the very top floor of the tower, and I was surprised there was no one else around. And although I thought I had come to see the eclipse, that is not the way it turned out.

As with the urge to climb over the railing of the theater balcony, I felt an equally irresistible urge to climb up onto the top of the retaining wall of Castle Craig. I didn't have to hang by my hands over the edge to challenge myself. It was enough to just stand erect on the very top of the wall and to look straight down. Castle Craig is tall in itself, but I stood on the side of the tower where there was a cliff right at its base. I knew that only a strong gust of wind stood between me and certain death. And the wind *was* blustering.

The stone wall was about two feet thick, and I had to keep both feet flat and firmly planted to resist the wind, which was blowing from my back.

I was asking myself, "Why am I doing this?" I didn't know what could be compelling me to stare death in the face, but it felt like something I had to do—*again*. I was telling myself that whatever it was that drove me to hang off the balcony years before was still active in me, like a dormant volcano still hot below the surface even when not erupting outwardly. I lifted my arms and hands directly over head and looked straight up for a moment. Then I lowered my arms for better balance since the wind continued to blow. Rather than a total eclipse, this was only a partial eclipse, so there was only a slight dimming of the already cloudy sky. Finally I carefully lowered myself back off the retaining wall and down to the safety of the top floor of Castle Craig.

I made my way back to my car and sat in the parking lot for a long time to ponder what had happened and why. Castle Craig has only been a drive away for years, so why did I wait until the sun was being eclipsed to climb to the top of it? I didn't know. Just like the last time I had intentionally confronted death, I let my thoughts wander to show me what had been percolating under the surface of my mind. Some of the same images of "dusty death" that had appeared years before resurfaced, but there were new images as well. Going far back in my mind to my earliest experiences, I recalled repeated childhood dreams of falling and then suddenly waking up in fear. There was also a dream of being in a burning building and seeing spiders running out of it.

There was a time in my youth when I was alone, and I picked up a banana and a big black spider appeared. I dropped the banana in fear, but went searching for the spider with a paper towel in hand. I found it, caught it, and squeezed the paper towel over it. I opened the paper towel to find the spider had escaped unharmed. In shock I dropped both the paper towel and the spider. After searching all over again, I finally found the spider and killed it. This doesn't sound like much of an event, but it made a strong impression on me at the time.

This led to another earlier memory of being in my childhood house in Meriden. The house, which was on a hill, had a cellar garage in the basement that could be accessed only from the backyard. It was used exclusively for storage, and I remembered a time when I was rummaging through old stuff that hadn't been moved for a long time. A giant thick black spider appeared, the largest I had ever seen, and I stepped on it. As I looked around, I noticed a set of large spider webs draped over the corner of one of the wooden double doors that opened out into the backyard. There were some matches nearby so I started to light matches and chase spiders with the flames.

I was called from upstairs and told to get ready to go to see a Dean Martin and Jerry Lewis movie with my brother, Rick, and Rick's friend, Butchy. Rick was forced to take me, which he would never do on his own. I was short and fat until puberty, when I suddenly became tall and thin. For the majority of outdoor activities I couldn't keep up with Rick and his friends, so most of the time I kept to myself. On this day I did my best to ignore comments by Rick and Butchy about my large rear end as I walked ahead of them on the long walk to the Capital Theater. As we were walking along Cook Avenue, a fire engine came roaring by. It wasn't until we got back home after the movie that I found out that the fire engine had come to our house to put out the fire that had originated in the location of the garage doors. I quickly confessed. I had only wanted to burn spiders, and in my memory there wasn't anything burning when I left the cellar. However, I was mistaken, and my parents certainly impressed upon me that I could have burned down the whole house. I expected to be hit with Dad's strap as I was usually disciplined, for example, when Rick and I got into an altercation. Nevertheless, this time I received only a severe reprimand, but that was all I needed to recognize the seriousness of my dangerous blunder.

Rick and I became close to each other when we got older, yet in my early childhood our relationship was like the New England weather— constantly changing. We were only a year and ten months apart, and I enjoyed his company when it was available. It appeared to me that our relationship was like a faucet that Rick turned on or off depending upon whether he wanted to play the part of Dr. Jekyll or Mr. Hyde. When he wanted to turn off our relationship, he resorted to calling me "Fatso," because he knew I was sensitive about my weight. But there were no arguments between Rick and me on the drive home after church on Sundays because we eagerly anticipated what was to come. Sitting around our beautiful wooden dinner table we would cut slices of still warm Italian bread, cover them with butter, and devour them, along with delicious homemade meatballs and spaghetti.

One time when Rick and I were very young, we were lying on the living room floor together watching a movie. As usual, Mom was on our left lying down on the couch, and Dad was on our right in his easy chair. We were watching a comedy, and right at the end two grave diggers were beginning to dig a new grave. Unexpectedly a scary ghost appeared, and both grave diggers ran off. The movie speeded up to exaggerate the effect of them running away—an ancient forerunner of today's special effects. However, Rick and I thought this was hilarious, and we were laughing in unison uncontrollably. Suddenly while laughing I unexpectedly blurted out a strange loud shriek and then stopped. It was as though this scream had been waiting under the surface for a long time to be released. This same shriek would be intermittently released on other such occasions of uncontrollable laughter in the future. As soon as it did come out, I would immediately suppress it because I was embarrassed by it. It was like a hidden terror in me that could only come out a few seconds at a time so I would not be overwhelmed by it.

Rick and I had played together in our early childhood, but things changed in my later childhood. Other than family events, Rick spent most of his time with neighborhood friends and kept me at a distance. I spent time playing with our next door neighbor, Ronnie, who was Rick's age, but who was mentally retarded. For the most part, though, I was alone, and I had two spots where I liked to go. One was at the top of a cliff near my home where I sat and dangled a certain kind of weed from my mouth. The weed had a white bottom section that was sweet, and I would eat it before picking another one to put in my mouth. The other favorite spot was in the local cemetery where there was a large group of pine trees. I would find a spot under a pine tree and just lie there and relax on a bed of pine needles. Both the cliff and the cemetery came to my mind as images somehow related to the Castle Craig event.

The next image that entered my mind was the time I was playing with my cousin Kelly. I was climbing in the strangely shaped pine tree in my front yard. It had a twisting trunk that appeared to screw itself into the ground. That day I fell out of the tree and hurt my right foot. Kelly laughed at me and wouldn't stop. I got very upset because I was obviously in pain, and that didn't seem to matter to her at all.

This event led to a memory of playing football with a bunch of buddies. I had been on the high school football team and played end—end of the bench. None of my closest friends had been on the high school football team, so when we got together informally to play football I was chosen as the quarterback. The other team had bigger and stronger linemen, and so to avoid the rush I rolled out to the right and lofted a very long pass in the direction of our right end, Dana. Then I completely blacked out. When I regained consciousness, Dana was in my face saying excitedly, "Don, I caught the pass!" But my attention was on my right ankle, which had been severely sprained. I had been hit from behind just as I passed the ball, and I couldn't even recall being hit. I limped my way home.

Then I remembered as a youth walking alone to an old, burnt, and abandoned building out on a peninsula at the beach. While walking back I cut the big toe on my right foot on a piece of glass and had to hobble my way back to our summer cottage.

Another foot-related incident then came to mind. My brother Paul once challenged me to use my ankles to lift my body up on my toes thirty times in thirty seconds. He promised that if I could do it, he would give me a dollar. So I tried, and he timed it. "Oh, too bad, you just missed. Try again," Paul said. So I gave it another try, and another, and another, and so on until my ankles hurt. I finally gave up. It did not occur to me at the time that having Paul as the time keeper was a big mistake. The next day when I woke up in the morning my ankles hurt even more, and the only way I could relieve the pain was to walk on my toes. As I was walking to school on my toes, I saw the words, "FUCK YOU," written on the sidewalk, and I was too young to understand their meaning. Even after school I still had to walk on my toes to get home, and on the way a little boy gave me a hassle about my weird gait. I told him it was none of his business, and he gave me the finger. I said, "You don't even know what that means." I confronted him because I didn't know the significance of that middle finger. I was hoping he would enlighten me, without me having to admit my ignorance.

He responded obligingly, "Stick this where the sun don't shine."

Perhaps the sexual aspects of this memory brought to mind the time when I was even younger and asked my mother, "Chickens come from eggs, but where do people come from?"

My mother, who was always so pleasant and composed, appeared visibly perplexed by my question and abruptly said, "When your father comes home, you will have to ask him about that." My mother was so obviously uncomfortable that I thought I had done something wrong by asking the question. I certainly wasn't going to make that mistake again by asking my father the same question. After all, since my father was a strict disciplinarian and often emotionally distant, he was not someone I would go to for a heart-to-heart talk. The answer to my "birds and bees" question would come many years later at the public library.

Next I remembered my resistance to being kidnapped as a fraternity brother at Central Connecticut, and after that my mind jumped all the way back to King Street Elementary School. I was standing in the playground and watching a large group of boys playing a new game they had made up. They were each taking a turn being dragged by all the others through the dirt. After each had taken a turn, they looked around, and one said, "Let's take him," pointing to me. It wasn't a request, and if it had been, it would not have been welcome. They ran toward me, and I ran as fast as I could away from the playground. But I was a slow runner, and they caught me. I began crying, and one boy said, "He's just a cry baby. Let's leave him alone," and so they walked away.

After a few moments of letting the magnitude of this humiliation sink in, I decided it would be better to submit to minor physical abuse rather than emotional abuse. I returned to the playground and told the boys I had changed my mind, and I let them drag me through the dirt. What I remember clearest of all is that after submitting to this dragging experience, one rather big boy named Roger approached me from behind. Without being provoked by me in any way, he put his arm around my neck expecting me to be easy prey for his showing off. However, I was infuriated, and I grabbed his arm and suddenly jerked my whole upper torso forward. His body went tumbling forward over my body, and he landed on his back on the ground in front of me. He was stunned and humiliated, since everyone could see what had happened. After that no one wanted to mess with me.

Next my mind wandered to a very different kind of dangerous situation. As a seventeen-year-old I had a girl friend who by her own admission was extremely frigid. Consequently she arranged for me to go out with her cute friend, Noreen, who had no such limitation. Noreen led me past a *No Trespassing* sign and into the old abandoned Belvedere Hotel, a short walk from the beach in Westbrook. I gathered she had been there before, and we found a comfortable bed in the barren condemned building. The condom I was using unexpectedly broke, and I asked her if she wanted to stop. Since the condom was already broken and had spilled its contents, she concluded rightly that it was already too late for there to be any benefit in stopping. I heard a sound and looked back over my shoulder and saw a big rat run across the room and out the door. She didn't ask what the sound was, and I didn't offer an explanation.

Then my mind fast forwarded to sitting on a couch in Noreen's parents' summer cottage where she took me on our next meeting. I stayed in the living room, as she went upstairs for a moment to make sure that no one was in the house. As I sat there, I was shocked to see a large rat run right across the living room floor and into a hole in the wall. I didn't say anything when Noreen took me by the hand, and we walked upstairs to her bedroom. She asked me not to bother with a condom this time, and I obliged in this pre-AIDS era. But after proceeding, we were interrupted by the sound of the front door opening downstairs. Noreen had me hide under the bed. She went downstairs and came back after a while. She said it was her older brother. However, he had just come in for a minute and then left. Noreen wanted to start up again where we left off. Yet after first seeing the rat and then hiding under the bed, I had lost my enthusiasm and insisted on leaving. That was the last I saw of Noreen. I heard months later that when I met her she was already a few months pregnant from a relationship with an acquaintance of mine. But I didn't feel these images of Noreen came to mind at this time because of the sexual nature of our relationship. These memories had presented themselves because of the fear of going into dangerous buildings or dangerous situations. That was the connection with climbing Castle Craig.

The thought of going into a forbidden building led me back to the memory of the first day of a summer job I had at a factory that made small wooden knickknacks. I was entrusted with taking a load of trash to the dump in the company truck. When I returned, my new boss wanted to know where the truck's spare tire was. I told him that because it was a bald tire, I thought it was part of the trash, so I threw it out at the dump. My boss was upset about my mistake and insisted that I go back and get the tire. When I got back to the dump in the late afternoon, it had already closed, but I just couldn't go back empty handed. I climbed over the fence and looked around. A fire was burning in the place were I had dropped the trash, and I couldn't find the tire.

There was a small building inside the dump, and through a pane of glass I could see the tire. Using poor judgment, I broke the glass to get the tire. I threw it over the fence and then scaled the fence and drove back to the factory, although by this time everyone had gone home. Then I went home also. A short while later the police showed up and took me with them. Someone had seen the vehicle license plate number and reported it to the police. With my father solemnly present, I explained my story with many tears to the police. The police checked out my story with my boss and confirmed that only a tire was taken, and finally I was released with a warning and a promise to pay for repairing the pane of glass. I resented my father's discipline at times as I was growing up, although in this situation I appreciated his support.

Like the experience with Noreen, this experience focused on going into a forbidden building. Then my mind was redirected toward an experience that seemed more related to the possibility of falling off of Castle Craig. I remembered the last day of my job as a pool attendant at an apartment complex. I was attending a party at the end of summer, and I had been drinking and was quite looped. After swimming in the pool and getting out, I tried to jump up backwards to sit on top of the retaining wall that ran around the perimeter of the pool. However, instead of my butt landing in a sitting position on the top of the wall, my whole body just kept on going backwards all the way over it.

From the inside, where the pool was located, the retaining wall was only about four and a half feet tall. Unfortunately the other side of the wall, where my body was falling backwards, was about twelve feet high. My body wasn't headed for a soft surface like grass; it was headed for cement. But there were cars parked below. My upper back landed on the very front of a car, my feet hit the wall, and my whole body folded in half. When I fell, it felt like I was floating. When I landed, there was absolutely no pain, probably because I was drunk. Even the next day there was not the slightest bruise on my body. If I hadn't been drunk and so loose, I would have gotten seriously injured or killed. Then again, if I hadn't been drunk, I wouldn't have so carelessly thrown my body over that wall. Nevertheless I wondered if it was more than the looseness of being drunk that had prevented injury. I wondered if there had been some sort of divine intervention that had happened without me knowing it, yet I was uncertain about this.

I was running out of memories that might have something to do with Castle Craig when some of my former art work came to mind. Specifically I remembered a series of abstract paintings in which spiders seemed to spontaneously emerge in the painting process. When this happened I would paint out such images, so it occurred to me that at that time I was reluctant to face the shadow side of my mind. There was also a period in the past when I made "process paintings," in which the goal was not to obtain a finished art object, but rather to just paint until I couldn't paint any more. This is similar to giving little children finger paints and having them paint and paint until all the colors mix into mud. My version was painting with darker and darker colors until there was only blackness left. This was my way of expressing depression, and it was how I felt at the time of these paintings.

The next image that came to mind was the drawing I had seen after hanging from the balcony at Central Connecticut. It was the image of a barren tree seen from below showing one last leaf falling toward the ground. For the first time I thought that the falling leaf was perhaps a symbol of a person falling from the tree. That thought came to mind because I had remembered injuring my right foot and my cousin Kelly laughing at me when I had fallen out of the pine tree. Then my mind quickly shifted to an etching that I called *The Lookout*. It showed the mast of an old style ship with a sailor on the top of the mast. The sailor is getting the best view of distant objects. The perspective of the picture is from the bottom of the mast looking upward.

That image led to remembering my painting of a man dressed all in blue standing on a pier (shown on page 48 and also displayed in color on the right side and in the middle of the back cover of this book). The perspective was an upward view, which showed the large wooden poles that held up the pier seen from below. The man stood at the end of the pier, which reminded me of my standing at the edge of Castle Craig. He had one hand held directly over his head, and in that hand he held a lamp that shined a light in the darkness of the night. He was a big man, yet one leg was oddly thin in proportion to his heavy weight. The right leg was wide at the top as would be expected, but from the knee to the ankle became extremely narrow. The upward perspective of the pier did not give a clear view of his feet.

CASTLE CRAIG

THE SEARCH

I named this picture *The Search* when I painted it during my college years. At that time I recognized my art work as an extension of myself, so I did have the passing thought that this picture must be about my personal search for meaning in life. However, the search for my own identity did not become an important and intense issue for me until after I left college. This painting coming to mind again after many years made me realize that the image of the man on the pier must be especially relevant to what I was searching for at the top of Castle Craig.

The final image that entered my mind was seeing myself in Mrs. Leary's high school science class. I raised my hand and asked her a question. I didn't remember the exact question, but it didn't matter what the question was. Mrs. Leary looked at me with that blank look of hers and said, "That's a good question." Then without answering me, she turned back to the rest of the class and asked, "Are there any other questions?" Without waiting for another question, Mrs. Leary continued, "OK, let's move on." This happened several times until I learned not to ask any more questions.

It seemed to me that my search for answers at Castle Craig was an attempt to complete a jigsaw puzzle that would give meaning to my life. My hanging from the balcony at college and my ascent of Castle Craig helped me to recognize that I was challenging myself to look at the pieces of this puzzle and see how they might fit together. However, there were actually two puzzles involved—a major one and a minor one. The major one might be called my "identity puzzle." Going through adolescence, everyone is confronted with the question "Who am I?" but at some point during adulthood most seekers become content with their answer to this question. I had already spent a great deal of time and energy as an artist and spiritual seeker struggling to discover my true nature, and I was generally satisfied with my conclusions about who I was. On the other hand, I felt that my identity is really a "life puzzle," and I would probably not be able to totally complete it until I had lived a full lifetime. For the time being I was ready to move on with my life without asking myself too many more disquieting introspective questions.

Nevertheless, by standing on the top of Castle Craig, I was giving myself the message that I could not put this question on the back burner, because I had left out many of the pieces from the shadow side of my nature. I called these missing pieces my "shadow puzzle," which I identified as my minor puzzle, within the major one being my overall identity. I realized I could not solve the larger question of my identity without first unmasking my shadow nature hidden in my subconscious mind.

I had been reading the writings of Thomas Merton, and I was concerned about his warnings regarding "false asceticism," in which the seeker divides himself into a "good self" and a "bad self." I called this the "saint and sinner syndrome," which involves wearing a saintly mask while suppressing the sinner impulses into the subconscious mind. The good saintly self goes to extremes in being spiritual or at least appearing spiritual. The bad sinner self that has been suppressed suddenly and unexpectedly pops into conscious awareness and sabotages those saintly appearances. This syndrome is seen clearly in some prominent religious figures, who are eventually exposed as having feet of clay. A non-spiritual example of this good/bad principle is the dieter, who goes on a very strict diet and then afterwards ends up binge eating to gain back all the weight that had been lost.

The bad or sinner side of our nature is not really a separate self, so perhaps a better name for this part of the mind would be the "shadow." It is the part of the mind that's unacceptable to us, such as strong emotions, unpleasant experiences, or guilt. Consequently, we have trouble seeing or acknowledging and accepting this part of the mind. Anyone who gets on the spiritual path will have to decide how to deal with this shadow. It becomes stronger through relying on the denial of unacceptable thoughts, impulses, or experiences and the suppression of these into the subconscious mind. The shadow can become a powerful subversive negative force in our lives as long as it remains hidden. But if it is brought into conscious awareness, the shadow can finally be recognized and accepted. Acceptance of the shadow helps us to learn how to express our feelings and impulses in a balanced way that is neither excessive nor too restrictive. This balance is needed in order to find wholeness and healthy self-love and avoid being divided into a good self, obsessed with being perfect, and a self-defeating bad self, racked with guilt.

What I called my "shadow puzzle" was my way of looking at this difficult challenge of accepting my shadow. Imagine that a jigsaw puzzle is in a locked box with a small hole in the bottom. Normally the task of solving a jigsaw puzzle lies in putting the pieces together. But in this case, there is also the challenge of shaking the box so puzzle pieces can fall out of the small hole. Only after all the puzzle pieces are shaken out of the box and seen can the full puzzle be put together and solved. The experiences in my life, such as hanging off the balcony and standing on Castle Craig, were examples of unacceptable parts of me coming from the hidden darkness of my subconscious mind out into the light of conscious awareness. Another example was the sudden anger that I felt when I grabbed Derek at work and when I fought the two hitch-hikers in my car. These experiences were a catalyst for realizing that the challenge of solving the shadow puzzle was something I could not ignore. I did not want to run the risk of the repressed shadow jumping out in an uncontrollable manner in the future.

Also, I did not want to put on a mask that would be needed to pretend that there is no shadow. If I truly wanted to grow spiritually, I would have to do more than just look at the bright side of spirituality.

I began to consciously look for shadow puzzle pieces to see if a theme might emerge. Some parts of the shadow I managed to uncover were a dangerous building, an injured right foot, cursing, and being insulted or ridiculed. Others parts were being kidnapped, punished, or harmed in some way by others. The image of the spider made a deep impression on me because of its ominous implications as a symbol of death. Perhaps all my dangerous puzzle pieces were summed up by this one central theme of the spider image—a tangled web of pieces pointing at danger or perhaps death.

However, there was another, related theme that seemed to be even more prominent than the spider. This theme revolved around three specific pictures that have noteworthy similarities—the tree with one leaf falling, the ship's mast with the lookout on top, and the man on the pier. Interestingly all three of these pictures were viewed from an underneath perspective. Another correlation was that all three pictures depicted a wooden pole or poles. I had drawn the tree's trunk to be as straight as a telephone pole; the large ship's mast was a pole; and the pier was held up by thick wooden poles. It did not take a rocket scientist to see the most important correlation between the tree, *The Lookout*, and *The Search*. All three pictures had a common meaning pointing in one direction. Furthermore, my hanging from the balcony and standing on Castle Craig pointed in exactly the same direction. This one unifying direction was the theme of falling or being in a high place and in danger of falling. This falling theme seemed to be related to the spider theme, because falling could cause death.

Yet zeroing in on the spider theme and the falling theme, which both represented danger and possible death, had not solved the shadow puzzle. Were the spiders and the falling to be interpreted figuratively or literally? I had no idea. Nevertheless, focusing on these two themes I felt was a significant step because it gave me a strategy for figuring out how the puzzle pieces fit together. If you start to see one or two particular images emerging in a puzzle, you can look for pieces related to those images and accelerate putting the puzzle together. Also, the spider and falling themes showed that my memories were not a series of disconnected events, but rather were all part of an interconnected wholeness. I thought if I could put most of the puzzle pieces together in a meaningful way, I would be able to find a new personal sense of inner wholeness. And with greater success at putting the shadow puzzle together, I would be closer to solving my overall identity puzzle and perhaps find an even deeper level of oneness and fulfillment.

I interpreted my final image of Mrs. Leary not answering my question as a sign that I wouldn't be able to find the solution at that point in time. It also occurred to me that the pieces could not be understood by themselves. Even a physical shadow cannot exist without a light source that casts the shadow. These negative pieces could only make sense within the larger context of my life as a whole, which would include many positive puzzle pieces as well.

Perhaps Mrs. Leary's typical comment of, "OK, let's move on," meant I should simply move on with my life. I decided to just allow events to unfold in my life and notice if any puzzle pieces came to my conscious awareness in my everyday living. Over the years I had learned to place my trust in the idea that life is like a river carrying me and everyone else toward a beneficial destination. All I had to do was swim or even float with the flow of this river, rather than swim against the current, which I believed would carry me closer to the solution of the shadow and eventually to a solution of the greater mystery of my overall identity.

---

1. Today Castle Craig is cut off from automobile access, so the only way to reach it is on foot.

5

SERVICE AND KARMA

≈ ◦ ≈

At the Integral Yoga Center in Hartford I met a married couple who told me that they belonged to the Self-Realization Fellowship. They recommended that I read the life story of its founder, Yogananda, so I read his book, *Autobiography of a Yogi*. In it I learned about Swami Pranabananda, the saint with two bodies, and Nagendra Nath Bhaduri, the levitating saint. I also read about Ram Gopal Muzumdar, the sleepless saint; Giri Bala, the woman yogi who never ate; and Rama, who was raised from the dead by Lahiri Mahasaya. Yogananda talked about his spiritual master, Sri Yukteswar, resurrecting and appearing to his disciples after death. A central figure was the spiritual master Babaji, who looked like a young boy, but who was said to be 1800 years old and living in isolation in the Himalayan Mountains.

Religion in the West seemed so sterile when compared to the direct experiences of the divine recorded in this autobiography. Was it all true? I wasn't sure, yet I was certainly open to that possibility. Although I had my doubts, what impressed me was the overall message that God wasn't just a presence that interceded in human history two thousand years ago. Yogananda's message was that God is available to us now and with His help anything is possible. Yoga disciplines seemed to offer the possibility of greater access to the divine. Here is Yogananda's description of his first opening to the divine:

> The unifying light alternated with materializations of form, the metamorphoses revealing the law of cause and effect in creation.
>
> An oceanic joy broke upon calm endless shores of my soul. The Spirit of God, I realized, is exhaustless Bliss; His body is countless tissues of light. A swelling glory within me began to envelop towns, continents, the earth, solar and stellar systems, tenuous nebulae, and floating universes. The entire cosmos, gently luminous, like a city seen afar at night, glimmered within the infinitude of my being.

The dazzling light beyond the sharply etched global outlines faded slightly at the farthest edges; there I saw a mellow radiance, ever undiminished. It was indescribably subtle; the planetary pictures were formed of the grosser light.[1]

From this perspective we are not inside the world. If we could expand our consciousness the way Yogananda had done in his vision, we would recognize that the world and the whole of the cosmos are inside of our minds. Everything we see here from the perspective of our bodies appears to be real, but is in fact *maya*, an illusion. In another vision, Yogananda was told by an inner voice that everything in the physical universe is a projection of light similar to the way a movie projector makes an illusion of forms on a movie screen. Yogananda was informed that a beam of light produced a picture of his body. He heard the words, "Behold, your form is nothing but light!"[2] Then Yogananda went into an ecstasy and experienced his apparently solid body dissolving into an expression of divine light.

If Yogananda was correct and this world really is an illusion, then the goal would be to wake up from this illusion. When we do wake up, we will realize that God, Who is Light and Love, has been united with us all along even in this world, in spite of outer appearances to the contrary. Generally speaking, this is standard Eastern philosophy. Yet from a practical side, as long as we perceive we are in bodies, we have to deal with living in this world, even if it is an illusion.

Yogananda recommended daily meditation as a means of expanding consciousness. He specifically advocated *kriya yoga*, literally meaning a cleansing yoga. I learned subsequently that this practice involved the repeating of a Hindu *mantra*, a holy word, in coordination with the breathing and with raising the awareness up and down the spine. However, the specific details of kriya yoga could only be known through a secret rite of initiation. This would involve a seeker being initiated by a teacher from the Self-Realization Fellowship. I was intrigued, but did not want to be initiated by someone who was not a follower of Christ. The Self-Realization Fellowship does honor Jesus, but he is not their focus. Also, I did not like the idea of secret spiritual disciplines that could not be freely practiced by everyone.[3]

Autobiography of a Yogi also talked about *karma*, the idea of cause and effect applied to the mind and to our deeds. Newton's laws of physics tell us that if we throw a ball at a wall with a certain force, it will bounce back at us with an equal force. According to karma, our desires, thoughts, and actions also have a bounce-back effect. Whatever we hold in our minds and also what we express outwardly all come back to us. I believed in the idea of karma because I saw it as a more detailed explanation of the Bible verse, "As you sow, so shall you reap."

Karma is the justification for reincarnation, in which souls come back to meet their karma. This explained to me that individuals born with handicaps, such as mental retardation or physical limitations, are meeting karma from a past life. I liked the idea that reincarnation contradicted the concept of living one's life with heaven or hell as the only two final destinations. Instead of being banished to hell by God, we would have endless opportunities to wake up from the illusion of this world. In the Catholic religion the place between heaven and hell, called purgatory, was where souls could pay for their sins with temporary suffering before being allowed to enter heaven. I came to believe that there is no hell and that this world itself is like a purgatory where we can face our karma through reincarnation until we eventually make our way to heaven.

The bounce-back of karma was not merely a theoretical idea in my mind. I had previously experienced situations in which I could see my karma coming back to me, which I had previously set in motion by my desires, thoughts, and deeds. The first time I saw this clearly was when I was playing touch football with friends and I was angry at one player on the opposing team. As I approached this opponent on the kickoff, I decided to block him by sticking my head into his stomach. In particular, I remember I had the desire to hurt him, which was unusual for me. At impact my cheekbone hit against his hipbone, and yet he kept on running as though I hadn't even touched him. I, on the other hand, had a broken cheekbone and needed surgery to have it repaired. I attributed this not just to a meaningless accident, but to my intention to hurt him bouncing back to me and hurting me instead.

Another example was my fight with Derek, in which I assaulted him from behind without his inviting a physical confrontation. My initiating of this assault had its karmic roots in the fact that I was holding on to my anger at my supervisors, who had inappropriately decided to welcome emotionally disturbed boys into a setting that had been designed to meet the needs of mentally retarded clients. Then after the assault, the karmic bounce-back happened that same night as I was driving home from work. Just as I had attacked Derek from behind, I too was attacked from behind, without having done anything to provoke this attack. The immediate and dramatic nature of this bounce-back was so clear and obvious to me that I could not ignore it as a perfect example of the validity of karma.

Karma is at times thought of as one thing, when actually there are three kinds of karma. An analogy from Vedanta scripture illustrates this: An archer carries on his back a bunch of arrows in his quiver. He has shot an arrow that is still flying in the air as he quickly grabs another arrow and is about to shoot it. The bundle of arrows in the quiver is *accumulated karma*, which consists of all the karma that has been acquired in one's past. Part of this accumulated karma is a person's character, which includes his desires, tendencies, talents, and personality. It is whatever you are holding in your mind from the past. The second kind is represented by the arrow that is in the air and cannot be stopped. This is the *fruit-producing karma*, which cannot be avoided since it is already taking effect and must be experienced. The third type, the arrow that is being held but has not yet been shot, is *new karma,* being manufactured now, that will be the source of future karmic effects.

I was interested in what these three karmas meant for me personally. The fruit-producing karma was my means of feedback for spiritual growth. I could see that whatever I was experiencing was something that I had caused by my past desires, thoughts, and actions. For example, I looked at my fight in the car as the fruit-producing karma that I had caused by the recently accumulated karma of my fight with Derek. If I did not want the fruit of being attacked in the future, I needed to release my desire to attack others. Seeing this cause of attack and the negative effect gave me the learning opportunity and encouragement to implement new and positive karma, which would produce effects that I wanted—instead of the negative effects that I did not want. In other words, if I didn't like the plants growing in my garden, I needed to plant different seeds. Understanding that all my experiences were personally deserved became my means of taking responsibility for my growth.

I also saw a connection between karma and my shadow puzzle. I had manufactured my shadow puzzle pieces by suppressing unacceptable experiences into my subconscious mind because I didn't want to look at them. But by understanding karma, I could take responsibility for them as part of my accumulated karma. I realized that whatever I had suppressed would become fruit-producing karma and thus bounce back into my conscious mind. The only question was how I wanted to face my karma. Did I want to welcome it or resist it? If I resisted the karma of my suppressed experiences, I felt that the bounce-back effect could, in a sense, "come out sideways," rather than directly. For example, if I suppressed anger from a past experience, my karma might come back to me as depression—anger turned against myself. In this case, the suppressed anger would not be released and depression would become a chronic problem.

Imagine that you are living in a house and you hear growling and roaring sounds. These are disturbing your peace of mind, so you begin to look for the source. It appears that they are coming from the basement, but there is no light there. You get a flashlight and go down into the cellar to investigate. You discover wild animals—a lion, a bear, and a tiger—locked away in cages. You become frightened and rush back upstairs and lock the door behind you. But now you know that you have a problem that won't go away and will continue to affect your peace of mind. Eventually you build up your courage and go back down into the cellar and open the lion's cage. The lion runs upstairs, scratches the furniture, and jumps out a window. On another day you open the bear's cage so it can escape, and finally you open the tiger's cage so it can escape. It takes courage to face the lions, bears, and tigers of our subconscious mind. Yes, the furniture gets scratched up, meaning our comfortable lives are upset temporarily, but at least the problem gets released and peace of mind results.

Why do I use the symbol of wild animals in this analogy? The root Sanskrit verb from which the word "karma" comes is "kri," and it means *to do*. Everything that we do, including the desires, thoughts, and expressions of the will in deeds, is part of our accumulated karma and produces *samskaras*, which are impressions left in the mind. Some forms of karma make deeper impressions in the mind than others. The kinds of karma that produce the deepest impressions in the mind are those that contain strong emotional content. Wild animals are used in the analogy to represent these kinds of emotion-laden karma. The karma containing wild emotions that we lock away in the dark cages of the shadow side of our nature, the subconscious mind. But instead of getting rid of the karma, emotional impressions remain active in the mind. These hidden impressions can chronically "growl" in the background of our minds, producing ongoing anxiety, sometimes depression, and other problems. Facing these caged emotional impressions by reexperiencing them can temporarily upset the conscious mind. Nevertheless, this inner confrontation has the effect of releasing these impressions from having any active long-term effect on the mind. Both present-life and past-life emotional impressions can be faced, reexperienced, neutralized, and released.

The *spider* and *falling* themes of danger in my shadow puzzle suggested unpleasant or perhaps traumatic experiences containing a strong emotional content of fear, anger, or pain. This emotional content I felt had to be brought out into the light and reexperienced. I decided it was better to invite my wild animals to come out so I could face my karma directly, because I felt that this was the best way to accept the shadow and release it. I added a very important Christian concept to my understanding of karma. I made a point of praying for the help of the Holy Spirit, my flashlight, in the process of welcoming my shadow pieces. I felt the Holy Spirit would assist me in facing my karma in the most gracious way so I could learn the lessons that would help me grow spiritually. Having accepted the cause and effect principles of karma, I studied yoga philosophy books that explained the specific form of yoga called *karma yoga*.

Karma yoga is the practice of working and living in accordance with the law of karma. The word "yoga" literally means union, and the ultimate goal of all forms of yoga is union with God. Consequently, the ultimate goal of karma yoga is divine union. According to yoga philosophy, the soul after death has three possible destinations. When the physical body dies, the vital forces of the body transfer to a more refined vehicle called the *astral body*. The astral body carries the karmic impressions recorded in the mind in a seed form. Those who have devoted their lives to God and done good works without selfish motives are guided by a perfectly awakened soul, who leads seekers to the sphere where they awaken to their oneness with God, achieving liberation. I could see Jesus fulfilling this role of being a guide, who helps souls to awaken fully to divine union.

The souls of seekers who have done good works, but who mixed these with selfish desires, can ascend to various astral planes or even to heavenly spheres where seekers receive the benefits of their good actions. However, when the merits of their good karma are exhausted, they must return again to earth in a human incarnation to continue with their spiritual evolution. Souls who have predominantly bad works with selfish motives can temporarily become ghosts or even demons in lower realms until it's time to come back to the earth in human form to have another opportunity to grow spiritually and eventually wake up to their oneness with God. In general this philosophy made sense to me because I remembered that Jesus had said, "In my Father's house there are many mansions."[4] Nevertheless, I gave no credence to the Hindu belief that very evolved souls could become "gods" in a celestial realm or very unevolved souls could be reincarnated as animals.

Seekers who understand that karma affects their spiritual growth and afterlife destination attempt to increase good karma and decrease bad karma. No actions are all good or all bad and more important than the actions themselves is the intention behind each action. No action can be automatically good or bad in itself. For example, a charitable work may be done for a selfish motive, such as power, pride, or praise, and lose some of its virtuous quality. A killing of a criminal who is about to kill a hostage can be a noble act of a policeman who is performing his duty as a service to others. Consequently, the good and bad values of karmic experiences are determined by the *motive*.

Imagine that a man asked two of his nephews to work in his field, and he offered to pay each of them $100 for one day of work. At the end of the day one nephew came to his uncle with his hand out and was given $100. Next the other nephew went to his uncle and said, "My dear uncle, this work is my gift to you. There is no need to pay me." The uncle hugged him, stuffed the money in his pocket, and said, "My beloved nephew, thank you for your gift. This money is not payment for your work. It is my gift to you."

Both nephews were given $100, but only the nephew who performed his work as a gift without thought of a return was practicing karma yoga with the necessary motive of selfless service. In this analogy the uncle represents God. Karma yoga is the practice of dedicating the fruits of one's actions to God. According to karma yoga philosophy, to overcome all illusions and awaken to union with God requires letting go of the desire for both the good and bad fruits of one's actions.

In contrast to the selfless motivation in karma yoga, I was faced with the fact that in my youthful twenties I had lived an almost entirely self-centered life. My immature work ethic could be summed up by one of Ronald Reagan's quips: "Hard work never killed anybody, but why take the chance?" Because of this, I found the ideal of karma yoga to be beyond my capabilities. I decided that it would be unrealistic and foolhardy to think that I could remove all my personal desires from my actions. Buddhism also advocates desirelessness as the way to overcome suffering in life, and I had attempted to manifest desirelessness in my past experiences but found that it was not helpful for my personal growth, so I did not want to go in that direction again.

I decided to focus on developing a less exalted form of karma yoga than totally selfless service, which requires saintly qualities. Just as a person can be a Christian without being a perfect follower of Christ, a person can be practicing karma yoga to a certain degree by any form of service, such as being a teacher or social worker, even if some selfish motives are mixed with unselfish motives. Karma yoga is sometimes thought of as the yoga of "work." However, it is more properly understood to be the yoga of "dedicated action." Consequently, any action, no matter how mundane, can be an expression of karma yoga, if that action is performed with a spiritual motivation.

Accepting responsibility for being the cause of our own karma encourages us to make good choices that will return good karma to us. Although karma literally means action or deed, karma is not limited only to setting actions in motion at the form level and reaping the concrete results of those actions. Karma, as the law of cause and effect, involves understanding that *thoughts* also act like a boomerang. Loving thoughts sent out to others come back as the non-physical mental karma of loving thoughts from others coming back to us. Unloving thoughts sent to others come back as the mental karma of unloving thoughts directed toward us. Jesus expressed this idea of mental karma by saying, "Judge not, and you will not be judged; condemn not, and you will not be condemned; forgive, and you will be forgiven."[5] Here Jesus is recommending a spiritual application of the law of attraction, but He is not recommending this law as a means of getting what you want at the material level.

Seeking an application of the law of karma that would be in accordance with the teachings of Jesus, I adopted my own variation of karma yoga, which I thought of as *Christian karma yoga*. Since I could not remove all my personal desires and seeking of the fruits of those desires, I decided to express what I called *enlightened self-interest*. I recognized that I had a goal-oriented personality and possessed the discipline necessary to achieve goals. Consequently, instead of trying to remove desires, I decided to choose goals that expressed spiritually oriented desires rather than the more selfish desires that I had chosen in the past. I still sought to experience the fruits of my actions, but I felt this was beneficial because I was seeking the fruits of the Spirit—"love, joy, peace, patience, kindness, goodness, faithfulness, gentleness, self-control."[6] Seeking such fruits was not entirely selfless from the perspective of karma yoga, but did express enlightened self-interest that would lead me in the direction of waking up to my oneness with God.

According to the philosophy of karma yoga the dedication of one's actions and the fruits of one's actions to God was an expression of worship. I didn't see my form of Christian karma yoga as a form of worship, but rather as an opportunity to ask for God's assistance. For me, dedicated action is not just about getting a spiritual result. It also meant including God in the process of that action by asking for His help either prior to or in the process of taking some action. This applied to asking for help in work situations, as well as asking for help in mundane activities. For example, I would often ask for God's help when I was doing something as ordinary as driving my car or writing a letter. Whenever I started a new project or wanted a new job, I would pray for God's help. However, my awareness of karma yoga helped me be less attached to whether my desires were fulfilled or not. I allowed my wanting to be tempered by the example of Jesus and by ending my prayer with the words, "Lord, not my will, let Thy Will be done." In spite of whatever I might think I might need, I felt only God knows what I really need.

I felt my Christian karma yoga of enlightened self-interest was supported by Jesus. Instead of advocating the seeking to fulfill material needs, for example through prosperity consciousness, Jesus taught what was worthy of seeking, by saying,

> And do not seek what you are to eat and what you are to drink, nor be of anxious mind. For all the nations of the world seek these things; and your Father knows that you need them. Instead, seek his kingdom, and these things shall be yours as well.[7]

I didn't have many life experiences of practicing service work, so I didn't consider myself to be a good example of my Christian karma yoga ideal, yet I wanted to move in that direction. So I took over the full-time duties of an elementary school art teacher who had left half way through the school year. I struggled with the demands of the job, especially maintaining class discipline. I became so focused on being a good disciplinarian that I was losing my enthusiasm for teaching and did not feel I was effectively serving my students so I decided to quit. On the day I planned to submit my resignation, a student came up to me and joyfully asked me to look at a little wooden plaque she held in her hands. Written on the plaque was a statement acknowledging her recent Catholic confirmation as a "soldier of Christ." As I read the words, my eyes began to well up with tears, and I felt God prompting me to resist the temptation to quit my job. It did not matter if I struggled with the job and could not do it perfectly. The important thing was for me to be a soldier of Christ. I rededicated myself to practicing Christian karma yoga for Christ. Strengthened by this experience, I was able to continue working and finish out the year.

I prayed for divine guidance on how to become a better Christian karma yoga worker and better person. Instead of changing my art teaching job, I changed my attitude and approach. I had been giving every class one project and felt I had to be a hard-line enforcer of discipline. I later loosened up and gave each class a choice of four or five projects, such as painting, block printing, stick sculpture, sketching, and clay projects. Students who wanted to do similar projects sat in small groups and talked quietly in a creative atmosphere. The students no longer needed rigid discipline because they were happier with greater freedom of choice and expression. The new approach required extra planning and coordination on my part. Nevertheless, I was happier too. Without needing to be a disciplinarian, I was free to focus on inspiring my students to explore various forms of self-expression.

My employment opportunities were providing important pieces to my shadow puzzle, even though I didn't always see it at the time. In the previous job with mentally retarded clients, I had felt oppressed by the poor decisions of others in authority. In this teaching position, I was the one in authority. At first I was oppressing others but then learned to let go of imposing my authority. How I responded to others being in authority over me and how I handled being in a position of authority did not seem like meaningful pieces of the shadow puzzle. However, I would find out in the future that the authority issue was indeed a significant part of it.

Some of the more obvious pieces of the shadow puzzle would take center stage in subsequent jobs. I did not feel called to a career as an art teacher, so I applied to be an aide in the recreation department of Gaylord

Hospital, a chronic disease hospital. I did not get the job, and normally I would have exercised non-attachment, accepting this as God's Will for me. However, I felt the job was so perfect for me that I uncharacteristically complained to God with tears that there must be some mistake here. A few weeks later I got a call from the hospital telling me that the job was being given to me because the person hired never showed up for work.

After I was hired, my supervisor, Suzanne Harsanyi, told me, "Don, I know you have been hired as an aide, but I am not considering you to be an aide. I can't increase your salary, but as far as I am concerned, you are a recreation therapist, just like everyone else in our department. We work as a team of equals and have equal responsibilities. Let me explain what it means for you and I to be recreation therapists. We are here to serve our patients. Every department in our hospital has a primary focus on physical healing. Our department assists in this physical healing by taking care of an undervalued and overlooked need—the need for emotional healing. Our patients come here and carry a lot of emotional baggage. Some of them are depressed. Some of them feel like victims asking, 'Why me?' It's our job to hopefully bring some joy, laughter, and hope into their lives.

"We aren't just a recreation department. We are a *therapeutic* recreation department. Our therapeutic recreation activities are working on improving a patient's attitude. A patient with a positive attitude will have the proper motivation for healing. He will want to heal and want to live a productive life. Our department has the essential function of nourishing this desire for healing. Recreation is sometimes thought of as an extra and unnecessary aspect of the healing process, but as far as I am concerned there is nothing more important than a patient's attitude toward his own healing process." I was very inspired by Suzanne, a wonderful example of a karma yogi, whose whole life revolved around service to others.

I encountered many patients who had become paralyzed and had come to Gaylord Hospital for recovery and therapy. One of the first patients that I met was Jasper, who was about ready to be discharged. We talked only briefly, but he told me how he had become a quadriplegic. He had dived into a pool, and tragically there was no water in it. I can't imagine the horror he must have felt when he realized that his body was flying through the air toward possible death or at least great injury. I felt compassion for Jasper. It occurred to me that Jasper was experiencing the results of his own former actions in this life or more likely the fruits of his karma from past lives. Obviously I said nothing of this to him since there was the danger of him believing that I was heartlessly blaming him.

The fact that Jasper's handicap was caused by a falling accident was a reminder for me of my *falling* and *spider* themes, since both implied danger and possible death. It did not seem accidental to me that I was confronted every day with people who had handicaps. I felt these people were reminders of whatever was lurking in the recesses of my subconscious mind, which I hoped would eventually emerge as pieces of my shadow puzzle. After all, what if my hands had loosened their grip while hanging from the balcony in college or what if my feet had slipped standing on the top of Craig Castle? I would have been a patient in a hospital like this, instead of a therapist. Upon meeting patients like Jasper I often thought, "There but for the grace of God go I."

Many of our patients had undergone an amputation and came to our hospital for recovery and therapy, including obtaining a prosthetic device. I remember a very young man named Harry who had lost a leg, and he discussed with me his anguish over why this had happened to him. I didn't have any answers that I felt would help him, and I didn't offer my own opinion, because that was not considered appropriate in my position as a recreation therapist. Working with patients like Harry, who were so young, increasingly convinced me of the validity of reincarnation. I could find no reasonable explanation for Harry's amputation other than it being the karmic result of his actions from a past life.

Another reason I couldn't tell Harry about my opinion was that he might feel I was judging him or blaming him for bringing this amputation upon himself through his own actions. An even worse outcome would be for him to believe me and then indulge in self-condemnation. Instead of leading to self-condemnation, understanding karma will hopefully help us come to a place of acceptance, in which we do not see ourselves as victims of outside forces. However, in Harry's case, offering what was in my heart was more helpful than offering what was in my head.

When I looked into the eyes of patients like Jasper and Harry, I asked myself, "Am I seeing a picture of myself in a past life? Or worse, am I seeing a picture of myself in the future? Perhaps I am just seeing a picture of my fears, and nothing more." In any event, I concluded that it was part of God's plan for my life to be working with the handicapped at this time. I could tell this work was important for my personal growth because I could see I was changing. I was becoming more loving, which was my goal for spiritual growth.

Yoga philosophy equated good karma with unselfish desires, thoughts, and actions and bad karma with selfish desires, thoughts, and actions. However, it was more helpful for me to associate good karma with *loving* desires, thoughts, and actions and bad karma with *unloving* desires, thoughts, and actions. It was easier for me to focus on being loving than on being unselfish. Unselfishness is more of a mental attitude than a feeling. Love is more of a feeling than a mental attitude. The idea of giving unselfishness to God felt less meaningful to me than giving my heart to

God, so the expressions of my heart were what I felt would nourish my personal growth. Consequently, my motivation for Christian karma yoga was *love*, and the fruits of the Spirit that I sought could be summarized by love as well. As love became more of my focus, I realized my practice was actually a hybrid of two paths—the selfless-service path of karma yoga and the path of love, which is called *bhakti yoga*. My personality was more geared to bhakti yoga, but I was hoping the influence of karma yoga would help me to let go of my past selfishness.

Mrs. Harsanyi later told me she was concerned about the large number of our emphysema patients losing the ability to expand and contract their lungs and in terminal cases slowly suffocating to death. These patients often could not or did not want to participate in regularly scheduled recreation activities. Mrs. Harsanyi was frustrated by her inability to come up with a recreation strategy for meeting their needs. I volunteered to provide an alternative for them by practicing what I called "conversational therapy," which was simply the practice of being a good listener. I listened patiently to my patients' stories, and often heard the same stories repeated over and over again. But that didn't matter because I wasn't there for my own entertainment. I was there to give love as a service but felt I was also receiving the love that I gave.

In this exchange, the patients were giving to me verbally, but my role was to give non-verbally by being fully present with them and by devoting my time with them to God. Since God is love, I felt I needed to not just listen, but to listen with my heart. I felt the best way to give the fruits of my work to God was to open my heart to each patient and look past the physical condition of the body before me in order to see the divine in each one. This expression of service and love also included an aspect of *jnana yoga*, which consists of discerning the real from the unreal, the inner divine spirit from the outer illusory form of the body. In this exchange, it appeared to me that patients could always tell that they were being accepted and loved in this simple act of my being totally present. I felt God was somehow working through me to bring healing to my patients—if not to their bodies, then to their minds.

Certainly I was experiencing a sense of fulfillment myself, which made me feel my conversational therapy was the most important function of my job, although it fell outside of the usual duties of a recreation therapist. However, the most difficult aspect of this job was the sobering feeling resulting from having a conversation with a patient one day and then finding out he was dead the next day. Some patients were prepared to meet death gracefully; others, however, were confused and frightened. Those who seemed least prepared were those who described their lives as a series of regrets.

The most striking example of a story of regret was Mr. Jackson. He was an elderly man who insulted me for wearing a beard and then another time for wearing Bermuda shorts. Although I wasn't affected by his insults, I finally stopped going to his room because his actions demonstrated that my presence was upsetting him. Several weeks later at an interdisciplinary meeting I learned from a nurse that Mr. Jackson had died. She told me he had driven away all of his family with his demanding and insulting behavior. When he realized that he was dying, he tried to get his family back, but they wouldn't communicate with him. In his final days he resorted to talking to strangers in the hallways in order to try to get them to come into his room to talk to him.

I was shocked and saddened to hear this. I wondered if I had made a mistake in discontinuing my visits to him, but I, like his family, had gotten the message from his actions that he did not want me to be around. If I had continued to see him when I felt he did not want me to visit, I would have been imposing my will on him, so I did not feel too bad about my choice to stop my visits. On the other hand, I wish I had known about his change of heart so I could have been of some minor assistance as a listener and friend before he passed away. The fact that Mr. Jackson had a dramatic change of heart just before his death made a deep impression on me. He wanted forgiveness from others, I assumed, to help him forgive himself.

While providing conversational therapy to other terminal emphysema patients, I felt I was learning important lessons from them. When their faces turned a bluish color indicating the end was near, they would often share with me a laundry list of "if only's" and "what if's." One of these was Willy, who told me about his estrangement from his relatives, especially his brother. Willy said, "It was all my fault. I wish I had acted differently." His questioning eyes told me he wanted forgiveness that he didn't think he deserved or could obtain.

"Could you contact your brother to tell him how you feel?" I asked.

"I don't even know where he is. It wouldn't do any good anyway. It's too late. I'm a goner," he said with a shaky voice because of his trouble breathing.

I didn't want to intrude, yet I couldn't help but ask, "Do you believe in a higher power?"

"I don't know. I'll find out soon enough," he said with an uneasy smile. I usually didn't talk unless I was guided to say something that would be helpful. I couldn't find any words to say to Willy that would help to relieve his obvious regret and guilt. Instead I mentally gave my forgiveness to him simply by seeing the divine in him that was his reality and disregarding his opinion of himself that was not his reality. I prayed for Willy because his assessment of his short time was accurate, and he did not seem prepared to face death. Not long after he passed away, I had a dream in which I saw Willy smiling broadly and waving to me. I felt reassured that he had found out there is indeed a higher power.

Patients like Mr. Jackson and Willy drove home to me the importance of finding forgiveness, especially self-forgiveness, long before death is just around the corner, when it may be too late. Of course, it is never too late to receive forgiveness directly from God. However, the problem is that if we don't get it from others, it is hard to conclude that we deserve to forgive ourselves and deserve to be forgiven by God.

It is logical to think that karma has no exceptions since it is generally considered to be a universal law and therefore we must always reap exactly as we have sown. However, God is not limited even by universal laws and so I believed that divine grace could intercede to overcome the cause and effect nature of karma. Under normal circumstances we can perform a bad action and can invariably expect to have that bad action returned to us as a learning experience to teach us to be more loving in the future. However, through divine grace we may not have that bad action returned to us as an equivalent negative experience. This experience of divine grace will not circumvent a learning opportunity; it will just allow that same learning to be experienced in a gracious way rather than a punitive way. Divine grace is God's version of community service replacing jail time.

The law of the Old Testament was based on a Jewish understanding of God's karmic justice expressed as "an eye for an eye, and a tooth for a tooth." But I felt because of Jesus we live under a new law, which I thought of as "the law of forgiveness" or "the law of grace." A funny thing happened to Saul (later to become St. Paul) on his way to Damascus where he was going to imprison the Christians just as he had already done in Jerusalem. He was filled with a dazzling light and heard the words, "Saul, Saul, why are you persecuting me?"[8] When Saul asked who was speaking to him, the answer came, "I am Jesus of Nazareth whom you are persecuting."[9] If karmic justice had prevailed, Saul would have been punished for persecuting the Christians in Jerusalem. Yet instead of a karmic punishment of justice, Saul received forgiveness. Saul did not avoid his learning opportunity to become more loving, but rather learned more about love through divine grace than he would have learned through the punishment that karmic justice required.

Saul's experience is a dramatic example of a less noticeable expression of the law of forgiveness that occurs in our daily lives today. God's grace brings into our daily experience opportunities to express love positively in order to learn the same lesson that the negative effects of bad karma would have taught us. The good news is that God gives us these Christmas presents of grace, perhaps even quite frequently. The bad news is that these gifts all too often go unnoticed and therefore remain unopened. I wanted to pay attention to God's Hand in my life. I felt that the service work before me at Gaylord Hospital was God's grace helping me to learn lessons in how to love that would make the return of some of my negative karma unnecessary. However, there was no way for me to know for certain if that was the case. In any event I felt it was important for me to take advantage of opportunities to express love, and I found these opportunities on a daily basis at work.

I mentioned previously that my shadow puzzle pieces, which seemed disconnected, had a common link of strong emotional content. It occurred to me that one emotion in particular was more prominent than any other— the emotion of fear. The spider theme and the falling theme both pointed to danger and possible death, which clearly related to this one emotion of fear. My puzzle pieces were suppressed into my subconscious mind because they were the parts of my mind that were unacceptable to me— in short, the parts of my mind that were fearful to me. I knew that the solution to my fears was to bring them to my conscious mind and face them. I asked myself, "What are the fearful things that I might want to suppress?" The answer I got was that these may be things that I felt guilty about. This raised the next question, "What do I feel guilty about?" In part, I felt guilty about my past because I hadn't yet completely forgiven myself for the self-centered years prior to giving my life to Christ. That is why Mr. Jackson's and Willy's struggles with guilt and seeking for forgiveness in the face of death were such a wake-up call for me, helping me realize my own need for forgiveness and the necessity for not waiting until it was too late to find it.

This awareness did not resolve the puzzle. It just made it clearer to me that the puzzle couldn't be resolved entirely on the intellectual level. It would require learning how to love and forgive others and myself. Sometimes people in helping professions are in denial about their own needs for help and healing. I was very aware of my needs in this regard. My service work was helping me to open my heart. However, I felt I had a very long way to go. I realized that firmly establishing an ongoing loving and forgiving state of mind could only be accomplished over time through encounters with others.

One of the most significant encounters I had in my recreation therapy work was with Mr. Days, an elderly black man. He was a tuberculosis patient who had relapses because he did not remember to take his medication at home. Consequently, he was in a chronic disease hospital only to ensure that he took his medication. I enjoyed my conversational therapy with him because he had a very upbeat personality. Leaving his usual cheerful tone, one day he said in all seriousness, "I want you to do something for me."

"What's that?" I asked.

"You see all these people in this hospital suffering. I want you to write a book to tell people how not to suffer."

"How do you know that I can do that?"

"Oh, I know you can do it. I can tell you can do it for sure. I have no doubt."

"Thank you for your confidence in me. I'm not sure if I can help people not to suffer at all, but maybe I can show people how to reduce their suffering by helping them find meaning in their lives. I will see what I can do about your idea," I said. My ego was flattered by Mr. Days, but I genuinely felt that the Holy Spirit had a hand in his words, which inspired me to start writing a Christian meditation manual and this autobiography. It would take a few decades before my first meditation manual was published and even longer for the autobiography, but I always remembered Mr. Days sharing his inspirational words, which gave me a very specific long-term motivation that made my own life more meaningful.

---

1. Paramahansa Yogananda, *Autobiography of a Yogi*, (Los Angeles, CA: Self-Realization Fellowship [1946] 1971), p. 149.

2. Ibid, p. 283.

3. The Self-Realization Fellowship has labeled its form of yoga as a secret, but methods similar to kriya yoga are described in *Kundalini Yoga for the West*, by Radha, a disciple of Shivananda, Satchidananda's guru. A preliminary technique leading up to kriya yoga, "Hong-Sau" mantra meditation technique, is noted in Chapter 7 of that book. A partial description of the initial stage of kriya yoga can be found in Chapter 9.

4. John 14:2, CCD.

5. Luke 6:37, RSV.

6. Galatians 5:22-23, RSV.

7. Luke 12:29-31, RSV.

8. Acts 22:7, RSV.

9. Acts 22:8, RSV.

YOGANANDA

PRACTICING THE PRAYER OF THE HEART

6

YOGA RETREAT AND
THE LITTLE ASHRAM

≈ ◦ ≈

Since I was learning how to balance my Christian faith with my yoga practice, I was excited to hear about a yoga retreat that Brother David Steindl-Rast was helping to coordinate. The retreat would be a meeting of East and West, of yoga and Christianity. It was called the "Yoga Ecumenical Summer Program" and was to be held in the Catskill Mountains of New York. While attending this retreat in 1972, I was inspired by meeting so many other seekers who were practicing yoga, not merely for physical health, but as a means of growing spiritually.

I struck up a friendship with a young man named Joel, who like me was practicing yoga as a way of opening to Christ. He was also repeating the Name of Jesus as a meditation practice. At the end of the retreat I was touched by his gift to me of the book entitled *Writings from the Philokalia on Prayer of the Heart*. I was inspired by these writings of early Christian monks, who described how to call upon the Name of Jesus as a devotional prayer. I found the following quotation from this Russian devotional classic to be particularly meaningful:

> Collectedness is given to the mind above all by our Lord Jesus Christ when we call on His holy name in our heart and faith. This natural method of descending into the heart by way of breathing, and seclusion in a quiet dimly lit place, as well as all other similar things, are merely certain aids to this.[1]

The technique of the Prayer of the Heart focuses on bringing your full attention into the heart and repeating the Name of Jesus in coordination with the natural rhythm of breathing. This technique of prayer, which I was practicing at the time, was similar to yoga practices of meditation. However, the success of this mental practice of attunement does not rest on the specifics of the technique, but rather on divine grace:

The first, or rather the greatest and most important, thing on which the success of this mental doing depends is help of Divine grace, together with a heart-felt, pure and undistracted calling on our Lord Jesus Christ....[2]

I wanted to emulate these early Christian monks—both in their practice of inviting divine grace and in seeking purity of heart—focusing on Christ as my primary goal, yet also open to yoga practices as a secondary influence. Prior to this retreat I had felt somewhat isolated, so I appreciated the fellowship of like-minded seekers. I recognized the benefit of receiving guidance from others who had walked the spiritual path longer than I had. While on this summer retreat I took advantage of the opportunity to seek advice from Brother David. I told him, "I don't love God enough."

He answered, "Well, what if you said, 'I love God enough'?"

"I didn't think of it that way. But how can I be more loving?" I inquired.

"Respond to God. Every person you meet is another opportunity to meet God. In every situation respond to God. As you respond to God you will grow in learning how to love. But don't be concerned with evaluating yourself. Perhaps you are like the person who wants to see if his flowers are growing, so he pulls them out by the roots and examines them. It's not so important to examine your growth on the path as it is to put one foot in front of the other and walk the path."

There were two other coordinators for the retreat. One was Swami Satchidananda, the founder of the *Integral Yoga Center*, which I frequented in Hartford, Connecticut. The other was Rabbi Gliberman. I recently came across a reference to him while reading *The Mystic Heart*, written by Wayne Teasdale, an *interspirituality* leader. I was surprised to learn that he had grown up in Hartford and had been inspired by a talk given by Rabbi Gliberman at the same local yoga center that I had attended. Brother Wayne felt that the Rabbi perfectly summarized the open-hearted attitude needed to bridge the gap between one spiritual tradition and another:

In exploring other traditions and in embracing them, remember, it isn't a question of *instead of*—Buddhism instead of Christianity, or Christianity instead of Islam—but rather of *in addition to*, that is, in addition to Buddhism, Christianity, in addition to Christianity, Islam.[3]

Because this quotation highlighted the same time, place, and sentiments that were so much a part of my own experience, it brought back nostalgic memories, yet its message is just as relevant now as it was then. In the 1970s I encountered many seekers who had given up Christianity entirely and replaced it with the yoga path. Back then there were only a few who wanted to synthesize the East and West in the way that Rabbi Gliberman so eloquently expressed. I sought this blending, as did Wayne Teasdale, but to my knowledge our paths unfortunately did not cross.

As the Ecumenical Summer Program was drawing to a close, I discussed with some other participants, Rusty, Ron, and Frank, how we might be able to extend the benefits we had already received through our spiritual fellowship. As a result of those discussions, we collectively decided to live together for eight months in our own little ashram, which we established in Milford, Connecticut, at a house right on the beachfront. Each morning we gathered together to practice the yoga disciplines of meditation, postures, and breathing techniques. However, I was the only one of our group who was committed to both yoga and following Christ.

I made Tiffany-style stained glass lampshades of my own design to support myself. Ron White was a craftsman who made fine jewelry. Frank Asch was a successful author and illustrator of children's books. My closest relationship was with Rusty Bush, who was artistic and perceptive. For example, he noticed that every time we went to the bank and I had money in my hand, I became nervous. It was true, yet I didn't notice this until he pointed it out. One day I conducted an experiment to look into this further. To get my own reaction, I took a twenty-dollar bill and burned it. The result was a feeling of freedom and exhilaration. Even though I needed financial resources for daily living, I viewed money with ambivalence because I saw it as a potential stumbling block that could derail my spiritual purposes.

As an additional means of financial support, I applied at this time for a counselor position at a home for disturbed boys. During the job screening, the interviewer gave me a psychological test and then explained the results. First he made sure I had understood the directions for the test to confirm that the results were accurate. Then he said, "You got the lowest score for ambition that I have ever recorded for this test. You have absolutely no ambition for any of the things most people want. Can you explain that?"

I told him my ambitions and goals were spiritual, not material, and that satisfied him. I got the job but didn't last long. The first day in the house six boys sat down for the dinner I had prepared. Before taking a single bite, they all simultaneously ran in different directions—running out doors and even jumping through windows. I got them all back after this intentional rite of initiation—designed just for me. However, I had to quit because I discovered that the job required me to physically restrain clients. Even though I could do this without harming them, I felt it was a form of forcefully imposing my will, and I could not reconcile this activity either with my karma yoga or my Christian spiritual ideals.

In our mini-ashram we identified four household chores, which we shared. We established a rotating schedule so each of us had a different individual chore every month. When we finally decided to end our temporary ashram, all three of my house mates admitted that they did not actually do their chores and that they appreciated that I did do them. All along I was fully aware that no one else was doing the chores and that I could have reasonably complained about this, but chose not to do so. Why? Because I thought of my mother. I recalled how she had been such a perfect model to me of the selfless service of karma yoga. And most importantly she never once complained to anyone about others, meaning me, not accepting responsibility. I consciously decided to follow her example, not with resentment, but with gratitude for being able to be of service, regardless of the choices of others.

Although the four monthly household chores were not collectively embraced, we did all take turns making dinner. One time when I was cooking, I was using a pressure cooker. When the food was cooked, I took the small metal rocker off the top of the pressure cooker suddenly releasing a stream of hot steam gushing straight up like Old Faithful at Yellowstone National Park. Observing this, Rusty exclaimed, "That's not the way you are supposed to release the steam."

I smiled and said, "Well, we all have different ways of letting off steam. This is my way of doing it."

"I see you are making a pun," Rusty acknowledged. "But the directions say that you are supposed to put the pressure cooker in water to cool it so there's no pressure left in the cooker."

"Do you always follow the appropriate directions in life? As long as you aren't hurting anyone, isn't if fun sometimes to just do what you feel like doing?" I asked.

"I thought that with mechanical products it's always best to follow the manufacturer's directions, but it actually never would have occurred to me to do what you just did. I guess it doesn't really matter whether the directions are followed or not, as long as no harm is done," he concluded.

"You just want to do what is right. But I think there may be many ways that are right. A lot of people are like sheep traveling along in life and doing what the directions of society tell them to do. My nightmare is to live an unconscious life like one of those sheep. But I don't have to tell you that. You usually question everything," I said, referring to his inquisitiveness during our many long talks.

Rusty was especially curious about divine matters, yet he described himself as an agnostic, even though he had been brought up in a Jewish household. He encouraged me to give him reasons why I believed in God, because he wanted faith, but could not believe in what he admittedly did not understand. I remember one conversation in particular in which I told him, "There was a holy man who was talking to an unbeliever in one room, and they went to a second room to continue their conversation. Finally they returned to the first room, and there was a large globe of the world on a table. The unbeliever asked, 'How did that globe get there, because it wasn't here a few minutes ago?'

"'It just appeared all by itself,' declared the holy man.

"'You must think I am a fool. It could not have just appeared. Someone must have put it there.'

"'Exactly! The world could not have just appeared. Someone must have put it here. Someone must have put you here, too,' asserted the holy man."

Rusty asked, "How about the scientific explanation of the evolution of life as the answer?"

"So you would rather believe in science than some other reason? Isn't there a scientific law that says for every action there is an equal and opposite reaction?" I asked.

"Yes. So what?"

"Then you believe in cause and effect, and that every effect must have a cause?"

"Yes, I believe in the law of cause and effect," Rusty admitted.

"The world is the effect. What is the cause?"

"As I said, how about scientific evolution and chance?"

"If this is true, where did the raw materials come from that allowed evolution and chance to produce the world? The raw materials of the universe are the effect, but where is the First Cause that produced these raw materials? If you believe in cause and effect, then you must also believe there was a First Cause that brought the raw materials of the universe into existence."

"How about the 'Big Bang'?"

"But who caused the 'Big Bang'? Can the universe itself be an effect without a cause? To be more personal, you are an effect. What is your cause?"

"I don't really know. That's why I'm an agnostic."

"You really only have two choices. Do you believe that you caused yourself?"

"No."

"Then the only other choice you have is that something other than yourself caused you. That something else is what is called God, who is the First Cause." I held up my right hand and said, "Look at this. Four fingers and a thumb, bone, skin, blood, capillaries, arteries, veins, tendons, nerves, nails, cartilage, and joints. If I cut it, it will heal. You and I both like to make art work with our hands, yet you and I will never make anything close to the masterpiece of this hand. Do you really think it is logical that evolution and chance made this hand?"

Rusty listened, but he was unconvinced. He generally concluded our conversations by saying, as he did on this occasion, "I don't know."

An experience at this temporary ashram gave me what felt like one more piece of the shadow puzzle, having to do with falling. In addition to regular sitting meditation I also spent time in lying-down meditation during part of each day. During one such time I suddenly realized I was floating above my body, which was below, still lying on my bed. The realization of having this experience, called *astral traveling*, made me fearful and shocked me immediately back into the body. My consciousness returned so quickly into the body that I felt a slight pain in my left shoulder. Afterwards I stayed in bed to ponder the experience. I recalled that in my childhood I had experienced this same kind of astral traveling.

I felt pride at having experienced astral traveling, but as the Bible teaches, "Pride goes before destruction, and a haughty spirit before a fall."[4] My bedroom was on the second floor, and I got out of my bed to go downstairs. However, I fell down the stairs and dislocated my left shoulder. It was the same shoulder that hurt a few minutes earlier after the astral traveling experience. I asked Rusty to put my shoulder back in, and I offered to tell him how. Nevertheless, he did not feel comfortable making the attempt because he was concerned he might do more harm than good, so I had to go to the hospital. I felt this experience of falling down the stairs was another in the growing series of life events that were hopefully leading me in the direction of solving the shadow puzzle.

I didn't tell Rusty about the astral traveling precursor to the accident since such experiences are by-products of seeking God and can be diversions from the real goal of direct relationship with God. Also I had learned that it's generally not a good idea to share spiritual experiences, because it encourages those involved to compare their spiritual progress. In addition, I was concerned about my tendency toward pride if I shared my experiences. Yet there were exceptions when I had a prompting from the Holy Spirit to share personal experiences. One such time occurred when I was having an intense conversation with Rusty. He couldn't understand why he was so uncertain about spiritual matters and why I seemed so certain.

"Let me tell you a story that explains my concern about spiritual belief," Rusty said. "Shiva and his consort were flying over the earth, and they looked down on a high mountain plateau. Shiva's consort pointed and said, 'There on that mountain is the holy man, Chandra. You are fortunate to have such a devotee.'

"Shiva said, 'Chandra is not a holy man. He has nothing to do with me.'

"'What do you mean?' asked his consort. 'He has devoted his whole life to you. He repeats your name constantly—Shiva, Shiva, Shiva.'

"Shiva insisted, 'I know nothing of Chandra. He knows nothing of me.'

"'But he is walking with his eyes closed seeking for you, calling out ceaselessly to you so he can find you.'

"'He doesn't want me. You are mistaken,' Shiva informed his consort.

"'Look!' she exclaimed. 'He is walking toward the edge of the mountain and will surely fall off. Rescue him.'

"'All right. When he falls off and calls my name, then I will rescue him.'

"Chandra with his eyes closed walked to the edge of the mountain. He fell off hollering 'Aaaahhhhhhhhhhhhhhh,' all the way to the bottom.

"Shiva said, 'Do you see now? If Chandra had called my name, I would have rescued him. I told you he was not my devotee.' So, Don, I don't want to be repeating some affirmation and not really believe in what I am affirming. I cannot be sure I won't be like Ganesh, seemingly devoting my life to God, and then finding out God cannot or will not rescue me. After all, many good people die without a definitive reassurance that God exists. How do I know I would not be devoting my life to an illusion that has no saving power? I cannot be sure that God isn't just an illusion or delusion that men make up to try to make sense out of nonsense. I know you repeat the name of Jesus, and I don't want to be disrespectful, but how can you be sure there is anyone out there at the other end hearing your prayer?"

I responded, "About three or four years ago I became interested in yoga at a time when I was still living with my parents. I was not interested in practicing *kundalini yoga* because I had heard that raising the kundalini could be dangerous. In particular I was aware of the danger of practicing advanced breathing practices before the body is ready to handle the energy that such techniques release. Nevertheless, even using the traditional form of yoga I was practicing, I made the mistake that many beginners make of presuming to be more advanced than I was. Consequently, I used common breathing techniques, which are normally beneficial; however, I neglected to practice these in moderation.

"One morning after completing a series of breathing practices in my bedroom, I stood up to do the sun salutation, with its sequence of twelve postures. At the beginning of it, I raised my arms overhead and looked up. Immediately I felt powerful waves of electric-like energy flashing through my body. This was the kundalini suddenly being released from the base of the spine upward. If you pump air forcefully into a tire tube with a weak spot, it will have a blowout. Similar to a tire tube with a weak spot, my body was not prepared to handle the force of the kundalini energy.

"The experience was extremely painful, and I felt as though I was being electrocuted since it would not stop. All I could do was repeatedly mentally call out the Name of 'Jesus' in the same way that a drowning man would call for help. Somehow I was still standing, but felt like I was surely about to fall since I had lost control of my body. When the electric-like shock waves didn't stop after invoking the Name of Jesus, I stopped calling His name, and I doubted just for an instant. Then with faith, knowing there was nowhere else to turn, I called out again with all my heart, 'Jesus.'

"Immediately after I reasserted the Name of Jesus, I felt the electric-like energy leave my body. I discovered my right hand was gripped around the glass knob on the door to my room. It seemed that the electric-like energy had exited through the right hand. But I had absolutely no awareness of putting my hand on the doorknob. I attributed the grabbing of the doorknob to an involuntary act accomplished by the Holy Spirit as an answer to calling out in prayer to Jesus as my Savior.

"You asked how I know that there is someone at the other end hearing my prayer. This experience is how I know. First I called His Name without faith and that did not work. Then I called His Name *with* faith and that *did* work. However, I don't think a *perfect* faith is required. In the Bible a man asked Jesus to heal his son, and Jesus asked if the man had faith. The man replied, 'I believe; help my unbelief!'[5] and his son was healed by Jesus. You can pray for faith. Once I made a sincere prayer to God in which I asked for a faith that could not be taken from me, because I was as uncertain about God as you are now. That prayer was answered in a rather dramatic fashion, which I do not want to get into now. But the point is that prayers are answered. They are not always answered immediately or in the way you expect, yet they are answered. You can ask for help from God with your faith, and I will be very surprised if your prayer for help is not answered." Subsequently I prayed for Rusty that he would, God willing, receive the faith that he sought.

This conversation, with the story of Chandra falling and my kundalini experience of almost falling, was another reminder to me of the shadow puzzle with its falling theme. It was one of the last conversations I had with Rusty. After we completed our eight-month commitment of living together, we went our separate ways. Rusty lived the little children's fantasy of running off and joining a traveling carnival. But the carnival life did not last very long. I got a letter from Rusty at a later date giving me the good and surprising news he had joined a non-traditional Christian monastic order.

---

1. E. Kadloubovsky and G. E. H. Palmer, translators, *Writings from the Philokalia on Prayer of the Heart*, translated from the Russian text, 'Dobrotolubiye,' (London: Faber and Faber Ltd., [1951]1971, 1975) p. 195 (also reprinted in 1992).

2. Ibid, p. 195.

3. Wayne Teasdale, *The Mystic Heart* (Novato, CA: New World Library, [1999] 2001), p. 49.

4. Proverbs 16:18, RSV.

5. Mark 9:24, RSV.

7

JERUSALEM

~ • ~

In 1973 when I arrived in Israel and stepped off the plane, instantly I got the strong impression that I was coming home. I wondered how many past lives I had spent in this holy place. At the time I was participating in the Hope Ecumenical Seminar, a six-week spiritual gathering of about seventy seekers from all religions and from all over the world. Somehow I was the only participant who didn't belong to some religious order or group. We spent equal time studying and visiting sites related to Christianity, Judaism, and Islam. Our itinerary ranged all the way from climbing Masada and swimming in the super-salty Dead Sea in the north to ascending Mt. Sinai and swimming in the crystal clear water of the Red Sea in the south.

However, much of the time was spent in the Old City of Jerusalem. It seemed appropriate that I had to bow my head to enter the cramped space of the Holy Sepulcher, where tradition says Jesus was buried. I kneeled and prayed there, but seemingly right away I heard a loud clanging sound. It was the attendant outside, banging his large cane on the stone floor to signal, "Get out of there so others can come in!" Our group also went outside the walls of the Old City to the reputed site of Calvary and then to the nearby Garden Tomb that many believe is the real burial place of Jesus.

In my unscheduled time I explored Jerusalem on my own. I went to pray at the top room of a building on Mt. Zion, which is believed to be the place where the Holy Spirit, appearing as fire in parted tongues, descended upon the disciples of Jesus. Right after that, at the suggestion of a fellow seminar participant, I went to a house near Mt. Zion to meet Sandra Barry, who was one of the best examples of love that I have encountered in my life.

Sandra explained, "I had been living a normal life in Ireland when one day I heard a voice speak to me. The voice told me to give love to everyone and not be concerned about any needs in the world, because everything would be provided. Nevertheless, I thought I might be insane or possessed by the devil. I prayed fervently for the voice to go away, but the voice would not stop. I was in great anguish and cried tearfully to God for help. I prayed for God to show me if the voice was from the devil or if I had some form of insanity. In response to my prayer, I was shown three bright lights. As I looked upon them, they merged into one glorious light. I was told that this was the mystery of the Holy Trinity. After this experience I never doubted that this voice was from a divine origin.

"Then one day the voice told me to sell everything and leave for Israel. I asked the voice why I was being guided to go to a foreign country, but was not told the answer. I was told only that I would be shown what I needed to know when I needed to know it. I gathered that I was being asked to have faith that God would be lovingly in charge of my life and the lives of my family if I allowed Him to be. My husband was skeptical at first, but after praying together, we decided to follow the guidance and trust in God. We sold everything and set out for Israel. But on our journey we ran out of money and only got as far as Greece. Then some kind people we met there gave us just enough money to complete our trip to Israel."

Sandra told me when I met her that God still hadn't fully revealed His Plan for her, her husband, and her children. However, she felt she would be starting some kind of spiritual community in the future. Through the generosity of others she and her family were given the place where they were living, which had only the barest of necessities. When I visited for the last time, I brought a bag of food for her from the Jerusalem market place. Sandra gave me a cup of hot tea. Not wanting to make her feel uncomfortable, I drank every drop of it without telling her how awful it tasted because of the poor quality of the tap water in Jerusalem. Sandra informed me that she had heard of an Arab boy who did not have a family and who had one leg amputated. No one wanted to adopt him, but she welcomed him into her life and home, even though her living space was very small and meager. She also invited me to stay with her, and I was tempted to stay because of the strong impression I had gotten on my arrival. I decided not to accept her offer, frankly because I lacked the humility to live in the cramped and poor conditions in which she lived.

In contrast to the loving symbol that Sandra represented to me, I also met her opposite counterpart in the seemingly innocent face of an Arab boy. On my own I went to the Old City and placed a written prayer in a crevice between the stones of the Wailing Wall. Afterwards I was browsing shops and bargaining with different shopkeepers for the best price on a gold Alexandrite ring that I had decided to buy as a gift for my mother. The boy came to me and insisted that he had a bargain down the street for me, if I just followed him. Something did not seem right, so I told him I preferred to stay in the area where I was. I went to another nearby shop, and the boy approached me a second time, but I declined his offer again. I went to a third shop, and the boy positioned himself near the doorway. Without prompting from me, the Arab shopkeeper told me, "There is a boy at the door. Don't listen to him if he talks to you, and don't go where he tells you to go." I thanked the shopkeeper and bought one of his rings. When I left, the boy again approached me. I declined his offer a third time without being rude to him, and this time he began cursing me and then ran away.

The most emotional experience I had on the trip occurred when I visited Yad Vashim, the war memorial honoring the Jews who died in the Holocaust. I saw the soap made from human bodies and the ovens used to incinerate bodies, yet I was most struck by a photograph. It was a picture of a single Nazi soldier pointing a rifle at a naked man and woman. They were clutching each other with utter horror on their faces awaiting the bullets that would soon end their lives. I began crying and went outside to cry alone.

Another place I wanted to visit was the Mosque of Omar. It is revered by Muslims as the place where the Prophet Muhammad ascended to heaven. It is honored by Jews as the location of the Holy of Holies in Solomon's Temple. The mosque is also called the Dome of the Rock—believed to be the site where Abraham, the father of both the Jews and Muslims, brought his son Isaac to be sacrificed and instead built an altar to God. The seminar organizers told us that it was inappropriate for our very large group of mostly Christians to go inside all at once. On one of my unscheduled days, I went to this mosque and performed the ritual cleansing and prayer that we had been taught in our lectures about Islam. Then I was allowed to go inside to see the exquisite craftsmanship of the mosque and to pray there.

However, I learned even more about Islam from another memorable event that occurred on my trip to the Holy Land. It was arranged by two Protestant ministers, Jason and Gerard, who had managed to schedule a meeting with the acknowledged spiritual leader of Sufism in the Middle East. Most religions have sects that center on experiencing the mystical side of spirituality, and Sufism performs that function within the larger context of the Islamic religion. I asked if I could come along for their private audience and the ministers agreed. At the meeting the Sufi leader inquired, "Why do Christians serve wine at their worship services when it is well known that wine causes men to do despicable things?" It was a logical question for him because traditional Islam bans alcohol.

Jason explained, "Alcohol, if used in excess can cause drunkenness, but in a Christian service only a sip of wine is taken. Christians believe that invoking the blessing of God makes this bit of wine into a spiritual food."

To elaborate on this answer I was going to say that snake venom is a dangerous thing if a person is bitten by a snake. However, scientists have discovered that snake venom can be administered as a form of medication for a certain type of rare disease. So the value of snake venom depends upon how it is used, and the same is true of how wine is used. But I never offered my explanation. As I tried to speak up, Gerard, sitting on a mat right next to me, poked me in the side. I figured maybe Gerard thought that because of my youth I might inadvertently say something offensive.

I noticed that the Sufi leader was fingering a set of beads while he was simultaneously fully participating in the conversation. Presumably, he was using the Islamic prayer technique of repeating the name of Allah. Similarly, I was mentally calling upon the Name of Jesus and was content to be a listener, not a speaker for the rest of the conversation.

At one point Gerard asked the Sufi leader, "Is there anything in your scripture related to what Christians refer to as 'the Apocalypse'?"

The Sufi leader responded, "We believe that there will be an Anti-Christ who will come. He will have a patch over his eye because he will be injured. He will appear to die and then reappear." I got the impression that without saying his name the Sufi leader was actually referring to Israeli General Moshe Dayan, who wore a patch over one eye. At the end of the private audience we thanked the Sufi leader for letting us visit with him. I felt that Gerard was trying to rush us along as we were leaving. We were already outside at a distance from the Sufi leader, who was standing at the doorway, when I waved goodbye and said loudly, "Shalom." As we hurriedly walked away, I asked Gerard why he had poked me in the side— apparently to keep me from speaking up. Gerard explained, "He thought you were Jewish. He had only agreed to meet some Christian preachers and had not agreed to meet with a Jewish person. Couldn't you see his expression? It was all he could do to contain himself."

Maybe he was praying on his beads so continuously just to retain his patience with me. I was wearing glasses, had a beard, and an olive complexion. When I introduced myself as 'Don Giacobbe,' the Sufi leader most likely did not hear an Italian American name. Instead, he probably heard the similarly pronounced Jewish name 'Don Jacoby.' According to Gerard the Sufi leader was already upset just by my apparently Jewish presence, but the absolute clincher happened as we were leaving. Gerard clarified, "When he heard you say 'Shalom,' he thought you were intentionally insulting him. As a sign of respect you were supposed to use the Islamic term, 'Salaam.'"

At age twenty-eight, I was the youngest participant in the seminar and obviously the most inexperienced. My immaturity also became apparent to me in my encounter with the elderly Archbishop of Israel. This Archbishop would be participating in a formal dinner held at the Tantur Ecumenical Institute, on the main road between Jerusalem and Bethlehem, where the seminar participants were staying. I volunteered to help with serving for the dinner. Half way through the dinner Sister Karen handed me a bottle of wine and instructed me to ask the guests if they wanted more wine. But Sister Karen specifically told me, "When you get to the Archbishop, don't ask him if he wants any more wine. If you ask him, he will say, 'No,' because in his position as an archbishop he will not want to appear to be immoderate. Instead of asking him, just go over and start pouring, and he will accept the extra wine and avoid appearing to be immoderate."

I nodded my agreement to her instructions and proceeded around the large room from person to person. I remembered what Sister Karen had said and intended to carry out her instructions, but when I got to the Archbishop, I felt like I would be imposing my will on him if I didn't ask. Just as I had asked everyone else, I inquired, "Would you like some more wine?" The Archbishop gave a gesture with his hand and a shake of his head to indicate, "No." It was only after he turned down the extra wine that I realized that I had made a mistake.

When I had gone all around the room, I returned to Sister Karen, and she confronted me sternly, "I told you he wouldn't take the wine if you asked him. Why did you ask him?"

"You were right. I should not have asked him. I thought maybe I would have been imposing my will on him by not asking, but I was mistaken. I am very sorry." Although Sister Karen accepted my apology, her face clearly showed her disappointment. To call this immaturity on my part would be an oversimplification. I really did not want to impose my will on the Archbishop, but on the other hand, I had given my word to Sister Karen that I would carry out her instructions in this situation. By overruling her will in my actions, I had imposed my will on her. Thus my excuse was a rationalization for my own willfulness. Reading the writings of the early Christian monks, I had often come across their emphasis on *obedience* as a virtue. I had always thought obedience was not an important character trait, but after this experience I took another look at this virtue.

I realized that obedience relates to a willingness to follow God's Will, which I consciously wanted to do. My lack of obedience meant I was giving preference to my own opinion without sensitivity to the opinions of others or to the "Opinion" of God. It occurred to me that my problem with obedience had its roots in pride, which was and remains an ongoing concern of mine. My saying "Shalom" instead of "Salaam" to the Sufi leader and my disregard of Sister Karen's wishes were similar mistakes. Both involved my lack of obedience in the sense of following my own will rather than seeking to respond to God's Will. It relates to the advice that Brother David had given me about responding to God.

In my unwillingness to respond to God, I think I was facing my past problems with authority figures, such as some past teachers, former bosses at work, and specifically my father. It was not that I was overtly antagonistic to authority, but that I had retained some past resentments and resistance. I have heard it said, "Whatever you resist will persist!" Consequently I thought I would have to face this problem again until I learned to accept authority graciously, without inner resistance.

A factor to consider here is the depth of my relationship with God. I mentioned earlier that after my return to Christ, I no longer had problems with my sexual impulses and I returned my heart to God and away from the distractions of the world. I considered the American dream to be just that—a dream of success at the form level. The dream could come true in the form of money, power, prestige, or sexual fulfillment, but all of these seemed illusory to me. After all, a dream that comes true is still only a dream, not ultimate Reality, and the Reality of God, the transcendental Ground of Being, is what I wanted. Jesus did not seek the illusions of the world, and I did not want to make these a priority in my life either. After a time of thoughtful consideration, I decided to increase my efforts to follow the example of Jesus by making a commitment to practice celibacy. I considered myself to be a *monk in the world*. (Specifically how this decision came about will be explained in a later chapter.) Since I was a monk, I thought of myself as being, in a sense, "married" to God, although I felt limited in my ability to love. Since God is the ultimate authority figure, I realized that my fear of authority was probably related to a fear of God. In the "Our Father" prayer, I was taught to address God as my Father, but because my human father had been such a fear figure for me, I couldn't easily equate God the Father with Unconditional Love. It was easier for me to accept love from Jesus, but I wanted to feel that same love directly from God. I felt I would have to resolve my issue with authority in order to increasingly open up to the love of God.

Although I had not yet received formal yoga teacher training, I taught yoga classes to other interested participants of the seminar. This karma yoga service of teaching was placing me in the role of being an authority figure myself, and this role reversal was a positive way of changing my perspective so I could see the value of authority. After all, the yoga class would not be effective if the participants were not appropriately obedient to my instructions on how to perform postures and breathing practices.

I didn't expect to see anyone I knew half way around the world, so I was pleasantly surprised to see Brother David Steindl-Rast again. He was one of the guest speakers for the seminar and talked to us about the meaning of the ecumenical movement. He pointed out that the word "ecumenical" was derived from a Greek word for "house," and then he elaborated upon the many different meanings of this word. Similarly he talked about the word "church" as meaning the Lord's House. In addition to the word *church* meaning a place of worship, it more importantly means the whole of God's people united by one Father. Brother David talked about the house and the church being the temple of each person's body, the dwelling place for our One Spirit that we all share. I cannot remember how Brother David marvelously interweaved all these meanings of house and church, but do

BROTHER DAVID STEINDL-RAST

JERUSALEM'S WAILING WALL AND MOSQUE OF OMAR

remember being inspired by his explanation of the ecumenical movement of which we were all a part. Like the seventy followers who were sent out into the world by Jesus to announce the coming of God's kingdom, we were each going to return to our separate houses on earth with the message that we are all part of God's world-wide community. Yes, we each have different rooms that expressed our distinctive sectarian callings to God, but all these rooms are in fact part of God's House where our spirits find Oneness, which transcends all sectarian boundaries.

I had a few private conversations with Brother David, who stayed with us for one of the six weeks. I followed his recommendation to visit a Zen Buddhist center in Jerusalem. When I entered this center, I forgot to take off my shoes and was quickly questioned by a Japanese monk. I could tell by the concerned look on his face that he wanted to know if I was a tourist intruder, who came to look rather than to meditate. I apologized for my mistake and reassured him that I had come to meditate. I was allowed to participate in a half-hour meditation and sat in full lotus as was my custom at that time. Although loud sounds could be clearly heard from the busy street traffic of cars and people, there was a serenity in this place of worship that could be felt, and I was grateful for my opportunity to visit.

Another of Brother David's recommendations that I followed was to visit a certain Englishman in Jerusalem. He was an Anglican priest named John, who practiced yoga as an expression of his Christian faith. To symbolize his joining of East and West he wore the saffron-colored robe of the *sannyasin*, the yogi who has renounced seeking the goals of the world. I visited him three times and was impressed by his spiritual dedication. I told him I was considering staying in Jerusalem and inquired about the possibility of staying with him, but he explained that his space was limited. We prayed together, and then he said, "I think you have the 'Jerusalem syndrome.'"

"What's that?" I asked.

"Visitors come to Israel, and specifically to Jerusalem, and become overwhelmed with the feeling that they have been here before. Some of them believe they are reliving past lives, but mostly it's a feeling of belonging and falling in love with this place. That's the 'Jerusalem syndrome.' It's a very common occurrence. Some visitors do belong and stay when they had no prior plans to do so. Other visitors get caught up in the illusion that Jerusalem has more of God than anywhere else. But whether you decide to stay or go, if your heart is set on God, you can be at home anywhere. After all, He is inside you." I felt the Holy Spirit was speaking to me through his words and decided to let go of my infatuation with Jerusalem. My return to America turned out to be a wise choice since I was able to avoid the Israeli and Arab conflict, called the Yom Kippur War of October 6, 1973.

8

THE HOUSE OF PRAYER

~ • ~

While I was in Jerusalem, Brother David gave me a third important recommendation, which provided me with a concrete reason for returning to America. He told me to consider staying at the House of Prayer he had founded as an ecumenical retreat center, designed to be a blending of East and West. After the seminar in Jerusalem, I lived for nine months in Gloucester, Massachusetts, at the House of Prayer, adjacent to a Jesuit retreat center, Eastern Point Retreat. The House of Prayer was run by four Catholic nuns, and one of them, Sister Sarah, was the director. She had an artificial leg that she often took off, but about which she never complained. One day at dinner I asked Sister Sarah if there was any meat in the soup, even though she knew I was a vegetarian. She told me there was no meat, yet as I was eating, I noticed a small piece of suspicious looking pink food floating in my soup. "This pink stuff looks like meat. Are you sure there is no meat in here?" I inquired.

Sister Sarah said with a smile, "Well, there is so little meat in there that it won't make any difference." I was dumbfounded. I stopped eating the soup, but I didn't say anything because I had learned to expect the unexpected from Sister Sarah. Another time she walked into the bathroom without knocking while I was taking a bath. She looked at me in a nonchalant manner, and I looked back at her in an equally nonchalant manner. Then she laughed and said pleasantly, "I didn't know anyone was in here," and slowly walked out.

One of the older nuns was Sister Jean, whom I called upon for guidance in helping me resolve a problem I had with Sister Sarah. I told her, "When we get together for dinner, Sister Sarah often makes humorous comments directed toward me in particular, but there is a judgmental edge to her humor. I thought I might talk to her about it, but I am concerned she might be defensive about my perception of her. Maybe you can give me a reality check. Do you see the same thing I am seeing or am I just imagining a slight sarcasm in her remarks?"

Sister Jean said, "I see what you are seeing. Her humor is sarcastic and directed toward you. I don't think she realizes exactly the impact of her words, but I do know that she genuinely cares about you. You can talk to her if you want to, but I am not sure she will be able to see what she is doing. If you are asking for my advice, I suggest that you handle it internally. Here is what I do when something like this happens. It's really simple. I just pray for the person and send that person love. When we are at the dinner table and she speaks with a bit of sarcasm, send her love. I will help you. I will send love to her too, and I will send love to you. How does that sound?"

"That's a deal. If this is the biggest problem I have, I will be very lucky. Thank you for your advice and your prayer support." Her advice worked and perhaps because of sending love in prayer, I noticed that Sister Sarah gradually reduced her sarcastic humor until it faded away toward the end of my stay.

The House of Prayer was located on a high plateau overlooking the sea below. On this plateau I could sit at the edge of a cliff and relax, just as I had done in Meriden. Also like my childhood experience in Meriden, I found a place to lie down under pine trees, even when there was snow on the ground. In addition to enjoying my solitude, I often took walks with Sister Laurette, who taught yoga classes to retreatants. She wore unflattering glasses that did not suit her face, but she was actually very pretty. On one of our walks she confided that she had not had a chance to explore life because she had entered the religious life at a very young age. Since she was still young and curious about life, she was in the process of considering leaving her religious order. I told her that she could dedicate her life to God whether she belonged to a religious order or not, as I had done. I suggested that we pray together and ask the Holy Spirit for guidance. However, by the time I left the House of Prayer, Sister Laurette had not made a definitive decision, and since then I have often wondered which direction she finally took.

While I was taking another walk with one of the other sisters, Sister Rogene, she remarked happily, "You are a real yogi!"

Instead of a quiet thank you, I responded with false modesty, "No. Not really."

Changing to an uncharacteristically serious tone, Sister Rogene asserted, "Come on now. What if someone were to say to me, 'You are a real sister'? And what if I would say, 'No. Not really'? Wouldn't that be false of me? Wouldn't that betray who I am?" I agreed with her and appreciated her confronting me. Her words helped me to take a closer look at my role as a yogi and as a Christian and at the example I could offer to others. After pondering her comments I decided that it would be easier for me to identify with being a "real yogi" if I could actually think of myself as a "real Christian yogi."

From a retreatant named Simon, I learned that many and perhaps most seekers think of being a Christian and a yogi as two distinctly different roles that are mutually exclusive. Simon explained that he was a Christian, but then he moved into a yoga ashram and disowned his Christian roots. He went to extremes with Eastern forms and ended up in a mental hospital. When I met him at the House of Prayer, Simon had returned to following Christ, and I enjoyed the opportunity to share with him. After leaving the House of Prayer, he sent me a letter telling me that he had made the mistake again of abandoning his Christian faith and going to extremes with Eastern practices. For a second time he ended up in a mental hospital. This time, against his will, he was given electric shock treatments. After being released from the mental hospital, he returned to Christ and was now committed to being moderate in spiritual disciplines, even in his Christian prayer life.

For Simon it was best to make a definitive choice between yoga and Christ, and fortunately he chose Christ. Simon had come to believe it was a contradiction in terms to be a Christian and a yogi simultaneously. Because he had given up all Eastern forms, he strongly suggested in his letter that I do likewise, in order to follow Christ completely. However, unlike Simon I had discovered that yoga was a means of deepening my relationship with Christ. Eventually I would become fully convinced that my life purpose was to set an example of how to be a Christian yogi so others will know that they do not have to choose between yoga and Christ.

My vision of combining yoga and Christianity, described more fully in Chapter 67, "Christian Yoga and Miracle Yoga," became more refined as I matured, but here in this chapter I would like to share with you my initial vision of how yoga can provide a means of following Christ. Before I do, let me clarify that having this vision of Christian yoga so early in my life didn't mean I was always able to live up to it. Nevertheless, I made progress in the manner of two steps forward and one step backward, with my vision serving as the direction in which I wanted to grow.

Until Eastern spiritual practices came into my life, I believed spirituality was something limited to Sunday mornings. Other than a Christian prayer at night, the rest of every day was spent in the non-spiritual activities that fill up daily living. Yoga can be just a set of postures and breathing practices that fills up the exercise category of life. But a deeper understanding of yoga reveals that life is not merely a collection of categories, with spirituality as simply one of them. Yoga teaches spirituality as a way of life that encompasses *all* daily activities.

I was personally moved by the following Bible quotation, which I took quite literally:

Behold, I stand at the door and knock; if any one hears my voice and opens the door, I will come in to him and eat with him, and he with me. He who conquers, I will grant him to sit with me on my throne, as I myself conquered and sat down with my Father on this throne.[1]

I felt Jesus was speaking directly to me in these words, asking me to open the door to Him. What is it about yoga that helped me then and helps me now to open the door to Christ that traditional Christianity does not? The key connection for me is the idea that yoga helps me to explore the presence of Christ within my physical body. In the West, Christ is apart from me, and I am worshipping someone, something outside myself. The East says Christ is within and can be experienced there as my own true nature. This difference is not just theoretical; it is practical. *Hatha yoga*, the yoga of the physical body, provides a practical framework for going within the body as an avenue for this direct experience. Hatha yoga disciplines consisting of postures and breathing practices help me to calm the mind and open the door to Christ better than an entirely Western approach, which leaves out an emphasis on the body. Yet hatha yoga is only a good beginning—part of a comprehensive framework that yoga provides for encountering Christ. This larger framework includes karma yoga (service), bhakti yoga (love and devotion), jnana yoga (spiritual discernment), and raja yoga (meditation). The combination of these forms of yoga helps me to work on my Christ connection in all the areas of my life, in contrast to the emphasis in traditional Christianity on spirituality for the limited time of Sunday worship.

In particular, I found the meditative aspect of raja yoga was the most helpful in fostering my inner exploration of Christ, providing a systematic structure for my spiritual life. I found yoga was a scientific means of opening the door to Christ—scientific in the sense of providing a structure that could be repeated by anyone and produce similar results each time. Yoga showed me that there was not just one door to Christ; there were seven inner doors called chakras, literally meaning "wheels" of energy and consciousness. A method called "Christian Yoga Meditation" helps to open all seven inner doors to Christ, and this will be described in Chapter 63, "Jacob's Ladder." In the West, connection with Christ is all about faith that does not require a direct "felt" experience to confirm this faith. I certainly feel faith is essential, but felt it was also necessary for me to have direct experiences of Christ. Yoga promises this direct experience, and after practicing it, I found that it delivered on this promise. Feeling the presence of Christ within is the nourishment that I needed to keep my focus on living a life devoted to God.

When I practiced these proven methods, I found that Christ did indeed come into my life through my invitation and daily renewal of that invitation. My Catholic upbringing had shown me the value of communion in Sunday service, but yoga, literally meaning "union," taught me how to find daily communion with Christ within—both in meditation and throughout the day. It was this intimacy with the divine presence that I found fulfilling and strengthening. In my vision of Christian yoga, I thought of my inner communion as not only walking in the light of Christ, but also as an opportunity to let that light shine outwardly. Thus inner communion led to becoming a spiritual vehicle bringing blessings to others and nourishing a sense of outer communion with my brothers and sisters.

Walking the path of Christian yoga, I sought the ideal of having a well-rounded practice, which included the selfless service of Christian karma yoga, the love of Christian bhakti yoga, the discrimination of Christian jnana yoga, and the meditation of Christian raja yoga. By accepting Christian yoga as my path, I had a perfect example to follow—Jesus. His life reflected a balance of dedicated action, devotion, knowledge, and contemplation. I felt Jesus was taking me by the hand, like a father takes the hand of his son, and was walking with me along the path. Also I remembered that I was never searching alone. I was joined in this search with my brothers and sisters since finding the divine within is the longing of every human heart either consciously or unconsciously. This collaborative adventure is part of a divine Plan of evolving spiritual consciousness. Jesus is in charge of this Plan, so I felt confident holding His Hand. I felt every step I took toward the Light, no matter how seemingly small, contributed to the overall spiritual growth of all conscious beings.

I especially felt at home at the House of Prayer because its purpose was to be a place of retreat for seekers like myself who wanted to find Christ within and to synthesize the East and West. Three times daily we meditated together on pillows in the chapel. One winter day while meditating in the early afternoon, I opened my eyes and was surprised to see that the room was filled with smoke, and all the other meditators had disappeared. I thought that the house must be on fire, yet was calm from having just meditated. During the meditation I hadn't smelled the smoke, but everyone else had, and they had left the room one by one. As I got up to see what had happened, Sister Sarah came back and told me that the smoke was caused by the kerosene burner in my room. Luckily there was not a fire, but the smoke filling the entire house was bad enough.

The kerosene burner was necessary since my room, affectionately called the "hermitage," was separate from the rest of the house. Calling my living space a room would be an exaggeration. It was actually the space at the bottom of a stairwell. I had been unwilling to live in the cramped quarters of Sandra Barry's home in Jerusalem, yet ironically I was living here in an even smaller space. There was just enough area to stretch out a cot under the slanting wooden bottom of the staircase hovering immediately overhead. The standing space was smaller than the size of a phone booth. In addition to the door at the top of the stairs that led into the House of Prayer, there was an exit door at the bottom of the stairwell, which was taped shut to hold in the heat. Brother David had visited the House of Prayer while I was living there, and he had advised me to make this place into my "cave," similar to where the early Christian monks had lived. I put up blankets to create an artificial ceiling to enclose the space, which made it even more cave-like and more able to hold in the heat.

I actually liked my cozy space, except for the difficulty I had in heating it. I was told that the kerosene burner was the only available way to heat this space. The day that the house filled with smoke I had lit the burner before leaving the room and had turned the wick down to a small flame. As sometimes happened, the flame grew larger after its initial lighting, only this time the flame grew much larger. Because we had all been meditating, the smoke had time to fill the house. Sister Sarah was the first to notice the smoke and correct the problem. When Sister Sarah returned to the chapel and told me what happened, Sister Laurette pointed to her face and laughed. Sister Sarah asked indignantly, "What are you laughing at?"

"You have funny black circles around your nostrils," Sister Laurette said.

Sister Sarah gave up her serious tone and giggled like a school girl, as she pointed at Sister Laurette's face. "You have them, too. Look! We all have black circles!" We had to clean the whole house from top to bottom. We had to wash all our exposed clothes, take showers, and wash our hair. I, of course, apologized for causing the problem and inconveniencing everyone. Making sure this did not happen again, we ran an extension cord from upstairs all the way down to the bottom of the stairwell in order to replace the kerosene burner with an electric heater.

Before using the cot, I had slept on a foam mattress on the floor. One night I woke up in a panic after an extremely vivid dream of black spiders crawling under my mattress. The dream seemed so real that I turned up the top of the mattress where my head had been, and sure enough there were black spiders. Even after cleaning under the mattress, there was an ongoing problem with spiders returning.

I remembered the incident in the cellar of my Meriden house, when I was trying to burn spiders and almost burned down the house. I realized there was a parallel between the cellar incident in Meriden and my living space at the bottom of the stairwell in Gloucester. Both places were lower levels of a larger building. Both locations involved incidents with spiders, a fire that could have burnt down the building, and extremely poor judgment on my part. I felt I was looking at pieces of my shadow puzzle, facing the same kind of issues I had first confronted hanging from the theater balcony and standing on Craig Castle.

My unresolved shadow puzzle had already threatened my life and the lives of those around me. Yet I wasn't overly concerned about the potential disastrous ramifications of continuing to leave this puzzle unsolved because I trusted that I and those around me were being protected by the divine within. Although I was aware of my great capacity for making mistakes, I felt God had an even greater capacity for limiting the harm I might do to myself or others. Also I trusted God would show me how to accept responsibility for my mistakes and help me to correct them in a gracious way. Since my shadow puzzle represented the fearful parts of my mind, I realized that entertaining fears of what might be hidden in darkness and what might happen in the future would only make matters worse. If I had given in to the temptation of fear, I would be walking in darkness, which is the opposite of my Christian yoga ideal of walking in the Light. Instead of giving power to darkness, I called upon my faith in the Light and intensified my spiritual disciplines. I invited divine assistance from the Holy Spirit in whatever way it might happen and felt confident the shadow puzzle would be revealed and resolved in its own time through God's grace.

Previously I mentioned that I trusted in the idea that life was like a river carrying me along for my benefit and that I was optimistic that this river would bring me to the solution of the shadow puzzle. I would like to now elaborate on that idea. This river of life has different names, such as dharma, the Tao, or the Way. In a Christian context it may be thought of as God's Will expressed as God's Plan.

God's Will is always to express love. Because of His Love, He has the desire for all of us to come Home, and we, as part of God, have that same desire consciously or unconsciously. This joint desire, which expresses God's Will, is the cause that will ultimately lead to the effect of us returning Home. God's Plan is His strategy for us to return to Him. This Plan includes our soul purposes, but places our individual purposes within the larger tapestry of His strategy for the salvation of all souls. The river of life, as God's Will activating His Plan, is beneficially carrying all of us, whether we realize it or not, toward spiritual growth and our ultimate awakening in Heaven. Each day this river guides us toward that final destination.

The cause and effect nature of karma plays a part in the river of life helping us to wake up. If we go against the natural flow of the river, we will be making bad choices that will produce negative karmic results, which can allow us to accept responsibility for our choices so we can make better choices next time. If we go with the flow of the river, we will be making good choices that will produce positive karmic results, which can encourage us to continue making those good choices. But the river of life does not rely entirely on karma to bring us Home because God and His Will transcend karma. Most importantly, God's Plan includes the intercession of divine grace, previously described as "the law of forgiveness," which allows us to learn some spiritual lessons without necessarily having to face all of our karma. Ultimately it is this indispensable divine grace that will bring us Home more than anything else.

Only God could coordinate how all our individual paths can most beneficially work together so we can all wake up. It was very reassuring for me to trust that God was in charge of not only my path, but the paths of everyone else whom I would encounter. Having this frame of reference I assumed that my shadow puzzle was part of God's Plan and that He would arrange my life and the lives of others in the best way to facilitate spiritual growth in general. I felt that by going with the flow of the river I would ultimately solve my overall identity puzzle and awaken to my true spiritual Identity in God. Along the way I felt that the unfolding of God's Plan would specifically resolve the shadow puzzle in a way that would be most helpful for me and for others. Instead of pushing the river by focusing on wanting to be further along than I actually was, all I needed to do was just practice my daily disciplines and simply take small steps each day in my walk in the Light.

In my disciplines I was inwardly nourished through devotion and meditation, yet also found reading to be helpful for inspirational purposes. Since I had already read many books about Christian saints, I focused on reading about Hindu holy men. I was deeply touched by the life of Ramakrishna, which was recorded meticulously in *The Gospel of Sri Ramakrishna*, which I eagerly devoured. Ramakrishna was a broad-minded and passionate spiritual seeker who worshipped God in both a personal and impersonal manner within the Hindu tradition. He often went into spontaneous ecstasies. However, I was most moved by how he clearly saw the divine in the world and in particular in each person he met. As a forerunner of the ecumenical movement, Ramakrishna saw all religions as the revelation of God presenting Himself in varied forms to meet the diverse dispositions of spiritual seekers. He would say that the English come to a water tank and what they take away is called *water*. What the Hindus take away is called *jal*. Just as the water is the same regardless of the name given it, God is the same Being regardless of the many names He is given.[2]

He set aside all forms of sectarianism, and he sought only the direct experience of universal God-consciousness. Ramakrishna devoted himself to following the time-honored spiritual disciplines of different religions, including Hinduism, Buddhism, Islam, and Christianity, and personally experienced the same divine presence within each one. For example, he explored Christianity through a profound personal experience of Christ. He was visiting the home of one of his disciples, and upon seeing a picture of Mother Mary and Jesus, he fell immediately into an ecstasy. For several days he became so totally absorbed in devotion to Mother Mary and Jesus that his followers were concerned that he might not come out of his ongoing ecstatic state of mind.

One of these followers of Ramakrishna was Vivekananda, who became the first spiritual teacher to come to America from India in order to bridge the gap between the East and the West. In 1893 he spoke inspirationally about raja yoga and yoga philosophy at the first Parliament of World Religions held in Chicago and was extremely well received. Subsequently he founded the Vedanta Society of New York, which is affiliated with the Ramakrishna Order of India and is still functioning today, dedicated to teaching the principles and practices of yoga.

Next I read about Swami Abhishiktananda, who was a Benedictine monk from France, but went to India to focus on Christ while absorbing Hindu spirituality. He wanted to 'Indianize' his contemplative lifestyle. He took on the role of the Hindu sannyasin. He let go of the European lifestyle by assuming the simple life of villagers, adopted a strictly vegetarian diet, and wore the saffron-colored *kavi*, identifying his role as a renunciate. He devoted most of his time to spiritual practices, such as worship, meditation, and the study of scriptures. He went to the East with the preconceived intent of Christianizing India. As a result of transforming meditative experiences in the caves of India, he shifted his focus to a true synthesis of the East and the West. The following quotation helped me identify with Swami Abhishiktananda because I could sense his passion similar to my own—a passion for experiencing the divine presence:

> ...the whole long history of salvation boils down to the blinking of an eye—a flash of lightning—an Awakening. It (the long history of salvation) has conceptual, mythical and sociological form only for one who is NOT awakened....[3]

Swami Abhishiktananda founded an ashram, which became a fully Christian and fully Indian contemplative community. Eventually he moved to a hermitage along the Ganges River, allowing Bede Griffiths, an English Benedictine monk, to assume responsibility for the ashram. Griffiths was a combination of mystic and scholar and published *Vedanta and the Christian Faith* in 1973. Although this book provided a valuable theological meeting ground between the East and West, I personally preferred the mystical aspect of spirituality over an intellectual approach. Nevertheless, I felt Griffiths valued finding the divine within his own heart just as I did because he loved to quote the following passage from the Chandogya Upanishad (8, 3):

> There is this city of Brahman (the human body) and in it there is a small shrine in the form of a lotus, and within can be found a small space. This little space within the heart is as great as this vast universe. The heavens and the earth are there, and the sun and the moon and the stars; fire and lightning and wind are there, and all that now is and is not yet—all that is contained within it.

The Western approach to spirituality focuses on the *transcendent* nature of God, Who is reflected in the universe, but Who is essentially above and beyond it. The Eastern emphasis is on the *immanent* nature of God, Who is directly present within each individual human heart, as is so wonderfully expressed in the quotation above. There were many inspired spiritual seekers from India who directly or indirectly influenced Western spirituality. I wanted to follow the example of those pioneers who committed their lives to the blending of the East and West. Indeed I felt it would in some manner be my destiny to do so.

However, that destiny would have to wait, considering my youth and spiritual inexperience. While living at the House of Prayer, I kept grounded by my mundane work at the adjacent Eastern Point Retreat operated by the Jesuits. Large retreats were regularly held at this center. I washed dishes and cleaned the bathrooms. I gave all of my wages to the House of Prayer to pay for my room and board. One time I was a week late in submitting my work hours to the Jesuit priest, and consequently the Jesuit priest refused to pay me. He said he had already paid me for the previous week, but he hadn't, and he absolutely refused to even discuss it with me anymore.

I apologized to Sister Sarah for not being able to give her the check. Nevertheless, I wanted her to confront the priest, because he was being unfair. She said, "The money is insignificant. You have already talked to the priest, and he will not budge. This kind of thing has happened before with this priest. I am at content. I won't throw away my contentment to fight for a few dollars. I am letting go of this. You have done everything that you can reasonably do, so you can let go of it now too." I could not reconcile this unfair situation with my idea of priests being held to a higher standard. After a good deal of prayer time, I was finally able to let go of my resentment. I accepted my responsibility for bringing this karmic situation upon myself due to my own mistake of submitting my hours a week late.

For the past several years whenever I had asked in prayer for anything that I wanted, my prayer was always answered. One exception was that I had asked for a resolution to my shadow puzzle and that prayer was not answered, but I still fully expected it to be answered in the future. I remembered my success with prayer when I was washing dishes one day and the cook burned his leg badly. He told me he was in pain, and I asked him if he wanted help. When he agreed, I placed my hand directly on the burned area. I prayed mentally, "Lord, please help," and then repeated the Name of Jesus. The cook exclaimed, "How did you do that?" because his pain had instantly vanished. I thought I could somewhat help his healing. However, I was as surprised as he was to find out that the healing was instantaneous. I had experienced healing of myself in the past, but this was the first time I experienced healing happening through me for the benefit of another person. I didn't really have a clear understanding of how healing happens. Subsequently I read about the Hindu belief that a person could heal another person by taking on their karma. From this I assumed that I must have taken the cook's pain away by taking on his karma.

Sister Laurette took me on a trip to Vermont to visit her brother, a monk who was staying at Weston Priory, which had become famous for its recordings of beautiful singing. I was tempted to stay there as a monk myself, in spite of the fact that I had no singing talent whatsoever. I first discovered this in elementary school, when a classmate stated admiringly, "You were really funny today in class."

"What do you mean?" I asked.

"When you were singing with our class, you were kidding—weren't you?"

"No, I wasn't kidding," I let him know that my "humorous" singing was not intentional, as he had assumed. That's when I learned that I was musically challenged. However, even a person with a tin ear like mine could appreciate the exquisite sound of the Weston Priory monks singing in praise of the divine.

While there I met Brother Percival, Sister Laurette's younger brother, who told me that he had been having a lower back problem for a long time. I prayed extensively and fervently for his healing. After I returned to the House of Prayer in Gloucester, I too experienced a lower back problem, not as acute as Brother Percival's, but which persisted for a long while. I attributed my back pain to the fact that I had taken the wrong approach in regard to the healing of Brother Percival. Influenced by the Hindu perspective of healing by taking on the karma of others, I had prayed to take on his infirmity, much like Jesus had sacrificed Himself for us. Not having contact with Brother Percival again, I did not learn whether my intercession had been of any assistance to him. Eventually my lower back pain disappeared. Nevertheless, I decided that there must be a better approach to healing than taking on someone else's karma.

While I was having a conversation with Sister Laurette and Brother Percival, he excitedly told us about a great movie with Robert Redford and Paul Newman that he had recently seen, which would in the future receive an Oscar for the best picture of the year. It was called *The Sting*, and it had a very dramatic surprise ending. One of my personal pet peeves was the thoughtlessness of someone revealing the ending of a movie and spoiling it for someone else. Just as I was about to speak up and tell Brother Percival to make sure not to tell us the ending—you guessed it—he blurted out the ending with unbridled enthusiasm. I let him know that he had spoiled the movie for me and possibly his sister, but I did not let on how upset I was and later had to pray to let go of my judgments of him.

On another occasion when all three of us were together again, I saw a paper resting on a desk that belonged to Brother Percival and asked him what it was. He said, "I am under-aged, and I want to take a trip, but I had to have my mother sign a permission agreement to allow me to go, and that's the consent form."

I took a closer look at his signature and his mother's signature on the document and said knowingly with a smile, "It looks like you and your mother have the same handwriting."

Sister Laurette quickly took a look at the signatures and said to him, "How could you?"

"Aaah, Sis. It's no big deal," he said, sheepishly admitting his forgery. Sister Laurette didn't want to make him feel bad so she played down the forgery after her initial shock.

Brother Percival had revealed the secret ending of the movie, and the karma wheel had turned to have someone else reveal his own secret. But I did not take myself off the hook for being the one who brought his karma to him. Just as it was inappropriate for him to reveal the secret ending of the movie, it was inappropriate for me to reveal his secret. After all, his mistake of exclaiming the movie ending was done unknowingly, and my mistake was worse because it was done knowingly. If I had to do it over, I would have been silent, just as I had wanted him to be silent about the movie. "I am sorry. I shouldn't have said anything," I said to Brother Percival seeing the obvious embarrassment on his face. He forgave me and that was the last time I saw him.

---

1. Revelation 3:20-21, RSV.
2. Mahendra, (anonymous author calling himself "M."), *The Condensed Gospel of Sri Ramakrishna* (Mylapore, Madras, India: Sri Ramakrishna Math, 1987), p. 119.
3. Abhishiktananda (Dom Henri Le Saux), *The Ascent to the Depth of the Heart: The Spiritual Diary of Swami Abhishiktananda (1948 to 1973)*. Selected and introduced by Raimon Panikkar; translated by David Fleming and James Stuart; published in Delhi, 1998, p. 319. Available through www.saujanyabooks.com.

9

YOGAVILLE ASHRAM

~ • ~

I learned more about healing in the next step on my spiritual path. In 1975 I moved to a new spiritual community, a yoga ashram called Yogaville in Putnam, Connecticut. I went there because I wanted to learn more about yoga and this was where the experts in yoga lived. I had given up my attachment to the Roman Catholic religion, which did not mean I rejected it as valueless. On the contrary, I saw it as a very helpful stepping stone. But now I wanted to go deeper in the direction in which it pointed, meaning to become immersed in Christ, with yoga as the means to that end. I had some reservations about going to an ashram where the seekers were devoted to a guru, in this case Swami Satchidananda, the founder of Yogaville. I was concerned that I might feel like an outsider due to my devotion to Christ. Nevertheless, I was excited about this new opportunity for higher learning—in spite of my previous disappointment with my college experience in which I lacked purposefulness.

Since my focus on Christ was internal rather than evangelical, I was welcomed as a yoga student and lived in the residential portion of the ashram, which was located in an enormous building on a very large estate. I was one of about seventy-five full time residents. Everyone worked, and I was assigned to do gardening, in which I had no experience and no interest, but for that very reason I figured it would be a good form of karma yoga that would teach me selflessness. Surprisingly one of the residents was a female medical doctor, who gave medical examinations including blood tests to new residents. My blood test revealed that I had a very high bilirubin count, which indicated a possible liver disorder, although I had no outward physical symptoms of sickness. The doctor made some dietary recommendations to address the problem. She insisted that I be taken off of any strenuous work assignments. As a result of her recommendation I was reassigned to work as an illustrator on the Yogaville Magazine. I made the drawings of different people on the back of the cover to illustrate the various aspects or kinds of yoga: someone meditating to represent *raja yoga*, working to show *karma yoga*, calling on the Name of God with prayer beads for *japa yoga*, doing postures for *hatha yoga*, reading scripture for *jnana yoga*, and finally someone doing devotional chanting to illustrate *bhakti yoga*, the yoga of divine love.

Swami Satchidananda advocated *brahmacharya*, sexual purity, and so obviously the single women and men had separate sleeping quarters. As at Gloucester, here too, I had a tiny living space. There were white bed sheets hanging vertically as "walls" to separate my "room" from the other "rooms." I had to get used to sleeping on my "bed," which was a folded blanket. In the space next to me was Margabandu, a massage expert. Margabandu had previously been a cook at the Hippocrates Health Institute. He said, "While I was there, they were obsessed with 'kitchen religion.'"

I asked, "What's 'kitchen religion'?"

He smiled knowingly and said, "It's worshipping the *food god*. I got caught up in it myself. There always seemed to be food missing from the kitchen. One time I noticed that a large new case of figs had disappeared. I couldn't find it anywhere. Then a month later it showed up in a closet, and there was only maybe a pound of figs left in the forty-pound box." While at the Health Institute, Margabandu went on a fifty-day fast. Fasting in moderation for a few days can be very helpful, but he found out that his extreme fasting was counterproductive. His digestive system became completely disrupted, and as a result he couldn't control his eating impulses. At his request I served him all of his meals, and he made a commitment to eat only the food that he was served, to help him overcome his impulses. Margabandu's recovery diet included mostly raw foods, such as salads, because, as he said, "When you're green inside, you're clean inside."

As it turned out, Margabandu would end up helping me much more than I helped him. Primarily he made me feel at ease by just being my best buddy in a strange new environment. On the practical side he introduced me to saunas followed by invigorating cold showers, which my young body found very invigorating. He showed me the yoga practice of cleansing the nasal passages by pouring water up one nostril at a time without gagging. In the future, if I ever felt signs of a cold coming, I would perform this nasal cleansing as a very effective means of avoiding sickness. Margabandu taught me all his massage techniques, but also his underlying approach, which was to feel God's love and to allow His love to overflow to others. Thus in learning how to give a loving massage, I also learned a new approach to healing. Another resident, Sukamar, who did landscaping at the ashram, was sick and confined to bed for a long time. When I visited him, he explained that Swami Satchidananda had told him the cause of his sickness. He was temporarily sick because of his karma from cutting down a very large tree on the property, one that he knew didn't need to be cut down. I did not pray to take on his karma, as I would have done in the past, because I had learned that healing a person by taking away his symptoms may not actually be helpful in the long run. Sometimes it is most helpful to encourage the person to face the consequences of his own behavior as a lesson in learning how to heal himself. As the old saying goes, "If you give someone a fish, you help him for a day. If you teach someone *how* to fish, you help him for a lifetime." To comfort Sukamar, I did give him the silver chain and cross I was wearing around my neck, which he returned a few weeks later after he had fully recovered.

Instead of taking on the karma of others, I learned from Margabandu that healing others is similar to giving a massage. First the person who wants healing has to request it. Then you have to ask the person who wants healing to focus on being receptive to God's love. Next, just as you would do for giving a massage, you feel God's love for you. As you feel God's love for you, you allow His love to extend through you to the one being healed. Since His love is infinite, you are not drained of your love or energy by allowing God's love to overflow to others. You really do not heal others. You are teaching others how to heal themselves with your assistance. Your own receptivity to love helps the person to be receptive and to heal themselves through their openness to God's love. I learned that healing should not be repeated—so that others learn to rely directly on God's love instead of relying on another person to be a channel for it. I found that facilitating healing came naturally to me through relying on God's love and my japa yoga discipline of calling on the Name of Jesus, which I did throughout the day.

Swami Satchidananda was one of the superstars of the many Indian gurus who were becoming popular in the 60s and 70s. In the late 50s and 60s Swami Satchidananda was the director of an ashram in the hill country of Sri Lanka. He initiated a modern approach to the ancient Hindu code of renunciates by driving a car, wearing a watch, and actively participating in question and answer sessions with seekers. This modernization was resisted by conservatives, who represented the conventional wisdom of India. However, the modern changes proved in time to be a necessary step in bringing the message of yoga to a greater range of seekers.

In 1966 Swami Satchidananda was invited to New York City by an American disciple, the artist Peter Max. Soon thereafter he moved to the United States permanently, to spread the yoga teachings of his guru, Shivananda. Swami Satchidananda first gained prominence in 1969 when he was the opening speaker at the historic Woodstock music and arts festival. His method of teaching yoga was called *Integral Yoga*. There were many Integral Yoga centers, but the main headquarters were in Yogaville at

Pomfret, Connecticut, although at a later date the headquarters would relocate to Buckingham, Virginia.

I enjoyed the daily schedule of getting up very early in the morning for group meditation and chanting, followed by my individual practice of postures and breathing. I had already served in the past as a yoga teacher, yet had not received formal yoga certification training. Consequently, at Yogaville I participated in and graduated from the intensive yoga teacher training program. My understanding of yoga was greatly accelerated, not just by this formal training, but by learning yoga practices from other residents. I learned how to do the difficult postures like the headstand and advanced breathing practices, as well as yoga cleansing practices.

There were also many special activities going on, including three-day and seven-day retreats, often at other locations. While I was at one of those retreats, I was meditating late at night and heard a steady humming tone, considered an expression of the spiritual OM sound. Although this sound was not unusual in itself, what was unusual was that the sound would not go away. I stayed awake all night listening to the humming sound, without feeling frustrated—I simply lay still and listened peacefully. The next day I felt energized rather than tired. The sound likewise continued all of the next day no matter what I was doing. In the evening I listened again, but this time I fell asleep, and the humming sound was gone in the morning.

In another special activity, the famous American seeker, Ram Dass, was speaking in Boston, and I had very much enjoyed reading his bestseller, *Be Here Now*, which taught the harmony of all people and religions. Ram Dass was generally recognized as a high-profile spokesperson for our generation. In the 60s my generation was the counter-culture hippie generation that had advocated "flower power" and experimented with free love and alternate lifestyles with the motto '*Turn on. Tune in. Drop out.*' Ram Dass had formerly been known as Richard Alpert, a Harvard professor, who along with Timothy Leary had led the way in delving into psychedelic drug exploration. Now, years later in 1975, Ram Dass had a different message: All that groping around at the physical level by the hippies was not merely dissatisfaction with traditional American culture based on materialistic success. Rather than just being a reactionary movement, it was a positive desire to transcend materialism itself and find the true meaning of life. Thus seeking an outer utopia of love based on the expression of individual freedom evolved into an inner journey. The groovy, free-and-easy, anything-goes attitude was set aside in favor of specific inner disciplines with the promise of replacing drug-induced highs with natural spiritual highs. The time-honored Hindu means of spiritual advancement based upon the guru and disciple relationship was held out as the holy grail of this segment of the hippie generation that wanted authentic spirituality based upon direct personal experience.

Ram Dass was uniquely positioned to articulate this transition from outer radicalism to inner transformation because he had gone to India to discover his own guru, Neem Karoli Baba, also known as Maharaji-ji. Ram Dass talked about opening to the direct experience of higher consciousness while also remaining grounded in practicing selfless service. He was not only informative; he was a very entertaining speaker, and I was aware that we had the same birthday of April 6. The most refreshing aspect of Ram Dass was that he was consistently up front about his own personal shortcomings. This unmasking of himself gave him more credibility than if he had pretended to be more spiritually advanced than he really was, and this endeared him to many seekers of my generation.

Almost everyone at Yogaville took off to hear him, and I was invited to go repeatedly, yet declined, even though I was definitely intrigued. Living in close quarters with so many people left me feeling that I could use a break to have some introspective time alone. I spent my time practicing my spiritual disciplines in addition to reading. I found a biography of Ramana Maharshi. He was only seventeen when he encountered the divine influence. He was alone when he was suddenly struck by an overwhelming fear of death. He was perfectly healthy, so it was purely a psychological state of mind. Yet, he thought he was going to die, and he felt he needed to confront the fear. This drove his mind inward to ask himself what it means to die. He decided to do role playing to get in touch with what happens when the body dies. He lay down on his back in a corpse position with his arms to the side and imagined his body was rigid and immobile. Then having decided in his role playing that his body was dead, he imagined his body would be taken and burned to ashes. The body being gone led to the question, "Am I dead?" He observed that his personality and the "I" in him seemed separate from this body that was inert. Ramana Maharshi concluded that he was the Spirit that transcended the body. Although the body died, his Spirit could not be affected by death. He identified thereafter with this deathless Spirit.

This was not merely intellectual conjecture. He felt he had bypassed the normal analytical thought process and instead directly perceived this as a living truth, immediately evident. He identified this inner "I" as his own true Self, his Spirit unrelated to body awareness. In fact, he felt this "I" was the only real thing about him. As a result of his experience of facing death, this "I" focused automatically on itself and became a natural inward condition. Gone for good was the fear of death. From this time onward his absorption in this Self became his continuous frame of reference. Other thoughts persisted in coming and going, yet the Self became the single dominating

SWAMI SATCHIDANANDA

RAMANA MAHARSHI

anchor for his awareness. No matter what he was doing at the form level with the body, he remained centered in this "I" of the Self beyond the body. Prior to this experience he had no consciousness of this Self, but afterwards he found himself dwelling permanently in this state of awareness. He moved to the holy mountain of Arunachala and stayed there the rest of his life, attracting many followers.

I was inspired reading about the life of this pure jnani yogi, who was able through spontaneous discrimination to directly perceive and hold on to his true Self. I decided to imitate his procedure of role playing to see what would happen. I allowed my body to become rigid, just as Ramana Maharshi had done. I felt myself allowing the physical form of the body to die. I tried to identify with my true Self, just as it was described in his life story and as it is similarly described in Vedanta. However, for me the true Self was identical to the Christ, or as I sometimes called it, the "Christ Self." Focusing on this true Self was a helpful learning experience, but lightning did not strike twice. Yes, I did have intellectual insight, yet not the direct inner awareness that Ramana Maharshi experienced. The jnani path of discrimination is not nearly as easy as it appears to be in reading this biography. In fact, there is even a danger of insanity with an extreme expression of following a mental path that attempts to transcend the world of form.

It takes a very unusual person with an exceptionally strong mind to follow a jnani path exclusively. Nevertheless, a certain degree of this kind of discrimination between the real and the unreal is necessary as a part of all other paths. I felt my experience of Ramana Maharshi's approach to spirituality was helpful as part of a balanced spiritual approach. In addition to using mental discrimination in jnana yoga, I was interested in bhakti yoga devotion, raja yoga meditation, and karma yoga service, but in my case all with the purpose of union with Christ.

Although my experiment to duplicate Ramana Maharshi's experience was not directly successful, there may have been a positive aftereffect. A few days later I did my morning yoga postures followed by my deep relaxation practice. I tensed up various parts of my body and released that tension in the body. Then as usual I entered a peaceful state of mind lying on my back. After lingering in this peace, I felt a great joy and could feel myself floating upward out of the body in an experience of astral traveling. Nevertheless, it was not a fearful leaving of the body like the one I had experienced at the mini-ashram in Milford. It felt as though some almost tangible personal divine presence, such as an angelic being or beings, was lifting me up out of the body. I felt protected by an envelope of love and was temporarily elevated into a blissful state. This ecstasy was very pleasant, but not the all-encompassing cosmic consciousness spoken of with reverence by spiritual aspirants. Then the uplifting divine presence very gently lowered my astral body back into my physical body. I looked upon this as a pat on the back from the Holy Spirit telling me I was on the right track in my spiritual path. I did not share this experience with anyone else, even Margabandu, because I felt it was a matter of spiritual integrity to remain silent in order to not let my pride get the best of me and not be the cause of provoking spiritual comparisons between myself and others.

This experience may seem totally unrelated to my Ramana Maharshi experiment. But I think it was Spirit's response to my desire to experience being freed of body consciousness. Perhaps my role playing of Ramana Maharshi confronting death and this experience of floating out of the body would be a preparation for my future passing into the next world. In any event I felt that both confronting death and astral traveling represented opportunities to make progress toward solving my shadow puzzle. Here were two examples of the two major themes of the shadow puzzle. The Ramana Maharshi experiment represented the spider theme of facing danger and death. The astral traveling experience highlighted the falling theme in the sense of overcoming the fear of falling. It was actually a reversal of the Milford experience of astral traveling, in which I became fearful and was abruptly and jarringly returned to the body. Right after this I had fallen down the stairs and dislocated my shoulder. In contrast to this fearful falling, the astral traveling at Yogaville was an experience of being lovingly lifted up to a spiritual height and then just as lovingly lowered, without any fearful sense of falling. If death is defined as a state in which the astral body permanently leaves the physical body, then the strong connection between the Ramana Maharshi experience and the astral traveling becomes clear: Both experiences addressed subconscious fears related to the transcending of normal body consciousness. The desire to be one with God is all well and good, but lurking in the shadows is the fear of this very union because it means overcoming our normal ego attachment to the body consciousness.

Each evening we came together for *satsang*, a gathering of spiritual seekers for fellowship and inspiration. The satsang room was always packed not only with the residents, but with the many devotees that lived in the community surrounding Yogaville. These meetings were opportunities to be close to the guru and be uplifted by his very presence, as well as receive his blessing. Swami Satchidananda had a palpable spiritual charisma, which his devotees felt and which I could feel, even without having any personal devotional feelings toward him. I could even see a glow of white light around his head, not on every occasion, but at these satsangs in particular. A guru overflowing with light and love was to be expected, but I was surprised to see the devotees equally filled with light and love. It seemed that at these spiritual gatherings Swami Satchidananda emanated a love outwardly to his disciples, who in turn enthusiastically sent love back to him. I got the distinct impression that all the love he was receiving from his devotees, he was radiating back to them. However, I was not sure whether he was doing this as a conscious loving practice or as a natural heartfelt expression without thinking about it. This love repeatedly sent out by him and continuously sent back to him produced a dynamo effect of amplifying the spiritual vibrations, noticeably uplifting even the less devoted participants, such as myself. The word "satsang" literally means "company of the holy." Indeed it felt like we were in the presence of holiness on these occasions. But I didn't feel the guru was the sole source of this holiness. Rather I believed the holiness was emanating from the collective spiritual intentions and innate divine nature of all those present.

I suppose all my insights about satsang could have merely been my imagination being influenced by my environment, but I felt my mind in general was being guided by the Holy Spirit through my intuition and in this specific case my intuition felt very strong. I had gotten an "A" in my college public speaking class, but I had learned only about the mechanics of how to present myself and clearly articulate ideas. I was never taught how to be a dynamic speaker who could uplift others. I made a mental note that if I ever got the chance to speak to spiritual seekers, I would make sure to send out love, receive love from the audience, and send it back out again as Swami Satchidananda had so effectively done.

At these gatherings Swami Satchidananda would answer audience questions and display his wonderful story-telling ability. One of his stories was about a boy with a puzzle, which he narrated as follows: "A boy was given a map of the whole earth, which he placed on the floor of his room. He left the room, and when he returned, he discovered that his older mischievous brother had ripped the map into many pieces. The boy tried to put the map together again but could not match the different parts of the world together. Out of curiosity, the boy turned over the map pieces. He recognized parts of a man's body on the turned-over pieces. He put together the man's body parts and taped them in place. After he had gotten the man together, he turned over the map and found that the world had been put together also. I am sure you see the moral to this story. First you put the man together and find oneness and peace. Having found oneness and peace yourself, you bring these qualities to the world too." I was impressed by this simple, yet graphic story, because I similarly felt I was putting together the puzzle pieces of my life.

Swami Satchidananda gave his students *mantras*, which were sound structures in Sanskrit and which were repeated during meditation as a spiritual discipline. He gave mantra initiation to almost all of the ashram participants, including even some of my Christian friends at the ashram. I considered him to be a holy man and thought that perhaps a Hindu mantra might help me. I felt that if I accepted this swami as my spiritual teacher, he would help me to reduce my reliance on my self-will and therefore gain humility, which I was concerned was lacking in me. Nonetheless, I had an uneasy feeling that I was disavowing my religious roots in Christ, especially since for a long time I had been repeating the Name of Jesus as my own personal mantra for meditation. During a private telephone conversation with Swami Satchidananda, I asked him about my concerns. He said, "You will not be abandoning your inner guru of the Christ Spirit because you have adopted an outer guru in the form of a human teacher. The outer guru is only the messenger of the inner guru, the Christ Spirit." I accepted this explanation and decided to receive mantra initiation.

My initiation was scheduled to take place on the eighth day of a ten-day silent retreat. I was sick every day for the first seven days of the retreat, and I had never been sick in this way before. There was a constant pain in the lower part of the center of the chest at the place in the body which in yoga philosophy is associated with the guru. Each morning I would have just enough energy to meditate and then do a set of yoga postures. After this I was so exhausted that I would have to go back to my room and rest for the remainder of the day, without being able to participate in any of the retreat activities. I kept thinking each day that the next day would be better, but each day was the same. I only remained on the retreat because of the upcoming initiation. When the initiation day arrived, I did actually feel better. I wore my white shirt and white yoga pants and brought some fruit and flowers, which were customary parts of the mantra initiation ritual. After a lengthy ceremony Swami Satchidananda walked around the room to individually initiate each participant.

There were many initiates, and when I saw Swami Satchidananda coming closer to me, a strong intuitive feeling suddenly came over me. I felt I was abandoning Christ, being unfaithful to Jesus. How could I have ever considered accepting a swami as my teacher to replace Jesus? How could I have thought that a Hindu mantra would be more beneficial for me than the sweetness and consolation of the Name of Jesus Christ? I was like Adam in the Garden of Eden, and I was trying to get something better, when I already had everything of true value.

As Swami Satchidananda approached I knew in my heart that initiation was out of the question. The person seated on the floor in front of me had a pencil and paper next to him, so I borrowed them and wrote a note stating, "I changed my mind about receiving initiation." When the Swami came to me, I immediately handed him the note.

Naturally he was surprised and asked, "You want me to read this *now?*" I nodded affirmatively. Without reading the note he said, "Wait here." He passed by and initiated the others. He read the note in the back of the room and then approached me from behind. He bent over and whispered quietly in my ear, "That's all right. I still like you," which I thought was kind of him to say. I asked if I could leave, and he approved.

I was emotionally shaken up when I left. I felt a deep certainty that I had done the right thing to refuse the initiation. However, I also felt that I had been foolish to have put myself in that situation in the first place. I continued to stay at the ashram for another month. One day when most residents were off the grounds, I happened to walk into the main ashram meeting area and saw two people at the opposite end of a hallway. There was Swami Satchidananda raising his voice in anger at one of the female staff, who was cowering from his words. As far as I could see, the ashram had always been immaculate; nevertheless, Swami Satchidananda raged at how this woman had been negligent in keeping the area clean. As if this raging was not enough, I was astounded to see Swami Satchidananda pick up a large potted plant and throw it with full force to the floor.

I felt like Dorothy watching Toto pull back the curtain to reveal that the great Wizard of Oz was actually an old man pretending to be something he was not. My image of Swami Satchidananda was smashed along with that pot, whose contents were covering the floor. I was the only witness of this encounter between Swami Satchidananda and his disciple, and I did not tell anyone else about it. With the memory of my own physical attack on Derek still etched in my mind, I could not very well sit in self-righteous judgment of Swami Satchidananda. I figured "there but for the grace of God go I." I could have been that disciple who was cowering, and this experience was a clear confirmation of the wisdom of my choice to refuse initiation. However, I was also concerned that some day in the future I could potentially put forth an image of being an advanced teacher and then fall short of living up to that perfect ideal. Many years later I found out that Swami Satchidananda, who was at that time in his early sixties, was giving some of his naive young female devotees a different kind of initiation—a "sexual initiation." As was reported in 1991 by the Associated Press, "Susan Cohen, a Connecticut mental health therapist, said Satchidananda took advantage of her when she was a student from 1969 to 1977. 'It would be very healing for everyone if Swami would address this issue publicly and stop denying it,' she said."

This same article stated that in 1971 Swami Satchidananda invited Sylvia Shapiro, age 19, to accompany him on a worldwide trip. She is now a New York lawyer, yet on that trip she served as a cook and photographer. In addition, she gave him massages twice a day. "'In Manila, he turned it from a massage into oral sex,' Ms. Shapiro said. 'I was upset. He didn't want to talk about it. He said he knew best, and I shouldn't worry about it.'" Ms. Shapiro maintained that the relationship continued for a year, but later Swami Satchidananda denied the relationship.[1]

The sex scandal that broke out in the early 90s caused many of his followers to leave Yogaville. Nonetheless, other devotees stayed, apparently believing the denials of their guru. When he gave a public speech in 1991, seven women protested, making sexual allegations.

> "I don't think it's as much the sex as the abuse of power," says a former Yogavillian also requesting anonymity. "With a guru, you have a trust," she says. "The Swami said he is a celibate." This former devotee talked to some of the women who claimed to have been abused and believed them. She says that not only was the Swami not forthcoming about the allegations, but he criticized his accusers. "I think an apology is what the women were looking for— an apology and an admission"—instead of "slandering them by saying, 'This is a crazy woman; she's disturbed.'"[2]

Regrettably Swami Satchidananda never admitted any wrongdoing. He passed away as an octogenarian in 2002.

I have come across similar reports of other gurus who have come to America from India and succumbed to this same temptation. There was also the temptation of materialism that many gurus could not resist. Apparently these Eastern spiritual teachers came with the good intention of bringing forth the exalted ideals of yoga, yet became seduced by sex, power, and position, so readily available in the West. However, the personal shortcomings of specific gurus, such as Swami Satchidananda, do not invalidate the value of the yoga disciplines they advocated, which do promote personal and spiritual growth.

In this autobiography I advocate the benefits of yoga, yet I also feel a necessity to provide a caution about the dangers of such a path if it involves a guru. That is why I have written about the character flaws of Swami Satchidananda and will describe similar shortcomings of other gurus in subsequent chapters to show how widespread the problem is. I hope this information will be helpful for seekers who might otherwise naively choose to follow gurus or spiritual teachers and be oblivious to their human frailty. Although these character flaws do not invalidate the genuine spiritual accomplishments of gurus, they do tarnish the example set for seekers, especially because of the tendency by such gurus to be in denial of their own shortcomings. Christianity has had its own problems with Catholic priests committing abuse; however, only a small percentage of priests have committed abuse with young, vulnerable boys. In the case of gurus, it appears that the percentage of abusing gurus is much greater, perhaps because there is less oversight in a yoga ashram, where the guru is considered divine and above questioning. Vulnerable young female devotees can be convinced by the guru that they are performing a "divine selfless service" as part of "divine play" on earth.

Such character flaws of gurus that abuse their power demonstrate an apparent inability of those involved to come to grips with the shadow side of their natures, which needs to be accepted and integrated into the spiritual path, rather than suppressed. It is this very suppression of the shadow and elevation of the outer "spiritual teacher mask" that produces these bizarre cases of abuse. Taking responsibility for one's misdeeds requires repentance or "metanoia," literally meaning "a change of heart." Repentance, properly understood, is not a call to guilt, but a call to humility and healing. This change of heart in order to come out of denial seems to be generally lacking in the case of the gurus involved in abuse. Also the victims need to take responsibility for a change of heart in order to find healing through forgiveness.

Because of the reprehensible nature of sexual abuse, it would be easy to forget the benefits many people have experienced in their spiritual life due to the positive influences of gurus, who are often flawed humans but still inspirational figures. The highest spiritual experiences are ones in which the seeker completely transcends ego consciousness and has a direct encounter with God. What is not well understood is that when that seeker returns to normal ego consciousness, his ego can remain largely untouched. Ingrained ego flaws need to be addressed at the form level in which they operate. I have no doubt at all that gurus such as Swami Satchidananda generally have had at least some types of genuine and profound transcendent experiences. In the case of those gurus who have had the very deepest spiritual experiences, just being in their presence is uplifting in itself. However, gurus who neglect to address the shadow side of their natures present a mixed bag that is neither all good nor all bad. Consequently, I look upon them in tones of grey, which recognize their walk in the Light that has uplifted many and their walk in darkness that has lead to bitter disappointment and disillusionment of others.

Most seekers who are attracted to gurus are young, impressionable, and naive about the fact that spiritual teachers can attain deep levels of higher consciousness and still retain unevolved ego characteristics. My concern about the naiveté of spiritual seekers is based upon my memory of my own naiveté in 1975, which was shattered in part by Swami Satchidananda's childish tantrum of anger. During satsang he had previously described the relationship between the guru and disciple by using the analogy of opening a coconut. He said the guru is like a hammer that smashes the coconut to pieces in order to obtain the white meat inside. The coconut is the disciple's ego, which must be shattered by the guru to reveal the divine essence within. This kind of analogy gave license for Swami Satchidananda to do almost anything and have it justified as a spiritual lesson for the disciple. I did not have any personal contact with the female devotee who had received Swami Satchidananda's anger, but it is most likely that she felt her guru was giving her a spiritual lesson, rather than expressing his own shortcomings. Imagine the lesson that he could have taught her by saying, "I am sorry. I lost my temper. Even gurus are human and fall short of their ideals. I don't want you to clean up this dirt and broken pot. I will clean up this mess myself because I made it. I hope I can salvage this living plant that I have traumatized with my unseemly outburst." Alas, the standard guru image of perfect spiritual attainment did not allow for such appropriate vulnerability that would have acknowledged the shadow side that even the guru must learn to accept and integrate into his personality.

Although the pot-smashing incident was a wake-up call regarding my own naiveté, I was still willing to dismiss Swami Satchidananda's mistake as a lone exception to his normal high character. I was willing to give him the benefit of the doubt because of my own shortcomings and because of seeing so many of my friends at the ashram who were obviously uplifted by his spiritual teachings. In fact, before I left the ashram, there was a special celebration called *Guru Purnima* to honor the guru as the embodiment of God Himself. At this joyous celebration some of my close friends, who had completed special training, were initiated as sannyasins and given the saffron robe to indicate their renunciation of the world. They were given the title of "swami," one who is at one with himself, to acknowledge their dedication to carrying on the direct teachings of Swami Satchidananda.

One of my close friends was Dharman, who later became Swami Dharmananda. He had what he called his *Ganeshmobile*, which was a van with a picture on the side of Ganesh, the elephant god. For a period of about a month I had a work assignment of driving with him to a distant college campus, and we would sell "Baba Burgers," soy burgers from his own special recipe. He would joyously sing his "Baba Burger Song" to attract customers, and sometimes I would join in the singing—off key, of course. Besides this work I had a lot of friendly social contact with Dharman because, as with Margabandu, only a sheet separated his "room" from mine. Once I gave him a massage, and afterwards he commented, "That was a good massage. I felt like you were a cook lovingly making a wonderful tossed salad."

By the twinkle in his eye I know that he meant he appreciated the massage, but he was also kidding me that I had used too much massage oil.

Consequently, I said, "Next time I'll use oil *and vinegar.*" Dharman was a delight to be with because of his infectious positive and playful attitude. Christianity overall is a bhakti path, and it is well known in yoga that bhakti seekers tend to be so lovingly attached to their chosen ideal that they think others *should* also worship their chosen ideal. However, I did not assume that my fellow residents would be better off if they were devoted to Christ as I was. I recognized the guru and disciple path that Dharman and other residents had chosen was right for them because everyone has a unique path up the mountain, although I felt we will all arrive at the same place on the very top in the Arms of God. You may have gotten the impression from my comments about Swami Satchidananda's shortcomings that I do not think he was divine. I do indeed think he is divine. It's just that I think that *everyone* is divine at the spiritual level and *everyone* is flawed at the human level of the ego, since all egos are illusory. The difference between the guru and the disciple is that the guru knows that he is divine and hopefully has had a direct taste of that divinity. When Ramakrishna met any new spiritual teacher, he would ask him, "Do you have the 'divine commission?'" He meant, "Have you had a direct experience of God that would qualify you to be a teacher?" Since a disciple generally has not had such an experience, he finds it easier to see divinity in his guru than he can see it in himself. I felt these guru and disciple relationships are karmic in nature, so I assumed Swami Satchidananda had been Dharman's guru in former incarnations. I was very happy to see Dharman enter his chosen life path to become a swami, but glad to be on my own journey following in the footsteps of Jesus.

I was grateful for the opportunity to live with so many truly dedicated spiritual seekers. Most of all I would miss Margabandu because we were best friends, and he was such a good example of love for me. Before I left Yogaville the doctor cautioned me that she thought I should stay until the bilirubin readings came down. Seeing that I was intent on leaving, she told me to make sure that I saw a doctor regularly for blood testing. Perhaps still remaining somewhat naive, I felt I had given my life to God and was not concerned about my health, so did not follow up with more tests. As it turned out, seven years later I did happen to have a physical exam and a blood test, which showed a normal bilirubin count.

Just before I left Yogaville, I was invited to have a conference with one of the mature female disciples with whom I had never conversed before. She said, "I hear that you are leaving us."

I said, "Yes, I have really enjoyed being here and have learned a lot. But I am devoted to Jesus and wanted to find a place for Christian fellowship. I am going to a Christian yoga center in California. It's called 'Jesusananda.' Have you heard of it?"

"Yes, I have. As matter of fact, I had heard through the grapevine that you were headed there. I wanted to caution you that the leader there could present a problem for you, so you may want to reconsider your decision."

"What kind of problem could that be?"

"I don't want to say anything unkind. Let's just say that he is a bhakti and sometimes bhaktis get carried away with their emotions. I just wanted to give you that caution for your consideration."

I figured he couldn't be any more emotional than what I had seen Swami Satchidananda display in his anger tantrum, but, of course, did not consider telling her about that. "Thank you for your caution. I will be aware of that when I go there."

She concluded, "I wish you well. But if things do not go well for you there, the door is always open for you to come back here."

---

1. Associated Press, "Swami's Former Followers Say He Demanded Sexual Favors," August 2, 1991, on this date first reported in the Richmond Times Dispatch. This article can be found posted on rickross.com/reference/Yogaville.

2. Lisa Provence, "Guru's Past: Yogaville Visit Opens Old Wounds," The Hook (Charlottesville's newspaper), April 21, 2005. This article can be found posted on rickross.com/reference/Yogaville.

10

JESUSANANDA

≈ ₀ ≈

Since my own life was a blending of Christianity and yoga, I relocated to Santa Cruz, California, to become part of a Christian yoga center called "Jesusananda," led by Demetrius Apollonius.[1] I was 30 years old, and Demetrius was only six years older than that. I appreciated that he was very spiritually enthusiastic. He was brought up in the Greek Orthodox tradition that values repeating the Name of Jesus, called the *Prayer of the Heart* or the *Jesus Prayer*. Demetrius explained, "I had been going to extremes with fasting and meditation. One day I lost control of my bladder and bowel functions. I was overshadowed by the Holy Spirit and I felt my heart beating very fast. Then I felt a divine presence and light expanding in my heart. I saw the word 'Jesus' in my mind's eye and suddenly experienced His Name being written on my heart with a blazing light."

I had already been practicing the Jesus Prayer and was familiar with the teachings of the Early Desert Fathers, so I felt comfortable with the teachings of Demetrius, who was a gifted speaker, as well as an excellent yoga teacher. His wife, Irene, and two children lived at Jesusananda along with his students. I was surprised that Demetrius had not attracted more spiritual seekers. His most devoted student, Otis, had been at Jesusananda the longest. Larry had been there the second longest. Edward, Alex, and Elizabeth were all under twenty-one and were newcomers like myself. All of us worked at the Jesusananda Health Food Store, which Otis managed. With our wages we paid for our room and board in the large house, which served as our home and the place where yoga classes were taught. The house had been donated to Demetrius by an anonymous benefactor.

The first week I was at Jesusananda there was a psychic fair in which the center participated. I was given several psychic readings, but none of these ego-flattering proclamations had the ring of truth. I was, however, interested in the Kirlian photography also being showcased at the fair. It's supposed to be a way of photographing the energy field around objects and people. The next two pages show two Kirlian photographs of my fingers.

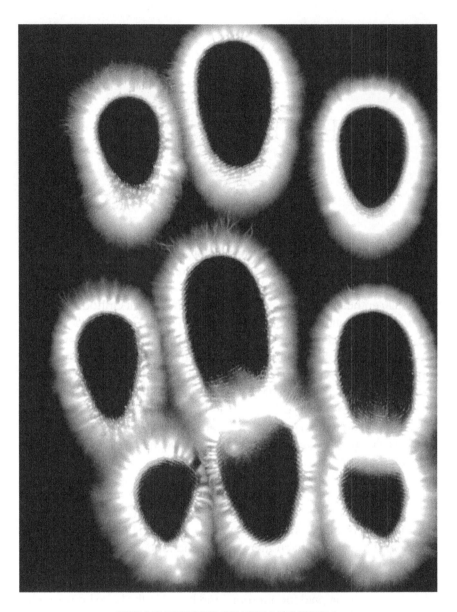

KIRLIAN PHOTOGRAPH NUMBER 1

Picture number one is a photograph of my fingers taken while I was completely relaxed. It is a picture of the energy field around the three fingertips of my right hand, and there are three different exposures. Notice how in this picture the energy field around each finger is thick and even throughout.

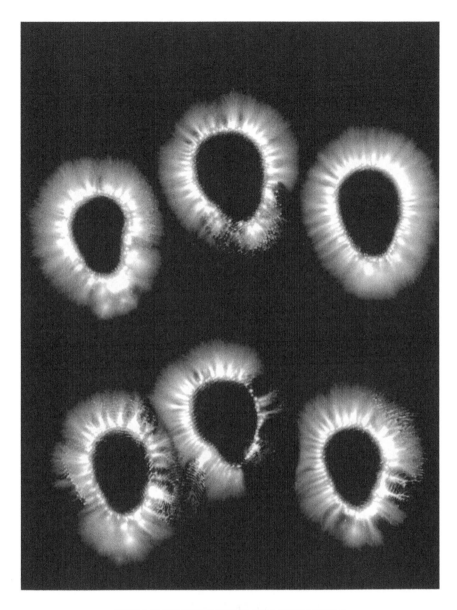

KIRLIAN PHOTOGRAHPH NUMBER 2

Photograph number 2 shows the same middle three fingers with two exposures. In contrast to the first picture when I was relaxed, during the second picture I was trying mentally to expand the energy field around my fingers for egotistical reasons. Notice how when I tried to exert effort to expand the energy field, the result was that the energy field was actually weakened, as can be seen by the breaks in the energy field. My effort and selfish purpose produced a tension preventing the natural flow of energy.

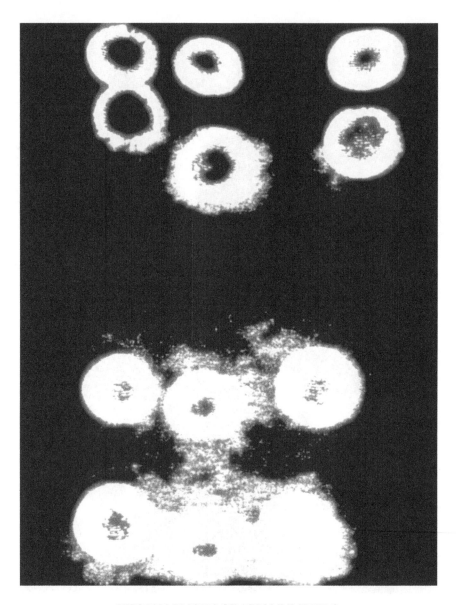

KIRLIAN PHOTOGRAPH NUMBER 3

I made friends with a woman named Ruth who told me about her own experiment with Kirlian photography. Photograph number 3 displays four exposures of Ruth's middle three fingers. The top exposure is a picture of her energy field when she was relaxed. The second exposure down from the top was taken immediately after Ruth began to pray for someone who had asked for her prayers. The third exposure was taken after Ruth had been praying for a while when she was fully focused on surrounding and filling the other person with love and light. The final exposure on the bottom was taken a few minutes later while Ruth was still concentrating on sending love and light to the other person. You can see how the bottom two exposures show a much more intense energy field around each finger than can be seen in the top two exposures. This example shows that sending prayers to others actually strengthens the one who is sending these prayers.

Later I learned that Kirlian photography research has been done on sick people before, during, and after receiving prayer healing. Before prayer healing, sick people had a broken and a very dim energy field around their fingers. During prayer healing, the energy field around their fingers was unbroken and very bright. After prayer healing, the energy field remained bright, but not quite as bright as when the prayer healing was being given. This demonstrated that sick people can increase their energy field during a prayer healing session itself and retain that increased energy field to a certain degree even afterward. Like the rest of us, Demetrius had a Kirlian photograph made of his fingers, and his picture was unlike anyone else's. On the positive side, there were very long extensions of light coming off of his fingertips, and these curled to the right or left. On the negative side, there were complete breaks between the light extensions, so the energy field was very uneven. I attributed this to Demetrius being a Scorpio with a lot of energy being sent out from his body. He was also an emotional person with strong fluctuations in temperament. When he was up, everyone was elevated, and when he was down, everyone was brought down. Most times he was uplifting and inspiring.

I had never seen Demetrius stay depressed for any length of time, but I had a hint of what that might be like when I met one of his former students, Lewis, who came back to the center for a brief visit. Lewis seemed disappointed when I told him that he would not be able to see Demetrius, who was out of town at the time. Lewis told me that he had what he called "an unfortunate disagreement" with Demetrius in the past. Consequently, he wanted to come back and give his best wishes to Demetrius. Later, I asked Otis about what happened when Lewis had lived at the center. He told me that Demetrius got the impression that Lewis was trying to be a teacher himself and was trying to steal his students away from him. Lewis and Demetrius had a physical altercation, and the result was that Demetrius became extremely depressed. He closed down the center for months and had recently reopened it before I and the other newcomers arrived. In fact, Otis said that our presence had fully revitalized and inspired Demetrius.

Likewise I felt revitalized by Demetrius. When I first arrived, he took me with him wherever he went so we could get to know each other, and we really enjoyed each other's company. Also I spent a lot of time with Edward and Alex, whose youthful enthusiasm was contagious. In the mornings we chanted the Jesus Prayer, meditated together, and practiced our yoga disciplines. We shared meals together, worked together at the health food store, took saunas together, and had many interesting conversations.

I especially enjoyed Demetrius's lectures. At one evening lecture, which was open to the public, he talked about the benefits of using a brain wave machine for meditation. He explained that the device is a biofeedback system to increase the depth of meditation by letting the meditator know what type of brain wave is occurring in the mind. Beta brain waves are 13 to 28 cycles per second and these are prominent during everyday living. Alpha waves of 8 to 12 cycles per second occur when you close your eyes and relax in meditation. Theta brain waves of 4 to 7 cycles per second predominate when the meditator sees visions. Theta waves also happen when the sleeping person is dreaming, thus having rapid eye movements, called *REM sleep*. Finally, delta brain waves from 0 to 3 cycles per second occur either during deep dreamless sleep or during very deep meditation.

Demetrius had purchased such a device, and during the lecture he put the device on his head to demonstrate how brain waves could be lowered through meditation. The device sounded out a different steady tone for each type of brain wave so the meditator could know the depth of his meditation. When Demetrius closed his eyes and meditated with the device attached to his head, we could hear the sound change from the steady tone for beta brain waves to a different steady tone to indicate alpha brain waves. After Demetrius showed us how to relax into meditation in this way, he wanted his audience to have a chance to use the device. Many were able to lower their brain waves from beta to alpha, although none were able to go to the deeper theta or delta levels. Everyone who wanted to use the device was allowed to do so, and the device was then given back to Demetrius, who handed it to me, gesturing for me use it. I deferred by saying, "I've already used it several times, so there's no need for me to use it now."

Demetrius persisted in a friendly yet insistent tone, "Come on, it's your turn," as he extended the device to me. After about two minutes of using the device, my brain waves went from beta, to alpha, to theta, and finally stayed at delta. You might think that my demonstration of reaching delta was a good thing, but it was a stumbling block. First of all, it was a stumbling block for me because it was a temptation for spiritual pride, which I understood was and remains my greatest weakness. I gave no outer signs of pride at that time, but I did not resist the inner temptation. Second, it was a stumbling block for both Demetrius and me because it was a temptation for comparison. It was the first time I realized that there was a subtle competition between us. After that night, I did not want to do anything that would make matters worse in this regard.

A few days later Demetrius gave me the brain wave device and told me he wanted me to mail it back to the manufacturer for a refund. "What reason should I give to the manufacture for why you are returning it?"

"It's malfunctioning," Demetrius said in an uncharacteristically abrupt manner. It appeared to me that Demetrius was distancing himself from me. I had been growing closer to Edward and Alex, and I got the impression that Demetrius was getting jealous of our closeness. I was concerned he might think I was trying to take away his students, as he had imagined Lewis doing in the past. To alleviate any potential concerns Demetrius might have, I offered to do promotional work that highlighted him as a spiritual teacher and so I wrote articles and sent out press releases.

I convinced Demetrius to hold a three-day Christian yoga retreat, and I did all the planning and coordination. We had a good turnout of twenty-five participants. Everything went like clockwork until a retreatant named Sam came to me for a private conference, which seemed a bit odd because it was a silent retreat like the ones in which I had participated at Yogaville. Sam spoke to me nervously, "I asked to talk with Demetrius alone and he agreed. I was critical of some things he said at his lecture yesterday about the Early Desert Fathers. He became angry and pushed me against the wall. He grabbed me by the shirt and then he walked away."

"Did you insult him or give him cause to be physical with you?" I asked.

Sam said, "No. I just told him I thought some of the Early Desert Fathers were too focused on maintaining spiritual disciplines. Then I said that I thought relationships are more important for spiritual growth than spiritual disciplines. When I told him I didn't think the Desert Fathers, who lived in caves, were the best examples for spiritual seekers today, he became irate and physical. Maybe he thought I was insulting the Desert Fathers. I didn't know what to do about it, so that's why I am coming to you."

"I don't know what to say or do, either. We both need to pray about this and ask to be guided." We prayed together and that was all that happened. I thought I was doing the right thing in this exchange, but I really had blinders on. In my mind I rationalized and made excuses for Demetrius. I was content to assume that maybe Sam had exaggerated the situation. Since it was a silent retreat, I used that as an excuse to not talk to Demetrius about this incident, and after the retreat I avoided bringing up the matter.

Later, another incident happened, this time with Larry, who was by his own admission a lukewarm spiritual seeker. I didn't see the incident myself, but Larry and witnesses who were present told me what happened. Demetrius was very loudly chastising Edward. Larry told Demetrius not to raise his voice. Turning away from Edward, Demetrius redirected his wrath toward Larry and enumerated his shortcomings. He criticized Larry for being late for morning prayer time and for snoozing instead of meditating.

Larry had heard enough and turned around to walk out of the room. Demetrius came at him from behind and sucker punched him in the side. Larry fell down in pain from the punch. Demetrius menacingly insisted that Larry apologize while he was still in pain on the floor. He wanted Larry to admit he should not have interfered with Edward being chastised and he should not have disrespectfully turned his back while Demetrius was talking to him. Larry apologized, but more out of intimidation than anything else. Demetrius felt no need to apologize for hitting one of his students.

After I had heard about this incident, I realized that there was indeed a problem with Demetrius's aggression, but I was still uncertain about what to do. Demetrius caught me off guard by coming to me, saying, "Everyone here respects you. It's important you speak up tomorrow morning at our regular meeting time to tell Larry that he must respect the authority of his teacher. The Early Fathers always respected spiritual authority."

Obviously Demetrius felt that hitting Larry was a justified disciplinary action because of his role as Larry's teacher. However, I knew that the Desert Fathers, who were noted for humility, would never have condoned any form of aggression. It was very clear to me that Demetrius was not open to accepting responsibility for his own shortcomings in this matter and that he would have resisted any attempt on my part to point them out. The next morning after our chanting of the Jesus Prayer and after meditation, Demetrius said, "I believe Don has something to say to Larry."

"Demetrius, you are an excellent teacher of the Jesus Prayer. I know that Larry made some mistakes, and he apologized for them. It's certainly understandable that you got angry at Larry because of his mistakes. Because of my own shortcoming of pridefulness, I need a teacher who can show me by example how to be humble. As my teacher, whom I respect, I am asking you to set the example of how to apologize when you have also made a mistake. I am asking you to apologize to Larry, not for pointing out his shortcomings, but for punching him. If you do not apologize, I will lose my respect for you and I will have no other choice than to leave the center." That is not what I actually said. It is what I *should* have said.

Instead I looked at Larry and said, "If you are walking along the path and see two snakes that are fighting, it is unwise to get between them. If you try to separate the snakes, you will probably be bitten yourself. It is best to keep your distance." On the one hand it wasn't what Demetrius had in mind for me to say to Larry. On the other hand it was not the highest road for me to take. It would have been better to directly confront Demetrius for his physical aggression right then, but instead I made this analogy in which I vaguely referred to Demetrius as a snake. I regret my weakness in not doing what was right. As a community we continued along with our spiritual disciplines and pretended that nothing was amiss.

At a later date I had a startling dream. I was riding on a three-seat bicycle, sandwiched between Demetrius behind me and Edward in front of me. I felt during the dream that I was protecting Edward in some way. Then the dream scene changed to a door that opened, and I carried a lighted candle as I passed through the doorway into a dark room. Suddenly the candle was blown out, and I was utterly surrounded by a totally evil darkness that filled me with terror.

I woke up from this nightmare with a strong impression of evil still present and was concerned about Edward being in danger. I felt compelled to wake Edward up so we could pray together for divine protection from evil, which we did for several hours with a lighted candle. Later in the morning at our meditation time I told Demetrius what had happened. He asked me why I didn't wake him up. I told him I did not feel comfortable going into his bedroom and waking Irene and him up in the middle of the night. I realized from the tone of his question that he suspected that this was an attempt on my part to steal the allegiance of one of his students, as he had imagined Lewis had done in the past. My response did not seem to alleviate his concern.

A few days later I walked into Demetrius's office, and he was loudly berating Edward. "I asked you to go to the store and buy two packages of toilet paper. And what do you do? You come back with two rolls of toilet paper. How long do you think these are going to last?" Demetrius asked with an unusual tone of disdain. Nineteen-year-old Edward looked confused and frightened. His father had forced him to come to the center because he had not done well in school. He was bright, but had a problem with self-worth, so talking to him in this degrading way was totally demoralizing for him.

In order to let Edward escape, I asked Demetrius if I could talk to him alone. After Edward left the room, I told Demetrius, "Edward is already uncertain of himself, so I think we need to look for ways to build up his confidence in himself."

"So now you are going to tell me how to speak to my students? Who do you think you are? You can't even follow the rules here yourself."

"What are you talking about?" I inquired. My mind instantly flashed on the incident of Larry interceding when Demetrius had been criticizing Edward. In this new situation Demetrius was redirecting his anger from Edward to me just as he had switched his anger to Larry during that previous incident. Only later did I recall the image of me sitting between Demetrius and Edward on the three-seat bicycle in my dream of evil.

"You've been eating while working at the health food store!" Demetrius exclaimed.

"No! That's not true," I affirmed. Demetrius had previously established a rule that we could eat any food from the health food store, without cost, as long as we ate only during breaks and not during work time itself. One day in the previous week I was on a break and popped an apricot in my mouth from the dried fruit bin just as Demetrius was coming into the health food store. Demetrius only stayed a few minutes and left without talking to me. I went to Otis, who knew I was on my break at the time when Demetrius visited, and I asked him to remember that I was on break. I explained to Otis that I was concerned that at a future date Demetrius would accuse me of eating while I was working. I wanted a witness to confirm that Demetrius had mistakenly perceived the situation.

"I saw you eating at work with my own two eyes," Demetrius reasserted.

"You saw me eat, but I was on my break. You can call Otis to confirm what I am saying."

"What a lame excuse!"

"Are you calling me a liar?" I asked.

"Yes, I am calling you a liar," Demetrius exclaimed in a loud voice.

"Call Otis," I asserted in an equally loud voice.

"Don't you tell me what to do," Demetrius angrily demanded. This time he raised both arms and made two fists in a threatening manner.

At this point I considered walking away to let tempers cool down. But I quickly dismissed that option because I remembered what happened to Larry when he turned his back on Demetrius and tried to walk away. I told Demetrius, "I won't walk away like Larry did and allow you to sucker punch me from behind."

This comment inflamed Demetrius even further. Inviting a physical confrontation, he hollered, "COME ON! Take your best shot." It was crystal clear that I couldn't walk away without getting punched from behind, yet I did not want to throw a fist at him, either. A fist fight is never a good idea, but is especially foolish for someone wearing glasses like myself. The option of taking off my glasses would mean not being able to see approaching punches. At this point all I wanted to do was to get away from this situation without any physical harm being done to either of us. I felt I could minimize physical harm by using skills learned on the high school wrestling team. Thus I jumped forward toward Demetrius and lowered my head below his fists so he could not hit me. Then I maneuvered to go behind his body, and I wrapped my arms and legs around him so that he could not punch me.

Our bodies were lying on a couch with my arms wrapped around his chest and my legs wrapped around his torso to prevent him from getting up and assaulting me. Once I had neutralized his ability to harm me, I was able to turn my focus to mentally repeating the Name of Jesus. Even though I knew Demetrius could not free himself, he was struggling vigorously to escape my grip and hollering at the top of his lungs. I told him I would let go of him if he promised to let me leave without harm. But he disregarded my offer and was hysterical in his anger. Hearing Demetrius hollering wildly, Edward came running into the room. He was shocked and stood there dumbfounded, not knowing what to do. I told him to get Demetrius's wife, Irene, which he did. When Irene came, I repeated my promise to let Demetrius up if he did not harm me. Irene pleaded with him to promise that he would not attack me.

"I love you, Demetrius. Please stop struggling, and Don will let go of you, and you can let him go away," implored Irene.

Edward said, "We love you, Demetrius. Promise to stop, and this will be over."

I added, "Demetrius, I love you too. I want to let go of you, and I want to go away. Let's end this." However, he would not stop struggling. I continued to mentally repeat the Jesus Prayer.

Finally Demetrius had exhausted himself in struggling. With Edward and Irene looking on, I said, "I don't want to hurt you, Demetrius, and I don't want to hold you down anymore either. I am going to voluntarily let go of you and hope that you have enough composure to not attack me. I trust you to do the right thing here when I let you up. I'm going to let go now." Then I took my arms away from his chest and released my legs that had immobilized his body. While my body remained on the couch, Demetrius stood up. He turned around to face me and grabbed at me, catching hold of the silver cross and chain around my neck. He broke the chain ripping it from my body. Then he uttered an incomprehensible groan. Turning his body away, he ran out of the office toward the kitchen. I was relieved it was finally over. I was shaken up, but considering the circumstances I was unusually calm inside, comforted by repeating the Name of Jesus.

I stayed in the office as Irene followed Demetrius to the kitchen. I kneeled on the floor and took off my glasses and wrist watch. Next I began to recite the Lord's Prayer. As I repeated, "Our Father, who art in heaven...," I felt I was giving myself and the whole situation into God's hands. When I finished the Lord's Prayer, I felt a strong impulse telling me to go to the doorway and look into the kitchen. I picked up my glasses, and when I got to the doorway, I saw Demetrius on the other side of the kitchen. He had grabbed the largest knife in the kitchen. Irene, normally a passive person, was right next to him, courageously grabbing his arm and screaming, "No," in a very loud, commanding voice. Demetrius was looking at Irene, and she managed to grab the knife out of his hand.

Just then Demetrius for the first time saw me standing at the doorway on the other side of the room and his eyes widened with rage. He turned, grabbed an acorn squash from the counter, and hurled it across the room at me. It hit the right side of my head. Up until that instant I was sure that I was protected by my constant prayer. Even when I saw Demetrius grasp the knife, I wasn't afraid. Yet when my head was hit by the acorn squash, I realized all at once that I was really in danger. I had a tremendous surge of fear and adrenaline and ran from the kitchen with Demetrius in hot pursuit. I ran perhaps the fastest I had ever run in my life and left him in my dust, even though under normal circumstances he was a much faster runner than I was.

The first thing I did after escaping was to go to a nearby church to pray. Fortunately, I had relatives from my mother's side of the family in Connecticut who had relocated to Santa Cruz. I called them, knowing I would be welcome to stay with them temporarily; however, I left out the details of why I was actually calling. One of these relatives was my fun-loving cousin, Ronnie. When I saw him for the first time in years, we laughed together over some of our childhood adventures. We vividly remembered our painting the outside shower building at my parents' summer cottage. We had playfully dueled each other with our brushes as swords and ended up with paint all over our clothes, even in our hair.

I stayed with my relatives for two weeks in order to conclude my service of teaching a yoga class at the local YMCA. Edward and Alex remembered my class and visited me there, even though Demetrius had ordered them not to see me. They explained that Demetrius was beside himself with anger after the fight. He expelled everyone from the center for that entire night and for the next couple of days. Then Demetrius invited everyone back and told them that I had attacked him without cause and wounded his heart area by scratching him with my fingernails. I told Edward and Alex that I had a watch on with a hand-crafted silver band. This specially made wristband had metal prongs that may have inadvertently scratched him, but, if so, it was without my awareness. Demetrius also quoted me as having said, "I am not cowardly like Larry." I explained to Edward and Alex that this was not actually what I had said, and I asked them to tell Larry that I was misquoted. I was gratified to hear that they believed my version of the altercation.

A few days before taking a flight to my parents' home in Connecticut, I went back to Jesusananda to pick up my belongings, yet did so with much trepidation. When I arrived, Demetrius said he did not want me to apologize to him; however, he asked me to apologize to Irene. I said to her, "I am sorry if I caused you any distress by my actions. I want to thank you for your courage and help in a difficult situation." In fact, she may have saved my life.

Then Demetrius and I went to talk privately in his office, the scene of our altercation. He started by saying, "You must have long fingernails because you put a deep gash in my heart area, and I had to go to the hospital to get stitches."

I extended my hands and said, "As you can see my fingernails are not long. You were probably scratched by the long metal prongs on my watchband, but I was unaware that this was occurring at the time." I showed him the hand position I used when my hands were wrapped around his chest. "This is how my hands were held and so my watchband must have been pressing right over your heart. However, even this would not have harmed you if you had not been struggling so vehemently to get away. It was your own struggling that must have created the digging effect into your heart area. I would have taken off the wristband if I had known it would be hurting you. But actually at no time did I have any intention to hurt you physically. I apologize to you for anything I did that may have caused you emotional or physical harm."

I waited, hoping that Demetrius would take the opportunity to also apologize, to whatever degree he was capable. The closest he could come was, "I talked to Otis, and he confirmed that you were on a break on that day when you had been eating at work." I thought it was too bad that he had not attempted to talk to Otis before things escalated beyond repair, yet I did not say that. Also I did not bring up the incident of his forcefully intimidating Sam over the issue of the Desert Fathers or of his punching Larry and feeling justified in doing so.

Considering the past ability of Demetrius to rationalize his behavior, I did not sense that he had the ability to apologize for his part in our confrontation. But I felt I needed to ask a few probing questions. "I voluntarily let you go. I did that because I trusted you. I trusted that you would let me go just as I had let you go. However, instead of letting me go, you grabbed my silver chain and ripped it away from me. Then you hit me with that acorn squash and chased me. Why couldn't you just let me go?"

To avoid answering the question, he half smiled and said, "I see you are learning to run faster." He was making reference to the times in the past when he had all of us doing running exercises outside, and I did not distinguish myself as much of a runner then.

I nodded my agreement as I silently repeated the Jesus Prayer. Yet I was not going to let the question go entirely. "You haven't addressed my question. To be more specific, why did you pick up that knife in the kitchen? What were you going to do with it?"

I knew he would not answer the question. To do so would have required an apology on his part, and he would not be interested in this kind of self-examination—at least not in a conversation with me. But I asked the question anyway because I wanted him to at least look at how far off the deep end he had been. I did not actually let him know what I was thinking, which was that during that altercation I felt he was temporarily possessed by evil—the kind of evil that would drive him to pick up that knife with the intention of using it.

I also did not tell him that the dream of evil I had a few days before was a precursor to our altercation. Some philosophies maintain that prior to every significant experience in our lives, we have a dream that prepares us for what is to come. I felt that was what had happened when I interceded between Edward and Demetrius—first in the dream and then in the office. Similarly, I faced evil in the dream and then again in this experience with Demetrius. Luckily, my prayers prepared me to face this danger, and without these prayers I may have given in to evil, as I believe Demetrius had done.

Normally evil is associated with wicked actions, but evil as an action is the result of evil as a thought. This evil thought is what I experienced in my dream of a terrifying darkness. In my opinion, evil in the form of thought is the very extreme belief that you are utterly alone and separate from God. There are disincarnate entities, called devils, who have devoted themselves to this belief. These negative entities can influence others to invest in this fearful idea and thus become vulnerable to harm. Nevertheless, this fearful belief itself is not true because God is always with you; yet the power of belief can make what is not true *appear* to be true. The belief in evil can make it seem very real and very fearful. If you give in to this belief in evil, it is because you are relying too much on yourself. If you are able to resist this belief in evil, it is because you are relying on God. If my prayer preparation—the result of my dream—had not happened, the experience could have ended even more tragically than it did. As it was, I felt fortunate that we had both escaped without serious physical injury.

However, there was serious emotional upheaval, and I was hoping that Demetrius and I could come to a deeper level of forgiveness than this conversation provided. With God's help I would have to find peace and forgiveness on my own and trust that with God's help Demetrius would find peace and forgiveness on his own.

To avoid addressing my question about why he picked up the knife and what he would have done with it, he answered my question with a question. "Why did you say, 'I love you too'?" He asked this question in a derisive tone, which implied that I was claiming to love him when I did not.

"I do love you, Demetrius. Even now in this conversation I am too afraid of you to fully feel the love I genuinely have for you. When I said, 'I love you too,' it was to acknowledge that you are my brother in Christ. Because of our fight, my fear didn't allow me to be as loving as I would normally be. But at least I held to the standard of never intentionally wanting to hurt you in any way. When we had the fight, all I wanted to do was to get away so neither you nor I would be harmed. Now I have the same goal—to be able to walk away without any further harm to you or me. We need time to be away from each other so we can heal."

"All your things have already been packed, so you are ready to go," Demetrius said as he pointed to my duffle bag in the corner.

"Did you find my silver chain and cross? When it was ripped off, it was left on the floor in this small room, so I assumed you would have found it."

Demetrius shrugged his shoulders, "No, I didn't find it. I don't know where it is."

"After our struggle, I took my watch off and left it in your office. Have you seen it?"

"I haven't seen that, either."

"I am owed three weeks back wages. Will you be paying me those?"

"Of course! I will instruct Otis to send a check to your parents' home in Connecticut."

We said goodbye as politely as we could under the circumstances. I picked up my duffle bag and that was the last time I saw Demetrius. Later that day I unpacked my belongings and was very upset to find that my writings were missing. Using a manual typewriter in those days before personal computers, I had written first drafts of a meditation manual and an autobiography. I was angry that all this work was gone. It was then that I remembered a vivid dream that I had on the night of the altercation. In this dream I saw a glass mirror being shattered, and I saw Demetrius throwing pages of paper into a flaming fireplace. When I woke up from the dream, I thought it was only symbolic, but after my manuscripts disappeared, I became convinced that Demetrius had destroyed my writings. Also, my silver chain, cross, and wristwatch could not have disappeared into thin air, so I concluded that he had also disposed of these. In addition to being upset about his destructiveness, I was upset at his dishonesty about what he had done and unwillingness to accept responsibility for his behavior; however, I did not feel that going back to Demetrius to confront him would produce any positive results.

After returning to my parent's house, the fact that Demetrius had been less than honest with me was confirmed by the fact that he did not send the check for my wages as he had promised. I would need to stay for three months at my parents' house to focus on recovering from my experience in Santa Cruz. During this time I learned to let go of focusing on what Demetrius had done inappropriately, and instead took responsibility for my own inappropriate behavior. Also I reminded myself of all the good times and positive experiences that had been temporarily obscured by the confrontation that had ended my stay at Jesusananda.

Demetrius had not believed me when I told him the truth, and his mistrust was the trigger for our confrontation. As part of my healing process I allowed my mind to recall other experiences in which I had not been believed. I remembered one of my previous art teachers, who accused me of copying a drawing of a man's head. I told him it was my original picture, but he refused to believe me no matter how vehemently I objected to his accusation. Then there was the time I was in the bathroom, and my sister Joanna wanted to come in—a common problem in a house with seven people and one bathroom. I informed her, "I will come out when I am done. I am doing number two."

"No, you aren't." Joanna surprised me by disbelieving me. "I'll give you a nickel if you can prove that you are really doing number two."

"You have a deal," I agreed. At my young age, a nickel was more money than I had at the time, plus I was offended that she would think I was not telling the truth.

Five minutes later I finished my business and automatically flushed the toilet, and then suddenly realized to my dismay that I had flushed away the evidence. The wheels of my mind started to turn to figure out what I could do to get out of this predicament. I couldn't tell the truth to my sister because she certainly wouldn't believe me now. I searched the medicine cabinet and was pleasantly surprised to discover some dark brown medicine in a tube just like toothpaste. I squeezed out almost all of it into the toilet bowl. It came out of the tube in one long, continuous, and very thin column. I opened the bathroom door and called out, "Joanna, come on in and see for yourself."

She took one look into the toilet and hollered from upstairs, "Mom!"

"What?" came my mother's reply from downstairs.

"There is a problem. You have to come up here and see for yourself."

I stood dreading what would come next. Sure enough my mother came up the stairs and exclaimed, "Oh, my God. What's the matter with your bowels?" as she looked upon the toothpaste-shaped brown droppings and then looked at me with genuine concern for my health.

To prevent a visit to the doctor for an invasive examination and to alleviate the fearful look on my mother's face, I had to admit the error of my ways. I pulled out what was left of the brown medicine and confessed only because there was no other option. "So your bowels are OK. What's wrong with your head? What were you thinking?" asked my mother, to which I shrugged my shoulders without a verbal response. The irony of the situation was that I had in effect lied—not verbally, but by my actions—to prove that I had originally told the truth.

Next I recalled a high school football practice in which, as a defensive end, I was running to block a punt. Roy, the halfback, made such a feeble attempt to block me that it was obvious he was only pretending to block me. I instantly concluded that this must be a fake punt and that the punter would try to throw a pass to Roy. Consequently, I stopped my run at the punter and stuck like glue with Roy to hopefully intercept the expected pass. However, I was surprised that this anticipated pass never came, and the punter punted the ball as usual.

At the end of the practice, Roy came over and asked me why I had not tried to run at the punter. He explained that the coach was considering, for the first time, starting me for the final game of my senior year, because of what had happened the day before when it had rained. Because of the rain we weren't able to have our usual outdoor practice, so instead we had an indoor wrestling tournament. Players competing for the same position on the football team were pitted against each other. The two players that the coach thought were the least skilled at their position wrestled first, and the winner went on to wrestle the next highest rated player on the couch's depth chart.

When the time came for the ends to compete, I knew I would be wrestling first because I was the low man on the coach's totem pole. I wrestled the other end, who also got very little playing time, and I won. Then I was matched against an end who got quite a bit more playing time than I did. Using the element of surprise, I suddenly charged him and pinned him in less than fifteen seconds. That gave me added confidence. Although I was a slow runner, that didn't matter in wrestling. Instead of running speed, I had agility, the ability to move my body quickly in short bursts of speed. The wrestling also showcased my will power and ability to out-think and out-maneuver my opponent, even if my adversary was stronger than I was. I proceeded to pin each of the other five ends, one after the other, finishing with pins of the two first-string players. Most of these pins were done quickly, in less than a minute. This was astounding to the coach and the players because I wasn't considered athletic, being such a slow runner. The coach must have remembered my wrestling performance on the following day when he was considering starting me. Roy told me that the coach had specifically told him not to block me out so he could see me run down the punter. But because I had stopped running at the punter, the coach concluded that I was afraid, and that is why he decided to not have me start the game. When I told Roy what had really happened, even he didn't believe me. Thus I went from being seen as a courageous wrestler one day to appearing to be a coward and liar the next.

Although I lost the opportunity to start in our biggest game at the end of the year against our arch rival from across town, at least I played in the second half, after the score was thirty-something to nothing. On one play I had an extremely clear and strong psychic impression that the play that was called was an end run to the right side where I was the right end. I hollered out as loud as I could, "It's an end run to this side," as the other team was about to hike the ball. The quarterback on the other team must have freaked out to hear me correctly call out the exact play he had called because he dropped the ball as it was snapped. It *was* an end run, but I headed for the quarterback, who was picking up the ball he had dropped. I got blocked by a player that I hadn't seen because he unexpectedly came from my left side, while I was looking to the right where the halfback and fullback were coming toward me as blockers. I got the wind knocked out of me by the block and fell down. At a later date, the film of the game was played for the team, and afterwards a coach came to me and asked why I had not gotten up on that play. I told him I was blocked and had the wind knocked out of me. However, the film actually only showed the top of my body and did not show the blocker who had knocked me down. The coach didn't believe me and thought that I had tripped and was negligent about getting up. I also told the coach that I had called out the play before the snap, but he refused to believe that either.

After reviewing these experiences of not being believed, along with my experience of Demetrius disbelieving me, I concluded that I could not allow other people's ideas about me, whether accurate or inaccurate, to determine my self-worth. I had invested in allowing other people, especially teachers, to become the eyes through which I perceived my worth. Instead of allowing others to determine my self-worth, I felt it would be better to invest in my opinion of myself. But relying only on my opinion of myself was not ideal either because of the dangers of denial and rationalization. In addition, relying on my opinion of myself led to comparing myself with others, which only resulted in the extremes of pride or self-belittlement. I needed to have a self-worth that was not based on special talents or abilities that some people have and others do not. I wanted it to have a deeper and more stable foundation.

I realized I needed to allow my self-worth to rest securely in the gentle, loving Hands of my heavenly Father. Understanding this intellectually was relatively easy, yet the practical application of basing my self-worth on a deeper and more loving relationship with God would take time. Of course, I had the example of Jesus to follow. I understood from my experience with Demetrius that above all I was being called to learn the true meaning of forgiveness. I had managed to come up with a forgiveness tinged with some lingering resentments, but what I wanted and needed was the kind of loving forgiveness that Jesus demonstrated.

I had already learned in the past from Margabandu how to heal others by feeling God's love for myself and letting that divine love overflow through me to others. I understood that manifesting love was my royal road to serving as a healer for others who specifically ask for healing. However, it did not occur to me that this same healing process could be applied to my relationships with everyone, even Demetrius. I wanted to truly love him, and I prayed for true forgiveness in our relationship. But I was painfully aware of my reduced ability to contact divine love myself, which limited my ability to heal myself and heal my relationship with Demetrius.

Living with my parents for three months was helpful for my healing. Repeating the Name of Jesus helped me in my healing process. I was inspired by reading about St. Seraphim, who was a famous Russian *Staretz*, or holy man and spiritual director. He was an Eastern Orthodox monk who practiced the Jesus Prayer. St. Seraphim's disciple Motovilov had wanted to know all his life what was the true goal of Christian life. St. Seraphim read his mind and told him that good deeds, fasting, and prayer were helpful as a means of spiritual growth, but that the goal was to acquire the Holy Spirit. He described how Moses glowed with a light so bright that the people could not look at him and how Jesus was transfigured with a dazzling light on Mt. Tabor. These examples illustrated the correlation between acquiring the Holy Spirit and being filled with a divine light.

When Motovilov was told this, he said he wanted a more complete understanding of what it means to acquire the Holy Spirit. St. Seraphim prayed for Motovilov to be given this understanding. Here is Motovilov's description of what happened next as he gazed at St. Seraphim:

> Then I looked at the Staretz and was panic-stricken. Picture, in the sun's orb, in the most dazzling brightness of its noon-day shining, the face of a man who is talking to you. You see his lips moving, the expression of his eyes, you hear his voice, you feel his arms round your shoulders, and yet you see neither his arms, nor his body, nor his face, you lose all sense of yourself, you can see only the blinding light which spreads everywhere, lighting up the layer of snow covering the glade, and igniting the flakes that are falling on us both like white powder.
>
> "What do you feel?" asked Father Seraphim.
>
> "An amazing well-being!" I replied.
>
> "But what exactly is it?"
>
> "I feel a great calm in my soul, a peace which no words can express."[2]

Reading about St. Seraphim was a significant reminder for me that all of my spiritual practices, including repeating the Name of Jesus, were simply a means of acquiring the Holy Spirit, or rather revealing the Holy Spirit that is already within each of us. Silent meditation in particular became my means of opening up to the experience of being filled with the Holy Spirit, with light, and with peace. I felt my heart opening again to divine love, and with it I felt I was healing my relationship with Demetrius. Yet a deeper, more complete healing of my relationship with him would take longer.

When I felt my time of living with my parents was coming to a close, I did one important thing just before I left. I went to my father and said, "In the Old Testament there is a tradition of children asking for their father's blessing. I'd like to follow that tradition and ask you for your blessing. I'd like to kneel and have you put your hands on my head for the blessing. You don't have to say anything. All you have to do is feel you are blessing me. Would you be willing to do that?" He was surprised at my unusual request but willingly complied as I knelt for his blessing. I did indeed feel blessed by him. I had resented his authority as I grew up and had never fully appreciated him. In asking for this blessing I was indirectly saying that I forgave him for the past and was asking for his forgiveness of me. I was belatedly accepting his authority as my human father. However, it occurred to me that at a deeper level I was accepting the Authority of my heavenly Father as well, and perhaps letting go of a chunk of my fear of God. Possibly in my time with Demetrius I unknowingly had carried with me my inner resentment of authority stemming from my father. I felt finding peace with my father and my heavenly Father as well helped me in my process of healing in relation to Demetrius. At the time, I believed that my confrontation with him and my process of healing were important pieces in my shadow puzzle. By facing the issues of confrontation, forgiveness, and healing, I felt I was coming closer to solving the shadow puzzle. I didn't know exactly why I felt that way, but it would take a change in the scenery of my life to find out.

Reading *Edgar Cayce: The Sleeping Prophet*, I was fascinated by the life story of this psychic. After placing himself in a trance, he told seekers about their past lives and explained how to bring about healing in their present lives. I made changes in my diet based on suggestions from his readings. I was encouraged by the fact that Cayce believed in Christ, yet he valued Eastern ideas related to reincarnation, meditation, and breathing practices. I called the A.R.E. (Association for Research and Enlightenment), in Virginia Beach, Virginia to inquire about the possibility of my teaching yoga there. I was referred to the Aquarian Age Yoga Center, and Jan, the director, invited me to come and take up residence there, which I did in March of 1976.

---

1. The names Demetrius Apollonius and Jesusananda are pseudonyms. This Christian yoga center was located in California, but actually not in Santa Cruz.
2. "The Notes of Motovilov" in Valentine Zander, *St. Seraphim of Sarov*, translated by Sister Gabriel Anne (Crestwood, NY: St. Vladimir's Seminary Press, 1975), pp. 90-91.
3. Photograph courtesy of the Edgar Cayce Foundation, A.R.E. at 215 67th Street, Virginia Beach, VA 23451, Tel. 800-333-4499 and 757-428-3588.

EDGAR CAYCE[3]

MEHER BABA

11

THE AQUARIAN AGE YOGA CENTER

~ ॰ ~

Ideally I wanted to be part of a Christian yoga center, but going to the Aquarian Age Yoga Center was a good second best alternative. Most ashrams have a bias toward the teachings of one charismatic guru or spiritual teacher, who serves as an authority figure and in some cases a cult figure. In contrast to this, the Yoga Center had a truly universal approach to spirituality that honored all spiritual teachers equally, both in theory and practice. Although I was devoted to Jesus, I admired certain qualities of some gurus. I liked Meher Baba's simplicity. His saying, "Don't worry, be happy" stuck in my mind. Remembering my own youthful tendency to say "I'm sorry" excessively, I adopted a variation of Meher Baba's quote. Whenever someone said "I'm sorry" about a minor matter, I would say, "Don't be sorry. Be happy." It usually brought a happy response.

Today there are many "lovers" of Meher Baba throughout the world. Some of these devotees belong to a subgroup called Sufism Reoriented. Unlike traditional Sufism associated with Islam, followers of this path "reorient" their lives to conform with Meher Baba's teachings of unselfish love, devotion, and service to others. These devotees believe in the evolution of consciousness through reincarnation and the involution of consciousness through inner spiritual development. They practice celibacy before marriage and often live together in communities.

I felt Meher Baba was a holy man, yet wasn't convinced he was an *avatar* or God-man, as his close followers believed. But I was encouraged to read in his biography that he taught that all seekers have a "divine vocation"—a calling to discover their true divine nature as part of God.

> Meher Baba says ... [to all others], "You, too, if you but knew it, are God: Why not wake up?" He claims no superiority for himself; for the entire essence of this knowledge is to lose every residue of self-importance. Any man freed from identity with his empirical self, thus being able to know his real self, could say as Baba says.[1]

Another thing I liked about this guru was that he had remained silent for 44 consecutive years. Although I had been on silent retreats in the past, I decided to follow Meher Baba's example of silence in everyday life. I set the goal of a three-day silence, and on the third day I was in the kitchen when I said to Jan, "Where's the...." I caught myself, but it was too late. Jan and I both started laughing, yet I returned to silence to finish out the rest of the third day. I had an increased sense of admiration for Meher Baba as a result of my experiment in "word fasting." We also upheld a Yoga Center tradition of fasting from solid food every Saturday. Some of us drank only water, while others fasted on juices or herbal teas. I liked the moderate aspect of this fasting, having seen some friends in the past mess themselves up by going to extremes. Unlike my experience with the residents of other spiritual communities, the residents here were rather uninhibited. For example, at night around 10 PM, we would all, men and women alike, go for a ten-minute walk to the beach in the cover of darkness and skinny dip in the ocean. Sometimes the unconventionality went too far. I found myself doing something I had failed to do with Demetrius. I went to Jan and said, "I know you and some of the other residents smoke marijuana together. I am not prudish and have done this myself before getting on the spiritual path. It is my feeling that marijuana weakens the will and lowers the attunement. I don't mind you smoking pot yourself. But I do not think it is appropriate for you in your position as a teacher and director of the Yoga Center to set this example for the other residents here."

Remembering the resistance to criticism exhibited by Demetrius, I braced myself, expecting the worst from Jan. "You are absolutely right. I am not setting the right example. I won't do it anymore," Jan said, surprising me with her humility and lack of defensiveness. She kept her word and did a complete about face. She was a remarkable woman from Australia, full of energy and enthusiasm. She was so good-hearted that when she came across Lily, a pregnant young lady who had no money and no place to stay, Jan took her in without hesitation. Jan had no regrets about her hospitality, even after Lily began to exhibit unusual behavior. At times Lily would get a strange look in her eyes and would speak incoherently. Then just as quickly she would snap out of this incoherent state and become normal again. Frequently she laughed out loud for no reason in a very silly tone. Her strange intermittent appearances included having dilated eyes, but there were absolutely no other indications that she was using drugs. It was evident to everyone at the Yoga Center that the vacant look she constantly had was due to possession. Often she would let me do the laying on of hands for healing prayer. I commanded the negative spirit to depart from Lily permanently, yet this produced no observable results. I made an inner commitment to do whatever I could, God willing, to help her heal.

Our Yoga Center sponsored a three-day retreat held out of town at a cabin in the country. At one point a snake came right through the open door of the cabin and into the very large room where we were congregated. Some retreatants wanted to do something to get rid of it. Hari, a former director of the Yoga Center, was leading the retreat, and we followed his recommendation to simply meditate. While we were meditating, the snake left the cabin. Later I felt I should capture the snake, but not harm it. I went outside, found the snake in a wood pile, and captured it. Holding the snake by its head, I held it up to show the others and then carried it off to the woods and released it. It occurred to me that the coming and going of the snake was like the possession that came and went in Lily. I also felt that by capturing and releasing the snake, I was symbolically doing something that would help release Lily from this condition.

Late that night I woke up. Sleeping retreatants were sprawled on the floor all around me. I quietly lit a large wide candle and felt moved to meditate. When I was finished, I bent forward as I usually did, yet this time I inadvertently put my face right into the top of the candle and put out the light. There was hot wax all over my face. However, I did not feel burnt or hurt in any way, just embarrassed, although nobody was watching. I felt that by putting out the light maybe something bad might happen.

The next day I intensified my efforts to focus on repeating the Name of Jesus. I reached a stage where I could consistently hold the Jesus Prayer, yet be relaxed, peaceful, and sometimes joyful. At one time I meditated alone near a stream. In the middle of my meditation someone came over and kissed my forehead and then left. I did not open my eyes to see who it was, but it was the kind of thing that Hari might have done.

When the retreat was over, I continued to repeat the Jesus Prayer while making the trip from the country back to the Yoga Center. I sat next to Lily in our van. Jan was driving, and Glenn, a black resident, was also with us. During the trip we stopped at a gas station, and the four of us all got out. Jan and Glenn were walking ahead, followed by Lily, and I was walking right behind Lily, still repeating the Jesus Prayer, and I felt a spontaneous urge to throw my arms into the air over my head. I immediately acted on this urge, and a flash of light and energy came over my whole body. There was no pain; however, I had no control over my body as it was falling forward. My arms lowered, and my body and hands landed on Lily. I felt the light and energy drain out of my body and go into hers. I was able to steady myself by bumping into her, so I didn't fall down. Lily maintained her balance and also remained standing.

My normal consciousness returned, and I righted myself as though nothing had happened. Jan and Glenn didn't see any of this. Lily tried to tell Jan what happened, but Jan ignored her, thinking she was just having an incoherent episode. And I certainly wasn't going to tell anyone what happened. After this incident, Lily's incoherent speaking, vacant looks, and strange laughing all disappeared so she became normal all of the time. Lily called her mother, who drove down from Ohio to pick her up. We heard later that she had delivered a healthy baby without any complications.

On the same day that we arrived back at the Yoga Center, I received a call from my mother in Connecticut. She told me that her brother, my Uncle Jim, had died on the same night that I had bent forward after meditation and put out the candle flame. When I was growing up, Uncle Jim lived right next door, and he spent countless hours with me playing cards. We played a game called *set back*, and he beat me almost every time. Nevertheless, I didn't mind because I enjoyed his company. He liked seeing Rick's and my excited and happy faces when he would take us out to eat as much ice cream as we could stuff into our little bodies.

In those playful days of my childhood while living in conservative Connecticut, I never would have imagined in my wildest dreams that I would one day find myself living at a yoga center and devoting myself to living a disciplined spiritual life. After morning meditation, I spent two hours doing yoga postures and breathing practices, plus an additional half hour of meditation. In the summer I would pick figs and persimmons that nobody else seemed to value from local trees, and there was, of course, swimming at the beach. Our neighbors next door had a fig tree and allowed me to take a shoot from it, which I planted in the back yard of the Yoga Center. Many years later the original fig tree next door had died. The transplanted shoot, however, had grown into a large fig tree. One of the few tangible reminders I have of these days is a snapshot (on opposite page) of me with a concerned look on my face as I was attending to a bird that was hobbling around on the grounds of the Yoga Center. I wasn't able to do anything for the bird other than give it some food and pray for it, but maybe that was enough because it was soon able to fly away.

Most importantly, throughout the day I constantly repeated the Jesus Prayer. Besides teaching yoga classes, I also had a weekly Jesus Prayer class open to the public for chanting and meditating on the Name of Jesus. I came to a deeper place of healing in relationship to Demetrius as I took on this new role of being a teacher of the Jesus Prayer. I was able to recall the many times he inspired me with his own enthusiasm and dedication to Jesus. The mistakes of Demetrius were a helpful reminder for me to avoid falling into the same errors. Above all, I wanted to be open and receptive to others and be willing to look at and admit any mistakes I might make.

Although I was practicing the Jesus Prayer in the form of an unceasing prayer as much as possible throughout the day, as the Early Desert Fathers had recommended, I took a less demanding approach in my teaching of

1976

others. I advocated the setting aside of regular meditation times every day because this lesser challenge was appropriate to most of the seekers who came to my class and wanted to simply learn how to meditate for a calmer mind. In these classes I often came across seekers who were not traditional Christian church goers, and I would reassure them that they did not have to be totally dedicated to Jesus in order to benefit from the Jesus Prayer. All they really needed was to be open to the divine influence. I recommended to these seekers that they simply sit in silence and focus on the Name of Jesus Christ, and that act in itself would bring the peace of mind that they were seeking. I suggested that each seeker choose a two-syllable word, such as "Jesus" or a few words, such as "Christ Love," that could be divided in half. The first half could be repeated on the inhalation and the second half could be repeated on the exhalation.

The awareness could be held in the heart—in the center of the chest or in the location of the physical heart. I was once asked, "Why focus on the heart? Wouldn't it be better to hold the awareness in the head?"

I answered, "Either location would be helpful. You are welcome to focus with the awareness in the head, if that is your personal preference or if you are guided in that direction. One yoga scripture defines yoga as 'the cessation of the modifications of the mind.'[2] Stopping the 'modifications' means stopping the *vrittis,* which are the thought waves that fluctuate in the mind, in order to experience the Spirit beyond all rational thinking. Consequently, some forms of yoga meditation focus on the center of the forehead in order to gain control over these vacillating thoughts of the mind. However, the early Christian monks were not interested in stopping the thought waves of the mind. Let me ask you to do something: Use your finger to point to yourself." When my questioner pointed to his chest, I asked, "Why did you point to your chest and not to your head?"

"It just seems more natural to point to my chest," he responded.

"Of course it does. We don't identify with the head because that's only where our thoughts are located. We identify with the heart because that's where we experience our feelings and desires. Jesus spoke of the heart as being the place where we keep our 'treasure.'[3] The early Christian monks formulated the Prayer of the Heart as a way of purifying their feelings and desires by becoming aware of the treasure of the divine presence in the heart. They wanted purity of heart not only to rid themselves of negative desires, but also as a way of fostering the positive desire for the love of God. Jesus said, 'Blessed are the pure in heart, for they shall see God.'[4] Certainly focusing on the Name of Jesus in the heart doesn't guarantee that you will see God, but it is a way of placing your *attention* on your *intention.* Nothing was more important to these early Christian monks than holding their pure intention for God in the heart. Even if this produced no noticeable experience of the divine presence, these monks felt fulfillment in this expression of their faith and commitment to God.

Often, beginning meditators today don't have the kind of devotion these early monks had. Nonetheless, some beginners find it is helpful to focus on the heart simply as a way of setting aside preoccupation with the mind. A year or two of daily practice of just bringing the awareness into the heart can bring a certain degree of inner stability and peace of mind even if there is no inner awakening of love for God and even if there is no conscious seeking for purity of heart. Yet I can tell you that the long-term benefit of consistently meditating on the heart is that it does very firmly establish your intention and desire for God and helps you become a more loving person—both in relation to God and in relation to your brothers and sisters."

Although I spelled out specific techniques that had been successfully used by early Christian monks, I emphasized that the real key to practicing meditation was not the techniques themselves. The important thing was to hold the spiritual intention of opening the heart to God's Love that is already within us, just waiting for us to recognize it and accept it. Any meditation technique that repeats the Name of Christ may be considered a version of the Jesus Prayer. Some of these variations focus on the heart or another part of the body, while others do not focus on any part of the body. For example, there is a form of repeating the Name of Jesus that is really a combination of six different techniques called "Christian Yoga Meditation," which will be described in Chapter 63.

In my Jesus Prayer class, after chanting variations of the Prayer of the Heart, we would meditate together for half an hour. However, I emphasized that the greatest benefit would come from meditating every day at a regular time, even if only for a short duration. Daily consistency is more important than anything else and gives a sense of inner stability and peace of mind. I enjoyed offering these classes free of charge, but Jan wanted me to charge a fee for my Jesus Prayer class, which was done for all our other Yoga Center classes. When I resisted this idea, she wanted me to at least put out an optional donation basket, and I reluctantly agreed.

Jan would soon have to return to Australia to attend to family matters, and she recommended that I become the new director. The Yoga Center was founded and owned by Jonathan, a spiritually oriented real estate agent, and he appointed me as the new director. I had been working at the local Good Will store to support myself but was able to quit that job and devote myself full time to yoga. For many years, the Yoga Center had lost money, but Jonathan used this as a business write-off for tax purposes. I was able to turn the losses into profits by expanding the services of the Yoga Center. As with all previous directors, I received room, board, and

1977

any other necessities, but no salary. In addition to classes at the Yoga Center itself, I taught yoga at Old Dominion University and created some new courses there. One of them was "Meditation around the World" in which I taught yoga, Zen, and Christian forms of meditation. Another new course was "Expanded Awareness Activities," which included role playing, past-life regressions, and even a laughing relaxation. For the laughing relaxation, I verbally guided the experience and then played a tape that induced laughter. The students would lie down on the floor in a circle with their heads on the stomachs of other students, which intensified the laughing. I later added yoga classes at the Armed Forces Staff College and at community centers, and I also taught spiritual art classes.

I grew a very long beard, which along with my facial features and olive complexion even made me look as though I could have come from India, the homeland of yoga. As a matter of fact, I appeared for an interview on the local Norfolk television show *Livas Live*, and Becky Livas, the host, asked me, "What part of India do you come from?" I was taken off guard since we had previously rehearsed all the questions she said she would ask me, and this was *not* one of them. Thinking quickly, I said, "I come from a far eastern state—it's called Connecticut," and that got a laugh from the audience, which helped me relax. So I added, "Becky, that's the wonderful thing about yoga. You don't have to come from India or bend yourself into a pretzel to gain the benefits of yoga. You can go at your own pace and practice yoga to bring health to the body and peace to the mind." Then I demonstrated several simple postures to show just how easy yoga can be.

As a teacher I had taken on the role of an authority figure, and in so doing I found myself letting go of my fear of God as the ultimate authority figure. In fact, I felt my heart opening to God's love for me, and I allowed that love to extend through me to my students. When I had been trained at Yogaville to become an instructor, I had been shown how to teach all beginning, intermediate, and advanced yoga postures and breathing practices, as well as the deep relaxation practice. However, I was given no specific instruction in the inner attitude that would be most helpful for the teacher. I developed my own inner orientation to teaching that represented a combination of the meditation of raja yoga, the love of bhakti yoga, the discrimination of jnana yoga, and the service of karma yoga.

Raja yoga was expressed in teaching because I considered my teaching to be a personal meditation, and I even sat in full lotus since that was the best posture for meditation. However, I kept a blanket over my legs, which effectively hid my full lotus posture so my students would not compare themselves with me. Also, I did not demonstrate postures for the same reason, but rather gave very clear verbal instructions. I advised students to raise a hand if they did not understand the instructions, and in that case I would immediately get up and go over to them and whisper personal instructions so as not to disturb the inner focus of the other students.

In addition to my own meditation, I conveyed to the students that they were to make the class a continuous meditation in which they could mentally focus on an inspirational word of their choice that would remind them of inner peace. Giving precise verbal instructions to my students required all of my attention. However, during the many pauses between instructions I focused meditatively on feeling God's love for me and allowing that love to flow through me to each of my students. As I called upon the Name of Jesus, I sometimes could even see them being filled with light and love. This loving expression of bhakti yoga was also an expression of jnana yoga, since I was discriminating between the unreal and the real through overlooking the forms of the bodies and seeing the divine presence in each person. I also felt the students being receptive to my love and sending love to me. Just as I saw Swami Satchidananda at satsangs absorb love from his audience and send it back to them, in my yoga classes I would return the students' love to intensify this loving experience.

My yoga teacher training courses were especially successful because they were an outgrowth of everything I had learned about teaching yoga. When I gave these training courses, I emphasized that teaching is a karma yoga expression of service and the best way to perform this service is to consciously send love to all the students throughout each class. New teachers that I had trained made monetary contributions from their classes to the Yoga Center, although these donations were entirely voluntary on their part. A newsletter was started, and more retreats were held.

Every Sunday we had a pot luck dinner open to the public, and I started a Sunday Christian service, which was attended by a small number of people. Because of my Christian orientation, the two Yoga Center activities I enjoyed the most were this Sunday Christian service and my class in the Jesus Prayer. When I taught this class, I discovered that there were many seekers who had given meditation a try and had decided it was too difficult for them. If you are one of these seekers or if you would like to consider practicing meditation for the first time, I would recommend reading Appendix A, "How to Meditate Using the Jesus Prayer of the Heart." This appendix provides more information about the Jesus Prayer in general, but focuses specifically on its application to meditation.

---

1. C. B. Purdom, *The God-Man*, (Crescent Beach, SC: Sheriar Press, 1971), p. 388.
2. Patanjali, *Yoga Sutras* 1.2, "Meditation," *The Encyclopedia of Religion*, edited by Mircea Eliade (New York: Macmillan, 1995), 9:327.
3. Luke 6:45, RSV.
4. Matthew 5:8, RSV.

12

SAY IT AIN'T SO, GURU JOE

~ o ~

After leading a massage workshop at the Yoga Center, Elizabeth, who was very attractive, informed me, "I would like to give you a full body massage, but I don't want to give you the wrong impression. I am celibate, and I want to stay that way. You can take all your clothes off if you like. It won't bother me."

She gave me a wonderful hour-long massage. It was actually the best massage I had ever received. When she was done and getting ready to go, I thanked her and said, "OK, it's your turn now." Elizabeth looked at me with surprise as I said, "I would like to give you a full body massage, but I don't want to give you the wrong impression. I am celibate, and I want to stay that way." I smiled and continued to parrot her words: "You can take all your clothes off if you like. It won't bother me." She looked at me rather apprehensively. After a slight, thoughtful hesitation she concluded, "Well, I guess I will just have to trust you." She took off all her clothes, and her trust was well-founded.

I had been celibate for more than eight years. Celibacy, in Sanskrit called *brahmacharya*, is sexual purity in thought, word, and deed. It is not merely an outer moral issue. When the sexual fluid is lost through intercourse or masturbation, there is a reduction in the ability to raise spiritual energy in meditation. It is possible to partially raise the kundalini while expressing the sexual impulse outwardly in marriage or through any other sexual outlet. However, a commitment to retaining sexual fluid accelerates the process of safely raising the kundalini. Celibacy is not a sacrifice if truly understood and if applied as part of a daily meditation practice. Those who practice celibacy without a consistent interior meditation life cause problems for themselves. The celibate person who fails to raise spiritual energy through meditation runs the risk of suppressing sexual energy, which is counterproductive to spiritual growth. I believe this is the underlying reason why some celibate priests exhibit deviant sexual behavior. On the other hand, celibacy that facilitates the raising of spiritual energy during meditation is a blessing. When the sexual fluid is retained, meditation can be enhanced, producing a deep inner feeling of divine communion and well-being. Having this feeling of inner completion is the reason why celibacy is not perceived as a sacrifice by an experienced meditator. Nevertheless, for this to happen requires not only sexual purity, but also overall purity of heart.

Even though I had become the director of the Yoga Center, I refused to participate in the chanting of the Hindu deities. This was due partly to my poor singing voice, but more so because I wanted to express Christian devotion exclusively. I was trying to build into my consciousness only the Name of Jesus, and I felt this chanting would build into me other vibrations that would only be a distraction. I sang only the Christian chants and let the other residents do most of the chanting. After my experience of almost being initiated by Swami Satchidananda, I was no longer tempted to move in the direction of seeking out a guru. Although I did not feel I would be helped by the relationship of the guru and devotee, in Sanskrit called the *chela*, I lived with and met many seekers who were on that path.

As the director of the Yoga Center it was important for me to maintain a universal tolerance of all paths. After living in Yogaville and seeing so many seekers and friends like Dharmananda and Margabandu flourish in that environment, I was well aware of the benefits of investing in the guru and disciple relationship as one's chosen path. Naturally I recognized the value of the teacher and student relationship, since I was a yoga teacher myself. My role as a teacher was to provide instruction to help others learn how to deepen their relationship with God. Nevertheless, I began to question certain aspects of the guru-disciple method of spiritual advancement because it went beyond the teacher and student parameters that focus on learning. Typically, the guru presented himself as God's representative and required the devotee to surrender the will to the guru as an indirect means of surrendering to God. Human intermediaries, such as gurus, send the message that the seeker is incomplete and must find his completion outside himself in another person. But the truth is that the seeker must accept the responsibility of looking within to find God. The seeker's completion can only be found in direct relationship with God, although genuine divine intermediaries, such as Jesus, can greatly assist in the seeker's awakening.

As far as I was concerned, the crucial factor in the guru and disciple relationship was the type of message the guru was conveying. I felt that ideally the guru would constantly remind the disciple to find wholeness and divinity directly within himself, so as to not become overly dependent upon the outer guru. My major concern was with the type of guru who would foster the idea of his own perfection, giving the impression that he is absolutely egoless at all times. It is appropriate to claim perfection in the sense that every soul is perfect because every soul is part of God. It is indeed the destiny of every soul to uncover this innate perfection that has been hidden, but not lost. However, I have a problem with the guru who claims perfection at the ego level. Part of the human condition is the possession of an ego, and we cannot be without it, but we can on a daily basis surrender the ego to the divine influence. The problem comes in when the guru claims that he does not need to surrender his ego on a daily basis because he has supposedly attained a permanent state of egolessness. Other than a true perfect master, as for example Jesus or the Buddha, such a perfect continuing condition of egolessness is not attainable. Claiming to have achieved this perfect state can only lead to denial and suppression of ego impulses that will eventually come out of hiding to reveal self-defeating behavior.

A guru who acknowledges that he has to surrender his ego each day to God can provide a useful example for his disciples to follow. Then if the guru makes an ego mistake, he can easily accept responsibility for that mistake and for correcting it, showing his disciples how to do likewise when they make mistakes. Openness of the teacher to his own self-correction is a necessary ingredient of the teaching relationship. Consequently, my primary reservation about the guru role was the promotion of the perfect master image that did not allow for self-correction. Ideally a guru would acknowledge his ego as imperfect and set the example of humility as the way to deal with it. However, because I did not see that approach by the gurus that I observed, I thought seekers needed to be cautious in their choices of a guru and hopefully find one who manifests the virtue of humility more than any other quality.

In contrast to my personal preferences, I welcomed gurus and swamis, as well as other spiritual teachers to come to the Yoga Center to give lectures and workshops. Swami Rama, the founder of the Himalayan International Institute, came and gave a talk about how he had lived in a cave in the Himalayas and was trained by a great, but little-known teacher. Swami Rama explained, "All the body is in the mind. But not all the mind is in the body." He informed us that he had proved his point at the Menninger Foundation where he had been tested extensively by Drs. Elmer and Alyce Green in 1970 and 1971. While being consciously aware of his environment, Swami Rama could at will manifest theta or delta brain waves, usually only experienced during sleep. He reportedly was able to demonstrate the telekinetic power of moving a knitting needle with the power of his mind. He shocked the doctors by stopping his heart for 17 seconds. He further perplexed scientific minds by inducing a difference of 10 degrees centigrade between his right and left arms. Traditional scientists had established that the body's involuntary organs functioned on their own without individual will being a factor. Research done on Swami Rama proved otherwise.

This discovery that the mind and will can influence the body led the way to biofeedback techniques. Most spiritual seekers are aware of biofeedback as a technique for deepening meditation, but research on Swami Rama was the forerunner for the medical application of biofeedback directed toward self-healing. Today patients can learn to use biofeedback methods for controlling high blood pressure and muscle tension.

Swami Rama brought with him to the Yoga Center an entourage of about ten devotees, and they noticeably beamed with light and love as he gave his lecture. Unlike Swami Satchidananda, he did not radiate light and love back to his disciples and create a dynamic exchange of giving and receiving love, which would have made for a truly uplifting satsang. I attributed this to my impression that he was mostly a jnani yogi, who was using his mind to practice discrimination between the real and the unreal rather than being centered on love. Although he did not significantly raise the spiritual energy level of the meeting through love, I still found his lecture to be inspirational because of the helpful spiritual principles that he advocated. He talked about the need to practice non-attachment as a means of purifying the ego. He expressed that expanded consciousness cannot be achieved unless the ego is purified. According to his teaching the ego needs to be purified in order to facilitate learning how to discriminate between the "real Self and the not-self." He elaborated that suffering is caused by failure to purify the ego.

After the lecture I gave him his percentage of the money that had come in, as was the long established Yoga Center custom. He looked at the small sum of money in his hand and declared firmly, "I was promised $500!"

"I did not promise you $500. Who made such a promise to you?"

"Jonathan, your founder."

"Jonathan did not tell me about this arrangement. You will have to get your money from Jonathan," I told him.

Speaking in a controlled yet obviously angry voice the swami insisted, "You are the director here. You have to honor the commitments of your organization."

I calmly reiterated, "We take in only a very small amount of money from free will donations. The Yoga Center is barely breaking even financially, so even if I consented to pay you, I do not have the money to do so. It is appropriate for Jonathan to take responsibility for making good on his promise." Swami Rama looked at me angrily and immediately left the building. Later Jonathan did in fact pay the swami the money that he had promised. However, what struck me was the contrast between his talk on non-attachment and his anger at the thought of not getting his money.

Instead of focusing on his shortcomings, however, I realized I needed to pay attention to my own need for non-attachment. In fact, I was angry at Jonathan for making this promise without telling me about it, and so I had to accept responsibility for my projection of anger. I talked with Jonathan about this, and he admitted that he had made a mistake. Yet his mistake did not make me feel that my anger at him had been justified. I was able to let go of my anger by surrendering my ego to the Holy Spirit in prayer and meditation to restore inner peace of mind.

I did not know at the time that Swami Rama, who had such exacting and unusual control over his body, could not control all parts of his body. On September 5, 1997 the Philadelphia Daily News reported, "Jurors decided the Himalayan Institute in Honesdale should pay $1.875 million in damages yesterday to a woman who was sexually assaulted by the center's aging spiritual leader."

The lawyer for the Himalayan Institute claimed the sexual relationship was consensual. However, a newspaper article by Richard Phelps states:

> Attorney John Humphrey said the Institute presented itself publicly as a center for holistic living, but beneath this veneer lurked "a very dark, dark secret, a cloud, a festering sore that was and is sexual abuse," he told jurors. Using his position as their spiritual guru to gain their trust, the swami convinced young women to submit to sexual demands, Humphrey said. The attorney described the sexual exploitation of his client as "spiritual incest," and worse than rape because she and other devotees viewed the swami as "a person approaching divinity."
>
> "It is just an absolutely gross, gross abuse of that trust," he said. More than 10 women have accused the swami of sexual abuse since 1979, he said, all of whom were ignored by the Institute.[1]

Seven years prior to this court decision "The Case against Swami Rama of the Himalayas" was published in the December, 1990 issue of *Yoga Journal* Magazine. This report was written by Katherine Webster after two years of extensive research. She included in her report the following quotation by one of the doctors who had tested Swami Rama at the Menninger Institute:

> Dr. Elmer Green says that he and his wife have heard from a number of women who said they were sexually exploited by Swami Rama. "If someone is a saint, celibacy would be his normal condition," Dr. Green comments. "A lot of people have confused the siddhis—the powers to control body, emotions, and mind—with

spirituality. But the siddhis can be an ego trip. A saint is a person who does what he says." Rather than being a saint, according to Green, Swami Rama is an advanced yogi and "a mortal with some ego problems."[2]

In addition to Swami Rama, another guru whom I met in Virginia Beach was Amrit Desai. He was the founder of a yoga center in Pennsylvania, which later relocated to Lenox, Massachusetts becoming the Kripalu Center for Yoga and Health. He was Hari's guru, and I knew many others who were his devotees. In 1994, many years after I met him, he resigned or perhaps more accurately was forced by his followers to leave the ashram that he had founded. Having been inspired by his lofty teachings, his followers became confused and disillusioned by his personal choices, which left a wake of betrayal, lies, sexual abuse, and abuse of power. "'He preached brahmacharya—celibacy for single people,' says a former Desai devotee. 'Yet he sexually abused a number of women who were his disciples.' All this allegedly while married with three children, says the disgusted former follower."[3]

The entire story hasn't been told because some followers sued and received a settlement, which prevents them from discussing the indiscretions of Amrit Desai. "'He exploited the disciples for millions, and then lied about it when confronted,' fumes another source, a Charlottesville nurse who lived at Kripalu for ten years."[4]

"When the nurse and now mother found out about the betrayals by her guru, 'I was furious and cried my head off,' she says. 'He's never apologized or owned up to what he did.'"

According to Lila Ivey at the Amrit Yoga Institution in Salt Springs, Florida, Desai wrote apology letters to every member. "Ivey doesn't deny Desai's mistakes. 'He owned up to them. He lost his life's work. He was sued and humiliated. It's amazing to see him hold that posture with dignity and grace.'"[5]

Amrit Desai's scandal is somewhat unique, not in what happened, but in the follow up. Although his first responses were denials, he eventually did acknowledge his improprieties and made an effort to apologize. Even though his belated effort to apologize may not be much of a consolation for some of his former disciples, this effort was remarkable when compared with the steadfast total resistance to rehabilitation exhibited by other, similarly tainted gurus. The other unusual follow up was the way in which Kripalu handled the transition to new leadership. In the past whenever a guru was discredited he would rely on continuing denial and remain in power. But even if the need for a new direction was recognized, the solution would be to appoint another guru to continue with the guru-disciple format for spiritual growth. However, Kripalu decided to experiment with a new approach to transmitting the authentic spiritual principles of yoga. Amrit Desai's departure from Kripalu was expressed in *Stripping the Gurus,* a revealing book by Geoffrey Falk:

> Following the departure, Kripalu restructured its organization to be led by a professional management team, "several of whom are former ashram residents." It has thereby become "the first traditional yoga ashram founded on the guru-disciple model to transition to a new paradigm of spiritual education. (*Kripalu,* 2003)[6]

I had a conversation with someone who had worked at Kripalu during the times of transition away from the guru model. She told me that in subsequent years Kripalu made a transition away from being a residential ashram and attracted a full spectrum of teachers and spiritual disciplines that included yoga, yet also went beyond the scope of yoga. Consequently the center became a better outreach for a wider range of seekers. She summarized her feelings by saying, "Amrit Desai leaving Kripalu was the best thing that ever happened to that center." Although Amrit Desai is no longer associated with Kripalu following his fall from grace, he is fortunately on the road to spiritual recovery by making public appearances to inspire seekers.

I wish I could say that the indiscretions of Amrit Desai, Swami Rama, and similar sexual-abuse incidents by Swami Satchidananda were isolated problems with a few gurus, yet unfortunately that is not the case. On the walls of our Aquarian Age Yoga Center meditation room in the 70s, we had placed images of a full range of gurus. A search of the internet will reveal the centers these gurus founded and their strengths and accomplishments, which include helping many people to make genuine leaps in their spiritual growth. On the other hand, most of these gurus have been accused of sexual improprieties or sexual abuse by former devotees. Some gurus who've been accused include Yogi Bhajan, Maharishi Mahesh Yogi, Muktananda, Bhagwan Sree Rajneesh, Sai Baba, and Sri Chinmoy. Geoffrey Falk's book *Stripping the Gurus* is a good resource for learning more about the indiscretions of these gurus. A search of the internet will also reveal numerous incidents of sexual abuse by gurus, but in many cases these are only unsubstantiated *allegations*, which have not been proven true in a court of law.

Fortunately Yogananda remained untouched by scandal. One of his disciples, Donald Walters, known as Swami Kriyananda, founded a community called *Ananda* as an independent offshoot of Yogananda's Self-Realization Fellowship. Donald Walters inspired many seekers and

Ananda was known as an excellent model of a cooperative spiritual community in the 70s and 80s. However, a decade later in 1998, Ananda lost a court case involving allegations of sexual improprieties by Donald Walters. Although he had presented himself as a celibate monk, he admitted his sexual activity in court, but characterized it as not being abusive. Nevertheless, he resigned from Ananda.[7]

In the absence of irrefutable evidence presented in a court case, the question of personal credibility becomes paramount. It seems to me that a guru who allows his followers to believe he is a perfect master already has a credibility problem. What would it take for longstanding and faithful disciples to radically reverse their thinking and become convinced that their guru is not in fact a perfect master? According to some devotees, it was sexual misconduct. I tend to believe these allegations are based on the truth. I believe boys when they say they were molested by their priests, so why would I not believe devotees who make claims of sexual improprieties by their gurus? These allegations have provided me and I hope others with a sobering caution regarding the merits of having a guru rather than practicing yoga without a guru.

The gurus who have been accused of sexual abuse remind me of a lecture I gave to a New Age group in my role as the director of the Yoga Center. To take the edge off of my usual seriousness I began light-heartedly by saying:

> Hello. I am Swami Propagananda. I can lead you from light to darkness, from the infinite to the finite, from the real to the unreal, and from graciousness to pettiness. If you want to be one of my devotees, I only require one thing from you—a frontal lobotomy! Then you will be able to follow me without any doubts. After all, I am Swami Propagananda, and being an all-knowing guru, I know what is best for you. I will relieve you of all your worldly possessions so you won't be held back by them. Now, how many of you want to become my unquestioning devotees? What? No one wants to be my devotee. OK, I confess—I am not Swami Propagananda. However, I am a teacher of yoga. My guru happens to be Jesus, but you do not have to accept a guru in order to benefit from practicing yoga.

Of course, I was making fun of the guru image, but I had no idea at the time that my jabs could apply to the wide array of gurus mentioned previously. After this silly introduction to my lecture, I proceeded in a more serious tone to describe and elaborate upon all eight components of Patanjali's classical yoga, which is *raja yoga,* sometimes called *ashtanga yoga*:

1. *yamas*, ethical restrictions
2. *niyamas*, ethical observances
3. *asanas*, body postures, part of hatha yoga
4. *pranayama*, breathing practices, also part of hatha yoga
5. *pratyahara*, the withdrawal of the senses from sense objects
6. *dharana*, concentration, intermittent focusing on one thought
7. *dhyana*, meditation, continuous focusing on one thought
8. *samadhi*, divine communion, "ecstasy," spiritual experiences

Most of my listeners were interested in hatha yoga, which includes the third and fourth steps of raja yoga, the "royal path." These two steps consist of the body postures, called *asanas,* and the breathing practices, called *pranayama*. Sometimes a student would ask, "How come you describe hatha yoga as a part of another yoga, raja yoga? Isn't hatha yoga a form of yoga in its own right, rather than a 'sub-yoga'?"

I would reply, "Much like the Hellenistic culture of ancient Greece, modern America worships the physical body as a humanistic ideal. Thus the American brand of hatha yoga today is considered to be the yoga of the physical body for the purpose of maintaining health. However, our Western culture has forgotten the origins of hatha yoga. I am asking you to look beyond the Americanization of yoga in order to understand what hatha yoga was intended to be. Raja yoga was codified by Patanjali in the second century BC. At that time, hatha yoga was not yet seen as a distinct form of yoga in itself. It was just the third and fourth steps of the eight-step process of raja yoga, which was an entire system for spiritual growth. In this classical raja yoga of Patanjali, the body postures and breathing practices of hatha yoga are only a means of preparing for being able to sit comfortably and practice the higher steps of yoga involving mental focusing and inner attunement leading toward divine union. However, hatha yoga became a yoga in its own right in the ninth and tenth centuries. At that time it was a small yoga sect that was considered heretical because of its focus on perfecting the physical body and obtaining magical powers. The idea was to balance the polarities in the body symbolized by 'ha,' meaning the sun, and 'tha' meaning the moon. The goal was not just balance the physical forces in the body, but rather to transform the physical body into the subtle divine body and awaken to one's true spiritual nature. Yet there was not the same focus on meditation as there was in the practice of raja yoga. As I explained it at the time,

> *Yoga* literally means 'union' or 'integration.' It means not only divine union, but also integration of the highest aspects of human and spiritual development with the lowest aspects. Consequently, the

physical health of the body is important, yet is considered a lower part of human development that needs to be integrated with one's higher spiritual development. Americans are correct in thinking hatha yoga is a yoga in its own right, but most Americans do not realize that it was not originally designed to be an end in itself for physical health only. The Americanization of yoga is really a diluting of the spiritual aspirations of hatha yoga and of raja yoga from which it evolved. My intention today is to help you realize that the physical postures and breathing practices of hatha yoga are simply part of a larger comprehensive way of growing as a whole person, physically, mentally and spiritually.

As always when giving a lecture on yoga, I cautioned my listeners to not make the mistake of skipping the first two steps of classical yoga and foolishly focus on just the higher steps. Apparently the dishonorable gurus identified previously failed to master the very first steps of classical yoga, which form the foundation for the higher steps. The first step is *yamas*, ethical restrictions. Some examples are harmlessness, truthfulness, sexual continence, lack of covetousness, and absence of greed. The second step is *niyamas*, which are ethical observances. These include purity, contentment, moderation, asceticism as guided by the Spirit, study, and surrendering to God's will in all areas of life. Both of these first two steps of classical yoga would fall into the general category of developing purity of heart. The tainted gurus emphasized the higher steps and did not pay attention to these lower steps, thus neglecting the development of the purity of heart needed for true spiritual growth.

But the shortcomings of unethical gurus taint, yet do not invalidate their genuine spiritual attainments and the good that is accomplished through them. Swami Muktananda is an example of the benefits and drawbacks of what gurus have to offer. Gerald Jampolsky, a medical doctor and psychiatrist, became interested in Kirlian photography, and he was invited to photograph the energy field around Swami Muktananda's hands. He mentally sat in judgment of the impressionable very young devotees who idolized their guru. While Dr. Jampolsky was visiting, Swami Muktananda touched him on his face, and afterwards had him escorted to a room where he was told to meditate. In spite of his suspiciousness of the whole situation, this is what happened:

After sitting quietly for five minutes, my body began to quiver and shake in an indescribable manner. Beautiful colors appeared all around me, and it seemed as though I had stepped out of my body and was looking down at it. Part of me wondered if someone had slipped me a hallucinogenic drug or if I was going crazy.

I saw colors whose depth and brilliance were beyond anything I had ever imagined. I began to speak in tongues—a phenomenon I had heard about but discredited. A beautiful beam of light came into the room and I decided at that moment to stop evaluating what was happening and simply be one with the experience, to join it completely.[8]

Dr. Jampolsky was surprised to discover that two and a half hours had quickly passed by when he was led back into the presence of Muktananda, who suggested he get a picture of Muktananda's guru as a focus for future meditation practice. Although he did not follow this suggestion, he noticed that in the next three months his energy level increased and he experienced a profound awareness of love unknown to him previously. This experience changed Dr. Jampolsky's ideas about what was real and what was unreal, as he had always been a skeptic about any realities beyond the physical world. In the future, while looking back on this experience with Swami Muktananda, he realized it had been an important turning point in his life that had prepared him to be open to accepting the spiritual principles of *A Course in Miracles* a year or so later.

If gurus such as Swami Muktananda have genuine spiritual experiences and can assist others in their own spiritual openings, how is it possible that such gurus become corrupted? If purity of heart is not a priority, gurus who have authentic spiritual awakenings may exaggerate these experiences in their own minds and even worse in the minds of their followers. Gurus tell their disciples that every person is divine; however, the distinct impression is left that gurus are "more divine" because they have realized their true nature. Gurus often assert, or at least imply, that they are both divine and *perfect*, which devotees all too willingly accept as a fact. Once the guru is accepted as divinely perfect and therefore "special," then any of his foibles or excesses are considered divine as well. Consequently this gives license to behavior that would normally not be tolerated by "ordinary" people. The assumption is that enlightenment automatically equates to virtue and therefore whatever an enlightened person does must be a virtuous action.

Not so, maintains former devotee Stan Trout, who served his guru Swami Muktananda for ten years as an ashram teacher and ashram director. Aware of sexual abuse by his guru, Trout, formerly Swami Abhayananda, resigned in 1981 from the SYDA Foundation, leaving behind his closest friends and life's work. His statement below refers to Swami Muktananda, but is cited here because in my opinion it applies to all corrupt gurus who have nevertheless had genuine spiritual awakening experiences:

> Muktananda's claim of "perfection" (Siddha-hood) was based on the notion that a person who has become enlightened has thereby become "perfect" and absolutely free of human weakness. This is nonsense; it is a myth perpetuated by dishonest men who wish to receive the reverence and adoration due to God alone. There is no absolute assurance that enlightenment necessitates the moral virtue of a person. There is not a guarantee against the weaknesses of anger, lust, and greed in the human soul. The enlightened are on equal footing with the ignorant in the struggle against their own evil—the only difference being that the enlightened person *knows* the truth, and has no excuse for betraying it.[9]

When a seeker progresses from one step of classical yoga to another, there is a tendency to acquire a certain degree of pride. Consequently, it is essential for the seeker to be aware of the need for humility, which is a requirement for developing purity of heart. Failure to develop purity of heart at the ego level does not invalidate whatever authentic enlightenment or awakening experiences a guru or any other person may have. The challenge after enlightenment is to fully integrate the elevated state of consciousness that transcends the ego with the world of form, which is the home of the ego. Misguided gurus unfortunately fail to successfully achieve this integration and instead allow the ego to remain intact. In addition, if a seeker raises too much of the kundalini before fully purifying the lower centers, there is the danger of accentuating the lower physical appetites, such as the sexual desires. This may have been a factor in what happened to these gurus, who most likely started out with high spiritual ideals.

Among the spiritual teachers depicted on the walls of the Yoga Center meditation room, only the "old school" gurus, such as Ramakrishna, Yogananda, Ramana Maharshi, and Meher Baba, have stood the test of time and been revealed as true saints, who practiced what they preached. Ramakrishna spoke simply, summarizing Hindu holiness by saying that the goal is to wholeheartedly seek God in all things inwardly and outwardly. He repeatedly warned his students to speak the truth and above all else to avoid "gold and lust." Modern day gurus came here to "spiritualize" America by bringing the wisdom of India to the West. Nevertheless, many of these gurus did not heed Ramakrishna's warning and ironically ended up being "Americanized" themselves in ways they did not expect.

Information on the internet reveals both the strengths and weaknesses of the many gurus, who accomplished much good while simultaneously falling short of their own high ideals. What can be learned from these gurus? Purify the ego or suffer the consequences. The wisdom of this advice has been proved true by those gurus who chose to purify the ego and has been equally proved true by those gurus who chose to suffer the consequences. None of the explanations of the gurus' behavior provided above are intended to condone their mistakes. Neither do I offer condemnation. The reason for avoiding condemnation is obviously based on my desire to follow the example of Jesus, but there is another reason that may not be so obvious.

A previous chapter indicated I did not make the mistake of surrendering myself to a guru. However, technically that is not true. I have adopted a persuasive swami. He told me he would be my intermediary standing in the place of God. He claimed that if I worship him, I would be worshipping God. He was lying. Even now I am still in the process of unraveling all his lies, which are too numerous to describe. Yet I remain attached to this swami, unable to let go of him. Who is this swami? This is my Inner Swami Propagananda, otherwise known as my *ego*.

Can I really condemn the egos of outer gurus in good conscience while simultaneously allowing my Inner Swami Propagananda to remain intact? I must be vigilant in limiting the power of this inner ego swami, who would totally dominate me if I let my guard down. Adding my own ego darkness to an already dark situation involving corrupt gurus does not bring the light. I would rather focus on learning how I can let go of my own pride and other ego shortcomings in order to prevent me from being sidetracked in my own spiritual journey. Consequently I call on Jesus, the Holy Spirit, and God to bring the light that is my true nature, in order to dispel the darkness.

The websites that reveal the mistakes of the gurus tend to represent everything in black and white terms. Generally the positive is minimized or not mentioned, and the negative is emphasized. However, this critical approach is balanced out by the official websites of these gurus that promote the positive and leave out the negative. Almost universally overlooked on these websites is the need for devotees to take on the responsibility of looking at their own shortcomings, which are certainly of a much less grievous nature than the gurus' missteps. I am concerned that what I am about to describe may be misinterpreted as a condoning of morally bankrupt gurus or blaming of devotees, yet neither is in fact the case. Devotees may not want to be told that they need to accept responsibility, because, after all, they consider themselves to be victims of irresponsible gurus who need to be held to a higher standard. When I watched television as a child, I learned very quickly that the cowboys with white hats were the good guys, and the cowboys with black hats were the bad guys. In some ways that is a comforting mind-set that simplifies choices in the world, but it is not based on the truth and therefore is not the way to find healing in our lives.

The truth, although it may be hard to hear, is that devotees make the mistake of personal disempowerment. They think of themselves as incomplete and so seek out gurus to get completion from them. When gurus fail to provide completion and indeed turn out to be scoundrels lacking in integrity, devotees understandably cry that they are victims. But assuming the role of a victim perpetuates the illusion of incompleteness. After dealing with the initial feelings of betrayal, at some point the devotee needs to reexamine the victim feelings of incompleteness in order to find healing. This reevaluation of feeling incomplete must extend not only to the devotee's reaction to the deception by the guru, but also to the original feeling of incompleteness that attracted the devotee to the guru in the first place.

Hopefully the devotee can learn over time to accept responsibility for his own inner feeling of incompleteness without blaming anyone else for it and most importantly without blaming himself either. The devotee can then turn to God for healing. When the devotee can free himself from focusing on the past, he can open directly to God within and allow Him to provide an inner sense of completion. I do not mean to oversimplify this by implying that this healing is an easy process. Overcoming sexual abuse or other kinds of abuse may take many years and many tears. However, blame of others or oneself is not the way to do it. Instead of surrendering to the guru as in times past, the devotee can correct that mistake by rightly surrendering to God. Is God not worthy of trust? Only He can open the heart and bring forgiveness.

Although I described my Inner Swami Propagananda as my ego, I actually have identified with all three roles mentioned here. The three roles are the corrupt guru, the devotee who is a victim of abuse, and devotee who is in total denial about any wrong doing by his guru. The corrupt guru represents my *idealized self*, which is the part of my mind that I like to show to the world in order to appear perfect. Hiding behind the idealized self is my *victim self*, represented by the abused devotee. This is the part of my mind that is angry for being abused by others and the world. Feeling anger is justified, the victim self next becomes my *victimizer self*, which ironically is represented by the corrupt guru, who is playing a dual role. Then, of course, there is the final role of my *denial self*, represented by the devotee in denial. This denial self is the glue of guilt that allows my subconscious mind to keep everything hidden away from conscious awareness. Of course, all these false selves are parts of my shadow puzzle consisting of the dark and unconscious parts of my mind. Obscured by all these false selves is my true nature in oneness with God. For me, Jesus represents this inner divine oneness, but other seekers may feel their true nature is symbolized by honorable spiritual teachers or gurus who have not been corrupted by worldly temptations.

When I lived at the Yoga Center, I still had not learned about how all the parts of my ego nature were functioning. I was especially having trouble with learning how to let go of my victim self. In particular, my previous experience of having an altercation with my teacher Demetrius was a stumbling block for me in learning to overcome identifying with my victim self. And there would be many other experiences of victim consciousness in my future. Having the intellectual understanding of the dysfunctional nature of placing myself in the victim role did not mean that I could automatically overcome the problem and prevent it from recurring. Upcoming chapters will revisit this issue describing my failures along the way. Many pieces to my shadow puzzle would have to fall into place before I could finally have the healing of my overall tendency toward victim consciousness.

---

1. Richard Phelps, "Woman Wins $1.8M from Lecherous Swami," *The Philadelphia Daily News National*, September 5, 1997, posted on rickross.com/reference/Yogaville.
2. Katherine Webster, "The Case Against Swami Rama of the Himalayas," *Yoga Journal* Magazine, December 1990 issue, posted on rickross.com/reference/Yogaville.
3. Lisa Provence, "Guru's Past: Yogaville Visit Opens Old Wounds," *The Hook* (Charlotteville, Virginia's newspaper), April 21, 2005. This article is posted on rickross.com/reference/Yogaville.
4. Ibid.
5. Ibid.
6. Geoffrey D. Falk, *Stripping the Gurus*, Chapter XXIII, "Up the Asana" (Amrit Desai), posted on strippingthegurus.com.
7. Helena Goa, "Sex and the Singular Swami," *The San Francisco Weekly*, March 10, 1999. This is a report about Donald Walters, a monk who was accused of sexual abuse. He admitted the sexual contact in court, but denied it was abusive. The Ananda Church for Self-Realization lost a court case in which Donald Walters was judged to have misrepresented himself as a monk and to have caused emotional trauma. Before the court case was concluded, Walters retired as spiritual director of Ananda.
8. Gerald Jampolsky, MD, *Teach Only Love: The Seven Principles of Attitudinal Healing*, (New York: Bantam Books, 1983), p. 12.
9. Stan Trout, "Letter from a Former Swami," placed at the end of *The Secret Life of Swami Muktananda*, by William Rodarmor. The book is no longer in print, but the letter can be read on leavingsiddhayoga.net/secret.htm.

13

USING DISCERNMENT

≈ ○ ≈

After having already revealed the disconcerting shadow side of gurus, I want to strongly emphasize that the high profile, corrupt gurus have given a bad name to those perhaps lesser known gurus who have remained faithful to their spiritual ideals and stayed above reproach. I assume that there are authentic, high-integrity gurus functioning now in America and perhaps very many more in India. I was fortunate to meet one such guru at the Yoga Center. His name was Swami Daya. He lived in India, but had come to America for a visit, arriving at our center with two close disciples. He was in his 80s and in good health. He gave a lecture about love, humility, and surrender to God, which enraptured our small audience. I was impressed by his very simple manner and felt he was an example of the love and humility that he advocated. At the end of his lecture, listeners were invited to come up one at a time and receive Swami Daya's spiritual blessing. Although I was firmly committed to Jesus as my personal guru and my suspicions about gurus had been raised in my time at the Yoga Center, I felt strongly prompted to come forward. On my knees I bowed down low, and he tapped my head with his blessing. I did indeed feel blessed by him and was very grateful for the opportunity to meet him.

Swami Daya did not have the charismatic aura of someone like Swami Satchidananda, but he did have a very peaceful presence about him. I was reminded of the story of a Zen roshi who was asked to speak to an American spiritual group. The Buddhist monks coming into the lecture hall were greeted by the American leader, who easily identified the roshi as the tall figure who radiated a powerful energy aura. He asked the roshi to take his place at the lecture stand, but was told by an embarrassed monk, "I am not the roshi. Here is my *sensei* (teacher)." There stood the roshi, an inconspicuous short man with nothing remarkable about his appearance. It's too bad that the flashy gurus of America have gotten so much attention while someone like Swami Daya would be largely overlooked. There are probably many more authentic gurus serving their students in obscurity. It is not unusual for a humble spiritual teacher to not want to be advertised so that whoever comes to him will be drawn exclusively by an inner divine impulse.

I don't know much about what gurus are available to seekers today in America, but I have heard a little about one guru recently. I have some friends who have become revitalized spiritually by having gone on retreats to this guru's yoga residential community. Their son was getting into all sorts of trouble during his teenage years, but he went to live at this yoga center and completely turned his life around. He lived there a long time, but then left to practice and teach yoga on his own. I asked him why he had left the yoga community, and he explained, "I was assigned to the karma yoga work of cleaning out the horse manure in the stables. I did not mind the humbling aspect of shoveling manure, but I kept asking myself why a guru who claims to be a holy man would need to own a stable of horses that he seldom rides. I could not stomach the contradiction between the guru's teachings and the extravagance of excesses like owning horses." His parents also stopped going to this yoga center. In the past they had benefitted by going to specialized yoga retreats, called "intensives," that involved many seekers developing a personal relationship with the guru and receiving *Shakti*, spiritual energy, from the guru. However, they were no longer nourished by these intensives and realized that they needed solitary retreats to find the divine within. I have not mentioned this guru's name because I haven't met him personally, so I am not in a position to evaluate his abilities as a teacher.

Like bees attracted to flowers, students will be attracted to and accept whatever teachers fulfill their needs. What they need spiritually may be a temporary boost to inspire them to then go on to find the divine within on their own. Or they may need a long-term relationship with a teacher. In either case, those who seek out gurus will have to consider two questions: Does the guru have true spiritual depth based upon his own direct personal experience of the divine? Does the guru have very high integrity and moral character consistent with his teachings? It can be difficult to answer these questions in order to discern between an authentic guru and an inauthentic guru. I am asking you now to use your imagination to participate in a little experiment to show you just how difficult this discernment can be. Imagine that you and a few friends go for a first-time visit with a guru. When you arrive, the guru greets you warmly. The guru specifically asks you to sing a spiritual song. You can imagine yourself to be a very good singer, and you sing with all your mind and heart. The guru lapses into an ecstasy as you sing. When your song in complete, he returns to normal consciousness and has a radiant smile. He makes a comment that you are beaming with a divine light. Your companions are surprised at his comment. You are wondering if the guru is prone to flattering his visitors or if he is actually seeing something in you that you cannot see yourself.

A short while later, the guru suddenly stands up and takes you by the hand. He leads you to another room where he and you are alone. Holding your hand, he looks at you and begins to shed tears of joy. He asks you why you have delayed your coming for so long and why you have made him wait for your coming. He continues to cry profusely, yet with joy, as he says these words very earnestly with tenderness as though you had been lifelong friends, when in fact this is your first meeting. Then the guru places his hands together in prayer position at his chest and salutes you as though you are a divine being. He says that you are an incarnation of a great sage who has come to relieve the sufferings of mankind. You have no illusions about yourself being a holy incarnation. You say nothing, but the thought comes to your mind that this guru must be insane. He asks you to wait in the room as he leaves and then returns with some small food treats. He puts the delicacies in your mouth with his own hand. You ask him to give you a bunch of these treats so you can give them to your companions. He steadfastly ignores your pleas saying that your friends will get some food later, but implores you to accept these delicacies for yourself. He asks you with a pleading tone to come again soon in the future, and you agree with some reluctance.

Finally the guru takes you back to rejoin your friends, and he welcomes questions to test him. Everyone asks him questions, and he answers each one with lucidity. He is very serene, showing none of the abnormal behavior he had exhibited when he and you were alone. He speaks only of renunciation and nothing you can see in his practical life contradicts his precepts. You ponder if your first impression of him as a madman could have been mistaken because his teachings seem illuminating to you. To test him you ask, "Have you seen God, sir?"

"Yes, I see Him just as I see you here, only in an intenser sense. And if you want to see, you too can see Him."[2] He continued, "God can be seen and spoken with, just as I am seeing you and speaking with you, but who wants to do so? People grieve and shed potfuls of tears at the death of their wives and sons and behave in the same way for the sake of money and property, but who does so because he cannot realize God? If anyone is really equally anxious to see Him and calls on Him, He will certainly reveal Himself to him."[2]

A short while later you leave, but before you do the guru asks you again to come for another visit in the future. Without making a full commitment you tell him you will try to do so. You leave with conflicting thoughts, wondering whether you have met a madman or a great spiritual teacher. That's the end of our little experiment with the imagination. With that being the only information you have to go on, what do you think? Have you met an authentic guru or have you met an inauthentic guru? Would you go back to see him again or have you seen enough to convince you to stay away? I am asking you to please use your discernment to make a decision now about your opinion of the merits of this guru before moving on to the next paragraph in which I will give you my own opinion.

Right now I will use my imagination, and tell you what I would have decided about this imaginary guru if I had done this exact same experiment just as you have. I would have concluded that his claim to actually see God sounded suspicious, so I would not have been convinced of his spiritual depth. I would have seen his emotionalism one moment and his serenity the next as a sign of emotional mood swings and possible instability. I would not have come back to see him for another visit. After all, why should I expose myself to a possibly deranged guru? This is what I would have decided if I had no more information about this guru than what I have described for you in this experiment. I feel I would have been right in my assessment in 99 out of 100 similar cases, but in this specific case, with this guru, I would have been mistaken.

There is more information about this guru that I did not explain to you. For this experiment you have been doing some role playing, like an actor playing a part. What I have not told you so far is that you have specifically been reenacting the part of Narendra in his first visit with his truly saintly guru, Ramakrishna. Narendra recalled the impact of Ramakrishna's words about seeing God by saying, "That impressed me at once. For the first time I found a man who dared to say that he saw God, that religion was a reality, to be felt, to be sensed in an infinitely more intense way than we can sense the world."[3] Narendra sang a hymn about the vision of God and one line was, "Behold, His Beauty is enhanced by fresh manifestations of Love! It throws into the shade a million moons! Verily, the lightning flashes out of His Glorious Beauty! The Blessed Vision causes the hair to stand on end." Ramakrishna, hearing these words, went into a blissful state in which his body became motionless, and his eyes were half closed and fixed as he beheld a vision beyond the world of form, described by a disciple as follows:

> The hair of his body does actually stand on end. His eyes are bedewed with tears of joy. The smile on his lips shows the ecstatic delight that he feels at the sight of the Blessed Vision. Yes, he must be enjoying a vision of unequaled beauty which puts into the shade the refulgence of a million moons! Is this God-vision? If so, what must be the intensity of faith and devotion, of discipline and austerity which has brought such a vision within reach of mortal men?[4]

In spite of Narendra seeing Ramakrishna obviously in ecstasy, he was still disturbed by the bizarre behavior that Ramakrishna had exhibited and was tempted to dismiss him as a maniac. Nevertheless the thought occurred to him, "He may be a madman but only a fortunate few can have such renunciation. Even if insane, this man is the holiest of the holy, a true saint, and for that alone he deserves the reverential homage of mankind."[5] Narendra's mind continued to waver back and forth, and so in making his second trip to Ramakrishna, he was determined to make a more definitive assessment of this odd guru. When Ramakrishna was in an ecstatic mood, he stammered some words and put his right foot on the body of Narendra, bringing him into an altered state of consciousness. He could see "with eyes open, that all things of the room together with the walls were rapidly whirling and receding into an unknown region and my I-ness together with the whole universe was, as it were, going to vanish in an all-devouring great void."[6] When Narendra hollered in distress, Ramakrishna laughed and gently touched his chest bringing him back to his normal awareness. Narendra no longer thought he could dismiss Ramakrishna as a madman, yet he still did not know what to make of this strange guru.

On another visit Ramakrishna talked about worshipping God in both his personal aspects and impersonal aspects. He explained the Vedanta philosophy of nondualism that maintains that God is the only Reality, and we are already united with God, but must uncover that awareness. He described the jnana yoga practice of discerning that every individual object seen is not the true Reality and by this process of negation the seeker comes to the realization of the impersonal Absolute.

> The Vedantist who seeks to realize God the Absolute reasons, saying, "not this, not this"; that is, the Absolute is "not this, not that"; nor any finite object; nor the individual soul; nor the external world. When as the result of this reasoning, the mind ceases to be moved by desires, when in fact the conditional mind vanishes, then is it that one can attain true knowledge, then is it that one's soul goes into *Samadhi* [transcendental ecstasy]. Such a man truly realizes God the Absolute and finds the phenomenal universe to be consequently unreal. He realizes that names and forms applied to finite objects are like dreams; that God the Absolute cannot be described by words; that one cannot, indeed, so much as say that God is a person.[7]

While in divine ecstasy, Ramakrishna himself spiritually experienced the transcendental nature of God as the Absolute and only Reality, but he also taught the value of worshipping God in a personal manner. He maintained that having an ego and living in the world of form necessitated that the

RAMAKRISHNA

NARENDRA BEFORE HE BECAME SWAMI VIVEKANANDA

seeker naturally thinks of himself as separate from God and feels a need to join with a Personal God. This dualism convinces the seeker that the world of form is real and not a dream. Dualists see all the forms of the world as the works of God, Who is in the process of creating, maintaining, and destroying the universe. The most advanced of these dualists see God within and without, manifesting in the individual soul and expressed in every part of the external world. The nondualists and the dualists in India stood in philosophical conflict with each other. Instead of siding with one philosophy or the other, Ramakrishna manifested in his own life and also taught others that both philosophies can be simultaneously accepted and integrated into one's spiritual life. He believed that the impersonal Absolute God and Personal God were one and the same and believing in one implied believing in the other. As with the nondualists, Ramakrishna could see that every object in the world is an illusion and God is the only One Reality. Yet, along with the most high-minded dualists, he could also see the presence of God in a personal sense in every object and person within this relative reality of the external world. Ramakrishna's acceptance of God as both personal in a dualistic sense and impersonal in a nondualistic sense helped me to formulate my own Christian synthesis of dualism and nondualism, which will be elaborated upon later in this book.

Most seekers can accept the ideas of dualism because the world appears to be so real and our ego condition convinces us we are now disconnected from God and must find union with Him. Narendra was brought up to believe in dualism. But his dualism was not high-minded enough for him to believe in seeing God's presence everywhere in the world and in every person. In addition, as a dualist it seemed to him that nondualism was blasphemous in asserting, "I am God." He could not believe that every soul is already one with God and needs to simply reveal this pre-existing union. Consequently, Narendra, who was still not yet twenty years old, could neither accept Ramakrishna's very high-minded dualism that sees the divine everywhere within form nor could he accept the nondualistic Reality of God that transcends form.

> One day at the temple garden he laughingly said to a friend: "How silly! This jug is God! This cup is God! Whatever we see is God! And we too are God! Nothing could be more absurd."[8]

Narendra did not know that Ramakrishna was within hearing distance of him. Ramakrishna could have potentially had some sort of ego reaction to his ridiculing words and could have verbally challenged him. Instead he responded in the most gracious, helpful, and surprising way possible:

Sri Ramakrishna came out of his room and gently touched him. Spellbound, he immediately perceived that everything in the world was indeed God. A new universe opened around him. Returning home in a dazed state, he found there too that the food, the plate, the eater himself, the people around him, were all God. When he walked in the street, he saw that the cabs, the horses, the streams of people, the buildings, were all Brahman [God]. He could hardly go about his day's business. His parents became anxious about him and thought him ill. And when the intensity of the experience abated a little, he saw the world as a dream.[9]

After a number of days, Narendra returned to normal consciousness with new respect for the teachings of Ramakrishna. But did these spiritual experiences convert Narendra into being committed to Ramakrishna as his guru? No. In spite of his dramatic spiritual experiences, he remained a skeptic for a very long time. Ramakrishna was not bothered at all by Narendra's reluctance to accept him, and in fact he welcomed the questioning minds of his disciples by saying, "Test me as money-lenders test their coins. You must not accept me until you have tested me thoroughly."[10]

Authentic yoga does not encourage blind and unquestioning followers, as the following story illustrates: A sannyasin saw three boys bowing down before a wall. There were four large "X" marks scratched into the wall. The sannyasin asked one of the boys, "What are you doing?"

The boy answered, "I am worshipping at my altar. A few days ago my two friends and I saw a sannyasin, like you, use a rock to scratch an "X" mark on the wall. Then he bowed down to worship, showing his reverence for the "X" mark. When he left, we imitated his example by making our own holy "X" marks, and we come here every day to worship at our altars."

The sannyasin pointed to a spot in the dirt in front of the "X" mark that the original sannyasin had made, and he asked the boy to start digging in that spot. The boy complied and was surprised to find a book covered by a cloth. The boy asked, "How did you know this book was here?"

"I am on a pilgrimage to several cities. On my journey a man asked me to do the favor of bringing this book to one of his family members who lives in my home town. The book was heavy so I decided to bury it temporarily while I continued my journey, and then on my return trip I could dig it up again. I was the sannyasin you saw previously who marked the wall with an "X." But I made that mark so I could find the place where I had buried the book. When you saw me bow down toward the wall and appear to be worshipping, you did not see that I was actually digging a hole and placing the book in the ground. It is good that you want to worship, but you should not worship mindlessly. Blind faith is not a virtue when you do not know with your reasoning mind why or what you are worshipping. As far as building an outer altar, you can do so if you wish. But always remember that the divine can be found within the altar of your own heart. You can always worship at that inner altar because God is within you."

Authentic yoga encourages seekers to conduct their own search for the truth. The guru may teach many different ideas, but asks the student to accept only the aspects of the truth which he can prove to himself through his own understanding and practical application. The deeper aspects of understanding will come to the seeker after first investing in service, devotion, and living a moral life. Each seeker must learn through his own experiences, and the questioning mind is a necessary part of letting truth be revealed from within. Narendra is a good example of maintaining this necessary inquisitiveness of the seeker. "He never abdicated his reason for a moment. He would accept nothing that could not be rigorously tested by reason."[11]

It took a long time of persistent questioning before Narendra was able to satisfy the concerns of his mind. However, mental reasoning was not the only criterion for discerning the validity of Ramakrishna. According to Narendra the key factor in him becoming bound to his guru was the intense love that Ramakrishna showered onto him and indeed on everyone.[12] In contrast to inauthentic gurus who want to be seen and worshipped by their devotees as divine, Ramakrishna saw and worshipped the divine in all the seekers who came to him. In a spiritual sense, charity is to see others as being further along on the path than they perceive themselves. Indeed Ramakrishna saw an ocean of goodness in the least of his disciples and in time they learned to live up to his exalted view of them. One of the many examples of this is Narendra himself, who would become the advanced spiritual teacher Swami Vivekananda and would bring Ramakrishna's teachings to the West.

Ramakrishna asked Narendra when they first met why he had taken so long to come because he had been given a prior vision that revealed their relationship as a karmic mission. In an elevated state of mind Ramakrishna was shown a transcendental realm and saw a great sage absorbed in deep meditation. Then a divine child appeared and sat on the lap of the sage. He whispered into the ear of the sage that he was going to be born on the earth and that the sage must come with him. The sage consented with a loving look. When I was reading about this vision, I figured that the sage must symbolize Ramakrishna as the teacher and the child must symbolize Narendra as his much younger disciple. But my assumption was mistaken. As I read on, I learned that the sage in the vision returned to meditation and Ramakrishna observed a part of the sage extend to earth to the place where Narendra lived. Consequently, on Narendra's first visit, Ramakrishna could see that he was the sage seen in his vision. Ramakrishna was so humble that even this vision depicted himself in the lesser role of being a child.[13] Although there has been some misuses of the guru and disciple relationship especially in America, the relationship between Narendra and Ramakrishna is a shining example of the best of what this time-honored tradition has to offer.

---

1. Gurudas Burman, *Sri Ramakrishna Carit* (Benegali), (Calcutta, India: Udbodhan Office), Vol. I, p. 212.

2. *Sri Ramakrishna, the Great Master*, translated by Swami Jagadananda, (Mylapore, Madras, India: Sri Ramakrishna Math, Second edition), p. 718.

3. Swami Vivekananda, *The Complete Works of Swami Vivekananda*, Vol. 9, Mayavati Memorial Edition, (Kolkata, India: Advaita Ashrama, 2002), p. 179.

4. Mahendra, (anonymous author calling himself "M."), *The Condensed Gospel of Sri Ramakrishna* (Mylapore, Madras, India: Sri Ramakrishna Math, 1987), p. 49.

5. Swami Prabhananda, *First Meetings with Sri Ramakrishna*, (Mylapore, Madras, India: Sri Ramakrishna Math, 1987), pp. 190-191.

6. *Sri Ramakrishna, the Great Master*, translated by Swami Jagadananda, (Mylapore, Madras, India: Sri Ramakrishna Math, Second edition), p. 737.

7. Mahendra (anonymous author calling himself "M."), *The Condensed Gospel of Sri Ramakrishna* (Mylapore, Madras, India: Sri Ramakrishna Math, 1987), p. 115.

8. Mahendra (anonymous author calling himself "M."), *The Gospel of Sri Ramakrishna*, translated by Swami Nikhilananda, (New York: Ramakrishna-Vivekananda Center, [1942] 1992), p. 58.

9. Ibid., p. 58.

10. Swami Ramakrishnananda, *Sri Ramakrishna and His Mission*, (Madras, India: Sri Ramakrishna Math, 1955), p. 46.

11. Ibid., p. 193.

12. Ibid., pp. 192-193.

13. Ibid., pp. 184-185.

14

UNUSUAL VISITORS

≈ • ≈

SUNRISE MEDITATION

In addition to the long-term residents at the Yoga Center, we had short-term residents. We charged only $8 per day, even though we were a ten-minute walk to the beachfront, where numerous expensive resort hotels were located. All participants were required to take part in the morning schedule. Everyone got up at 5:30 AM and a half-hour later chanting began, followed by group meditation, yoga postures, and breathing practices. Sometimes we meditated at the beach in the early morning as shown above.

SUFI DANCING AT THE YOGA CENTER

The Yoga Center sponsored events and workshops from many different disciplines and teachers. Every week there was something new to learn and enjoy, including tai chi, massage, psychic readings, scream therapy, and Sufi dancing. One workshop in particular comes to mind which focused on free-form body movement. We watched as each participant took turns moving around the room in an uninhibited display of spontaneous body movement. I even surprised myself by taking a turn that helped me overcome my self-consciousness about my musical and dance limitations.

A Hindu dancer came and gave a wonderful performance at the Yoga Center, but what I recall most about him was that he was sixty-five, yet he looked like he was forty. I asked him his secret, and he said, "Every morning I squeeze a whole fresh lemon into a gallon of water. Then I drink the water. Finally I throw up the water. This cleanses the stomach and keeps me young." At the Yoga Center he did not find any converts to his fountain of youth.

A group of visitors from India came and told us they wanted to perform a very important Hindu fire ceremony, called *Agnihotra*, in our residential house behind the large Yoga Center temple where the classes were held. To be hospitable, the other residents and I agreed to have the ceremony in our living room. The visitors took cow dung, placed it in a bowl, and set it on fire. They seemed delighted as the smoke filled the house from top to bottom. The other residents, one by one, excused themselves, suddenly remembering important engagements elsewhere. However, I had to stay, since I was the director. When the ceremony was mercifully over, the visitors were genuinely pleased to have had the opportunity to pass along this purification blessing to the Yoga Center. I respectfully thanked them for their gift. In addition to smoke, they left behind what they told me was important literature that they asked me to post. The literature elaborated upon the merits of eating bits of cow dung to cure many kinds of sickness. I know the cow is considered a sacred animal in India, but some things can be carried a bit too far.

For some sleep-over visitors there was no charge. An example was one penniless young man who came to the Yoga Center. I naturally asked him, "What's your name?"

"I don't know," he answered in a monotone voice with a blank look on his face.

At first I thought maybe he was kidding, yet there was no indication of that. He didn't appear to be speaking deceptively, either. He looked like a lost soul—something I too had experienced at one time during my spiritual seeking many years previously, although I always knew my name. "Since you don't know your name, I don't know what to call you. Tell me what I should call you."

"I don't know," he repeated.

"Just make up a name. I'll call you whatever you want me to call you."

"You give me a name," he said quietly.

I decided, "OK, you are 'John.'"

"I am John," he said, and that is what we called him.

On the day he was leaving, he came to me and gestured for me to follow him. He walked over to the place near the door where we had placed our shoes, since it is a yoga practice to walk barefoot inside. He pointed to my shoes and speaking in his expressionless voice he said, "I want your shoes."

"I need my shoes," I responded.

"I want your shoes," he repeated, as usual in his monotone voice.

"They are the only shoes I have, so I need to keep them." I opened the refrigerator and told him, "Look, you can have whatever food you want out of here."

He had shoes himself, but he still persisted, "I want your shoes."

"I need them. Here, take this food instead," and I loaded him up with food, and he finally accepted that he would not have the shoes. Almost immediately after he left, I regretted not giving him my shoes. In fact, I *still* regret it.

Another example of regret occurred when Darryl came to stay at the Yoga Center. I already knew him from the times he had come to my Jesus Prayer classes a year earlier, and I had previously visited him when he was living in an extremely hot and cramped attic during the summer. Darryl's friends had requested that I visit him because they were concerned about his welfare. At that time I asked him, "What are you doing up here? It's like a furnace."

With several gallons of water beside him, Darryl asserted firmly, "I have water. I am going to stay up here until I reach Christ Consciousness."

"Or until you have to go to the bathroom." Darryl seemed a bit too solemn, so to loosen him up I said, "I once heard that a great philosopher remarked, 'Men are Gods who *shit*'" This did not have the desired effect, so I joined Darryl in his seriousness by saying, "Enlightenment is a worthy goal. Christ Consciousness is a worthy goal. However, even the Buddha gave up asceticism and only was enlightened after following a path of moderation. I tried to go to extremes too, and it's a dangerous path."

"Nothing you can say will change my mind," he affirmed, and that was the way the conversation ended. Next I learned from a friend that he had allowed Darryl to visit with him for an agreed upon period of time. When the agreed-upon time for the visit was completed, Darryl refused to leave. After exhausting all other options, my friend went to Darryl's room and poured ammonia all over the floor so Darryl was forced out by the vapors. That is when Darryl showed up at the doorstep of the Yoga Center. I told him we normally would allow anyone to stay for just one night without cost, but in his case I would give him three days to stay. After that he would have to leave. To emphasize the point, I said, "I know how you left your previous place. Before I let you move in here, you have to promise me that you will leave in exactly three days without causing any trouble."

"I promise," he said.

Darryl chose to participate in my Jesus Prayer class again, as he had in the past. As an experiment I had been conducting for about three months, I was holding a class in Zen Buddhist meditation that Darryl also began to attend. In this class I asked students to meditate upon a koan, either "What is my true nature?" or "Who am I?" Along with the koan, I taught the other traditional practices of Zen meditation that I had studied, including the sitting position, the walking meditation, the hand positions, and the bowing-forward gesture.

However, I introduced two very non-traditional elements as part of the experiment. One of these was to raise my voice very loudly to the point of screaming. The other was to curse at the participants in that loud voice. Traditional Zen practice includes hitting students with a stick on the muscles that lead from the neck to the shoulder. Instead of being a punishment, this hitting is done to increase awareness and stimulate meditation. Likewise, my experiment with loudness and cursing was implemented for the purpose of improving mental focusing in meditation, rather than as a punishment. I carefully and thoroughly instructed students that I would yell and curse, and I explained why.

I also told them that their purpose was to not allow the yelling and cursing to affect them in any way. Instead they were to focus ever more strongly on the koan. If they had any emotional reaction to the yelling or cursing, they had been instructed prior to the Zen practice to ask within themselves, "*Who* is having an emotional reaction? *Who* is this 'I' that reacts emotionally? *Who* does not like yelling? *Who* does not like cursing? *Who am I?*" Everyone understood, at least intellectually, that this was just to stimulate their practice.

Then during the session itself, right after I yelled or cursed, I would say, "Are you upset? *Who* is upset? Are you angry? *Who* is angry? *Who* are *you?*" No one ever complained to me about the format because everyone was forewarned exactly what to expect. Many told me that they learned to be detached from their own emotional reactions and to let go of those ego reactions, so they were less likely to reappear.

One day after teaching a yoga class, a student inquired, "Do you have a rule about no students going to your residence in the back?"

"No, people are always dropping in to visit unannounced. You are welcome to come any time," I reassured her.

"I don't know if I should tell you this. I went to your residence, and I went inside and someone screamed, 'You asshole,' at me so I ran out of there as quickly as I could."

I laughed out loud and said, "That was me, but I wasn't hollering at you. That yelling and cursing was actually part of our non-traditional Zen meditation class. The students in the class know that I am just stimulating them to ignore my outbursts and to meditate more deeply. I'm sorry if I scared you, but I'm glad you told me about this so I could explain it to you."

Darryl told me he really liked the Zen class because he felt it was like therapy for him. He was facing some childhood memories of situations in which others had yelled at him. When the third day came and it was time for Darryl to leave the Yoga Center, he would not go. I waited one extra day, and then I went into his room carrying a full bucket of water which I emptied onto him as he lay on his bed. It was perhaps a harsh thing to do, yet he got the message. After a short while he came to the kitchen to say goodbye. Feeling guilty about taking such a drastic measure, I handed a glass of water to him saying, "Here. You can throw this at me."

Darryl handed the water glass back to me with the words, "You will have your turn, but not by my hand. The universe will pay you back by someone else's hand."

"You are probably right. I was just hoping I could get my karma now when I can see it coming, rather than later. However, you know that you made a promise to me to leave when the three-day limit ended."

"I know I promised, yet I felt I was making so much progress here that I was hoping to stay."

"I'm sorry, Darryl. I wish you well wherever you go." We hugged, and that was the last time I saw him. A few years later I heard that Darryl had gone to extremes and had died, although it was uncertain whether his passing was accidental or suicidal. This news made me feel guilty about my part in having forced him to leave the Yoga Center, where he felt he was making progress. I still regret not letting him stay. Several years later I was at the A.R.E. summer camp in the country, and a prankster came up from behind and threw a full bucket of cold water on me. I was chilled to the bone, but then smiled as the image came to mind of Darryl telling me that the universe would repay me.

After the three-month experiment with Zen meditation at the Yoga Center, I no longer engaged in this teaching method, for two reasons. One reason was that it seemed too forced. I felt as though I was trying to make fruit ripen by some artificial means rather than allowing time and sunlight to take their effect in a natural way. The other reason is that the yelling and cursing seemed not the most loving approach and that teaching in this way threw me off of my Christian focus.

15

FORGIVENESS

≈ ∘ ≈

Many seekers came to the Yoga Center not just for the learning of yoga disciplines and philosophy, but also for forgiveness and healing. Some seekers were struggling with alcoholism. I remember one person who came to yoga classes only intermittently. Unexpectedly he stumbled his way into my bedroom while I was asleep in the middle of the night. He woke me up and, of course, startled me. "You scared me," I said. "What do you want?"

He came close to my face so I could smell the alcohol on his breath and mumbled, "Nothing. I just wanted to visit."

I could have been indignant; however, I remembered how drunk I used to get as a college student. "I wouldn't mind talking to you now, but in the morning you wouldn't remember anything I might say. Go home and sleep it off. Come back in the daylight tomorrow, and we can talk then."

He said, "All right," and staggered off.

For some seekers, the Yoga Center held out a unique opportunity for approaching life differently. For example, Glenn wanted to take up residence with other yoga seekers in order to firmly establish a new lifestyle after being in prison. He had fallen in with the wrong crowd and had been imprisoned for armed robbery. While in prison he discovered yoga and meditation. Being a black man, he had experienced discrimination in the past, and former convicts often experience discrimination when they come out of prison. He, like all of us, wanted the simple gift of acceptance and love, which he had learned to give and receive. Sometimes a meditator will experience a jolt of energy that jerks the body in various ways. Glenn and I shared this common experience during our morning meditations.

One morning I was sitting at the round, wooden kitchen table, which Glenn had skillfully resurfaced as a service project for the Yoga Center. Glenn brought me a little health food cake and said lovingly, "This is a gift for you. I don't have a reason for this. It just seems like this cake has your name on it." I, of course, happily thanked him for his gift, but did not elaborate on why his gift was so appropriate. I marveled at Glenn's gift because it was my birthday, and he could not have known because I had not told anyone. After Glenn left the Yoga Center and started his own woodworking business, I donated all my long-unused stained glass equipment to him and trained him how to use it.

Like Glenn, I too had come to the Yoga Center for forgiveness and healing, in the aftermath of my experience with Demetrius. I found that I felt forgiven and healed by forgiving and helping to heal others. I found out that in some way the director was similar to a priest, whom others sought out to confess their shortcomings. Many of these confidential confessions concerned sexual impropriety, such as adultery. One temporary visitor, a young man, came to me, and speaking nervously he told me, "Last night I met a woman at the beach and took her to the Yoga Center temple, and we had sex there. Actually, we had sex right in front of the altar."

He scanned my face apprehensively. He could see my questioning face, as I asked, "Why are you telling me this?"

"I am not sure. I guess I feel guilty about hiding it."

"Why did you choose the altar area? There are a lot of other places in the temple that you could have used."

"It felt like a compulsion. I was drawn to the altar like a magnet. It felt like we were having sex in front of God—whether He liked it or not."

"I am not too certain what to say. There is a rule that there is to be no sex in the temple or in our living quarters in the back building, but there's no rule about sex outside of the Yoga Center. I am disappointed that you had sex in the temple and in front of the altar. Nevertheless, I am not going to get upset about it. If I were to get upset, I would be defiling God's altar that is inside of me. The altar in this building is only a symbol of God's altar inside of you and me. Should I put a sign in front of the altar that reads 'NO SEX IN FRONT OF THE ALTAR,' or will you promise me that you will have your future sexual encounters some other place?"

"Yes, I promise."

I assured him, "I forgive you if that is what you want. I do not want you to feel guilty because that usually serves no useful purpose."

"I have never really resolved my feelings about sex and guilt, and I am not sure how."

"I was brought up a Catholic, so sex and guilt went hand in hand. When I had my hormones running through my body at puberty, I made a promise to God in prayer that I would express my sexual feelings in whatever way I wanted to, but that when I resolved these feelings, only then would I return to Him. To make a long story short, now due to meditation I can raise up the sexual energy and offer it to God for spiritual purposes. This ability to raise up sexual energy enables me to maintain celibacy. However, if a person is not yet able to raise up sexual energy, the energy will have to be expressed in some manner. I cannot tell you what is the appropriate way to express this energy. It is a personal decision you will have to figure out yourself. What I can tell you is that guilt only makes matters worse, not better."

On another occasion I returned to our living quarters, and a temporary resident, Babette, had a man I had not seen before in her room. They both acted so guiltily that it was obvious that the house rule on sex had been violated. It was also obvious to Babette that I knew, so I decided that it would be better not to add to her guilt by making a verbal accusation then or even later after her friend had gone.

Because I had not confronted her, Babette trusted me enough to come to me at a later date and ask me to give her a healing session for her knee that was not healing. She had gone to the doctor, and he told her that X-rays showed she had torn cartilage in her knee and that surgery would be required to repair it. I did the healing prayer of the laying on of the hands and called on the healing power of Jesus. At a later date she went back to the doctor who took more X-rays and discovered that the cartilage had in fact healed, although he did not understand how this could have happened without surgery.

There were always residents coming and going, but Bhavani, Usha, and Judith formed a permanent core of spiritual seekers. They worked at outside jobs to pay for room and board and also actively supported the Yoga Center through teaching and service projects. At a meeting with the owner, Jonathan, these three female residents proposed that I step down as the director. They wanted to have someone else be the director or have a group of joint directors. I was initially shocked and hurt to hear about their proposal because their concerns had never come up before in any of our conversations, and I felt close to the women. Jonathan asked me what I thought of this proposal, and I said, "I am a bit surprised because I haven't had a chance to process this. I feel I have done a good job of bringing our organization from red ink to black ink for the first time."

Judith spoke up, "But one of the reasons why you have been able to make ends meet is that we pay for our room and board, and that money every month keeps us afloat. In addition to our outside jobs we also teach some of the yoga classes and do a lot of the upkeep around here. If we didn't have to pay room and board, we could do a lot more for the Yoga Center." Bhavani and Usha expressed similar sentiments that they would like to do more, yet their outside jobs were a limiting factor.

I listened attentively and then said, "I have learned not to go against the flow of the river, so I don't want to resist a change if that is what needs to happen. I propose that for today and for the next few days we pray and meditate together about this. I think we all want to do God's Will. Hopefully we can all get clear on what would be for the highest good of everyone." My proposal to defer a decision on this matter for a few days was accepted.

BHAVANI AT LEFT AND USHA ON RIGHT AT YOGA CENTER

After getting over my initial hurt feelings, I remembered how Demetrius felt when he suspected that I was trying to take his students away and usurp his authority. In that case I wasn't even trying to take away his role, yet he reacted to me as though I was. In this case the women really were trying to take away my role, but even so I did not want to react in the same jealous and defensive way that Demetrius had. I did not want to become so attached to a role that I forgot to be loving, which is my true calling as a follower of Christ. It would be easy to blame my confrontation with Demetrius on his ego; however, the fact is that it takes two egos to have a conflict. I felt this was an opportunity for me to look at my own ego attachments and let go of them. I also felt that this whole situation was another step in the direction of solving the shadow puzzle.

To help me let go of my ego attachments, I consciously tried to perceive the situation from the women's perspective. They felt they should get more authority or more compensation for all the work they were doing and in fact doing so well. Seeing the situation from their perspective helped me to gain a deeper appreciation for all of their contributions to the Yoga Center. Instead of trying to come up with a form-related resolution to this dilemma, I decided that my lesson was to surrender my role to God and to send light and love to each of them. I made the choice to trust in God and that choice in itself felt healing for me both in respect to my past with Demetrius and in respect to this situation.

The next day was Saturday, and with Bhavani and Usha off from work we and additional friends went to a farm for strawberry picking. Of course, the best part of strawberry picking is that you eat as much as you pick. Sitting in the middle of the farm we set aside all differences and joyfully chanted, "Amen strawberries, Amen strawberries, Amen strawberries, Amen, Amen, Amen strawberries." It was a delightful outing. The next morning after our regular chanting and meditation in the temple, I left the meditation area. But then I had a strong intuition that I needed to go back to the meditation room where the three women were still located. I followed this guidance and after returning said, "I had to come back because I feel there is someone here who wants to say something to me."

Judith spoke up, "You are right. It's me. I do want to talk to you."

I had been standing at a distance, so I came closer and sat down. Judith continued, "I know you were upset about us asking you to step down as the director when we talked Friday with Jonathan. However, since then you have been so kind to us. Yesterday at the strawberry patch we were so together and joyful. I feel guilty because it was my idea to ask you to step down." She began to cry and said, "I want to apologize to you." I too began to cry, first a little bit, and then a lot. Judith came over to me and put her arms around me and hugged me and then all four of us hugged as a group. This was the simultaneous giving and receiving of forgiveness and healing that I needed for this situation, but also for my past with Demetrius.

After the crying subsided, the women confirmed as a group that they wanted me to continue as the director. I also let them know how grateful I was for all the service work they did. I said, "I want to give you the opportunity to tell me how I can make things easier for you. Yes, I know I don't do much chanting. I still don't want to chant if my heart isn't in it. Yet maybe there are some things I can change that I am not aware of. I am open to whatever you want to tell me."

Bhavani spoke up hesitantly, "There is one thing. When you ring the bell in the morning at 5:30, you ring it too loud."

"Really? I had no idea. You mean the sound is too loud?"

"It's not just the sound. It's the way you ring it so insistently."

"Well, I could ring it more quietly. I would be happy to do so. But how about if each person has their own alarm clock? Would you prefer that?"

Everyone agreed that it was best for each person to be responsible for waking themselves with an alarm. However, I would still have to use the bell for visitors sleeping over, who did not have an alarm.

"So what else do I need to hear to make things better?"

They looked at each other and then back at me, and Usha finally said, "There isn't anything else."

Even though they did not say so, I was aware that my lack of chanting had been somewhat of a sore spot, at least in the past. The next morning I wanted to show my willingness to be more open so I participated in one Hindu chant, which is truly universal. I chanted the Sanskrit words of the chant that we typically used to end our chanting session. The English translation is:

Lead us from darkness to light.
Lead us from the unreal to the real.
Lead us from the fear of death to immortality.

16

RELEASING
INNER BLOCKS

~ ๏ ~

Occasionally I attended the meetings of a New Age group called the Fellowship of the Inner Light. This group, years later, would buy the Yoga Center property to set up its own headquarters. At a Fellowship meeting which attracted many Christian seekers, I first met Dylan, with whom I felt an immediate rapport. One day I walked over to his rented house near the Yoga Center. I asked him about his background, and he explained, "I went to Youngstown University and received a B.S. in chemical engineering. I was into the college scene, but I knew there must be more to life than having fun by going to parties and drinking. I wondered what was the purpose of it all. So in the library I found metaphysical books, especially Eastern philosophy, that made sense to me. When I read about Edgar Cayce, a new dimension opened up for me. I felt he spoke the truth.

"I began practicing meditation and did a lot of yoga breathing practices. I think I went too far with the breathing methods, and one day I was totally overwhelmed by a great energy that I could not control. It was probably a kundalini experience. So I learned to not go to extremes with breathing techniques. Gradually I have been developing my psychic ability, but I think it is important to use that ability to help people.

"I wanted to be of service, so I volunteered for Vietnam service as a medical specialist and worked at the hospital base camp in Vietnam. It helped me to face reality. I saw the world as it really is. When I returned, I had a high-salaried management job in chemical engineering in Salem, Ohio. However, because I wanted to help others, I quit and got a job as a social service worker. After several years I realized that social work doesn't really solve people's problems. I felt that the best way to help people is to help raise their consciousness. As a result I felt guided to resign my job and come here to Virginia Beach. Since I have been here, I have been experimenting with the use of light and sound to help people to change for the better. If you want, I can arrange to give you a light and sound session so you can see the benefits for yourself."

I accepted his offer and set up an appointment for a future session. Before leaving, we meditated together. Afterwards Dylan asked me if I had a good meditation, and I told him, "During the meditation the crown of my head felt as though it was opening up. It was like there was a circle on the top and back of my head that opened to infinity. It felt like that opening was being filled with light and love. It was very joyful. In fact, I still feel that joy. Maybe it has something to do with you and me meeting."

"That confirms what I heard during my meditation. An inner voice said, 'You can work together to help others.'"

As I walked back to the Yoga Center, I remained in a very exhilarated spiritual state and felt that we would indeed work together to accomplish spiritual purposes. I returned to Dylan's house in the Yoga Center van on another evening, and I had the promised light and sound session, which I found to be very uplifting. This kind of light and sound session heightened all of my spiritual senses and brought me into an otherworldly state of mind. However, the downside of this unusual state was that I could not stay grounded in the functions of the everyday world. Consequently on the way back to the Yoga Center I drove right through a stop sign that I did not even see. Out of the corner of my eye I saw a jeep coming straight at me from the left side. The oncoming car almost hit square against my driver's seat, but because I was moving forward, it hit right behind my body in the middle of the vehicle, caving in a portion of the left side of the Volkswagen van. My left shoulder was hurt, although not seriously enough to warrant a trip to the hospital. The two people in the other car were not hurt, although their car was also seriously damaged.

Because of the experience at Dylan's house, I was not as grounded as I would normally be. Nevertheless, I couldn't understand how I could have missed seeing the stop sign. After the accident I walked over to take a closer look and discovered that there was a large tree branch that blocked out the sign. When the police officer came, I made sure that he could see that the view of the stop sign was obviously blocked.

The next day I called Dylan, and he came over and gave me a healing session for my shoulder, which did recover quickly. Later I went back to the scene of the accident and took a photograph of the branch in front of the stop sign. I went to the city workers who were responsible for handling signs to have them make a written statement about the inappropriateness of the sign. They refused to do so, but they did respond immediately in another way. The next day I drove by the sign and discovered that the city workers had cut down the branch.

I had gotten a ticket for going through a stop sign, so I brought the photograph to court. I showed the photograph to the judge and naturally asked him to dismiss the ticket. The judge firmly responded, "Somebody has got to pay for this ticket." I was dumbfounded. I thought in my mind, "How about justice? Let the City of Virginia Beach pay the fine for not removing that branch from in front of that stop sign." However, due to my fear of the judge I never got the words out, and I was, of course, the "somebody" required to pay the fine. Fortunately, our insurance company paid to repair the Yoga Center van. The agent told me their investigation had discovered that the other driver had been smoking marijuana, so they came to a settlement with the insurance company of the other driver.

I didn't resort to blaming Dylan for my accident. In fact, I still felt very supportive of his work, although I suggested he tell future subjects to be extra careful driving home after a light and sound session. So we could work together, I invited Dylan to become a resident of the Yoga Center. He agreed, and I gave him yoga teacher training so he could assist others in learning how to practice yoga. Dylan and I began to offer what we called the "Light and Sound Course," which was a series of six different sessions over a six-week period. Because of Dylan's psychic ability combined with his scientific background, he was able to provide the structure for the course and the equipment needed to produce the light and sound effects. He used a synthesizer for sound effects, but also designed and built unique devices to produce specific light and sound effects. My contribution to the sessions was to lead participants step by step through guided meditations and other activities designed to enhance the experience.

Participants who completed the entire course found that some sessions were more effective than others. For example, Jim Mustin, a counselor who worked for the Juvenile Domestic Relations Court, did not feel the impact of the experience until the second class. That was when he was able to loosen up and let go of emotional problems. He explained, "I was carrying around a lot of tension. When I found out the source of that tension, I found myself relaxing."[1] He summarized his impressions by saying, "It was terrific, a powerful experience."[2] However, he felt that the class especially benefitted those who had previous meditation experience and those who had set meaningful spiritual goals for themselves. In fact, these were the kinds of seekers who were attracted to this course.

After completing the course, participants were given an evaluation questionnaire and were asked what changes they had experienced. Jeffrey, a school teacher, wrote:

> The most notable experience I had was a real feeling of peace (after shedding some tears). I've learned to go deeper within. The greatest change I have undergone within myself is that I have noticed a big increase in love. That includes all I have come in contact with, not just my family.

Sally, a dental technician, told us:

I experienced an increase in awareness of Oneness with All. There is an almost overwhelming sense of home-coming and well-being. As a result of the light and sound experience I have an overall sense that everything is OK now—no matter what the outer circumstances. I have a clearer picture of where my blocks are, what my work is, and how to do it. Confidence has increased greatly. I use my talents in a way I never could before.

We invited a newspaper reporter named Helen Crist to one of the sessions. Helen was not what you would call a New Age person. She was a middle-aged woman who seemed conservative and reserved. Before the session, she told me she would write a newspaper story about whatever she experienced, but she cautioned, "I'll have to be objective." The following is a description of her experience in her own words:

I found myself repeating over and over, "I am sorry, so very sorry." An electronic sound seemed to float around my head like a butterfly fluttering about. A burst of glorious organ music consumed me, and a Christ-like figure beckoned to me as I walked up the aisle of the cathedral. The voice said, "Come to me, my child. I forgive you."

I found my hands forming over my breast in the manner of prayer. The music filled my entire being. Quite peacefully I realized that all thoughts of negativity were swallowed up by the loving presence which said simply, "I forgive." I was filled with an overwhelming sense of love and purification, joy yet sadness.

Flashes of past lives emerged. Tears flowed constantly and noiselessly, continuing as I returned to this time and place. The happiness remained with me. There was an inner joy and peace that others sensed and responded to. Later as I talked on the phone, I observed that my speaking voice had lowered. It was musical and loving, free of tension.[3]

Marilyn, a psychologist, wrote in her evaluation:

My anxieties have been reduced, and I feel more confident in counseling and teaching, knowing that I can tap a source within. There has been a feeling of joy in being alive and being able to help others experience this joy.

In general I felt that this course was a very important experience for me. It has released a lot and made me more aware of other people's problems (as I work with them). I seem to tune in more quickly, but I don't get wrapped up emotionally to a point where I get drained.

The questionnaire asked participants to identify the most helpful and significant aspects of the course, and Marilyn gave a typical answer:

The most significant experiences dealt with reliving past life scenes, which were relevant to this life and my work as a counselor.

Although I led guided meditations and gave specific instructions during the sessions, these never included any promptings telling the participants to experience past life scenes. Nevertheless, the Light and Sound Course often elicited scenes of past lives. Not only were these visual experiences; they were a reexperiencing of the emotions that had occurred in those past lives. Usually this reexperiencing was both emotional and physiological. For example, a participant named Harry told me that in one of his sessions he felt energy go down his arm, yet he felt the energy stop at his wrist. In the session he had a vision of his hand being cut off, which he thought was related to a past life. Simultaneously he experienced his wrist getting extremely hot and painful like it was burning up. Then the energy cleared through his wrist and into his hand, as he felt he was reexperiencing and releasing fear and anger from that life. Afterwards he felt a tremendous sense of relief and peace.

The universal experience of all the participants in the Light and Sound Course was the healing of inner blocks. There are seven basic spiritual centers in the body, called *chakras*. Energy naturally flows upward in the body from one chakra to another, but there are usually blocks that stop this natural upward flow. Certain sound waves and sound frequencies, in combination with specific colors, can loosen these blocks so they can be released. Normally, these obstructions are rigid and locked into certain parts of the body. Sometimes these blocks were caused by traumatic past life experiences or by repeated negative emotional responses over time. The effect of the light and sound on these blocks is a little like adding water to clay to make the clay pliable so it can be easily molded. By loosening up the blocks, the light and sound experience released the natural spiritual forces within. The result was the elimination of these inner obstructions and the emotions related to them. Participants experienced healing and a feeling of freedom and inner harmony.

It is very difficult to understand the intensity and transformative effects of the Light and Sound Course without having that direct experience yourself. With that in mind, I asked Darius Firestone, who was a biomedical technician, to write a description of his experience:

> The course was given by a chemical engineer in Virginia Beach, who became a psychic and started channeling data on how light and sound effects the release of energy in the body. He was given specific frequencies and colors to use in opening specific energy systems to get rid of negative energy patterns.
>
> With this he designed his own equipment, which was used in the six- week course. We were given an introductory session, and at that session and at the beginning of each subsequent session we were told we had to go with the emotion. If we wanted to cry, or yell, or scream, we were to allow ourselves to express this feeling, so those energy elements "could leave the body." This was continually harped on. Something at each session happened to me—from sweating, to a moment in a 16th Century castle where a type of minuet was being played and danced to, to a total emotional blowout, which occurred in the fifth session and which we were told was the most important one. A newspaper woman also attended that session and wrote a major article concerning the course.
>
> The Fifth Session: We were told the previous sessions tended to open us to the point where we might experience major releases, and we had to go with the emotion. In many of the other sessions "I" tended not to go with the emotion because "I" could override it. Because "I" did not think it was necessary to scream and all that other stuff—it was to a degree not needed—or so I thought.
>
> I now had a session where there was no control. We sat on a floor in a circle. Light phonograph music that was pleasing was played. We had to keep our eyes closed. I could feel the colors bombarding me, and I could feel a change in intensity. Ten minutes into this, the girl across from me starts whimpering. In two more minutes I start to think that her whimpering is the funniest thing I ever heard and start to giggle out loud because I could not control it. The more she whimpered, the more I giggled, which then turned into full-blown laughter.
>
> In my head there were thoughts that I really had to control this obnoxious display because the girl will think I'm laughing about her, and the others will think I'm an idiot. At that point others, very large men, started to cry, which really made me laugh. The more I tried to control it the worse it got. Then I went from wildly laughing to

hysterical crying, and a strange sweat soaked my entire body. At that point I did not care about who or what anyone thought. I was hysterically sobbing and out of control. And I could hear everyone else experiencing their degree of release. At this point the music stopped, and high resonant frequencies were being leveled at us from what looked like a space gun. With each step in increase of frequency it tended to grab something inside and made it worse. Talking to others later, they would all say the same thing—there was absolutely no control in any degree.

For the second part of session number five we had to lie on our backs on the floor with our knees up in the air with our arms resting on the floor over our heads. The psychic information said this position was important for the release of negative energy patterns. There was no music on this one—just loud varying frequencies along with associated colors bombarding us. I started to sweat again in this very cool Yoga Center, and the sweat appeared "thin and strange," not like usual sweat. It was strange rubbing it, and it was different. The impression I had was that it was from the nervous system. In a very short time my clothes were saturated with this strange stuff. Several people started to scream. I didn't feel any of that and just laid there hoping this would soon be over. In about ten more minutes strange things started to occur. "<u>Things</u>" started zooming out of me. They were coming from my solar plexus area, and, as they moved, they appeared to follow an energy pattern outside my body. They moved always from the solar plexus area up to the head area and zoomed out into space. The smaller they were the faster they went. I could tell the exact size. They moved up just inches away from the physical body, and, as they zoomed into space, they went faster. The larger they were the slower they moved up. I could have in one minute a dozen or so little ones while larger ones were less frequent.

I just laid there realizing this tremendous phenomenon when something dramatic started. Something "BIG" started to come out of the stomach area. I could not move my fingers. I noticed my heartbeat increased, and the sweating increased. This thing started to scare the daylights out of me, and I believed if I didn't get out of that room I might die. I tried to roll over so I could crawl out of there, but I could not move. I was paralyzed. I felt I was "giving birth" to something that scared me. I could not yell or move, and the screaming around me went out of focus. It seemed the room was not there. I felt as if I was in a cloud, and no one could detect the tremendous trauma I was in.

At this point I could feel the pulse in my throat slow down. I thought I could at that point move my arms, but was not sure what was moving. I realized I could not escape from this and had to totally accept what was occurring. At that point this thing broke out of my body and very slowly moved up and out of my outside field. The more it moved away from me the louder the room became and my awareness increased. The sweating ceased, and I felt I had delivered a baby elephant.

The large thing that came out of me had stopped all the smaller things from moving through me. But after the large thing left, smaller and moderate size things started coming out of me at an increased tempo. At this faster rate every conceivable size was represented, from button size to baseball size. There were about one to two dozen every fifteen seconds, and this went on rather heavily for nearly fifteen minutes. I just lay there marveling at this. Near the end of the session as the sound was being lowered, this cleansing process slowed down considerably. When the equipment was turned off, two to four things per minute were released until the process stopped.

Near the end a lot of the participants really started yelling for maybe ten minutes. When it was over, we were told to remain and compose ourselves. No one moved for half an hour. When I got up and walked, it was as if I was not touching the ground. I was in love with the world. I felt so good I wanted to be around people. We stood outside talking about this. The newspaper woman came out and asked how we felt. I asked her about her experience and she said that all she did for two and a half hours was cry. She was supposed to interview the engineer, but in her state of mind all she wanted to do was to go to sleep, even though it was about 3:00 PM.

It took courage for Darius and the other participants to face these inner negative emotional patterns and to release them. The Light and Sound Course was not for everyone because not everyone is ready or willing to face what has been built within. The mind is the builder, and whatever is in the body is the result of the mind. The negative emotional or energy patterns lodged in the body are caused by negative thoughts of the mind. Healing requires a change of mind. The change of mind allows the negative thoughts and the negative emotional patterns in the body to be released.

The Light and Sound Course created an optimum environment for having a dramatic change of mind, but was by no means the only way to bring that about.

There were two other kinds of experiences in my own life that had produced a similar opportunity for having a significant change of mind.

One was an extremely expressive form of group psychotherapy that I had experienced when I lived in New York City after graduating from college. The other transformation experience was a six-day Zen Buddhist retreat in which I meditated for more than eight hours each day. These experiences of emotionally expressive group psychotherapy and extensive hours of intensive Zen meditation were both means of reexperiencing and loosening up negative emotional patterns. With these patterns becoming malleable, there was the opportunity to have a change of mind. The reexperiencing allowed the realization that let me tell myself, "Yes, I made this emotional pattern with my mind." With this same realization came the opportunity to change my mind—to say, "No, my mind no longer wants to keep this emotional pattern or energy pattern."

But in my experience of these two earlier transformational experiences, more emotional patterns were brought up than I could release, in large part perhaps because of my own immaturity at that time and my lack of preparation. By the time that the Light and Sound Course came into my life, I had already done a lot of raising up of inner energy, so I was better prepared to face and release inner negative patterns. In addition, the Light and Sound Course itself was extremely effective in facilitating the process of having a change of mind and releasing inner blocks. The inner blocks were sometimes experienced as emotional releases and often experienced as just energy releases without any attending emotion.

There is a river of events, called by the Chinese the "Tao" or the "Way," flowing in your outer life to produce harmony. Similarly, there is a river of energy or life force inside your body that is flowing to produce harmony. The kundalini is not just the overpowering energy locked up at the base of the spine. The kundalini more importantly is this inner river of energy and life force that is flowing upward in the body. The purpose of the kundalini is really to cleanse and create inner balance. When the inner blocks are loosened up, this river will cleanse and release these blocks, similar to the way water from a shower washes away dirt once it is loosened up by soap. The soap that can loosen up inner blocks can be meditation all by itself. This soap can also be the experience of light and sound designed for this purpose. The Light and Sound Course incorporated inner attunement and focusing to enhance the effectiveness of the light and sound.

There was a feeling of responsibility that I had in leading the participants through this cleansing process. I first experienced this sense of responsibility when I became a hypnotist in my late teens and early twenties, which was before my involvement with any conscious spiritual purposes. Having had this experience of hypnotism was an asset in leading the Light and Sound Course. Since I was leading the guided portions of this course and giving functional instructions to the participants, it was necessary for me to control my voice and to maintain my composure throughout all the sessions of the many Light and Sound Courses that were given. If participants were all screaming collectively, I had to be centered on facilitating the process, just as Dylan had to be focused on operating the necessary equipment.

Like Dylan, I was constantly exposed to the transforming effects of the light and sound experience. Nevertheless, I was able to resist being overcome by emotional patterns during light and sound sessions because of my past experience practicing hypnotism, which allowed me to remain in control of myself. I was not influenced by suggestion, by imagination, by what others were experiencing, or by any external stimuli, such as the light and sound. An even more significant factor in maintaining my composure was what I had learned through being a yoga teacher. When I taught my yoga classes, I learned to actively give instructions to the students and simultaneously feel a deep inner attunement. Especially during the silent moments, I felt light and love rising within me, and I extended this light and love to my students. I guided the Light and Sound Course in the same way, by focusing on blessing all the participants in their time of openness and by calling upon divine assistance. In this way, each guided session of this six-week course was actually an internal meditation experience for me and an extension of the fruit of that attunement experience to others.

Another reason why I was able to resist being overcome by emotional patterns while facilitating this course was that I gave myself solitary light and sound experiences on a regular basis. It was at these private times, without the responsibility of leading a group, that I was able to experience the release of emotional patterns. But even in these private sessions, I never really let loose emotionally, and most releases were just of energy patterns without an accompanying emotion.

On a daily basis it became easy for me to raise up the kundalini energy in a safe and controlled way. Often this produced an immediate inner revitalization at all levels, which was usually experienced as a feeling of well-being. Nevertheless, sometimes there was a temporary period of disorientation. For example, when a large inner block was raised up and released, it would take me perhaps a day or two days to adjust to this inner change. Because the Light and Sound Course participants would be releasing very significant inner blocks for the first time, they were given only one session per week, which allowed them plenty of time between sessions to allow the inner changes to be fully incorporated into their daily lives.

---

1. Helen Crist, "Metaphysical Peace at the Beach," in the Beacon section of the *Ledger-Star*, Norfolk, VA on Tuesday, November 8, 1977.
2. Ibid.
3. Ibid.

17

PSYCHIC EXPERIENCES

~ ∘ ~

I thought all the releasing of inner negativity that was occurring in me might lead to revealing the answer to the shadow puzzle. Since the time when I hung from the theater balcony and first challenged myself to face identity issues, I felt the solution to my puzzle could be found by uncovering hidden memories that went all the way back to my early childhood. But living at the Yoga Center, I realized that revealing subconscious memories of my life couldn't fully resolve the puzzle because these were not going back far enough. After seeing so many Light and Sound Course participants relive past life scenes and emotions, I wondered about my own past lives. I realized my shadow puzzle might have something to do with emotions, decisions, and events from past lives, and that is why it was so difficult to solve. In this sense my dilemma was similar to the problem encountered by some of my former hospital patients, who had serious diseases, disabilities, or accidents which could not be attributed to anything that they had done in this lifetime.

Unlike so many of the Light and Sound Course participants, I did not have any past life scenes emerge either in group sessions or privately. In order to get some clarity on past lives, I experimented with psychic readings, but was generally disappointed. One psychic told me I was St. Peter in a past life, and there were other flattering readings, yet these readings did not seem genuine to me. I did ask one psychic to comment on my experience in Santa Cruz without giving him a clue about what had occurred. He said, "A negative spirit interfered between you and another person, causing problems," which seemed to be an accurate assessment. But even this psychic seemed inaccurate in answering other questions.

The one psychic that I did trust was Jim Branch, because he spoke of things in my current life that he could only have known psychically. Consequently, I tended to believe in the past life that he identified:

This one sojourned in the time of the Christ as one of the Seventy who had contributed in the formation of the beginnings of the Church of the day. This one was called by the Christ, not with the word as heard with physical ears, but by a simple beckoning.

According to Jim, this entity was named Percephas, and when he was very young, he received training in healing and raising inner attunement. He became a teacher for others in how to integrate the body, mind, and spirit and how to raise vibratory influences, which interestingly sounds like a description of the purpose of yoga. Percephas helped others to remove subconscious blocks and improve inner alignment in order to become open to higher realms of consciousness in accordance with God's Will. A key to assessing the validity this kind of information was the degree of my emotional response to a particular past life. I had two readings by Jim, and in each reading, when Percephas was mentioned, I was emotionally overcome with a strong tearful reaction and with a feeling of being blessed.

In addition to the various positive descriptions of contact with Christ, one reading indicated that this lifetime of Percephas was a time of "intense trial," which I gathered included some form of physical disability and suffering. Percephas would have withdrawn the life force from his body and ended that lifetime, but did not do so because of the influence of the Master. Consequently, he met and overcame many inner blocks and served as an example for others to do likewise.

A possible clue to the source of this suffering was provided in an unusual way. I was in my room in the Yoga Center, and I heard someone come into the house. People were constantly coming in and out of our residence, so this was hardly unusual. But for this one and only time, I had a sudden feeling of fear and the thought of being physically harmed by whoever had entered the house. Jim Mustin, who was mentioned earlier as one of the Light and Sound Course participants, made his way to my room and asked if he could talk to me. Jim explained, "I wanted to come to you to tell you about a past life I experienced during one of the sessions in the Light and Sound Course. I was a Roman soldier, and in the scene I saw myself riding a horse. I had placed a rope around a person, and I was dragging him with my horse. I don't know if I killed him; however, he was being harmed. I came to you because it appeared that the person I was injuring was you."

I explained to Jim my fearful response when I heard him come in. Nevertheless, I told him I appreciated him coming to me. "If I was that person being injured, I forgive you," I said. "But it is more important for you to forgive yourself, because guilt won't help you to be more loving. Soldiers are subject to orders from those above them, and that Roman soldier could have just been carrying out orders. Also, if I was harmed in that lifetime, it could very well have been because I had harmed someone else in a lifetime even earlier." I think Jim was relieved to know that I would not be angry at him and that I appreciated our conversation. We prayed and meditated together briefly to focus on each of us being at peace about this potential past life encounter.

This past life event was a piece of the shadow puzzle related to being dragged as a child in the playground and other hazardous situations. For example, it reminded me of being in danger of falling when I had hung off the balcony and when I had stood on the top of Craig Castle. However, my past life experience with Jim, if it did occur, did not seem to be a big deal to me. On the other hand, if Percephas was really my past life, the influence of Jesus and the importance of forgiveness felt like extremely important aspects of my life, and perhaps a significant part of the shadow puzzle as well. Yet in a way it did not matter if the specific lifetime of Percephas was revealed to me or not. I already knew that I had some kind of contact with Jesus in a past life, even if my specific name used in that lifetime had remained hidden.

One day, Dylan came to me and asked me if I wanted a psychic reading from him. He did not usually do individual personal readings. Nonetheless, he made the suggestion to be helpful, and I accepted his offer. Dylan's reading did not involve any use of light and sound devices, but my previous experiences with them had brought me to a place of readiness for his psychic reading. We sat cross-legged on the floor facing each other in our residence at the Yoga Center and held each other's hands. Dylan opened himself up to my mind and in particular to my past. He described what he sensed: "It's outdoors. There's a boy in shorts—maybe located in Scotland or Ireland. He's running. He stops running. Now he is in an old, damaged building. Something happens. The floor is weak, and he falls through the floor. It's dark. Very dark. Blackness." Dylan spoke calmly. "He's in pain. His leg hurts. Spiders. He can't get away. It's so dark. Spiders everywhere."

I started screaming. *Loud* screaming. Dylan stopped talking, because no more talking was needed. I was there in the blackness. There were no images, but I was reexperiencing the emotion—terror, unending terror. The screaming did not stop. I held nothing back. I couldn't hold back, even if I had wanted to. There was no control over this continuous, full-blown screaming. It must have lasted at least twenty minutes. In my group psychotherapy years before I had experienced excessive screaming as an emotional release. However, that screaming always had an element of control. With this screaming, I had not even the slightest bit of control, as if it were happening all by itself. All I could do was experience it coming through me as an involuntary event.

When it finally stopped, I noticed that I was still holding Dylan's hands with my hands. He looked shocked, and I must have looked the same way, because I certainly felt that way. Neither he nor I had any idea that this kind of extreme experience could have resulted from this reading without having the light and sound components present. After I stopped screaming, I sat for five minutes in a stupor and totally exhausted. I would have liked to lie down and rest, but I did not have that option. Immediately I had to drive to Norfolk to teach a college yoga class at Old Dominion University.

Although I was in a very fragile state, I managed to pull myself together and teach the class. Afterwards I was sitting in the Yoga Center van when a young woman from the class came over to my van door and started a suggestive conversation. She was very pretty, very young, and her obvious flirting was telling me she was very available. Normally, students talked to me in the classroom right after class. They don't follow me out to my vehicle unless there's another agenda. This kind of thing is an occupational hazard for yoga teachers, but I was also a celibate monk. I was in such a fragile condition that it would have been easy to give in to temptation and use the artist's line of "showing her my etchings" in the back of the van. Luckily, I was able to politely resist this temptation. I pretended I was oblivious to the flirting and gently excused myself without offending her.

It would take a long time to process the psychic experience with Dylan. The images of the old building, darkness, a leg being hurt, spiders, and falling were all images I had in the past considered as pieces in my shadow puzzle. But prior to this psychic reading, I had not told Dylan anything about my past experiences related to the shadow puzzle. I did consider the possibility of having been carried away by suggestion and a runaway imagination, yet my experience as a hypnotist had shown me that I was not suggestible. Even if I had been suggestible, this experience was so off the charts that I could only conclude it was an authentic reexperiencing of a past life. Confirming this assumption was the fact that the experience was a gigantic piece of the shadow puzzle, fitting right in with many other puzzle pieces. It even seemed at first glance like the possible solution to the puzzle.

Yet I felt there was more of that lifetime that I needed to uncover. Through meditation, dreams, and my own psychic impressions, I began to piece together a picture of that frightened boy's life and his adult life as a man. The boy was warned not to go to a very old, partly burnt, abandoned building, but he went there anyway. He fell through the floor into a cellar area, dislocated his left shoulder, and badly injured his right foot and lower right leg, which was broken and bloodied. He couldn't get himself out, and he screamed for help; nevertheless, no one came. It was dark and spiders were attracted to his blood. As he blindly swatted at hungry spiders in the darkness and wondered if he would ever be rescued, he was overcome by pain, panic, and despair.

Finally his father and others came and found him. He was brought back to his home and placed on a table. His left shoulder was put back in place, but his right leg was too badly injured to be repaired and thus was amputated below the knee. In later life he fell in love with an attractive woman whom he could never hope to have as his wife. Finally he became hopelessly depressed and threw himself off of a pier into the sea and drowned. Since no name was given for the boy who grew up only to commit suicide, I call him "Spider Boy." The way Spider Boy ended his life came to me when I went to a pond near the Yoga Center. I began crying and found myself walking with a limp in my right leg, even though there was nothing physically wrong with that leg. I was recalling the end of Spider Boy's life and reexperiencing the emotions of Spider Boy's suicide.

The death scene reminded me of one of my painting, called *The Search*, which depicted a man with an apparently withered right leg standing on a pier. This is the same picture (shown in Chapter 4) that had also come to mind after standing on the top of Craig Castle. I recalled as well the woodcut of the boy's face in despair and the picture of the depressed figure bent over his legs. And I remembered the drawing of the man with the fearful, spider eyes.

Also coming to mind were some images related to old buildings. There was the cut on my toe after visiting the old burnt building on the peninsula at the beach. There was the image of Patty and me, trespassing to go into the condemned building where the rat appeared. There was the junkyard that I trespassed and the shack that I broke into, for which I was arrested.

My memory went back to my former bedroom at the little ashram in Milford. My thoughts focused on how in a sense I "fell" from being astrally projected above my body, and landed back in my body, hurting my left shoulder. Immediately after this, I had fallen down the stairs and dislocated my shoulder. I recalled the incident at the fraternity dance when I was lying down on a table and became very afraid for no apparent reason. I also remembered the story my parents told me about being on a rocking chair and falling over backward and being taken to the kitchen table for stitches. There was the time I went to the cellar in my parents' home and killed spiders with fire, almost burning down our house. There was also the emotionally charged dream of experiencing a terrifying blackness and evil darkness prior to my conflict with Demetrius.

One significant recollection was remembering my parents taking a drive to the House of Prayer in Gloucester in order to pick me up for Christmas. I took them down the long staircase that led to my "room" in the tiny space at the bottom of the stairwell. My mother and I reached the bottom, but my father remained on the steps because there was not enough room for three people to stand at the bottom. Both my parents looked like they were sucking lemons. "You can't be living here! Are you sure you are all right here?" Mom asked as my father looked on sternly without saying a word.

"I'm fine," I reassured her without telling her about my only concern— the spiders, which were a constant problem.

"We'll get you back to Meriden today and get you into your nice warm room," Mom asserted with the implication of rescuing me from disaster. On the trip to Meriden my parents took turns reminding me that there was no need to come back to Gloucester, since I could stay in Meriden instead. The night when we arrived in Meriden there was a devastating ice storm that knocked out both the electricity and the gas in the house. We had no heat. My parents went over to a relative's house that did have heat, while I chose to stay for three days in the dark and cold house. Looking back on this now reminds me of Spider Boy in the dark and cold cellar where he was rescued from danger by his parents. But when he was taken home, instead of the complete rescue that he had hoped for, he had to go through the additional trauma of having his leg amputated. What also crossed my mind was that I may have had the very same parents when I was Spider Boy as I did in this lifetime. If so, when I brought my parents to see my room at the bottom of the stairwell, perhaps they too were subconsciously recalling the danger of that past life and were attempting again to rescue me.

I could clearly see that all of these images, drawings, and experiences in my life were pieces of the puzzle, which now fit together and made sense in the context of Spider Boy's life. With the revealing of Spider Boy's lifetime, I was satisfied that the shadow puzzle had been solved, but I still felt the need to be healed. My visits to the past were neither for nostalgia nor for ego purposes of self-glorification. Reexperiencing the past was only useful if it could lead to healing in my present life. It was not enough to solve the shadow puzzle intellectually. I had to bring all of my hidden emotions back into conscious awareness in the present moment. If these emotions could be fully faced and consciously released, I would be healed.

When I relaxed completely in a lying down position, I could tell that I was still not completely healed. I could feel harmony and energy in all parts of my body, except for one. The one area where there was no energy was my right foot. This had been true for me for the past several years and was always an indication for me that even though my right foot was physically healthy, there was still a subtle inner problem of some sort that needed healing. I thought that when the shadow puzzle was fully resolved, the confirmation would come as an inner healing of the right foot. Thus I believed that this reexperiencing of Spider Boy's past life would have that result, but this healing did not happen. I assumed I must be continuing to hold on to negative emotional patterns stemming from Spider Boy's life. I realized I needed to focus on forgiveness, if I wanted to find healing, and this would just take time.

18

MORE REVEALED

~ • ~

A few weeks after discovering my past life as Spider Boy, I was satisfied I didn't have to be concerned any more about uncovering past lives, since the shadow puzzle had been solved. In my daily private sessions of light and sound, I focused on letting go of the past and accepting divine love and forgiveness in the present moment. But Dylan came to me and asked if I wanted another reading from him. I was surprised and asked him why he was making the offer. He said, "I think there is something more there."

I deferred to his judgment, although I did not have that same feeling. We went to the same room we had used before, but this time I made sure I did not have to go off to teach a class right after the session. Dylan told me, "The last time we did this I was holding your hands the whole time. It was hard on me to be bombarded with the psychic energy of screaming that was coming out of you. I didn't want to let go because you were in such pain. This time I think it would be better if I sit on one side of the room and you sit on the other side."

I agreed to this simple request, yet I really didn't think there was any cause for concern because I assumed there couldn't possibly be another such traumatic experience in my psyche. Dylan and I meditated silently for a few minutes. Then Dylan spoke, "I'm sensing an incline like a mountain of rock or a building of stone built on a slant. It's in ancient times, but I don't know where. A man is on his back or leaning backwards. He is holding on to a pole of some sort. If he lets go he will fall. If he falls, his body will be ripped to shreds."

I was listening attentively, however there was no emotional response within me. Dylan continued, "There are people watching and ridiculing him. He is angry at them. Some of the people watching are cursing him while others are laughing at him. He curses them and even curses God. There is anger in his eyes—very intense anger. Now he is in pain. The pain is becoming unbearable. His grip on the pole is weakening. He can't hold on much longer."

Suddenly it was no longer a story that I was intellectually hearing. I was there. I was this man. Exactly like the previous reading, I screamed just as strongly and just as uncontrollably. There was only the screaming. I didn't see anything. I didn't get any intellectual insights because my mind was in a state of terror. All I could do was let the screaming come through me. It must have been all of twenty minutes of screaming. When it had all been poured out, I was completely spent. I had to lie down on the floor to recover my strength, and after about fifteen minutes I heard Dylan getting up to walk out of the room. Without opening my eyes, I said, "Thank you." After he left, I remained lying there on the floor for another half hour. When I finally got up, I was still exhausted and disoriented, but I felt something had changed for the better inside of me.

Upon reflection I understood that this was it—the real root of the shadow puzzle. The Spider Boy lifetime was not the source of the shadow puzzle. It was the result of this just revealed root cause of the mysterious man on a pole. Who was he? Why was he on the pole? Who were the people who were watching? Where and when did this happen? I felt I needed to answer these questions. I was intellectually curious, but on the practical side I felt I needed to have these answers in order to help me heal.

However, part of me had already been healed. One observable result of the healing was that my voice changed. It was deeper and more resonant. An inner tension within my voice was gone. When I really laughed in the future, I would never again let out a weird scream as had happened in the past. Although I was still a poor singer and chanter, I could sing and chant much, much better. Even other people noticed the voice change and asked if I had a cold because my voice sounded so different.

I meditated and devoted my private sessions of light and sound to the purpose of revealing more of the lifetime of the man on the pole. It was obvious he had been placed on the pole as a punishment for something. He was surely taken against his will and by force. He was probably imprisoned before this punishment. I sensed that he was also injured and bleeding, which made it difficult to hold on. I felt that before he had been placed on the pole, his right big toe had been cut off. He may have been castrated as well. I also got the impression that this man did not think that he was being punished for a just cause due to his own wrongdoing. His cursing and hate were directed toward those who had brought about his punishment, but he was particularly upset because these were people he had considered friends at one time. He felt terribly betrayed, and his curses were made with the strong conviction of his innocence and righteous indignation that these tormenters were the ones who deserved punishment.

Since my conclusion was premature in regard to Spider Boy's past life being the solution to the shadow puzzle, I again began to review additional puzzle pieces that seemed to be relevant to the man on the pole. When I wanted thoughtful solitude in Meriden and even in Gloucester, I chose to sit at the top of a cliff or to lie under a large pine tree and look up at it, like this man must have looked up at the pole while hanging onto it. I remembered my drawing of the barren tree with the perspective of looking up from below. The trunk could be seen as the viewer looked up and saw only one partially broken branch. Falling from the tree was only one leaf as it twisted and turned while it fell. It was the last leaf to fall from the empty tree, and the branch looked more like a pole than a tree branch. It seemed the last leaf falling could have symbolized the man falling from the pole with his body twisting as it fell. This idea called to mind Kelly laughing at me as a child after I fell out of a tree and hurt my right leg. I recalled how angry I was at her for laughing when I was in pain, similar to the way this man was angry at his tormentors for laughing at him and celebrating his pain.

There were the puzzle pieces that involved direct conflict. One example was the high school fight with Brian that involved an accusation of cursing and my refusal to forgive until he told the truth, which sounds like the righteous indignation mentioned above. There was the fight in the car, in which I was punched from behind, and reacted with righteous indignation by striking back. There was the experience of not being believed by my own football team members, by my coaches, and even by my art teacher. Significantly there was the very recent fight with Demetrius stemming from being accused of eating inappropriately at work, which was in fact not true.

There were the two times of being kidnapped in college and the strong resistance to this happening. There was the childhood event of the other children chasing me in order to drag me through the dirt. Also, there was my crying at being ridiculed by them and my subsequent choice to let them drag me through the dirt. Then I was grabbed from behind for no reason by a boy in the playground, a surprise attack I strongly resisted.

There was also the falling backwards over the pool retaining wall a long distance down and miraculously not being hurt. All these experiences relate to standing on Craig Castle to face the potential of certain death below and to hanging from the theater balcony, and in that situation I was holding on to two wooden poles that held up the balcony rail.

In addition to the puzzle pieces I had already assembled, I encountered one more very important piece after experiencing Dylan's second psychic reading. I had a very vivid and dramatic dream that was directly about this past life. The dream revealed the portion of the experience that Dylan did not quite get to in his psychic reading. It was what happened when the man let go of the pole. In the dream there was falling—like the falling that occurred so many times in my childhood dreams. But in this dream I was only an observer of the falling, rather than experiencing the fall directly. In this dream I observed the body hit something solid, and then it rolled over and over and over again. Later this reminded me of the many times as a child when I rolled my body down the grass hill in my Uncle Jim's back yard next door. Then there was the observation in the dream of a mangled bundle of flesh, blood, and bone that was all that was left of the body when it stopped rolling. Finally in the dream came the very clear words, "Allan Greene,"[1] and then the word, "Benedict."[2]

I gathered that the most significant part of this past life was that this man, whom I will call "Pole Man," was not prepared to face death. He met the most important moment in his life with fear and anger. This reminded me of the story Rusty told me about the holy man, Chandra. During Chandra's life he called upon the name of Shiva, yet when he actually faced his own mortality, he forgot to turn to his spiritual ideal of Shiva and instead gave in to his fears. When the Pole Man faced death, he was not a common criminal, but rather was a high-principled man, perhaps a spiritual leader of some sort. Yet he failed to hold to his high spiritual aspirations at the time of death and instead descended into cursing others. While on the cross, Jesus said, "Father, forgive them, for they know not what they are doing."[3] Can you imagine Jesus cursing his tormentors? If this had happened, all the good of Jesus's life would have been overshadowed by this single moment of faltering.

Unlike Jesus, Pole Man died cursing others around him. I wouldn't be surprised if Pole Man actually called them "spiders" as a curse. But there is a universal law that we must reap whatever we sow, so he would have to meet the anger he had sent out. Living a life of spiritual ideals and in the end throwing them away was a mistake, yet it was even more unfortunate for him to repeat his mistake. Pole Man had the opportunity to meet himself again as Spider Boy and to make changes. Nevertheless, he carried his anger, fear, and pain right into Spider Boy's life and could not face and overcome these strong emotions. His mistake in both past lives was not that he had angry, fearful, or painful feelings, because being devoid of these emotions would be unrealistic. His mistake was to repeatedly fail to offer his anger, fear, and pain to the divine within and to trust in divine help.

Since I have concluded I was Pole Man, my challenge was and is to learn from my past life mistakes and not repeat them. I believe that I, as Pole Man, faltered not because of the faults of others, but because of my own shortcomings. Pole Man blamed others for his own faults, yet more importantly he blamed God. Because he blamed God, he could not very well turn to God for divine help. Having lost his faith, he could not say in his pain, as Jesus had done, "My God, my God, why hast thou forsaken me?"[4] Because I thought the failure to turn to the divine within was Pole Man's biggest mistake, it became my goal not to repeat it.

Pole Man was betrayed by his own faults, so I needed to learn to take responsibility for my own faults. It seemed to me that pride was probably at the top of the list of my past life and present life faults, and so I would have to learn how to be humble by following the example and guidance of Jesus. Perhaps I would even have the opportunity to meet the ones I had cursed as Pole Man, so I could respond differently—so I could withdraw my curses. I hoped to forgive them for their actions and forgive myself for my own inappropriate actions and reactions.

It was for this reason that the specific names were given to me in the revealing dream of Pole Man's death. I did not know anyone at all named Benedict, so I didn't focus on that name. However, I knew Allan Greene. I had met Allan at the Fellowship of the Inner Light; yet he was just a passing acquaintance.

After the Pole Man revelation, I went to Allan's apartment, and he let me in. Allan shuffled his feet in small steps, the only kind he could manage without falling over. His hands were curled up and stayed that way. He had once been physically normal, but was slowly losing the mobility of his legs and hands. "So what's happening?" he asked.

"Have the doctors been able to figure out the cause of your condition?"

"They aren't sure. They are still trying to come up with a diagnosis," Allan said.

"Rose told me she really appreciated you giving her the gift of taking her and a group from the Fellowship to Israel," I mentioned to make small talk.

"Yeah, I got an insurance settlement so I used the money to celebrate, and Jerusalem seemed like the best place to have a celebration. I thought for sure if I bathed in the Jordan River, I would be healed. I wasn't healed. Nevertheless, I was very glad to go anyway. So are you and Rose good friends?"

I answered, "Yes, Rose is my good buddy. She is very easy to talk to. Rose also told me that you gave her a car as a gift. She calls her car *Amazing Grace*. She said that the name came from you as well." There was an awkward pause of silence, which sometimes happens when two people don't know each other very well. "I actually came over here today to tell you about some experiences I have had." I proceeded to review the psychic reading experience of the man on the pole and the subsequent dream which revealed Allan's name. "I think I was the man on the pole, and I think I knew you in that lifetime. I believe you were involved with putting me on that pole, and I think I in turn cursed you. I think the condition you are in now is due to the karma of what happened in that past life. I believe that we hated each other in that life and in order to heal we have to come to a place of forgiveness. What do you think?"

"I don't know what to think." Allan spoke objectively without any emotional response. "What you say may be true. But it could just as well be untrue. I have no feeling about it one way or the other."

I said earnestly, "I wish I could let you know how important this is for you and for me. I am convinced this happened. It is your opportunity for healing and my chance for healing, too."

"That may be true, but I can't say I believe something that I do not believe," he concluded as he shrugged his shoulders, and that was that.

"I understand. I have come to you and told you this fantastic story, and I can't expect you to believe me just because I say it's true. You need to have your own inner realization. At least you know about it now, so maybe in the future you will get some of your own guidance on this matter." There was nothing more to say, so I excused myself and let myself out. Although I wasn't angry when I talked to Allan, I walked outside, sat down on the curb, and got very angry. I really did intellectually understand that Allan could not easily accept this story, but my anger was coming right from my past life. I realized my motivations were not pure. I knew I needed to forgive him. However, first I must have wanted to blame him and make him feel guilty, before I could forgive him. I had to go home and meditate to release my anger and improper intentions. I had to ask Jesus for humility.

At a later date I called Allan and talked to him about the Light and Sound Course. I invited him to come to a free light and sound session, and in this session I also offered to start with a personal healing on his behalf. I explained to him that this was as much for my sake and healing as it was for his. Allan accepted my invitation and was assisted to the session by his close friend Martin. I had a short break when I was not leading the group, and I devoted that time to Allan's healing. He was lying down during the session, and I tuned into his body to assess where I felt healing was needed. It was clear to me intuitively that his problem was in his neck, so I placed my hands there and prayed fervently. A tremendous force was raised up in me and through me. At one point the healing reached a very intense level, and I let out just one very loud scream.

I was not sure if the scream was for my personal sake to release a block within me or for Allan's sake to help clear a block within him. I hoped it was a helpful release for both of us. I did all I could do for this healing time, but I had to return to leading the entire group. Shortly, Allan signaled Martin to take him out, so he did not stay for the entire light and sound experience. I was disappointed that he left early but was glad I had the opportunity to provide a healing opportunity. I felt at this point I had to let go of any attachment I had to working out my past through Allan and trust that God would give us both whatever we would need in the future to find resolution.

---

1. His real name.
2. Not the actual name, for the sake of confidentiality.
3. Luke 23:24, CCD.
4. Matthew 27:46, CCD.

19

THE LAW OF
MINIMAL RESPONSE

~ ● ~

I felt it was time to leave the Yoga Center and to hold the Light and Sound Course in a neutral location, so I gave my notice to Jonathan. He gave me a thousand dollars as a going away gift, which was not expected, but certainly much appreciated. Dylan and I rented half of a duplex outside of town and held the Light and Sound Course there. I had a dream in which I slid down a steep incline. When I got to the bottom, I looked at a piece of paper in my pocket that read, "December 10 will be a bad day." Afterwards I forgot all about this dream.

Dylan and I sat together for a meal one day and Dylan said in a matter of a fact manner, "I received psychic guidance that there will be an earthquake on December 19, and this will produce a tidal wave that will hit Virginia Beach."

"So what should we do about it?"

"Nothing. What can we do? Nobody would believe me anyway."

"We have got to do something. A lot of people are in danger. I would hate to think that so many of my friends would be harmed and that I did nothing to help," I asserted.

Dylan looked at me questioningly, "I am not sure this is a good idea."

"It would be selfish to not share this information, if we could possibly save lives. It doesn't matter if people don't believe this or not. We have to tell them at least. Then people can get their own guidance to decide for themselves if this is true." After similar conversations we finally decided to put out a written disaster warning and post fliers on local community bulletin boards. I remember leaving our duplex and locking the door with my key as we were about to go off and post the fliers. As I locked the door, the key broke completely in half without any undue pressure from my turning it. I should have been alerted to the possibility that this was a warning not to proceed.

Another day, forcing a carpet into Dylan's small VW beetle, I threw out my left shoulder and had to wear a sling afterwards. This shoulder dislocation occurred on December 10, and only later did I remember that this was the date indicated in my dream as a "bad day." In hindsight, in addition to my key breaking, I should have interpreted both the dislocating of my shoulder and the fulfillment of my dream as two more signs for me to stop promoting the disaster warning prediction.

As a result of the flier, a group of at least twenty-five people gathered together to pray about the possibility of this disaster really happening on December 19. Dylan and I did not attend the meeting since we were not even aware that it was being held. After praying and asking for guidance, the group left town before December 19. Similarly Dylan and I left town and stayed in a distant motel. We waited. Nothing happened, although the weather conditions were extremely bad that day, with rain and unusually high tides. Dylan and I resisted the temptation to blame each other or to fall into despair.

Months before, I had arranged to make an appearance on December 20 on the local television talk show *Livas Live*, as I had done before. Although I was scheduled to do a yoga demonstration, I was not able to do so because my left arm was still in a sling. At the studio I asked if Dylan could join me and if we could talk about meditation and the Light and Sound Course. Becky Livas, the host, agreed, and so there we were on TV the very next day after having been proved inaccurate in regard to our disaster warning. I heard later that many people were irate, thinking that the disaster warning was an intentional device that we had used to draw attention to the Light and Sound Course, just as this TV appearance was an attention-getting device. I realized that my own poor judgment in regard to the disaster warning had brought me into a position in which such ridiculous accusations could seem plausible to others.

Immediately after "the disaster that didn't happen," Dylan and I put out fliers saying, "We apologize." The Light and Sound Course was a radical approach to transformation because of the channeled light and sound information and because of the strong emotional releases and reliving of past lives that were generated. It had been successful entirely because of word-of-mouth recommendations by satisfied participants. But because of the disaster warning and TV show, we lost all credibility and were out of business. It was even worse than that. Many of my old friends avoided me altogether or began talking to me in a guarded way that made me feel like a stranger with the plague. Subsequently, I went to a service at the Fellowship of the Inner Light, and I felt shunned. Only two people at the meeting greeted me in a loving manner the way they had in the past. Some people actually looked at me with fear in their eyes. I got the impression from others that they thought I was seriously unbalanced mentally.

Previously I had asked for humility to overcome the karma of Pole Man and could not have been given a more humbling experience! With my role as a spiritual teacher evaporating overnight, I discovered just how much pride I had invested in this role. I went from being respected in the inner community of spiritual seekers to being totally rejected. It occurred to me that I was experiencing what Pole Man had experienced in being accepted and then rejected by his community. I did not want to make the same mistakes that Pole Man had made, by his not accepting responsibility for his own mistakes and by rejecting those who had rejected him. I accepted that I had gotten myself into this situation because of my own bad choices. However, now I could make better ones. I reminded myself to not be discouraged, but rather to turn more fully to God's love for me and let God's love continue to flow through me to others. I would continue to live a life of service to others and sought guidance in how to proceed.

Although the Light and Sound Course was dead, Dylan and I kept our focus on our inner development. Of course, daily meditation and yoga practices continued to be central. Prior to finding full-time employment, Dylan and I decided to use our free time to help each other to grow spiritually by experimenting with various forms of creative expression. For example, we conducted improvisational sessions, such as acting out scenes between characters in the Bible, like Moses confronting Aaron after coming down from Mt. Sinai with the tablets of the Ten Commandments. We did improvisational dances and then gave each other feedback on how to express greater freedom of movement. We went to the woods to get in touch with nature and at other times to have emotional releases through scream therapy.

This experimenting with our own personal growth activities ended when we both found full-time employment in service work. Dylan got a job as a social service case manager. I found a job as an aid at the local training center for mentally retarded clients. It was a large state institution—the type of facility that in the future would be phased out of existence, giving way to community-based residential programs. This institution was not one big warehouse of people, but consisted of many small group cottages for children and adults. I started in a children's cottage in which I had to fasten cardboard tubes onto the arms of one child, Kevin, to prevent him from licking his hands, because this was the program that had been written up for him by my supervisor. What I remember most was a couch that absolutely reeked of urine, and much of my job was about cleaning up the urine and feces of profoundly retarded boys and girls.

Needless to say, this wasn't an uplifting environment for either residents or staff. Still, it was service work that I felt could help me grow spiritually. However, I could not see how I was making a positive difference in the lives of these children and requested a transfer to a cottage with adolescents. The female worker I was replacing had gone out of the cottage to look for Clarence, a nonverbal black resident. But he had jumped from the roof of the cottage onto her and injured her so badly she had to quit the job. At the cottage, Clarence got a lot of time-outs in a locked room. Having time-outs in a locked room is considered by today's standards to be abusive and a violation of residents' rights yet was standard procedure at that time. Clarence would often run outside and climb high up in the trees and stay there for long periods of time until he got hungry. He did not seem to receive any positive reinforcement, so he appreciated it when I gave him back rubs. In fact, the back rubs calmed his hyperactive nature down considerably. He responded to me positively and learned to trust me, and in general stopped being physically aggressive. I was next promoted to the position of recreation technician, which meant I could bring some joy into the lives of many of the residents.

I also had a part-time job for Interact, the after-hours component of the state social services department. I worked on weekends or after regular work hours for any emergency situations and also manned the social services counseling hotline. A co-worker, Nathan, taught me his counseling philosophy, which was similar to the ancient medical mandate, "Do no harm." His counseling version of this was to "let the problem resolve itself by you not interfering with the solution." In effect, this meant to do only what was absolutely obvious and necessary—no less and especially no more. This might be called "the law of minimal response." He said, "I can't tell you how many times I have seen workers trying to do more than the situation required, ending up creating a much bigger mess. In most cases, if you do nothing, the universe will resolve the problem for you. On our evening shift all we have to do is stabilize the situation until the daytime workers can take over the next day."

One time, for example, Nathan and I got a call to go out and make an initial investigation regarding alleged abuse of an adolescent boy. In our visit to the home we determined that abuse appeared to have occurred. Consequently, immediate removal of the child was warranted for his protection until a complete investigation could be initiated the following day by the full-time child protective service worker. We took the adolescent boy from his home and escorted him to our car, and we all got in. However, the boy immediately jumped out of the car and quickly ran down the street. I was about to run after him when Nathan said, "No. Don't run after him. That's not our job. Our job was to pick him up, not run down the street after him. Were you going to grab him and physically restrain him? Maybe he would get hurt. Maybe you would get hurt. This is what I meant by not doing more than is required, because you could make things worse. Right now it is a police matter. We will call the police. If any physical restraining needs to be done, they will do it because that is their job. Actually, before he ran away, we had a problem because we had no foster care alternative available where the boy could stay tonight. Now the universe has resolved that problem for us by his choice to run away. If you had caught him and brought him back, we still would not know where to put him. But now it is the problem of the daytime regular social worker to figure out where to put him, once the police find him."

Nathan also explained that when he was responsible for answering phone calls on the counseling hotline, he would get very few calls because he meditated and his mind was at peace. He named a couple of the coworkers, whom he described as hyperactive personalities. He said that when they worked, they attracted the most numerous calls and the most serious calls because like attracts like. Since the job required working in pairs, Nathan and I chose to work together, and we did have mostly quiet nights or weekend days. I also discovered that the problems we did encounter had a way of consistently resolving themselves.

One day I had taken a walk and was on the way back to my duplex when a dog approached me from the front. As I looked at the dog, he walked around me and went out of my line of sight. Then he came up from behind me and bit my right leg once and ran off. The bite broke the skin, yet it was not a serious injury. I was irate and went back to my apartment and had to spend a good deal of time turning to God to release my anger. If I had gone to the animal control department and shown my bite, I could have forced the owner to put down the dog. However, I decided to do nothing, based on what I had learned from my work with Nathan. Also, my own inclination was to offer everything to God's will, and if something did need to be done, I would be shown what to do.

The dog belonged to Benjamin, who shared the other half of our duplex. Two weeks after I had been bitten by his dog, Dylan and I heard noise outside and we peeked through the closed blinds. We saw Benjamin on our side of the duplex pulling at electrical wires that led into our house. Benjamin was obviously very upset and angry about something. We decided to sit down and pray for him, sending him light and love, and soon he went back inside his side of the duplex without actually having been able to completely pull out the wires. The next day when Dylan and I were coming into our duplex, Benjamin approached us at our door and told us that his dog had died and had been poisoned. He asked if we had seen anyone who could have poisoned the dog. We told him we hadn't seen anyone who could have done this and offered our condolences. He looked at us suspiciously but did not accuse us of poisoning the dog, although that is clearly what he thought. I didn't know if Benjamin knew his dog had bitten me two weeks earlier, and I did not want to add to his suspicions.

Subsequently, the children in our neighborhood started calling us gay names. Dylan and I concluded that Benjamin, thinking we had killed his dog, had told the neighborhood that we were gay. It was not bad enough that we had the inner spiritual community of Virginia Beach disrespecting us, but we had somehow managed to attract disrespect from our physical neighborhood as well. We even attracted someone who was intermittently siphoning gas out of our cars parked in the driveway. One night I actually saw a man lurking outside and came out of the house hollering. He left his gas can behind and ran off into the trees at the end of the street. In the darkness I did not get a good look at him. It might have been Benjamin, although that was uncertain. Whoever he was, he did not come back in the future for more gas.

Several years after I had left that area of the city, Benjamin approached me in a food store. He told me that he had thought I had poisoned his dog and that he was very upset at me at that time. However, he said he went to the trouble and expense of having an autopsy done and found out that his dog hadn't been poisoned after all, and it didn't appear there was any foul play in regard to its death. Benjamin then looked me in the eyes and said, "I am sorry. I wasn't a very good neighbor to you. Please forgive me for misjudging you." Of course, I accepted his apology, which was very genuine and totally out of the blue. When he said that he "wasn't a very good neighbor" to me, I knew he meant he did things that he regretted, but was too embarrassed to specify them. I mentally forgave him for that also. What struck me about this is that if I had reacted to him previously by saying or doing anything overtly negative to him in any blaming fashion, he would not be apologizing at this later date. It was only by my turning to God and doing nothing at the form level that this later resolution could happen. Perhaps I was learning from the mistakes of Pole Man and so was not repeating them.

Nevertheless, I had not entirely overcome the past because I was still attracting black spiders into my bedroom. Dylan's bedroom and even the rest of the house had no spider problem. I decided that they were coming in from the two windows in my room. Because I was not able to stop all the cracks in the windows, I covered the whole frame around both windows with clear plastic and tape. This worked, yet resulted in a constant and unwanted view of numerous spiders. They were able to get by the window cracks and then got stuck on the inside of the clear plastic. Nevertheless, they were unable to enter the room due to the tape holding the plastic in place. I accepted that this spider issue would be an ongoing problem that I would have to face until I could release the underlying blocks. Symbolic of this was that there was still an energy block in my right foot. However, I did make progress in partially clearing the block so that at this time the major part of the block was focused mostly on the general area of the right big toe.

My mind drifted back to a casual conversation I had years before at Yogaville with Margabandu about the body. He said, "It's kind of strange that we think we are inside the universe, but the universe is inside our bodies—the sun, the moon, the stars—all inside of us. The most earthly things are in the lower part of the body. That's where we store our worst earthly problems."

I said, "Whenever I do the deep relaxation part of my yoga practices, I feel that everything within is at peace, except for my right foot where there is an energy block."

Margabandu nodded knowingly and said, "Our worst problems are the karma we have the most trouble facing. We try to distance ourselves from those problems so we push them as far away from the head as possible because we think we live in the head. The feet are the farthest distance from the head, and we walk on our feet so that's our contact point with earthly things. You can be sure that's your worst problem right there in your foot. When you clean out that problem, you'll be really happy." I wasn't convinced that everyone pushes their worst problems into their feet, but at least it seemed to be true in my case. Because of my faith in God's grace, I felt that the happiness of resolving the foot problem would certainly come—but I had no idea how long it would take.

20

OPENING TO PERSONAL RELATIONSHIPS

≈ • ≈

Like the *Odd Couple* movie and television show, Dylan and I had housekeeping issues in which I was the clean one and Dylan the sloppy one. For example, Dylan would crack nut shells to eat the nuts and leave the shells on the kitchen table—for days. When I attempted to draw this to his awareness, he felt I was trying to control him. I explained my request for a clean table was a common courtesy, not an outlandish imposition of my will. The nut shells remained. I decided to let go of my reminders, and as I had learned at work to do nothing to force a resolution of a problem, I even decided it was not my problem but Dylan's. He would resolve it when he was ready to do so—which did happen later in a different living situation.

Dylan was uncomfortable in social situations and more introverted than I was. He was more of a head person than a heart person. I had been that way too when I was younger, but I had learned to open my heart, mostly due to my seeking and to divine grace. One day Dylan confronted me, "I feel like you are putting out a pleasure-seeking vibe—for example, like that *Annie Hall* movie that you suggested that we go see. It seemed out of character for you."

"Well, you are entitled to your opinion." I said nothing more, yet thought it was too bad that he did not open his heart more. He was right about my unusual pleasure-seeking vibe, but wrong about what it meant. It was my birthday. That's why I wanted to celebrate and go to a movie. I didn't tell him that it was my birthday, because I did not feel it was my responsibility to tell him. He was present when my previous birthday was celebrated at the Yoga Center, and if he had wanted to, he could have made a point of remembering the date. I had learned that Dylan just did not have a lot of social graces, though I accepted him as he was, not as I would have liked him to be.

Dylan himself was aware of his problem in learning how to open his heart. One day while he and I were talking in a parked car, I made some comment about my own need to learn how to be less judgmental and more loving. Dylan stated flatly, "You are not the one who is judgmental and unloving. I am not a loving person. You are a loving person. In many ways you have shown how loving you are." He elaborated and gave examples. He talked about how his heart felt closed and how he wanted to open it, but couldn't. I just sat and listened. Then suddenly he put his hands to his heart and made an expression of being overcome by some sort of energy as I looked on with concern. He said, "You are healing me."

"I'm just listening to you," I said.

"I feel you are affecting me. Your heart is healing my heart. It's still happening now," he said with assurance.

"I'm glad to hear your heart is being healed. I'm not sure that I can take credit for it. But if that's the case, I'm glad for you and for me too," I said while mentally sending him a prayer of blessing. Dylan's nature was not radically transformed by this one healing; however, it was a significant step forward for him in the direction of learning to open his heart.

Actually I had been told in a Jim Branch psychic reading that I could help others to release inner blocks through consciously directing my mind in prayer. More pertinent to this healing incident with Dylan, I was also told I could facilitate the spontaneous removal of blocks in others without consciously directing my mind to do so. The way I look at healing is that when people are healed, they are always just opening themselves up to their own inner divine Source from which all healing comes. But another person, by their loving presence alone, without conscious effort, can remind the one being healed of the divine within themselves. This reminder is enough to trigger their own inner healing of themselves.

An unusual thing happened one day when Dylan and I had gone to the beach. We were sitting on a bench watching people passing by on the boardwalk. A total stranger walked up to me and said, "Hey, man. Do you want a drag?" as he extended to me a marijuana roach.

As if that was not surprising enough, I replied, "Sure!" as I took one nice deep inhalation and held my breath, not really expecting one puff to have much of an effect on me after all these years of being drug free.

The stranger offered Dylan a drag, but he declined, and the stranger left. Then Dylan turned to me and said, "Are you crazy? Why did you take that pot?"

"I didn't even think about it. I just responded spontaneously. It felt nice just accepting something the universe was putting right in front of me."

Dylan said in a serious tone, "You would throw away years of discipline for one puff of pot?"

"Actually to tell you the truth, there is a part of me that really enjoyed doing it because I knew it would shock you," I said happily without the slightest bit of contrition. In fact, I was feeling quite good from that one drag.

"Ah, that sounds like the truth," Dylan acknowledged without any of the previous serious and judgmental tone.

"Now it is your turn. You tell me something truthful," I said.

"OK. You see all those people out there on the beach? What I see is a bunch of Christmas presents with problems inside. When I see you, I see problems too, but without the Christmas box and wrapping."

"Is that good or bad?" I asked, still feeling light-hearted.

"Oh, that's good—really good. You see, all those people out there are totally concerned with the Christmas wrapping and the bow to cover up the box and cover up the problems inside the box. All they want to do is hide the problems inside the box, so they don't have to deal with solving those problems. When I look at you, I don't see that box. Ironically you appear to be worse off than those people, because you don't have that shiny Christmas wrapping to hide behind. But actually you are better off, because you are able to face your problems and let go of them. This makes you look outwardly more shaky at times, when inwardly you are getting stronger all the time. Other people think life is about showing off their outer box. However, for you life is about removing the inner problems, even if it makes you look bad outwardly. Does that pass the truth test?"

"Yes, it's true, but I can't take credit for what you are saying. I would probably like to have a Christmas present wrapping like everybody else; however, I am just not very good at covering myself up. I do have a defensive exterior, yet I am totally transparent. Whatever is there inside just comes out, whether I want it to or not." Still feeling the pot, I offered, "I am going to give you a chance to ask me any one question you want. I will tell you the absolute truth without pulling any punches. But don't ask unless you really want to have a truthful answer, whatever it may be."

Dylan asked, "My question is, 'What is my worst quality and my best quality?'"

"Your biggest strength is that you have a deep intuitive ability to see into other people. Your penetrating insights make everyone transparent to you. When you see all those people on the beach you can see through all those Christmas wrappings and through the box to what is inside of them. You can even accurately articulate the exact nature of the inner problems that other people are inwardly dealing with. It's like everyone is wearing emperor's clothes, so they think they are covering up, but your inner sensitivity gives you insight into what lies beneath the surface masks. Your ability extends to your perception of yourself, at least in some areas. You can sense some of your own inner problems so you can face them and overcome them. On the other hand, some of your inner problems are blind spots that you have not yet revealed to yourself and therefore cannot release. You are also deeply dedicated, more than anyone I know, to transforming yourself by overcoming your inner problems. How is that for the truth so far?"

"That's good," Dylan acknowledged. "So what is my worst quality?"

"Your greatest strength is your greatest weakness. Seeing into everyone's inner hidden problems can be somewhat of a curse. It can be depressing to see people as being a collection of problems. In a way you see too much, being unable to just look at pleasant Christmas wrappings. But your real greatest weakness is that you see too little. There are three levels, and you are only looking at the top two. Your weakness is that you are not looking at the third and deepest level. Below the first level of the Christmas box with its wrappings and below the second level of the problems is the Christ. If you want to overcome this weakness, you will need to change your focus. You will have to learn to see the Christ in everyone. That means you will have to allow your sensitivity to not stop at the problem level. You cannot focus on problems in other people and also see Christ in them at the same time. Christ doesn't have any problems, so you will have to overlook them. You will see whatever you value. If you value problems, you will see problems. If you can open yourself to valuing Christ more than problems, you will see Christ and not the problems."

Dylan and I had a common understanding of the word "Christ" in our conversation. He knew that I was not talking about seeing Jesus when I described seeing Christ. He knew I was saying that the Christ presence is already within everyone. It's just that the Christ is hidden from view because of the masks—pretty or ugly—that we have placed over the Christ. Mystics from every spiritual path have directly awakened to the universal Divine Light, which I consider to be the Christ Light. But for most of us, we could use the indirect means of discernment to see the Christ presence within each person. What Dylan did not understand is that motivation is everything in regard to seeing, because you will see whatever you are truly and sincerely looking for. Most people want to see the masks because they believe the masks are real and the masks are their identity. Only a very few can see the Christ because only a very few want to see the Christ and believe that the Christ presence is in everyone. I asked Dylan, "Do you want me to elaborate on how to see Christ in others?"

"Go right ahead," Dylan stated.

"To see the Christ you have to look past problems. How you do this with other people is by disregarding their problems. You may not be able to entirely avoid seeing problems, but you can ignore them. What you see is determined by what you want. Make your wanting for seeing Christ in others greater than any other wanting. Then you will be able to see Christ and not the problems. When you try to see Christ in yourself, you may see problems instead. However, you can still *look* for the Christ. You can bring any of your problems to Christ and see them being dissolved by giving them to Christ. So what do you think?"

"That sounds right to me. Maybe you should smoke pot more often," Dylan offered lightly.

"I'll probably never have another puff the rest of my life," I said, which turned out to be true. "Let's go to the park off of 64th Street," I suggested, and that's where we went. We took a walk on the nature path at the park, and everything before me became filled with light. Even the dirt beneath my feet was transformed, into a crystal path radiant with light! As I looked ahead, everything in my vision began shining with the same bright light. It was like stepping into another world where everything was filled with a translucent light emanating from within. I assumed the pot was still affecting me, and likewise my talk with Dylan was also affecting me. I had told him to look for the Christ. By giving him this advice, I had become alerted myself to seeing the Christ, which could be seen in people and even in the world around me.

When everything became filled with light, the colors all faded away. Everything that formerly had color became a shining white light instead. Actually, I had experienced this before while sitting still in meditation or sitting motionless in church. I had experienced white light in objects, and also I had seen people transformed into light. However, in this experience what was unusual was that the whole panorama was changed into light, and I was walking instead of being perfectly still. This vision of light everywhere lasted for about fifteen minutes and then stopped. Of course, Christ is spiritual and not physical. I realized that this kind of seeing light in physical forms was only a *symbol* of Christ and demonstrated that I was at that time opening to divine love. In spite of my one puff of pot, I want to emphasize that I am not recommending the use of drugs and that seeing the symbolic light of Christ can be accomplished and developed through natural means.

Dylan said that he was going to let go of his attachment to celibacy and be open to relationships. His decision encouraged me to consider the same option after having been celibate for ten years. I knew celibacy had helped me to raise up my inner attunement, but perhaps I had become too closed off. I decided to go ahead and open up. For my first date I asked out Angela, a very attractive lady. She had a house out of town, and she offered to drive to my house, and then I would drive us to Norfolk to take her to the movie theater. When she came to my house, I introduced her to Dylan. After he met her, he said to both of us, "Can I go to the movies with you." I was dumbfounded. Yes, this was the same Dylan that did not want to go see *Annie Hall* on my birthday! My first date in ten years and Dylan wanted to weasel his way into going with us to the movies. I would put this in the category of a father asking his son and daughter-in-law to come on the honeymoon. This is what I meant above about Dylan lacking in social grace. "Dylan, you are a jerk to ask such a very thoughtless and selfish question!" That is what I was tempted to say, but instead I said, "OK." In spite of my inner resentment toward Dylan, I was as gracious that night as I could be under the circumstances.

Fortunately, on my next date there was no chance of a repeat of the problem with Dylan because Angela invited me to her house for dinner. I liked Angela and felt the feelings were mutual. Later that evening we made our way to the bedroom. She gave me a massage, and I gave her a massage. Similar to the way light and sound can loosen a person's inner blocks so they can surface, a massage can sometimes produce the same effect. Angela had a psychic release, and as part of that release, she became very vulnerable and cried while talking about past experiences related to her father. While she was still in a vulnerable state of mind, I pursued a more intimate encounter. When we had our clothes off, I reassured her, "We won't go all the way." Nevertheless, we did go ahead and initiate sexual intercourse. I had an immediate ejaculation, but that would not normally be a problem because consistently in the past I had been able to have two erections.

However, there were two problems this particular night. One was that as soon as intercourse was initiated I was overcome by the regretful thought, "I am abandoning Jesus." All I could think about was Jesus and how I was throwing away my vow to be a monk for God. Consequently, there was no way I could continue. In addition, I had said we wouldn't go all the way as a promise to reassure her that it was all right to continue to be intimate. Then I broke my word at a time when she was very vulnerable, having previously had an emotional release regarding her father. It was similar to a counseling therapist taking advantage of one of his clients who was vulnerable because of psychotherapy. I had to reconsider my disbelief of Dylan's earlier contention that I was in a pleasure-seeking pattern. In spite of the fact that I felt very bad about my multiple mistakes with Angela, I failed to confess or even address my shortcomings with her. I slept over that night. After Angela made breakfast, she lent me a book on the sexual techniques of tantric yoga, and I left.

It was very unusual for me to get sick, yet I got sick and remained sick for a week with flu-like symptoms. I attributed my sickness to my mistakes with Angela. After I recovered, I called her to apologize. Before I could say anything, though, Angela told me she had also been sick for a week and it was clear that she did not want to talk to me. Several months later, when I was dating someone else out of town and near Angela's house, I called and asked if I could drop by her house just for a minute to return her book. It was a convenient excuse to see her so I could apologize in person. When I arrived at her house, she called for me to come in and was on the top of a ladder painting. She did not come down, probably as a way to keep me at a distance. I talked to her from below and explained what had really happened. She did not know I had even been a monk and was struggling with breaking my vow. But most of all I told her how sorry I was that I broke my promise and that I took advantage of her when she was in such a vulnerable state of mind after having had an emotional release. After she heard my apology, her voice tone changed, becoming mellower, and she came down from the ladder and thanked me for my apology. We hugged, and I left for my date with another lady friend. Angela and I never did go out again, but years later I accidentally ran into her at the A.R.E. She told me that happily she had become a professional practitioner of what was called "Psychic Massage," a means of using massage to help a person have psychic releases of inner blocks.

21

THE HIGH POINT HOUSE

~ ⚬ ~

Dylan and I ended up moving into a house on High Point Road where my good friend, Rose, lived. I was glad to finally be away from the spider problem at my previous home. One day I was lying on my bed and thinking of how I had become so immersed in the concerns of the world including my work that I had lost some of my spiritual focus. I began praying to God asking for Him to help me. While I was praying, something crawled right on my forehead, and I was startled. I immediately jumped up and saw what it was. On the bed was the largest spider, other than a tarantula, that I had ever seen. I hollered, "Oh, my God."

Normally I would have killed it. However, I remembered I had been praying for God's help, and maybe I could respond differently, at least this time. Mentally I projected the thought to the spider, "I am not going to kill you. I am going to take you outside, but I don't want you to come back." Then I reached out my hand without covering it with anything and took the spider outside. Next I took a shower as a symbol of cleansing, and happily there was no spider problem in the house after that.

Rose and I living together for the first time provided an opportunity for us to experiment for a short time with having a more intimate relationship than friendship. We only got as far as a little cuddling. We got along terrifically socially, intellectually, and spiritually, yet unfortunately neither Rose nor I had a sexual attraction to each other. As far as my outward appearance, I did not present a very masculine package. In fact, I liked to think of my inner personality as a balance of masculine and feminine, expressive and receptive qualities, so I did not feel I should go to the trouble of projecting a masculine image. Long before baggy pants came into style, I liked them because they felt comfortable. I was always pulling up my pants, because my belt was too loose. I even liked to wear shirts with flower decorations on them. But Rose convinced me I was sending out the wrong message. Consequently, I enlisted her much needed help and good taste in revamping my wardrobe, showing me what to throw out and what to keep.

Rose and I often had silly conversations in which we laughed and even giggled a lot, which is a side of me that usually only a woman could bring out. One day we challenged each other to a gross out talk in which we educated each other on root chakra nuances. Rose anointed me with the title of "Grand Exalted Gross-Outer." In turn I placed a lampshade on her head and crowned her "Queen Grossalot." Of course, this experience was not gross by my college standards, but would qualify as a temporary harmless detour from our normal expression of our high ideals.

One day Rose, Dylan, and I were trying to meditate at the end of one of our house meetings, but instead we took turns giggling. Then we all laughed out loud to surrender to our inability to focus. I picked up Dylan's nearby magazine and asked, "If you are done with this, can I have it?"

Noticing the glint in my eyes, Rose shook her head in a "no" gesture to Dylan, who then said, "No, I think I should keep it."

"OK," I said with smile and put it down.

Seeing me being so agreeable, Dylan changed his mind and said, "Go ahead. I am done with it. It's all yours," and he handed it to me.

"Great!" I said and promptly and gleefully ripped it in half.

Rose grabbed what was left of the magazine saying, "You can't tear this up because I want to do it." She tore it to shreds. We each grabbed handy old newspapers and ripped them apart laughing and throwing shredded papers all over. We pretended that the shredded paper was money and started stuffing it inside our clothes. That led to throwing giant newspaper spit balls at each other. Before it was over, we were mimicking Marilyn Monroe's slow, saccharin-sweet singing to John Kennedy, "Happy Birthday, Mr. President. Happy Birthday to you," and doing paper dances around the room, imitating Gypsy Rose Lee's striptease fan dance.

Other than exceptional times of ridiculousness, my friendship with Rose was based on affirming to each other, "I see the Christ in you." We saw through the outward masks of imperfections and perceived the Christ nature in each other. Whatever you see in another person, you strengthen in both the other person and in yourself. We strengthened the awareness of Christ in each other and in ourselves. That was the gift we gave to each other. Since we had joined for the common purpose of seeing Christ in each other, we had formed what I later would understand was a "holy relationship."[1] We did not realize that by sharing the one goal of seeing Christ in each other, it would help each of us to set aside our ego-based sense of separate interests and enable us to generalize our goal so we could grow toward seeing Christ in everyone. At that time we did not know it, but we would remain steadfast friends and continue to nourish each other in this way for all of our lives. Although we were not soul mates in the sense of being lovers, we were and continue to be "spiritual soul mates."

If we did have a sexual relationship, it potentially could have ended badly. We could have lost our lifelong spiritual friendship, which would have been very unfortunate. As it turned out in our living arrangement, Rose did not get along with Dylan very well at first, but that would change for the positive over time. At our meetings we agreed occasionally to have a "confession" time in which we took turns revealing our own shortcomings. We learned to set aside the temptation to blame or judge one another. Also instead of telling others what they should do, we presented our own problems and needs to each other. Without imposing our will on others, we could request others to respond to our needs out of love.

For example, Rose once said, "I don't like going into our common bathroom and seeing beard hair from shaving in the sink. That hair just looks awful, so I don't feel comfortable leaving it there. I've been cleaning it up almost every day, but I wonder why I should have to clean up after another person's mess. I don't know what to do because I don't want to impose my will on anyone. On the other hand, the mess itself is an imposition of another person's will on me. Also I don't want to be quiet about this problem and build up resentment against anyone. What do you think is the most loving thing for us to do about this situation?"

At the meeting Rose tactfully did not specifically single out Dylan as the one leaving hair in the sink. However, she had told me previously that she knew Dylan was doing this. I advised her to bring the issue up in our house meeting because Dylan would probably respond better in the group, if we could focus on our common spiritual goal of expressing love. Although Dylan had been unresponsive in the past to my similar promptings of cleanliness at the previous residence, in this new situation he accepted his need to make adjustments in his actions. As a result of our meetings, Dylan learned that such requests were not attempts by others to impose their will on him, but rather were ways of asking for common courtesy that expressed the high ideal of divine love in a mundane, tangible way.

On Christmas Dylan was surprised when he opened his present, a very nice camera, which I had given to him. He looked at me with a combination of confusion and happiness, because it was such a wonderful and unexpected gift. As I looked on, I felt my heart open in joy for him, and I was so happy I started to cry. Simultaneously Dylan was very touched and cried too. He said, "I suddenly realized how much you love me, and I feel like an ass that I hadn't seen it before." He initiated a hug, and we stood hugging for a few minutes while crying some more. We had never cried with each other before, and Dylan did not think he was capable of it any more. Also Dylan in the past would always hug without putting his heart into it. His hugs were superficial and very quick. But this hug was a true heartfelt hug without fear.

Three days later at one of our "confession" portions of our household meetings, Dylan admitted, "I did not realize until recently, on Christmas, just how much I had been rejecting your heart energy in the past. In the last place where we lived I was upset that our neighbors thought we were homosexual partners, so I was not receptive to your heart energy because I was afraid of homosexual connotations."

As he spoke, I started to cry from hurt, not joy. I said to Dylan, "I'm sorry. I can't respond right now in a loving way to you. What you have said had brought up in me all the times in my life when I had wanted to express love and been turned off by others." I could barely speak. Dylan looked totally confused because he was trying to be loving, and ironically I couldn't accept his love. Rose was able to explain in a very loving way to Dylan why I couldn't respond. Finally I said to Dylan, "These hurt feelings were not limited to you. They go all the way back to my stern father, who couldn't express love, and even back to past lives." Then I couldn't speak any more because of the hurt feelings and tears. Rose got up and hugged me. When she hugged me, I realized I wanted Dylan to hug me too, and he did. This was my healing, and afterwards I was able to let Dylan know that I certainly did appreciate his openness in regard to what he shared. At subsequent meetings, Dylan was able to discuss and better understand other ongoing blocks that prevented him from giving and receiving love, most notably the stumbling blocks of judgment and pride that every seeker must face.

After an initial adjustment period, Rose and Dylan got along just fine, and their relationship blossomed into much more than a friendship. In the future the two of them would live together in their own apartment for a time until the relationship ran its course. When Rose and Dylan first became a couple, she and I also needed a little time to adjust to this new relationship and to reassure each other that we would remain friends as always. I bought a cassette tape recorder for Rose for Christmas, after first haggling with the store manager over the price because it was a demonstrator model. Then the recorder was stolen before I could give it to Rose. Instead of getting upset, I decided it happened because I shouldn't have bought a demonstrator, and a low-end product at that. I reexamined the way I was looking at money and decided to think in terms of giving. I ended up buying another recorder that was the top of the line, three times more expensive, and I felt joyous about giving it to her.

Not long after this I went to Rose's bedroom while she was sitting on her bed and handed her $400 in one dollar bills. I explained that I was giving her the money because I knew she was having trouble making the rent. In sheer joy she threw the money up in the air as we celebrated together. In subsequent months it became clear that Rose was so burdened with work that she couldn't get what she really needed, which was a healing and inner cleansing at all levels. I volunteered to give her $100 every week so she could quit her job and get the necessary healing.

Rose made significant progress in facing and overcoming emotional karmic patterns originating from past lives, and her health improved. She possessed a great deal of spiritual depth and insight into her karmic patterns, and we often shared observations and feedback in a mutual exchange regarding our patterns. By the time Dylan and I had moved into our new High Point home, we had both felt that we had gotten as much out of our light and sound experiences as we possibly could, having removed our most traumatic patterns from past lives. A reading from Jim Branch had given me the impression that I no longer needed very intense emotional releases such as those provided by light and sound, but rather would benefit most through raising energies during my meditation and by learning to more deeply relax and thereby let go of inner tension.

However, I felt that perhaps the light and sound experience might be helpful for Rose in clearing away patterns related to past-life traumas. Dylan and I would have been willing to take our equipment out of storage and show Rose how to use it, but I got the impression that light and sound was not her cup of tea. For one thing, when the Light and Sound Courses were held in the past, she never expressed even the slightest interest. Rose had her own way of facing and dealing with her inner problems, and she said she wanted her process to be respected. At times when she was going through a difficult time in dealing with deep karmic patterns, she didn't want intellectual, spiritual, or psychological suggestions about the nature of her problem or recommendations on how to "fix" her. All she wanted was to be hugged and loved in the moment. She felt this alone would support her in her own internal process of healing. If I did feel guided to tell her something, I focused on speaking from my heart rather than from my head.

My goal was to be fully present with her and accept her just as she was. Rose was so sensitive that she could tell if my attempts to help were generated by a desire to relieve her upset feelings or a desire to remove my own uncomfortable feelings. If I was trying to take away her pain so I would not feel my own inner pain, that would hardly be helpful or healing to her. Fortunately I was able to accept her intense emotional distress without flinching from it and without being adversely affected by it myself. I felt my role was to be at peace myself and not get caught up in her emotional state of mind. In order to be able to accept her, I would focus on God accepting and loving me. Then I would feel God's love flowing through me to extend acceptance and love to her. One of the most beneficial things that I learned from hugging and accepting Rose in these situations was that even in her worst moments of distress, I could still see beyond the mask of appearances and see the Christ in her. By doing this, I was perceiving her true inner wholeness, rather than focusing on her apparent limitations, and felt I was helping her indirectly to open to divine healing from within herself.

In the springtime Rose fell off her bike and injured her right leg, which is interesting in light of my own psychically revealed experiences of falling and injuring to my right leg. The cut in her leg went right to the bone, and it was still oozing blood after three days. I firmly suggested she go to a doctor. She objected to my suggestion, noting rightly that I avoided doctors at all costs myself. Since Rose was open to assistance in the form of love, I offered to give her a healing session that might help her to open up to her own inner source of healing. When I prayed over her leg, I held my fingertips around the wound. I felt some energy come out from the wound into my hands. Next I felt a lot of energy going through my whole body into my hand and then right into Rose's body. I experienced some spontaneous involuntary hyperventilation and felt energy waves passing through me to her.

Simultaneously, Rose was experiencing emotional releases, and she got in touch with the feelings behind her wound related to past experiences in her life. The next day the wound had for the first time formed a scab and was able to slowly heal. On that next day I noticed red bumps on my left hand and felt these bumps were a result of the healing. I didn't ask to take on any karma, but this may have inadvertently occurred. If I'd taken on Rose's karma, I didn't mind, since I felt I could release this problem more easily than she could. Then she gave me an oil massage. The following day red bumps like the ones on my hand appeared on her arm, and the red bumps on my hand disappeared. I felt that she had taken back the negative energy I had removed from her leg and had allowed it to manifest on her arm. Subsequently the red bumps on her arm also disappeared.

In Virginia Beach, we often went to a public garden that consisted entirely of different colored roses. We felt this was the perfect place, as the saying goes, "to stop and smell the roses," and while savoring their fragrance, we enjoyed each other's conversation and company. Once, when we went to a sidewalk art show in Norfolk, I bought her a photograph of a white rose, which she kept on her altar for many years.

When we moved into the house on High Point, she generously allowed me to have the large bedroom that I requested from her. As a gift to help decorate my room, she even gave me curtains, which she handcrafted herself. We shared a connection with Mother Mary, so the color of the curtains was what she called "Mother Mary blue." I still have those same blue curtains in my bedroom thirty years later. These form-related tokens of our friendship are reminders of the bond we have with each other. But I feel at a loss to convey in words how deep this bond goes, except to say that Rose is the most thoughtful and loving friend I have ever known.

---

1. The term "holy relationship" is used in *A Course in Miracles* to indicate a relationship in which two people join in a common purpose and consequently the Holy Spirit comes into that relationship.

22

NEW JOB AND NEW RELATIONSHIPS

~ • ~

I was able to help Rose financially because of a job upgrade. I had left my job at the training center when I got a better job with Volunteers of America as a counselor in an independent living program for emotionally disturbed adults. Later, the position of Supervisor of Residential Services for mentally retarded adults opened up. I applied and was hired, at least in part because of having traded in my long fluffy beard for a clean-shaven young professional look. I was the supervisor for an apartment program and a group home designed to promote independent living. The twelve-person group home, called Baker House, was a new program, and I wrote all the policy and procedures manuals to comply with state regulations. I hired all new staff. One new person, Dolly Anderson, was not working out very well. She had been trained like the other staff, but unlike the others she did not retain what she was trained to do. I asked her to come to my office, and when she arrived, I said, "I noticed that you are not following through with a lot of the things you have been asked to do."

She cut me off before I could continue, and she stood up and actually began screaming at the top of her lungs at me, "You aren't helping me. You haven't given me enough training."

I waited until she stopped screaming and looked at her as she stood defiantly while I remained seated. I said quietly, "If you had not interrupted me, I was going to tell you that I had called you to my office now for another training session. I thought maybe the previous training sessions were not adequate to explain your duties. However, if you raise your voice like that again, I will have no other choice than to let you go. But I want you to succeed here, and I will give you as much training as you need." She apologized, and I gave her the additional training. Nevertheless, she continued to fail to meet the requirements of the job and did other things she had been told not to do. For example, in training sessions she had been told our clients are adults and need to be treated in an age-appropriate manner. But Dolly talked to the clients as if they were little children, and she even gave them children's toys as "gifts." Eventually I realized that her failure was not due to inadequate training; it was a matter of intentional noncompliance. Yet I wanted to avoid firing her, and I felt committed to working with her.

Toward the end of one of our work days our staff went to an agency meeting, which was held at a disco place. One of my co-workers gave me a glass of wine, which I accepted, even though I knew that even a very little alcohol could make my act silly. At home that night my silliness kicked in as a delayed reaction. I was engaging in double talk with Rose and Dylan, and I put a light wicker chair on my head. Just then I got a call from work and put the phone to my ear while still balancing the chair on my head. I used my serious work voice in talking to my staff member to resolve an issue that had come up at the group home. I was able to maintain my serious voice tone in spite of the fact that Rose and Dylan were still laughing and carrying on in the background. I found out much later that the staff member misinterpreted the laughter in the background as my encouraging others to ridicule our mentally retarded clients, and shared this misinterpretation with other staff members, causing staff discontent.

While I was dealing with new relationships at work with staff, I was also meeting new people in my personal life. There was a studio apartment adjacent to our house at High Point, which our lease required us to rent. One potential renter was a single parent, Pamela Malone.[1] As I showed her the apartment, her small son, Torey, crawled at my feet, untying my shoe laces. She did not rent the apartment, but I recall how she looked standing outside just before leaving. She was like the ancient Egyptian Nefertiti, tall and elegant, and she was not wearing makeup. A friend of mine named James liked to say in jest, "The first five times I saw Pamela, I did not remember or even see her face," implying his attention was otherwise directed at her skimpy outfit. What I recall about her is that instead of standing there pridefully, she was a woman seemingly oblivious to her own innate beauty, which only increased her attractiveness to me, as did her slightly stooped shoulders, suggesting a sense of feminine vulnerability.

I later had two dreams about Pamela, both of a sexual nature. Since I did not normally have sexual dreams, I felt I was being guided to pursue a closer relationship with her that might evolve to more than a sexual relationship. As a date, I took her and her son out to dinner. She had been hurt in the past in a relationship and was very reserved. I visited her at her apartment, and as I was at the door in the process of leaving, I gave her an impulsive and quick kiss on her lips. She was not expecting the kiss and was taken aback. In hindsight the kiss was something I never should have done at that time and in that way. However, what I remember is that the kiss itself felt very sweet to me. Pamela called me later that night and told me, "I want to be your friend, but I don't feel comfortable being more than that." I took her at her word, figuring she did not have a sexual attraction to me. Also there was an age disparity with her being 22 and me being 36. I was certainly attracted to her, although not infatuated. Consequently, I was disappointed, yet not crushed. Right after that we went to the movies as friends to see *The Empire Strikes Back*, and we would remain friends.

Pamela and I participated in a play held at the Fellowship of the Inner Light, which was now located in the former Yoga Center's temple building. The play was called *Genesis* and was an allegory of the fall from heaven and the return to heaven. I played the part of "Whispering Spirit," who is the first of the seekers to turn on his light and trigger others to turn on their own light to return to heaven. Although we only used flashlights as outward props in turning on the light, I was inspired by playing this role to remind me in my personal spiritual life to be aware of inwardly opening myself up to the Christ Light and letting that light shine through me to others.

The writer, director, and producer of the play, was David. The surname he had been raised with as Wyatt, but he had renamed himself David Sunfellow[2] as the result of an inspiring dream related to the sun and to letting his own light shine. The play was about a conflict of good and evil characters and portrayed David's vision of all souls, both good and bad, returning to the divine Light in heaven. His play gathered together a group of spiritual seekers as actors and collectively inspired them and many other spiritual seekers who came to see the play.

David's life itself was inspiring in terms of his sincerity and dedication to doing God's Will. First, he was guided on an inner journey of discovery that required almost total isolation from society, except for a few personal contacts. Later when I met him he was just beginning his public phase, in which his activities burst onto the scene inspiring many to become more personally connected to each other, to God, and to the signs of the times.

On a Saturday morning in May of 1981 I had a dream about going on a vacation in the mountains of North Carolina with David. I went to where David was sleeping in the summer in a tiny beach cabana. It was about the size of my former room at the bottom of a stairwell in Gloucester. When I told him of my dream, he agreed with the idea of us both going to the land trust of the Arthur Morgan School, where his brother, Walter[3], was living and working as a counselor. After informing my work associates of my sudden decision to take a two-week vacation, we went to North Carolina. We traveled in my car, since David had no means of transportation, and I enjoyed getting to know him along the way.

At my request, we made a detour to Swami Satchidananda's Yogaville, which had been relocated from Putnam, Connecticut to Buckingham, Virginia. I didn't feel any particular need to see Swami Satchidananda, but I did want to see some of the residents that I had known previously. However, upon our arrival I was surprised and disappointed to find out that Margabandu, Sukamar, Dharman, and my other close friends had all left the yoga community. I guess I shouldn't have been surprised, because yoga ashrams in America generally tend to attract young idealistic students, who are very dedicated for a time, but then fairly quickly move on to other growth experiences.

When we first arrived at the site of the Arthur Morgan School in North Carolina, I spent some time socially with David and Walter, but I soon felt a need for inner spiritual nourishment. I am not much of an outdoor person, but I challenged myself to spend most of my time alone, camping in a tent in the woods on a spiritual retreat. I continued doing my yoga postures and breathing practices every day as I had been doing for years, but this was a time to greatly increase and intensify my emphasis on meditation. I fasted on grape juice and refocused on the Jesus Prayer. For my affirmation I used the words, "Jesus, humble," because I felt pride was my biggest problem.

At a time when I was doing a meditation lying down, because my legs could endure only so much sitting, I heard beautiful music. I felt inwardly absorbed by the sound itself, without reflecting mentally on the experience. When my reflective mind kicked in, I wondered where was the radio producing this sound, and then the sound instantly disappeared. I popped up looking for a radio, although I did not have one in this isolated spot in the woods. But there was no radio. I could only conclude that this is what is called "the music of the spheres." At the end of my camping experiment I was spiritually revitalized. Also I felt a deeper connection with David and felt we would work together in the future to accomplish spiritual purposes.

When I returned to work in Virginia Beach, I carried a typed letter of resignation with me. Nevertheless, I couldn't bring myself to submit it. I felt guided to quit, but was too attached to the money and the position of authority. Sure enough, problems bubbled up at work, and there were simultaneous changes in my home. Just before this retreat, I had moved out into the studio apartment, originally to have more solitude. However, after coming back, I invited David to live with me without cost, and in fact I gave him $35 a week, which I made him promise he would use only for buying food. David pitched a tent outside in order to still remain close to nature. Unlike Dylan in the past, I did not have to be concerned about David making a mess because he was even more conscientious about cleanliness and orderliness than I was. With Rose and Dylan's relationship growing stronger, my partnership with Dylan was waning and being replaced by an informal partnership with David.

Not long after this, David began dating Pamela, and I felt fine about it. I did notice their relationship was a repeat of the same pattern that had occurred when I approached Rose initially and then later my roommate, Dylan, formed a relationship with her. One day, David and I went to see a movie called *The Man Who Fell to Earth*. It was about a high spiritual being who came from outer space to earth and established a financial empire with the help of a partner. But he lost some of his high ideals and got enmeshed in worldliness, making him vulnerable to lower forces. Finally, the time came when in the middle of the night a group of conspirators killed his partner by throwing him out of a tall building, similar to the Pole Man falling to his death. This group of murderers took away all of the man's empire, leaving him in utter despair in the end. Also, the main actor, David Bowie, had David's name. I wondered if something like this happened to the Pole Man and if David had been involved as a helpful partner, since I felt close to him. *The Man Who Fell to Earth* was an appropriate title for the movie, and an equally fitting description of the Pole Man, so I thought this might be the uncovering of another missing piece of my shadow puzzle.

At first glance it would appear that David and I had little in common. Like Dylan, David relied on his mental abilities and was often distant, aloof, and hard to read. I was more heart-oriented, accessible, and easy to read. However, my feeling of closeness to David had nothing to do with the usual formula for friendship, which is based on similar personality traits. We got along very well and joined with each because we had a common purpose of deep spiritual intent and desire to be of service. In addition, we had similar spiritual practices of meditation and watchfulness of dreams. Like me, David was also drawn to Virginia Beach in 1976. For the previous five years he had been led to spend a lot of time by himself in wilderness settings in order to pray and meditate, so he would be shown how to do God's Will. David, along with his brother, Walter, spent the winters with little food, camped out in cold nearby forests.

David felt certain this solitary experience was preparing him to one day start a spiritual community. I was open to this because I had been told in a psychic reading by Jim Branch given at the Yoga Center that I would be involved in the future with a spiritual community. According to this reading, I would be a slightly older person living among younger community members, and I was nine years older than twenty-seven-year-old David. As a step in the direction of drawing people together for a spiritual purpose, David was going to lead a conference about earth changes at the A.R.E. summer camp in the Blue Ridge Mountains of Virginia. But it looked like I would not be able to attend because of growing work concerns.

---

1. Actual name.
2. True legal name of David Wyatt and David's actual chosen last name of Sunfellow.
3. The name of David's brother, Walter, is a pseudonym.

23

DOLLY

≈ ∘ ≈

At work Dolly asked me if the clients could have a dog as a pet, and I told her that the executive director, Neal, had said he did not want pets in Baker House, because that is what my supervisor, Austin, had told me. At that time I didn't tell her that I also didn't want pets in the house, although I realized the therapeutic value of pets. The reason for my reluctance was that the dog would add another responsibility to the staff workload at a time when Dolly herself was already not fulfilling all of her responsibilities.

A week later Dolly brought her large black dog to work, and she left it outside. I thought that perhaps she did this just to reopen the issue of having a pet at the group home, yet I decided to give her the benefit of the doubt. Not wanting to overreact, I remained silent because I did not want to make an issue out of this one time occurrence of bringing the dog to work. The next day when I walked into Baker House, I saw Dolly walking down the hall with her big dog beside her, before the residents had come home from their day program. I told her, "I didn't say anything about bringing your dog to work yesterday, but I don't want to have your dog in this house."

She responded, "Why did the executive director, Neal, say we can't have a dog?"

"I said, '*I* don't want your dog in this house.'"

Dolly came back saying, "But you said Neal didn't want us to have animals. One of us asked Neal, and he said he didn't care one way or another. He said it was your choice to decide on pets."

"Austin told me that Neal did not want pets, so there was no need to tell you my personal decision. Since Neal does not care, and it is my decision, I am telling you right now that I do not want pets here. However, what I am really upset about is that you have brought your dog in here to try to intentionally confront me with what you thought was a lie on my part."

Dolly said, "I was traveling with the dog in my car, when I realized that I would be late for work if I went back home. I brought the dog with me today so I would not be late for work."

"I would accept that excuse at face value today if you hadn't also brought your dog to work yesterday. And don't bother to give me an excuse for bringing your dog to work yesterday." I was infuriated that she would go to Neal, who is my supervisor's supervisor. I was also irate that she had intentionally brought the dog into work just to force me to reopen the pet issue and to confront me with what she thought was my lie. I restrained my rage enough to not raise my voice, but with a controlled and yet obvious anger I told her, "I want you to drive your dog home immediately—right now!"

As a diversion, Dolly said, "What's that?" and she moved quickly to the windows. "Look at that hail! I've never seen hail that big. I can't go until the hailing stops." The sudden onslaught of hail was unusual because it hardly ever hailed, and up until this moment it was a sunny day without a hint of precipitation. The furious hail started from the moment I told her to take her dog home and ended three minutes later, at which time Dolly took her dog home without further incident. I wondered if the explosion of anger that happened within me, though expressed with control, had somehow caused this outburst of hail, even though it seemed extremely unlikely.

A few days later I had promised another staff member, Jake, that he could take a client to the Tidewater minor league baseball game, so Dolly would have to work alone on that one evening. On the afternoon of Jake's outing, Dolly came to me saying she wanted to go out for an important church function that she had planned long in advance, but which she had neglected to tell me about. Since a worker was needed later that same day, there was no time to find an available fill in. If I had to choose sides, I would pick Jake because I had already promised him and his request was made on behalf of meeting a client's need for socialization. On the other hand, I was reluctant to disappoint Dolly. I took some time alone to pray about this situation. Then I told Jake and Dolly that neither of them had to stay at Baker House because I would work the second shift, even though I had already worked the first shift.

The next day another staff member, Hannah, told me she wanted to tell me something but only if I told no one else, not her coworkers and not the supervisor above me. I agreed to abide by her need for confidentiality, so Hanna told me, "Remember that business card you found on the kitchen table that said, 'Anderson, Sales Associate,' and you asked Dolly about it since it had her last name on it."

I said, "Sure, Dolly told me that it was her uncle, Samuel Anderson's business card for his boating business."

"There was a picture of a boat on the card, so she told you it was a boating business belonging to her uncle. Actually it was an insurance agent's card that belongs to Dolly Anderson, not to her uncle. She laughed about it after you left because she could see you believed her. Have you noticed her $300 dresses? She is going out with an insurance agent, who is giving her those dresses. He is her boss, and she works for him full time as an insurance associate."

I said, "Of course, she knows that our company policy does not allow her to work full time at another job."

"Sure she knows. Do you know why you have gotten complaints about people calling Baker House at night and always getting a busy signal? It's because Dolly is on the phone making insurance business calls all night. She has Jake buffaloed into doing all the evening work, because she knows he has a crush on her."

"So why have you decided to tell me all this now?"

"I think the ladies and men here are being short changed. She is still talking to them as though they are little children, even though you talked to her about being age appropriate. She doesn't care about anyone but herself, and yesterday is when I decided to tell you. Dolly insisted to Jake that he not go to the baseball game with our client so she could go out instead. Jake for the first time stood up to her, and that is when she came to you. It was really kind of you to work a double shift yesterday to allow both Jake and Dolly to go out. However, Dolly did not go to a church meeting that she told Jake she wanted to attend. She went to an insurance business meeting."

Of course, I was very upset at hearing this and decided Dolly no longer deserved second and third chances. The next day I went to my supervisor, Austin, and told him that I found out she had a full time job against our policy. I explained that I was going to fire her, but I could not tell him that Hannah had been the confidential source of my information. I also gave him many other reasons to fire her. However, Austin told me emphatically that he would not allow me to fire her, in spite of the fact that my job description gave me full authority to hire and fire. He told me to follow her in my car to monitor her going to her other work office. I told him I did not want to do this, but he insisted. At that time I was not aware that Austin was influenced by Dolly, who had come to him to complain that I had a vendetta against her. Apparently he lost his faith in me, thinking I had lost my objectivity. Possibly Austin, who was a lady's man, had lost his own objectivity through the influence of Dolly's feminine charm and beauty.

To make a long story short, I did end up firing Dolly, but in the process the other staff found out that I had followed her in my car. Consequently, my staff lost all trust in me, thinking that they had to look over their shoulders to see if I was following them. On the day when a staff meeting was scheduled, I sprained my right ankle and stayed home. That evening there was a lightning storm. The very large tree in the front of the High

Point house was hit with lightning, and a third of the tree broke off and landed on the house, damaging it. When I went to work, I stopped at the main office to see Austin, who told me that he had held the scheduled meeting himself with the staff. The staff told him they did not trust me, and so he decided to ask for my resignation. I could have told him that the staff had lost trust in me because he had unwisely instructed me to follow Dolly in my car. Yet I refrained from any recriminations and gave absolutely no resistance to his request for my resignation. I told him I appreciated his initial faith in me, which he demonstrated by hiring me for this job, and then I wrote out my resignation.

I remembered that Pole Man had cursed everyone who had opposed him, and I felt it was extremely important for my growth to respond with love and forgiveness in this critical situation. By mutual consent I was relieved of my duties that very day. I made a point of going to Baker House and talking to each staff member individually. I told them that, in spite of their lack of trust in me, I very much appreciated them both as service workers and as people. It was obvious that they were pleasantly surprised at my leaving so graciously.

At a later date I accidentally ran into Austin, and he said he misjudged the situation and overreacted. He said that when he met with the staff, they exaggerated the problems at Baker House, making it sound like the program was in total disarray. But after I left, he found out that all the clients' needs were being met, and the program was actually very well organized. He said that he did not believe me when I first came to him to fire Dolly. He admitted it was a mistake on his part to prevent me from firing her at that time, and it was a mistake for him to insist that I follow Dolly in my car. Later, I found out Austin and Hannah began dating after I left, and she must have finally told him what really happened, because I never betrayed her confidentiality.

I also met Jake later and he told me, "I was wrong about Dolly and wrong about you. She visited Baker House after you left, and I told her not to talk to a new client, Matthew, because if she talked to him, he would have an emotional outburst. I left the room, and when I returned, Dolly was talking to him. He immediately went berserk and started screaming, and it took me a long time to calm him down. I told Dolly off and told her to leave. That was the first time I realized how defiant she was and what you were dealing with when she was working here. Although I thought you were the problem, she was really the problem and I couldn't see it. I am sorry, Don. I was taken in by her because she was so pretty, and I was infatuated with her."

That evening I cried just thinking about Jake's apology. When he first started his job, he missed an important meeting and did not call in. I found out Jake had a drug problem, and I confronted him, but told him that I would not hold the past against him. I told him I expected him to stop the drugs, and I trusted that he would. I told him he would have to get his act together to serve our clients. He lived up to my trust in him and was an outstanding worker after that. Because I trusted him when he needed someone to trust in him, I had been disappointed that he did not trust in me when I needed his support. However, I was deeply gratified that he offered this unsolicited apology, which came about by my not making the same mistake of blaming that the Pole Man had made.

I really wanted Dolly to succeed at her job, and I cannot attribute her failure to succeed to her just being a "bad apple." Obviously Dolly made mistakes, but I made mistakes as well, so I do not feel justified in my actions in regard to her. My dad used to say, "Two wrongs don't make a right." Consequently, my own inappropriate emotional reactions to some of the things she did were entirely my responsibility. I did the best I could at the time; nevertheless, I was too emotionally reactive to respond to her in a truly loving way. For many months I tortured myself over the fact that I had been incapable of living up to the challenge of loving her. It was necessary for me to pray over a long period of time in order to forgive her and forgive myself for my shortcomings and finally come to a place of peace. Of all the people that I met at this job, there is just one that I still remember to bless every day in my prayers, and that is Dolly.

From my relationship with her I learned the importance of forgiveness. I thought that I had been doing a good job of putting the puzzle pieces of my life together, but all of a sudden everything fell apart because of a dispute with one person. As Jesus had said, we must make peace with our brothers and sisters before coming to the altar for devotion to God. At those times when I was caught up in my negative emotions toward Dolly, my peaceful attunement in meditation disappeared. From this I realized that forgiveness of others was actually a form of enlightened self-interest. Nevertheless, it did not occur to me that my thought system in regard to the nature of forgiveness was still faulty. Years later, I was able to radically change and improve my perspective on the meaning of forgiveness, as will be explained in later chapters.

24

THE LIGHT HOUSE

≈ • ≈

Having been released from my work responsibilities, I was free to attend a week-long conference and retreat coordinated by David at the summer camp of the A.R.E. This structured retreat was entitled *The Earth Changes and Transformation of Man Conference*. On the fifth day of the conference, I was lying on my lower bunk bed in the cabin I shared with several other participants. I mentally saw a clear image of a large bell directly above me. Later that day, I was introduced to a new addition to our cabin, who that evening would sleep above me in the upper bunk bed. Her name was Janet *Bell*. She was a reporter for the *Movement Newspaper* and had come for a portion of the conference to write an article.

After the conference I enjoyed reading her story, seeing the conference through her eyes. While in Virginia Beach, she had been exposed to conservatively dressed and often older A.R.E. people. In contrast to the Virginia Beach main offices, considered to be the "head" of the A.R.E., the camp at Rural Retreat, Virginia, was thought of as the "heart" of the A.R.E. Here at the conference, Janet encountered jeans with holes, work shirts, outdoor boots, and sneaks. There were men with beards and long hair and women without cosmetics. She thought that coming from a big city she would feel out of place, but that feeling of being an outsider lasted only about an hour. She was warmly welcomed and caught up in the action-packed events of each day.

Janet was impressed with David's creativity and spiritual dedication. He had very carefully, even meticulously, planned the conference for a long time without financial compensation. In fact, he had set aside working for money for the last nine years, trusting that if he dedicated himself totally to God, then his needs would be met, and they were. She felt David expressed himself with love and a desire to be accommodating to everyone's needs. She noticed he willingly and without attachment set aside some of his plans to let a few rebellious retreatants have their wishes granted.

Janet was apprehensive about the doom and gloom aspects of possible earth changes, such as predictions of her home state of California slipping into the ocean. However, she was relieved to hear David say, "The basic essence of the whole thing is seeing the earth changes as a message of hope and not fear. It's not a fire and brimstone doomsday end of the world, but rather a transformation going on—like a birth process. It is essentially a spiritual transformation, and the first thing that needs to be done is for souls to get themselves together within themselves, learn to love one another and all creation, and go within and ask God what to do in all matters and concerns."[3]

Janet participated in several activities—a dream preparation, called a "dream incubation," a guided "reverie" of visual images led by David; the creation of a sacred "dream charm"; and a purification ceremony around the evening campfire. She wrote about her experience of the fire ceremony, which helped participants bond together as a group with the common purpose of spiritual upliftment:

> After dark, we all, about sixty of us, met at the back of the dining hall. There in silence (per previous instructions), we made a chain holding hands, and moved in runs and walks through the dark meadow and through a small path of trees to a large campfire in the center of the circular meditation grove. We formed a double circle and sat around the fire.
>
> This ceremony was to be one of purification for the night of dreaming ahead. We had been told to look within and find things that we wanted to offer to God. They could be qualities we wanted to give up or problems that had not been solved. This offering could take any form—written, verbal, silent, or one of our own choosing.
>
> One by one people rose to offer what they had to the fire. Most of us were silent, though one woman sang an incredibly prayerful melody. The atmosphere was extremely intense and very serious. It reflected the quality that comes to mind most often when I think of the people at the camp—dedication. There was a sincerity present, a very deep longing for God that I had experienced in few of the other groups I had participated with in my years on the spiritual path.[4]

Janet was excited in the morning to remember a significant dream that addressed an important concern she'd been struggling with. The morning was spent in silence, meditation, and energizing exercises, followed by breakfast. Then there was a group discussion of dream discoveries, showing forth the conscientious seeking for the divine by all participants.

The next portion of the conference consisted of the sixty participants dividing into smaller activity groups. These groups focused on a variety of special interests, such as holistic healing, relationships, music, drama, attunement, and outdoor survival. The most adventurous souls chose the

RESUME PHOTOGRAPH

JAMES GREGORY

survival group. Their hardy, good-natured leader was James Gregory, who brought the survival group into the forest for an outing of being "lost" without sleeping bags and without food. They learned survival skills, such as how to forage for food in nature and how to start a fire without matches.

Janet liked the food at meals and noted it was in keeping with the Edgar Cayce readings. I was pleased to hear her feedback since I had made up the menu at David's request. Janet appreciated the overall sacredness and seriousness of events, but one of the highlights of the camp conference for her was the performance of "Sixty Centuries," a comedy written and directed by David. In this play, a team of TV reporters conducted interviews inquiring about earth changes. I was interviewed as Rama, one of two warring leaders from the lost continent of Atlantis, where the prophecies about earth changes were unfortunately disregarded. A "reporter" then solicited opinions on the coming New Age changes from others, including an extraterrestrial from the Pleiades, the Anti-Christ, and a nature spirit and a ridiculously oversized "rose" from the Findhorn Community garden.[5] A reporter in scuba diving equipment reported on California being under water. James, having been the leader of the survival group, came on stage and showed his extensive camping survival equipment. Next, I followed him onto the stage carrying a briefcase with a sign on it saying "Survival Tool." I opened it and pulled out a large pillow. I sat cross-legged on it and chanted "Om." Janet and the rest of the participants found the production to be a hysterical spoof of the whole world of psychic phenomena that often takes itself much too seriously.

On Janet's last day at the conference, she participated in a service at the circular meditation grove. She wrote, "I was almost immediately filled with the loving presence of spirit (sounds trite, yet as I write this, tears come to my eyes as I recall the scene). I quickly saw the past three days fly through my mind and thought of David's words the day before: 'There has never been a question as to whether or not the earth changes are coming. They come to all souls who reach a certain stage of development. The only question is the degree and the degree is determined by how we respond, how much we learn to love and allow God's grace to flow through us.'"[6]

The dramatic earth changes that were predicted by Edgar Cayce and other prophets never did occur, at least not yet. But "inner, psychic earth changes" that occur when souls are ready to be transformed certainly did happen in my own life. The revealing of the Spider Boy and the Pole Man were examples of my inner earth changes, and another such unexpected transformation would happen shortly after the conference.

The A.R.E. camp program director, Calvin, and his wife, Evelyn, came to David and me and proposed that we all live together when we returned to Virginia Beach. We rented a large brown house together, but at a later date, Calvin and Evelyn offered to assume all the rent responsibilities. Their generosity was greatly appreciated, since I was out of work and David relied only on free will donations from his projects and plays. As a spiritual foundation for our household, we meditated every morning and again before dinner. On Saturdays we had a family entertainment night, which included movies, games, or other activities that we all enjoyed.

The house was at first called the "Brown House," because of its color, but was later more aptly called the "Light House." It formed a base for David Sunfellow to let his "light" shine through his plays, conferences, and projects. David used his artistic and writing skills to illustrate and publish newsletters, including the *Vision Quest Quarterly* and the *Forerunner*. In addition, he played the guitar and wrote and sang inspirational songs. Through all of his various projects, David had managed to bring together a collection of spiritual seekers. However, he wanted to take this teamwork one step further by establishing a service group, which he called the "Core Group." David asked me, "What do you think the purpose of this Core Group should ideally be?"

I spontaneously responded, "To prepare the way for the Second Coming of Christ." David immediately brightened up as though a light had come on within him resonating with his own yearnings, and so that became the stated purpose of the group along with a dedication to doing God's Will.

I had a dream in which a group of people were asking the question, "What is the best way to prepare for the Second Coming of Christ?" Many answers were given, yet not the correct one. Finally someone said, "The best way to prepare for the Second Coming of Christ is to express love now." With this answer everyone in the dream cheered their approval.

After many discussions, the Core Group could not adopt a unified theological perspective about the Second Coming. But we did agree upon the fundamental idea of "expressing love now," as had been emphasized in my dream. The Core Group of about ten members was not publicly known as a group. We performed selected projects behind the scenes, without drawing attention to ourselves, in order to express love through selfless service. For example, we would show up as a work group at the local food coop building. Of course, there were David's plays and annual A.R.E. conferences, which continued to draw the Core Group into closely coordinated activity, which helped us to bond together as unit. There was always the hope we would eventually evolve into a full-fledged community.

Pamela continued her relationship with David. When I had moved out of the studio apartment, she had moved into it. Then when her relationship with David deepened, she moved into the Light House. One day something sudden and strange happened that would qualify as my next inner psychic earth change. For no apparent reason I was completely overcome by a psychic awakening distinctly different from any before or since. A door to my past was opened and rushing in came an awareness of a long-hidden, all-encompassing love for Pamela. It was not just an infatuation, similar to the ones I had experienced before with other ladies after directing my heart in their direction. This was entirely different in both quality and intensity. A flood of such strong loving emotion consumed me so I could not function normally and had to lie down. But it was not blissful. Instead I was thrown into total turmoil. It felt like the inner parts of my psyche were reorganizing themselves, like the earth rearranging itself after an earthquake.

After this opening, I told Pamela what had happened to me. I explained that before this psychic event I had fully accepted her relationship with David and had not consciously stimulated this psychic experience by coveting her. I let her know that my feelings were caused not by my current lifetime, but rather by a past life in which presumably we were married. The details of that past life were not revealed to me, just the intense emotions.

Pamela looked at me confused and disconcerted, "I don't know what to say. I don't have any feeling for you in terms of a relationship. Are you sure this isn't just a sexual thing?" she asked.

"Sure, it's a sexual thing. A man and woman relationship is always sexual. But that is not what this psychic opening is about." I proceeded to explain the two sexual dreams I had before I dated her. One was a scene showing the widening eyes of her son, Torey, as he looked into the back of a hay wagon. The dream gave the distinct impression that Pamela and I were embracing, but without our bodies appearing in the dream. The other one was about Pamela preparing to make bread by stirring eggs, which had sexual implications. I informed her I had not had any such dreams since. Finally I said, "I don't think I can even explain to you how deep this psychic experience goes. I know you are not attracted to me. However, I had to tell you about it anyway. I had to let you know my feelings, although nothing can come of it. I apologize for putting you in this awkward position."

Later I found out that Pamela was pregnant with her first daughter, Jeremia, which I was not aware of at the time of our conversation. Time heals everything and the intensity of these deep, psychically released emotions could not have lasted anyway. I did a lot of praying and meditating to release any inappropriate emotions and lingering relationship attachment to Pamela. I was able to close the psychic door that had temporarily opened. I never did release the idea that I did in fact have a past life relationship with Pamela that was a deep, genuine, and pure love. I became satisfied that this love relationship would remain in the past and not manifest again in this life. I felt that I had a past karmic relationship not only with Pamela, but also with David, and that it was important to continue to deepen my friendship with both of them.

The next play that David offered at the Fellowship was *The Messiah Is Coming*, and I volunteered to play the part of a wise elder. In my important scene, a Roman solder, played by James, knocked me down to the floor. Rehearsing this scene required being knocked down over and over again. One reason I found this difficult was the falling aspect that reminded me of the falling of the Spider Boy and Pole Man. Making these rehearsals more difficult to accept was my impression that James was actually enjoying knocking me down. I confronted him about this. He said it was true he enjoyed knocking me down, but he felt he was just doing "method acting" by getting into his part. I told him that I did not mind being knocked down in the actual play, yet I did not want to be knocked down repeatedly in the rehearsals. James agreed. However, in a subsequent rehearsal he knocked me down anyway. He said he forgot his agreement with me. At first I was angry, but knowing James had meant no harm, I forgave him for knocking me down. Nevertheless, I decided to withdraw from playing that role.

After giving up the wise elder role, I took a minor role as one of many rioters, who would raise their arms for their crowd scene. When my arms were raised, David, who was next to me with his arms raised, accidentally bumped my left arm and dislocated my left shoulder. I lay down and an ambulance was summoned. While I waited for it to arrive, I focused on mentally repeating the Jesus Prayer. Then the entire cast gathered around me and started doing a Jesus chant on their own initiative. It was as if they could hear my inner repeating of the Name of Jesus, and followed suit by offering the comforting Jesus chant, as follows:

> Jesus, Jesus,
> Thank you for your love of us.
> Show us God's Will for our lives.
> We love you, Lord.[7]

Just before the ambulance arrived, I called David over and told him, "I know it was an accident. I love you, brother."

He responded, "I love you too, Don." I felt it was very important for me to share my love and concern for David in this situation to relieve any potential guilt on his part. I knew David had been very upset because of my approaching Pamela about my psychic opening of loving her. However, he and I had not discussed it. I felt this injury was an outward expression of his anger, but I was absolutely certain that it was not done consciously. It was most likely an expression of a subconscious karmic undercurrent between David and me. Also I realized that the way to overcome such patterns was to disarm them by responding to them with love.

When the ambulance arrived, I was placed on a stretcher. As I was carried out of the building, the entire cast was still singing the Jesus chant. I thought of the Pole Man, who had been hurt and had responded negatively by cursing his community and cursing God. Then I considered the sequence of recent events that included being knocked down by James during rehearsals, being injured by David in this rehearsal, turning to God after the injury, giving a blessing to David, and being blessed by this spiritual community. I felt this whole series of events was a healing of the projection and blaming that had occurred in my past life as the Pole Man.

My left arm was placed in a sling, but because of previous dislocations, I was concerned that I would have a trick shoulder that would come out very easily. In order to heal completely, I decided to immobilize the arm to the point of spending almost all of my time in my room resting, which I did for six weeks. The positive side of this was that the shoulder did heal solidly; the down side was that the shoulder joint became very rigid from lack of use. I thought it might never return to full range of motion, yet Calvin very kindly came to my rescue. On a daily basis he prayed over me, massaged me, and gave me physical therapy by rotating the arm to return full range of motion. Previously, I had a dream about Calvin in which he was a spiritual being who blessed me, and this experience was a fulfillment of that dream. Of all the people I have met in my life Calvin is the one person I most admire, partly because of his spiritual dedication, but most of all because of his humility. He is the most truly egoless person I have ever met, and egolessness is the truest test of spiritual advancement.

As I was leaving my previous job, I had begun inventing and illustrating a personal growth card game, called the *Starlight Game*, as a business venture. But subsequently I was concerned I would not be able to finance it. Calvin was going on an out-of-town business trip, and I hugged him as he left. When I got back to my room, I discovered an unexpected gift of a $500 check from him—and he was already generously paying for the rent. I fell on my knees crying, not for the money itself, but because of how much I felt God loved me and how little I had done to live up to such love.

Before my shoulder had healed completely, I was doing a lying down meditation and repeating the Name of Jesus when suddenly I was no longer in the body. I was in the full lotus position and floating around the room in my astral body. I observed my physical body still lying on the floor. I was floating in a circle, with my face always turned toward the center, where a small, joker-like figure sat with an insipid smile on his face. As I continued to repeat the Jesus Prayer during this experience, I wondered what would happen if I stopped repeating the affirmation. So I did stop repeating the Name of Jesus, and immediately the impish figure jumped at me. As his figure hit my astral body, it felt repulsive, and I instantly found myself firmly back in my physical body. I had the impression that this figure, in spite of his smiling face, was an astral entity who was trying to influence my mind with negative spiritual suggestions. I would cling ever more firmly to the Name of Jesus as a result of this incident.

In the springtime, long after my recovery, I experienced three days of continuous spiritual upliftment. Perhaps this was the fruit of spending so much time in solitude and silence in my room during the previous winter. I had devoted myself so much to repeating the Jesus Prayer that during this time I was feeling God's presence wherever I was and whatever I was doing. This state of mind was described by the monk Brother Lawrence in his book, *The Practice of the Presence of God.* For these three days I felt like Brother Lawrence, in that I could see God in everyone and everything all the time. I had fallen in love with God and was carried away with divine infatuation. The more I loved Him in everyone and everything, the more I felt totally loved myself. I felt God was guiding me inwardly in every situation with every person. It felt joyful to know I was doing God's will in every mundane activity.

I remember the exact time when this cloud of love evaporated. I hadn't given much thought to my business venture of the *Starlight Game* in those three days, but I decided that I needed to call a particular person to see if he would be interested in promoting it. Anticipating making the phone call, I began thinking about this person, about the game, and about my financial needs. I had shifted my focus from allowing God to be the doer in my life to the self-consciousness of me being the doer. After this change in my awareness, I could not return again to my former continuous loving state. However, as an aftereffect I did find that I was able to feel greater devotion and opening to divine love during the times I set aside for meditation.

When my birthday came around in April, no one at the Light House knew about it. But on that day David and Pamela came to me, saying they were grateful I had been letting them use my VW beetle. They noticed that the extra use was putting a little wear and tear on the vehicle and wanted to acknowledge their appreciation, so they handed me a gift of $100.

---

1. Janet Bell, "A.R.E. Camp: The Heart of the Matter," *Movement Newspaper*, Vol. 7, Issue 1, January 1982.

2. Ibid.

3. The Findhorn Community, on the northeast coast of Scotland, is noted for its gardens, which produce giant plants despite the harsh conditions. Community members attribute the great size of the plants to the assistance of nature spirits.

4. Janet Bell, "A.R.E. Camp: The Heart of the Matter," *Movement Newspaper*, Vol. 7, Issue 1, January 1982.

5. The actual Jesus chant lyrics began with "Jesus, Jesus," but the rest of the chant is my own variation of the original.

25

LEE

~ • ~

As an aftereffect of my psychic opening to a past life with Pamela, I felt unresolved and unfulfilled regarding the emotions that had been awakened. Perhaps it was inevitable that I would meet another person who would help me sort out the male/female issues that had been revealed. This person was Lee, whom I met at the Fellowship. She had decisively separated from her husband in New York, where they owned a jewelry store. Having difficulty adjusting to her approaching divorce, she came to Virginia Beach for healing, along with her six-year-old daughter. She was intelligent, tall, thin, and pretty. We became friends and eventually more than friends. We then decided to live together.

Rose and then later Calvin's wife, Evelyn, had previously noticed the shortcomings in my wardrobe, and Lee now brought them to my attention. In particular, Evelyn had joked with me about my baggy, loose-fitting pants. (If I had known the future, I would have told her that I was ahead of my time in this respect.) She felt I was pushing ladies away by my sloppy dressing. Tight fitting clothes are frowned upon in yoga because they restrict the natural breathing so at the Yoga Center I got accustomed to wearing very loose-fitting yoga pants. After leaving the Yoga Center I continued that loose-fitting style of dressing because I felt I was making myself physically comfortable, without realizing how this appeared to others. Fortunately Evelyn had a way of telling me about my shortcomings with a light touch. In fact, she would often manage to make me so silly that I would laugh with my whole body. Then she would even make fun of the way I laughed with my whole body, which only made me laugh more. Lee handled this sensitive clothing issue by stroking my ego, telling me that in bed I was very masculine, being lovingly in charge, which she liked. However, then she made it clear that my loose-fitting clothes made me look weak and not masculine. Consequently, she insisted on treating me to a shopping spree, which naturally included buying a new pair of jeans that actually fit my body.

Lee and I had sex every day for many months. One night after I had briefly started foreplay, I told her I really did not feel motivated on this particular night, so I wanted to stop. She wanted me to continue because of having already been activated. I complied, but not wholeheartedly. The next day, Lee insisted that we break up because she said I was not enthusiastic the night before. Generally she felt that she, being a Scorpio, liked sex more than I did. I asked her, "Don't you remember last Saturday night?"

Her eyes lit up, and she smiled, "Ah, you remember that!" obviously pleased that I recalled our sexual experimentation with a new position. I explained that it was true that we were having sex every day because I knew that is what she wanted. I told her I did like sex, but I also knew it lowered my ability to raise up energy in meditation. If it was entirely my decision, I would probably not choose to have sex every day. She still wanted to break up, so we made plans to go our separate ways in the near future. However, shortly before our planned separation, we decided to stay together after all.

I had recently met a Norwegian visitor, Sympher, who could not speak English very well, so it was hard to make himself understood. Yet he was very intuitive, and I liked him. Lee, Sympher, and I were going to go to David's second A.R.E. conference, called *The Essenes and the Second Coming of Christ*, but there was a problem. A friend named Rita had a dream of a person at the conference, possibly Sympher, having a bad experience. Rita said that she didn't specifically see him in her dream, but she was aware that a well-known local psychic had made a judgmental comment that he felt Sympher was "mentally unstable." David was asked to determine if Sympher should be allowed to attend the conference. A meeting of interested parties gathered to discuss it, and I stood firmly in support of him. I expressed my opinion that he was being perceived with suspicion merely because he was a foreigner and that the dream and the labeling as mentally unstable were both without merit. David decided to allow him to attend.

At the conference, when we sat in a meditation circle in the evening, we could hear someone moaning and obviously emotionally distraught. The dream that predicted someone would have a bad experience at the conference was accurate. But the troubled person was not Sympher, who had no problems there. I went to the woman who was in distress and felt guided to sit on the ground in front of her. I placed my hands on her feet to provide a grounding effect and invite God's help. Then two other participants came also and did the laying on of hands for the upper body. The distress passed, and the woman was able to continue at the conference without further incident.

I had told Lee that I viewed this conference as a retreat and wanted to be in solitude and communion with God as much as possible. However, I felt it was important to participate in the group activities, including a leadership activity of my teaching the Jesus Prayer. Although Lee said she understood my need for solitude, toward the end of the conference she came to me in an anxious state of mind. She said she saw other couples being together a lot and therefore felt I was ignoring her unnecessarily. At first I was unsure how to respond. I felt my need for solitude was designed to honor the spiritual purposes of the conference, but I did not want to be insensitive to her need for companionship. Finally I led her to a barn with a loft for privacy, and we had sex. As Lee and I left the barn, another couple was walking to the barn hand-in-hand with apparently a similar motivation. I felt that I had perhaps made a mistake and set a bad example for others in terms of the spiritual priorities of the conference.

That evening we were sitting by the campfire participating in a cleansing activity in which we offered ourselves to God and purged ourselves of our perceived shortcomings—a process similar to the fire ceremony described by Janet Bell in the previous chapter. As I was prayerfully searching my mind to see what I needed to surrender to God, one camper spoke up ominously, saying she could see the face of a devil laughing in the fire. Perhaps this psychic impression was nothing more than an overactive imagination, but it triggered in me the strong feeling that I had let down the conference's spiritual purposes by having sex with Lee earlier. David had given me some leadership responsibilities in the conference, and in that role I felt it was important for me to devote every ounce of my energy toward spiritual purposes, not personal sexual satisfaction. The next morning I came to David and told him what happened. I apologized to him and started weeping uncontrollably. David, whom I had never seen cry, was as comforting as he could be, yet I sensed he felt awkward because of my vulnerability and the intensity of my crying. To make matters worse, there was no way I could discuss this with Lee without her feeling personally rejected and blamed. I did not think she would understand why I felt distraught, just as she had not understood my need for temporary solitude during the conference.

When Lee, Sympher, and I drove back to Virginia Beach after the conference, Sympher and I wanted to stop for a visit at the Fellowship headquarters in New Market. Although Lee objected, she was overruled based on two outnumbering one, so we did stop briefly. We got back that night, and the following day Lee told me she was furious that we had stopped there, especially since it was her car we were driving. She told me that she was breaking up with me. I accepted her decision, though I had a very different perspective on why we were separating. I felt that the real problem in our relationship had to do with not having the same degree of single-minded spiritual dedication. All along I had felt that if we both placed God first in our lives, we would stay together. When we had initially decided to live with each other, we had agreed to meditate together every morning. At a later date Lee backed out of this arrangement, and that change in priorities was a caution sign to me that we would not have a long-term relationship.

It was agreed that I would stay until I could find a new living situation, hopefully within a month. Before I moved out, Lee told me that her period had stopped and the result of her pregnancy test was that "the rabbit had died." Around dinner time, she explained that the conception had happened on the retreat. "Weren't you taking your birth control pills then?" I asked.

"I discontinued using the pill because I didn't expect to have sex during the conference," Lee said.

"That's reasonable considering that I told you I wanted to have solitude so I could be centered on God during the retreat. But if I had known that you were off the pill, I would never have pursued having sex that day. What I want to know is, when we were in the loft together, why didn't you tell me then that you were not taking the pill?" I asked.

"I didn't think of it," Lee said.

"I don't understand how you could *not think of it*," I said with a look of disbelief.

"What's done is done," Lee said with an obvious sense of finality. Then there was what could be called quite literally "a pregnant pause" in our conversation.

I resented that she had not told me she had discontinued her birth control pills. I did not tell Lee that I had cried bitterly with David the day after our sexual encounter because I regretted failing to devote myself entirely to God during the retreat. If Lee had told me the truth back then, there was no chance that we would have had sex. Even in this pause in our conversation, I felt she was not telling me the whole truth. I could have pursued the matter further—hoping to hear from her a more believable reason why she didn't tell me she was off the pill. However, she looked so desperately vulnerable telling me she was pregnant with our child that it did not seem right to force the issue. Instead, not knowing what to say, I just looked at her with a dumbfounded expression on my face.

Finally Lee broke the silence, saying, "I'm not going to have the baby. So that's that." It was clear from the way she expressed herself that her decision to have an abortion was not negotiable. Although my relationship with her was not a union of deep love, I still felt we had joined, at least initially, to explore the sacred within each other. Sex itself is a biological act, but can become a sacred act if offered to Spirit. Even if both partners do not hold sex in a sacred place by offering it to Spirit, it can, nevertheless, still sometimes produce a sacred result—the miracle of a new life. This sacred result is expressed beautifully in the words of author Marjorie Holmes:

> What is an act of love but a fusion? Of bodies, yes, but of souls as well. The secret hungering essence of self seeking to find itself and lose itself. Seeking to vanish and begin again. This is true in the perfect and rapturous sense when the two people deeply love each other. But even when they don't, when on the common, everyday plane they may be miles apart, the mystery of sex can provide an instant out of eternity in which there is genuine union, and out of it a new life can come.[1]

In spite of my recognition of the sacredness of a new life, in one of my lowest moments I failed to speak up for saving this child—potentially the only child I would have in this life. Undoubtedly, Lee still would have had the abortion no matter what I had said, but at least I would have done the right thing by advocating for saving the child. Perhaps because I genuinely regretted my failure, the universe provided an opportunity to do the right thing in the future, when I unexpectedly got a job advocating for the welfare of vulnerable children, a story I will tell in an upcoming chapter.

Lee told me she wanted me to pay the $600 fee for the abortion. Being unemployed at the time and still resenting the fact that she had not told me she was off the pill, I took the low road here, too. I told her I did not have the money and would not pay it. She started screaming, "Get out! Get out, you adulterer!" It was evident that she meant *now*. To her credit, she did not curse, but I was shocked that she called me an "adulterer," since that word had never even occurred to me. In my mind she was free from any commitment to her husband, even though the divorce had not yet been finalized. She would not stop screaming, expressing her anger at the top of her lungs, but I remained silent. When she finally ran out of gas, I said in a quiet voice that I would leave immediately, as she demanded. Not owning a car, I called a friend to come over. After stuffing all my belongings into the car, I left to stay temporarily with my friend.

The next day I went back to visit Lee, and I apologized for saying that I would not pay the $600. I told her I did not have the money, but would pay her when I got it. I gave her some valuable personal objects to show my good faith. Then I was surprised to receive an unsolicited check from a relative for about $500, which enabled me to pay her sooner than I had expected. After some time passed, we were able to come to a place of forgiveness for each other. She said she appreciated that I did not scream back at her when she hollered at me. She had a dream when she first came to Virginia Beach about an elevator that went to many levels and a janitor who cleaned out all the levels. In our last conversation she acknowledged feeling that I had served her as that janitor. She felt my influence had helped her to clean out at many levels within herself, after the emotional turmoil of her separation, which did eventually lead to a divorce.

I had a feeling and a desire that my relationship with Lee would be my last sexual relationship. I wanted to be a monk again, totally dedicated to God, but my problem was that I did not feel I was worthy of returning to being a monk because of having previously already broken my vow of celibacy to God. I moved into a two-bedroom apartment with Bruce Shelton, a probation officer and a friend from my Yoga Center days and from the Fellowship. At a time when he happened to be out of town, I met a stranger named Manuel who needed a place to stay for one night. I invited him to stay at my apartment, just as I used to invite strangers to sleep over at the Yoga Center. During his visit he told me about a very recent spiritual experience of his:

> While I was meditating, I felt a sudden opening of tremendous energy at the base of my spine. The energy slowly crawled up my back. As the energy rose to my heart level, my hands involuntarily came together in prayer position at the chest. The energy moved up my back through my neck and into my head. I felt myself blissfully filled with divine love and overcome with gratitude. It seemed like I stayed that way for a very long time. Finally, the energy slowly descended in reverse order of its rising, until it returned to the base of the spine.

After describing this obvious kundalini experience, Manuel said that as an aftereffect of his spiritual opening, he felt a lingering pain in his lower back. I had been experiencing a lower back pain myself for a few months, but without mentioning my own condition, I asked him if he wanted me to give him a prayer healing session for his back. He welcomed this session, and afterwards we hugged goodbye because he told me he would be leaving very early in the morning before I would awaken. I went to sleep that night, and the following morning I was lying in bed on my stomach, which was a very unusual position for my sleeping body. I was just beginning to wake up when I felt a hand holding my left wrist and another hand planted at the base of my spine. Still groggy and not quite awake, I felt I was being held down by someone behind me. Consequently, I twisted my upper torso to the right and raised my right arm to push away this stranger. As I turned and my arm was already in motion to swat at this person, I was shocked to see a figure of a man consisting entirely of shining blue light. As my right arm, still in motion, hit the glowing figure, it instantly vanished.

Coming to my senses, I realized that the figure was nothing like the negative astral entity that I had seen during the astral traveling experience at the Light House. I only had an instant to look at this glowing blue light figure, but I recalled it looked very beautiful. It occurred to me that I was not being held down to restrain me; rather, that I was receiving a healing from a spiritual entity, most likely an angel. I felt foolish having swatted away an angel and healer, who had probably come to help me because I had been so willing to help Manuel the day before. In fact, I had previously gone to several chiropractors for help, and this had only made my lower back worse. However, after this healing, the lower back pain disappeared.

I sat in bed for about ten minutes pondering the significance of my healing visitor and then fervently asking for forgiveness for so rudely striking at him before I knew what was happening. Then I heard a voice, as clear as a bell, say the words, "Do you want to be a monk?"

I immediately responded "Yes" mentally and then quietly said "Yes" verbally as well. I felt this was the confirmation that I needed to tell me that it was all right for me to be a monk now, even though I had broken my vow of celibacy in the past. I have faithfully remained a celibate monk ever since, convinced that I have truly been called to this vocation.

---

1. Marjorie Holmes, *How Can I Find You, God?* (New York: Galilee Doubleday, a division of Bantam Doubleday Bell Publishing, 1998) pp. 22-23.

26

SPECIAL
RELATIONSHIPS

≈ ◦ ≈

In the future, I would learn from studying *A Course in Miracles* to look at my relationship with Lee as an example of a "special love relationship," which is the most common type of relationship. In contrast to a "holy relationship," a special relationship is one in which the motivation is for each partner to become special by being with another person who is seen as special. This specialness is based on the premise that people are not equal and must try to be better than others to find happiness. In the special love relationship, partners come together with separate interests and therefore do not have a common purpose. This is the opposite of partners in a holy relationship, who recognize common interests and consequently have a common purpose. For example, my relationship with Rose was and is a holy relationship with a common interest in spiritual growth and a specific common purpose of seeing Christ in each other.

The special love relationship seems necessary because each partner has feelings of guilt, unworthiness, and incompleteness. These negative feelings are within and can be overcome by taking responsibility for one's own false perceptions and by looking within for divine assistance to heal the mind. However, in the special love relationship, instead of looking within, partners focus on getting help from outside themselves. Partners feel they have special needs for overcoming what is lacking within. These special needs are separate interests that cannot be shared, rather than common interests that can be shared. In a distortion of the true nature of love, each partner with separate interests uses the other as a means of getting their own special needs met.

The special love relationship is a bargain in which specialness is the commodity exchanged. This exchange of specialness will seem to solve the hidden inner feelings of guilt, unworthiness, and incompleteness, as long as each partner feels the other is giving a fair return of specialness. But when partners feel they are not getting enough specialness to meet their special needs, blaming will occur. When partners blame each other for not giving enough specialness to fulfill the bargain, the love can quickly change to hate. This reversal, in which love becomes hate, is a sure sign of the special love relationship being revealed for what it is—a bargain. This bargain is what passes for love in this world, yet true love is based on *giving*, rather than *getting* through bargaining.

To give a very simplified example, imagine that a woman feels inferior about her intelligence so she has a relationship with a man who offers to her the specialness of his high intelligence. Similarly this man feels inferior about his physical appearance and so he enters this relationship because she offers him the specialness of her beauty. They each feel they have obtained a "trophy" partner that fulfills their special need to compensate for their own shortcomings. But then the woman gains weight. Her partner thinks she is not holding up her part of the bargain, so he blames her for losing her beauty. The woman feels the man is using his mind to criticize her. Since his intelligence is being used against her, he has lost his appeal of specialness that originally attracted her. Both partners then feel they are not getting their special needs met and that they have made a bad bargain. Consequently, love turns to hate and they mutually decide to end the relationship in order to find someone else to meet their special needs.

In my relationship with Lee, she had a feeling of inferiority about her level of spiritual development so she was attracted to the specialness of me having devoted myself to spiritual growth. I felt inferior because of my inability to bring about an intimate relationship with Pamela so I was attracted to Lee as a sexual partner who could give me the sense of intimacy and healing I was seeking. I was able to inspire her spiritually, and we meditated together. She gave me the intimacy that I was seeking. Initially, we both felt we were getting our special needs met.

My original spiritual encouragement became less appealing to Lee in time, and she lost interest in our practice of meditating together. And I found that sexual intimacy was not fulfilling in a holistic way because it lacked a deep love connection that would give it meaning beyond physical satisfaction. I was faced with the fact that it was inappropriate for me to cast Lee, whom I did not genuinely love, in the role of being a substitute for Pamela, whom I did love. Neither of us felt that our special needs were being met and our separation became inevitable because we were both focused on what we were getting (or *not* getting) rather than on what we were giving.

In special relationships, the mind becomes occupied with the concerns of the world and focused on having one's own special needs met. In addition, there is also the desire to meet the partner's stated special needs. The focus is primarily on fulfilling one's own individual will and only secondarily on carrying out the partner's individual will based on fulfilling separate needs. Consequently, the partners become unconcerned about doing God's Will and ignore the goal of waking up spiritually. At some level I knew all along that in this relationship, I was putting God in the back seat rather than letting Him be the driving force in my life. But the misplacement of my priorities only became painfully clear to me when I confessed to David with tears that I had inappropriately chosen to have sex with Lee while on our retreat dedicated to God.

David told me once, "What I am afraid of is that I will one day become like a sailboat floating around aimlessly without my sail up. I don't want to ever fall asleep spiritually." I felt my time with Lee had been helpful in sorting out all the feelings left over from my psychic opening in relation to Pamela. In the aftermath of our separation, Lee told me that our time together had helped in her process of healing emotionally, following her separation from her husband. In spite of some good that came out of the relationship, the down side for me was that I had been slowly falling asleep spiritually. At first I didn't think I was worthy to rededicate my life to God because of having broken my vow of celibacy, but after the experience I described in the previous chapter, I felt I was again called to be a "monk in the world" devoted to God. As a monk in the world, relationships were very important to me, and I wanted my relationships to be a reflection of my relationship with God.

As an outgrowth of my refocusing on spiritual ideals, I wanted to address the issue of the danger of specialness and the importance of equality. My biggest problem had always been pride. If I could let go of specialness and instead value equality, it would help me to overcome my pride and make God, rather than ego gratification, my top priority.

The issue of equality had already come up some years before. Right after returning from my retreat in North Carolina, I visited an open-hearted friend of mine, Patience. Coincidentally she was the supervisor of the mental health unit of the Volunteers of America, where I also worked. From my Yoga Center days I remember a few conversations with her in which she would fill up with overflowing joy. Smiling broadly, she would beam so much spiritual light at me that I had to break off eye contact, not being used to receiving so much love. I have never met anyone else, before or since, who had that effect on me. She asked about my retreat in North Carolina, and I shared with her my renewal of the Jesus Prayer. However, when I mentioned that I had traveled with David, her face displayed a sour look. I asked her what that expression was all about, and she said, "Well, you know how David is," as though I should know exactly what she was talking about.

"No, I don't know what you're getting at," I said, genuinely perplexed.

She hesitated thoughtfully. Choosing her words carefully, she said, "David has very high spiritual ideals, and he does everything he can to live up to them. But his ideals are so high and so pure, where does that leave other people? Do you get what I mean?"

"No, I don't know what you mean, and I don't want to know," I said, although it seemed she was implying he was judgmental of others who don't measure up to his high standards. "I don't think you know David as well as I do. David has inspired a lot of people, and I am one of them. David is my friend, and I don't want to talk about him behind his back. Let's talk about something else." I was taken aback by Patience's comments because she normally spoke positively about other people, and I respected her opinions, but in this case I dismissed her conclusions as totally unwarranted.

At a later date I attended David's first A.R.E conference, the one that writer Janet Bell attended. I completed the nine-page T.A.P. questionnaire. "T.A.P." stood for Talents, Abilities, and Life Purpose Workshop. David had devised this as a tool to help seekers find and focus on their spiritual ideals. One of the workshop activities involved sharing our life stories with others. Since David and I were busy during the conference, we decided to share our stories on the first day after it was over.

Starting first, David told me his story in confidence, so I am not at liberty to share the details of what he said. However, I can say that hearing about his life helped me to understand the forces that molded his strong and often stoic character. As a result of his life experiences, he learned to place his full trust in himself—in his intellect, resourcefulness, and abilities. In regard to spiritual matters, he was entirely self-taught and managed to find God and devote himself to high spiritual ideals. In stark contrast to my youthful experimenting with drugs, David said he never touched them. He never even had a cigarette. I marveled that he was like a lotus flower rooted in the mud of the world, yet rising up through the murky water to float on the surface, displaying its beauty in the sunlight.

When David finished his story, I told him how much I appreciated him sharing so much of his personal life. I realized from his generally aloof manner that it was quite unusual for him to open up in this way. David and I were already joined together because of our common spiritual purposes, but I had always felt he held me at a distance emotionally. After hearing his life story, I understood why his personality was so different from my own. In sharing my life story with him, I wanted to be as open as he had been by making sure to tell him not only my most meaningful spiritual experiences, but also by sharing with him my numerous shortcomings and failures. I made a point of speaking from my heart. I hoped our mutual sharing would draw us closer together in spite of the distance I felt in our relationship.

When I finished my story, I looked at David, expecting some kind of positive response, but instead he said bluntly, "I got the impression you thought you were being my teacher." That was hard for me to swallow because I had just shared with him the most intimate details of my life. I remembered that David was almost entirely self-taught in spiritual matters. Perhaps he was put off by my talking somewhat authoritatively about the nature of my own spiritual experiences. One of David's favorite sayings was, "Those who know, don't say. Those who say, don't know." Because I had said so much about spiritual experiences that were deeply meaningful for me, perhaps he thought that I was among those who really "don't know." Whatever reason he had, I felt I needed to give him the benefit of the doubt. After all, in listening to my narration he was probably rightly sensing my own attachment to specialness and pride. However, his conclusion that I was thinking of myself as being his teacher did not make sense to me because it was not my intention, and I had spoken from my heart. I told him, "I'm sorry you feel that way. I feel people always come together to learn from each other. But that's quite different from one person presuming to be another person's teacher. I can assure you that I have no intention of being your teacher."

David said "OK" and that he had to go out. As he prepared to leave, I walked to the bathroom, but then turned around and said, "I just want you to know that there is no question in my mind that we are equals. I assume you feel the same way, don't you?"

I thought David would immediately say, "Of course, we're equals." Instead he said, "I have to go." He withdrew from the apartment, but I could tell from his voice tone and manner that he had already withdrawn emotionally. We didn't have a follow-up discussion. After that, I recalled Patience's opinion of David that implied he was sitting in judgment of others who don't live up his high ideals. Although David did not come right out and say it, I did get the impression that he was looking down on me in a judgmental manner and did not see me as his equal.

I gathered that David was viewing equality in terms of equality of talents manifested in the world, similar to the abilities identified in his T.A.P. questionnaire. In that sense he had more expressive qualities than I had. Because of his abilities, he was much more of a leader than I was, and I was perfectly willing to defer to his leadership at times, especially at the form level of navigating in the world. However, I was viewing equality in terms that had nothing to do with personal abilities. For me, equality meant equality in Christ, as I had experienced in my relationship with Rose. In any event, I felt that there was not the openness at that time to pursue the issue further.

After moving into the Light House and having lived there for a long time, I asked to have a talk with David. After a short meditation together, I reminded him about the equality issue that was raised in my mind after we had shared our life stories. I asked David to address this issue. He paused and then spoke solemnly. I sensed he was trying to respond honestly when he said, "I've been very successful in my life when I compare myself with other people. In a way, my success has become a problem, like the problem of Lancelot in the story of King Arthur. Lancelot is so successful in everything he does that it becomes his curse. He defeats everyone he meets, which leaves him invulnerable and without challengers. I would love for someone to come along to challenge me, but it just hasn't happened."

I didn't think David was bragging because that wasn't his style. He explained that when he compared himself with others and saw others coming up short, he was just using objective discernment to observe facts, rather than being subjectively judgmental of others. The quality I admired most about David was his purity of purpose—his desire to do what was right before God with uncompromising integrity. Consequently, I did not question his sincerity in believing within himself that he was not being judgmental. Nevertheless, I felt he had a blind spot about the issue of equality that he just couldn't see. I would realize later that I had an equally large blind spot, but at the time I started to cry as he talked because I felt this tremendous gulf between us that could not be breached. I felt that he was looking down on me, and there was nothing I could say or do that would enable him to see us as equals. In fact, what made me cry even more was that he was looking down on me right then for crying, seeing my vulnerability as a defect. In spite of my emotional reaction, I realized David was still very much my friend and my equal in Christ, even though this blind spot happened to bother my ego, thus obscuring my ability to see Christ in him with the same clarity that I could see Christ in Rose.

Living in the Light House with Calvin's wife, Evelyn, we confided in each other and compared notes on our viewpoints of David. We both admired his many obvious expressive gifts but experienced similar concerns about his apparent lack of receptivity. We felt that at least in some areas he was so rock-solid strong in his self-confidence and so convinced of the correctness of his thinking that it prevented him from being open-minded and receptive to others. We attempted to discuss our concerns with David, yet met with defensiveness and withdrawal, so the topic was quickly dropped. We should have realized that if we were correct about David lacking receptivity, he would naturally not be receptive to us telling him that he lacked receptivity. In general, telling another person about your perception of their shortcomings seldom produces positive results, unless that person is asking for such feedback—and David was not asking. I just had to accept the fact that on this issue David and I would not be able to find common ground.

At a much later date I would learn from *A Course in Miracles* that there was a better way to deal with the perception of a fault other than bringing it to the other person's attention. Instead, I could *make a space for the other person to be OK, even if he has the fault I see*. Seeing the other person as OK allows me to stop judging and then to see the light in him. If you would like to try this out, choose someone you're having a problem with. In prayer or meditation, make a space for that person to be OK (and from Christ's perspective he is). After you do this, ask to see at least a small light in him. If you truly want to see it, you will. This request is always honored because you are opening your mind to forgiveness that leads to love.

In the future I would learn to think of forgiveness as the process of "looking and overlooking." The *looking* portion of forgiveness is looking for the divine reality—perceiving the holiness of Christ in another person. The *overlooking* portion of forgiveness is looking beyond errors—past the ego mask without allowing one's perception of the divine in another person to become distorted.[1] Once I could do that, I could perceive faults as not part of that person's true nature in Christ. I could see errors as neither good nor bad, but merely meaningless because they do not come from the divine Source of meaning.[2]

This forgiveness process of seeing Christ in others brings healing to the mind. From the Course I would learn that, ideally, forgiveness involves releasing errors of the ego right in the beginning, before becoming preoccupied by them. In later chapters I will talk more about the dynamics of forgiveness that involve letting go of our illusions of guilt that we project onto others so we will not have to face the feelings of guilt within ourselves.

Unfortunately I did not yet have this higher perspective that would have helped me to overlook the faults in David and look for the holiness of Christ in him. Consequently, I felt it was easy to see blind spots where David needed growth, but I could not see my own. Instead of asking David about his lack of receptivity, it would have been better for my own growth to focus on why I was so prone to tears and expressions of vulnerability. Looking back on this now, I can see that David was actually correct in seeing a shortcoming in my vulnerability, which I had mistakenly seen at that time as a virtue. The good side of my vulnerability was emotional openness, but I was tearfully carrying even this positive quality to an inappropriate excess. The downside to my vulnerability was an attachment to self-defeating victim consciousness. However, I wouldn't become aware of that blind spot until much later, and I will save my discovery of it for a later chapter. Although I couldn't see my victim consciousness at the Light House, I was aware that I wanted and seemingly needed David's approval, just as I had sought Dylan's in earlier days. Apparently, David did not have a reciprocal need for my positive feedback, and it appeared he was not concerned about my need for his approval. My need was not exactly a blind spot because I was aware of it and willing to admit that it was inappropriate. However, I could not grasp *why* I was so needy for approval, and that lack of awareness *was* a blind spot.

The approval issue came to a head for me when David asked me to write an article on meditation for the quarterly magazine that he published. After I submitted my writing to him, he informed me that instead of using my article, he was going to write his own article on the subject. I wasn't a great writer, but good enough a few years later to be paid to produce weekly articles for a local newspaper. And in this case I was writing about the subject of meditation that I knew very well. Yet even in this area of expertise my writing wasn't up to David's high standards.

I was upset at the time, but looking back now, I can see that behind those upset feelings was my own sense of unworthiness—and the other side of my pride pattern. In seeking David's approval I wanted him to meet my special need to compensate for my own feeling of unworthiness. It seems I was seeking a form of special relationship in order to get specialness from David. In other words, I was foolishly being influenced by my ego to seek self-worth from others, rather than looking for the divine within for my sense of self-worth.

This need for David's approval persisted and remained unfulfilled for many years. Eventually I became spiritually stronger within by relying on God's love for me as the only assurance of my worth that I needed. Thus I was able to increasingly heal my own sense of unworthiness, and I slowly outgrew the need for David to appreciate me.

Although David did not intend to be my teacher in this, he was my teacher in how to let go of approval by refusing to play the specialness game with me. This was ironic because I can see with hindsight that by spurning my attempts to engage him in giving and receiving approval, he was actually preventing me from making our relationship increasingly *non-equal* through the medium of specialness.

Although I had resented his emotional distancing and considered it a fault, David was inadvertently my teacher in this also. In the future I would get a job in which a specific form of emotional distancing was a necessity. In this job, that I will describe later, I needed to step back from emotional outbursts by my clients, but it was not just for withdrawal alone. The withdrawal simply enabled me to not get caught up in the client's emotional turmoil, and by preserving my calm mind I could then see the Christ in my client and send him love. From this I learned that emotional distancing can actually become a virtue as long as it is strongly linked with compassion.

Although I felt that David lacked compassion for me in many of our early exchanges, with each advancing year he has learned to open his heart increasingly to others and has today become a much more loving and compassionate person. Indeed, whenever I see him now, I can tangibly feel his warmth and love for me and mine for him.

Long before I had overcome my special need to seek external forms of specialness from others, I was already gaining an appreciation of the importance of equality, so I was inspired to write a short play entitled, "Learning How to Be Ordinary." The story was a fable about the giving up striving for specialness—letting go of the desire to be set apart and above others, which is an expression of pride. The main character was "Big Lion," who turned down the specialness of being the king of the jungle in order to tell everyone that they were ordinary and equal. He encouraged everyone to understand that they could love and accept themselves just as they were, as ordinary, and that they could love each other by seeing each other as equals, rather than as competitors for specialness. Just as Jesus came with the message of love and met rejection from many of His own people, Big Lion met resistance from those who wanted to protect their claim to specialness. Big Lion was persecuted, but in the end was rewarded for letting go of specialness.

From time to time, I was invited to speak at the Fellowship for Sunday service. For one such occasion, I decided to put on this play. I played Big Lion, and David volunteered to play Little Lion. We had newly purchased gold bathroom rugs for our manes, and we looked ridiculous in our full body outfits. In order to enlist audience participation, I told everyone to think of an animal that they would like to be. In the middle of the play, Big Lion was looking for an animal that is ordinary, but every animal said that he was special. Playing the part of Big Lion, I asked audience members, "What animal are you and are you ordinary or special?" I had prompted the audience before the play started to give the answer in the following form: "I am a (*name of animal*), and I'm special because (*description of special qualities*)." Everything went fine with the audience participation until one lady that I called upon couldn't speak, and she began crying. Perhaps the issues of ordinariness and specialness were difficult for her to face. If I had thought quickly, I could have said, "Oh, I know what animal you are. You are very special because you are a wise and mysterious animal. You show your wisdom through your silence." But instead of saying the right words, I did something even more important—I came over to her in my silly outfit and hugged her. She hugged me back and stopped crying, and I could see her eyes saying "thank you" as we moved on with the play. The play was very effective and easy to execute with audience participation. The script can be found in Appendix B, "An Ordinary Play."

The play is included here not for reading but in case any adults or even children would like to put on this play with their church or other spiritual organization as an allegory of the life of Jesus and as a way of emphasizing the significance of equality.

The play was not only entertaining and informative for others; it was beneficial for me as well. I felt it was a reminder and even a reenactment of the life of the Pole Man, and I wondered if David too was reliving a corresponding past-life experience of his own at the same time. However, this was more than just a reenactment for me. It was a symbolic correction of the past. The Pole Man brought his traumatic experience upon himself and was unable to meet death gracefully because of his own sense of specialness, which led him to pridefully think he was better than others. This play was an opportunity to correct the mistakes of the Pole Man by symbolically acting out the letting go of specialness and the acceptance of equality.

This kind of reenactment and correction of the past occurring in the present moment was what I would learn in the future to call a "memory walk from darkness to light." This awakening of the divine within may also be called a "memory walk to now"—a remembrance of the past to heal the present. Recalling the past, such as my writing of this play or becoming aware of past lives, can unfortunately be done to exalt the ego and remain locked into the guilt of the past and fear of the future. But for the recalling of the past, however it occurs, to be considered a "memory walk," it needs to be a healing experience. Consequently, a "memory walk" is an opportunity to let go of the ego and of past guilt, which brings you to *now*. Now is the present moment in time where you can find a taste of eternity and a taste of heaven, and it is this eternal now that brings divine healing with it.

The real test of the healing value of this play as a "memory walk" was to allow my emphasis on equality and letting go of specialness to carry over into my daily life. I needed to learn how to respond differently in my relationships with others so that I could let go of specialness. My experience working with Dolly at Baker House had shown me that I had a long way to go before overcoming my attachment to specialness. At least I had my holy relationship with Rose, which I continued to nourish, to help remind me of equality by seeing Christ in her. Because of our common purpose of seeing Christ in each other and seeing each other as equals, it made it easier to increasingly see Christ in others and see others as equals. Rose became my anchor, so that whenever I got sidetracked into specialness, our interaction reminded me to refocus on attempting to see Christ in others and valuing equality. Ideally I would have been able to generalize this seeing of Christ in Rose to similarly seeing Christ consistently in David and indeed in everyone, but due to my ego blocks I was not yet able to do that.

I wanted to see the Christ in Allan Greene more than anyone else, but I had lost track of him. After I had that dream of being given Allan's name and after confronting him about my thoughts that he was one of those responsible for the torture of the Pole Man, I had felt unresolved. Why would I be given his name if we were not able to come to some common understanding regarding the past life of the Pole Man? I wasn't sure what he needed, but I felt I needed to learn to completely forgive him. Rose told me he was living at the Mayflower Hotel, a high-rise in Virginia Beach, and so I went to see him. He had gained weight, and I could hardly recognize him as he sat in bed. His hands had shriveled up, becoming unusable. His legs were immobilized as well, so he had lost the little mobility that he still possessed when I last saw him. I asked, "Allan, what happened to you?"

Allan explained, "Remember you put your hands on my neck when you gave me that healing session at the Yoga Center. You were tuning into a problem in my neck that the doctors told me needed surgery. The doctors said that after surgery either one of two things would happen. Either I would be healed or dead." Allan smiled without self-pity and said, "You see they were wrong," and he tilted his head slightly to the side and shrugged his shoulders, which was just about the limit of his mobility.

"I'm sorry to hear that, Allan."

"Are you still doing your Jesus thing?" he asked.

"Sure, Jesus is still my joy," I shared.

Allan said, "I don't have a personal relationship with Jesus, but maybe someday I will."

"I like to think that Jesus has a personal relationship with everyone. He is like a long lost relative that we don't know about, and then one day He unexpectedly comes into our lives. When He appears, we suddenly realize He has been our relative all along and He was loving us even when we were not aware of Him."

"So I guess I'll just have to wait until my long lost 'Uncle Jesus' makes an appearance in my life. Actually maybe He has already appeared because He is in *A Course in Miracles*."

"So you are reading the Course. Are you finding it helpful?"

"I sure am. My favorite section is called, 'I need do nothing.'[3] Nothing is a good thing for me to do, because I can't do anything anyway."

I asked, "And what does 'I need do nothing' mean?"

"It means I am already the holy Son of God, so I don't have to do anything to earn salvation. All I have to do is nothing, but simply accept what I already am. Of course, everyone else is the holy Son of God, too."

"Well, that sounds good to me. I guess our seats in heaven are already reserved, and we need do nothing to pay for them." I was wondering if Allan had given any more thought to the possibility of a past life in relationship to the Pole Man, but I didn't want to put him on the spot by asking him.

However, Allan must have anticipated my unasked question, because he offered, "I haven't gotten any guidance about that past life thing, but if I do I'll let you know. I don't really get much guidance these days and haven't been able to remember my dreams lately."

"If it's important, you will get guidance eventually. I'm sorry if I was so insistent previously about the past life scenario, and right now it doesn't seem that important." Actually, it was still important to me, but it didn't seem important for us to discuss in light of Allan's physical deterioration. Instead of focusing on what Allan knew or did not know about the past, I had shifted my focus to my forgiveness of him. This visit was an example of a "memory walk to now," because in our exchange I was revisiting my memory of the Pole Man's life for the sake of healing in the present moment. My prior experience of working with the mentally retarded, who often had physical as well as mental disabilities, had helped to prepare me to look past Allan's outward mask of physical limitations. I was able to affirm my equality with him, and I was able to see Christ in him in the present moment.

---

1. C-In.2:56, p. 77 (p. 73). For those not familiar with Course references, the C stands for the "Clarification of Terms" found at the end of the book.
2. T-9.IV.4:4-7, p. 169 (p. 157).
3. T-18.VII, pp. 388-390 (pp. 362-364).

27

CREATIVE EFFORTS

~ o ~

In addition to my relationship with Rose, I had another significant holy relationship, an outgrowth of my efforts since the early 70s to write a meditation manual. I had written about Christian meditation without reference to yoga and Zen meditation practices, which might be offensive to some Christians. However, the meditation techniques that I developed integrated Eastern ways of focusing on certain parts of the body to raise up creative energy with the specifically Christian invitation to the Holy Spirit to enter into every aspect of one's being. Out of the blue, I received a phone call from Stuart Dean, whom I had known only as an acquaintance at Fellowship meetings. Stuart said, "I was meditating, and I was asked by Spirit to help you with your writing. Are you writing something, and would you like my help?"

I was naturally surprised and pleased that he had been spiritually prompted to help me, so I accepted his offer. Stuart at that time was an editor at the A.R.E., and he provided editorial feedback. I appreciated his insights and the way he always offered me editorial options without attachment. One day we got into a discussion about judgment. Stuart affirmed, "We aren't really equipped to make judgments."

I asked, "What do you mean?" Stuart pulled out a copy of *A Course in Miracles* and asked me to read a paragraph in the section entitled "How Is Judgment Relinquished?" Below is the paragraph I read, which identifies the goal of learning set by the Course, as follows:

> The aim of our curriculum, unlike the goal of the world's learning, is the recognition that judgment in the usual sense is impossible. This is not an opinion but a fact. In order to judge anything rightly, one would have to be fully aware of an inconceivably wide range of things; past, present and to come. One would have to recognize in advance all the effects of his judgments on everyone and everything involved in them in any way. And one would have to be certain there is no distortion in his perception, so that his judgment would be wholly fair to everyone on whom it rests now and in the future.

Who is in a position to do this? Who except in grandiose fantasies would claim this for himself?[1]

After reading this paragraph, I said, "I may not be equipped to make judgments, but how do I navigate through the world without making judgments to determine what course of action to take?"

"Go ahead and read the next paragraph, which answers your question," Stuart said, and so I read the following excerpt:

> Remember how many times you thought you knew all the "facts" you needed for judgment, and how wrong you were! Is there anyone who has not had this experience? Would you know how many times you merely thought you were right, without ever realizing you were wrong? Why would you choose such an arbitrary basis for decision-making? Wisdom is not judgment; it is the relinquishment of judgment. Make then but one more judgment. It is this: There is Someone with you Whose judgment is perfect. He does know all the facts; past, present and to come. He does know all the effects of His judgment on everyone and everything involved in any way. And He is wholly fair to everyone, for there is no distortion in His perception.[2]

I inquired, "Who does the Course say is this, 'Someone with you Whose judgment is perfect'?"

Stuart responded with his own question: "Who do you think this is?"

"For me it's the Holy Spirit, of course," I affirmed.

"It's the Holy Spirit in the Course, too. We are not equipped to make judgments by ourselves, but we can ask the Holy Spirit for guidance in the events and decisions of life and allow judgments to come *through* us rather than *by* us."

"Although I don't know much about the Course, if it encourages us to rely on the Holy Spirit for guidance in regard to judgments, then it sounds like it rests on solid ground spiritually." Looking back on this conversation about judgment, it seems ironic to me now that I immediately went ahead and made a judgment on my own without relying on the guidance of the Holy Spirit. I could see that the Course might be helpful for Stuart and others; however, I made the judgment that the Course would not be helpful for me. Relying on my own judgment, I was not really open to another New Age philosophy after having previously investigated many psychically channeled sources that fell short of my ideal of single-minded focusing on Christ. I had heard that the Course was dictated by Jesus Himself to a psychic channel; nevertheless, I had made the judgment that the idea of Jesus being the author of the Course was just too incredible to believe. I did not even consider the possibility that my judgments about the Course might be wrong, and so I did not bother to ask for guidance from the Holy Spirit.

In addition to my book writing, which continued for many years, I also worked on my creative game projects. After my self-publication of the *Starlight Game*, I promoted it as a "the positive self-image game" and as an educational game. The object of playing the game was to spell "STAR" by collecting four cards with the letters S, T, A, and R on them. But each of the four letters had to be a different color. A unique aspect of this game was that the cards were arranged in a pattern that was used as a makeshift "game board," which allowed players using game pieces to acquire needed cards. To obtain the S card, standing for *silence*, players listened to others tell them about their positive qualities. To receive the T card, representing *talents*, players acknowledged their own positive qualities. To get the A card, standing for *acceptance*, players chose areas in which they would like to increase self-acceptance. To obtain the R card, representing *response*, players responded to a question. I went to local schools and gave the game to teachers and school counselors for them to use with their students. A local newspaper woman took a photograph of my friend Bruce Shelton and me playing the game and wrote a story about the *Starlight Game*, which included the following testimonials:

DON AND BRUCE SHELTON PLAYING THE "STARLIGHT GAME"

Old Donation School for the Gifted was receptive. Jane McClellan said: "The game has a lot of value for increasing student self-awareness and as a listening activity. It can be a springboard for many discussions. It can encourage good feeling among members. We will continue to use it with students in our gifted program."

Glenda Anderson, proprietor of Montessori Institute of Tidewater, was equally receptive. "The kids love it. It's in line with our policy of tolerance and bringing up emotions they might otherwise be afraid to express. They do this in a non-threatening game-like setting."

I also worked on weekends as a recreational therapist at the Peninsula Psychiatric Hospital in the adolescent unit, and the patients enjoyed playing the game. When giving lectures to New Age groups, I described the game from a spiritual perspective. In the talk below I focused on the identity issue that had dominated by own spiritual life, relating this to the *Starlight Game*.

I would like to share with you three stories that have a common element. I'll begin with a true story told to me by a friend named Jim Deleo. He went to a bank in Washington, D.C., to take out a loan. He was directed to the woman who specialized in taking care of loans. As he approached this woman, he inquired, "Are you the loan arranger?"

She said, "Yes."

"Well, I'm Tonto!" Jim said. She frowned. He quickly added, "It's a joke! You know—the Lone Ranger and Tonto."

"I don't think that's very funny at all," she snapped. Jim just stood there looking kind of limp. That's the first story. The next story is a variation of a story about Mullah Nasrudin, who was a modern Sufi teacher. A man enters a bank, and he goes up to the teller, who says, "Could I see some identification?" The man looks around in his pockets and can't find his wallet. Finally he pulls out a mirror and holds it up. He points to his reflection saying, "That's me!"

This same man is in my third story. He walks into a store and goes up to the clerk. He asks the clerk, "Did you see me come in?"

The clerk responds, "Yeah, I saw you come in."

The man says, "How did you know it was me?"

Would anyone in the audience want to venture a guess as to what is the common element in all three of these stories?

Answering my question, a man in the audience proclaimed loudly, "None of the stories are funny!" Everyone laughed, including me, and then I continued with my lecture by first telling the man in the audience:

That's very good. Go to the head of the class. I know you meant my stories weren't very funny, but even in the stories the characters themselves didn't see anything funny happening. The loan specialist didn't laugh at Jim's joke because she took herself and her role too seriously. I am sure the bank teller and the store clerk didn't laugh either because they were similarly stuck in their roles.

Can anyone here tell us what is another common element in each of the three stories?

In response to my question, a woman in the audience spoke up simply saying, "Identity." I acknowledged her insight:

Yes, identity. Now, there's a lady with a sharp mind. Identity is indeed the basic question in each of these stories, and I think it is a question worth asking. If we want to make life a joyful harmony, we first have to answer the question, "Whose life?" In other words, "Who am I?" In order to answer that question, we usually give ourselves a role in life. The choices we make to define this role of who we are often do two things. First, our roles limit who we are. Second, they make us serious. After we place ourselves in roles, we can't find joy in our lives because we feel we are that role. The loan specialist, the bank teller, and the store clerk responded as they felt their roles required them to respond.

The great psychologist, C. G. Jung, once indicated that life can be divided into two parts. Part one is about finding one's place in the world, which is a building up of the ego and defining one's role. Part two is about answering the spiritual questions of life, which ironically involves the letting go of the ego and earthly roles. This second part of life is about answering the basic question of "Who am I?" in relation to God. I think the first thing we have to do to answer that question at a deep level is to admit that we don't know. As long as we think we know who we are based on our roles in the world, how can we find out who we really are?

A man lost a coin. After the sun had set, he went outside to where the streetlight was shining. He was standing on the curb looking for his coin. A stranger came up and asked, "What are you doing?"

The man answered, "I'm looking for my lost coin."

"Where did you see the coin last?" the stranger inquired.

"I had it in my house."

The stranger was perplexed and asked, "In that case why are you searching out here, instead of looking in your house?"

"Because the light is better out here."

This story illustrates that we sometimes look for the answer to who we are where the light seems to be brightest. It's often the light of our rational mind that seems to be the brightest, and so we ask our rational mind, "Who am I?" The only problem is that the rational mind will say, "I am who you are." However, we are in fact more than just the rational mind. If we fail to realize the limitations of the rational mind, our analytical mind may take us in one direction one day and in another direction another day until we are going around in circles. The rational mind is valuable, but we must pierce beyond our analytical thinking in order to answer the fundamental question, "Who am I?" We must find our identity in our experience of the divine. In particular I recommend finding our identity within our experience of God's love for us.

The remainder of this talk addressed the identity question in relation to the four aspects of the *Starlight Game*. At the conclusion of my lecture I summarized them:

> The four principles that help us answer the question, "Who am I?" are silence, talents, acceptance, and response. Through silence we can listen to God, which we call meditation. When we listen to God, we experience an increased awareness of what He says to us eternally, which is, "I love you." Thus we can answer the identity question by saying, "I am one whom God loves." Our talent is the strength God gives us by loving us, so we can say, "I am one whose greatest talent is to give love, just as God gives me love." Through acceptance we can love ourselves in a healthy non-egotistical way and say, "I am one who loves himself even when I make mistakes." In response to others we can say, "I am one who loves others even when they make mistakes."
>
> At the deepest level we will probably not discover who we are in this lifetime. This is because we are part of God, and for us to truly know ourselves, we must know God as He is, face to face. This is a mystery, which will be resolved only when we give up all our worldly roles and are transformed in divine union with God. However, until that time comes we need a working definition of who we are that will bring us closer to God and therefore closer to our true nature in Him. Since "God is Love," we can be satisfied with a perspective that allows love to be the answer to every question, even the question of our identity. For the time being we might choose to answer the question of "Who am I?" by simply saying, "I am a being of Love."

CHILDREN PLAYING THE "GOOD NEWS GAME"

In spite of the good response I received from those who actually played the *Starlight Game*, I was not successful in marketing it. I also self-published a Bible game called the *Good News Game*, which focused on love. I drew better illustrations for this new game, and it had a more professional look than the *Starlight Game*. Neither one brought much financial reward, but both were very satisfying creative projects.

I was always glad when I got guidance about my projects, even when it came belatedly, such as occurred when I was reproducing a picture of Jesus. I planned on using the picture as Christmas cards and as a gift to participants of the "Christ Centered Meditation" workshops that I had recently begun to teach. I was told that a local psychic had taken a photograph with his camera, but the resulting picture was unexpectedly a likeness of Jesus. I thought the picture was beautiful and had five hundred 5 by 8 cards printed up. The night after picking up the pictures from the printers, I had a dream in which the holy man Padre Pio took the picture of Jesus and ripped it up. From the dream I gathered that the photograph of Jesus was actually a hoax so I immediately dumped all five hundred pictures in the garbage. Hearing about the beautiful and expensive pictures being discarded, David, usually sparing with his compliments, told me,

1982

DRAWING OF JESUS

"I've seen how faithful you are to your guidance in the past and I think it's wonderful. You get very enthusiastic about doing something and go full steam ahead, but if you get the message from your inner guidance that you are off base, you turn on a dime one hundred and eighty degrees and correct yourself."

Although I always sought guidance in decision making, I did often fail to make wise choices and needed correction. But knowing the Holy Spirit was not keeping score of my failures, I learned to think of myself as being successful as long as I held fast to my pure intention to seek God and do His Will. My guidance seemed to only kick in with any strength and clarity as a correction after the fact, pointing out mistakes in my decision making. Nevertheless, my guidance actually did work precognitively in an incident involving another picture of Jesus. Even in this case I had planned to move in a particular direction, but my guidance helped me *before* making a mistake, rather than correcting a mistake already made.

After discarding the fabricated photographs of Jesus, I proceeded to print up another five hundred pictures, but this time I used one of my own pictures of Jesus. It was a drawing I had made years earlier. I was going to give this picture that I had framed to a friend as a gift. When I arrived at his house, I reached out to pick up the drawing and felt strongly guided to not give it to him. I couldn't fathom why I would get this guidance, but I had learned to not go against my intuition when it was as strong as this. Later I found out quite by accident through a third party that my friend had intentionally deceived me about a matter that would affect others and affect me negatively. I was able to forgive him by seeing that he had only caused harm to himself, which had manifested as a financial downfall. Considering his deception, I was glad the way things turned out in regard to the drawing because instead of it going as a gift to my friend, it became available to reproduce and give as a gift to many others. The photograph that was a hoax and the experience with the drawing were lessons reminding me that because it is easy to be deceived at the form level, I needed to always be open to guidance, as well as guidance correction. Consequently, I needed to follow the advice of Jesus to walk through the world being as "wise as serpents, and guileless as doves."[3]

---

1. M-10.3.1-7, p. 27 (p. 26) This is the first reference in this autobiography for the Manual. For those not familiar with references to *A Course in Miracles*, M-10 is the Manual's tenth section, 3 indicates the third paragraph of that section, and 1-7 represents the first through the seventh sentence in that paragraph. The quoted reference can be found on page 27 of the second and third editions of the Course and page 26 of the first edition.
2. M-10.4.1-10, p. 28 (pp. 26-27).
3. Matthew 10:16, CCD.

28

PREPARATIONS
FOR COMMUNITY

≈ • ≈

The conferences that David had been holding every year at the A.R.E. summer camp evolved into smaller meetings called "Family Gatherings." The idea was to build toward establishing the long held goal of a spiritual community. The gathering in 1984 was held at a wooded rural property owned by John, a Core Group member. John was a very openhearted person, who had once been a member of Rev. Moon's Unification Church.[1] His real life experiences in the Moon cult were almost a carbon copy of the plot of the 1981 movie *Ticket to Heaven*. John had been entrenched in the Moon community and had been so brainwashed that he was without a personal identity and had lost his freedom of choice. Fortunately his family became involved. They actually had to physically kidnap him, and then through personal intervention they deprogrammed him from the teachings of the Moon cult.[2]

Even though that experience of a cult community had been disastrous for John, he was enthusiastic about our efforts toward building a new community that would preserve freedom of choice. After we collectively discussed community possibilities, we had an inspiring ceremony in which we waded into a river on the property and had a symbolic baptism in our own Jordan River. A group of us stood in a circle up to our chests in water and horizontally lifted the body of the one being baptized, and we prayed. The person being baptized would say his or her name and make some verbal prayer, after which he or she would be lowered into the water, be submerged for a few seconds, and reemerge, symbolically spiritually cleansed.

Pamela, David, and most of the others were baptized ahead of me. I took my turn at this baptism very seriously and had prepared for a new start in my life by shaving my head. To let go of the past and start anew, I had dropped my last name and used the name "Don James," since James was my middle name. When I was lifted up by my brothers and sisters, I said, "I am Don James. Oh God! Into your hands, I commend my spirit."

The words came out spontaneously with great emotion, as if I was actually facing death, not a symbolic baptism. It was a "memory walk to now," a journey into the past for healing in the present moment. I was reenacting the death scene of the Pole Man, but with the difference being that in this reenactment I was being totally supported and loved rather than being cursed and cursing back. Perhaps even more to the point, I was also reenacting the death scene of the Spider Boy, since as a man he died by drowning himself, thinking himself to be unlovable. During each of these past lives I made the mistake of not commending my life or my death to God. This baptism experience provided a healing that cleansed the past and affirmed God's rightful place at the center of my life now.

The next person being baptized was James Gregory, who was a Core Group member and the survival specialist at the A.R.E conferences. When his body was raised up horizontally by the group, James proclaimed joyously, "Thank you, Lord, for your many blessings. I am *James Don*!" Our seriousness evaporated into laughter, because we knew James was jesting by reversing my "Don James" name, and we continued to laugh as we lowered James into the water for his baptism.

James had lived with us at the Light House during the second year we were there. Before he moved in, I didn't know him very well and was wary of him because he had unceremoniously knocked me down as the soldier in David's play. I was afraid he might be overbearing and challenging to live with, but I was pleasantly surprised to discover he was easy going and had a heart of gold. James was a good photographer, and he kindly volunteered to take pictures of me for resume purposes. He had always been self-reliant, working for a long time as handyman and jack of all trades. However, he told me he was learning how to rely entirely on God, allowing Him to lead the way in all things. We enjoyed each other's company for leisure time activities, and James would give me updates on his progress in making faith in God the center of his life. His consistent example was a reminder for me to continue with my own practice of asking for guidance from the Holy Spirit throughout the day—even in small matters such as what to eat for a particular meal. Eventually James was guided to return to his homeland of Canada to be with his ailing father, but our paths would cross again in the future.

We hoped our family gatherings would bring about the long-awaited goal of a community that David had wanted to establish, yet no community manifested. After the mini-community living situation at the Light House disbanded, David and Pamela found themselves on the move from one temporary living situation to another. Finally, David and Pamela moved to Celo, North Carolina to consider becoming part of an already established intentional community, where David's brother, Walter, lived with his wife.

David and Pamela concentrated attention on their children and their own relationship, which previously had taken a back seat to David's projects in Virginia Beach. He and Pamela made some friends; however, they did not feel connected to the spiritual ideals of the Celo community. They missed the enthusiasm and purposefulness of their time in Virginia Beach, and they wondered, as I did, what went wrong with their hopes and dreams of starting their own spiritual community.

In addition to David's inclinations toward community, Pamela had also received her own inspiration about it. In 1981, she had a vision in which she saw Jesus come to her and take her on a journey, which led to the top of a hill. From the top of the hill a beautiful city vibrant with life could be seen in the valley below. Jesus informed Pamela that it was her purpose to help this city become a reality by watching over it with her prayer and protection. At first she thought this vision related to ushering in a new life within herself and being in harmony with the coming new age in the world. But eventually she came to feel that she was being called to help usher in a new community of people dedicated to God and led by Jesus.

David and Pamela were already living in Celo when the final few Family Gatherings took place, and the last gathering was in the summer of 1985. Three of the participants were Robert Perry, his wife Wendy, and their friend Sarah. They lived in California in their own three-person community, and after the last gathering they expressed their interest in having David and Pamela join their spiritual community. However, David and Pamela received guidance about moving to Arizona. Pamela woke up one morning and heard the word "Arizona" being spoken. While looking at a globe one day, their son, Torey, put his finger on one spot and asked, "What country is this?" Pamela was surprised to see his finger resting on Arizona. Years earlier, when David had a dream about his future in spiritual communities, the dream included the words, "A desert will be very important to you." The growing guidance received by David and Pamela coincided with a psychic reading that had previously been given to Robert and Wendy. This reading said that their future community would be located "within Arizona to the north of the city of the bird coming from the fire (obviously meaning north of Phoenix)." Robert, Wendy, Sarah, David, and Pamela all discussed community building, sought further guidance, and eventually came to believe they were being drawn together to become one spiritual family. They decided they would communicate regularly until there was specific guidance about when to make the move to Arizona.

To renew my connection with David and Pamela, I visited Celo a few times and discussed with them the possibility of moving to Arizona with them as part of this community building. David and Pamela were unsure about exactly where in Arizona they were being guided to go. I was asking for guidance about my own role in this community, and subsequently I had a dream in which I was given the name "Sedona," a tourist city in Arizona known for its beautiful red rocks. Most of this city is surrounded by mountains and located in a valley similar to the valley Pamela saw in her vision. I felt guided to join in the effort of community building. Later Sarah received guidance for me that camping in Celo would be a very good preparation for my future adventures, which presumably would include camping out in Sedona. Following this advice, I went to a forest in Celo in order to camp out and fast for an extended period of time.

One memorable day I was sitting on a rock formation and meditating when I was prompted to open my eyes. About a yard away from me I saw a large gray snake with a triangle-shaped head, which meant it was poisonous. We gazed at each other, but neither of us moved. I closed my eyes and continued to meditate, although this quiet time was more of a prayer time calling upon God's blessing and protection. When I finished meditating, the snake was gone. I was not naturally an outdoors person. However, this time alone helped me become better prepared to meet the challenges of camping in Arizona, which would surely include more than its share of crawling creatures.

My final visit to Celo was in the fall of 1985. Since winter would be coming soon, there were no plans to move to Arizona right away. David and Pamela were attending the Quaker services on Sundays, and I joined them. We liked the Quaker idea of sitting in silent prayer, although we were not committed to that form of spirituality. Quaker church members are encouraged to be moved by the Spirit to speak out spontaneously during the service, and we were not inclined in that direction. I noticed that in the times of silence during the service, it was easy for me to see a glowing white light around the heads of church participants.

Subsequently, I came across a book by George Fox, the founder of Quakerism, called *The Journal of George Fox*. I was impressed by his direct experience of seeing the Light of Christ and his emphasis on encouraging others to find Christ within. He wrote:

> "Now the Lord God opened to me by His invisible power that every man was enlightened by the divine Light of Christ, and I saw it shine through all;...."[3] and also "...all things, visible and invisible, are seen, by the divine Light of Christ,...."[4]

I could certainly identify with George Fox in that he did not fit in with the commonly accepted understanding of what it meant to be a follower of Christ. He was rejected by traditional Christians, who relied on the outer forms of worship, but who could not understand his emphasis on being open to the Light of Christ within.

At the end of my visit with David and Pamela, as I was about to leave Celo, I was feeling guided to either return to Virginia Beach or go to a community named "Christ Land" in New Market, Virginia. Because of my curiosity and interest in Christ Land, I had written a letter to this group. I told them I had no money for rent, but I asked if I could come to live there anyway for a while to learn more about their group. While I was still in Celo, they wrote back and welcomed me to come. I was unsure about where to go and finally decided to return to Virginia Beach and forget about Christ Land, since it seemed out of the flow that was pointing to a future community in Arizona.

On my drive back to Virginia Beach, I decided to give myself a break, as well as rest my blue VW bug, "Chapel," so I stopped at a highway rest area in Hickory, North Carolina. I parked the car in the back, and didn't see any other cars there. I went to the men's bathroom, and as I was finishing up washing my hands, a stocky man with a ruddy complexion came in. He smiled and said, "Hi!" I didn't smile, and I didn't say anything back. Men just don't generally smile or say hello to other men in the men's room. Being suspicious, I just wanted to get out of there as quickly as possible and be on my way. I went outside and only got about five steps away from the door, when I heard the stranger call out, "Maybe you can help me!"

I turned around, and there he was with a very pleasant voice saying, "I want to get to Front Royal, Virginia. Do you know how to get there?"

In the middle of the stranger's chest there was a four-inch-long silver cross, which seemed a little ostentatious because of its size. Nevertheless, the sight of this Christian symbol quelled some of my suspicion. "I have a map in my car. If you wait right here, I will get it and bring it back here." I could have had him walk with me to my car, but I thought I might be inviting too much familiarity. I thought maybe he was gay, and I didn't want to give him the impression of interest in that direction.

"I will wait right here for you," he said and smiled broadly.

I went quickly to my car in the back parking area and returned with the map. I opened the map to right where Front Royal was and handed him the map to look at himself. I told him, "You are really lucky to ask me about this now because the next exit after Hickory is the one you need to take to go north to Front Royal. If you missed this exit, you would have gone far out of your way."

He said, "I see it right here on the map," and he put his fingertip right on the map to show me. I expected to see his finger touching Front Royal, but instead his finger was right on New Market. He smiled again very widely, as I looked at him with a bit of shock, because Christ Land is in New Market, and I felt he was literally pointing the way to go there.

I said, "You have your finger on New Market. Front Royal is over here," and I put my finger on the right spot, which was an inch and a half away from where he had his finger.

"Oh, you are right!" he said and smiled again.

Mentally I was thinking, "You did that on purpose, didn't you?" But I did not say the words out loud. Instead I asked, "Why are you going to Front Royal?"

"I'm going to visit my brother," he said in a happy tone.

"I hope you have a nice visit with him. Just take the next exit north, and it will take you where you are going. Bye and good luck."

"Thanks for your help. Bye," he said raising his hand to wave goodbye. I raised my hand to wave also, and I turned around to go back to my car, thinking this was certainly a strange encounter. After taking no more than ten steps, I decided to look back at the stranger. But he was gone! He didn't even have time to get in a car, let alone drive off, and there were no cars driving off anywhere. Then it occurred to me that he must have gone back into the men's room. As I walked to the men's room, I asked myself, 'Where is his car?' I had the only car at the rest stop. After looking in the men's room and not finding him there, I looked in the only other place he could possibly be—the ladies' rest room, yet he was not there either.

Was this smiling stranger, who was not handsome and somewhat on the pudgy side, really an angel? I thought he was an angel; however, there was a simple reality check that I could use as a test. Angels are messengers, and the message of this messenger was for me to go to New Market— presumably to go to Christ Land. The angel test would be to see what happened after arriving at Christ Land. Going to that place in particular must be very important, otherwise an angel would not have been sent to give me a course correction. On the other hand, if nothing significant happened on my visit to Christ Land, then it would probably be a mistake to think this stranger was actually an angel. So I set aside my firm plans to go to Virginia Beach. I took the next exit north, the way to Front Royal, but also the way to my new destination, New Market and Christ Land.

---

1. See cultnews.com.

2. See rickross.com, cultnews.com.

3. George Fox, *The Journal of George Fox*, edited by Rufus M. Jones (Richmond, IN: Friends United Press, 1976), Chapter 2.

4. Ibid.

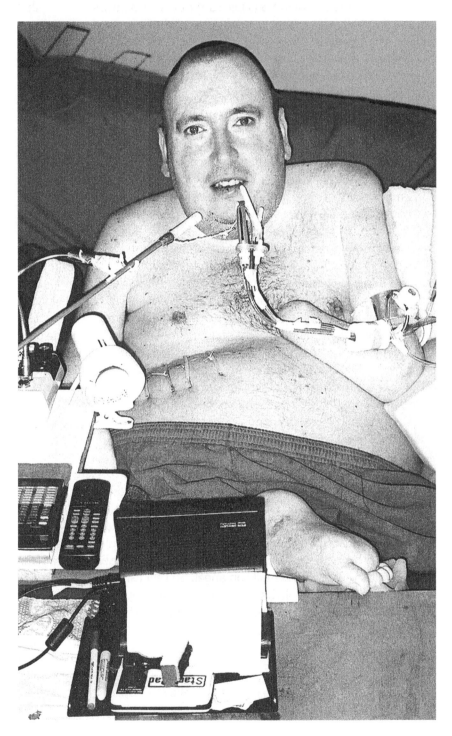

ALLAN GREENE

29

UNEXPECTED
MEETING

≈ ◦ ≈

Rain was coming down as I made my way to New Market and finally arrived at Christ Land and met Floyd and Kathryn, who owned this large tract of land dedicated to Christ. Kathryn explained, "We had hoped to start a spiritual community on our farm land. So far we have not been successful. Quite a few people have come, but have not stayed. There is only one person staying with us now." Kathryn did not tell me anything about this one person; she simply led me to his room to introduce me. She opened the door and said pleasantly, "Don, this is Allan." And there was Allan Greene, and I was certain beyond doubt that the stranger I had met in Hickory, North Carolina was indeed a divine messenger.

"Hello, Don. What brings you all the way out here?" Allan said with obvious happiness to see a familiar face.

"I must be here to see you, but I didn't plan it this way," I answered.

"You know each other?" Kathryn inquired.

"We go way back—way, way back," I said to her and then looked at Allan with a smile. "However, I think both of us are surprised to find each other here." It was obvious that Spirit had set up this meeting for us to have an extended period of time together for healing, but it also became a time for the nourishing of friendship. At Christ Land I had time to be alone and do my daily meditation and yoga practices, and I also helped with harvesting food from the farm. That left a lot of free time that I spent with Allan. As a quadriplegic, Allan could not feed himself or take care of eliminations, so I volunteered to assist with these duties, as well as miscellaneous needs as they arose.

Allan's appearance had changed because of gaining more weight, and he was beginning to remind me of the Jabba the Hutt character from the Star Wars movie, *The Empire Strikes Back*. But his mind was undiminished by his physical limitations, and it seemed even sharpened by his continued study of *A Course in Miracles*. He talked a lot about it, and I listened politely to honor his interest, although my heart was not in the Course.

Knowing my allegiance to Jesus, Allan explained, "The whole Course is supposed to have been dictated by Jesus to a 'scribe,' named Helen Schucman, with the encouragement of her colleague, Bill Thetford. Helen and Bill were psychologists who joined in a 'holy relationship' for the common purpose of finding a 'better way' to get along with each other. Because they had a common purpose, with common interests, the Holy Spirit entered the relationship to produce the Course as the means of finding a better way to live. If the message of the Course could be summarized in one word, it would be *forgiveness.*"

I offered, "Maybe you and I could have a holy relationship. We can join for the common purpose of forgiveness. I know you don't know what to make of my past life story, but even if it is not true, we can still join for the purpose of forgiving each other. What do you think?"

"That sounds terrific to me. I still don't know about past lives, because I have enough to handle in this life. However, the more forgiveness I have in my life, the better," Allan agreed. "But there is another thing you can do for me. You can remind me of my long lost relative, 'Uncle Jesus.'"

"Hey, you remember 'Uncle Jesus'!" I said, appreciating the fact that Allan thought that our conversation of a few years ago about Jesus was significant enough to remember.

"Sure, I remember Him. I wouldn't want to forget one of my relatives, especially one who is loving me even though I have paid no attention to Him. Actually my idea of God has always been impersonal. Nevertheless, I have felt there is something missing. I would like it to be more personal, so I am attracted to the idea of Jesus. When I see you, you remind me that a personal relationship with Jesus is still possible. So I like to hear you talk to me about Jesus."

"I'm always happy to talk about Jesus. What I would like to do is look through the Course and find the parts that discuss Him. Then I can talk to you about Jesus in the context of the Course." Allan liked that idea, and he let me borrow a paperback copy of the Course. The paperback contained about twelve hundred pages. I didn't want to read them all so I focused on the few sections that had "Jesus" in the heading.

The next day, I was glad to tell Allan, "I found my favorite section of the Course. The heading is 'Does Jesus have a special place in healing?' Here is what it says in reference to Jesus:

> There is now no limit on his power, because it is the Power of God. So has his name become the Name of God, for he no longer sees himself as separate from Him.
>
> What does this mean for you? It means that in remembering Jesus you are remembering God.[1]

"This section seems to be saying that the impersonal God that you have always been comfortable with can be reached by remembering the personal Name of Jesus. This next quote explains more about the Name of Jesus:

> The Name of Jesus Christ as such is but a symbol. But it stands for love that is not of this world. It is a symbol that is safely used as a replacement for the many names of all the gods to which you pray. It becomes the shining symbol of the Word of God, so close to what it stands for that the little space between the two is lost, the moment that the Name is called to mind. Remembering the Name of Jesus Christ is to give thanks for all the gifts that God has given you.[2]

"I don't know much about what the rest of the Course says, but at least this section convinces me that there is some good stuff in it, and I see why you like it. I like the way it confirms the value of calling upon the Name of Jesus for meditation," I concluded.

Allan said, "I have trouble focusing my mind for meditation. You are probably good at it. I know you have been practicing spiritual disciplines for many years. I was wondering about something. How did you get interested in following a spiritual path?"

"OK, let me give you a choice. I can tell you the bare-bones story of how I became interested directly in spiritual things, such as when I started to practice meditation for the first time. I can tell you a medium-length story that gives you a little insight into my background that led up to me spiritual interest. Or I can give you the long version, the whole story of my life experiences from my youth. The long version would include my college years and living in New York City. That way I could tell you about all the experiences that were not spiritual in themselves, but which indirectly led up to me later consciously seeking spiritual growth. So do you want the short, medium, or long version?" I asked.

"I am not going anywhere. I'd like to hear the whole story."

"Well, since you want the whole story, I'll start with my college years, but I want to caution you. My first life experience that would prepare me for choosing the spiritual path much later certainly wasn't anything uplifting—far from it. It was actually rather psychologically painful and depressing. But although it was a negative experience in itself, it had the positive effect of making me give up on seeking worldly goals. I suspect many people get their initial spiritual motivation from being disappointed in what the world has to offer. I had a bad experience with two of my college teachers. I had planned on being a teacher myself, but after my encounter with them, I gave up on that goal for my life. Another result was that I felt alienated from other people and from the world. My feelings of anger toward those teachers have never been fully resolved. I understand that my unresolved resentment is a form of blaming, and blaming others allows me to avoid taking responsibility for my own feelings. Blaming these teachers makes me think I am justified in being angry. Yet it doesn't really matter what these teachers did. I know now, at least intellectually, that my anger is not justified. My anger is always my own choice and my responsibility, but I haven't yet really reached a place of forgiveness. I know I will have to eventually learn how to forgive them for the sake of my own peace of mind. Also, I don't want to pretend that I am further along on the spiritual path than I really am. Given my ego shortcomings, when I talk about these teachers to you now, I won't be able to do it without that blaming mentality that I had back then and haven't fully released. Here's what I am getting at. Do you mind if I do a little subjective ranting, even though I know it's really not justified?"

Allan responded, "I don't mind. The Course says, 'If you point out the errors of your brother's ego you must be seeing through yours…'[3] so you won't be able to tell me about the errors of these teachers without your ego doing the speaking. But from what you said, I think you know your ego is involved and at least you will not be in denial about it. I feel my job is to not sit in judgment of your ego, or then I will be seeing you only through the eyes of *my* ego. Even while I listen to your ego speaking, my job is to look past your ego and see the holiness in you, because you are really the holy Son of God, just as I am. That seeing past the ego and instead seeing holiness is what forgiveness is. The Course tells me that my purpose in life is to let go of judgment and extend love and forgiveness to other people. Because of my physical limitations, I am not able to extend and serve other people as much as I would like. In fact, for the most part, people are serving me. So now I have an opportunity to serve you. The reason why I think this is a service is that it sounds like you just want to get some things off your chest, and my listening will help you do that. Am I right?"

I admitted, "Yes, I think you are right about me getting things off my chest. I haven't talked about this old stuff with anyone. It's been hiding in a dark corner in my mind, so talking about it will help take it out of hiding. Maybe if I let off a little steam, it will help me to move in the direction of the forgiveness that I would like to eventually reach." With Allan's openness to my unvarnished sharing, here is the story I told him:

I went to college for two years at a school which did not offer a major in art. To become an art teacher, I transferred to Southern Connecticut State College in New Haven. In the previous school I was in a fraternity with a lot of wild socialization; however, at the new school I didn't know anyone. I became very withdrawn and focused on my art work. This was similar to my childhood when I was left alone and I would spend my time drawing. In high school I was voted the class artist, in spite of the fact that I never actually did any painting other than some watercolors. In college I was excited about the prospect of learning how to paint in acrylics and in oils. I lived at home and commuted, so I would set up still life compositions and paint them. This was the first time I learned how to really focus my mind, and I think it prepared me for learning how to meditate later in my life. In a way, my painting was a form of inward seeking, and in that sense it was actually a form of meditation itself, although that thought didn't occur to me at the time. Just as in meditation, time would literally stand still, and before I knew it, a few hours had passed. I found that I liked focusing my mind more intently than ever before.

I immediately developed a style that was dark and realistic, similar to the way Rembrandt's paintings look.[4] The second painting that I ever made, *Brown and Red Still Life*, is a good example of my dark painting style. My first painting teacher said that he liked my style, but he encouraged me to experiment beyond what I could already do, in order to improve my artistic skills. I took his advice and learned how to paint in many different styles.

BROWN AND RED STILL LIFE

For example, *Blue and Green Still Life* demonstrates a lighter painting with free-flowing brush strokes. My second-semester painting course was in watercolors exclusively, and the teacher, Mr. Todd, also told the class to experiment instead of trying to create a unique style. Taking this to heart, I made a point of making each painting distinctly different. I tried my hand at doing landscapes inspired by Turner, as well as still lifes inspired by Cézanne. I did wash watercolors and dry brush watercolors and even went outdoors to do watercolors from nature like the Impressionists. In addition, I liked to do seascapes, which reminded me of the happiest times of my childhood—summers spent at our cottage at the beach.

I had been warned by classmates that Mr. Todd played favorites. If I sucked up to him, that would guarantee a good grade; if I did not, it would be much harder to get a good grade from him. I knew I didn't want to suck up to him, but I didn't want to antagonize him, either. I had heard that in the previous year a student in conflict with Mr. Todd had been thrown out of the art program. One student in my watercolor class had the same style in the beginning of the course as at the end, which was the technique of using ink drawings over watercolors. He constantly sucked up to Mr. Todd, so I knew he would get an A even though he did none of the experimenting with different styles that we were told to do.

At the beginning of the course Mr. Todd described one of my landscape watercolors as "subtle, lovely, and lyrical," with a "wonderful dreamlike quality." Mr. Todd didn't know me at the beginning of the year, so he made this initial evaluation based on the quality of the picture itself as a work of art. That watercolor showed a country path. Consequently, I privately titled it *The Road Less Traveled*, because I considered myself to be somewhat of a maverick. At the time, I was reading about the beatniks living in New York and the hippies gathering in Haight-Ashbury in 1966 and admired their nonconformity. I had no intention of following their example by going to the extreme of dropping out of normal society, but I was well aware that even mild forms of nonconformity were frowned upon in conservative Connecticut. Consequently, with the idea of restraining my maverick tendencies, my strategy in relation to Mr. Todd was to have as little contact as possible with him during his class in order to not draw attention to myself and thus prevent any potential conflict with him.

In addition to limiting my verbal contact, I decided to also limit visual interaction by wearing sunglasses to avoid eye contact, yet that was a miscalculation on my part. Wearing sunglasses indoors seemed innocuous enough to me, but in this regard I seriously underestimated Mr. Todd's degree of conservatism. He didn't verbalize any objection to me, but I recognized right away that the sunglasses were enough to sour his attitude toward me, although out of stubbornness on my part I continued to wear

BLUE AND GREEN STILL LIFE

THE ROAD LESS TRAVELED

them anyway. His change in attitude toward me was confirmed by the fact that after this point my watercolors no longer had any appeal to him whatsoever. For a final review at the end of the course, I submitted all of my work for Mr. Todd's assessment. He looked at *The Road Less Traveled* again, and in this second examination of the same picture he described the watercolor as "blurry and undefined," totally contradicting his initial evaluation. Then he went on to summarize his criticism of all of my paintings by saying that I did not have a "style."

For the first time I offered a verbal objection to him, "You told us to experiment and not settle on one style."

Mr. Todd explained, "I told you that at the beginning of the course. By the end of the course, I expected you to have a style." I looked at him incredulously and incensed, but for the time being held back the temptation to confront him further by asking why he never told us he expected us to have a style at the end of the course.

My lack of respect for Mr. Todd finally boiled over on the last day of the class in a final written test. On the essay part of the test, I wrote that I felt he was a "phony" who judged art work based on whether he liked the student or not at a personality level. Before he read my test statement, he asked to talk to me privately, and for the first time I directly confronted him. But based on his reasonable responses to me in the conversation, I decided that I had unfairly judged him, and I told him so. I shook his hand and felt we had resolved our differences. However, it did not occur to me that he hadn't yet read my written test. I got a phone call at home a few days later: "I read your test and that you called me a 'phony.' I know I told the class that everyone would get an A, B, or C, but I am going to make an exception in your case and give you a D."

Although I was upset, I spoke surprisingly calmly, "I wrote that you were a 'phony' *before* we had our conversation in which I told you I had misjudged you. I would not have written that word *after* our conversation. Unfortunately, by your decision now, you are showing why I said you were a phony in the first place. Instead of judging me by my pictures, you are judging me by my personality." I waited for him to respond. However, there was only silence. I waited for him to hang up, but he did not. Finally I said with an even tone of voice, "Why are you waiting and not hanging up? If you are waiting for me to get angry or curse you, that will not happen. I would not give you that satisfaction." Then he hung up. I'm sure that if I had sworn at him, he would have used that as an excuse to give me an F instead of a D.

In high school I never got lower than a B for a final grade and did very well at the previous college. However, this incident turned me against caring at all about what grades I got. After this point my grades in credit courses suffered because I did only the bare minimum of studying needed to get a passing grade. I decided to really take a 'road less traveled' by putting the full force of all my energy into my own personal painting, even though I no longer had any painting classes for credit. After a summer of transitioning from realistic art to abstract art, I came back to college in the fall and informally showed all my recent art work to my former acrylic painting teacher. He was very impressed with the work that I was doing on my own, but then asked, "Did you make someone in the art department angry at you?"

"I had a run-in with Mr. Todd," I answered. "How did you hear about that?"

He looked at me, pausing momentarily to consider what he should say. He cautioned me, "You better watch your back." I gathered he did not want to say anything more, yet at least he was kind enough to give me a warning.

Suddenly I was called into the administration office. I was told that they had examined my former courses at Central Connecticut and would not accept the transfer of any of my credits from art courses taken there. Before I had transferred to Southern Connecticut, however, I had made sure to obtain the administration's approval of all my transfer credits. Now no one would tell me why they made this reexamination, but it seemed to me to have Mr. Todd's fingerprints all over it. I complained and very fortunately found a signed document that proved that the administration had already given me written approval for all of my transfer credits, and then the administration backed off. If I had not been able to find that document, I would have been required to stay in college for a full additional year in order to graduate.

Mr. Brand, a friend of Mr. Todd, was my teacher for teacher training, and right away he made a point of singling me out for criticism. I had tried to avoid being outspoken in Mr. Todd's class, but in this new class I could not avoid speaking up because of Mr. Brand's challenging remarks directed toward me. For example, on one assignment I make a crayon drawing on the rough side of a masonite board. Mr. Brand critically drew the attention of the whole class to the fact that my signature was very large. He did not like it when I told him that the crayon media and rough texture would make a small signature illegible. Another time, Mr. Brand decided I had to bring in a cardboard box the size of a refrigerator for a group mural project, without giving anyone else an assignment. I couldn't find such a box, so I brought in a wooden door instead, and he ridiculed my failed assignment, even though the door worked well for the group mural. Later, I had a clay project that was not quite dry, so I placed it on the ledge of an open window to dry overnight. It rained that night, and the project got soaked, so

I had to bring the project in even though it was totally wet. Mr. Brand didn't believe my story about the open window and the rain, and he spoke about my project sarcastically and disgustedly to the whole class.

One time he asked me a challenging question, and I said, "I would rather be silent and thought a fool, than to speak up and remove all doubt." The class laughed at my quote of Abraham Lincoln. Nevertheless, Mr. Brand looked angry at my response, especially because of the laughter. Mr. Brand's class had two one-hour sessions and a fifteen-minute break in between. During one of these breaks, I met Susan, a free-spirited student I knew and liked. She suggested we take a ride, so I did not return for the second one-hour session. If anyone else had come to the first hour and skipped the second hour of Mr. Brand's class, he might not have noticed the absence. But because I sat right in the center of the room in his line of sight and because of his tendency to single me out, I was sure at the time he would notice I was missing from his class. I knew he would be upset about it, but I threw caution to the wind, figuring he would just verbally embarrass me in front of the class the next time I saw him. But that verbal reprimand in class never came.

Mr. Brand assigned me to go on student teacher training in Westbrook, Connecticut and another student to do teacher training in West Hartford. I went to the other student, and we agreed to switch our assignments. During the class I told Mr. Brand about the switch and explained that by switching, we each had much shorter trips. I would save an extra thirty minutes, and the other student would save forty-five minutes. Mr. Brand said, "Your trip to Westbrook is not one hour and fifteen minutes. It's only forty-five minutes."

I contradicted him, "My parents have a summer cottage in Westbrook, so when I said that the trip is an hour and fifteen minutes, I was basing it on my own personal experience." He was obviously very upset because I had made the switch, and in front of the class I was able to reasonably refute every objection that he made.

A few days later I was summoned to a meeting with the head of the art department and a group of art instructors. The only teacher present with whom I had a class at that time was Mr. Brand, who spoke up first, saying that I had cut his class and when I did show up I was uncooperative. But then surprisingly he said, "We were going to throw you out of the art department. However, I looked at your records at your previous college and your grades were exceptional. Why aren't you doing as well here with your attitude and your grades?"

I felt I was being railroaded, and I knew his friend, Mr. Todd, had a hidden hand in this. I was actually very quiet and reserved in most of my classes. In Mr. Brand's class I was much more outspoken because he was repeatedly baiting me with critical remarks, which elicited responses from me. Mr. Brand had probably told the other instructors in this meeting that I was a loudmouth who was always drawing attention to himself. He certainly did not tell them he was the one pointing out my shortcomings to the class and inviting and often requiring a response from me. However, in this unfair situation, if I complained about Mr. Brand's baiting of me, it would be the end of my hope to be an art teacher. I started crying and said, "I have had a hard time adjusting to a new school. But the real problem is I have fallen in love with a girl. The one time I skipped out on your class, it was because she asked me to go with her. I couldn't turn her down. But she doesn't feel the same way about me as I do about her, so I've been depressed about that." I did like Susan, but I wasn't in love with her. Although my story was a lie, it sounded sincere and seemed to satisfy them.

Mr. Brand said, "We are going to give you a chance to go out on student teacher training, but if you make one mistake, we will yank me out of the program."

For elementary school teacher training in West Hartford my master teacher was Mrs. Marlin, and she was absolutely a lifesaver for me. After successfully completing my training, she told me, "I want you to know I gave you a grade of A, but Mr. Brand overruled my grade and gave you a B, and he was not supposed to do that."

I reassured her, "That's all right. I don't care that he lowered the grade."

Mrs. Marlin continued, "Mr. Brand also went around to all three of the elementary schools where we teach art and told each one that you were argumentative and had a very bad attitude. He said he expected you to fail and told them to let him know as soon as you make the slightest misstep. The people at all three schools told me that they did not know what he could have been thinking because you have been a terrific art teacher."

After I made it through the student teacher training, there was a greater challenge awaiting me. In order to graduate I needed to take a meaningless class called "Art in the Home," and the only one who taught this course was Mr. Todd. Beforehand, I wondered if I would have the restraint to hold back my negative feelings toward him. I still thought of him as a phony, but if I sucked up to him in order to hide my anger, I would become a phony myself. When I finally took the class, I was successful in avoiding the two extremes of being openly hostile and being inappropriately ingratiating.

The most difficult challenge for me was listening to Mr. Todd when he found excuses to talk about Yale University, which he had attended as an art student. He was particularly enamored with the architectural beauty of the Art and Architecture Building. As he told us, "The architectural challenge was to come up with a design that would fit into the historical context of the traditional Yale landscape and at the same time come up with a design that was thoroughly modern. This building was a marvelous solution to problem of blending the old and the new." An isolated and informative comment such as this one certainly wasn't the problem. It was Mr. Todd's tendency to continually return to his praise of Yale.

In the future Southern Connecticut State College would become a university, but it was thought of then as only a mediocre teacher's college, at the lowest rung of higher education. At those times when Mr. Todd began talking about Yale, I felt he was gloating by reminding us lowly students that he attended an elite university. On the last day of the class I brought in my final project, a miniature model house with the unusual design of a three pointed star. Mr. Todd said, "I like your project very much. Can I have it as a model to show future classes?"

I immediately realized Mr. Todd had intentionally and manipulatively placed me in a crisis of decision. On the one hand, if I gave him the model house, he would put me in the position that I hated of sucking up to him, which is what he wanted me to do. In turn he would probably give me an A, not for my work, but for sucking up to him. On the other hand, I needed a good reason to explain why I could not give him the model. This was necessary because I did not want to be outwardly rude to him, which would reveal the true hidden contempt I still had for him. I knew without a doubt that he was not telling the truth when he said he wanted the model, and that his request was actually designed to make me either suck up or reveal my hidden hostility. I decided to meet his deception with a deception of my own. Thinking quickly, I said very pleasantly, "I would really like to give this model to you. However, my mother told me she loves this model, and I already promised it to her."

Mr. Todd was stunned by my response and did not utter a word. His face showed obvious disappointment, not because he wouldn't get the model, but because I had neither sucked up nor revealed my hostility. Of course, he knew that I was lying; nevertheless, he was powerless to do anything about it. I added, "It's too bad that I can't give this to you; however, I do appreciate your high opinion of my work." I smiled when I said this, yet it was a phony smile. Although I had avoided sucking up, I had become somewhat of a phony in the sense of hiding my real feelings and of lying to him in response to his lying to me.

In the hallway outside the classroom there was a large metal trash barrel, and I dumped the model there and walked off. Mr. Todd predictably gave me a B because I had not sucked up. Although I did not get the A that I deserved, I was able to maintain what little was left of my self-respect. Unfortunately I was so burned out by my experiences with him and with Mr. Brand that I felt dead inside. Although I had obtained a teaching degree, my heart was closed to pursuing a career as a teacher.

After telling my story, I asked Allan, "I am feeling a little uncomfortable rambling on, giving such an extensive monologue. I know I asked you if you wanted the long version. But I am giving so much detail that I want to make sure you are not losing interest. I need to get an update from you. Do you still want the long version, which I have made into a marathon monologue?"

Allan said, "As far as I am concerned there is no problem with you just saying whatever you want about your life. I enjoy listening. Eventually you'll get around to talking more directly about the spiritual things that happened to you. But telling me more of your life story will help me to get to know you better as a person. I don't have an extensive social life and so just having someone to spend time with is great. I want to tell you something right now so you won't have to ask me again. Whenever you want to talk about your past—any part of your past, whether it relates to spiritual things or not—go right ahead without any hesitation and talk as long as you want. I will be able to see you are in a 'monologue mode' and I will automatically and gladly shift into a 'listening mode.' So in the future you don't have to ask again if it is all right for you to ramble on.

"OK, and I'll do my best to keep it interesting. I'll tell you what—I'll give you my permission to fall asleep if I am not successful."

"Fair enough," Allan said.

"Then I guess we have a deal. Thanks for listening." I felt the service of listening that Allan was offering and would perform for me on many occasions in the future was a result of my good karma. It was the karma of my recreational therapy practice of serving my patients in the hospital with conversational therapy, in which I was in what Allan called his "listening mode."

Allan asked, "Do you mind if I tell you what the Course calls your relationships with Mr. Todd and Mr. Brand?"[5]

"Believe it or not, I actually can listen as well as talk, so go right ahead," I said.

"They are called *special hate relationships*. These relationships are like scapegoats for our own problems. In ancient times on the holy Day of Atonement (Yom Kippur), the priest would lay his hands on the goat and confess all the faults of the children of Israel. Then the goat would be driven away into the desert, and symbolically the goat would carry away the sins and guilt of the people. This is where we get the word 'scapegoat.' When we have a special hate relationship, we find someone we dislike, and we deny our own guilt and problems by projecting them onto this other person. This other person then becomes our scapegoat. This projection is made possible by thinking that we are the victim of the other person, so it is only natural to feel justified in hating that person. Of course, denial and projection of guilt works both ways. You were using both Mr. Todd and Mr. Brand as scapegoats for your problems and thinking of yourself as a victim of them. In turn they were using you as their scapegoat for their problems, all the while thinking of themselves as victims of you. The special hate relationship continues as long as both sides continue to hate. The way out of this relationship is forgiveness. Speaking of forgiveness, I hope you will forgive me if I am getting too psychological for you."

I said, "That's all right. Actually I like it. Can you tell me more about the special hate relationship?"

"Sure. Each partner is trying to obtain specialness. Specialness is the ego's substitute for love. It is a form of self-worth based not on equality, as love is, but on being better than someone else. The most common special relationship is the *special love relationship*. In this relationship, both partners feel deficient inside. To fill that void inside themselves they have a transaction or bargain in which they each acquire specialness from the other. Unlike the outwardly friendly and willing exchange of the special love relationship, the transaction in the special hate relationship takes on the antagonistic nature of stealing. This theft is justified by each partner thinking the other has attacked first and caused injury requiring retribution.

"For example, in your special hate relationship with Mr. Todd, you felt when he talked about Yale or gave you a lower grade than you deserved, he had stolen your specialness and thus had taken your self-worth from you. Consequently, your hate was saying to him, 'You are guilty of stealing my specialness and so I am perfectly justified in stealing it back from you.'[6] So what you were doing was looking down on him by projecting guilt onto him, so he gets your guilt. Denial allows you to not see the guilt within yourself, and projection allows you to see guilt only in him. At the same time that your guilt is going from you to him, you are taking back from him the specialness that he took from you. He in turn was doing the same process in his mind of projecting guilt, looking down on you, and thus acquiring specialness from you."

Listening to this explanation of my relationship with Mr. Todd, I nodded affirmatively and smiled broadly.

Allan continued, "Unfortunately the acquiring of specialness based on being better then someone else provides only a false sense of self-worth that is unsatisfying compared with true self-worth based on love. Also, the problem with projecting guilt in order to give it to someone else is that you end up actually *keeping* the guilt that you thought you sent to the other person. Consequently, projecting guilt makes you feel *more* guilty, not less. That's why special hate relationships are so unfulfilling and painful.

"A lot of people only want to read about light and love in the Course, but get turned off by reading about the dynamics of the ego. Yet we can't get to the love without first 'removing the blocks to the awareness of love's presence.'[7] The ego is the source of the blocks to love because it is an unloving idea that says each of us is a separate self, limited and alone. There is no use fighting against the ego because it's part of our minds. However, because it is only a false idea about ourselves in our minds, we can simply change our minds and accept who we really are. The easiest way to do that is to look past the ego masks in our brothers and sisters and see Christ in them. That's what forgiveness is. If we can forgive others by looking past their ego masks, we can learn to let go of our own ego masks and accept our true nature in Christ."

I said, "I would like to be able to see past the ego masks of the difficult people I have encountered in my life, but I'm just not there yet. At least I can see Christ in our mutual friend Rose, and she can see Christ in me, so that's a start. Also you and I can see Christ in each other in our holy relationship. You look a little tired. Is this a good time to stop?"

"Yes, but before we wind up, I want to ask you something. At one point when I was talking about special hate relationships earlier, you seemed to light up, and a big smile crossed your face. What was that all about?"

I replied, "I was smiling because you're more right about my psychology than you know. Tomorrow I'll tell you the rest of the Mr. Todd story, and then you'll understand what I mean. Thanks for your insights about my story and my psychology. I like to figure out what is happening in my subconscious mind beyond my everyday awareness. I'll think about what you said and pray about it as well." I accepted Allan's description of my relationships with Mr. Todd and Mr. Brand as examples of special hate relationships, and I also put my former relationship with Dolly in that same category. In my prayer life I focused on forgiving these people so I could let go of the past and find peace. Although Allan's insights helped my intellectual understanding, my habitual reaction patterns were so ingrained that I found that in a practical sense my ego was still very much in charge in my future relationships.

---

1. M-23.2:6-7, 3:2, p. 58 (p. 55).
2. M-23.4:1-5, p. 58 (p. 55).
3. T-9.III.3:1, p. 166 (p. 155).
4. Here I am referring to how Rembrandt paintings look *now*. Rembrandt used linseed oil which darkens with age and exposure to ultraviolet light so his paintings are darker today than when they were painted.
5. "Mr. Todd" and "Mr. Brand" are pseudonyms.
6. Not an exact quote. The ideas expressed in this paragraph are best understood by reading all of the section entitled "The Laws of Chaos" and the following: T-23.II.11:4-9, 12:1-12, 13:1-13, pp. 491-492 (p. 457).
7. T-In.1:7, p. 1 (p. 1).

30

AFTER COLLEGE

~ • ~

After talking to Allan about Mr. Todd and Mr. Brand, I realized that these past figures in my life were still influencing me negatively. Clearly I had not resolved the intense emotions that they had generated in me. It occurred to me that in my college experience I was reenacting my Pole Man lifetime. First there was risking my life by hanging from the balcony at Central Connecticut, just as the Pole Man had hung off a pole holding on to his life. Then with the two teachers at Southern Connecticut there was the feeling of being unfairly persecuted by others who exerted control over me. I felt Allan had been a victimizer in the Pole Man's life, and I had to forgive him in this lifetime, just as I had to forgive Mr. Todd and Mr. Brand. I didn't feel the need to explain all this to Allan, since I didn't want him to think I was blaming him. I felt that Allan, by his simple gift of listening to my story, was ironically and appropriately helping me to forgive and find healing. In addition, I felt grateful for Allan sharing the psychology of special hate relationships because he was giving me insights into my former past life hate directed toward him, which would help me let go of that ancient hate. It became clear to me that both learning how to forgive and improving my psychological understanding of my subconscious mind would eventually help me to put together the pieces of my shadow puzzle.

Continuing my talk with Allan on the next day, I said:

Yesterday I told you I became disillusioned with teaching, and then I generalized this into being disappointed with life. Even before my bad experience in the last two years of college at Southern Connecticut, I had a growing sense about the meaninglessness of life. I was in a fraternity my first two years at Central Connecticut. I had a lot of friends to keep me occupied, but I still felt a deep sense of aloneness, adding to my feelings of meaninglessness. Back then I even allowed myself to hang over a balcony in the college theater, risking my life to give myself the message that there was something wrong with my life that made it seem senseless to me.

In my experience at Southern Connecticut, I was too immature to realize how I had acted inappropriately. I think you were right about me forming special hate relationships with my teachers by making them scapegoats for my problems. I had problems with both Mr. Todd and Mr. Brand because they were each arrogant. However, I was equally arrogant, making conflict inevitable. For my graduation in 1967 in New Haven, I brought a suitcase with me, and after the ceremony I informed my parents I was moving out of their house right then. I did not know how ungrateful and rude it was to say goodbye and leave them there. It did not even occur to me at the time that my parents had planned a celebration back at our home in Meriden, which I only found out about much later.

In New Haven I moved in with a girl friend, Gail, who had a six-year-old daughter. I had almost all my paintings with me, except for the ones I had given away. But the only painting I did at that time was covering Gail's VW beetle with bright red, yellow, blue, and orange paint. After having my first experience of smoking pot, I remember being in a mellowed out altered state lying down on the linoleum floor of the kitchen with my shirt off. Finally when I went to get up, the skin of my back rising up from the floor created a suction effect and produced the sound of passing gas. Then I continued making these passing gas sounds thinking it was hysterical. I found out that pot made me listless affecting my will and specifically took away my motivation to paint.

In order to graduate I had to conform and knuckle under to Mr. Brand and Mr. Todd, when what I really wanted to do was tell them off. Not wanting and not able to take full responsibility for my own shortcomings, I blamed them for imposing their will on me. I felt emasculated by the whole process of having to appear compliant and agreeable, when I really wanted to rebel. I thought maybe I could put the past behind me in this new living situation, but I was still steaming inside because I felt they had stolen my self-respect and life seemed meaningless to me. I drew a self-portrait that was not intended to be a realistic rendition, but rather to express the feelings of depression and alienation that I was experiencing at that time.

I decided I needed to do something to at least symbolically take back what I felt had been stolen from me. I happened to be living in a house right near the Yale Art and Architecture Building where Mr. Todd had studied. I remembered his glowing commentary about Yale and about this building in particular, which we registered as an elitist slap in the face to the students at our lowly state teacher's college. One day, I walked over and wandered around in the building. It's considered even today by many experts to be an example of great architecture, but from the inside, seeing cement everywhere, I was struck by its cold drabness.

At this point I didn't know quite what I would do, although I was intent on hatching some sort of mischief, which I hoped would present itself. I happened upon an area where student paintings were stored. I expected to see some students, yet there was no one around, perhaps because it was summertime. I also anticipated seeing outstanding paintings by promising young artists—after all it is a well-known fact that Yale attracts the best and the brightest. However, I was surprised when I pulled out a painting that was about five feet by seven feet. Imagine a large canvas filled with muted pastel-colored acrylic paint applied by a house painter's roller, with colors separated by using masking tape. That is what this canvas looked like—a particularly bland and unremarkable attempt at a work of art, devoid of any redeeming quality. Its only prominent feature was its sheer size, which merely proclaimed its shortcomings all the louder.

In the mediocrity of this canvas I saw the opportunity stretched out before me to accomplish my mission of mischief symbolically directed toward Mr. Todd. The thought crossed my mind that I could take a large canvas like this one and cut it up to make at least ten authentic works of art. It was a short leap from that thought to entertaining the idea of becoming a Robin Hood of art—stealing from the elite rich and giving to the poor common man—myself, of course. I laid down the canvas and, finding a nearby tool, unstapled the canvas from its frame. Then I did likewise with five or six other similar canvases by the same art student. Next I rolled up all the canvases like one would roll up a carpet, and I walked out of the building with enough canvas material to last me a very long time. In spite of the fact that Mr. Todd would never know about my symbolic act of protest, I imagined I was walking away from his beloved university with a measure of my lost self-respect stolen back.

Now you can see why I was smiling yesterday when you were talking about how partners in special hate relationships feel justified in stealing back the specialness and self-worth that they thought had been stolen from them. Of course, Allan, at that time you didn't know I had stolen these paintings as a way of getting back at Mr. Todd. Consequently, I was amazed at the remarkable accuracy of your insights into my warped psychology. In fact, I was so impressed that it made me think there is more depth in the Course than I had first thought.

At the time of my theft, I felt justified; not only because of Mr. Todd, but because of the pathetic quality of the art work I had taken. I did feel a passing pang of guilt, yet quickly dismissed it by reminding myself that I would never have taken these paintings if there was any merit in them as works of art. But looking back on my theft now, I feel embarrassed. Nothing justifies stealing. I know that an artist's work—even an inept artist's work—is like his children and to take a person's creative work is to steal something that is sacred to him. Even after all these years I regret this terrible mistake. Yet at the time I did not care about sacredness or spiritual ideals. I was glad I had successfully eluded the punishment of law enforcement and escaped the embarrassment of being caught in my theft. But there was a higher law at work that I had not accounted for—the karmic law of cause and effect.

After living with Gail for a month, she and I took a one-day trip out of town to visit a relative of hers. We came back the next night, and the house had been destroyed by fire. We walked inside and went to the second floor of the house where we had lived. Standing in the bedroom, all I could see was black burnt wood, and it was hard to believe. Most startling of all was the view. I looked up and saw the blackness of the sky and the stars shining, because the roof had been burnt away. It was like a surreal painting come to life. I was struck by the temporary nature of all that had seemed so solid and permanent a short time before. This experience confirmed my worst fears about the meaninglessness of life. Almost all my paintings were in the house and were destroyed, which heightened my sense of meaninglessness. Most sorely missed were my best paintings, to which I was very attached. Trying to make some sense out of this senselessness, I concluded that the universe was telling me that because I took someone else's paintings away, it was necessary for my paintings to be taken away from me.

Gail's former husband, who had just gotten out of a mental hospital, showed up and confronted us, saying, "You think I did this, don't you?" We denied his accusation, but it had crossed our minds. Later I heard that Gail had been doing ironing and had left the iron on when we left for our trip. The fire department determined that the iron was the cause of the fire. I returned to my parents' house, not mentioning anything about the fire.

I considered going to live in New York along with a friend, Hal. But I decided to apply for a local job as a social worker. Without studying in advance, I got a score of 85 on the state employment test for the social worker position and was hired for the job. I was on a date with a friend and said to her, "My friend Hal and I were going to go off to New York to live. I was going to be an artist, but I decided to take the social worker job."

She said, "I know why you aren't going to New York. You are afraid!"

It was like she shot an arrow in my heart. I knew for a fact that she was right. One of the abstract paintings lost in the fire was a picture of a white figure leaping from one world to a larger world. In the belly of the figure there was a gaping open mouth and large red tongue screaming in fear. I wondered if this was the symbol of my fear of going out into the world. If I stayed in a small town in Connecticut, I might end up living a life of conservative conformity—a life of jumping through hoops to meet the expectations of other people. I decided to change my plans and give the big city of New York a chance and not let a little fear stand in my way.

Hal and I made our way to a hotel there, and Hal's radio was stolen out of our room because we didn't give a tip when we arrived. We later found an apartment at 68 West 10th Street, between 5th and 6th Avenue in

Greenwich Village. I naively thought I could get rid of the roaches in our apartment and made my best effort at exterminating them. Our short, overweight landlady raged at me for being sloppy, because my neighbors complained that roaches were coming into their apartments from ours. I told her it was happening because I was the only one trying to kill them, and the roaches were seeking less hostile tenants. Normally, you don't see roaches unless you are trying to get rid of them, but it was a losing battle.

A few years younger than me, Hal had bright red hair, fair skin, and a studious appearance. He always seemed to think things out methodically, and he appropriately got a job as a trainee in the new field of computer programming. He wanted to get ahead in the world, which I did not. I got a job as a guard at the Museum of Modern Art. Each day I was assigned to a different part of the museum. I was fascinated by a temporary special exhibition of the ancient Egyptian treasures of King Tut (Tutankhamun).

Once I was working in a room with a painting titled *Hide-and-Seek*. This large painting by Pavel Tchelitchew has a gigantic tree in the center and hidden in the tree trunk is an unmistakable image of an erect penis. Most visitors passed by the picture without noticing anything unusual. One pretty young lady came very close to the picture and stared for a long time right at the tree trunk. She looked over at me, perhaps wondering if I knew what she had discovered. I smiled knowingly. She smiled back. Then she walked over to me and batting her eyelashes asked, "Do you have the time?"

"I'll have time after work," I wanted to say happily with a wink, because her expression showed she was obviously flirting. Instead I looked at my watch and told her the time. Recently I had been on a New York bus and had tried to strike up a conversation with a beautiful woman who looked like a model. She told me loudly and coldly, "Shut up!" That kind of experience made me a little gun shy. Even after I told the time to the young lady in the museum, she paused as if waiting for me to speak up. I let her walk away without saying anything. I was following one of the guard rules, which was to avoid engaging in conversations with visitors. But I spent the rest of the day kicking myself, wishing I had broken the rules in this case.

As a museum guard, I was expected to follow and enforce the rules. Museum visitors were often tempted to touch the displays. One of my job responsibilities was to make sure that no touching occurred. One day when I was working in the architecture and design section, I was tempted myself to not only touch a work of art, but to *sit* on it. The enticing display was the life-size "chocolate chair" sculpture, entitled *Armchair* (shown on the opposite page).[1] The outer form of the chair was made of dark brown poured polyurethane, which because of the color made it look like it was poured chocolate. I knew I would be fired if I was caught, but I wanted a little excitement in an otherwise boring job. After the museum closing time, I boldly went past the restraining ropes and sat on the enticing chair. I sank down very fast, and air came suddenly gushing out. Instantly I was filled with the fear that the chair was going to fall apart from my weight, leaving a scrap heap of broken plastic left behind. I jumped up and was greatly relieved to see the chair return to its former shape. However, to leave no trace of my indiscretion, I wiped away my footprints leading up to the chair.

I woke up one morning with the distinct impression that I was supposed to quit my job at the Museum of Modern Art, so I gave my two-week notice. Next, I got a job as a guard on the day shift at the Whitney Museum. When not working, I became totally absorbed in my painting and stayed up all hours of the night. Not getting much sleep, I found myself repeatedly late for work in the morning. My boss came to me and very angrily exclaimed, "You are an asshole! Do you know that?" I could tell that he was expecting me to object, and then he was going to immediately fire me.

I smiled, saying, "You are right. I am an asshole," which caught him off guard. "I want you to put me on the night shift, so waking up in time won't be a problem." Since he had planned to fire me, he was reluctant to grant my request. But he agreed to give me a chance to work the late night shift.

To balance my inwardness of painting and the reclusiveness of being a night watchman, I felt I needed to do something outwardly to socialize. Wearing a white shirt and a red corduroy jacket, I went to the nearby fountain at Washington Square Park to meet young ladies. I met Lydia there, and using a line similar to the artist's classic invitation to see his etchings, I brought her to my apartment to show her my paintings. We lay in my bed with a wooden chair suspended horizontally over our heads. The legs of the chair were fastened to the wall at the end of the bed where our heads were. Fastened to the seat of the chair was a light socket, which had a red light bulb in it. The red light lit up Lydia's face as she said, "Before we get started, I want you to know I have a steady boy friend. This will only be a one time thing. Also there is a possibility I might have some sort of venereal disease. Is that all right?"

A CALLOW YOUNG MAN IN 1967

"Sure," I said. Of course, this was before the aids era, and I had not been in the sack for a while. We had sex, and she was very good looking, but what I remember about her is that her body was so perfectly shaped and velvety to the touch. As I looked at her face in the red light, it suddenly flashed into a green light and then back to a red light. It startled me at first, until I remembered something from my art studies. If you expose your eyes too long to one color like red, it will tire the cones in your eyes. The result is that you will see the opposite or complementary color, or green in this case. The next day when I returned to the fountain at Washington Square, Lydia was there with another man, and we pretended we didn't know each other.

At a later date I noticed a bump on my penis and went to the free clinic at St. Vincent's Hospital. I was told I had gonorrhea, but fortunately had caught it at a very early stage. The doctor gave me a penicillin shot, which took care of the problem.

One day when I was walking, a woman introduced herself to me—very unusual because the unwritten rule on the streets of New York is to walk straight ahead and don't talk to anyone and don't even look at anyone. She said, "I like you. I have only one problem. I am married. If you don't mind that, we can get together if you want to."

"You are very attractive. Thank you for approaching me, but I don't get involved with married women. I'm sorry." This may sound strange since I didn't seem to mind a little venereal disease. But I wanted to avoid the guilt of breaking the Catholic taboo on adultery. I walked away, but then I stopped and gazed back at her as she was still looking at me. I was tempted and stood there hesitating for a minute before finally walking away.

Having different work schedules, Hal and I hardly saw each other, which was fine since we had little in common. I didn't have many friends. I went to a bar on a night off from work. The bartender told me about a lesbian bar he was going to after work at 1 AM, and he agreed to take me along. I don't remember much specifically, except it was an eye opener seeing so many people who, like me, did not want to conform to society.

Out of boredom I put an ad in the newspaper offering private hypnotism sessions on a donation basis. Josh, the only person answering the ad, asked me to put on a demonstration for some of his friends. I agreed although I had never before given a hypnotism performance for a group. A week later six strangers showed up at my apartment, yet Josh wasn't with them. Finally Josh knocked on my door a half hour late, but he left when I didn't answer the door. Unfortunately I couldn't let him in because I was already totally focused on hypnotizing a gay actor named Terrance. Once he was hypnotized, I told Terrance he was in the tropics and had him unbutton his shirt because of the heat. Next I told him that he was at the North Pole, and he began to shiver until I said he was in a room with a normal temperature.

Then I gave him a slice of potato to eat, but told him it was a sweet and juicy peach. As he was eating I exclaimed, "Oh, I gave you a slice of lemon by mistake." His mouth immediately puckered up and his whole face wrinkled up. Finally I gave a post hypnotic suggestion that when I told him to open his eyes, he would see that everyone in the room is naked and he would think that is very funny. I added that after fifteen seconds he would see everyone as fully clothed. Then I told him he would forget everything that happened, although he would feel relaxed and happy that he had come to this gathering. When I instructed him to wake up, he had a surprised look on his face and began to laugh. He was surely seeing naked people, but then he abruptly stopped laughing.

Afterwards I talked with Terrance to make sure he was all right, and he told me he had a friend who could take professional photographs of me in case I wanted to go into modeling. I told him I wasn't interested in modeling, but I would like to have some photographs taken. That's how I met a gay man named Dane, who was in his early twenties. He said he would take some photographs of me, which he insisted would not be nude or gay in nature. I agreed after making it perfectly clear that I was straight. He worked at a professional studio and made large prints which I saved as an ode to my ego. On one of my visits to my parents in Connecticut, I showed my mother two of the pictures Dane had taken. My mother framed one of these pictures and put it up on the wall. I was surprised that she chose the picture of me with the proud look of a callow young man (shown on page 308). That was certainly part of my character, yet for display I would have chosen the other picture that looked more like a serious young artist (shown on the opposite page). However, neither photograph captured my self-image as well as a simple charcoal drawing I had made (displayed on page 312). The drawing was a self-portrait that was intended to be more expressionistic than realistic. My eyes are dark brown, but the irises were intentionally drawn lightly to reveal in my questioning eyes that I was a young fellow confused about my identity.

If I got lonely, I would visit Dane. He told me he was a child prodigy with the piano and for years practiced until he had his great opportunity to do a solo performance at a top showplace—a place like Carnegie Hall. Yet on the day of the performance, he became so overcome with fear that he just didn't show up, and that was the end of his piano career. He and I played chess together. My own strategy was always to expect to win and don't be afraid to lose, because fear attracts losing. So I always played conservatively and patiently, waiting for the other person to make a blunder. Dane would always start off the chess game very well, and once he even took my queen in the beginning. But he would always find a way to make a mistake and lose the game, which reminded me of his piano story.

A SERIOUS YOUNG ARTIST

SELF-PORTRAIT IN CHARCOAL

On one of my visits, he pleaded with me to put on some black leather pants that he had, and finally I agreed. Then when I came out of the bathroom and showed him the pants, he said he wanted me to pull down my zipper and expose myself. I had always been clear with him about being friends, yet not gay friends. But this was the first time I realized he did not understand. I told him, "That's the end of the fashion show. I've got to go."

Later he called me on the phone, and I thought he would apologize for stepping over the line in our friendship. Instead he said, "I know you were teasing me and laughing at me because I'm gay. Also you are a chess expert. You toyed with me there, too. You would let me take some pieces at the beginning of a game, and then you would come back and demolish my pieces. I won't let you torment me any more." I tried to explain that I didn't win the chess games; he lost them. I told him that he had a self-defeating pattern of throwing the game away even when he was ahead. I told him I wasn't attempting to tease him sexually. However, he did not believe me and said he did not want to continue to be friends.

I had another friend at work, Joe, who worked the evening shift with me. He was an unusual character with a North Carolina accent. Of all things, he often talked to me about Zen, of which I knew nothing. He would see my drawings that I did at work to occupy my time, and he would ask, "Do you save these?"

"Of course I save them."

"That's too bad," and he would shake his head mockingly because he knew he was confusing me, which he enjoyed doing.

"What do you mean by that?" I inquired.

"In Zen, you gain by what you let go of, and you lose by what you keep," Joe answered with a smile and walked away with an obvious air of intellectual superiority.

Another time he showed me a five-line Zen haiku poem about a flower being run over by the wheel of a cart, and he said, "Do you see?"

I replied, "That's interesting," which Joe knew was my way of saying that I didn't have the faintest idea what he was talking about. Joe liked to make fun of my lack of knowledge in matters that he understood. Now I have more knowledge about what he was saying, but even so, the way he was saying it clearly demonstrated that he didn't respect me. I told him that I did not like his disparaging remarks about me or my art work. I advised him not to continue, implying there would be consequences if he did. Subsequently, he made a sarcastic remark to me with a derisive laugh and walked off. His remark really ticked me off, so the next time I saw him I talked to him in an exaggerated North Carolina accent. I made fun of the way he extended certain vowels and fluctuated his voice. He was upset, yet tried to pretend that this didn't bother him. Nevertheless, I wouldn't stop.

The only way I would talk to him after that was with a wildly fluctuating North Carolina accent. I knew it was eating him up inside that he was getting the ridicule that he had thoughtlessly heaped on me. Eventually Joe asked almost pleadingly, "Will you stop doing that?"

Inwardly I weakened for a second and almost stopped. However, I remembered how I had asked him to stop talking to me in a degrading way, and he didn't stop. Consequently, I said, "Whaaat do you meeean? Ah alwaaays taaalk like this." Joe's face dropped, and I could see he was hurt, but I felt he deserved it for making me feel that way in the past.

Finally he came into our little night watchman office and sat down right next to me and said, "I want you to punch me in the face right now."

I asked, "Are you sure about this?"

He said, "Yes, I'm sure." So without hesitating, I punched him on the right side of the jaw. It was a quick short punch. I did not pull the punch, but it wasn't a round house punch intended to do serious damage, either.

Joe's head was snapped to the right from my right-hand punch, and he brought his head to center in a bit of a shock. "You really did it! That was a real punch. I didn't think you had it in you. What you were doing by making fun of my North Carolina accent was hurting me much more than any punch you could give me. That's why I gave you the opportunity to get out your anger by punching me. Do you know what I would have done to you if you had refused to hit me? I would have ridiculed you mercilessly for being cowardly enough to hurt me with words and not courageous enough to hit me. You saved yourself a lot of grief," he said with noticeable admiration.

I smiled and said jokingly, "Do you want another one?"

Joe laughed and said, "No! One punch was enough." After that we had no problem about mutual respect. However, there was still a sense from Joe that he felt he was more intelligent than I was. Consequently I challenged him to figure out a puzzle that I gave him, and he accepted the challenge. I told him that I had figured out the puzzle in three days, so if he could figure it out sooner, he would be one up on me. Susan, the young lady who had convinced me to cut Mr. Brand's class in college, had given me the puzzle. I was motivated to solve it to impress her because she did not know how to solve it herself. It was a Chinese puzzle in the shape of a cross.

The puzzle is shown in the diagram (on the opposite page) with the pieces indicated as 44 black circles. If you want to try your hand at it, you can make your own version by cutting up 44 small pieces of paper or you can even use 44 dominoes, 44 checkers, or 44 pennies. A solution can be found at the end of this book in Appendix C, "Solution to the Chinese Puzzle," although there may be other solutions of which I am unaware.

THE CHINESE PUZZLE

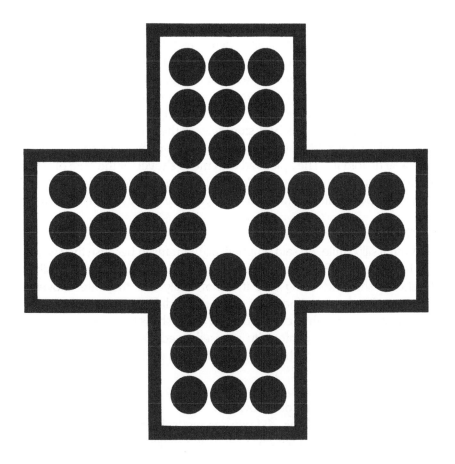

I continued my narrative:

I struggled obsessively for two days with the puzzle, and on the morning of the third day the answer immediately presented itself. This spontaneous solution gave me the distinct impression that a higher awareness in my subconscious mind had solved it that night when I was sleeping. That day I went to show the answer to Susan, but I couldn't find her. I found out later that she had broken into the college traffic department to rip up a ticket she had received and apparently didn't get caught. It seems she had to withdraw from school for some other reason and return to New York where she lived. It was too bad, because I was very attracted to her and wondered what happened to her. I got her address eventually and mailed her a letter with the solution of the puzzle, but she never responded.

Joe thought he could figure out the puzzle, but eventually came to me and said he could not. After that he never again gave out the aura of having the upper hand mentally. There was a feeling of equality, and he was more willing to talk about his personal life. He told me he had asthma as a child, and once he had a breathing attack, in the middle of which he had an inner realization that he was in complete control of his breathing. So he consciously stopped the breathing problem right then, and it never came back again. However, his best story was of the time his school visited a farm, and he was told that it was his job to shovel the manure in the barn. The way he told it, "They pleaded with me to shovel for the sake of school spirit and for the American flag. And I told them I wouldn't. They told me it was my responsibility. I refused, and do you know why I refused?" he asked me.

"No, why did you refuse?"

With a silly smile, he said emphatically, "I refused because they wanted me to shovel *shit*. People are always being told that it's their responsibility to shovel shit and being told it is not really shit they are shoveling. However, I knew even then that shit is shit. I did not want to shovel shit, and there is nothing they could do to get me to shovel shit." Because of my own struggle to avoid conformity imposed by educational systems, I find it amusing just to think of the way he said it with such obvious joy.

I broke off my monologue to ask Allan, "Do you think this would be a good place to stop until tomorrow?"

"Sure. Speaking of shit, did you see my 'shit happens' poster?" Allan pointed out a poster on his wall with witty sayings that all began with the words, 'Shit happens when....' I didn't find much humor in the list, but Allan thought it was worthy of displaying, so I read it politely without comment. Then I suggested we watch TV, which was Allan's favorite pastime. Some nights I would suggest we meditate together. The last thing I would do with him each night was the ritual of carefully adjusting his pillow and assortment of cushions. This might take several minutes as he was very particular about the pillow and cushions being just right, since he would not have anyone available to make adjustments for the rest of the night.

---

1. Anderson, Gunnar Aagaard (1919-1982), *Armchair*, 1964, Poured polyurethane, 29 1/2 x 44 1/4 x 35 1/4 inches. Manufacturer: Executed by Dansk Polyether Industri, Denmark. Gift of the designer (720.1966) to the Museum of Modern Art, New York, NY. Digital Image © The Museum of Modern Art/Licensed by SCALA / Art Resource, NY. Reference: ART175853.

31

MARIE

~ o ~

At the time when I was painting in New York City I had no conscious awareness that there was a Pole Man or Spider Man lurking in the hidden corners of my mind. Nevertheless, the dark nature of my art work itself revealed the need to pay attention to something in the shadow side of my personality. Although I had not yet made the conscious decision to solve my shadow puzzle by putting together the elements of my subconscious mind and making sense out of them, I did feel I was searching for the meaning behind the challenging images that were emerging in my paintings.

At my next conversation with Allan I talked again about my painting as my form of meditation:

My painting was becoming an increasing obsession, monopolizing most of my time and energy. I was developing my meditation ability in the sense of learning to focus my mind toward the placement of paint on canvas. Yet I was not aware at the time that this focusing would lead eventually to meditation itself. In addition to being a form of meditative focusing, my abstract expressionistic painting produced an emotional catharsis, and therefore was my form of psychotherapy.

Two artists whom I very much admired were Vincent Van Gogh and Jackson Pollock. I could identify with the fact that these were two tortured souls. Each used different means of expression, but both captured in their painting the same intensity of their struggle with the dark side of their natures. Van Gogh used familiar realistic forms, yet his unique brush strokes and use of bold colors conveyed a strong emotional content characteristic of expressionism. On the other end of the spectrum, Pollock was entirely liberated from any familiar realistic forms. Instead of using paint to represent objects or people, he used his application of paint to represent paint itself. Pollock's pouring and splattering of paint on canvas was his form of totally abstract expressionism, which appeared to be entirely spontaneous, yet contained a somewhat structured pattern.

My abstract expressionism was half way between the forms of Van Gogh and the formlessness of Pollock, containing elements of both. In my abstract paintings, which contained both spontaneous and methodical aspects, I allowed forms to emerge. These forms were coming forth from my subconscious mind and were jumping onto the canvas through the media of paint. Common symbols often included sexual forms. However, I was surprised at how often symbols of death, danger, and isolation emerged, such as graves, ominous buildings, and figures in darkness. [Two examples of these dark pictures are *Grave* and *Burial.*] Sometimes as I painted the forms of spiders emerged. The spiders frightened me so I painted over them. I vaguely recognized that these spiders in particular represented the hidden corners of my mind that I was not yet ready to face. [It would be years later that I would discover that the source of my fear was in the subconscious memory of my past life as Spider Boy.]

The paintings were dark with some indications of light and color used for contrast and as a focal point. I painted on canvases size 18 inches by 24 inches, and I still have some of these. However, I transferred many paintings to very large canvases 5 feet by 8 feet or larger, and I don't have any of these today. On the larger canvas only the one small area of the original 18 by 24 picture would have a strong contrast of color and light. The great expanse of the canvas would be very dark, usually brown, perhaps symbolic of the great darkness in which I felt I was living. An artist named Ad Rhinehardt had popularized a movement called "minimal art" since there was minimal contrast in his paintings, and he used the phrase, "less is more." I called my work "maxi-minimal art" because in the large expanse of my work there was minimal contrast, but in a small area, usually in the center or at one of the corners, there was maximum contrast. On one such large canvas I installed a coin machine device in the center with a small red light bulb behind it as a representation of a prostitute's vagina. However, most works were entirely paintings using paint only.

An interesting effect of this maxi-minimal art was that the viewer approaching a large painting was invariably drawn into close proximity to the small area of maximum contrast. Then at his close location the viewer would be able to examine the detail of the smaller area of high contrast containing light and dark forms and brilliant colors. Next the viewer was almost compelled to look at this small area of high contrast, which is right in front of his eyes, in stark contrast with the vastness of the totally dark area that seemed to overwhelm him because of his positioning. The purpose of these paintings was to entice the viewer into this form of comparison and participation in the art work. This placed the viewer in a position to experience the level of darkness that I was experiencing in my personal outlook on life at that time.

GRAVE

BURIAL

SEXUAL COMPOSITION

Most of my paintings had a sexual content, which is not surprising since painting is often considered a sublimation of the sexual drive. [An example is *Sexual Composition*, which is shown on the opposite page.] However, the direction of my personalized abstract expressionism was not what could be called the cutting edge of art in the 1960s. Marshall McLuhan made the famous statement that "the medium is the message." He meant that the media of advertising and modern technology had become both the new means of artistic expression and the message of that expression. America had become world famous for being a manufacturer of objects, just as for centuries artists had been the makers of works of fine art objects. But the age of industrialization that focused on objects was giving way to the age of technology that focused on managing information. The media of paint and canvas was being replaced by the images of advertising, television, and later computers, which took over the art world. Andy Warhol was one of the clearest examples of the fact that "the media is the message."

I interrupted my monologue to ask Allan, "Are you familiar with Andy Warhol?

"Sure, he's the guy that said that 'everyone will be world famous for fifteen minutes,' but I am still waiting for my fifteen minutes. Wasn't he also the guy who painted Campbell's soup cans?" Allan asked.

That's exactly right. His work was appropriately called "Pop Art." He used popular advertising images like Campbell's soup cans, or even images of popular personalities, like Marilyn Monroe and Elvis Presley. His training was in graphics, so his paintings were actually graphic arts statements transferred to large canvases. For him the media of graphics and advertising itself became his message. Andy Warhol not only glorified American media advertising, but he himself became an advertisement. Ever since Andy Warhol, the art world is no longer about the object of the work itself. It's about packaging. It's about ideas and information. Artists who can articulate their work well and place it in some kind of avant-garde context can succeed in the art world.

Although Andy Warhol popularized popular art, he cannot be accused of originality. This distinction goes to Marcel Duchamp, the father of "found objects." He found an ordinary porcelain urinal, turned it upside down, placed it horizontally, and called it art. Duchamp entitled his found object the "Fountain," signed it with the pseudonym "R. Mutt," and entered it in an art show in 1917. It was dismissed as a vulgar desecration of art at the time; however, now is recognized as a legitimate attempt to liberate art from form. To Duchamp the art was not in the art work itself, as a manipulated and manufactured form, but rather in the mind of the artist. Just as beauty

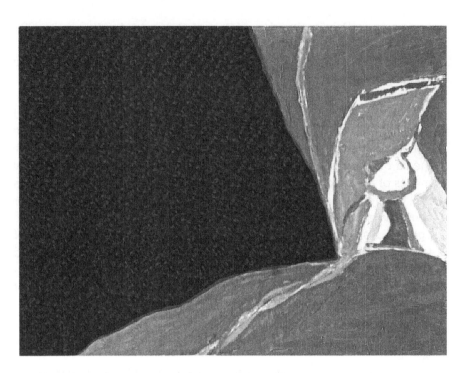

MALE EXPRESSION

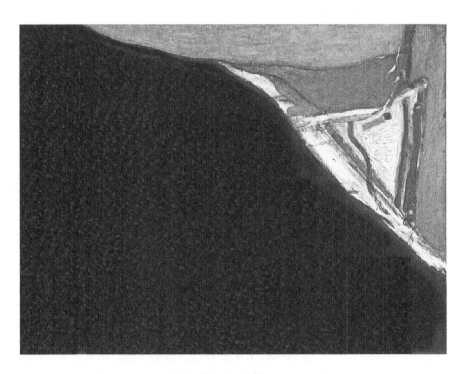

FEMALE DESIGN

is in the eye of the beholder, Duchamp maintained that art is in the eye of the artist. The artist's vision enables him to see art even in ordinary "readymade" objects, just as they are, by looking at them differently— seeing what is normally overlooked by undiscriminating minds. Duchamp challenged the institutional framework in which art works were judged, yet he had to be actively engaged in dialogue with that institutional framework, even if he was in conflict with it.

My problem with the art of Warhol, and even the art of Duchamp, is that to follow in their path would require me to be extroverted enough to be engaged with the institutional framework of art. I actually made one concrete attempt to do this. One day I came into the Whitney Museum when I was not working and went up to the administrative offices. I asked the secretary if I could see someone on the staff who would be willing to talk to me about my paintings. I was seen by a distinguished looking man wearing an expensive suit. I described my maxi-minimal paintings, which were too large to bring with me. Then I showed him some 18 by 24 inch paintings. I don't remember which ones I brought with me, but there were probably some pictures containing mostly sexual imagery. [Three examples of these kinds of abstract paintings are *Male Expression*, *Female Design*, and *Female Composition*.]

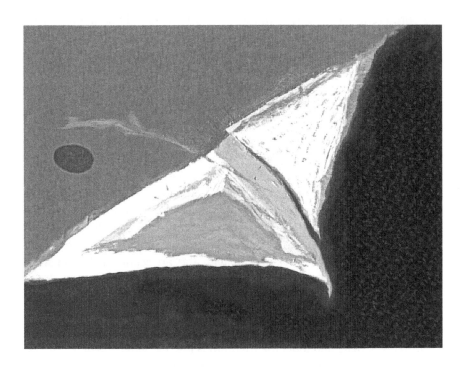

FEMALE COMPOSITION

He asked, "What do you want from me?"

His condescending tone of voice showed me that I had made a mistake in coming to see him. Nevertheless, I said, "I just want to ask you if you have any advice for me that you think may be helpful."

He paused for a long time and looked distressed that I was even talking to him. Finally he said, "I don't know what to say. You just have to do what you think is right." I thanked him for seeing me without any notice, and I got out of there as quickly as I could.

That night my supervisor cornered me when I arrived at work and angrily blasted me for having the nerve to impose myself on this Whitney administrator. I gathered that my supervisor had been roasted by the administrator because one of the insignificant guards had the boldness to inappropriately approach him. I promised my supervisor that I would never make that mistake again, but I had already made that promise to myself.

At first I was upset because I felt like a lowly plebeian approaching an aristocratic representative of the elite art world. Upon further reflection I was more upset with myself than with the administrator. When the administrator had remarked, "You just have to do what you think is right," he was merely trying to get rid of me, however his words made sense. I did need to do what was right, which meant to me that I had to be authentic—true to myself. My coming to the administrator was an inauthentic act on my part. I reminded myself that the one positive thing I had learned from my experience with Todd and Brand was that I could not seek some kind of outer approval from others for my art work. What makes an artist into an artist is that he works on his art, not that he is recognized for his art.

I had to admit to myself that using the name of "maxi-minimal art" to describe my painting style was my feeble attempt to position my work in the world of art philosophy. Nevertheless, I realized that my heart was not genuinely invested in that kind of promotion. I guess by working in a museum I had been influenced to come up with my own pretentious art philosophy so I could fit into the art world. However, there is no art world— at least no art world that is real. And reality is what I wanted—specifically, the discovery of my own reality, my identity. Although I did not know my identity, what I did know about myself was that I did not really care about the outer world of art or even about the outer world of everyday life. Consequently, I never got involved with the art scene in the sense of seeking out galleries to show my work and sell it, because that wasn't my interest. I became resigned to the conclusion that my art work would never be valuable in the institutional art world, yet I was just as certain that my art was immensely valuable to me in my process of self-discovery.

Instead of believing that "the medium is the message," I believe that in art "the messenger is the media." Art consists of the footprints of the artist, who is the messenger. The artist acts as a messenger by looking at his footprints in order to give himself the message of his own identity. In addition, hopefully his footprints will be a message that will inspire others to seek their own identity.

Although the name "maxi-minimal art" was pretentious, my paintings themselves were not. They truly portrayed the footprints of my *psychic sweat*. For me, painting was my form of therapy and search for meaning in life. I was certain that my paintings, which depicted a bit of consoling light in the midst of massive darkness, were indeed valuable as an accurate record of my search. My painting didn't give me answers to the meaning of life, but the action itself of painting was a kind of answer for me. When it was the only answer I had, it held me together with the thought that at least I was an artist, who was seeking his identity. Eventually I would find that "meditation is the medium" for my self-discovery. However, first I needed to become obsessed with painting as a transition activity from form to the formlessness of meditation.

Painting obsessively was making me increasingly withdrawn, and my work as a night watchman was also isolating, especially after my co-worker Joe left. To save money, the museum eliminated Joe's position; so instead of two night watchmen working together, I was the only one on duty full time. Fortunately someone came into my life to draw me more out into the world. That person was Marie.

Hal and I went out to do laundry one day and met Debbie and Marie. Hal ended up going out with Marie on one date, and afterwards I told Hal I wanted to take her out. Hal said, "How about if you give me two cigarettes, and that will satisfy me?" and I handed him two cigarettes. Marie, who was 19, and I became close. She explained, "Debbie and I met at a psychiatric center. We both had tried to commit suicide and failed. I was in love with my boy friend, Billy, and it didn't work out. There was no reason to live. The psychiatric center was a joke. It didn't help at all. But Debbie was my savior, and I was her savior. We discovered that there really is such a thing as love. We learned about love because we loved each other. Not lesbian love. Just love. That love is what helped us recover so we both wanted to live again," she said with a smile, the most beautiful smile I had ever seen to go with a pretty face.

Marie wasn't tall and thin the way I liked, just average height and a nice figure and very long brown hair. She made me laugh when I took myself too seriously, which was all the time. She drew me out and liked me to go with her to socialize with friends, but my focus was still on painting. We drew closer, and I told her I wanted to love her, yet felt blocked inside. I didn't know if I could really love someone. She wanted to know about the first woman I had sex with, and I told her that story.

I was sixteen, and I went out with a girl my age who had a very bad reputation. She had glasses that detracted from her looks. However, without the glasses I thought she was cute. A friend of mine came to me and told me not to go out with her because I would be ruining my reputation. But I told him, "What's a good reputation for unless you can ruin it," which made no sense, yet it shut him up.

I didn't have a car so I would walk to her house and visit with her there. Because it was the wintertime, there was no place to go without a car. I could tell she was getting infatuated with me, and I was beginning to like her too, but sex was really my priority. I felt bad that I was making her fall in love with me, even though I only wanted sex. We double dated with a high school buddy, Douglas, and in the back seat of his car I had my first experience of touching third base. Third base for a sixteen-year-old youth is like an exotic foreign territory forbidden to outsiders. Suddenly getting a visa to this mysterious destination was a revelation, confirming through firsthand experience that all the rumors about this place were actually true. We steamed up the windows of the car, yet that was about as far as it went. She had study hall with me, and I passed her a note that said, "Will you do it with me?"

She passed back a note she had written that read, "If I do, will you leave me?"

I wrote back, "No."

She wrote back, "Then yes!"

I arranged a double date with my friend Douglas, and we went to an Elvis Presley movie at the drive in theater. She and I had sex in the back seat. It was an extremely inept attempt at sex on my part with a quick ejaculation ending it. She didn't care because she loved me. I became immediately guilt ridden for two reasons. One reason was that because I had grown up as a Catholic, it had been drilled into me that sin and the resulting guilt are the path to hell. The other reason is that I knew I had been deceptive with her and felt bad about it. That evening after we let our dates off, Douglas drove me to our old junior high school to talk. I was upset, and I threw a rock at a glass window, breaking it.

I had used a condom, but I could not forget that a friend of mine had gotten his girl friend pregnant on his and her first experience of sex, and he had to marry her. The day after I lost my virginity I felt I had to do the most difficult thing I had ever done. I called her up and told her our relationship was over. Then I really felt guilty. The guilt of causing her this pain and the pain of facing my own insincerity stayed with me. I felt only an evil person would make someone love them and then throw them aside like I had done. So I concluded I must be a bad person, which hindered my feelings of self-worth and affected other relationships in the future.

PENCIL DRAWING OF MARIE

MY LOVE

So that was the story I told Marie, and when I finished the first thing Marie asked was, "What was her name?"

I half smiled and half frowned and said, "Her name was *Marie.*" I would not have told her if she hadn't asked. Her expression became completely blank. She didn't say a word, got up from the bed where we were, and walked into the bathroom. I waited a minute, and then I figured I better follow her. I opened the bathroom door, which she had left ajar. She was standing behind the door with her face to the wall, crying. I tugged at her to turn around, and I hugged her. I said, "So you both have the same name. I'm not trying to deceive you about loving you. If I wanted to deceive you, I wouldn't have told you the story. Give me time. I care about you. Let me have time to learn how to open my heart." Actually right then my heart did go out to her, but I still couldn't say, "I love you." It occurred to me that in the future if we broke up, she would have to be the one to break it off, because I wouldn't be able to face the guilt of hurting her by ending it myself.

[I made a semi-realistic portrait of Marie, using mostly green and some blue paint to depict her hair, which was actually dark brown. The design was slightly influenced by the Egyptian headdress of King Tut that I had seen at the Museum of Modern Art. Although it was hard for me to tell Marie that I loved her, later I gave this painting the title *My Love.*]

Hal brought home some reduced strength LSD one day. I hadn't been smoking pot since the few times when I lived with Gail after college, and I had never taken LSD. However, I decided to try it for the first time and so did Hal. We didn't hallucinate, yet all our senses became very finely tuned, and we became very happy. We both enthusiastically engaged in breaking eggs over each others' heads and throwing glassfuls of water at each other while laughing uncontrollably. We decided to explore the great outdoors with a few tomatoes in hand. We ran down the street still silly and after heaving the tomatoes at the side of a building returned to our apartment. It was the most fun Hal and I would have.

The silliness wore off, but the drug was still affecting my senses later that day when I went out on a date with Marie to the movies. We saw an Ingmar Bergman flick, *Hour of the Wolf,* about an artist who was tempted, deluded, and destroyed by a society that he could neither fight nor escape. I hoped it was not an omen of my future; however, it certainly was an impressive movie to watch on acid. A theme of the movie involved the artist symbolically leaving behind his conscience and childhood innocence. In one shocking dream-like flashback, a child was hit in the head and killed by a man with a rock. During this scene, Marie, who had not taken a drug, suddenly let out the loudest blood-curdling scream I had ever heard. Then she covered her face, and I thought she might want to leave, yet we stayed. Although Marie would get very afraid at times, her fears would give me an opportunity to reassure her that everything was all right.

But I had my own fears to deal with. I got a call to appear for a draft physical, and I had to go back to Connecticut for it. It was the Vietnam War draft, and people were arguing over whether it was a just war or not. The term "just war" may be an oxymoron, yet many people felt it was their duty to fight. I had a friend from Connecticut, named Freddy, who served in Vietnam because he felt it was the right thing to do. When he returned, he wouldn't talk about what he experienced. I admired his courage to go.

At the time of the draft I felt the way that my night watchman friend, Joe, felt when he was told to shovel shit. I don't like to use the word "shit" or any curse words. However, it's the best word to describe this. Just as Joe was told to shovel manure for the sake of school spirit and for the American flag, I was being told that it was all right and even my duty to shoot a rifle and kill people who disagreed with American foreign policy. I had no doubt that I was being asked to shovel shit, and like Joe I knew it was shit.

Killing other people was the worst kind of shoveling shit, but the truth is that I felt every aspect of being in the army itself would be one long nightmare of shoveling shit within a system that suppressed my individual freedom of choice. I had already shoveled shit for Mr. Todd and Mr. Brand in order to get a degree and be part of the system. But after shoveling their shit I found out that I no longer wanted to be a part of a system that required me to shovel shit. I was a night watchman, instead of a school teacher, precisely because I wanted to drop out of the normal dog-eat-dog society where sheep are herded along in single file and told they have to shovel shit. By having a nothing job, at least I wouldn't be subject to paying the price of jumping through hoops of shit. And the draft would drag me back into a system of great conformity, where shoveling shit was a way of life. I could not allow myself to be led along as a good little sheep.

This draft physical was actually my second notice. I had already taken a draft physical six months before in New Haven. At that physical I focused on the fear of having my life taken over by forces beyond my control, and my two blood pressure readings were so high that they put me up at the YMCA, to test me again the next two days. At the Y, I met Martin, a friend from high school, who was also being detained. He told me he was eating salt to get his blood pressure up. We went out to a restaurant and ordered only mashed potatoes. We each found full salt shakers and emptied the contents into the potatoes. It tasted terrible, so we added ketchup, which didn't help. Martin said being tired would help, so we did all sorts of exercises to tire ourselves out. I failed the two tests the next day and the two tests the following day. Afterwards there was no celebration—just a bitter relief that it was over, at least for the time being.

I dreaded this second draft physical. I failed two blood pressure tests on the first day and was sent to the YMCA again. This time I met Adam, a friend from Westbrook, and he was using drugs to get out of the draft. In the past he had experimented with a lot of different drugs and also natural herbs just to see how they would affect him. The strangest effect he experienced was ironically from a common herb, but he had to eat a very large quantity of it. He said it made him completely desireless. Adam used to like sports, sex, money, and riding his motorcycle. However, he didn't care about any of those things anymore. He said, "I didn't know who I was anymore. It was a terrible state of mind. I didn't even really care if I lived or died." In fact, he didn't care about anything because he had absolutely no emotions whatsoever and no purpose or reason for living. It took him months to start to like anything. Gradually, the effect of the herb wore off and he recovered his emotions and desires.

Allan, you are probably wondering about the name of that herb, but I can't tell you. Adam told me its name, but he said it would be very bad for anyone to take this herb in the quantity he used. I don't think you would take it, Allan, yet you might tell someone else, and I don't want to be responsible for someone taking it. Anyway, I'm getting off track. I didn't think I needed drugs to fail the physical. I went in the morning of the second day to take the blood pressure test. After the test the examiner said, "Great! One more good reading this afternoon, and you will be in the army." He smiled.

I stood up and started hyperventilating. I started hollering hysterically, "I'm scared. I'm scared." I *was* afraid of going into the army, but I was faking this outburst. I figured a short time of humiliating behavior would be better than two years of being controlled and dehumanized. One of my former fraternity brothers was there as a witness, to add to the humiliation; yet I didn't care and kept hollering. A doctor came over and tried to calm me down, but I kept intentionally alternating between hyperventilating and screaming. I was physically restrained and forced onto a table for the doctor to examine my eyes to see if they were dilated, which would mean I was on drugs. I kept breathing heavily and quickly and continued screaming and struggling.

[As I talked to Allan about my screaming, fear, and being physically restrained on a table, I suddenly became conscious that I had been reliving my past lives. I was reexperiencing the Spider Boy's experience of first being very afraid and screaming and then later being restrained on a table by a doctor, who amputated part of his leg. I had also been reliving the Pole

Man's experience of being physically restrained by others and hollering in fear. Of course, at the time of the draft physical I had no idea that these subconscious factors were a motivating force behind my emotional reactions. I didn't share these insights with Allan because I didn't think I should keep bringing up past life issues with him. I appreciated his attentive and patient listening to me, and I didn't want to give him the impression that I was blaming him for the past.]

Finally the doctor brought in a guard and told me I was going to be arrested if I didn't stop struggling and allow him to examine my eyes. It was an idle threat, but I was so excited, it didn't occur to me that the doctor wasn't telling the truth. I was afraid that my parents would find out I was arrested, and so I stopped. The doctor was able to examine my eyes, which were not dilated. When he was done, I said, "I don't want to come back here again."

The doctor said, "No, you won't have to come back here again." They let me lie down for a while alone. After I sat up, an army staff member, not the doctor, came over and told me, "You have to come back in the afternoon for another blood pressure test." I was too worn out to complain that it was the opposite of what the doctor had told me. I came back for that test and for two more the following day. The readings were all high, probably because I was exhausted.

I paid a stiff price for failing the draft physical. I was very depressed, as well as physically and emotionally drained. I wondered if I should have been a conscientious objector, based on the fact that I didn't feel the government gave me the right to kill another person. The charade that I had put on didn't seem worth it, even though I wasn't drafted. As an aftereffect, I felt like a bug. I remembered the other fellows who were there, looking at me with pity. They thought I was either crazy or a coward. I wondered if they were right. Although I had thrown the fit intentionally and could have stopped at any time, wasn't that a crazy thing to do? Was this my selfishness and strong will preventing me from being manipulated by others? Or was my deception really a deceiving of myself? Was it an action of a weak-willed person and coward? Guilt and self-doubt followed me back to New York.

Marie set up a gathering of friends as a celebration to welcome me back. I told everyone what happened and how cowardly and crushed I felt inside. They all were supportive and encouraged me to feel good about escaping from the army. However, I still couldn't feel justified in my actions, and even now I don't feel justified in what I did. It was a cowardly thing to do, but there was some good that came out of it. It made me realize I had a problem. This recognition would eventually lead me to be willing to make changes in my life to correct what I felt was broken inside of me.

I moved out of my living situation with Hal, who was himself planning to move to Denver. Marie's friend, Janet, let us live with her for a few months until we could find a place of our own. There were no roaches at Janet's, but there was soot on the window sills. It was an apartment at 13 Saint Mark's Place, right next to the *Electric Circus*. Of course, the *Electric Circus* wasn't a circus at all but a rather famous nightclub. It was one of the reasons why New York is called the "city that never sleeps." In fact, all of Saint Mark's Place was a street that never slept.

The next summer I took a two-week vacation and went to my parents' cottage in Westbrook. Marie came with me for one of those weeks, since she could get only one week off from her secretarial job. My parents were conservative, so I did not tell them we were living together. My parents, Marie, and I were playing a card game, when Marie made a remark about us not being able to see the sun coming up in the morning. I kicked her under the table, and my mother changed the subject after giving a knowing look to my father.

Back in New York after the vacation, Marie asked me to come into the bathroom to help her. She asked me to look very closely at her vagina because there was an irritation, and she could not see what the problem was. There was a small white speck I saw, and then it moved. "This little white thing here is alive, and it looks just like a crab. I think you have the crabs. And if you have them, I must have them too." Trying to figure out how this happened, I called my best buddy at the beach, Richie, and he told me he had them too. When I was in Westbrook, I had slept over in a bed at his house, and that is how I got the crabs, which I then gave to Marie. We had to shave off all our pubic hair and wash every bit of our clothes to finally get rid of them.

I asked Allan, "Should we stop here for today with the crabs? Is this a little more information than you wanted?"

"I'd rather hear about them than find out about them the way you did. I'm surprised those little critters actually look like crabs. I'm looking forward to the next installment."

32

OPENING UP

~ o ~

Picking up my story where I had left off, I told Allan:

I was home alone one day, and I came across a record of Beethoven's Sixth Symphony, which I played. Even though I wasn't interested in music at all, I decided to just lie down and listen to it. I suddenly began crying, and I was not sure why. Then I felt it was just because it was so beautiful. That was a sign for me that I was changing and starting to open up a bit. I started to listen to popular music, too. I really liked the sound of "Monday, Monday" by the Mamas and the Papas, and from a photograph I made a charcoal drawing of Michelle Phillips, one of their singers. I even went out and bought my first record, "The Sounds of Silence," by Simon and Garfunkel. The singing was good, but I was really attracted by the lyrics, which reminded me of the darkness I had experienced in my life and expressed in my paintings. I remember some parts of the song:

> Hello darkness, my old friend
> I've come to talk with you again....
> In restless dreams I walked alone
> Narrow streets of cobblestone....
> People talking without speaking
> People hearing without listening....
> And people bowed and prayed
> To a neon God they made....

My opening to music corresponded with my becoming more open to Marie's influence in my life. It was kind of Janet to let Marie and me stay at her Saint Mark's apartment for a couple of months until we found a new place to live in Astoria, part of Queens, which was a short subway trip from Manhattan. We lived in the second story of a house where the conservative landlord lived on the first floor. I told him that Marie and I were married, to get him to allow us to live there. With our own place and an extra room for a studio, I was able to go back to painting.

MICHELLE PHILLIPS

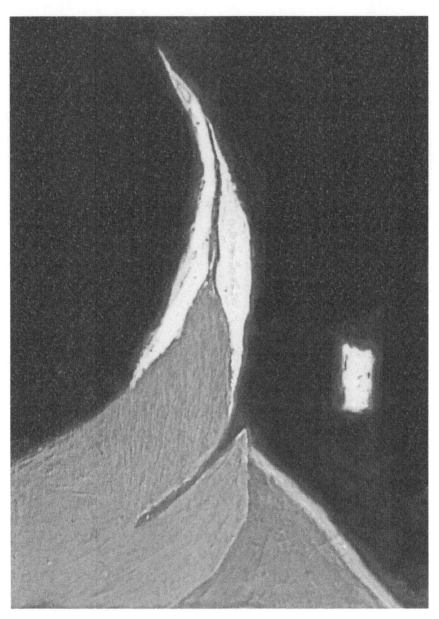

MAN ALONE IN THE DARKNESS

Although I had originally come to New York with Hal, I still felt I was alone and alienated. I had tried to fill that void through new acquaintances, but was only partially successful. I would not have felt lonely if I had looked within and found God's abiding presence, which could have let me know that I am forever connected to all my brothers and sisters in the universe.

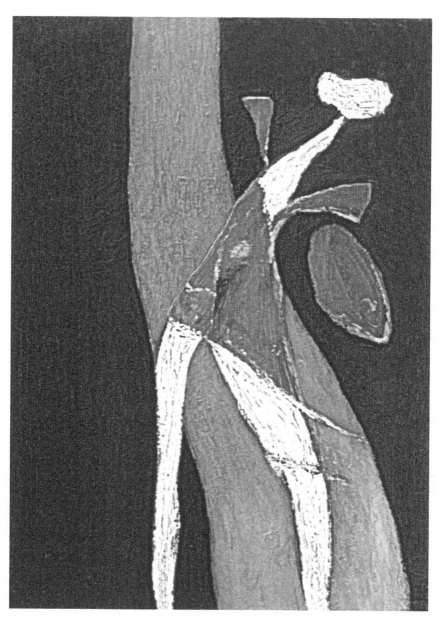

WOMAN ALONE IN THE DARKNESS

However, I had no inkling that such a deep inner relationship with God was possible. When I looked within all I saw was darkness, which was reflected in all my paintings. Sometimes to specifically express my loneliness I made paintings showing a solitary, alienated figure. [Two examples are *Man Alone in the Darkness* and *Woman Alone in the Darkness*.]

TWO FLOWERS

Marie coming into my life had helped me to overcome my sense of loneliness. Now that we were living together in a place of our own, my new paintings often showed two images to symbolize my relationship with her. [Three examples are *Two Flowers* (on the opposite page), *Two Lovers* (on page 341) and *Together in the Light* (on page 342).] There were still some representations of sexual imagery, but I no longer made paintings that were exclusively about sexuality as had been the case in the past.

Marie was going to a psychotherapy group, and she finally convinced me to go too, although not to the same group she attended. This form of psychotherapy was an outgrowth of the practice of psychiatrist Dr. Daniel Casriel, one of the original founders of Daytop, a drug recovery program.[1] This therapy involved expressing extreme emotions. The premise was that when emotions such as fear, hate, and pain are not allowed free expression, a person becomes out of touch with his own feelings. The end result is that these unexpressed emotions "come out sideways" as personality problems. The objective was to contact your feeling nature and get past the negative emotions so you could then experience the love that is the deepest part of your nature.

Participants were discouraged from intellectualizing. The question that was always being asked was, "What are you feeling right now?" For example I might say, "I'm angry." I would briefly tell everyone why, and others might ask questions to draw me out. Then I would repeat the words, "I'm angry," to each person in succession and maintain eye contact. I might be sitting or standing. My voice would get louder and my anger deeper. I might express some anger at the throat level and then reach a deeper level of anger by involving the chest. Other members of the group, especially the leader, a former group member, would shout encouragement or insults, whichever was more effective. If I got really mad, I would be expressing anger from the gut level so all parts of my body would be involved. Every muscle and nerve and my whole being would vibrate with anger.

The idea was to be authentic about your feelings and after fully getting out one feeling, this would make room for another feeling to surface. After expressing anger, I might feel fear or pain and express that feeling. Finally I might feel love and want to hug someone in the group. Or I might just feel relieved and calm and consequently stop. But oftentimes the emotions did not come out so neatly and were only partially expressed.

Because of my limited income, I was able to attend group sessions only once a week, but still made some progress in my therapy. However, whenever I was in these sessions, I felt I was in a way performing to meet the expectations of the group. I wanted to get to a deeper level of letting out my emotions. I wondered what would happen if I didn't have an audience, so I took what I learned about expressing emotions to my work place.

Every day thousands of people came to the Whitney Museum to look at the art work. But at nighttime I had the building all to myself—or almost all to myself. The museum employed an engineer who also worked the night shift. Usually I saw him on the top floor where he stayed. This would happen on the beginning of my rounds when I would take the elevator to the top floor, and then I would walk down through each floor to finally arrive at the basement.

One particular night after completing my rounds, I went to the bathroom in the basement. I stared at myself in the mirror. I was looking intensely for something in the mirror, perhaps in my eyes, but I didn't see what I was looking for. I wasn't sure what I was looking for.

I opened my mouth and screamed, "I'm afraid! I'm afraid! I'm afraid!" I kept screaming the same words as loud as I could until my body was shaking all over. What was I afraid of? I didn't know. However, after a while, I didn't feel any more fear.

Then I changed to shouting, "I'm angry! I'm angry! I'm angry!" My face flushed red as hate welled up within me, and I continued to vent. For a while the anger gave me an intoxicating feeling of power. What was I angry at? I didn't know. The anger too ran its course.

Then I felt an emptiness inside and began hollering, "I hurt! I hurt! I hurt!" I started screaming assertively in the loudest voice I could muster, with both feet planted solidly on the floor and with an air of defiance. Maybe I thought I could shout away the emptiness like I had shouted away the fear and then the anger. But the emptiness didn't go away, it only got bigger. As it got bigger, my voice lowered more and more until it became a whimpering, "I hurt. I hurt. I hurt." Along with the words lowering in pitch, my body lowered as well until I was rolled up in a ball on the floor. Then I couldn't speak at all except for moaning. I wept uncontrollably. I felt a pain deep inside that I had been carrying there perhaps all my life, yet never knew it was there before. But feeling emptiness and pain didn't make them go away. I asked myself in my mind, "Why? Why? Why? Who am I? Why am I doing this? Where does this pain come from?" I had no answer, just more groaning.

My wallowing was interrupted by a noise from outside the bathroom. I jumped up with all the speed of molasses. The dominant part of my mind realized the need to avoid being found weeping on the floor, and that part of my mind dragged up the rest of my mind that didn't give a damn what anyone thought. My mind was too foggy to consider that it was very strange that anyone would be coming. I turned a faucet on and threw some water on my face to cover the tears, just as the engineer casually strolled into the bathroom. "They have bathrooms on top. What's he doing down here?" I wondered, but didn't say a word.

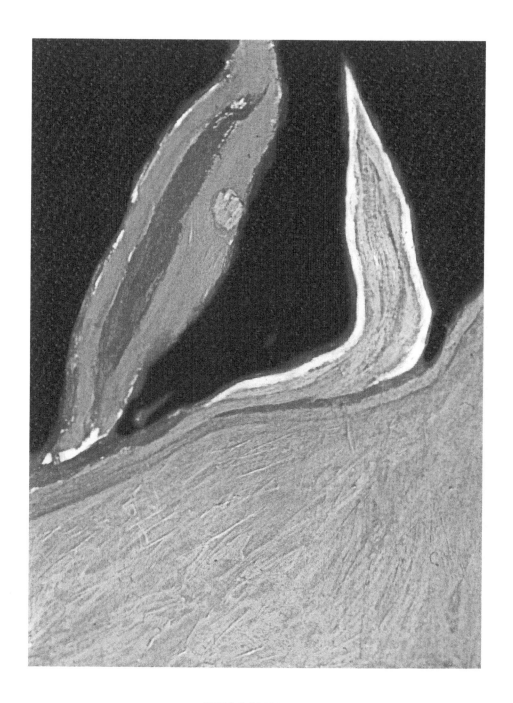

TWO LOVERS

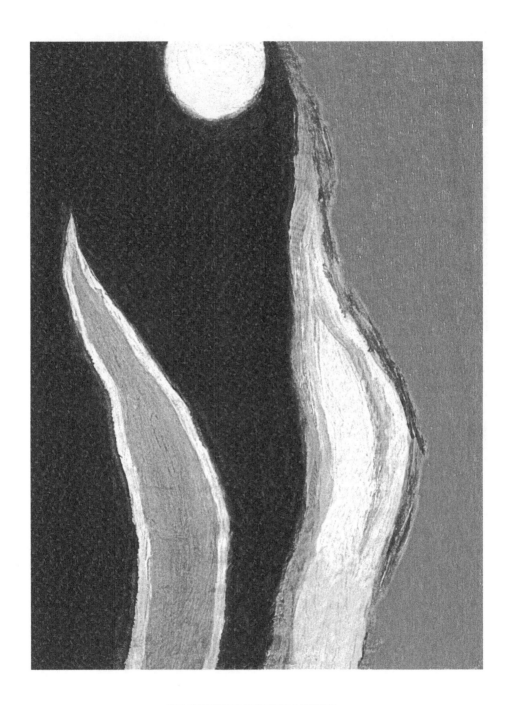

TOGETHER IN THE LIGHT

He nonchalantly greeted me with a wave of his hand while walking to the toilet stall. I walked out and hoped he hadn't heard any of my sounds. His unexpected interruption wouldn't stop me in the upcoming weeks from having similar sessions every night. These solitary sessions were much more emotionally charged and challenging than my group therapy. Sometimes there were insights of former guilt or an awareness of wallowing in self-pity or self-hate that would become apparent. However, the root problem I kept coming back to night after night was the question, "Who am I?" During group therapy the deepest question that was asked was, "What do I feel?" Sure, I could feel emotions, but, "Who is having this emotion?" I had reached a much more fundamental question than the group therapy normally addressed. This problem of identity tormented me, and at its deepest level it always brought up extreme pain. The pain was about not having an answer to the question, "Who am I?"

I remembered a time when I was satisfied with an answer. In an English course in my first year of college I was asked to write the answer to the question of "Who am I?" I was told I had to give three quick answers to this question—the first three answers that came to mind. My answers were: I am Donald James Giacobbe. I am an intelligent, independent individual. I am a creative artist.

At that time I was satisfied with these answers. However, when I was reduced to a moaning bag of flesh on the floor of the Whitney, these intellectual answers were meaningless to me. I wanted to *really* know who I was. I wanted to *experience* who I was. I groaned for the answer. Emotions came and went, but I was convinced these were not the answer. The deepest feeling I had was pain. There was also a pain about why I was even asking. Only crazy people don't know who they are. I had to face the possibility I might be insane to be asking such a question that no one else seemed to be asking, at least not with this degree of obsession. The closest I got to an answer was, "I don't know," and this would cause more pain. I intentionally felt the pain of not knowing as intensely as I could. I decided that the dull daily pain of being a stranger to myself was worse than this acute pain that might let me know more about my identity. I didn't tell anyone about what I was doing—not even Marie.

After this kind of grueling self-confrontation, which was usually about 3 or 4 AM, I would walk back to my regular first floor station and do a few pencil drawings to relax my mind. These weren't artistic masterpieces, just doodles for fun. Sometimes I would read, and one book I recall was *Summerhill*, about a radical school in England that truly respected the child and allowed the child to be in a position of choice, instead of being boxed into a canned system of learning. After reading this book, I concluded that my childhood might have been more messed up than I had thought. I loved

LINCOLN SELF-PORTRAIT

my parents, but was aware of some dissatisfaction with them, especially with my father. However, this book intensified those feelings.

There was an expression of this dissatisfaction with my parents in my painting titled *Lincoln Self-Portrait*. I portrayed myself to look like Lincoln because I admired him, but also because of the sadness often seen in his photographs. In this painting, made during my college years, my facial expression and the green, orange, and yellow colors in my face were intended to show my feelings of depression at the time. Attached to my neck in the picture was a single face that was divided into two halves. The left half represented my mother's face in profile and the right half stood for my father. I was consciously aware of inserting this image to symbolize my feeling of being attached to my parents in an unhealthy way at the time when I was still living with them. In my weekly group therapy sessions, I focused on expressing anger toward my father, and to a lesser degree toward my mother, with the idea of getting my suppressed feelings out in the open and hopefully releasing them.

The year before, when I lived on West 10th Street, my parents visited me and were totally shocked to see what my apartment looked like, and they probably didn't even see the roaches. They couldn't get out of there quick enough and took me to a restaurant for dinner. I later received a letter from Dad, who had not written me before. In his letter he told me that some very strange things were happening. Mom was doing some cooking when an explosion happened in the oven. The explosion was dangerous in itself, but as an aftereffect her blood pressure suddenly skyrocketed so much so that she had to be temporarily hospitalized. Dad also wrote he was growing *purple hair* on his tongue. Strangest of all, my conservative father was telling me that he felt *I* was somehow responsible for these things, even though there was nothing logical to substantiate such a conclusion.

However, then I realized that in this psychotherapy I was working with mental, emotional, and psychic forces that could have such unexpected and unwanted consequences. In a way, the emotional expression might be thought of as "anti-prayer," directing the mind negatively. But at the time I was not careful about how I directed my emotions, because I thought it was only therapy with no outer consequences. I could not dismiss my father's conclusions in his letter because I knew the intensity of emotions I had directed toward my mother and father. On the other hand, it seemed a bit far fetched to think that my emotional expression could have that kind of negative impact on my parents.

I came back to Connecticut to visit my family for Christmas. While we were watching TV, I was talking to Mom when Dad angrily said, "shush," to shut me up as he would so often do as I was growing up.

"Don't say 'shush' to me!" I snapped back for the first time ever.

Dad immediately stood up and hollered, "I'll say anything I want to you!"

I stood up and said, "I won't be told to shut up any more!"

"Who do you think you are, talking to me like that?" Dad spouted with a red face.

I asserted, "I don't deserve to be told to shut up, and I won't put up with it any more."

I had never challenged my father directly so this was strange territory for us, and neither of us was backing down. My mother was in shock and crying, "You stop talking to your father that way. I am so disappointed in you." My oldest brother, Paul, was visibly angry at me, and he left the room. He told me later that he left because he was tempted to physically come after me.

Then my anger evaporated, and I was left with all the hurt feelings that I had stored up in my childhood from my relationship with Dad. We were still standing face to face, and I started to cry and just blurted out, "All I ever wanted was for you to love me."

Then the most astonishing thing happened. Dad started crying, and then he put his arms around me and hugged me, and I hugged him back. Dad never hugged me, so then my tears expressed my appreciation of his embrace. After our hug, we both turned to look at my mother, who was still crying, and she said to me, "Don't you ever do that again. You have to respect your father." What could have been a terrible situation ended as well as it possibly could, and I felt a healing occurred for both my father and myself.

But it was not quite over. The next day, just before I was going to return to New York, I was down in the cellar, and then started to go back upstairs. I forgot to lock the cellar door. Dad came down to the cellar and made a derisive comment. It was something like, "You damned fool! You don't even know how to lock the door."

"Don't talk to me that way!" I demanded.

"I'll talk to you any way I want!" he hollered.

Although I challenged Dad the night before, I hadn't really let loose my anger. This time, though, I didn't hold back and screamed, "No, you won't!"

There was so much force and emotion projected toward Dad that for the first time I actually saw fear on his face. It was like the great and terrible Wizard of Oz being revealed to be an ordinary man. I realized that all these years Dad had made me afraid. However, it was all a pretend mask of intimidation. He said with an attempt at forcefulness, "As long as you live in my house, I'm the boss."

He was so shaken by his fear that he momentarily forgot the obvious fact, which I told him, "Did you forget? I don't live in your house anymore!" I didn't have to holler. I was no longer afraid of him, after seeing his fear.

He backed down and said quietly, "OK, let's make peace. Try not to do anything more that upsets your mother."

I agreed, "I don't want to upset her either," and that was the end of our confrontation. After that experience, my father didn't change drastically, but he mellowed considerably over time, and we never had another standoff with each other. He still had moments of angry irritability directed toward me. One time at a later date he spoke disrespectfully toward me, and to avoid a confrontation I walked out of the house and cried outside. He came after me because he knew he had spoken inappropriately. He meekly asked me to come back in the house, which was as close as he ever came to apologizing. Even though he continued to speak disrespectfully to me at times, I just learned over time to accept that it was his shortcoming and not my problem.

Blaming my parents for my problems was just a temporary phase that occurred as part of my psychotherapy. Later, when I became involved with spiritual growth, I learned to take full responsibility for my own experiences and emotional reactions. I began to see my parents not as my parents but just as people like me, who have their own problems not related to me. They had given me an example of a relationship in which the man is dominant and the woman is submissive, yet I found out quickly in my relationship with Marie that these roles would not work in our relationship.

Marie and I had a lot of ups and downs. When she showed me a set of earrings and told me she had gotten this jewelry by shop lifting, I got on her case. One day Marie found a roach in her dresser drawer, and she freaked out hysterically. She seemed to overreact with fear at times, and she lacked self-confidence. I had experience with hypnotism and knew the power of suggestion, so when she had just gone to sleep one night I decided to give her the suggestion that she would be able to more easily let go of fear and have more self-confidence in herself. She had a dream about a mouse talking to her, and she was upset about the dream. I told her I was probably the mouse and told her what I had done with my hypnotic suggestion while she slept. She was very upset, and rightly so, because I should have gotten her permission in advance. Another time when we were walking in Manhattan, Marie handed me a gift. Opening the box, I found white boxer underwear covered with red hearts. Instead of appropriately thanking her, I made the mistake of saying, "Gee, why didn't you get me pink, silk panties? I'm sorry. I can't wear these things." She got upset and threw them down the steps leading to a lower level apartment. I apologized, but the damage was already done.

At this point I asked Allan, "Do you want to stop now, and tomorrow I will move on to how I got interested in meditation?"

"Yeah, that sounds good. Do you know what Popeye said when he was eating a sweet potato?" Allan asked with his usual smile when he was speaking in jest. His humor was usually on the silly side, but that didn't matter. What I appreciated was his intention to loosen me up when I was getting too serious.

"No, what did Popeye say when he was eating a sweet potato?"

"I yam who I yam!" Allan said with obvious satisfaction, gently making fun of my identity search.

I responded, "Are you ready to meditate and tune into the Great, 'I Yam who I Yam'?"

"Yes, I yam," he said emphatically, and we closed our eyes for our attunement. As I began to meditate I was reminded that my agonizing about the question, "Who am I?" at the Whitney Museum was the first time I was trying to directly answer the question of my identity. My paintings were a search for identity in the form of images, but in my emotional torment at the museum I consciously realized just how important answering this question was to me. Years later, this questioning would crystallize into the challenge of solving the overall identity puzzle for my life as a whole and more specifically solving my shadow puzzle by uncovering the pieces of it hidden in my subconscious mind and putting them together in a meaningful way.

---

1. Daytop Village, or Daytop, was founded in New York in 1963 by Dr. Daniel Casriel, Father William O'Brien, Dr. Alexander Bassin, and several others.

33

THE NEW WORLD
OF MEDITATION

≈ • ≈

Continuing my narrative, I began:

Allan, we've finally arrived at the direct answer to your original question about how I got interested in following a spiritual path. It actually started with headaches that I began to have for the first time in my life. I went to a medical clinic to find out what was wrong. The doctor told me my body was healthy, so I figured it must be something wrong with my thinking or emotions. My psychotherapy group was addressing my emotions, but I felt I wanted to change the way I was thinking. I discovered that the mind set and attitudes that worked for my parents in their relationship did not work for my relationship with Marie, so I had to find a better way of thinking. My Catholic spiritual understanding was limiting me and making me feel increasingly guilty, so I sought a different spiritual outlook. Plus, confronting my emotions alone at the Whitney Museum brought up the larger question of "Who am I?" I thought maybe there was a missing spiritual element that could help me find the answer.

My first encounter with spirituality in New York came while I was out walking and was approached by a Krishna devotee. He was standing outside of a yoga ashram, and he invited me to come inside for a dinner that was about to be held. Although I hardly ever acted spontaneously, my curiosity got the best of me, and I made my way to the second floor of the ashram. I felt I had time-warped into some ancient culture where people were dressed in very loose-fitting white or many-colored clothes wrapped around their thin bodies. They moved slowly and spoke in subdued voices with an ever-so-pleasant tone. In contrast to the business and no nonsense of New York, they seemed to have found some secret for being at peace, or at least appearing at peace. However, I felt as though I did not speak the language of this foreign country, which made me feel uncomfortable.

We had to wait to eat until the guru presented himself and gave the blessing. Apparently this was a special celebration because the head guru of

KRISHNA

the Krishna movement was in town. When he arrived, I asked the person next to me who he was. The reverent answer was, "He is Krishna's representative here. He is Swami Prabhupada. He will talk to us about Krishna, and then we will eat." There were many enthusiastic "Hare Krishna" chants, which I listened to politely as I gazed upon the glowing blue body of Krishna displayed on a large poster. The guru, whom I irreverently thought of as the *Grand Poobah*, looked solemn and sour in contrast to the glowing faces of the devotees. He talked about how we are not material bodies at all and cannot be because we are spiritual beings.

[I don't remember Swami Prabhupada's exact words, but here is what he wrote about this idea:

Actually, the first lesson of *Bhagavad-Gita* is, "I am spirit soul. I am different from this body." I am a living force, but this material body is not a living force. It is dull matter, and it is activated only because spiritual force is present. In the spiritual world, everything is living force; there is no dead matter. There, the body is totally spiritual. One may compare the spirit soul with oil and the body with water. When oil is in water, there is a distinction and that distinction always remains. In the spiritual sky, there is no question of oil being placed in water. There everything is spirit.[1]]

The idea that spirit is distinctly different from matter and must always be different made some sense to me, at least intellectually, but I couldn't see what could possibly be the practical application of that idea. Then he said, "Following Krishna is the path of perfection." He talked at length about the goal of becoming "dear to Krishna" and ended his discourse with reading the chapter from the Bhagavad-Gita about, "The Yoga of Devotion," meaning devotion to Krishna.

[This is a portion of the chapter he read from:

> One who is free from desires;
> Who is pure, wise, impartial, and free from anxiety;
> Who has renounced all undertakings;
> And who is devoted to Me [Krishna], is dear to Me.
> One who neither rejoices nor grieves,
> Neither likes nor dislikes,
> Who has renounced both the good and evil,
> And who is full of devotion, such a person is dear to Me.
> The one who remains the same
> Towards friend and foe, in honor and disgrace,
> In heat or cold, in pleasure or pain;
> Who is free from attachment; and
> The one who is indifferent or silent
> In censure or praise, content with anything,
> Unattached to a place, equanimous,
> And full of devotion; that person is dear to Me.[2]]

From what he said it seemed to me that quite a lot was required of a devotee in order to become "dear to" Krishna. Since I had none of the virtues described in the chapter from the Bhagavad-Gita, I didn't think I would be very pleasing to Krishna. But instead of looking to Krishna as a representative of God, I felt I didn't have to look any further than to my own mother. After all, I could count on her loving me no matter how many mistakes I might make. I could see where it would be nice to be devoted to God or a divine representative of God, who loved me like my mother. Or at least I would want my God to not keep score of my trespasses, but from my Catholic upbringing I wasn't sure if that was possible.

After reading the quotation, the swami explained that everything we do can be spiritualized by our devotion to Krishna. Turning toward the food that we would soon be eating, he asked, "What is the difference between this holy food and ordinary food? This is like ordinary food, but because it is offered for Krishna's satisfaction it becomes spiritualized." Then he gave

SWAMI PRABHUPADA

the blessing of the food, and we ate. The food left a good taste in my mouth, but the rest of the experience left a bad taste. It's not that anything specifically negative happened. In fact, everyone was very kind, perhaps too kind. It's just that I didn't feel I belonged nor did I want to be converted to worshiping Krishna or his guru representative, Swami Prabhupada. I wondered if this was a cult and if they were all hypnotized through mass suggestion into being so sweetly disposed.

The truth be told, I would have probably been just as uncomfortable if they were all worshiping Jesus. I did not consider myself to be a particularly religious person, and it was challenging to be exposed to so many people who had devoted every aspect of their lives to religion. I was still curious about gaining individual spiritual understanding, but I could do without religious "groupiness."

I heard from an acquaintance that Scientology could raise my individual consciousness. I went to a Scientology center in town and was given a test with electrodes attached to my hands. I was asked questions to see if I had responses that would register electronically. Any response meant that presumably I had a problem related to that question. I was told eventually I could make progress and become a "clear" person, who had no responses that registered electronically. I asked to talk to someone who was advanced and was allowed to talk to the head man. But he gave me what sounded like canned answers to my questions, and he talked in a monotone. I could understand why he would have no electronic responses if he was tested by the electronic machine, since he seemed like a robotic machine himself rather than a genuine fully-present person. Learning to be emotionally unresponsive so there was no reaction to anything did was not appeal to me.

Since I wanted knowledge, I thought the best place to go would be a bookstore. The first book that attracted me was *The Tibetan Book of the Dead.* It talked about the afterlife and how it was important to look for the white light. The book described many potential afterlife places, and each place was related to a different color. These afterlife places followed the sequence of the spectrum with the least evolved place being red. Next was orange, and then each successive color followed, leading up to the higher levels, such as purple, and finally the highest, which was white light. The book also spoke of talking to the person who is dying and verbally telling him to look for the light, even if he is not fully conscious.

I thought all this was fascinating, especially the idea of seeing white light as the highest attainment. However, since I would have to die to see the white light and since I did not plan on dying any time soon, I was looking for something that could help me now. While at the bookstore I recalled all those stories Joe told me about Zen Buddhism. Consequently, I looked at the Zen books and was drawn to *The Three Pillars of Zen*[3] by the roshi, Philip Kapleau, and my life would never be the same again.

The biggest immediate change was that I started to look at the world differently. Growing up in my Western culture, I had always believed in the unquestioned reality of the world. I was caught up in what appeared to be the very real drama of everyday living, which sometimes involved a rollercoaster of emotions. But after reading this book I began to consider the radical question, "Could my whole frame of reference regarding the world be merely a mistaken assumption?" Not being previously exposed to yoga or Eastern philosophy, this was the first time I was presented with the idea that this world I inhabit is not real. The Zen Buddhist idea that the world is an illusion was difficult to swallow, but I was intrigued simply by pondering something I had never before even considered a possibility. I felt I had been presented with a puzzle, the most all-inclusive puzzle possible— the enigma of "What is the true nature of reality?" I liked puzzles and Zen Buddhism welcomed my doubts, my questioning mind. Instead of requiring me to accept any idea on blind faith, this philosophy said I could solve this puzzle myself if I was willing to make a commitment to practicing Zen disciplines involving extensive meditation.

According to Zen Buddhism, the true Self is Buddha nature or Mind, which is the origin of this world and which transcends this world of illusions. Everyone already has this Buddha nature or Mind, but this true Self is hidden from ordinary everyday awareness, which is based on ego consciousness. Zen Buddhism wouldn't specifically describe this illusory world as a prison, yet my interpretation was that perhaps I had been in prison all these years and did not know it. I was not convinced that I was in fact in prison, but was determined to do everything in my power to find out. I understood there was a way to escape this prison, and that gave me a purpose I had never had before. It changed what I felt was a meaningless life into a meaningful life. And the book gave very practical steps for how to escape from illusions and called the goal of escape by the name of "satori" or "enlightenment." There were even stories of ordinary people who had walked this path and who had found enlightenment. I figured that if they could do it, maybe I could, too.

The most appealing aspect of seeking enlightenment was that it was the answer to the question, "Who am I?"—the same question with which I had been struggling in my solitary form of psychotherapy at the Whitney Museum. There really was a Self that went much deeper than just my emotions. I was this Self that could be experienced after all, although not through the methods I had been using with psychotherapy. Surprisingly, there was even a practice described in which some seekers could ask themselves the question, "Who am I?" as a technique of awakening to enlightenment. This is a question, called a *koan*, that cannot be answered intellectually, but can be answered by the experience of enlightenment.

Most amazing to me of all was that the book maintained that everyone is already enlightened. How could this be? It is as if we were in a dark prison, and we think we are locked inside. But really it is only dark because we have our eyes closed. We are locked inside only by our minds. Actually the doors to this prison are unobstructed doorways that anyone can walk through. Enlightenment is merely an opening of our eyes to what already is. Consequently, enlightenment is not really a change. Enlightenment reveals our true nature the way it is now, always was, and always will be.

This idea that enlightenment is not a change is best illustrated by the parable of Enyadatta, which is recounted in Kapleau's book.[4] It's been a long time since I read this book, so I don't remember all parts of the story. Nevertheless, I'll make up my own version in order to give you the basic message:

In ancient times Enyadatta was a young woman who every afternoon looked in her full-length mirror to admire her beauty. One morning her mother came to her bedroom when she was gone and cleaned her mirror. After she was done, she absentmindedly did not hang the mirror on the wall where it had been, but just leaned it against the wall so it was left almost a foot lower than before. That afternoon when Enyadatta walked over to her mirror, she didn't even notice it had been lowered because she was half-witted. When she looked in the mirror she could see only as far as her neck and nothing above it. Not seeing the reflection of her head, she exclaimed, "I've lost my head! What will become of me? I will surely die. Where is my head? I must find it." She ran around frantically and became hysterical, screaming, "I've lost my head! Have you seen it?"

Everyone she met said reassuringly, "Your head is right there above your neck where it has always been. You haven't really lost your head." But Enyadatta did not believe them, insisting that she had indeed lost her head. She sobbed uncontrollably as she ran here and there looking for it in a frenzy.

She lived in a community of compassionate people. They gathered to decide what they could do to help her. A wise man said, "Poor Enyadatta is running around exhausting herself with her tears and fears. The best thing we can do is to tie her up so she will not hurt herself. That will calm her down, and then maybe she will listen to reason." So they tied her up, and she did calm down. With soothing words they kept telling her over and over again that everything was all right because she still had her head. They gently told her that she was unfortunately deluded. They explained that the problem was with her mind and that she could change her mind and realize she hadn't lost her head after all. Their loving words started to sink in, and she pondered, "Could I be mistaken? Maybe they are right." She partially believed them, but she was not convinced that she still had her head. Then one day she was visited by the same wise man who had suggest that she be tied up. He brought a stick with him and hit her on the head with it, saying, "That's your head!"

"Oh! I do have my head!" she hollered. Realizing that her head was not lost, she was overwhelmed with great joy. The wise man immediately untied her since she was no longer in danger of hurting herself. But then she started to run up to people saying, "I lost my head, but now I've found it. Isn't it wonderful?" She wanted everyone to celebrate with her.

However, everyone she met told her, "You never lost your head. You always had it. It's not really so wonderful that you have a head. Everyone has a head. There is no reason to celebrate because it's quite normal to have a head. It's still part of your delusion to think that you are somehow *special* because you have a head. Although Enyadatta had been overjoyed at first because she felt she had found her head, eventually she calmed down, realizing that she had not really gained anything new or out of the ordinary. Accepting the having of her head as quite natural, she settled back into a very normal life.

That's my variation of the parable. Now I'll give you my interpretation of the meaning. Enyadatta represents the seeker of today who feels there's something missing in his life. He runs around haphazardly in the world trying to find what's missing. He may try drugs, sex, power, or materialism and can totally exhaust himself or even hurt himself seeking to find what's missing. Of course, none of these outer things can fill the void to supply what's *really* missing. In the same way that Enyadatta didn't actually understand her problem, the seeker does not realize that the problem is in his own mind. Enyadatta being tied up to calm her down is an analogy for the seeker attempting to restrain and control himself through practicing meditation, which calms both the body and the mind. Then the mind becomes open to reason offered by others. The loving community symbolizes the teachings of Zen Buddhism and the testimony of those who have practiced it. Just as the community convinces Enyadatta that maybe she had not lost her head, the seeker learns from Zen teachings and from others who have walked this path that maybe his true nature has not been lost. Seekers begin to ask, "Is it possible that my mind is wrong about who I am?" Similar to Enyadatta wondering and half-believing what she was told, I also started opening up to the idea that maybe I do have a true nature that I never lost. Finally I got to the point where I believed in my true nature enough to be willing take steps to find out if I really had one.

The wise man in the story is the one who helps Enyadatta come to her senses by hitting her in the head with a stick. He stands for the Zen teacher who has experienced his own true nature and can help others do the same. A Zen teacher will sometimes hit a student with a stick, not to hurt him, but to stimulate his meditation practice and help him in his quest to experience enlightenment. Enyadatta running around overwhelmed with joy about finding her head is like the seeker who becomes enlightened for the first time. He can become prideful, thinking he has done some extraordinary thing, when in fact all he did was discover the same true nature that everyone already has. In the end, Enyadatta realizes that finding her head was not a discovery as much as it was a letting go of her delusion and accepting the very natural condition of having a head. The seeker who becomes enlightened can come to the same realization that there is nothing special about himself. He can see his enlightened condition as a perfectly normal state of mind within everyone, whether they are aware of it or not.

I really like this parable. The Zen approach teaches humility. It focuses on discovering how we are all really equal and there is no specialness about our true nature that would make us in any way better than anyone else. I knew I was prideful, but since it never made me happy, I admired this emphasis in Zen on equality.

After reading this book, I wasn't sure if I could become enlightened, but I felt at least I could change my perception to allow me to experience the world differently. The only thing that prevents enlightenment from dawning is the ego, the idea of a separate self. Whatever ways I could let go of the ego would bring me closer to waking up. Since the ego is the idea of separation and therefore only a thought in my mind, releasing the ego is related to letting go of the thoughts of the mind. This calming of the thoughts of the mind is the practice of meditation.

I learned the Zen method of meditation, called *zazen*, by following the step-by-step instructions for beginners provided in Philip Kapleau's book. At the start, I focused the mind on what is called the *hara*, an area just below the navel. First I meditated on the inhalations and exhalations to calm the breathing, which helped calm the mind. Later I focused on just the exhalations and still later on just the inhalations. I used the practice of "counting the breaths" from one to ten, and then back to one. This counting procedure is a means of focusing on the neutral thought of numbers in order to let go of the other thoughts in the mind. After counting the breaths came just following the breath—fully observing the inhalations and the exhalations without counting. In the traditional practice of zazen, the eyes are held just partially open, with the gaze downward at about a forty-five-degree angle. The eyes are kept unfocused on an area a few feet in front of the body, with the body sitting and facing a wall.

Marie was away visiting her parents for several days when I started to apply these directions. After meditating for the very first time in the evening, I lay down to go to sleep that night in my usual position, lying on my right side with the legs together. My hands were placed on the right side of my face and with the palms together, forming a pillow for my head. When I woke up in the morning, I was in the exact same position, which made me think I had not moved all night. I had none of the grogginess that I typically experienced from sleep, and my mind was unusually clear, even crystal clear. On subsequent mornings, there was less grogginess than usual, although not the absence of all grogginess. Greater mental clarity continued, although not to the degree I experienced that first morning. Right away I felt as though I had taken a step out of prison and was in somewhat of a new world. I was convinced that meditation really could change my life because I felt it was already having that immediate effect.

Marie had promised to temporarily take care of a friend's very young cat, but while she was gone, that responsibility shifted to me. The cat and I had a mutual dislike for each other, so we got along by staying out of each other's way. However, whenever I practiced meditation in a cross-legged position on the floor, the cat suddenly became my friend. The cat would crawl up onto my lap, which is where the hara is located. So that's how I learned that cats are attracted to the vibrations of meditation, which is not too surprising, since their purring is a form of meditation. Before sitting down for my practice of zazen, I would usually lock the young cat into the bedroom, but sometimes I actually let it cuddle up and purr in my lap while I meditated.

In order to sit in the cross-legged position, I had to stretch my knees, which were initially stiff. Because the full lotus was the recommended body position, I meditated that way. However, it was quite painful before the legs stretched properly. But I decided to simply confront the pain and not give in to it. At first I meditated for a short time and then increased the time. I used a timer and vowed not to move until the timer went off, no matter how painful the legs felt. I felt this physical pain was not nearly as painful as the emotional pain I had experienced in the past. In fact, I found this encounter with pain to be rewarding and confidence-building for me. I felt that by enduring the pain I was overcoming some deep emotional patterns. The result was that I was feeling cleansed inside.

When Marie finally came home, I was so exhilarated and happy to see her that she was shocked. In the past I had been rather reserved in my demeanor, and now I was very excited and even joyful. I spoke to her glowingly about my adventures in meditation and how I was changing for the better. I spontaneously picked her up and carried her off to the bedroom, and we had sex. It was the most remarkable sex I had ever experienced. My whole body was completely alive like it had never been before. Marie was not just Marie; she was like a female goddess of femininity. Confronting all that pain had made me feel inwardly that I deserved pleasure, and for the first time I felt completely open to sharing joy.

I felt so dramatically different that I was open to changing my entire diet. I became a vegetarian overnight, since this was recommended as a way to deepen meditation and promote good health. I had been a light smoker, and I gave up smoking cigarettes. The biggest change, though, was emotional. I felt a tremendous burden had been lifted from my shoulders. One day I remember being higher than I had ever been on drugs. I was happy all day. I tried to figure out why. Then I realized that there wasn't a reason, and there didn't need to be a reason. As I walked down the street I felt that I was literally in a movie. Everything in this movie was perfect, and everyone was perfectly cast for their parts.

When I went to a fruit market, I carefully observed the man working there as he weighed the vegetables. I saw him with clever sleight of hand hold down the scale to make the vegetables weigh more than they should. In the past I would have spoken up to express an emotional reaction, but instead I remained silent and at peace. Actually I was amused. Of course, this state of mind didn't last. Nevertheless, I realized I had dramatically changed for the better.

Another time I went to a movie, and what I saw was a flat white screen with colors floating over it. It was just an illusion seen as an illusion. Those floating colors were not really people on that screen. This was a remarkable illusion to see, yet a terrible way to watch the movie. Half way through, I forced myself to pretend that those really are people, and I allowed the normal illusion of the movie to take over so I could be entertained again. However, this experience made me realize that perhaps there are two ways to look at the world. In one way of looking, I could be caught up in the illusion. In the other way, I could see through the illusion and see what is behind the appearances of colored shapes. After all, it is only the colored movie film that makes the illusions, but behind the film is the pure, formless white light of the movie projector. Perhaps in the world, too, there is a real formless White Light behind the illusory earthly forms that I normally see in everyday life.

During my nights at the Whitney, I practiced meditation while also continuing with the daily emotional self-confrontations about which I told no one. But eventually I came to feel that the method of deeply penetrating my emotions in a solitary manner would not give me the answer to my persistent question of "Who am I?" In fact, if I continued with this solitary emotionalism, I felt that it would be just too exhausting emotionally and

PATH TO THE LIGHT

physically, and I was not even sure anymore if it was helpful. It seemed in conflict with the peaceful sitting of meditation that was producing such good results. So I just limited myself to the one group therapy session a week, with the support of others as a more moderate approach to expressing my emotions.

I still had my art work as my other form of therapy and self-discovery. Immediately after beginning to practice meditation, my art work improved noticeably. My painting began to reflect my new direction by consistently including expressions of light. In the past I had often used the image of the moon, but this image of light took on the new connotation of spiritual seeking. The moon image remained in some paintings, but in others gave way to the larger light of the sun.

I made a painting called *Path to the Light* that's the best example of this new direction. This painting is displayed on the opposite page. But before reading the following description of its symbolism, I suggest looking at the color version of the picture, which can be seen on the bottom and in the middle of the back cover. At the top of the picture there is an image of the sun. Also at the top is a blooming flower, which represents reaching the end of the spiritual path and truly finding the Light. The stem of the flower symbolizes walking along the spiritual path toward the flowering of spiritual growth. Unlike real flower stems that always rise upward toward the sky, this expressionistic stem forms a *horizon*. However, unlike a typical *horizontal* horizon, the stem forms a *diagonal* horizon. This narrow green border line rises from the lower left to the upper right, between the sky and the earth, touching both, yet not fully invested in either one. Thus the line of the green stem divides the dark blue sky above (mostly on the left side) from the muted yellow ochre earth below (mostly on the right side). This boundary line symbolizes walking along the spiritual path, maintaining a balance between reaching for heaven and being rooted in the world. The diagonal nature of the horizon is intended to give the impression of viewing only the left side of a steep mountain. Consequently, the top of this mountain, where the flower is fully blossoming, stands for the summit of spiritual growth.

On each side of the stem, there is a very large leaf—one rising above the diagonal horizon and the other descending below it. The leaf above is red and is surrounded by the blue darkness of the sky, but it points toward the light of the sun. It is an image of me as the seeker walking on the path. The leaf on the other side of the stem, extending below the diagonal horizon into the earth, also represents me. However, this dark blue leaf is the negative image of me, formed by the light hitting the red leaf and casting a shadow on the ground. This shadow leaf represents the dark side of my psyche in my subconscious mind that I take along with me as I walk to the

Light. This dark side is the source of all other images of fear, pain, danger, and death that had appeared in my previous paintings.

[Many of my past paintings were completely dominated by ominous images coming from the hidden corners of my mind, but here in this picture the dark psyche was reduced to its proper place as only part of a larger context. Consequently, the negative image of the shadow leaf represented, in just one small symbolic form, what I would later call my shadow puzzle. The painting as a whole, with all its forms, partially represented what I would call the identity puzzle of my entire life. It was not a complete representation of my identity puzzle because there were no images of my fellow seekers—those teachers and examples of spiritual attainment whom I would follow on the spiritual path and those who would walk with me on my journey to the Light.]

I made a whole series of these flower paintings, but also made other paintings about seeking the Light. Some of my earlier art work had actually frightened me by their images of darkness and death, but these new paintings were soothing to my psyche, expressing a sense of hope and even optimism. Although my paintings improved in regard to my understanding and my enjoyment of them, I lost my one-pointed obsession with creating works of art. Eventually, I valued my meditation more highly than my art work, realizing that my painting had been functioning as my means of meditation and self-discovery all along. Meditation now seemed to be a more direct means of focusing and self-discovery.

Feeling I had talked long enough, I suggested to Allan, "I would like to tell you about Marie's reaction to all these changes in me due to meditation, but that might take a while. Maybe we can defer that to tomorrow."

"It sounds like your experience with meditation was quite dramatic, so I see why it is so important to you. I look forward to hearing about how all this affected your girl friend," Allan said with his characteristic enthusiasm.

---

1. A. C. Bhaktivendanta Swami Prabhupanda, *The Path of Perfection*, (Los Angeles, CA: The Bhaktivedanta Book Trust, [1979] 1985), p. 4. I have used this quotation from Prabhupada's book as a representation for his words at this time when I met him.

2. Bhagavad-Gita, XII:16-19. This particular quotation can be found on the internet at www.santosha.com/philosophy/gita-chapter12.html.

3. Philip Kapleau, compiled and edited with translations, introductions, and notes, *The Three Pillars of Zen* (Garden City, NY: Anchor Books, 1980), p. 239.

4. Ibid., "The Parable of Enyadatta," p. 57-59. My version is a variation of this parable, with some parts added and other parts paraphrased.

34

BREAKING UP

≈ • ≈

I explained to Allan:

I have an epilogue to answering your question about how I became interested in spiritual growth. Sometimes opening up spiritually can produce unexpected consequences. Not too long after I had begun practicing meditation, I was talking to Marie on the phone and when I hung up, I started to cry uncontrollably. I didn't know why I was crying. Later when Marie came home, she gave me more information that explained for me why I had been crying. She said, "Just before I called you on the phone, I had been in my group therapy session. The group told me that you were using me, and they convinced me to leave you. However, when I was talking with you on the phone, I couldn't go through with it."

This gave Marie the opportunity to tell me for the first time about her experience of my transformation. She could see that I seemed happier. However, she felt that when I sat alone for meditation, I was separating myself from her. She had tried meditation herself. Nevertheless, she didn't see any value in counting numbers. I couldn't express love to Marie in the past, so when I did become more loving because of my meditation, it was too much for her to accept. The changes in me were so dramatic that I wasn't the same person, so she didn't trust me. I felt hurt because, although I was able to give her love that she deserved and always wanted, she couldn't believe it.

Marie suggested that we have a private consultation directly with the psychiatrist Dr. Daniel Casriel. I told him, "I am making a lot of progress by meditating, and it's helping me to love Marie more."

He replied, "There really isn't much merit in sitting silently. Marie is getting the impression that you are withdrawing from her because meditation is a form of withdrawal from the world. The benefits that you are experiencing from meditation are because you are feeling confident that you are doing something on your own. Because of your tendency toward withdrawal, I believe what you need is to be with other people—lots of different people. But on the other hand, I believe what Marie needs is to learn to stand on her own two feet. She needs a time alone to find herself. So I am recommending that you separate for a year in order for you both to grow. Then after a year you can get together again and see if you still want to pursue your relationship. What do you think?"

Right away, Marie said, "That's a good idea. Let's do that."

I was stunned, hurt, and angry. I couldn't understand how she could so instantly throw away our relationship because some authority figure recommended it. Since Marie had already said that she wanted to do this one-year separation, I felt that I couldn't reasonably object. I halfheartedly said, "If that is what you want to do, we can do that." Shortly after we left Dr. Casriel's office, I got in touch with how furiously angry I was feeling. I said, "I am really upset about this. I don't really want to break up."

"Why didn't you say so in the meeting?" she reasonably asked.

"I was too angry and hurt by you so quickly agreeing. I think you are too influenced by this psychiatrist and by your therapy group. Can't you think for yourself?"

"I am thinking for myself. And I think this will be good. We'll only be separated for a year, and then we can get together again," she answered.

"Look, we can make a commitment to contact each other in a year. Nevertheless, I think this psychiatrist knows that you and I will each find new friends. He knows that it is unlikely that we will be reunited, but he put out this carrot of reunion to make the separation look appealing. However, it is an illusion."

"It doesn't have to be an illusion, if we don't want it to be. A year is a short time, and afterwards we can get together again," Marie offered.

"Separating doesn't feel right to me," I said, "but I can tell you really want to do this. I promise to meet you after a year. Nevertheless, I am concerned that a lot of unexpected things can happen in a year."

"I do believe, like the doctor said, that I need to learn how to be more self-reliant, and this will give me time to do that. Maybe I'll even have an apartment by myself. Then we can get together again," Marie affirmed. We tried to separate as gracefully as possible. I rationalized by deciding that at least I didn't have to feel guilty about being the one to break us up. Marie and I decided to live together for one more month to make the transition smoother.

At Marie's urging I had already signed up for a marathon, and I decided to go through with it. A marathon was an intensive group therapy session lasting thirty-eight hours. The idea was to use fatigue to reduce the effectiveness of normal defense mechanisms. The marathon I would be attending had twenty members instead of the usual smaller size of our regular therapy group. I was nervous since I didn't know anyone in the group and only was in one previous session with the group leader, Jarvis.

As the marathon began, Jarvis asked who wanted to start first. Lyla, a woman with long black hair, said she had a feeling she wanted to express. She got out of her chair and turned directly to me and hollered, "I'm angry. I'm angry at you." I could hardly believe she was singling me out for her anger since I had never seen her before in my life. She continued to express her anger at me. Then she said I reminded her of her anger at her parents, so she switched to expressing her anger at them.

After she finished, Jarvis asked me, "Don, do you have any feelings you want to express?"

"No, not really," I said evasively.

Jarvis challenged me, "Don, I saw the expression on your face when Lyla was hollering at you. How about getting out some of those feelings?" Consequently I took a turn in which I expressed my anger at Lyla because I felt she was angry and critical of me for no good reason—just like my father. This led to being angry at my father. My anger was coming from my throat and then my chest, but not yet from the gut level. To help intensify my anger, I was given a pillow and told to imagine that the pillow was my father. I got to the gut level anger and started acting out the stabbing of my father with an imaginary knife. Then I became very dizzy, and at the same time I felt a sharp pain in my stomach. I stopped and said I didn't want to go on. The group insulted me for giving up and insisted that I continue. However, I would not express any more anger toward my father and refused to continue.

After I sat down and another person took a turn, I got up to leave the room to go to the bathroom. Jarvis, who was sitting near the door, intercepted me. "You aren't leaving, are you?"

I reassured him and walked out. Someone was in the bathroom, so I lay down on a nearby couch. My whole body began to shake, and I was still dizzy and felt like throwing up. What really upset me was that I felt I wasn't supposed to be stabbing my father with that imaginary knife. Something inside told me right then that my father was correct about what he wrote in his letter. I was in fact responsible for strange things happening to my parents because I had been projecting anger at them. But I knew the group would think this was just an excuse to avoid confronting my feelings. Plus the extreme negative reactions in my physical body confirmed that I really had to stop even if my stopping looked bad to the group.

I was still very dizzy for a while after returning to the group, but later was able to help other participants to draw out their emotions in their turns. Most participants took two turns. After twenty-four hours of continuous group therapy, we took a six-hour break in which we were allowed to leave and sleep. Then we returned for the second half, which was eight hours that included feedback in which each participant received feedback from every other participant. I was one of the first people to receive feedback, and the first person giving me feedback was Lewis. He was someone I liked, and he said he felt love for me because I had helped him get out his feelings. The next few people were polite, yet vague. Then it was Jarvis's turn, and he said, "Don, I don't like you, and I don't trust you. When you had your turn to talk, you stopped. You could have gone on, but you just gave up. You didn't even try. Although you could have come back later, you didn't do that, either. You didn't make the effort. And that's not fair to the rest of us."

Then there was a succession of others that said they didn't trust me. One woman, named Florence, said gently, with a caring tone in her voice, "I really appreciated how you helped others here. You were fully present for them. You helped them get out their feelings. But how about getting out your own feelings? This might sound strange, yet I have the image of you standing at the very edge of an abyss. You're looking down at a deep, black, bottomless pit. You are frozen there in fear. You are terrified of taking a step for fear of falling in that pit."

[Florence's description of me standing at the edge of an abyss struck me at the time as starkly truthful. I had tried to give myself the same message four years earlier when I hung over the balcony in college and looked down at imminent danger below. Yet secretly lurking in the back of my mind was the Pole Man, who was fearfully holding on to the pole and looking down at the prospect of certain death below. Of course, I had no awareness of my past lives when I was at the marathon, but Florence's comments were particularly striking to me anyway because she had spoken so compellingly and compassionately from her heart. The benefit of the marathon was that it brought out in the open the hidden pieces of what I would later call my shadow puzzle. However, the session didn't help me make sense out of the dark fragments of my subconscious mind that were revealed.]

Lyla, who had hollered at me at the beginning, gave her feedback next. She finally explained more clearly to me what upset her about me, "Look at yourself! You wear a black hat, a black scarf, black gloves, a black coat, black pants, black shoes, and a black moustache. You even trim your sideburns into pointed, sharp daggers. You make yourself look like an evil bad man in the movies."

When everyone had finished, it was my turn to say something about the feedback. I tried to form words, but I was so devastated that all I could do was lift my head up and groan loudly from deep within me. I had no idea I was projecting a bad man image. When Lyla pointed it out, I could see she was right. I felt it was an expression of my guilt, especially the guilt I still felt about the first Marie in my life, whom I had deceived into loving me and whom I had left so cruelly. It was also an expression of my guilt about getting out of the draft. Confronted with all the guilt in me, I felt like crawling under a rock and hiding. However, there was nowhere to hide. When all participants had taken a turn in receiving feedback, everyone was getting up and hugging everyone else—except me. I wanted to leave, yet I didn't. Then finally Florence come to me and hugged me. After her hug I felt a little better, and then Lewis also came over to give me a hug.

The whole experience shook me up considerably. Signing up for a marathon meant taking on a commitment to meet each week on an ongoing basis after the marathon was over. When I originally signed up, I could meet that commitment, but then with my subsequent plan of separation from Marie, my plans changed. I decided I was going to leave New York City, yet I didn't inform anyone before the marathon that I wouldn't be able to go to the follow-up meetings. In this sense I was dishonest and deserved not to be trusted by the marathon participants. At the second follow-up meeting I informed the participants that I was leaving and that this would be my last group meeting. I explained that I was relocating to Rochester, New York, to be closer to the Zen center run by Phillip Kapleau. Jarvis said he was disappointed in my decision and said, "It takes a lot of inner strength, courage, and discipline to practice Zen meditation. I don't see that you have what it takes to benefit from Zen. I think you would gain more growth by staying with this group and getting in touch with your emotions." There were no warm goodbyes from the group.

I gained a lot from the group therapy, but it was only as a stepping stone, not an end in itself. Some participants treated this therapy as if it was a religion that answered all the questions of life. I made no attempt to explain that I was concerned that emotional projections directed toward another person actually go to that person and affect that person adversely. I didn't explain that I thought acting out of stabbing my father may really hurt him. When my father had many operations under the knife subsequently, I felt somewhat responsible. Later I would learn that when a person continually expresses his emotions outwardly, it can exhaust his inner spiritual energy and that negative emotions like anger can produce poisons in the body. Also, this therapy perpetuates the illusion that anger is justified because of what others have done to you to make you a victim. Eventually I came to understand that anger is never justified and being a victim is an illusion, although it is a particularly hard one to release. I still haven't been able to release this victim pattern myself.

[When I was sharing my story with Allan, I was referring to my Spider Boy and Pole Man victim patterns without telling that to him. My early abstract paintings were visual representations of this victim pattern, even without any human images in them. For example, one of my paintings I called *House of Pain*. It's a picture of the house in which the Spider Boy fell through the floor. I titled another picture *House of Terror* because it scared me to look at it. It depicted a dark maroon house with a drumstick-shaped form attached to it. A sharp, knife-like image was cutting into this drumstick form. It was an illustration of my leg being amputated in my past life as the Spider Boy, yet at the time I painted it I was only aware of the fear I felt in depicting it. Another painting I called *Cutting Edge*. This painting is shown on page 370, but before reading the section below, I recommend looking at the color version in the lower right hand corner of the back cover. Brightly colored forms of high contrast would grab the attention of most viewers of this picture. Nevertheless, the title of the painting came from the less conspicuous green and brown form at the far right, which appeared to be a broad-bladed cutting tool. Looking like an elongated blade of a butcher's knife, this tool seemed to be slicing into a large red image. At a later time with hindsight, this too seemed to be a symbolic representation of the amputation that occurred during the past life when I felt as though I was a victim. Since that Spider Boy lifetime involved being traumatically cut by a knife, it becomes even clearer why, during the marathon, I was so reluctant to act out the stabbing of my father.]

To conclude my story, I explained to Allan, "Marie and I had enough time to adjust to the separation, and we were resigned to it. I said my final farewell to her at Janet's apartment so she would have some emotional support. She was crying when I left the building and went off to Rochester. So that is the last installment of my long involved story of how I got started on the spiritual path."

"I have one final question. What happened with Marie and you? Did you contact each other after a year?" Allan inquired.

"I called her after a year, and a man answered the phone. I said, 'Is Marie there?' and he hung up. Then I called again, and the same thing happened. I wrote her a letter saying I had returned to Christianity and was interested in becoming a monk, but was clear that I very much wanted to see her in person to talk to her. I gave a suggested date, time, and place for me to visit with her in New York City. She wrote back that she did not want us to meet. She said her therapy group felt that because I was thinking of being a monk, there was no point in us meeting. She said she was not convinced there even was a God, so she felt we did not have enough in common with me to meet. I was very disappointed because, even if we did not get together, I wanted to see her in person and wish her well. Because of my spiritual seeking, I felt more open-hearted, and I realized how much I really loved her."

HOUSE OF PAIN

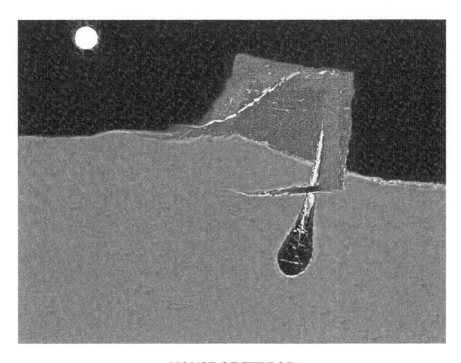

HOUSE OF TERROR

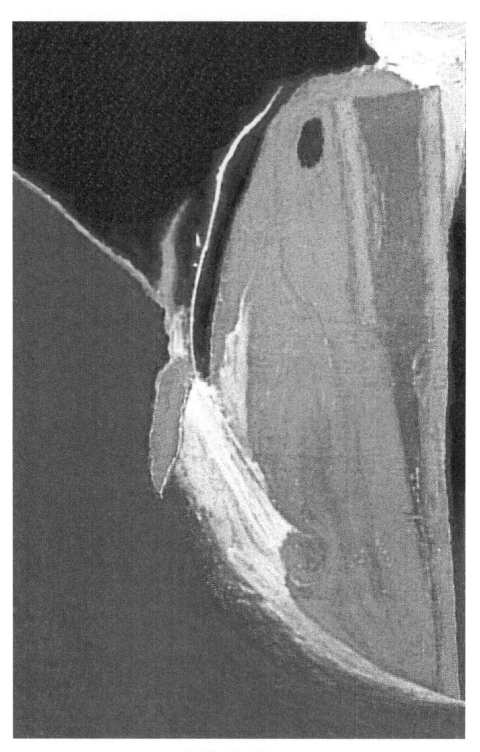

CUTTING EDGE

Allan asked, "Did you ever think about what might have been?"

"Sure, but we don't get to go back and rewrite the script of our lives. However, there was something I wondered about. Several years later I had a psychic reading that said, 'You have a boy who is inwardly close to you.' That made me wonder if I had a child by Marie, so I tried to contact her again, but was unable to find out where she had gone. The only other young children I was close to was my brother Rick's sons, especially his oldest, Jimmy. I was his godfather, yet I seldom saw him because he was living in another state. So that's my story. Of course, there is always more to tell, but I think that's enough for now," I concluded.

After a couple of months I felt that my stay at Christ Land was almost completed. I told Allan about my plan to leave, and he said, "There's something I want to share with you before you go. We all have a disease. Do you know what it is?"

"No, what's the disease we all have?"

"It's called *guilt*! It's a 'dis-ease' of the mind. At first glance, it seems quite innocuous. Yet this mental discomfort is the root cause of all physical ailments."

"I can see where guilt can cause some problems, especially mental problems. But I don't understand how it would cause *all* physical problems. How is that possible?" I asked.

"Let's consider what guilt is," Allan suggested. "It's the idea that I've done something bad and so I am bad. Because I am bad, I deserve to be punished. When a mind feels that it deserves to be punished, what do you suppose it will do?"

"I guess your point is that a guilty mind will be so upset that it will punish the body," I responded.

"Exactly right! The guilty mind will punish the body perhaps with a headache or a broken leg, maybe with a cold or even with cancer—all varying degrees of the same self-imposed punishment. You may not believe this, yet everything starts with the mind. An unhealthy mind will produce an unhealthy body—even a quadriplegic body like mine. The reason why I am telling you about this is that you have shared in your life story a lot about your past experiences of guilt. I don't want that guilt to come back and bite you in the future, so I want you to know there is a cure for this disease of the mind. According to *A Course in Miracles* that cure is forgiveness, which is the great need of the world. Forgiveness removes guilt and returns peace to the mind. Forgiveness will not always heal the body because, for example, I will always be a quadriplegic. However, the purpose of life is not to heal the body. The real purpose of life is to heal the mind so it is ready to wake up in heaven. Forgiveness offers this healing that prepares us for heaven. But we will only consent to forgive ourselves if we believe in God's unrelenting Love for us. All spirituality must lead to this awakening of God's Love. The reason why I always remind myself that I am the Son of God is because I am claiming the Love that God has for His Son, bringing eternal forgiveness. But accepting forgiveness is not just about accepting God's Love. Do you know what else is important?"

I replied, "We have to accept love from other people and give love to them."

Allan nodded his head affirmatively and said, "Yes, specifically we have to forgive others by seeing them as part of God and worthy of love. When we see another person as being guilty of something, we will think they are not worthy of love. The price we pay for seeing guilt in others is that we will see ourselves as guilty and not worthy of love. When we forgive all others of guilt, we simultaneously forgive ourselves of all guilt. You may never become a Course student since there are many different ways of finding our way back to heaven. But I do feel you need the central message of the Course, which is forgiveness. I know you have forgiven me, but I am concerned more about you learning to forgive everyone and especially yourself. I hope you can learn to let go of all guilt and totally forgive yourself. I just wanted to share that message with you before you go," Allan concluded.

"Thank you. I will take that to heart," I said. "What I want you to know before I go is that you are right—I have forgiven you. It does not matter if you remember our past life together, and I suppose there is a possibility I could be mistaken about our past together. What does matter is that I forgive you now, and I see you as the holy Son of God. Now I have to, as you say, come to a deeper level of forgiving everyone, including myself. You have told me that I remind you to think of Jesus, and now when I think of you, it will remind me to focus on forgiveness."

"And we can also remind each other that we are each the holy Son of God," Allan affirmed. I learned a lot from him, but nothing more important than the message of forgiveness. Perhaps the most impressive thing of all about Allan was not what he said, but what he did not say. He never uttered a world of self-pity so there was none of the "Why me?" that I had heard so many times while I was working as a recreation therapist in a hospital setting. Allan had made peace with himself, which was inspiring for me. He showed me that we can find contentment in our lives no matter what condition we find ourselves in. I was very grateful that Allan and I had formed a wonderful friendship, and I was certain that's why I had come to Christ Land. I felt the experience was healing for both of us. Next I returned to Virginia Beach to prepare for the transition to community living out West.

1986 IN VIRGINIA BEACH AFTER LEAVING CHRIST LAND

35

MOVING OUT WEST

~ ∘ ~

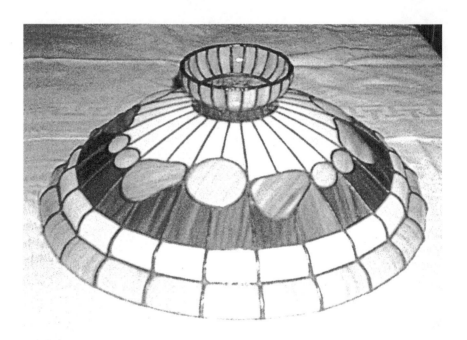

After returning to Virginia Beach I lived with my good buddy Chester Hatstat, who let me stay in his trailer for half a year without paying rent. Rose was still living with Dylan, and during this time I was able to reconnect with her again both socially for entertainment and spiritually in order to see the Christ in each other. I also offered prayer healing to people who wanted this service. Chester and I had long spiritual conversations, and before I left to go out West, I gave him my best Tiffany-style stained glass lampshade. It was my original design, with every single piece bent in my own kiln with molds I had specially carved for this purpose. It was the most beautiful piece of art work I had made, and it took me a full month of working seven

CHESTER HATSTAT

STUART DEAN

hours a day to complete it. I wanted Chester to have it because he had been so loving and generous to me in allowing me this time to prepare for my new adventure of community building.

I also gave a lampshade to Stuart in appreciation for the gift of his time and effort in helping to edit my book on Christian meditation. It was at this time that Stuart told me one of his own spiritual experiences: "I was very upset at one time in my life about the idea of my relationship to God. I had a lot of spiritual doubts, but then I had a vision of a gigantic matrix of lights all interwoven with each other. I felt I was one of those lights with a certain eternal place in the divine pattern. I realized that I am already that light, even though I have not yet awakened to the full awareness of it. After this vision, I no longer doubted by place in God's Light." Stuart talked to me again about *A Course in Miracles*, just as Allan had done, and I politely listened. I could not refute anything he said. However, I did not feel I needed a new spiritual philosophy. Having acquired a variety of spiritual ideas over the years, I was happy with my philosophy that focused on Christ, yet included influences from yoga and Zen.

In preparation for going to California to join with others for the next phase of my spiritual journey, I decided I needed to slim down and let go of some of my art work. I had already mailed some paintings to my brother Rick in Illinois and given others away. But I still had many paintings I had made in New York City years before, and I dropped them off at the local Goodwill store. At the time I thought this was a lesson in nonattachment—after all, these were my "children" I was giving away. However, looking back now, it's something that I regret, since these paintings were a tangible record of my spiritual journey. Nevertheless, the silver lining was that at least I had taken photographs of most of them, so the record was not totally lost.

In July of 1986 I left Virginia Beach by plane and arrived in Anaheim, California to be part of building a spiritual community. I immediately offended Robert, Wendy, and Sarah by implying that the real community formation would be now, which in their eyes trashed all the hard work they had already done in building their own three-person community. I soon discovered that I was not the first to open this can of worms, because David Sunfellow had already set off similar fireworks of his own. He and the whole Sunfellow crew of Pamela, their three children, Torey, Jeremia, and Shawna, along with their dog had appeared on the scene a month earlier after driving cross country in their beat up 1968 VW van. Since the arrival of the Sunfellows in June, a tug of war had been set in motion between what was dubbed the "Anaheim Half" and the "Virginia Beach Half."

So far I have mostly addressed how David, Pamela, and I, forming the Virginia Beach Half, worked together toward the goal of building a new community. At this point it may be helpful to describe the Anaheim Half in more detail. Sarah had grown up in Southern California expecting to live a conventional life based on American materialism. But in the summer of 1983 she was feeling a sense of the meaninglessness of life, and she had no spiritual aspirations. She was given a set of meditation tapes by Roy Masters and very shortly felt dramatic changes in her consciousness. Sarah recorded one specific experience:

> God has spoken to me. I can still feel His Presence and hear His words. I saw Jesus coming toward me from the light. He said, "Be not afraid, My child, for I am here." I dropped to my knees and began to repent for my sins. I told him that I had done bad things in my life. The Lord told me that I need not repent. He said that I had only been caught up in human endeavors, and that it did not matter anymore. He said that He and I were one now, and that He would be with me forever.

Sarah felt changed by her divine encounter, and as an aftereffect she found that she could hear what she called the "Voice of God." She described her transformation of consciousness in this way:

> My whole perception of reality changed. I felt like I had joined with God in some significant way, and that all He wanted me to do was love other people, situations, and myself. I felt extremely free, bound to the laws of God rather than man. There was a distinct feeling that all my life I had been searching without even being conscious of it, and that now my search was over.

Sarah's opening to the divine presence was exhilarating and joyful. She had a continuous awareness of the divine life flowing through her, but this higher state of consciousness soon wore off. Having experienced this elevated awareness, she was upset to find that her deep connection with the divine was lost, and she became inwardly confused. She felt guilty that she might have done something wrong to disconnect herself from God and felt discouraged because of her inability to regain her former high level of consciousness. Although she retained her ability to hear God's voice, she had serious doubts about the authenticity of this inner voice. Nevertheless, her guidance told her that in the future she would regain her experience of unification with God, and she hoped this would happen in spite of her reservations about her abilities.

To make sense out of this contrast between her former elevated state of consciousness and the darkness in which she found herself, Sarah visited her friend, Robert, who along with his wife, Wendy, was living in San Jose. A casual friendship between Sarah and Robert changed into a deep spiritual connection. After returning to Southern California, Sarah received visions of a spiritual community, which she called "Our Home." Sarah resisted talking about her visions because they were so sacred to her. Finally, after some weeks, she told Robert about her visions of a spiritual community. Robert explained to her that he and Wendy had previously received their own guidance that they would be part of a new spiritual community. Sarah and Robert realized that their common guidance about a future community was a divine prompting. Robert in particular felt inspired by the thought that God was providing signs to pursue the spiritual community that he and Wendy had been preparing for since they had received their psychic reading a few years earlier.

Based on their joint guidance, Robert and Wendy relocated to Anaheim, California to start a spiritual community. With high expectations, Robert enthusiastically invited friends from his former Edgar Cayce study group to join in this new community adventure. However, he was surprised and disillusioned by their total lack of interest. For the practical purpose of finances, Sarah was invited to live with Robert and Wendy to share expenses. Only after Sarah moved in did they realize that this in fact was the start of their planned spiritual community, which was the direction in which God had been guiding them all along. Since Sarah's move-in date was January 15, 1984, the Anaheim Half celebrated this date as the birthday of their community.

Robert discovered interesting parallels between his newly founded community and the celebrated spiritual community located in Scotland called Findhorn. Both communities had three founding members that seemed to symbolize the mind, heart, and will. Also both communities had their cornerstone relationship include a strong male figure who brought the community vision into manifestation in the world, and a strong female heart-centered person who received divine guidance for the community.

The male figure at Findhorn, Robert Caddy, was represented in the Anaheim group by Robert, who was intellectually brilliant. Before beginning this community Robert had planned for a career along the lines of a modern-day philosopher. But he was redirected by a combination of the community and a growing interest in *A Course in Miracles*, of which he would become an authoritative teacher and spokesman. Robert, like Robert Caddy, was emotionally distant. Robert fulfilled the role of being the interpreter of the divine plan as it unfolded in their community. He drew upon direct guidance, as well as parallels, like the one with Findhorn, to help highlight the divine hand that was at work in their lives.

The female figure at Findhorn, Eileen Caddy, was represented in the Anaheim group by Sarah, who was all heart. Her heart allowed her to open up to pure divine inspiration and hear the Voice of God, and also to connect at the heart level with other people as an expression of love. However, her elevated heart could also descend into emotional extremes in which her natural loving nature closed down. Robert reminded Sarah to use her reason for necessary balance, and Sarah reminded Robert to use his heart as a balance to his rational thinking.

Wendy represented the will and would get things done in the world of practical, everyday living. Wendy liked to take action and be in control to accomplish goals. She had difficulty adjusting to the fact that God was intervening in her life, which at times made her feel resentful that God was taking over control of her life. Nevertheless, Wendy had felt from her youth that she had a calling to one day become a minister.

Sarah was not the only one to hear an inner divine voice. Wendy could hear what she felt was Jesus speaking to her, and this first occurred a short time after Sarah moved into their house. In the garden one day, a heated argument broke out between Wendy and Sarah. At a loss for what to do, Wendy asked for inner guidance on how to proceed. She heard a voice say, "Tell her that you love her." So Wendy followed the advice, and surprisingly it worked. Wendy and Sarah were both redirected toward what mattered, which was love, and the form-related problem was amicably resolved.

Nevertheless, not all future community disputes would be so quickly resolved. One issue that was consistently controversial was, "Who founded this community?" Did the Anaheim Half start the community? Robert, Wendy, and Sarah felt they had a special place as the founders of this community and therefore were concerned that the newcomers from the East would disrupt what they had set in motion. The Anaheim Half felt that they knew better how God's Plan should unfold for the community.

On the other hand, the Virginia Beach Half felt that in prior years they had already been participating in God's Plan for community building. The joining of David, Pamela, and me in the Light House started in 1981, predating the Anaheim joining by three years. The Virginia Beach Half felt that they had years of experiencing attempts at community building and that they were being prepared all along for a future community that God had planned for them. However, not even recognizing that God had been the true founder of the community could resolve this dispute. Instead of valuing the gifts that each half had to offer, there was an overall lack of trust and suspicion between the two halves.

The relationship between Robert and David symbolized the differences and lack of trust between the two halves. Robert and David engaged in a verbal wrestling match, with neither side giving in. Robert focused on what he considered the blind spots in David and presented these as the problems that David needed to address. David likewise offered what he considered Robert's blind spots to him to look at and correct. Each denied that they had such blind spots, and each considered that the other was seriously mistaken. Neither would make any concessions. Out of futility they both had to call a truce and take a step back in order to ask God to reveal what would be most helpful.

This ongoing confrontation had simmered down considerably by the time I arrived. At first I thought that Robert was representing the Anaheim concerns and that David was representing the Virginia Beach concerns, including my own interests. But after a while, I no longer felt David was advocating for my concerns. This tug of war appeared to me to be simply a power struggle for leadership of the community. By engaging in a standoff, Robert and David neutralized each other, creating a leadership vacuum. How to resolve this leadership issue would be a long-standing concern, and over the years the community went through many phases of attempting to resolve this problem.

After Robert and David finally disengaged from their combat, there was a general understanding that firmly holding to one's own individual perspective would not work for a community. So we tried to come into each other's world to see from the other person's perspective. We held group meetings every day to listen to each other and to learn how to open ourselves to each other. The stated goal was to become more loving, yet often there was only more confusion. We tried to create a safe space for everyone to share their deepest feelings. However, this was difficult because of mistrust.

At one of these meetings I shared what I was feeling. "I am here because God wants me to be here, and that is the only reason. This community is like an 'arranged marriage,' not just for me, but for all of us. God has thrown us together with people who are very different from ourselves, and we have to learn to make the best of the arrangement." The idea of an arranged marriage would thereafter often be quoted by many of us to describe how we were being forced to be in relationship with people whom we did not choose based on our own personal preferences.

I elaborated by saying that this marriage arranged by God is supposed to be a marriage of equals, but it did not feel that way to me. I felt that Sarah, Robert, and David were first-class citizens in the community, while Wendy, Pamela, and I were second-class citizens. I explained that I actually felt like even less than a second-class citizen. Looking at each person, I said, "I am finally part of a spiritual community, and as I look around this room, who are my friends? I have a relationship with David because I was attracted to him, not because he was attracted to me. I have a relationship with Pamela because I was attracted to her, not because she was attracted to me. A friendship is based on mutual attraction, and I have not felt that here. The fact is, I don't have any friends here." I began sobbing.

David spoke up. "There is something wrong here."

Was David right that there was something wrong here? Yes, he was correct that I had a shortcoming in regard to why I was crying. I was claiming to be a victim and indirectly blaming others for my feelings, and I would continue to do so in future community situations. Eventually, after many years, I would come to realize how I could overcome this feeling of being a victim and blaming of others, but I was not yet ready to see how I manufactured this pattern. Also in my subconscious mind there were still the Spider Boy and Pole Man experiences of perceiving myself as a victim who engaged in blaming. The Pole Man experience in particular seemed to be a time of being rejected by a whole community of people and in turn rejecting that community. If I could express my hurt feelings of rejection to this new community and if I could be loved and supported anyway, it would go a long way toward healing my Pole Man experience and my victim pattern.

Although David was intellectually right to notice there was something wrong about my expression, he was emotionally wrong to be pointing that out to me when I was in a weeping emotional state. In addition, the idea of us sharing with each other was not to make judgments on the nature of each other's problems, but rather to open up our hearts to each other. After David's judgment, Sarah immediately countered, "Let Don have his feelings, even if you don't agree with what he is saying."

After the meeting I talked to Robert privately. He said, "Did you notice how after David said, 'There is something wrong here,' everyone shut up, and no one ventured to express any more feelings. Judging someone while they are having feelings, even if they are speaking inaccurately, is a killer for creating a safe space for us to share with each other."

I explained, "David doesn't really understand vulnerability. It makes him feel uncomfortable because he sees it as a weakness, not a strength. David talks about equality, but he doesn't see me as an equal. I believe David looks down on me because I am too vulnerable—too quick to cry. I don't think he has the ability to be receptive to me and to come into my world. Consequently, for us to connect I have to be receptive to him and come into his world and be reasonable, rather than emotional. He has a real purity about him and a total dedication to God. My admiration of those qualities helps me to come into his world and communicate with him. Actually I feel closest to him when I meditate with him, rather than when we talk with each other."

One of the things that we came to learn as a result of these community sharings was that others could really see our shortcomings better than we could see our own. David had already gotten a glimpse of these problems in Celo, North Carolina, before coming out West. Looking back on this time of living in Celo, David wrote:

> There was a lot of tension—tension in both my relationship with Pamela and my relationship with my brother, Walter. Although they expressed their concerns in differing ways, they both were saying essentially the same thing: "THEY DIDN'T FEEL LOVED BY ME."
> At the time this was an extraordinary thought. It simply didn't register. How could they possibly say, think, or feel that I didn't love them after all the time, energy, and life blood I had given them? I had shared with them both all the main things I knew about God— and lived these things with them. Their concern escaped me. I tried to understand what they were saying and feeling, and lamely tried to ease their minds, yet I essentially concluded it was their problem, not mine. They did, of course, both have major problems they were working on and bouncing off me, but their essential insight that I didn't really love them, I later realized was painfully true. But at the time as close as I could get to this major realization was that I needed to spend more time with Pamela and the children (and also my brother, Walter).

It was as a result of David's participation in our new community that he realized that his challenge was to come to a deeper level of learning how to give and receive love. Of course, he was not the only one who had lessons to learn. We were all in the process of learning the same lesson of how to love. David liked to tell the following story: "A group of people, who thought they were in hell, sat before a large table overflowing with delicious food. However, they had very, very long spoons taped to their hands. They could scoop the food up, but it was impossible to bring the spoon to their mouths to eat it. Then they decided to feed each other and discovered that they were in heaven, not hell."[1] We too needed to focus on what we were giving to each other, rather than focusing on what we were getting. If we could learn to appreciate others and give love to others, we would likewise feel appreciated and loved ourselves.

---

1. This is a paraphrasing of the story, "A Parable of Heaven and Hell," from the writing of Lionel Blue and June Rose in *A Taste of Heaven: Adventures in Food and Faith*, published in 1977 by Darton, Longman & Todd, Ltd.

36

COMING TOGETHER

≈ ◦ ≈

The war of words between Robert and David created a lot of polarizing between them about many issues. Robert was an advocate and teacher of *A Course in Miracles*, and David set his mind strongly against it. Robert saw no problem with computers and other technology, and at that time David preferred natural forms of expression that were non-technological. David would churn out dreams that confirmed the specific problems that he had discussed with Robert. On the other hand, Robert took the position that David's dreams could at times be divinely inspired, but could also simply be reflections of his own judgments and prejudices. There was no way to resolve these intellectual differences. The additional opinions of the other four community members contributed more confusion and lack of unity in the community.

To help us gain clarity on these and other issues we collectively asked for divine guidance and discussed each person's individual guidance. The Virginia Beach Half relied mostly on intuitions and dreams, as well as how the course of events seemed to be revealing what the next step would be. Sarah and Wendy had their inner voices, and Robert felt he could read God's Plan by watching for patterns and parallels that presented themselves in our daily lives. Also our discussions about the guidance itself was a form of guidance in which we could share our understanding and personal experience as a way of coming to a consensus on how to proceed. Even the attempt to function as a team rather than as separate individuals was a worthwhile direction for building within ourselves the trust that we could actually be a spiritual community.

However, we even had a controversy about guidance itself. Sarah became a focal point of this controversy because her guidance was playing a central role in our group. David raised the issue of how much trust should be placed in any single person's guidance, and Sarah herself had doubts about her guidance. We drew upon everyone's guidance when we collectively wanted to address a particular issue of concern for the community. Yet often we would turn to Sarah's guidance whenever we came to a standstill and didn't know what to do. Sarah's guidance consistently reminded us to focus on the content of love and to let go of form-related concerns.

At times when I felt I needed to be by myself, I walked to a nearby church to pray and meditate. On one such occasion a man approached me and told me his wife and children were stranded and needed help. I brought him to a local Catholic social service agency and stayed with him after they told him they could not help him. After turning within and asking for guidance, I gave the man $65. I had only $77, so that left me with only $12 to my name and no job. When I got back to the house, the others told me that I had acted foolishly because often con men go to churches to convince naive worshipers to give them money.

I had given the man my address in case he needed additional help, and he showed up at our house and saw me in the back yard. He came over and asked for more help. Even though I accepted the assessment of other community members that he was a con man, I did not feel it was my place to harshly judge him and to confront him. I told him to wait there, and I went into the house. I returned with two pears, which I gave to him. I explained I could not give him any more money, and he left eating a pear. I said a prayer for him because it seemed to me like a terrible waste of a life for him to think he could gain something of value by being a con man. Then community members were upset that I had given out the address of the house to this stranger.

I was already being looked down upon for a lot of reasons. I wasn't very much concerned about form-related issues and appearances, like my baggy pants not being held up by a belt. I was not accustomed to stacking the dishes in a giant mountain formation as was the household custom. Consequently, whenever I washed the dishes, which I volunteered to do often, I would end up breaking a glass or a dish, which became a joke told behind my back. There was also a whole bunch of items precariously balanced on the top of the refrigerator. I managed to dislodge them, and they came crashing down onto the kitchen floor, drawing more attention to my bungling. I never had such a problem before or since, so I had a sneaking suspicion that this was my subconscious way of acting out to express my feeling of being rejected.

At this time I was 41 years old, David was 32, and everyone else was in their twenties. Let's suppose, for example, that I made a comment that I was in a college classroom when I first got the news that President Kennedy was shot, since the date November 22, 1963 was burned into my memory. But what could that date mean to the Anaheim Half? After all, at that time Wendy was four years old, Robert was three, and Sarah was one. Robert was kind enough to alert me to the fact that some of my remarks dated me, creating a distance between me and others, so I learned to not make references to the past. There was a lot of bantering and sarcastic jokes between the Anaheim group members that made me feel like I was trying to join a clique. However, I didn't know the social interaction rules of the group. Also when I had been part of spiritual groups in Milford, Pomfert, Santa Cruz, and Virginia Beach, the seekers were already just as removed from being in the everyday conventional world as I was. The Anaheim Half had spiritual ideals, yet their personalities were very much into the conventional world. For example, in past communities I could offer to exchange massages as a way of connecting, but I got the impression that a massage would be a little too "touchy feely" for the Anaheim Half. I was familiar with seekers who would have no reservations about dancing around a room spontaneously or participating in a structured Sufi dance, activities that would be considered targets for humor by the Anaheim Half.

In addition, my monk identity created distance, although it was not intended to do so because I considered myself a "monk in the world." Everyone was married except for Sarah and me, and Sarah was engaged to Barry and would soon be married. I was told by one community member, "I am not upset about you being a monk. It's how you carry it." I could assume from this that my spiritual pride was oozing out of me, in spite of my best efforts to hide it. Whenever questioned about this, I had no problem openly admitting my spiritual pride without trying to beat myself over the head with it. I was told by one person that by symbolically representing meditation and its importance to the community, I was threatening this person's freedom of choice not to meditate. All of this mystified me since any other spiritual community in which I had been involved held meditating and the ideal of being a monk in very high esteem and did not require any justification.

I did not ask the community to appreciate the outer monk in me, which included my ego attachments to being a monk. From my perspective, whether I presented an acceptable or unacceptable outer monk was beside the point. I was married—to God! I had chosen to be a monk to remind myself that my life was not about external appearances. The real value of my life had been placed on my inner world, where outer appearances were not very important to me. However, they were important to others, especially the Anaheim Half. I asked them to see through the outer mask that I presented and to see the Spirit inside of me. It would be an ongoing request on my part, because I was asking for more than they were capable of giving. I wondered if the Pole Man had been spiritual and if he was misunderstood and rejected because of his spirituality. If so, then resolving this issue with the community would help me to heal the past as well as the present.

I was asking the community and in particular the Anaheim Half to see the divine in me for my benefit and healing. But I was also asking this for their benefit as well. It occurred to me that although they had practiced prayer and meditation and some had heard a divine voice, they must not have an inner world like mine. They did not seem to understand that there is a place of profound peace within me. Of course, they certainly had the same deep and fulfilling peaceful place within themselves, but they just didn't have access to it yet. If they could not acknowledge and experience this inner world within themselves, then how could I expect them to understand or appreciate this inner world in me?

On the other hand, if they could somehow believe I could experience this inner world, then that might be the motivation for them to trust that they too could find peace and nourishment in the inner world within themselves. However, I could not bring myself to describe my sacred inner world to them, because I felt it would be like "throwing pearls before swine." I did not think they would understand or believe me, and I did think they would turn on me and perceive only the spiritual pride in me that was indeed an already obvious shortcoming of mine.

Instead of wanting to live in a hermitage apart from the world, I wanted to be a monk in the world because I wanted to not only see the divine within myself, but also see the divine within the world and specifically within other people. In the past I had been able to see through the masks of others in order to see the Christ in them, and I felt it was my calling to eventually be able to do this consistently. However, at that time I was having trouble seeing the divine in those who were making judgments of me, which in turn led to my making judgments of them. It would take a long growth period for me to get over the pattern of judging others for judging me. I did not feel satisfied with seeing the divine in others only when they weren't judging me. I felt that my long-term challenge was to be able to see the divine in others precisely at those times when they were judging me, which was the standard that Jesus had set for His followers.

When I was labeled as foolish for throwing away my last funds to a con man, it was the last straw in a series of rejections that were weighing heavily on me. Just as the community as a whole turned to Sarah to resolve unresolvable issues, I asked Sarah to consult her inner guidance on the issue of me giving money to the man who requested it. Her guidance indicated I had acted in a responsible manner because I had asked for inner guidance and had expressed love to the man based on the best of my understanding. The implication was that even if I was mistaken about this man, it did not matter. What mattered was that I had sought guidance and was attempting to express love. As would often happen, Sarah through her guidance had come up with the remedy that satisfied everyone.

The message from her guidance that always came through was to become vehicles of love, and it was the one common goal that we all accepted. None of us was a shining example of living up to this ideal, but just agreeing on it was an accomplishment in itself for our community. I once tried to take this a step further and see if we could come up with a common word or words that we all could use as a meditation affirmation to help us draw together at a deeper level spiritually. Nobody liked the idea, and even if the idea was accepted, it would have been virtually impossible to come up with a word or words everyone could agree upon.

In spite of our differences we made enough progress in our sharing together to finally shift our focus toward finding how to get along with each other and function collectively. We turned our attention toward sharing what our individual spiritual purposes were that we wanted to manifest in our group and in the world. We took turns in sharing symbolic visual images that represented our individual spiritual purposes. Representing the intellect in our group, Robert possessed the ability to absorb a great deal of detailed and confusing information. He could find the underlying pure principle behind various seemingly unrelated manifestations, and then clearly help others see and understand the truth for themselves. He shared images from a reading by Sarah, as follows: "Robert is standing at a podium, talking and lecturing to an audience in an auditorium. He is saying important things. But he's light and laughing and being humorous. He is getting through to people with his sincerity and helpfulness. After he finishes, the people come up and hug him, and he hugs them. They thank him for what he's doing. He feels warm and fulfilled. He's writing—writing a book. It seems like the lecture has to do with the book. It's about his ideas, spiritual stuff, and how that can help people."

Representing the heart, Sarah had the ability to communicate love to others by connecting with them at the heart level. However, she also served as a hub between people, helping them connect with each other and connect with God. She saw herself in this way: "I'm walking in a field with tall grass all around me, gently swaying in the cool breeze. I am just walking slowly, but most importantly, I'm feeling God around me and within me. I'm feeling completely loving and at peace. I am with God."

Representing the will, Wendy was talented in regard to bringing things into material manifestation and bringing spiritual enrichment to people's lives through ministry. She described her image: "I see a woman under a big tree on a bright, clear day, speaking to a fairly large group of people. I am expressing my thoughts in a clear, vibrant, and loving way. Afterward, a few people walk with me, talking, and I am understanding, accepting, and compassionate. The people feel drawn to me because of how loving I am, because of the peace within me."

Representing the nurturing influence, Pamela had a mothering quality oriented toward serving and grounding others to help them find harmony in life by becoming part of the whole of the earth, including, of course, the human community. She perceived her image, as follows: "Native American Indian seeking to be in union with the Holy Spirit. To be in tune with all life. Honoring Mother Earth and helping heal her pain."

After the foundation for Findhorn was established by the three original members, a fourth member, named David Spangler, was attracted, and his coming initiated the extensive expansion phase of Findhorn's growth. David Spangler embodied the synthesis of all the qualities of the original founders, so he represented a harmonious balance of inner and outer qualities needed to provide leadership for Findhorn's expansion. Robert, noticing parallels between our community and Findhorn, felt that David represented this balanced one man culture and felt that David would spearhead our community expansion in the future, just as he had accelerated spiritual growth for many seekers in Virginia Beach.

David had already demonstrated the ability to fuse all the elements of life into a simple, pure, and total orientation toward God in his own life. He saw himself leading others to give up their old ways and to unify all the various aspects of life into one holistic approach to God and Christ. His symbolic image of himself was described as: "Moses leading the Jews out of Egypt (physical, emotional, and mental bondage to the world), through the wilderness (of inner and outer earth changes, representing purification), and into the Promised Land (of Christ Consciousness) by doing God's Will and following in the footsteps of Christ."

I was the only community member who practiced yoga daily, and my greatest strength spiritually was my inner attunement. Consequently, in our group I represented divine attunement, especially related to meditation and the awareness of Divine Light, which I also call the Christ Light. I shared the following symbolic visual image with the community: "I am one of six people sitting in a circle and meditating. A dove is in the center of the circle high overhead. The dove is the Holy Spirit, who sends a ray of Light straight downward. The single ray divides into six rays that go to the head of each person meditating. I have an innate yearning for and awareness of oneness with Divine Light and an ability to channel that Light into conscious awareness. I will become increasingly conscious of the Divine Light expressed in the earth and in people and help others become consciously aware of that Divine Light."

This visual image shows six people in a circle because of the six people joining in our community, but the image could be of a limitless number of people. The light coming down in the middle is One Light, and although it divides into six rays, it still remains One Light—pure and undiluted. The people in the image may have different individual talents. However, the light manifests in each one to exactly the same degree, and therefore in the light everyone is equal. The only variable is how open the seeker is to becoming aware of this pure Divine Light. To see the Divine Light means to see your own true nature—to see the Christ in you, which is always present, whether recognized or not. Potentially you can become aware of the Christ within yourself directly through meditation or other inner experiences. But you can also see the Christ in others, which enables you to indirectly recognize the Divine Light within yourself. This is the service Rose had provided for me and I for her. I wanted to grow in the direction of seeing Christ in all my community relationships, but I was hoping that eventually I would be able to generalize this awareness to many others and ideally perhaps to everyone I met.

Our collective community visions of the future were our ideas of our individual purposes in the earth. However, since we were in a community, we discussed at length how we could assist each other in accomplishing our purposes. This orientation helped us to come together in a closer union and prepared us for having a ceremony to express our commitment to God, to our community, and to each other individually. We felt that this was like a spiritual marriage ceremony in which we were giving our lives to each other. In this unifying ceremony we each lit candles from one central source, symbolic of our inner light, and made our community commitment in the following words: "I promise to do God's Will to the best of my ability."

We wanted to come together and resolve all past differences, but we also had to learn to be patient. David had a dream in which St. Peter stood in the middle of a corn field. Raising his arms, St. Peter commanded the corn with the word, "Ripen!" Naturally the corn was not ready, so it did not immediately ripen as commanded. Then a voice in the dream said, "Band together now in patience and in love, and know that it will take time for you to ripen, too."

Although a lot of questions, issues, and grievances remained unresolved, we had made the crucial joint decision to come together for the common purpose of building a spiritual community and doing God's Will. Robert, Wendy, and Sarah were happy because after a long time others had finally come to join with them. David, Pamela, and I were gratified that after so many failed attempts at community, we were finally going to experience the real thing. Everyone felt that we were ready to learn how to increasingly cooperate together as a spiritual family. We expected future fights because that is a part of family life. But we were hopeful that with God's help we would persevere and that God's Will would be accomplished through living our lives dedicated to Him and to each other.

37

ON TO SEDONA

≈ • ≈

The original plan had been for David and Pamela to stay in Anaheim for two weeks in June before moving on to Sedona. However, it was the middle of August before they were able to set off for their new home and establish a foundation for the future work of the community. The Anaheim Half would support this effort through prayer, financial help, and frequent communication by phone and mail. The plan was for the Anaheim Half to take up residence in Sedona at a future unspecified date in order to fully reunify the community. Although I wanted to go to Sedona immediately, I understood it would be better for the Sunfellows to travel ahead first. After all, David and Pamela were traveling with the children, Torey, Jeremia, and Shawna. All the Sunfellows and their belongings, as well as their dog, Chewy, were squeezed into their willing, yet sometimes cranky VW van. They arrived on August 14, which had been a significant date of healing in my life, as I will describe in later chapters.

I stayed back in Anaheim for an additional eight days—long enough for me to meet Findhorn's Peter Caddy, who was visiting and sleeping over at our house at Robert's invitation. Robert was churning out more parallels of how it was that this founder of Findhorn had arrived at our house just as our community was experiencing its own growth spurt. On the same day Peter Caddy came, I was able to meet Barry, Sarah's future husband, and his friend, Mark, who together had just succeeded in riding from coast to coast on bikes. I felt connected to them right away, and I marveled at their achievement. Perhaps strangely for a monk, I had always been a sports fan. I appreciated athletic accomplishments, although I was not athletically inclined myself. In fact, I would even have a hard time adjusting to the physical challenge of camping in Sedona. At least I consoled myself with the comforting thought that it would only be a short time of camping in the desert. Surely we would make friends and become involved with all sorts of spiritual endeavors in our new home.

When I arrived in Sedona on August 22, I found the rock formations more beautiful than I expected. The first camp site that David and Pamela came upon just happened to be in the shadow of a bell-shaped mountain

BELL ROCK

of red rock, appropriately called Bell Rock. It was one of the many esoteric "vortexes" of energy in Sedona. For the sake of privacy, I set up my tent and camp site at a distance from David and Pamela's site. I set up a candle in my tent for night reading and meditation, and the next day went out with David and Pamela to explore Sedona. There were plenty of New Age centers, bookstores, restaurants, and health food stores that served as gathering points for seekers who had been attracted to Sedona, often without knowing quite why they had come. Around every corner it seemed there was a psychic channel of St. Germain, a spaceman, brother rabbit, or some other-worldly entity.

We met a lady named Ariel and we suggested having a meditation time together. We closed our eyes expecting to enter into inner silence and experience the divine presence. But Ariel launched into verbal channeling, and she wouldn't stop. Finally other people came over and interrupted her monologue. Later that day when I returned to my tent, my candle was bent completely over—melted from the summer heat. That's when I realized that this camping experience would be more difficult than I had expected.

The next day Pamela was frightened when she walked near a rattlesnake and it rattled ominously. However, David came to the rescue and with a stick carried the poisonous snake away, something I would see him do on several occasions. David was a consummate outdoorsman, familiar with wilderness living in extreme climates, so it was comforting to have his leadership. I admired his courage, strength, and determination physically, mentally, and spiritually. Even though our situation was a difficult one, David was best equipped to cope with whatever might come our way.

Gazing up at Bell Rock, which looks like a giant bell from a distance, I decided that I would challenge myself by climbing this rock formation and sleeping on top of it for one night. The only book I had brought along with me to Sedona was the *Ascent of Mount Carmel*, the famous guide for the spiritual life written by St. John of the Cross. My mini mountain climb would symbolize my attempt to ascend the spiritual growth mountain described in this book. Because David looked down on my lack of physical prowess and Pamela looked down on my lack of grounding in the earth, I felt this attempt at physical accomplishment would show them that I was willing to stretch beyond my normal comfort zone and go the extra mile to adjust to this new situation.

I climbed up by myself and encountered a difficult point in which the only way to proceed upward was to climb between two very large slabs of rock that went straight up vertically. There was a distance of a yard between the slabs, so I had to wedge my body against both slabs simultaneously to lift myself up beyond this vertical wall of rock. Finally I succeeded in reaching the very small plateau, which was my goal and which was just below an unreachable pinnacle. After darkness came, I stayed up to look at the sky, which is crystal-clear in Arizona, making it a prime site for astronomical observatories. I saw a shooting star and decided that I wanted to see two more to confirm that I would be able to accomplish the spiritual purposes that I had come into the earth to manifest. I meditated and afterwards indeed did see two more shooting stars. When I woke up in the morning, I looked over the edge of the steepest side and said goodbye to my glasses as they fell off disappearing into the rocks below. The glasses could not have survived the fall, and I would not be able to find them on the steep side. I climbed down the mountain, again wedging my body through the vertical crevice and made my way to the bottom.

I didn't see any of the "etheric spaceships" that were said to be hovering over or inside Bell Rock according to various channeled sources in Sedona. However, I had accomplished the feat of ascending the physical and symbolic mountain and expected David and Pamela would be appreciative of my willingness to extend beyond my normal limits. Right after my return to our camp site, I asked David for a comb and was unceremoniously greeted with, "Can't you get a comb of your own?"

"I know we are low on money so I didn't want to ask for money to meet that need," I said, since we held all money in common.

Pamela told me, "A comb would cost very little, and it would make you more independent so you won't have to rely on us for something you can have yourself."

I certainly agreed with them about the cost of buying a comb, but I wondered where were the congratulations for the independence expressed in climbing Bell Rock by myself. It was then that it first struck me that not only would this be a physical struggle for me, it would also be an emotional struggle that would test my patience and limits. Then again, if I really wanted to ascend the mountain of spiritual growth described by St. John of the Cross, I would have to live up to the words of Jesus, "If anyone wishes to come after me, let him deny himself, and take up his cross, and follow me."[1] And David and Pamela would have to do likewise for their own spiritual growth.

But denying ourselves was not on the top of our list of goals for Sedona. We had come in order to make connections with fellow seekers and groups and to get on with our real spiritual work, similar to the work we had done together previously in Virginia Beach. Surely God had already brought seekers to Sedona who were just waiting for what we had to offer. While in Anaheim, David had a series of dreams that made it clear to him that our trip to Sedona would be a time for furthering the work of preparing for earth changes and preparing the way for the Second Coming of Christ by drawing people together for spiritual projects.

We put out a flier all over town to invite like-minded seekers to meet with us and hear our plans for assisting in giving birth to Christian spiritual transformation. But no one came. Actually Dirk came, whom we had met earlier that day in the library, but no one came because of the flier. It was discouraging. Sedona was a magnet for seekers, so it had been reasonable to expect to find some who honored Jesus as we did. But in Sedona where did Jesus fit in? He was just one of the many "Ascended Masters," who were a dime-a-dozen, arrayed among spirit guides, discarnate entities, and space brothers. Some psychic channels saw Sedona as a gathering place of the 144,000 seekers mentioned in the Book of Revelation. Some local seekers felt they would be beamed up to heaven by UFOs that regularly patrolled the Sedona airspace. In contrast to the New Age hodgepodge of seekers without a Christian focus, there were small, yet dedicated groups of fundamentalist Christians. These fundamentalists felt it was their calling to rescue the New Agers, headed for hell from following the work of the devil.

Between the eclectic Jesus of the New Agers and the hell-fire Jesus of the fundamentalists, we offered a Jesus who could be encountered in the silence of prayer and meditation. We hoped to find at least some who wanted to join with us in this form of inner attunement to the divine. However, the various spiritual groups we visited, although interested in prayer and meditation, did not share our Christian focus and appreciation of silence. We told one Science of Mind minister about our interests, and he said, "I've seen a lot of people like you come to Sedona. Do you know what Sedona does? It takes people in and then spits them out. There is only one thing for sure—within six months you will be gone." Ironically it was the minister who was gone in less than six months.

But how long would we last? Money was running out, and we were not connecting with anyone. We were concerned that our interim period of adjustment would be longer than we had anticipated. Regarding the current situation, David had a dream that portrayed Sedona as a circus. Another one of David's dreams symbolized Sedona as a New Age Las Vegas in which the inner Christian divine life could not be found. We had been certain that we were in Sedona to do God's will and carry out His Plan. Nevertheless, we had to reconsider our beliefs. Maybe we had mistakenly been carrying out our own plans instead. David had to reinterpret his dreams about going public with Christian rebirth and transformation. He concluded that the dreams must have meant that he needed his own inner Christian rebirth and transformation. Perhaps it was God's Plan all along for each of us to transform ourselves through relying on God alone and helping each other to grow.

The immediate task before us became obvious. We simply had to learn how to live together in an extremely inhospitable environment and still hold on to living out our spiritual ideals. With money and food scarce, we had to deal with spiders, rattlesnakes, scorpions, mosquitoes, and tiny no-seeum insects. Some days the temperature soared above 100 degrees, so we felt like we were in a sauna even when we were in the shade. Then there were days of rain, which produced thick red mud to contrast with the usual red dirt and dust of Sedona. Winter was approaching, which would bring new challenges of snow storms and freezing temperatures. Drinkable water was hard to find and bathing presented a difficult challenge.

Of course, a major concern was the children, who required a great deal of supervision, attention, and care. David and Pamela, and I to a lesser degree, needed to adjust our lives to meet their basic needs. David and Pamela found it difficult to find time alone as individuals and as a couple. I gave them a breather by watching Jeremia and Shawna for an hour each day. Our time together was usually dedicated to making up magical adventure stories sprinkled with talking animals, fairies, princes and princesses, as well as dragons and monsters. I would start the story, and they would each have to contribute to the story telling. I also spent time with Torey for half an hour each day, with a conversational walk, a game, or another activity such as throwing rocks at a selected target.

My short time with the children was a drop in the bucket compared to the tremendous amount of time and energy they required. Their needs included feeding them, keeping them clean, meeting bathroom needs without a bathroom, maintaining appropriate playing time and socialization, and providing educational opportunities. Meeting children's needs in a normal household situation is difficult enough, but in a continuously unpredictable camping environment, everything was greatly intensified. David and Pamela went to extraordinary lengths to care for and love the children. I marveled at the fact that the children themselves were generally cooperative and thrived in circumstances that I found extremely difficult.

It would have been wonderful if we could have just set up one camp site to give us a sense of stability. But sooner or later a forest service ranger would come along. His visit was especially embarrassing when he would find me lying down and resting in my underwear because of the heat. Typically he would stick his head down to the screen door of my tent and say, "Did you know you can only stay here for fourteen days?" He did not mean fourteen days in this one spot; he meant we were limited to fourteen days per year anywhere in the Sedona forest land. Of course, I would act surprised, as though this was my first encounter with a forest ranger. Then he would write out a warning that gave us a few days to get out. Luckily our roving camp site was discovered by a different forest ranger each time. The trick was to hide so well that we would not be found, but it gave us a sense of continually playing the part of Harrison Ford in *The Fugitive*.

There was no prospect of any of our camping conditions improving. In fact, there was the distinct possibility of our situation getting worse—such as the potential of sickness or having absolutely no money or food. Could all this possibly be the fertile ground for us to grow spiritually? David, Pamela, and I had very different personalities. Nevertheless, we had always gotten along in the past. Then again, we had always had normal living conditions, which allowed us to maintain our comfort zones. But our circumstances had propelled us out of our comfort zones, which intensified everything about our personalities, bringing out both our strengths and weaknesses—especially our hidden weaknesses.

The situation brought out David's leadership strength along with his single-minded trust in God and likewise revealed his weakness of being emotionally distant. Pamela could draw upon her intuition, appreciation of nature, and nurturing qualities, yet she was discouraged by feeling disconnected from God. She used her intuition, but often felt like a victim of God's Will, since she found it hard to make sense out of the demands of daily living placed on her by this precarious camping lifestyle. I, like David, had no problem with being connected to God and being dedicated to God's Will, but I was very challenged by the difficulties of living outdoors.

In normal circumstances we did not have to address our weaknesses, but here we were faced with the dark sides of our egos, which we could no longer keep hidden. I hoped this whole situation of being in the desert with David and Pamela might assist me in solving my shadow puzzle, since I was facing the shadow parts of my psyche. But that hope was of no consolation to me at the time because, in spite of my best intentions, the dark side of my personality was gaining the upper hand in this situation. As the physical hardships affected all of us and as the loose screws in our personalities started to fall out, we gave in to the temptation to sit in judgment of each other. Because of our judgments, we each found ourselves overreacting to what someone else had said or done. For example, one of my less than shining moments was when I went to eat soup that Pamela had made for us and asked, "Is this the same bowl that Chewy ate out of?"

"Yes, but it's the only bowl we have to hold this soup!" Pamela replied.

I was offended by having to eat out of the dog's bowl and not too pleasantly let Pamela know how I felt. In turn, she let me know that she did not appreciate my attitude. Of course, we mended our fences. However, this pressure-cooker situation brought out unloving ways of thinking, acting, and feeling. These kinds of strong negative reactions we had to one another revealed that we each had very serious problems that we needed to overcome. After all, if we truly wanted to follow Jesus, we would have to learn how to love others, especially those closest to us.

---

1. Matthew 16: 24, CCD.

38

DOING GOD'S WILL

~ • ~

In spite of emotions boiling over at times and voices being raised at times, there was one good thing that we took for granted back then, but now seems remarkable: No curse words crossed our lips at any time. Speaking civilly was a form-related expression of our spiritual aspirations, but it wasn't much consolation to us. David, Pamela, and I fully agreed that if we wanted to live up to our spiritual ideals, we would need to learn how to love one another. The problems we were having in our relationships served as a mirror reflecting back to us that we were failing miserably to love one another and that we obviously needed to make changes. On the one hand, we would have to let go of our judgments of each other and realize that we were engaging in denial and projection. Denial allowed us to disown the shadow within each of us, and projection enabled us to see the unacceptable aspects of each of our psyches as shortcomings in others rather than taking responsibility for them within ourselves. We would also have to be patient with being judged by others and try not to use their judgments as a justification for judging in return, which was a trap that I constantly fell into. On the other hand, we could also learn some important lessons from the strong negative reactions of others. Even if their reactions revealed their problems, we learned to ask ourselves, "What am I doing inappropriately that is attracting these kinds of negative reactions?" The overall idea was to learn how to become fully responsible for all of our own emotions, regardless of what the other person said, did, or thought. We realized, at least intellectually, that our real work was to change ourselves, rather than trying to change each other. Nonetheless, we would often fall back into projection and forget to take full responsibility for our own emotional reactions.

At first we did not enthusiastically embrace the need to recognize and overcome the dark sides of our personalities as the true purpose for our living in Sedona. Sure we wanted to change and become more loving people, yet we thought maybe there were more gracious ways of doing that. Pamela had gotten a part-time job at *Food Among the Flowers*, a restaurant in town. I had already accepted a six-week contract from Goodwill Industries to provide training services for Graham, a mentally retarded client. I worked right alongside him sorting clothing and gave him staying-on-task objectives, which helped him to eventually do the job independently. As Graham and I sorted through incoming donations, I set aside wool blankets for myself because I knew I would need them to keep me warm in my tent during the upcoming winter months. Sam, who did the pricing for the store, charged me all of 50 cents per blanket because he knew we were camping out. One day at Graham's team meeting, the state developmental disabilities worker, Mark, showed up in his tailor-made suit. It occurred to me that I had the training and experience to do his job. I thought it would be wonderful if I could somehow find full-time employment, hopefully in a service-oriented job, before the winter came so I could support all of us on my salary.

After camping for three months we were enticed by the tantalizing possibility of having a roof over our heads with warmth, no insects, running water, and comfortable spaces to lie down without the fear of forest rangers coming to dispossess us. Then we had encouraging dreams that seemed to indicate that we could start a church—a church where followers of Jesus could come for devotion and attunement to God. We were hopeful that our anticipated house could conveniently be our church as well as a meeting place for like-minded seekers.

We were faced with two choices—a grueling winter camping or a radiant church and house dedicated to God and Jesus. We had a meeting one night in which we made a firm decision collectively to actively pursue both a job search for me and house hunting in order to start a church. The very moment when this meeting was concluded, we looked up and saw a shooting star. It was not one of those tiny falling stars that last for a few seconds. It was a gigantic falling star close to the earth that streaked across the sky for a half a minute with a long tail of blazing light. Of course, we decided this must be the hand of God confirming the correctness and inspiration of our decision, so we proceeded enthusiastically.

Although we found a house that we thought would be ideal for our spiritual purposes, somebody else rented it. My search for a full time job was no more successful than our house hunting. Sometimes interviews went very well until I would have to do "a song and dance" explanation of why I had no telephone. "Can I call you in a few days to see if I have the job?" was not the best way to end an interview. Then we found out that our sign from God wasn't a shooting star after all, but a returning Russian satellite burning up as it re-entered the earth's atmosphere. Next David got dreams about us "rushing ahead" to do what God had not planned for us and that my efforts at finding a full time job were "polluting" the work God really had in mind for us. We were shocked at this turn of events. David and Pamela were discouraged, yet rebounded relatively quickly and accepted their fate of camping out in the winter.

On the other hand, I remained confused. I could no longer trust my dreams. I was starting to believe that Robert was right that our dreams can be inspirations from God, but they could also be reflecting back to us our own hopes, fears, and judgments. In this case, were the inspired dreams the first dreams that guided us toward a church? Or were the inspired dreams these more recent dreams that told us to stop? In spite of having my own dreams that showed me my fears, I could not gain clarity. I felt frustrated by David and Pamela feeling guided to stop considering options that would give relief to our precarious situation

I had already gone to extremes in making adjustments to my life far beyond what would be reasonable for my physical constitution. Before me were even more intense challenges that would be presented by a winter of living in a tent. I had reached my limit. I told David and Pamela that I had decided to leave Sedona and go stay with my sister, Joanna, in Las Vegas. I was thinking of coming back at a later date when the cold weather had passed. David and Pamela felt that my decision was not the best choice, but they graciously drove me to Flagstaff where I caught a bus to Las Vegas. While sleeping in a warm and comforting bed in Las Vegas, I woke up in the middle of the night with a vision of the Sunfellow crew riding in the van and all happily greeting me. The warm bed did not feel so reassuring to me after all in light of the fact that I had left my friends and fellow seekers behind. Most of all, I remembered that I had made the community vow, "I will do God's Will to the best of my ability," and I felt I could not break my vow. In addition, I felt that it was part of my destiny to be in the desert with David and Pamela and that I needed this difficult experience to reveal more of the elusive pieces of my shadow puzzle.

After being gone two weeks, I drove back in a car that Joanna's friend Russ had given me for $700, to be paid back at some unspecified future date. I came back on Christmas day and wondered how I would find them since they had probably moved. But as I drove into town I saw the familiar rusty VW van parked in front of the Sugar Loaf Inn. The Anaheim Half had paid for the Sunfellows to have a motel room for a few nights of relief on the holiday. I was welcomed back even though I still wanted to get a job and pay for a house and use my car for transportation. Yet I didn't even make it to one more interview. It suddenly dawned on me that the essential lesson for me to learn was that we were all in this together to accomplish a common purpose. Whatever I was going to do had to be done as part of a unified effort with David and Pamela. So I resigned myself to a winter in a tent and trusted that God would help me to meet this challenge. I drove the car back to Las Vegas to return it and then came back in a bus to my unpredictable camping situation, yet with renewed determination.

I had physical limitations that made my winter experience especially difficult. I had an enlarged benign prostate, so that even in warm weather I had to get up about three times in the night to urinate in a jar. The cold weather made it more difficult to deal with this common prostate condition, necessitating approximately six interruptions to my sleep each night. Then I got prostatitis, an inflamed prostate, so there was pain in the perineum, especially when sitting on a solid surface. Going to a doctor was out of the question because I did not want antibiotics in my body. I used prolonged fasting instead and trusted in prayer and natural healing, which eventually cured the inflammation.

At times it was so cold when I woke up in the morning that my drinking water had frozen overnight. I had a piece of foam, my wool blankets, and a sleeping bag for warmth, but I had a pain in my right hip that just wouldn't go away. Because of the pain, it was hard to go to sleep, and in the morning the hip was especially sore. I continued to do my yoga postures and breathing practices. However, a temporary lower back pain limited my normal flexibility. I was frustrated by my physical limitations and asked for God's help to heal or at least for patience to deal with the situation as gracefully as possible.

Since the outer work of a mundane or spiritual nature was deferred, we could proceed to do our true work of facing self and learning how to love. One way of learning to love was investing our trust in God, which was most challenging for Pamela. When we were camped off of Schnebly Hill Road, it had snowed quite a bit and with the snow melting, the dirt road became a river of mud. Unfortunately we were totally out of money. The van's gas meter was on empty. Nevertheless, David thought there might be just enough gas to get into town, but probably not enough to get back. Pamela in particular was greatly discouraged by the apparent hopelessness of the situation. David reminded Pamela of the many miracles of the past in which, just when our resources ran out, something unexpected would happen to rescue us. We set out driving up Schnebly Hill Road through mud and snow and had difficulty doing so. This steep and winding hill had no guard rails, presenting the possibility of sliding off the road to the right and tumbling over the edge of a cliff. For safety reasons and to make the van lighter, David drove alone through the most dangerous stretches of the upward climb, while the rest of us walked. When we reached the top, David put the van in neutral in order to save gas. Then we coasted down the other side of the hill, which was paved and which led to the post office at the end of the road. There in our mail box was another miracle—a gift of more than two hundred dollars from the Anaheim Half.

Learning how to love by trusting in God was easier than learning to trust in each other. We had hoped to be of one mind. Even in the cold of winter we managed to meditate together outdoors in order to join in the Spirit as the sun rose over the mountains of Boynton Canyon. However, the problems began when we tried to communicate verbally. Pamela did not like a lot of verbal processing so she would excuse herself if we talked too long. David and I would have lengthy conversations in which we would often find ourselves on opposite sides of philosophical issues.

I felt we needed to learn acceptance and give up judgment. David was aware that judgments could be negative, but he maintained that there was a positive side of judgment called "discernment" of the truth, which he considered to be as important as acceptance. I was aware of the Eastern description of discernment as the ability to discriminate the real from the unreal, or in other words distinguish between the True Self and the ego. From my perspective, seeing the faults of others was a subjective process of judgment and projection. It was the imagining of the unreal, the ego, to be real, which is the exact opposite of discerning the real from the unreal. David felt he was "discerning" what was objectively there in another person's ego, which to my mind was a convenient excuse for indulging in judgment. David felt that blanket acceptance, without discernment, would be condoning other people's inappropriate behavior. We both did agree that there had to be a way to let each other know how we were impacting each other's lives, yet it was hard for us to find a way to do that lovingly.

A factor that influenced me greatly in the controversial discussions with David about judgment was that, in addition to the immediate ramifications affecting our current nomadic lifestyle, I was also contending with issues of judgment going all the way back to past lives. When spring came, I discovered numerous black widow spiders on the underside of my tent. Their distinctly characteristic asymmetrical and disjointed webs bore witness to the fact that these spiders had been there very close to me, and yet hidden, for quite a long time. Being so close and so hidden, they were symbolic reminders that I could not run away from the Spider Boy lifetime. That past life ended in suicide from an inability to cope with the very same issues of being judged and being found wanting in the eyes of others and in my own eyes. Even more to the point, the Pole Man died as a result of others who had made judgments with which he no doubt disagreed. So in polarizing with David, I was really trying to work out those deeper unresolved issues that were a life and death matter in my past lives. Sometimes there was anger in me. But usually the deeper feeling of despair and unworthiness would come out when I found myself reduced to tears, which happened a few times in David's presence and occasionally when I was alone after an argument.

The trigger for my private weeping outbursts was not what David or anyone else had said or done. It was my own feelings of failure that I was not living up to my high ideal as a monk of following the example of Jesus. Instead of expressing love, I was playing the ego's game of judgment myself. My ego objected to various community members judging me, yet did not hesitate to sit in judgment of them for judging me. I could not see my way out of this hypocrisy. After all, the very people I thought were judging me were the people I most respected for their determination to do God's Will above all else. Knowing God's Will is to express love, I could see clearly my own failure to meet the challenge of living out my spiritual ideal. If I could not love my friends who held high ideals, how could I possibly learn to love everyone, as Jesus does and as I am called to do as well? I blamed myself for this failure, which reduced me to tears, because I could see no way of overcoming my ego. I did not realize it at that time, but what I needed was a whole new thought system that would help me let go of judgment and see things differently with a forgiving mind. I was so invested in wallowing in my shortcomings that I did not even consider the possibility that studying and applying *A Course in Miracles* could show me a way out my dilemma.

After my occasional private crying sessions, I always retreated to my inner spiritual world. Just as a crying boy is comforted in the arms of his precious mother, I too would receive a reassuring divine embrace. From my direct experience it was crystal clear to me that God was the initiator of this inner love, and I was the recipient, blessed by His grace. Yet even this grace I could not communicate to David. In fact, it would become a bone of contention between David and me, focused on the issue of grace versus self-effort. I considered that grace was the most important element of spiritual growth, while David gave more weight to developing one's own talents and abilities. For example, I said, "God loves us first, and His grace and love enable us to respond with our love for Him."

David responded, "We have to love God first. It is up to us to take the initiative in love." As far as I was concerned, God's eternal Love is always with us, and all of spiritual growth is simply a matter of waking up to His unconditional Love. I would have been better served by seeing and rejoicing in the Love of God within David and me, rather than arguing, which only succeeded in closing my own heart. My understanding of God's ever-present Love did me no good since I could not apply that awareness to my relationships. Furthermore, I compounded the problem by blaming myself for my failure to love.

Because David and I found ourselves butting our heads together on these kinds of issues, we gradually learned to agree to disagree without trying to change each other's mind. We tried to focus as much as possible on the things that all three of us held in common. We certainly agreed to make loving one another into our primary work. We also agreed that we could learn how to love by following the example of Jesus. It became apparent to all of us that the specific example that Jesus gave to us was taking up his cross—denying self, which is the letting go of the ego. The teachings of St. John of the Cross were helpful in this regard because he taught how to let go of every ego attachment in order to seek God alone.

One of the hot issues that arose was how many possessions we should be taking from one camp site to another. It was pointed out that I had too many possessions. This was a concrete example of the philosophical tension between David and me. Was this subjective judgment, as I maintained, or objective discernment of the truth, as David advocated? I had a tent, two suitcases, blankets, a foam mattress, tarps to screen out the sun, and not much more. By any normal standards this was not a whole lot of possessions. But this was not a normal situation. With our constant moving, my possessions did impact on David and Pamela in regard to the limited space of the van. With a heavy heart I reluctantly I threw away about half the items in both suitcases, including numerous photographs from my past. That was a concrete example of an attempt to deny myself, at least at the form level, and to be responsive to David and Pamela, rather than reactive.

Unfortunately, all my excess baggage was not physical and thus not so easily thrown away. I didn't think judgment was a healthy practice but couldn't stop indulging in it. We didn't fully understand projection, so we indulged in it in spite of our best efforts to be loving. We just couldn't keep ourselves from looking at each other's blind spots. Sometimes we thought it was helpful, even loving, to tell the other person about his or her blind spots so they would change and correct their shortcomings. We didn't realize that by focusing on the other person's faults, we were avoiding taking responsibility for our own faults, such as judgment. We didn't understand that by judging others negatively we were encouraging and strengthening the quality of negative judgment in the other person and in ourselves. However, if we could look past each other's shortcomings and instead see the divine in each other, we would be strengthening the awareness of the divine in ourselves and in each other. Because of the extreme stress of camping, we could not overlook each other's faults. Nevertheless, we did the best we could at denying ourselves and really did attempt to cooperate together and function as a team. Even when we failed in loving, which was often, we knew that we were at least sincerely attempting to love one another to the best of our understanding.

39

VISITORS AND FRIENDS

~ o ~

As we made loving each other and denying ourselves a priority, we found that people we knew started showing up. One day I was walking a lonely stretch of road in Boynton Canyon, not far from our hidden camp, when I was surprised to come across Roger, a friend from Virginia Beach who just happened to be visiting Sedona. I invited him to stay over at our camp site, but it snowed heavily that night, and he left. Pamela's mother came to Sedona to visit us. While we were all in the van, we drove to the post office, where a letter from Stuart was awaiting me. He was still editing my Christian meditation book, which I had titled *His World* from a vision I had of those words while resting in my tent. As I read the letter in the van, I welled up with tears while attempting to hide my face. Luckily, Pamela, her mother, and the children got out of the van at a stop, and David and I were left alone. David had noticed my crying and asked, "What's the matter?" I told him I was crying because I was so inspired by the letter. Stuart's words that struck me the most were, "I think that, ultimately, all we can do is to inspire someone to *want* to be 'in His World.'" I was deeply touched that the book I was still writing might have that effect on some people.

I was also keeping in touch with Rose, whom I would call from a pay phone and then give her the number so she could call me back. Rose was my spiritual lifeline. Even over the phone we could do for each other what no one else could—we could overlook the shortcomings in each other and instead see the Christ. This reminded me of what I wanted to do with David and Pamela—to see the Christ in them, even if I was incapable of doing so at that time. I felt I needed someone else to see the Christ in me so I could see the Christ in that someone. I thought I needed David and Pamela to see the Christ in me and then I could see the Christ in them. Conversely at those times when I felt (rightly or wrongly) that I was being judged, I felt justified in judging in return. Intellectually I knew I was mistaken to think in terms of "you scratch my back, and I'll scratch your back," but this bargain was all I was capable of manifesting at the time.

Then another visitor came, one who helped me to step outside the box of loving the Christ in another person *only* when my love was returned and to let go of judging in return when I felt judged. This visitor was Tom Dunn, a friend from Virginia Beach. He was passing through town on his way to California, and we had only a day and a half together. Tom's background was in counseling and psychology. He had just read *A Course in Miracles* and was exuberant about his recent spiritual insights. Allan, Robert, Stuart, and many others had advocated the merits of the Course as a means of understanding the nature of the ego creating an illusion of separation from God and as a means of finding forgiveness in relationships.

When Tom was sharing, though, I felt he was trying to force the Course on me. I told him my concern in a caring way in order to point out that no book or method can replace our own inner prompting from Spirit. Since I didn't feel an inner prompting to study the Course, I felt I couldn't move in that direction. Tom acknowledged that he realized he was subtly imposing his will on me and so he backed off.

However, we did continue to discuss a basic concept of both the Course and Eastern philosophy, which was that the ego hides our true nature, our nature in God. We talked about ways we might take off our ego masks in order to see the Christ in each other. I said, "The ego literally 'feeds' on our thoughts. If we could silence our thoughts in meditation, we could in a sense 'starve' the ego, at least temporarily."

Tom pointed out, "That's true. Yet when we come back to the everyday world, the ego will merely reassert itself again. There has to be a way in addition to meditation to transform our awareness so we can simply change our viewpoint. The ego is like seeing through a small hole in the wall. Why not just expand your view so you can see out of a window? Why not just take down the whole wall? The ego isn't real. I know this body you see isn't me. I am the Christ, who is the real me that is here."

"I know the ego is just a false thought about yourself," I replied. "But I don't think it's *easy* to change that false thought. To claim to be the Christ within we have to go deep within in meditation and then experience that presence, rather than just making an intellectual statement about being the Christ. If we claim it before we experience it, we may manufacture a false self-image that claims to be the Christ, yet is just a prettier false mask."

"I still don't think meditation is the only way to recognize the Christ," Tom asserted. "I think we can simply change our minds and perceive the Christ presence. It may not be a direct experience of the Spirit. However, it can be an intuitive feeling that says He is there in me and in you."

As Tom said these words I remembered that when I saw the Christ in Rose, it was just as he described. So I agreed, "You are right. Meditation is not the only way. You can have intuitive awareness of the Christ. Maybe all that is required is a change of mental attitude to be open to that intuition." As I was speaking it occurred to me that maybe I could have that change of

TOM DUNN

DON IN 1988 — ONE YEAR AFTER TOM'S VISIT

mental attitude right then in my conversation with Tom. I felt prompted to hold a loving attitude toward him and to repeat the Name of Jesus. As I looked, I could see a glow of light around Tom, which was like the light I used to see around people when I was sitting still in church.

Since I was content to just look at him in love, I could just be receptive and let Tom say whatever he wanted. With his psychology background, Tom started to tell me his insights into my psychological makeup, even though I had not invited this. Normally, I would have put up a stop sign like I had earlier when I felt he was imposing the Course on me. But I felt this interaction with Tom was both a test and an opportunity to have a change in mental attitude, so I let him go on talking. I continued with the Jesus Prayer, and he continued to glow in my sight.

Tom pointed out my spiritual pride, my biggest shortcoming without a doubt. He also mentioned my judgment, saying, "You are judging me right now—not so much with your words, but by your thoughts about me. I don't mean to hurt your feelings. I am just saying what I believe is true."

This circumstance seemed very ironic to me because here Tom was saying to me exactly what I had said to the individuals in the Anaheim Half before leaving California. In addition, I had been saying the same thing in different ways to David and Pamela. In my conversations recently, with David in particular, I would tell him he was judging me and that my judgments were only in response to his judgments of me. When I indulged in this finger pointing to make others feel guilty for their judgments and to condone my own judgments, I was giving in to my victim pattern. I had been greatly discouraged by my repeated inability to communicate and my obvious lack of love, so I would often end up in tears before David and Pamela, or privately wallow in tears.

Here Tom was saying that he was the victim of my judgments, and I could have responded by claiming to be a victim of his judgments. I had no doubt that he was making judgments, but what was really strange was that his judgments didn't matter. I discovered I could love him while he was judging me. I thought that, as was the case with Rose, I needed someone to see the Christ in me in order for me to see the Christ in them. What I learned in that conversation was that I could see the Christ in Tom even when he was seeing my faults and telling me about them. In addition, the glow around him was getting bigger and filling him, so he was glowing all over with a white light. I felt my heart was opening to him regardless of what his mask looked like. The love I was feeling for Tom was a divine grace—probably a result of calling on the Name of Jesus, which I could do most effectively when I was listening rather than speaking.

I could see the victim pattern Tom was describing so clearly that I didn't want to respond in my old ways. I was having the very change of mind and attitude that we had just talked about. I explained to him, "As you are talking, I feel my ego mask wanting to ask you questions, such as: 'Why are you saying this?' or 'Aren't you judging me?' Also I feel my ego wanting to defend itself by saying, 'I admit I have pride, but you do, too,' or 'Your intentions for sharing aren't pure, as you say they are.' Yet at the same time I am having an inner realization that it doesn't matter what your intentions are. That is your concern. I don't have to defend my ego mask by showing you what I think are your faults. I accept everything you are saying because it's true. Yes, pride is my number one fault. Yes, I was judging you because you are not as inclined toward meditation as I am."

"That's right," Tom agreed. "It doesn't matter if my intentions in sharing are pure or impure. In either case you don't have to defend your ego mask." As I listened to him speaking, the glowing white light in and around him continued undiminished. In this elevated state I was still aware of my ego, but not afraid of it. I didn't have to hide it or protect it because it didn't have any power. I could see that my ego wasn't me. Because my ego wasn't me, I could take it out of hiding and admit everything Tom said about it. I felt free and joyful. In addition, I could see that Tom's ego wasn't him, so I didn't have to react to it or analyze it.

With my ego no longer threatened, I felt no need to manipulate or control Tom or to defend myself, so I welcomed him to talk more about the Course, which obviously meant so much to him. He began, "The whole Course is summarized by the two lines, 'Nothing real can be threatened. Nothing unreal exists.'[1] The ego in you and in me is threatened because it isn't real. Because the ego is unreal, it doesn't exist. However, you do exist because you are not the ego. You are part of Christ. Your true Self is in God—unseparated from God. The ego is the belief in separation. But since separation from God is impossible, the ego is not real. It only seems real because you believe in illusions that don't exist. When you dream in your sleep, you believe the illusions you see in your dream. Yet when you wake up, you realize that your dreams weren't real and none of your dream images really exist."

I observed, "Because of the references to the ego, the Course seems to have a strong Eastern flavor, which is unusual for a Christian philosophy."

"You're right. I like that it reinforces so much of what I've learned in Eastern philosophy, which emphasizes the importance of having a direct experience of reality. For example, what do you think of this Course quote: 'A universal theology is impossible, but a universal experience is not only possible but necessary'?"[2]

Before saying a word, a whole series of thoughts flashed in my mind. It occurred to me that various paths have different ideas about reality, but there is really only one reality. Consequently, the ultimate experience of that reality must be the same for everyone. That universal experience of transcending the ego is called samadhi by Hindus, enlightenment by Buddhists, illumination by Christians, mystical ecstasy by Jewish Kabbalists, or union with Allah by Muslim Sufis. Since Tom was well aware of all those names, I simply said, "I like that idea. That universal experience you are talking about has been given many different labels, but is almost always described as an all-encompassing experience of the White Light. It's a profound experience that transcends sectarianism because God Himself is nonsectarian. But I once heard a monk named Brother David [Steindl-Rast] say, 'There are many paths, but *you have to get on one of them.*'"

"I agree with that," Tom said. "There is a perfect path for each one of us. It is the path that has been *perfectly assigned* by Spirit to suit each of us individually. The Course says that Spirit has given everyone a 'special function.'[3] It's a specific role for each of us to play in God's Plan, one that only we can play. The point is that it's important for each of us to be true to the path we are called to follow, whatever it is."

"In the end we all get to experience the same one reality. The only question is how many lifetimes we want to have before we finally wake up to the White Light," I said, knowing Tom believed in reincarnation as I did.

"The Course agrees with you, Don, that the only question is whether we get to heaven sooner or later. As for me, I don't want to come back again. I want this to be my last lifetime—the one when I fully wake up to my true nature in the White Light."

I thought it was ironic that I was seeing a symbolic reflection of the White Light in Tom as he spoke about waking up to his true nature in that Light. But another sort of irony entirely escaped me. I hadn't asked myself why I was seeing Tom in the light on this particular occasion, but had not seen him like this the many other times we had met and talked. Although Spirit certainly had gotten my attention, I wasn't getting the full message. It didn't occur to me that the Course, clearly part of Tom's path, could possibly be part of the path the Spirit had already assigned to me, without me yet knowing it. I was pridefully sure I had already figured out everything I needed to know about my path.

"I want this to be my last lifetime, too," I added. "My path is a little unusual because it is a combination of yoga and Christianity. However, I have only one goal, and that's to wake up to my Christ nature. I know you are as enthusiastic and dedicated as I am in following the path you've been given. And I am happy for you, because it looks like you have found and are walking your path of following Christ through applying the Course principles, and being open to Eastern philosophy as well."

Tom agreed, "Yes, and you and I have the same goal of awakening to our true nature in the Christ."

After this point, our conversation continued to be a marathon, but I mostly listened. I thought the shining light in and around Tom would fade away after a short while. Nevertheless, it lasted that whole day and into the next day. This experience was a longer version of the time I took a puff of pot when I was with Dylan and walked in the park in Virginia Beach to discover a world of light before my eyes. At some points when listening to Tom the shining light extended all around. However, most of the time the light remained centered on Tom as I continued to stay completely receptive to him and to the divine grace that was making this vision of light possible. Finally at the very end of our sharing, when Tom was about to leave, we reached a climax in which Tom told me, "I feel my mission will be to be a spokesman for God and to open people's hearts to Christ. I know you still think I need to go deeper within in meditation before going out in public for God. You are still sitting in judgment of me. I know it shouldn't be important to me that you won't accept me just the way I am. I have to accept myself whether you accept me or not, but...." Then he started to cry and through his tears said, "I wish I didn't care what you think, but I guess I do care because I'm crying. Why can't you just accept me?"

Although I was still seeing him in the light, I was dumbfounded. I had been in tears myself many times recently, especially over this very issue of wanting approval from another person—specifically David. I had wanted David, and before that others, to see through my mask and accept me. I realized just like Tom that I needed to fully accept myself and not let my self-worth rest on someone else's approval. However, the flip side of my pride was my feelings of unworthiness, which caused me to break up in tears at not being accepted. But in this situation with Tom, I was on the other side of the approval equation, being asked to accept him without judgment. I wanted very much to accept him completely, yet I couldn't quite give up the thought of judgment that he really did need to go deeper within before going out and preaching to the world. Suddenly I felt my heart open up, and I could feel myself in his place. It did not matter what I thought—good, bad, or indifferent. Tom was really saying to me by his tears, "I am not this weeping mask you see. I am really the Christ."

Then I started crying too, but these were tears of joy to see the Christ in him. I said nothing of the light that I had seen in him the past two days and even in this situation. I reached out my hand to his hand, and we cried together. A healing took place at that moment in what I found out later the Course calls a *holy instant*, which is an exchange of love that the Course refers to as a *miracle*. The Holy Spirit came into each of us by our invitation to deepen our relationship with each other and with God. The Holy Spirit touched each of our hearts, allowing our masks of separation to fall off, even if only temporarily, so we could each see the Christ in the other.

Afterwards, in the spirit of unmasking his own ego, Tom explained without prompting from me that his previous intentions were not pure in pointing out my faults. He acknowledged that because I had not defended my ego by attacking him, it enabled him to see his own mask more clearly. When all was said and done, we both were able to see we had used judgments to support the ego mask and to separate ourselves from others. Since there are no accidents in the universe, our Anaheim community members came on their first visit to Sedona while Tom was there. Tom met them and especially enjoyed talking with Robert about their common interest in the Course.

Tom had studied *jnana yoga* based on Hindu Vedanta, and he could appreciate elements of Eastern philosophy in the Course. Tom had also read *Autobiography of a Yogi* by Yogananda and was inspired by his life story, just as I had been. Yogananda started the Self-Realization Fellowship teaching seekers to practice *kriya yoga*. When Tom left Sedona, he went to San Francisco to live at the yoga community called *Ananda*, which was an independent offshoot of the Self-Realization Fellowship founded by a disciple of Yogananda. I had no doubt that wherever Tom went, he would turn people's hearts toward Christ, since he had already been a catalyst for me to open my heart more fully to the divine presence.

Of course, my time of elevated consciousness during Tom's brief visit evaporated quickly, and I descended back into my old unhealthy patterns of judgment and victimization. Nevertheless, I had learned from my experience with Tom that it was possible for me to let go of judgment and see the Christ in others even when I was being judged by others. A temporary effect of my interaction with Tom was that when I talked with Robert on his visit, I felt less defensive about my ego mask. Consequently, I invited Robert to tell me my faults so I could become aware of my blind spots. Two things stand out about what he told me. One was that I seemed too needy of other people's approval, which had also been revealed in my talk with Tom. Robert described my other significant shortcoming in this way: "I know you call on Jesus, and I consider Him to be our community leader, too. Yet there is a down side to that. You have placed Jesus on such a high pedestal that your valuing of Him has devalued your idea of yourself. The problem with traditional Christianity is that on the one hand Jesus is God and on the other hand His followers think of themselves as being unworthy. If you focus on yourself as being unworthy and not deserving of being in God's presence, how can you approach Him?

"Although you are not a Course student, you may want to consider the way the Course looks at Jesus and at you. According to the Course, Jesus is an elder brother who has awakened in heaven and realized His Oneness with God as the Christ. But Jesus considers you to be His equal. Only your attachment to your ego makes you think you are unworthy. In fact, there is one Christ, who is the one Son of God. Yet the Course also maintains that we are all Sons of God. We are all equal parts of the one Christ, which means we are equal parts of the one Son. That's why the Course states, 'Christ is the Self the Sonship shares, as God shares His Self with the Christ.'[4] So there are no small parts in the Christ, who is the Son of God.

"If Jesus is the only Son of God and if the rest of us are less than that, then God would be unfair because he would be giving some of his creations more love than others. You and Jesus are both Sons of God and parts of the One Christ. You can still honor Jesus as your elder brother, who shows you the way. But maybe you can learn to identify more with your own Christ nature as His brother, not as an inferior. When you can identify more with your true Self in Christ, you won't be so needy of other people's approval."

I said, "I understand the idea that Jesus and I are brothers and there is some basis for equality because we have the same Father, Who has given us both the same Light and Love. I know the awareness of my true nature is hidden within me waiting for me to uncover it. But the fact is that Jesus is fully awakened to His Christ nature, and I am soundly asleep in my Christ nature. Consequently, it seems arrogant for me to claim equality with Him, and doing that would be totally lacking in the humility that I feel I need."

"Your equality with Jesus is not based on how well or poorly you are functioning in the world now. Obviously you fall greatly short of Jesus in that respect. Your equality is based on the idea that you just said—that you both come from the same Source of Light and Love. We understand the idea that Jesus is the 'light of the world,' but the Course says that you and I can also be the light of the world by letting our light and love shine into the lives of others. Here is a Course quote you may want to consider:

> But the ego does not understand humility, mistaking it for self-debasement. Humility consists of accepting your role in salvation and in taking no other. It is not humility to insist you cannot be the light of the world if that is the function God assigned to you. It is only arrogance that would assert this function cannot be for you, and arrogance is always of the ego.[5]

Robert explained, "The Course is saying here that we become the light of the world by letting the light and love of Christ within us shine into the lives of others through applying forgiveness in all our relationships. This is our function that God has given to us. If we debase ourselves by saying, 'I am not like Jesus. I don't have the light and love of Christ in me,' then we won't let our light and love shine."

I was able to hear his feedback without the usual defensiveness of the past, and I appreciated this somewhat new perspective. I had already been aware of my true Self in God and aware of all my brothers as my equals. I did believe that there is only one universal Christ that we share equally. But in spite of my belief in equality, it was still difficult for me to specifically accept that Jesus is my equal. Even if it is true that Jesus is my equal in the White Light, that is merely a philosophical idea, which doesn't help me in a practical way. Here in the earth, I am obviously light years behind Jesus. Furthermore, I very much need the help and guidance of Jesus to navigate through the world and to grow in the direction of fully awakening to the Light. I liked the idea that Robert shared about letting my light shine into the lives of others through forgiveness. I felt Jesus was helping me do that through my love of Him and His even greater love for me, which was and is so spiritually nourishing for me. But was I devaluing myself by valuing Jesus too much?

As I pondered this question, I remembered a related story I had heard:

> A Zen Buddhist monk went to a temple and walked up to the altar. He placed his hands together in prayer position and bowed forward before the statue of Gautama Buddha with all the reverence he could muster. As he stepped aside a second monk stepped forward and spit on the Buddha statue. After leaving the silence of the temple, the first monk confronted the second one, asking, "Why did you spit on the Buddha?"
>
> "I didn't spit on the Buddha. I spit on a *statue!*" came the reply.
>
> "Even so, you have dishonored the memory of the Buddha," the pious, yet angry monk protested.
>
> "That statue won't help me to wake up. The memory of the Buddha won't help me wake up. And even if the Buddha himself should suddenly appear before me right now, he couldn't grant me enlightenment either."

The epilogue to this story is that the second monk did indeed eventually wake up to his own true nature. However, the first monk did not receive enlightenment because he had elevated the Buddha to such a lofty status that he had discounted his own ability to uncover his own Buddha nature.

This story doesn't fit neatly into a typical Christian context because it emphasizes only self-effort and doesn't account for the divine blessings of God. Maybe the Buddha couldn't help the Zen monk to wake up, but I still fully believed that Jesus, through the Holy Spirit and God's grace, can and will help me to eventually wake up—either as I walk along my path or at the end of my journey. However, the thought-provoking part of the story was the pious monk giving too much deference to the Buddha, resulting in the devaluing of his own ability to wake up. Similarly, I wondered about Robert's caution that I was placing Jesus in such a special, exalted, and unreachable divine category that I had been inadvertently devaluing myself and creating a self-image of unworthiness. I could see that my pride was a way of counterbalancing this hidden unworthiness. In addition my approval-seeking and tearfulness in response to lack of acceptance were showing me that I had been fostering the idea of my unworthiness.

I began to at least consider the possibility that Jesus already saw me as His equal in Spirit and that Jesus wanted to help me to take my place as His equal in the *Sonship*, which is what the Course called the collective parts of the one Christ. I continued to call upon the help and guidance of Jesus, which was also a part of the Course teachings.

The ideas Robert related were not entirely new to me. One concept that is presented in the Course and difficult for traditional Christians to understand is that there is one Christ that we all share and we find our individuality in that one Christ in which we live and have our being. Jesus perfectly embodied the one Christ, the one Self, that we all share, which I sometimes call the "Christ Self." Having been brought up as a Roman Catholic I had originally learned that Jesus is the one and only Christ. Prior to coming across the Course I had already been gradually exposed to the new idea that there is only one Christ, one Son of God, which is shared by all seekers, who are equal expressions of one God. While I was reading the writings of the Trappist monk Thomas Merton, I first seriously considered the unusual idea that there is one Christ that we all share. I came across this quotation that summarizes our true relationship with others and with Christ:

> When you and I become what we are really meant to be, we will discover not only that we love one another perfectly but that we are both living in Christ and Christ in us and we are all one Christ. We will see that it is he who loves in us.[6]

After reading Merton's quotation, I was inspired by St. Symeon the New Theologian's thoughts on spiritual identification with this one Christ. For example, he wrote, "We become members of Christ—and Christ becomes our members...."[7] Also I noticed there were some Biblical quotations that reminded me that we are all parts of the one Christ, such as, "Now you are the body of Christ and individually members of it."[8] My ideas about there being one Christ that we share evolved over a fifteen-year period before coming across similar ideas in the Course. At the beginning of my spiritual search, my experience with Eastern practices exposed me to the idea of the Self or *Atman* in the yoga scripture of Vedanta and to the idea of Buddha nature in Zen Buddhism. These Eastern ideas affirmed that there is one divine nature we all share equally. This understanding served as a foundation for later accepting the very similar idea of the one Son, the one Christ, shared by all seekers. I felt it was vitally important for me to clarify the nature of Christ because I saw this understanding as crucial to helping me awaken my own Identity in God.

Having already been exposed to the idea of there being one Christ that we share, I was open to Robert's suggestions in regard to letting go of my sense of unworthiness. While still being committed to honoring Jesus as my guide, I was open to the idea of becoming more aware of my equality with Jesus in the one Christ. As a Christian philosophy the Course was unique in that it focused primarily on the seeker changing not just particular thoughts, but changing his frame of reference for perception. The new perspective of worthiness is one example of how the Course shows the seeker not so much what to think, but how to perceive himself differently so he will have a new way of thinking in all situations. The Course student is confronted with the choice of two overall ways of thinking. The standard way of thinking is to think with the ego. The new way of thinking encouraged by the Course is to think with the Holy Spirit.

Why then didn't I want to become a Course student? I felt I was already aware of the struggle between being guided by my ego or the Holy Spirit. I knew I needed help in that struggle, yet I wasn't convinced I could get that help from a book—any book of ideas. Because I considered this an inner struggle, I thought I could go within in prayer and meditation and find all my help there. I was concerned I might become rigidly dogmatic if I ever accepted any one specific set of spiritual principles. Also I didn't want to admit that my current thought system was inadequate when I had so carefully assembled it from different Eastern and Western spiritual sources over many years. I was touched by the passion Tom displayed in talking about the Course. In addition, I was intrigued by the thought-provoking concepts that Robert shared with me from the Course. However, I was not motivated enough to become a Course student.

---

1. T-In.2:2-3, p. 1 (p. 1).
2. C-In. 2:5, p. 77, (p. 73).
3. T-25.VI.4:2-3, p. 530, (p. 493).
4. T-15.V.10:10, p. 314 (p. 292).
5. W-61.p1.2:2-5, p. 102, (p. 101).
6. Thomas Merton, *New Seeds of Contemplation*, (New York: New Directions, 1972), p. 65.
7. St. Symeon the New Theologian, *Hymns of Divine Love*, translated by George A. Maloney, S. J., (Denville, NJ: Dimension Books) Hymn 15, line 151, p. 54.
8. First Corinthians 12:27, RSV.

40

COMMUNITY BUILDING

≈ • ≈

Our time in Sedona was planting the seeds for our future community, which we hoped would eventually become a full-fledged community with land and spiritual endeavors that God would reveal to us in the fullness of time. But a first giant step toward giving birth to a community would happen in the most natural of ways—the birth of a child. With all the challenges already facing Pamela, I found it remarkable that she gave birth to her fourth child, Rayel, in a tent in the Sedona wilderness. We were camped in a secluded spot near a dried up river bed. David's visiting brother, Walter, and his wife, Sheila, a midwife, were nearby and available for assistance as needed.

This was the monsoon season, and the hard soil did not absorb water very well, making the desert land subject to flash floods. Shortly after the birth, a downpour created a flash flood that suddenly wiped out the brand new birthing tent. Two other tents, containing children napping and important possessions, came within inches of being washed out as well. David figured that he could discern the signs of any future flash flood, so he set up another tent in the same place where the first tent had been. After making sure he could quickly take down the tent, David boasted to his brother, Walter, that he would never be caught off guard again by another flash flood. Walter, an experienced wilderness camper himself, predicted that it was foolish to plant the second tent where the first one had been so quickly demolished.

A few weeks later there was another rainstorm. The wind in the previous downpour was blowing in a direction that produced a flood that started slowly, providing a warning of greater flooding that would follow. However, the wind in the second rainstorm blew from the opposite direction so there was no initial buildup like David reasonably expected to provide a warning. Instead there was just one roaring wall of water that gave no warning and blew away everything in its path, including the second tent. When Walter arrived on the scene, he exercised his brotherly prerogative to laugh himself silly at David's best laid plans. Walter knew how much of a perfectionist David was, especially about being thorough and prepared in a camping situation. He rightly figured he would never have another opportunity to have a laugh like this at his brother's expense. In contrast to Walter, we weren't inclined to see the humor in the situation because we were so focused on just surviving. Nevertheless, to David's credit he graciously accepted Walter's brotherly ribbing.

An important part of our community building was for the two halves to keep in communication by telephone, through the mail, and through praying for each other. But most interesting was that each half was getting the same spiritual messages. Soon after getting my own vision of the term *His World* as the title for my book, I received a letter from Sarah in which she used the exact same term, and I found out it was a term that had come to her through her inner voice. As the Virginia Beach Half, which had now become the Sedona Half, was getting the message to *deny yourself*, the Anaheim Half was getting the same emphasis to set self aside. And, of course, we were consistently getting the same guidance to love one another and to follow the example of Jesus.

Both halves were also becoming aware of the value of *unknowing,* as it is best expressed in *The Cloud of Unknowing.*[1] This classic book describes how to set aside the normal intellectual process in order to draw closer to God. We were also familiar with *The Practice of the Presence of God*[2] by Brother Lawrence, who had the ability to be aware of the divine presence even in the ordinary duties of everyday living. The excerpt below is from my letter to the Anaheim Half written shortly after Rayel's birth regarding my attempts to learn how to be more open to God's healing love as exemplified by Brother Lawrence:

I decided to write a little more here about being aware of God's presence all of the time. First I am aware of how little I am capable of knowing and of how I have even less capability to practice what little I do know. Yet I have found that trying to be completely unknowing is not quite what I need to do. I am applying my unknowing toward others so I really feel I don't know what's best for someone else. For myself I feel I must claim a few things that I do know to help me be aware of God unceasingly. They are:

1. I know God loves me.
2. I know God is present always—whether I choose to be aware of Him or not.
3. I know that I can not be aware of God's presence all of the time except by God's grace and by asking Him for help.

Consequently, I am focusing on asking this God, Who loves me and is always present, to help me to be aware of Him. I talk to Him and ask Him to help me to continue to talk to Him so I won't forget that He is present.

I don't want to claim any victory here. I just want to say that I feel He is helping me to be aware of Him to the degree I rely on His grace, not my ability to hold a particular attitude toward Him. In this, my incompetence is not a stumbling block, but rather a reminder of Him and of how much I need His help.

While asking for His help to be aware of Him is my priority in this practice, which is I feel an exercise and strengthening of faith, the other aspect I find helpful is thankfulness. So when I talk to Him I not only ask Him for help, but also thank Him. The thankfulness is an acknowledgment of receiving help, as opposed to asking and not expecting help, and is just an appropriate response to the Love that He is.

Other subsidiary aids have been repeating the Jesus Prayer and at times talking to Jesus, or talking to Mary, or addressing the Holy Spirit and inviting that presence. Also helpful has been seeing God as the One Friend—my best friend. Everywhere, in every person I meet the same One Friend.

Although living outdoors was extremely stressful at times, being free from the concerns of working at a job allowed me to become increasingly aware of God's presence. During meditation I focused on acknowledging my oneness with Christ as my true Self, and in the everyday world I focused on being aware of God's love. A side benefit was also a new appreciation for the beauty of Mother Nature, which can easily be seen in Sedona, in spite of the hardships of survival.

I had managed to survive for a full year and was fully committed to persevering through a second winter. Nevertheless, the Sedona Half made a trip back to Anaheim in the fall and what was expected to be a short visit extended into a six-month stay in Anaheim. I had been looking forward to getting back into a warm bed to relieve the persistent pain in my right hip. Because of space limitations, however, I had to continue to sleep in my tent out in the backyard. One night I was meditating in my tent lying on my back, even though I usually sat cross-legged. As I was opening to the loving divine presence, I saw a bright inner light that came over me momentarily and then disappeared. I felt I had received a divine blessing and the hip problem, which had been getting worse, felt noticeably better, though it would take months of gradual improvement until it was fully healed.

The day after I saw the light, Robert asked, "Did you see that bright light last night?"

I wondered how he knew I had seen a light the night before, but without mentioning my experience, I inquired, "What light are you talking about?"

"It lit up the whole back yard. You must have seen it."

"You mean a car's headlight?"

"No, a car couldn't have done that. The entire back yard was lit up very brightly. By the time I got out of bed and walked over to the window to take a closer look, it was gone. What do you think it was?"

"I guess it will have to be a mystery," I said, which was true as far as it went. I was reluctant to talk about mystical things with Robert because he tended to be very logical and would view my interpretation of the event as just another way of propping up my ego. Years later, I asked Robert again about this bright light in the back yard. With his logical mind he attributed the light to a problem with the electrical transformer on the nearby telephone pole, although that had not been mentioned by him when we first discussed this. If it had been an electrical problem with the transformer, I believe the light would have been a sudden flash, but in this case the light lingered momentarily before it quickly disappeared.

(In this writing I have often made other community members appear to be one-dimensional. I feel limited in my ability as a writer to do justice to their uniqueness and ask you to keep this in mind as I describe the spiritual journey we shared with each other. A specific example of my presenting one-dimensional community members is my description thus far of Robert as being logical and not emotional. In fact, Robert and each of our community members were many-faceted. In the next few pages I hope to provide a broader portrait of Robert's character.)

One day Robert, David, Barry, now Sarah's husband, and I went to a local pool in Anaheim. They wanted to play a game in the water called "Marco Polo" in which the one who is "it" has to keep his eyes closed and yet be able to find and touch someone else, who then would become "it." When I became "it" rather quickly, I couldn't find anyone and had to quit after becoming completely exhausted. After the game I went to urinate, and blood came out in my urine, a condition that soon healed itself. I was pathetically overmatched not just by age, but by athleticism. Even if I had been as young as the others, there would have been no difference in the outcome. Afterward I went to Robert and told him that, in spite of my interest in sports competition in the past, I felt there was something intrinsically wrong about competing with other community members. Robert told me he felt it was just a game that we played in the pool, yet I still felt something was wrong. The competition just did not feel loving, at least to me. When I thought about it further, it dawned on me that the fault was in myself because of what I had been doing all along in the community. I had been exhausting myself in competing, especially verbally with Robert and David. I realized I didn't want to invest in that direction as I had been.

Our community met regularly to share and draw closer together, and we now entered a very important phase of learning how to express our true feelings in an atmosphere of acceptance, by listening to each other without making judgments. During our morning meeting in late January of 1988, Wendy expressed her fear of being controlled by the group and of having her free-will choices limited. David shared his fear of the group going astray and explained how this fear had led him in the past to try to control the situation or the group

I admitted that I had also been suppressing my feelings and expressed my anger about previous occasions with the group when I felt not accepted and not loved. At earlier meetings, when this kind of anger was expressed, a defensive attack would predictably follow, but because of our progress as a group there was no emotional retaliation this time. As I was allowed to expose this anger without being attacked, I felt fear emerging. I told the group that my fear was about expecting to be attacked for expressing my feelings.

[I once told Robert that when I looked at his face in the straight ahead position, it reminded me of Byzantine icons of Christ I had seen. Even in the slightly turned position of the head in the photograph of Robert on the opposite page, I can see some of the features of an icon of Christ in his light, clear skin contrasted with his dark eyes. Robert thought my comment about his face was odd since the idea of looking like an icon had never crossed his mind. I got the impression it was not a thought he would give credence to in the future. I could always count on Robert thinking and then doing what he felt through his guidance was the right thing to do. In this sensed, it would be truer to say, Robert was more Christ-like in his mind than in his face. His focus on holding to what is right, did not prevent him from making mistakes. But it did allow him to do the right thing by admitting his mistakes whenever they come into his conscious awareness, even if the truth proved to be embarrassing, as in the example below.]

Speaking up next, Robert stepped out of the box that was normally assigned to him as *Mister Mind,* and he too expressed his feelings. Robert addressed me saying, "I sense that below your feeling of fear there is the pain of feeling unloved. I feel guilty because I feel I have caused some of that pain. I haven't been fair to you. I know you are the Son of God. But I haven't been making the effort to see you as the Son of God. I'm going to try harder." I was deeply touched by his words, yet much more by the fact

ROBERT PERRY IN 1988 DURING THE ANAHEIM VISIT

THE SUNFELLOW FAMILY: DAVID, PAMELA,
TOREY, JEREMIA (top left), SHAWNA (far right), RAYEL (bottom)

that he was speaking vulnerably with many tears in his eyes as he opened his heart to me. I cried with Robert, and we embraced. I felt a healing took place for Robert and me, similar to the healing that had taken place the previous spring between Tom and me. (Coincidentally, Tom had called a few days previously and would be visiting our community in a few weeks.) Since Robert could break out of his box, I felt any one of us could do likewise, and that was the direction the community was taking little by little. After this encounter, Robert made a greater effort to reach out to me by initiating one-on-one walks with me for us to improve our communication and friendship.

With the stress of camping out in the Sedona desert set aside for the time being, the Sunfellows were flourishing as a family. The photograph on the opposite page was taken in the early part of 1987 during the Anaheim visit, and it shows the happy faces of the Sunfellow family. (Shawna is impishly making a funny face in the picture.) In addition to the main house at Anaheim, there was a cottage available in the back that provided a temporary home of their own for the Sunfellows. Pamela even had time to help out with the community garden in the back yard, because she really enjoyed keeping close to the earth through gardening. In the past when I played a variety of simple one-on-one games with Torey, I had routinely played badly to let him win. But now he became more confident in himself, and I found that he could win on his own without any help from me. Rayel remained a happy six-month-old baby, proving to be equally at ease with outdoor camping and indoor living. Shawna and Jeremia loved all the special attention lavished on them by Sarah, Wendy, and Robert, who spent time with them individually and went out of their way to make all the children feel comfortable.

David was changing, too, becoming more loving and more focused on Jesus. I had always had a personal relationship with Jesus as my guide and master, and assumed David had the same relationship. But I learned that he viewed Jesus in an impersonal way as an elder brother who had himself taken the path all the way to God and therefore is our example to do the same. David did not see Jesus as someone who enters his life in a personal way and leads him back to God.

However, David was open to learning more about the role of Jesus in his life and in the community. Robert suggested that they both visit a bookstore in Los Angeles that is owned and operated by followers of Da Free John, who claimed to be a "perfect master." Robert felt there were some valuable central teachings presented by this American spiritual teacher, and David found to his surprise that he agreed. David disagreed with some peripheral teachings but found the basic message to be very helpful in rounding out the teachings that he was already familiar with, such as those of St. John of the Cross and the Course.

But David then read Da Free John's biography and saw the way he projected himself in photographs. He listened to the way Da Free John talked about himself as a perfect master and examined the words his followers used to describe him. David finally concluded that the images Da Free John projected of himself were, in David's words, "dripping in ego." No matter how elevated the teachings were, the man as a person was obnoxious to David.

David's perception was made even without awareness of the sexual improprieties that would be alleged in later years. There is an online article by the well-respected spiritual philosopher, Ken Wilber, acknowledging that Adi Da (a later name for Da Free John) possesses the extremes of profound spiritual insights on the one hand and deeply flawed personality traits on the other hand.[8] Recently I talked with a female friend, whom I will call Tiffany, about her life as a member of Da Free John's community in California. She explained, "Da had nine 'wives.' That says a lot right there. Da might tell his followers collectively to be celibate for a month. Then he might tell them to have sex with their partners every day for an extended period. Next he might instruct them to have sex with the partner of their best friend for a month. He told the women to surrender to their male partners and the males to surrender to him. He said that the men had the right to be physically or sexually abusive to their female partners. He told the women to be submissive to their husbands even if they were abusive. I know about that from first-hand experience because I was married to an abusive husband in the community.

"I had a close friend who was one of the privileged females allowed to go on one of Da's trips to Fiji. Da forced her to have sex with him on that trip. She was very upset, and when she told her husband after coming back to California, he also became outraged. She filed a lawsuit against Da. Some community members came to me to ask me to also file a lawsuit. I would have been fully justified in filing abuse charges, but I decided to leave the community instead. I don't even like to talk about that time in my life because I've moved on," Tiffany concluded. Sexual allegations were one of the reasons why Da Free John closed the California community and moved to Fiji.

Tiffany told me she did not want me to use her real name, but she did want me to quote her. She wanted me to relate her experience so that youthful and naive seekers would be aware of the potential danger of giving over their personal power and decision-making to another human being just because that person has taken on the role of being a spiritual leader. She felt that sometimes common sense is a more reliable guide to navigating safely in the world than lofty spiritual ideals. Acknowledging that she had been naive herself in the past, Tiffany did not want others to make the same mistakes that she had.

In my previous encounters with Tiffany, I had noticed that one of her outstanding qualities was her sense of personal empowerment. She consistently spoke the truth as she saw it with quiet wisdom. I mistakenly assumed she had always been so independent-minded and self-assured. When she told me about having lived with an abusive husband in an abusive spiritual community, I was very surprised because there was not the least trace of naïveté in her current character. Her revelation put a personal face on the bizarre stories I had heard about abusive gurus. It was reassuring to see firsthand that growing out of a bad situation, an originally naive seeker like Tiffany could avoid wallowing in victimization and instead could make personal empowerment into one of her strengths.

During our extended stay in Anaheim when Robert had talked to me about the Course, he explained that victimizers and victims as equally responsible for their dysfunctional symbiotic relationships. It appears that the victimizer is attacking the victim. However, the Course maintains that the victimizer is actually attacking himself by selecting his victimizing role, and the victim is attacking himself by choosing his victim role. Both the victimizer and the victim are experiencing what they have chosen for themselves. Although both the victimizer and the victim are experiencing an attack on themselves in the illusions of the world, neither one can change their essential reality as Sons of God, made in the image and likeness of His Love. Even though I was not a Course student, I could accept all this philosophy on an intellectual level.

On the other hand, my prior programming, especially my emotional programming, was resistant to this higher intellectual understanding. In particular I had a problem with the idea of abuse of any kind—but especially abuse related to the responsibility of a spiritual teacher to his students. I had an initial visceral reaction to the discovery of so many corrupt gurus who had apparently thrown away their purity of heart, which is at the center of the sacred function of being a spiritual teacher. In my mind I held gurus to the standard that Jesus established for spiritual teachers when he said, "...to whom much has been given, much will be required."[9] As disheartening as it was to see so many advanced spiritual leaders fall short of their high ideals, there was a sobering and helpful lesson that their negative example taught me. What I learned was that I could not afford to sit back on my laurels of self-satisfaction and through spiritual sloth lose vigilance for awakening to the kingdom of God. Otherwise, I too could fall even though I considered this as an extremely unlikely possibility. Adding to my concern was the memory of my past life as the Pole Man, who, for whatever reason, literally and figuratively fell from grace. I did not want to duplicate that fall because of any spiritual neglect on my part.

Closely aligned with the issue of guru abuse is the troubling aspect of deception involved in that abuse. I felt it was important to share with others here in my autobiography the deception of fallen gurus so others would not be similarly deceived in the future. But in the process I didn't want to be deceived myself, either. I had come to believe the world is a dream. Yet I didn't want to be deceived into thinking that the darkness of the deeds of corrupt gurus was any more real than any other illusory dreams of the world. In spite of that, my heart went out to the deceived victims who were apparently victimized by fallen gurus. Yes, I did intellectually believe that victims need to accept responsibility for making themselves vulnerable to being victimized. Yes, I accepted that such victims and even corrupt gurus can never lose their true nature as children of God. However, that understanding could lead to the mistaken idea that nothing matters here at the form level. This world is indeed a dream, but dream pain still hurts in a dream world. I felt a responsibility to caution others, when appropriate, on how to navigate in the world to avoid dream pain. Consequently, I have felt an obligation to explicitly describe in this book the shortcomings of unethical gurus. My goal has not been to condemn and demonize these gurus, falsely imagining that they do not deserve the same love and forgiveness that is rightly due to every child of God. Rather my single motivation had been to warn youthful and naive seekers in order to help them avoid unnecessary dream pain. The sacred responsibility that spiritual teachers have to their students is similar to the sacred responsibility that parents have to their children, although children are even more susceptible to abuse than naïve, youthful students. In the future I would find myself in the position of protecting children from potential abuse, and that experience, which will be described in a later chapter, intensified and crystallized my sense of compassion and protectiveness for any victims of abuse. Also my desire to protect others from being exposed to victimization was fueled by my own past struggles with victim consciousness.

Even without the awareness of any abuse issues, David's impressions of Da Free John caused an upheaval within him. If David had known the inner workings of Da Free John's community, he would have been even more disturbed than he was. He was perplexed by the sight of apparently very valid teachings emanating from someone who had become caught in the web of his own ego. It occurred to David that he as well might gain the essence of the spiritual life and be able to promote true spiritual teachings and yet might fail to be an example of it. What if he too became convinced he was a perfect master, when in fact he was not? Or worse, what if he knew he was not a perfect master and promoted himself as one anyway?

David became concerned about how he could possibly avoid all the pitfalls of the spiritual path presented by his ego. However, his concerns were resolved by the realization that he really did need help from a True Perfect Master. After all, Jesus had demonstrated His perfection by overcoming every temptation of the ego. Rather than exalting Himself, Jesus humbled Himself in every possible way. David then opened his heart and mind much more fully to Jesus. He commented on his change of heart by saying, "I marveled at myself for thinking I could do what He did without His help."

Previously David had thought that it was primarily his job to find his way back to God and that it would be wrong to shift that responsibility on to Jesus. But his new realization enabled him to see that if left to his own devices, he might never find his way back to God. He needed to take the hand of Jesus and allow Him to lead the way out of his ego labyrinth and into his true Home in the presence of God. As I was learning to not value Jesus so much that I devalued myself, David was learning the opposite lesson of elevating Jesus to the position of being his personal Master.

Our extended stay in Anaheim proved to be a time of consolidating the gains of the community as a whole and to strengthening the bonds between individual members. There were still conflicts that flared up and then subsided, only to return at a later date because they had been temporarily managed but not resolved. However, in spite of these weather storms of emotions, there was a noticeable shift in the community. There was more of a feeling of God and Jesus shepherding our community toward denying ourselves and learning to love one another. Just as it was not David's job alone to find his way back to God, it was not our job to manufacture a community. It was God's community, and His Plan being carried out. God through Jesus was personally directing and assisting us in the formation of His community. Earth changes, the Second Coming, and other concerns were set aside because that was not the direction shown to us at the time. How would our community destiny unfold? We did not know, yet felt God would reveal what we needed to know when we needed to know it.

---

1. *The Cloud of Unknowing* and *The Book of Privy Counseling*. These two books by unknown authors have been incorporated into one edition by Father William Johnston, who edited them and wrote the introduction. (New York: Image Books, a division of Doubleday and Co., Inc., 1973).

2. Brother Lawrence, *The Practice of the Presence of God*, (Springdale, PA: Whitaker House, 1982).

3. Ken Wilber, *The Case of Adi Da*, October 11, 1996, shambala.com.

4. Luke 12:48, CCD.

41

RETURN TO ARIZONA

~ o ~

David, Pamela, and I were revitalized by our time in Anaheim. We knew that the challenges before us in Sedona were still going to be formidable. However, we had proved we were survivors and felt we would continue to grow in learning how to love one another. In May as we were leaving, Tom, who had visited in February, was returning again to Anaheim to seriously consider the possibility of joining our community, which he eventually did.

The first time we had gone to Sedona it was with preconceived ideas about what we wanted to accomplish. Historically, why did people go to the desert? It was because there was nothing there. The early Christian monks all the way back to St. Anthony went to the desert because there was nothing there to divert them from finding God. This time, our goal in going back to Sedona was to have no expectations—attempting to be open and allowing God and specifically Jesus to lead the way. After starting out well in our interactions with each other, we discovered that old negative patterns started to re-emerge, but we very much attempted to respond differently, with more flexibility and love.

We were each trying to break out of our molds. David was changing from an "always-in-control" type into a person who allows others to take over his controlling functions. For example, I drove the van for the first time, instead of David, in order for Pamela and me to work together to do errands. This in turn gave David extra time to catch up on writing letters. Pamela had often been reluctant to express herself, but she was being transformed from an "I-want-my-own-space" type into a person who spoke her mind. She allowed me in particular to be more a part of her world. I was learning how to give up my "I'm-in-my-own-monk-world" frame of reference to being more flexible and responsive to the world in which David, Pamela, and the children lived.

My past fear was that David would try to control me and that Pamela would isolate herself from me. I was grateful this was not happening, but I had not forgiven them for these past patterns, and my unforgiveness carried a blaming energy. My unforgiveness blocked me from being loving and responsive to them in a way that would help them to let go of their old patterns and respond with love to me. Realizing this, I focused in prayer on learning to find a deeper level of forgiveness for David, Pamela, and also for myself. On the practical side, I attempted to be more aware of the ways I contributed negatively by my inappropriate actions that triggered their patterns. In spite of my best intentions, I found myself at times having the opposite effect from the one I had intended.

One old pattern we could not seem to overcome was our dysfunctional dynamics around job hunting. David abandoned his former strategy of just waiting for a job to come his way and initiated an active job search. He even applied as a gas station attendant, but our collective attempts at job hunting failed. David proposed the idea that we were too tense about the issue and needed to release this intensity and fear in order for us to be truly open. Pamela couldn't at first accept the idea of loosening up because she was becoming increasingly concerned that our money and food were quickly disappearing. However, we tried our best to make our relationships more important than job seeking.

Similar to Pamela, I felt a sense of urgency about the job seeking, but a dream helped me realize that David was right about our need to let go of our fears. In the dream a group of fishermen caught a gigantic load of fish in their net, and Pamela tried to catch fish like the fishermen, yet couldn't catch anything. She was on the wrong side of the net and scared the fish away. I was helping the fisherman distribute the fish. I saw some dead fish, and I was told this kind of fish pretends to be dead, but is really alive. I picked up a big one of these fish and put it on shore.

In my dreams, fish symbolize Christ and His work. I felt the dream was saying that we were doing the work of Christ. Nevertheless, we needed to let go of our fears so the work could be accomplished. Also, the fish that appeared to be dead meant that we were accomplishing Christ's work even though outwardly what we were doing appeared to be lifeless.

Although Pamela intellectually agreed about the need to relax and trust, she was increasingly becoming unglued due to the stress of raising the children, campsite living, lack of finances and food, and feeling isolated. She was being intensely challenged in her weakest area of growth—trust in divine providence. For example, she broke down and finally bought disposable diapers, but then immediately felt guilty almost to tears about possibly wasting food money since our finances were so low. Self-doubt set in, and she wondered if, in choosing her, God had picked the wrong person to be in this situation.

Aware of Pamela's difficulty, we gave her more time and space to be alone and tried to lighten her load of responsibilities. Also we made a conscious effort to let her know how much we appreciated all the wonderful ways in which she really did contribute to all of our lives. We also reminded her of all the progress she had made in communication. In the past she would be unclear and somewhat confused, and after trying to bring up her ideas, she would quickly give up and withdraw into her own world. However, she had now learned to listen to the concerns of others while still presenting her ideas clearly and persistently until her concerns were eventually acknowledged by others. She had learned how to be assertive without being offensive. She was able to agree with some portions of what others told her and disagree with other portions. Nevertheless, one problem she still had was that she seemed to magnify her shortcomings in her own mind and overlook the importance of the gains in her growth.

Our money ran out at the end of May and, facing a desperate situation, money arrived from Wendy. Then we had to move again, but this move was better than in the past. I had learned how to more efficiently break down my camp site and reestablish it in a new location, and I had gotten rid of some of my belongings to make moving easier for all of us. Yet I was so exhausted from the move that temporarily I didn't want to watch the children. Because this made things harder for David and Pamela, we talked about it. The result was that I learned to be more conscious of how difficult it was for David and Pamela to take care of other concerns if they could not find a time of relief from watching the children. David and Pamela learned how much my physical limitations affected me on those occasions when I had to physically exert myself and how many times in the past I had helped out even though I felt very tired from the activities of the day.

Although the issue of watching the children was quickly and amicably resolved, Pamela was triggered by the fact that we had run out of money before Wendy's money arrived. She asserted that our decision to let go of focusing on getting a job right away was wrong. David and Pamela argued about this issue with equal vehemence. Finally Pamela agreed with David that we should not intensely pursue a job with a feeling of desperation. On the other hand she affirmed that we should not just wait for a job to fall in our laps. Finally, we agreed to be more open to job possibilities without doing so in a fearful way.

I decided to pursue a full-time job as a supervisor of a top local hotel, on the graveyard shift. I suggested I could drive the van to work and David and Pamela could move out of sleeping in the van and sleep in tents instead. In the evening when David and Pamela heard about this job and how it would impact on their lives, David was very disturbed, and he argued with me. But Pamela was even more upset. We were all still upset when I went to my tent to sleep. Finally Pamela told David she had reached the end of her rope and was ready to pack up the van and leave Sedona with the children. The next morning we resumed our talk about the job, and I found out Pamela was serious about leaving Sedona for good.

I had figured that if I could get this job, it would be best for David and Pamela as well. However, I now knew that David and Pamela didn't like how the job impacted them, so I saw them as obstacles to my getting a job that we all needed. Consequently, I had made getting the job the goal and made David's and Pamela's feelings a secondary concern. In the course of the conversation, however, I admitted that the better solution for this job and any other job hunting was for me to reverse my priorities. I had to make David and Pamela my number one priority and make any job a secondary concern. Instead of taking things into my own hands, I learned to draw upon David and Pamela as resources to discern what kinds of jobs would be best for all of us. This reestablishment of our priorities based on loving one another helped to stabilize the situation.

Nevertheless, later that day Pamela got into a disagreement with David about his job hunting and complained that she was not being included in his process. Pamela told him that he was not open-minded in regard to his job hunting, just like I had been telling them the day before that they were both too closed to the idea of my finding work. David refused to look for work with a fearful state of mind and would not allow a desperate money situation to influence him to take a job that he felt God did not want him to do. We talked about this together and decided again, as we had earlier in the day, that we needed to all work together. Consequently, we decided to read through the newspaper want ads together and would collectively agree what jobs to pursue. We made some telephone calls, and although no jobs resulted, we were all happy with the way we were finally on the same page.

That night I had a dream I felt confirmed we had finally gotten on the right track. In the dream, a judge had several million dollars that he was about to give to some people, but he told them that because they were arguing, he had decided they wouldn't get any of it. The people realized that they wouldn't get anything unless they came to agreement, so they made a greater effort to work together cooperatively and resolve their differences. Obviously, the dream meant that unless we continued to come together as a group with greater harmony, our financial situation would remain bleak.

A couple of days later our camp site got tagged again by the forest service after only one week, and we were on the move again. We decided to be more invisible at our next site. My tent would be well hidden and the only one standing in a very remote place. David and Pamela left no tents or other things at our camp site during the day when the forest rangers were out. Each evening they would set up for the night and pack up again in the morning, leaving no trace of having been there.

David found a little temporary work pulling weeds, but a job did not open up for me. In my secluded camping spot, I focused on inner and outer purification. I regularly fasted on water for three days at a time and used an enema bag. After one of my fasts I passed a black slimy substance. When not fasting, my diet was sparse and the same every day. I had fruit in the morning. For lunch I had some lettuce, carrots, sunflower seeds, twelve almonds, a few pumpkin seeds, a pinch of spirulina and gelatin, and a bit of bee pollen. For dinner in the late afternoon I had a fruit meal—usually one type of fruit per meal, alternating apples, oranges, peaches, or melons. If I felt protein starved, I would occasionally have a can of sardines.

I resorted to this raw food diet because I was having body aches and pains that I was concerned might become a chronic condition. Indeed, this fasting and restricted diet, along with continued yoga practice and more meditation, did improve my physical constitution. While I was on an extended apple fast, I found that my feces were colored yellow, not brown. It literally did not smell, negating the rhetorical question, "I suppose yours doesn't smell?" Nevertheless, there must have been some smell because hungry squirrels somehow managed to find the spots where I buried this pure food by-product. We all buried our feces, but in my case I also had to cover the burial spots with heavy rocks. Perhaps all this information is more than you are interested in hearing. However, it gives you an idea of how we had to pay attention to every little detail of our physical surroundings and the surprises that came our way. One day I came back to my tent and found a squirrel size hole in my tent, yet that was nothing compared to the ant invaders that came and required a complete tent renovation.

During my focus on healing through external means such as fasting and a limited diet, I also confronted issues related to learning how to love. I read about Anatoly (now called Natan, his Jewish name) Sharansky, the Russian Jew who spent nine years in Russian prisons before being released to Israel. I was inspired by his determination and courage, which encouraged me to continue with my fasting even when I was dizzy at times.

In addition, I read about Mother Teresa, who disregarded her own heart condition in order to serve others. In her seventies she plugged away at teaching people how to give their lives to Jesus by seeing His eyes in every poor and dying person whom she and others served. I cried in reading about the love manifested by these servants of the poor and sick. When I looked at myself, I saw by contrast how much I was falling short of my own calling of being a giver of love. Nevertheless, in my prayers, when I was most inspired, I felt Jesus loving me at my deepest core, and I focused on that love penetrating me. I was sure of His love for me (and the love of God and Mother Mary). That assurance within me was my rock bottom sense of security, among all the insecurities that were present in my outer camping life. I was in the process of learning how to feel about myself the same way that Jesus feels toward me—to love myself.

42

JOBS OPEN UP

≈ • ≈

David, Pamela, and I hadn't been consistent about practicing group meditation, but since the end of May we had decided to make a greater effort to have an attunement together every morning as the sun rose. At the same time, we were cooperating more harmoniously throughout the day by all contributing to the care of the children, doing errands together, and being of assistance to each other. Also we asked for the Anaheim Half to send us their prayers and expressed to them that we also felt we wanted to be of one mind with them. We hoped these sincere efforts toward greater unity would culminate in bringing relief to our external circumstances through a job or jobs opening up for us.

In the middle of June a job finally opened up for David at Beverly's Market, a health food store, and we made friendships through that work situation. David made a strong connection with a co-worker named Kerry, and they felt their hearts opening to each other to experience a kind of love that neither had experienced before. There were no sexual indiscretions, but the love they felt for each other had both romantic and spiritual aspects, and the intensity of their love created obvious problems, since they were both married. Remarkably, Kerry's husband Carl remained calm and chose to support Kerry in her need to explore the love that she was experiencing.

Pamela, however, was devastated, and David made no attempt to hide the love relationship. He felt he had a deep spiritual connection with Kerry, which to him was important to nourish, so he spent a great deal of time with her. Pamela felt that she had given her heart to David. Nevertheless, he had never felt the deep, overpowering infatuation for her that often initiates relationships. Ironically, I had expressed this kind of powerful love for her when I had my past-life opening years earlier. Fortunately, that love in me for Pamela had long ago been locked away somewhere in my psyche, where it remained hidden. Of course, she wanted and felt she deserved that kind of love from her husband, even if it was only a temporary romantic opening of the heart that faded away as time passed. She had hoped all along that David would one day give her this gift of love, but now it was being given instead to Kerry. In addition, Pamela felt her responsibilities in caring for the children were increasing with the time David spent nurturing his relationship with Kerry.

From David's perspective, he felt he was finally opening up and learning how to really love. He felt that his flowering of love would manifest in all aspects of his life and in his future work in Sedona. He wanted Pamela to appreciate this opening of his heart and support him by sacrificing her own personal feelings for the sake of the greater good that would come out of this opening. David also felt that the love he was experiencing through his relationship with Kerry, if nourished, would allow him in time to open his heart to Pamela.

Pamela felt she had already sacrificed her life and personal interests to help manifest David's projects and live up to his spiritual ideals, such as doing God's Will. She did this more out of a personal love for David than for any lofty ideal, and she consoled herself by knowing she was the primary woman in David's life. Now she was being asked to sacrifice even this, and it was too much for her to tolerate. She reacted emotionally, alternately with anger or tears. She felt David was looking down on her as being emotionally immature and unable to rise to the occasion as Kerry's husband Carl had been able to do. David dealt with Pamela's reaction by withdrawing emotionally from her, which in turn made her feel isolated and even angrier. Pamela, who had never even had a formal wedding, gave back David's ring to signify a separation in their relationship.

At this point Robert, Sarah, and Tom arrived on the scene in Sedona to be mediators. They were uniquely qualified for this service because the Anaheim Half had already gone through their own similar circumstance. When Sarah moved in to live with Robert and Wendy, the obviously profound and loving spiritual connection between Robert and Sarah blossomed. This sent Wendy into a tailspin and created upheaval in all of their lives. Indeed each of them experienced great pain working through this situation in order to preserve the sanctity of the marriage between Robert and Wendy, the holiness of the true spiritual relationship between Robert and Sarah, and the friendship between Wendy and Sarah. It would take a lot of processing, prayer, and time to come to terms with this situation and find peace.

What made the Anaheim three-way relationship resolvable was that there was a clear understanding that the priority was with the marriage. There was the recognition that God had ordained the marriage as a means of two partners making each other the center of their lives. In this context, a spiritual relationship with a third party could play a very helpful secondary influence. What made the Sedona three-way relationship more difficult to resolve was that David was making the spiritual love relationship the priority and was putting the marriage into a secondary position.

From David's perspective he was attempting to act very honorably and conscientiously all along and as always very much wanted to do God's Will. Because of their own similar experience, Robert and Sarah in particular were able to help David to see more clearly that he needed to reestablish his marriage as his priority and that he could still preserve his loving spiritual relationship in a lesser role. Once David realized he had been off center, he apologized publicly to Pamela and to everyone else for his misunderstanding of the situation. Because David returned to making his marriage his number one priority, it was easier for Pamela to see the value of David's spiritual relationship with Kerry.

Immediately after this unsettled period, Pamela was asked to apply for a position with the Montessori School of Sedona, and she in turn asked me to apply. She even gave me an application, which I decided *not* to fill out because I felt my previous teaching of Torey was about all I wanted of teaching children. Two weeks later I was driving the van and turned down the wrong street. Pamela noticed that the Montessori teacher, Eunice, had her home on this street, View Street. (I had grown up on South View Street in Meriden, Connecticut.) Eunice had previously invited Pamela's children to come over anytime to play with her own daughter, so Pamela suggested we drop in. During the visit I struck up a conversation with Eunice's daughter and made a pencil drawing of her face. Eunice thought the drawing was a good likeness of her daughter and said, "Why don't you apply for the assistant teacher job? I think you would be great with the children. You can still apply today, even though this is the last day to submit applications."

I felt I was being tapped on the shoulder by God, Who was making it hard for me to refuse, so I applied and was hired. I felt this would be a learning experience in how to love, but what I didn't anticipate was that this would be a lesson in being grounded in the practical aspects of life—my weakness and Pamela's strength. Up until this point, camping was my idea of an ultimate grounding experience. However, I learned children can be a grounding experience as well. I remember coming home after my first day of work, and Pamela asked about how it went. I groaned, "I feel *shell shocked!*"

Finding humor in my situation Pamela smiled knowingly and said, "Now you can see first hand what I have been dealing with in raising children." The children I was working with were ages three to six, in the range of her own children, Shawna and Jeremia. With Pamela's interest peaked she said, "Tell me more about your adventures."

I explained, "God really does have a sense of humor. I had asked Him, 'I want to be a monk and to rise up into heaven, so give me a worthy teacher.'

"Of course, God always answers our prayers, so He said, 'I'll give you many worthy teachers. If you want to go to heaven, you first have to sink your feet down into the earth. The scorpions, tarantulas, black widow spiders, and rattlesnakes will be your teachers, so go live in a tent in the desert and let them teach you how to be grounded.'

"After two years, I said to God, 'I am tired of the scorpions, tarantulas, black widow spiders, and rattlesnakes being my teachers. Send me new and better teachers.'

"So God, Who, as I said, always answers our prayers, said, 'Why don't *you* be the teacher? Go be an assistant teacher at the Montessori School, and you will find what you are looking for. If you can't learn how to be grounded there, you can't learn anywhere.' God tricked me into taking this job by making me think I would assist in teaching these children. However, He turned the tables on me and made me the student and these little ones have become my teachers. I am facing 'self' in ways I would never have chosen consciously. It's very humbling. I had a dream a while back in which I was told, 'All growth is a lowering of self.' Now I am finding out first hand what that means."

Of the fifteen children in our class, we had about eight hyperactive ones, who each felt the whole world revolved around them. Three boys in particular gave me the impression they had been feeding on Mexican jumping beans all their lives. In the middle of each day, Eunice would have me take these three boys out of the classroom in order to do playground activities designed to burn up some of their nearly inexhaustible energy.

The following is an excerpt from a letter Pamela wrote to the Anaheim Half after they returned to California and shortly after I started my job on August 22, exactly two years after my original arrival in Sedona:

> So much has happened since Kerry has entered our lives that it is hard to record it or even understand it all. The most recent thing that can be recorded is a funny occurrence that happened the day before yesterday when Don was talking about his job. As he was describing his experience at the school, all of us began to laugh. Don explained how much he realized he is the student and the classroom and children and school are his teachers, instead of the other way around. He continued to explain that one of the main themes in the classroom is to teach the children how to deal with practical life skills with grace and calmness. Everything has to be precise, graceful, and smooth in the Montessori method of teaching. You also need to be totally into the children's world and relate to them in a very direct and present way.

So, as Don was talking about going to school every day, he was realizing how God arranged this job situation to continue his own personal growth process in the area of being grounded! I'm not doing justice here, and I'll leave it up to Don to fill in the rest. The point I am trying to make is that all of us here are being guided by certain things God has arranged in our lives in order to face our greatest weaknesses. Not that we haven't been working on them— it's just that things have been arranged a little differently on more intense terms.

Don has also been very supportive to me throughout this whole relationship thing between David, Kerry, and me. His strength came out in terms of being supportive and compassionate. David and I have healed our relationship to a large degree. If it hadn't been for Don, I'm not sure I would have held out.

By David and Kerry discovering their special relationship, they have exposed all the cracks in me and in my relationship with David. It has made each of us work on our weakest areas: I need to work on self-worth, clarity, and knowing myself; David needs to realize how he needs to consider others and how he affects them. He needs to learn how to come into their world and see from their perspective. It's encouraged us to grow more than ever and clean up the old, if we can manage to do so. The main thing I felt to communicate is that all three of us here are being placed by God in a position to see ourselves in a very interesting way.

Seeing our community as a whole—at work with all our talents present a few weeks ago when we were together—is something God is helping us recognize. He is helping us all realize our stuff and how we need to clean it up. But many blessings are present. When we worked together on the dynamics present here, a great clarity and strength were revealed.

It's been the most intense time in both David's and my life. In fact, David is sick right now, to the point of total breakdown and exhaustion. He is resting and recovering and things are up out of the pit, but not totally balanced. We still continue to grow, and David and I are doing better as a couple. His relationship with Kerry is still a concern, and he is trying to see how it needs to be. Overall David is much more extending and loving toward me.

A house feels close, as though something will happen soon. This is a feeling we share. We shall see—it feels like a certain kind of arrangement by God is happening.

Indeed a house did manifest shortly, which removed the ongoing stress of constantly being uprooted and exposed to the unpredictable elements of nature. A new, stable place to live also helped us all face and deal with the intense challenges that had just come to a head and needed to be sorted out and slowly healed over time. Our new home was an older model trailer in a mobile home park. We often took a short walk from our home to the Verde River at Red Rock Crossing where Cathedral Rock stood majestically. Because of its exquisite beauty, this mountain of red rock with water flowing near its base is the most photographed site in Sedona, and some say the most photographed natural formation in all of the United States.

Before moving into our new home and while we were all in the soup of coming to grips with the relationship issues raised by David and Pamela in regard to Kerry, another important, though less dramatic, community issue presented itself. Robert had earlier told Sarah he felt it might be time to write a statement of our community identity. Sarah responded that to do so we would need a name for our community. The community did agree upon a name and then a set of guiding community principles. As a result of the process of coming up with a community identity, it became apparent that the community represented a synthesis of the East and the West. How our community found its identity and learned to see itself as an expression of a marriage of the East and West is presented in the upcoming chapters.

RED ROCK CROSSING AND CATHEDRAL ROCK

43

THE MARRIAGE OF
THE EAST AND WEST

≈ • ≈

When Robert raised the issue of choosing a community name, Tom offered the suggestion that the community name should come from the New Testament. Immediately Robert's mind went to one of his favorite sections of Revelation, the beginning of Chapter 21. He specifically thought of the first two sentences that included the idea of "a new heaven and a new earth,"[1] but he could not think of an appropriate name. On Monday morning, August 15, Robert asked David if he could think of a name for the community from the New Testament, and David quickly came up with "New Jerusalem." Robert realized that the very next verse, after the two that had already come to mind, included "...the holy city, New Jerusalem, coming down out of heaven from God."[2]

Later that day Robert came across a book by David Spangler entitled *Revelation*. In it, Robert found many phrases about "the new heaven and the new earth," and this was yet another reference to the beginning of Chapter 21 of Revelation. In addition, David Spangler was playing the same symbolic leadership role in Findhorn as David Sunfellow was playing in our community, which gave weight to David's suggestion of "New Jerusalem."

This same day I was told I had been hired for the job at the Montessori School. That day in the evening, we had a community meeting in which everyone present agreed to accept our new name—the "New Jerusalem Community." Robert subsequently wrote about the new name in our community journal, which was a written record of all of our community communications, ideas, and the events in our lives. Robert described the biblical reference to "New Jerusalem" as an extension of the idea of Israel, a people chosen by God to be an embodiment of the true relationship between man and God. Just as the Jewish people were called by God to carry out His Plan of salvation, our community was being called, along with many other seekers, to participate in this Plan. The "New Jerusalem" marks the end of the historical stream of the Judeo-Christian tradition, by pointing

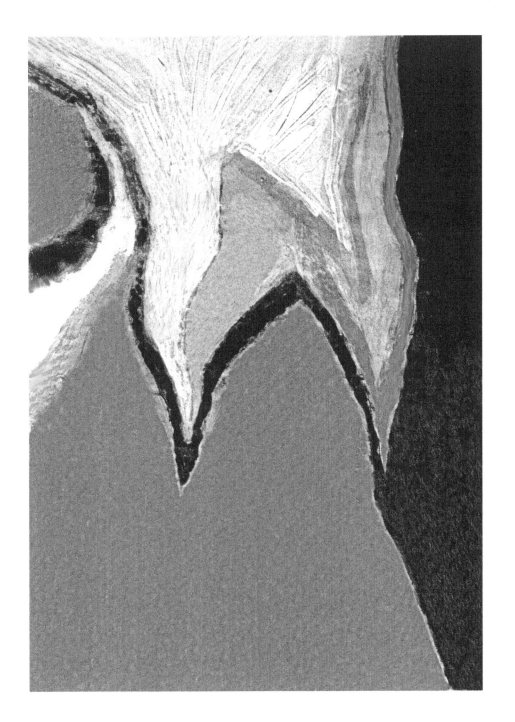

DAWNING OF THE NEW JERUSALEM

to a climactic time in the future. And just as two thousand years ago Jesus experienced a personal death and rebirth as a spiritual transformation, so in modern times the earth itself is expected to experience some sort of apocalyptic death and rebirth. These apocalyptic changes will bring forth the New Jerusalem, representing the final spiritual transformation stage ushered in by the return of Jesus Himself. The New Jerusalem represents the historical culmination point of Western spirituality in the world.

But there is an equally important interpretation of the New Jerusalem that is related to Eastern spirituality. The best known explanation of this meaning can be found in the readings of Edgar Cayce. According to this interpretation, Revelation itself is a description of the individual journey of spiritual awakening. This Eastern perspective interprets the seven churches mentioned in Revelation as the seven chakras. Similarly, the opening of the seven seals in Revelation is interpreted as the opening of the seven chakras from the base of the spine upward. In this interpretation the New Jerusalem represents the culmination of the individual's journey to God. The Eastern view of individual divine union is that the seeker is already united with God now, yet is invariably unaware of this oneness. Spiritual awakening is then a realization of the seeker's pre-existing condition of union with God, and this realization is symbolized as the New Jerusalem.

Although the interpretation of the New Jerusalem as the climax of Western historical spirituality has received the most attention in our culture, the lesser known interpretation of the New Jerusalem as each individual's awakening is equally important. Certainly Jesus Himself, as a model for mankind, achieved this full opening to divine awareness in his own lifetime, thus demonstrating each person's individual potential for transformation. Indeed Jesus, through His own attainment, is able to assist each seeker to awaken to the divine presence. With the exception of Jesus, the best example of the realization of the New Jerusalem state of consciousness was Mother Mary. She was transformed in consciousness and taken up into heaven during her Assumption, which is celebrated by the Catholic Church on August 15. Since this was the same date that the community named itself the New Jerusalem Community, I proposed to the community that we celebrate August 15 as our community birthday.

In my mind, birthdays and receiving a name went together. My parents had agreed that my name would be "Peter" long before my birth. But when I finally arrived on my birthday, my mother told my father, "His name is Donald." When my father asked for an explanation, my mother said that she couldn't explain it, except that she just knew the name was Donald. Ever since I have been trying to figure out who this Donald is. In my earliest photograph (shown on the opposite page) my questioning eyes seem to already be asking, "Hey, who am I and what am I doing here anyway?"

Because we receive our names at birth as our first step in learning who we are, it seemed appropriate to me that our community name and birthday should go together as a celebration of the attainment of the New Jerusalem, as exemplified by Mother Mary's Assumption. Just as Mary gave birth to Jesus, David and Pamela left Anaheim to give birth to the beginnings of our community in Sedona. They arrived in Sedona on the Vigil of the Assumption (August 14), and their first full day was the Assumption (August 15, 1986).

I sent a letter to our Anaheim Half to recommend August 15 as our New Jerusalem Community birthday. What I did not know at the time of writing the letter was that in Lubbock, Texas, a miraculous appearance occurred, which included visions of Jesus and Mary. The people there reported the vision of a giant light in the sky in the shape of a cross. Some claimed that the metal portions of their religious items, such as crucifixes and rosaries, were transformed into gold. This extraordinary event occurred on August 15, 1988, the same date our community received its name.

David and Pamela thought the idea of having the community birthday of August 15 was inspired. However, the Anaheim Half wanted to have the community birthday fall on January 15 because that was the day Sarah moved into the Anaheim home of Robert and Wendy. David and Pamela proposed that January 15 could be considered the conception of the community and August 15 could be the birthday, but the Anaheim Half would not buy into that. As with many issues between the two halves, we did not come to agreement.

The remainder of this chapter and the next two chapters discuss the relationship between Eastern and Western spirituality. This information at times does not relate directly to events in my life, so you may wonder why in this autobiography there is such a great emphasis on the East and West. The reason is that the essence of a person's life is his *purpose*, rather than simply being a collection of memorable events. In my case, digressing from the outer occurrences of my life allows me to focus more directly in these pages on my life purpose, which is strongly linked to the synthesis of the East and West.

At this time it may be helpful for you to know that I believe I had a past life in India as a spiritual teacher. This was first revealed to me in the early 70s after returning to America following my trip to Jerusalem. Perhaps the overseas travel opened my mind to a broader perspective beyond my American upbringing. I mentioned previously that the shadow puzzle consists of all the hidden pieces of the subconscious mind. In addition to the fearful images lurking in the dark corners of my mind, there are also positive images from this life and past lives. My past life in India is an example of a very significant positive piece of my shadow puzzle. Nonetheless, I decided it would be unwise to share with others the uncovering of my Hindu past life since my goal was to set aside the ego, not magnify it. This past life was an undercurrent and motivating force in my teaching of yoga when I was the director of the Aquarian Age Yoga Center in Virginia Beach. At that time a psychic reading by Jim Branch mentioned my purpose of transferring the cultural influence of the East into the West. The reading stated, "This one would find self with the duties of— if there were drawn the parallel in the musical—transposing those spiritual forces through one cultural influence to another." There are many forms of sectarianism in both the East and West. This same reading went on to describe my desire to overcome these dividing influences while remaining firmly focused on Christ:

> This one would transfer understandings, which are latent in each and in every one, expressing the Creative Forces through the organized in the religious or the like that there might be seen shining through all the eternal light of God the Father. This one through the activities shall seek to overcome all obstacles that might impede regarding sectarian influences, dividing forces, and the like.
>
> Then this one shall seek at times an apparent paradox—to call no name except One Name, and then to lay aside those secondary influences of naming that there not be raised up in words the making for the dividing or the apartheid influences. This will make for greater unity and in such finds within self the reverberating vibratory influences generated through the naming of the Name of the Christ. This anointed consciousness, this loving merciful awareness, is the root of all intent in spiritual pursuits, regardless of their name.

At the Yoga Center my two traumatic past lives as the Pole Man and Spider Boy first surfaced consciously, and at that time I was able to release many pent up emotions from my mind. After this venting of inner tension, the influence of my Hindu past life became even stronger. This past Hindu lifetime is still affecting me now just as it inspired my aim at the Yoga Center to demonstrate in my own life how to walk the path of yoga with Christ as the goal. Also my vocation as a Christian monk carries an Eastern influence into my Western culture. In India many monks are wandering *sannyasins*, renunciates, who are not affiliated with any formal religious organization. My vocation of being a monk in the world does not follow this example of uncompromising renunciation. However, it does carry over the Hindu idea of a monk devoted directly to God without requiring an affiliation of a religious order, as is traditionally required of a monk in the West. Both as a monk and as an example of Christian yoga my mission in my current lifetime is to be an embodiment and example of the marriage of the East and West. Consequently, I cannot truly share my life story without emphasizing the blending of the East and West as I will be doing here in the upcoming pages.

[This marriage of the East and West is visually represented by the back cover of this book. The paintings on the right side of the back cover symbolize forgiveness, which is emphasized in Western spirituality. The paintings on the left side of the back cover symbolize spiritual awakening to one's own true nature characteristic of Eastern spirituality. This inner spiritual awakening is depicted in the abstract expressionistic painting *Dawning of the New Jerusalem*, which is shown at the beginning of this chapter and also displayed in color on the left side and in the middle of the back cover. This painting represents not only one's individual spiritual awakening but also stands for the anticipated future event of the collective awakening of mankind as a whole.]

It was certainly no accident that I found myself in a community that encouraged me in my goal of bridging the gap between two different cultural influences. At the same time we were talking about the issue of a community birthday, Robert initiated another dialogue, expounding at great length in the journal about our community being a true synthesis of the East and West. An example of that synthesis was the dual meaning of the New Jerusalem as the culmination of both Eastern and Western spirituality. Robert saw the spiritual energy coming in through the East and the West as two seemingly different impulses, but which were actually the two halves of a single divine Plan. Each of these spiritual impulses was born, grew to adulthood, and then left its birthplace to go out into the world to do its work.

According to Robert, the Eastern birth was the early Vedas of 1500 BC and the Western birth was Abraham, around 1800 BC. The Eastern early maturity stage was the Upanishads of 800 BC, and the Western early maturity stage was Moses of 1200 BC. The Eastern adulthood stage was the Buddha of 500 BC and the Western adulthood stage was Jesus in the early AD years.

India was the birthplace of the Buddha and Buddhism, just as it had been the birthplace of yoga. From this common starting point, Eastern spirituality expanded as missionary movements throughout the East and in modern times have influenced even the West. The simple premise of the Eastern impulse is that the spiritual centers within the body can be opened and inner spiritual awakening can occur. God in yoga or the Buddha Mind in Buddhism represents the divine essence as reality itself—the only reality there is. The world is only an illusion—a dream that feels and appears real in our ego condition. But in reality we are not limited egos; we are part of the ultimate reality. Our goal is to awaken to this truth. We can use disciplines like yoga and meditation to help us awaken. However, when enlightenment finally comes, we will realize that we were existing in reality all along and had never been separated from our true divine nature in eternity, beyond time and space.

Jesus was born in Israel, the birthplace of Western spirituality, including Islam, Judaism, and Christianity, as all three religions trace their descent from Abraham and the belief in one God. From this birthplace, missionary movements spread all over the West and have influenced the East as well. Eastern spirituality is primarily an upward impulse toward God in order to escape from the illusions of the world and awaken to divine union. In contrast, the Western impulse is a downward and outward movement of God's influence in the world, producing a transformation of our daily lives. God communicates His love through meeting our needs even at the form level and guiding us to live meaningful lives in the world. The goal is to allow God's Spirit to flow through us as ministers, prophets, healers, counselors, spouses, friends, and fellow seekers to bring divine love to others. The most important aspect of life is expressing loving relationships in which love is received from God and extended to others. The same loving expression is intended to be carried out by religious groups that are carrying out God's Plan throughout history. The overall goal is to lead mankind toward salvation, culminating in transcendence of the world and mankind into a "new heaven and a new earth."

The problem with an entirely Western approach is that the seeker feels separate from God, so he is trying to become united with God. His feeling of separation from God appears to be his reality. This is expressed by his belief that he is a very limited being, with all sorts of faults, which makes him feel unworthy of God. On the other hand, he desires to become united to God, who is seen as all loving. The Western seeker therefore is a walking contradiction. How can he seek God wholeheartedly when half of him wants God and the other half feels unworthy of being in God's presence? He is bound to feel conflicted because he desires God, yet he has an image of himself as being weak and undeserving of divine love.

The problem with the entirely Eastern approach is that the seeker may meditate and have exalted spiritual experiences, which temporarily transcend the ego without transforming it. When the seeker returns to normal awareness, his ego remains intact, along with its attachments and selfishness. If the ego is just ignored, by relying only on meditation, the ego, which is the very idea of separation, will keep asserting itself as a barrier to awakening to the seeker's true nature of oneness. The missing piece of the

Eastern approach is its lack of emphasis on relationships. After all, each seeker, who is already in union with God, is also in union with his brothers, who exist in union with God with him. How he sees his brother is how he will see himself. If he does not see his brother as part of himself and part of God, he will not be able to invest in the truth that he is really in union with God and with his brothers in God. Consequently, it is important for a seeker to serve his brother and help his brother to awaken to the divine. In so doing he is letting go of his own ego idea of separation and reinforcing his awareness of his own true nature in God.

Eastern and Western impulses have both gone out into the world as somewhat separate forces. However, these are actually complementary movements intended all along by the divine Plan to be married to each other. Through His resurrection, Jesus embodies this marriage of the East and West—a marriage of spiritual seeking to transcend the world and the historical movement of God in the world. Jesus expressed the Eastern goal of Self-realization by raising His own individual consciousness to a state of perfect divine union. Also Jesus extended love to others by doing God's Will and is still participating in fulfilling God's Plan for the world. Thus Jesus manifested the accomplishment of the Western goal of fostering loving relationships and raising the collective social consciousness of mankind. Following the example of Jesus is really the uniting of the East and West to bring about spiritual fulfillment that could not be found otherwise.

The Eastern and Western impulses have very often been thought of as contradictory and incompatible. But the marriage of the East and West harmoniously joins elements from each impulse to produce a balance and wholeness that neither could achieve separately. This marriage contains the following premises: We already exist in divine union with God, and this world really is a dream. We are going through a divinely inspired journey leading to the time when we will wake up and realize that we are spiritual beings outside of time and space. However, instead of setting the goal of escaping the world, we can use our awareness of our union with God as a means of allowing God's love, which is always with us, to be expressed in our relationships. We can perceive the world through God's eyes as a reflection of heaven, and that divinely inspired perception allows us to let go of our ego idea of separation. We can meditate in Eastern fashion to set aside the ego temporarily and experience God's presence more directly than would otherwise be possible. But we can also serve others and express love in Western fashion to help us let go of the ego's attachment to selfishness. By combining these Eastern and Western approaches to egolessness and finding love both within and without, we can best find salvation as individuals and as groups.

Of the many journal entries that Robert offered to the community for consideration of the East/West ideas, the following entry in my opinion was a particularly insightful observation concerning the marriage of the East and West:

> Not only does it seem time for a spiritual revolution on the earth that would involve the whole earth, but East and West have been courting each other for a while now, intermingling culturally. Also, it seems very significant to me that the two ancient mother countries, India and Israel, both went through the dramatic and symbolic process of regaining their independence this century—in fact, a year apart, in 1947 and 1948, respectively. Both threw off the yoke of the modern, secular world—symbolized by British rule—in a reassertion of their ancient spirituality. Israel regained the land God promised them and India's Gandhi used spiritual principles to chase out the British. Those two events are highly suggestive and could easily symbolize something new and important about to unfold between these two streams those countries represent.

How this marriage of East and West related to our new community name Robert described as follows:

> Although we as a community seem more directly related to the West, that does not at all exclude a strong relationship with the East. To use the analogy of our name, the old Jerusalem is a place torn by division, separated into Jewish, Christian, and Muslim quarters, and totally separated from the East. The true interpretation, I feel, is that the idea of the "New Jerusalem" is that it is to be a higher expression of that same tradition, in which God's Western child had grown up and is ready to join with God's other child, the East, to marry and together give birth to a truly whole expression of God's Will for our planet. In other words, our name can be taken to signify a point of synthesis, rather than a strictly Christian development. As is obvious, I feel that we [along with many others] are being raised to be an instrument of this marriage and this birth. From my point of view a greater function could hardly be imagined.

Robert also felt that the best theological synthesis of the East and West so far presented to the world has been *A Course in Miracles*. At a future time Robert came to the conclusion that the Course, authored by Jesus, was in a sense another "incarnation" of Jesus. Robert saw the Course as an embodiment in book form of Jesus coming into the world of form again—

a mini-version of the Second Coming, as perhaps a foreshadowing of the apocalyptic event. The Sedona Half was particularly attracted to the possibility of preparing the way for the Second Coming, but the New Jerusalem Community was not a Course community. David acknowledged the value of some Course principles. Nevertheless, he in particular did not want the Course philosophy to dominate our community. Generally, however, we were open to the Course philosophy, and eventually the majority of community members would become Course students.

The community as a whole accepted Robert's basic premise regarding the joining of the East and West outlined above. The New Jerusalem Community members felt that we were a part of the marriage process that the world itself is in the process of undergoing, as will be increasingly revealed in the future. The term New Jerusalem is usually identified exclusively with the Western Christian tradition, but our community felt that the name New Jerusalem represented a synthesis of the East and the West—the direction in which our community seemed to be growing along with the world as a whole.

I thought at first that maybe the Eastern influences of the community should not be overtly expressed when we wrote our New Jerusalem Community mission statement, in order to not offend Western seekers. In my own life I had struggled in the past with how to balance my Christian faith with my background in Zen meditation and yoga disciplines. The way I had learned to deal with this struggle was to highlight my Christian focus and to keep my Eastern inclinations and disciplines as part of my inner spiritual life, but otherwise somewhat hidden. However, through this community dialogue and specifically the influence of Robert, I realized how important it was to acknowledge the synthesis of the East and West in the community. Over time it would become increasingly apparent to me that the proper balance between the East and West would be important not only as an outward expression in the community and in the world, but also as an expression in my own individual life as I followed the path of Christian yoga, blending Eastern practices with following Christ.

---

1. Rev. 21:1, CCD.
2. Rev. 21:2, CCD.

44

GUIDING PRINCIPLES

≈ • ≈

Once the name of our New Jerusalem Community had finally been established, we were ready to consider a community mission statement of our guiding principles. Considering our past failure to come to consensus on one philosophy, we were surprisingly able to agree upon three spiritual principles that we could all support. Just as our community was a joining of the East and West, similarly these principles were a combination of a Christian approach and Eastern philosophy. A story will help to illustrate the first two principles:

In the Middle Ages a woman was caught sneaking out of a cathedral carrying her newborn baby boy on one arm and in her free hand a golden chalice she had stolen from the altar. She was taken to prison and a local official asked her for the name of the baby's father, since he didn't want to put the child in jail. The father was actually the elderly local magistrate who would decide how many years she would have to spend in prison for her sacrilegious act. But the woman was afraid that if she named him, he would deny it and give her an outlandish twenty or thirty-year jail sentence. The woman claimed that the hermit living on the hill, Brother Bernard, was the father. Subsequently she was given a five-year prison term.

The town official brought the baby to the monk's small home and confronted him, "Are you the father of this child?"

"Not my will, let Thy Will be done," Brother Bernard said.

The official said, "Ah, you don't deny it!" Not being familiar with the Bible, he misunderstood "Thy Will" to be "thy will." Thus he said, "Oh, you want me to decide what to do. Well, here is my decision!" Without saying another word, the official placed the baby on the floor and abruptly left.

Brother Bernard picked up the baby, and looking into the boy's eyes, he said, "Not my will, let Thy Will be done." It was unusual for the monk to say these words aloud because he lived alone in silence most of the time. However, the words themselves were exceedingly familiar because he had made a habit of repeating them over and over in his mind throughout every day as the prayer he had chosen to unite himself with God. The monk was not disturbed about the new challenge before him because he felt God's Will is often expressed through the decisions of others, outside his control. He called the boy "Jonathan" because it meant "God has given." Not knowing how to entertain a child, Brother Bernard read to him every day from his prized one-of-a-kind Bible that was a colorful and elaborate hand-made illuminated manuscript. Surprisingly, the boy was often soothed by this reading, perhaps more by the loving tone of the monk's voice than the inspiring words. But sometimes the boy cried wildly and even reading the Bible had no effect. The hermit taught himself how to play the lute in the hope it might pacify the child when he cried. He could play only simple tunes, but he found one melody along with a two-line chant that worked wonders at calming the boy's crying tantrums.

All went well for the five years the woman spent in prison, but with her release she immediately went to the hermit's home. She barged in and claimed, "You have stolen my child. What do you have to say for yourself?"

"Not my will, let Thy Will be done," came his reply.

She too did not understand that "Thy Will" meant God's Will, so she said, "Of course it's my decision!" She grabbed the boy and carried him off while he kicked and screamed uselessly. The monk immediately directed his mind to repeat, "Not my will, let Thy Will be done," as a single tear dripped down his face.

Twenty years later, the boy Jonathan had become a young man and had studied the Bible but rejected it. Instead, he had become a thief, going from town to town looking for stealing opportunities. One day he returned to the same town where he was born, but by then had forgotten all about his past. He was told by a local person about a hermit who had been offered forty pieces of silver for his Bible but refused to sell it. He made his way up the hill to the monk's home and introduced himself as Samuel, although that was not his real name. He told Brother Bernard, "I would like to learn more about God. I can read and have read some of the Bible, but I would like you to teach me more. Can I visit with you and learn from you?"

The monk said, "Not my will, let Thy Will be done. Welcome to my home." The monk's words sounded strangely familiar to Samuel as he went inside. The two lived together for five days, but then Brother Bernard had to take his once-a-week trip into town for supplies. The hermit returned as it was getting dark outside and a full moon had risen. When he entered his home, he expected to see Samuel, but he was not there. Immediately it became apparent that the precious Bible was gone as well. Brother Bernard looked out his window at the exquisite full moon above, and thought to himself, "Samuel took the Bible, yet too bad I could not have given him the Light as well." He meant he would have liked to teach him not only the appreciation of the great beauty of the light in the sky, but he would have liked to help him become aware of the Christ Light within. Then the monk returned to mentally repeating, "Not my will, let Thy Will be done."

Samuel ran off to a neighboring town with the Bible and brought it to a local merchant. He said, "My name is Samuel, and this is a family heirloom, but I must sell it. It's worth forty silver pieces."

The merchant said, "If it is worth that much, I will give you thirty pieces of silver so I can gain a good profit. However, I don't know if it is worth that great a sum. Will you let me take it for three days so I can evaluate its worth?" Samuel reluctantly agreed to let the merchant take the book, and he returned to the merchant three days later. The merchant informed him, "It is worth forty pieces of silver just as you said, so I will give you the thirty pieces of silver I promised you."

As the merchant began to count out the silver pieces, Samuel asked out of curiosity, "Why did it take you three whole days to make your decision?"

"I had to travel to the next town to show it to someone who knows all about Bibles."

"What's the name of this person who evaluated the Bible for you?"

"Brother Bernard. He's a hermit."

"Didn't he say anything else about this Bible when you showed it to him?" Samuel asked.

"He said that this is a fine Bible and I would be wise to purchase it."

"Nothing else?"

"No, nothing else. Why do you ask?" Samuel suddenly burst into tears, and the confused merchant asked, "What's wrong?"

Samuel said, "I've changed my mind. I've decided not to sell it after all," and he quickly departed with the manuscript. He made his way back to Brother Bernard's home and was welcomed in. Samuel said, "The merchant in the next town told me that he showed you this Bible, and you said nothing about owning it. Why didn't you tell him that I had stolen it from you?"

"You didn't steal it from me." Brother Bernard opened the cover of the Bible and there was a letter. He said, "This letter was written by my teacher when he gave me this book. I want you to read it now."

"All right," Samuel said, and he read, "'Dear Brother Bernard, I needed this book to help me grow, but now I can see you need it more than I do. This book is being given to you to use while you still need it. At some future date you will meet someone who will need it more than you do. You will know when the time comes for you to pass this book along to another.'"

Brother Bernard said, "When I noticed the book was missing, it was clear that you needed it more than I did, so it's yours now."

Samuel began sobbing and held the book out, "Please take it back."

"I can't take it back. If my teacher were alive today, what would he think of me if I would take this book back? It is God's Will for you to have this Bible."

But Samuel was inconsolable and said, "For this book I was going to take from the merchant thirty pieces of silver—the exact payment Judas received for betraying Jesus. I couldn't keep this book. Please take it back."

"There is no way I can take the book back," the monk said. "But I have a solution. You can keep the book and stay with me. Then we can both read from it. How about that?"

"Yes, yes, I would certainly like to stay. But I am not worthy to be here in your presence," Samuel cried.

"Nonsense! There is no more God in me than there is in you," the monk insisted.

"I am not worthy," Samuel reasserted, still weeping uncontrollably, so much so that his body was shaking.

The monk reached for his lute and began to sing the simple two-line chant that he hadn't sung in years: "Not my will, O Lord, God of heaven and earth. Not my will, let Thy Will be done."

Samuel was startled by the singing and the melody that seemed so strangely familiar, and he stopped weeping right away, just as he had stopped crying as a baby. Suddenly his mind opened, and he remembered something he had long forgotten. He recalled that his mother had told him that a monk had raised him for the first five years of his life, but she had not said who it was. He blurted out, "Could you be the monk who raised me for the first five years of my life?"

"Jonathan! How wonderful! Your name means 'God has given,' and now He has given you to me again. You do not realize how much you have given me. Before you came into my life, I lived alone so I had no close relationships—no one to love. Yes, I loved God. But you gave me the opportunity to extend my love to you, and that opened my heart more than I can tell you. Isn't our God gracious?" Brother Bernard proclaimed with tears of joy.

"Yes, He is gracious. My name indeed is 'Jonathan.' The name 'Samuel' I made up, liar that I have been. But with your help and with the help of God I promise to mend my ways." Brother Bernard extended his arms and they embraced. Jonathan did indeed keep his promise.[1]

This tale illustrates the practical application of our community ideals. Brother Bernard did God's Will by allowing His Spirit to be the parent force in his life and in his journey back to God. He allowed this Spirit to enter his life and become the author, the inspiration, behind all that he said, did, had, thought, felt, and was. On the level of his outer life, God's Spirit guided his decisions, arranged his situations, and supplied all his material needs. On the level of his inner life, this Spirit entered his heart and transformed it into a reflection of God. This is an example of the real heart of God's activity, the work of His Spirit to transform hearts and minds.

Once God's Spirit flowed into Brother Bernard's heart, love flowed through his heart out to others. This blessing accomplished two things: It awakened others to God, and it was the primary means through which Brother Bernard himself discovered love. This kind of love was not a human love that was manufactured by the mind, but was a touching of God within him and awakening to God in others. This kind of love inspired by God also motivated Brother Bernard to actively confront and relinquish his ego-boundaries, which resulted in an experience of joining with God in another. Through this love he recognized and joined with other individual aspects of God and thus prepared himself to eventually join with all of God Himself. Loving others, therefore, was Brother Bernard's primary means of relinquishing his ego and discovering God.

The preceding two paragraphs were Robert's descriptions of our first two community spiritual principles, which I have partially rewritten to apply specifically to the life and example of Brother Bernard. These guiding principles are summarized in the following two sentences:

First principle: We do God's Will by allowing His Spirit to fully enter into our lives.
Second principle: Manifesting loving relationships is our central spiritual practice.

There was an understanding that these principles would work together. Applying the first principle of expressing God's Will would naturally lead to the second principle of loving relationships. Then the second principle would lead to a third principle, which addressed our relationship with God. Just as the community was a balance of the West and East, the first two principles represented the Western and Christian viewpoint and the third principle expressed an Eastern perspective. The third principle identified our ultimate goal related to God. This goal is illustrated by the tale of Indra, which I had heard at a lecture by Swami Satchidananda. Here is my altered version of that story:

Indra lived a life of perfect peace in heaven among his many friends, but he was not completely content. He went to Brahma, the Creator, and said, "Is this all there is? Yes, it is continually blissful here in heaven, and all my friends are satisfied. However, I am not satisfied. Since you are the Creator of all that exists, You can do anything. I want more than you have already given me."

Brahma replied, "You have been given eternal joy. What more could you want? I have already given you everything. How can I give you more than everything?"

But Indra persisted, "I insist that you give me more. I know there is some experience You haven't given me, and I demand that You give it to me now. If you don't give me what I am asking for, I will leave heaven and I will search out and find that missing experience somewhere else."

"Since you 'insist' and 'demand,' I will let you have the new experience you want. You cannot have this experience in heaven, but you do not have to search for it yourself. I will send you to the place where you can have this missing experience, but you can stay away from heaven only for one year. Then you must return to your home in heaven alongside all your friends."

Indra was greatly pleased. "Thank You."

"There is no need to thank me for your leaving heaven since I am only giving you what you want, but you can save your 'Thank You' for when you return," Brahma said.

In the twinkling of an eye, before Indra could say another word, he was transported to the body of a sleeping pig. When Indra opened the pig's eyes all he could see was his pig world, and he lost all memory of his life in heaven. Now as a pig, Indra accepted his duties as a father pig with a wife pig and twelve little piglets. He became attached to his family and enjoyed lying down in the mud and delighted in bathing in the warmth of the sun.

A year passed by, and Vishnu, having been sent by Brahma, appeared to the pig, and said, "I have come to bring you back to heaven. After all, you are Indra, and we miss you in heaven."

"Who are you?" Indra asked.

"I am your friend, Vishnu. Indra, I want you to come back to your rightful place in heaven."

"My name isn't Indra. Can't you see I am a pig? I don't want to go to heaven even if you could take me there. Look at my lovely porky wife and adorable twelve piglets. You are a deranged person. I won't go with you."

Disappointed, Vishnu returned to Brahma and reported, "Indra is caught up in the illusions of the world. He no longer remembers that heaven is his true home. He refused to come back with me. What do you want me to do?"

Brahma handed him a sword and said, "Indra's time of illusions up! Do what you must do to bring him back from his dreams."

Vishnu appeared again to Indra and said, "I know you think you are a pig, but you are not actually a pig. You are a celestial being, Indra, and you must return to heaven where you really belong."

"I belong right here with my wonderful pig family and pig friends. I'm going to lie down here in my favorite mud hole and close my eyes to enjoy my sun bathing. When I open my eyes again, I want you to be gone and never come back again to bother me with this nonsense about me belonging in heaven," Indra said while reclining into his familiar mud hole, and he fell asleep.

Not to be detoured, Vishnu took out his sword and with one fell swoop cut the pig open from top to bottom. Out popped Indra with his heartiest laughter, "Ha, ha, ha! It's amazing! I really thought I was a pig. I'm sorry I didn't believe you, Vishnu, when you told me the truth. I loved my pig wife and pig children, and it was an interesting experience, but I wouldn't want to repeat it. Let's go back to heaven. I want to talk to Brahma."

When they got back to heaven, Indra told Brahma, "Thank you for giving me what I asked for, but I've learned my lesson. I don't ever want to leave heaven. I promise I will never again ask for more than everything you have already given me. I apologize for insisting and demanding to leave in the first place."

Brahma replied, "No apology is needed because no harm has been done. You just temporarily fell asleep in a pig's body. Now you have fully awakened from your slumber and are again in heaven. Let's celebrate!"

In this tale, Brahma as the Creator represents God the Father.[2] Our community understood that we are all spiritual beings that are equals as children of one Father. Indra manifesting inside the pig's body symbolizes *every* seeker who is in the process of discovering his true identity. In the earthly world of form each seeker finds the human body as his frame of reference and his identity, instead of identifying with his true home in heaven. In the story Indra didn't lose his established and eternal place in heaven just because he was temporarily in a pig's body in the earth. Similarly, our eternal place in heaven is waiting for each of us, although we have no awareness of it while in the earth. This tale of Indra demonstrates the third community principle:

Third principle: Awakening to our pre-existing union with God is our ultimate goal.

With a general awareness of the beliefs of most community members, Robert was the one who first came up with the three ideas of GOD'S WILL, LOVING RELATIONSHIPS, and UNION WITH GOD, which he believed expressed our community principles. He saw the application of these three principles as a process of transformation in which we increasingly open up to the influence of God's divine Light. Robert described the transformation in this way, "It is a process of God's Light entering the world and little by little spreads out growing brighter, shining away all shadows and all boundaries until the Light shines without obstruction and becomes fully the only thing there is. Our only job in the process is to direct all of our activity and all of our passivity toward receiving this Light and letting it do its work in us and through us."

According to Robert, the sequence of the first two principles—expressing God's Will followed by loving relationships—leads to the third principle of union with God. The first two principles are the means, and the final principle is the end, the result, the goal. God's Spirit flows down to us as the first principle of God's Will and out through us as the second principle of loving relationships. As His Spirit moves downward and outward, more and more of God is entering us and the world. This ultimately results in two things: God fully manifests inside of us and God fully manifests in the world. And, of course, eventually the whole thing disappears into oneness with God. This union with God is not a true outcome of the first two principles. They do not produce it; they simply awaken us to a pre-existing condition. They are processes that awaken us to what is beyond process, to our unconditional divine Reality—to our true nature in God.

This sequence of principles from the first to the second to the third may give the impression that the third principle as the goal was not actively involved in the transformation process. However, the third principle of union with God was not inactive, just waiting for the other principles to be implemented and then result in the goal being accomplished. The third principle, signifying a pre-existing union with God, was the motivation for our spiritual growth. We did God's Will and expressed loving relationships because the desire for union with God was and is motivating us.

But an ultimate union with God in heaven was not our only motivation. The other motivational factor was our faith that we were already united with God in reality. We did not think of ourselves as limited and unworthy people who were separated from God and from His love. Instead we trusted in our ever-present union with God, which inspired us to open our hearts and minds. Knowing God's love is within us, we let His love extend through us out to others to remind them of God's presence within them.

The first two principles of expressing God's Will and loving relationships were what Robert identified as the "downward and outward dynamic of God's Spirit." The third principle implied that this world of apparent unworthiness and separation from God is illusory and we need to wake up to our pre-existing reality in God. The first two principles represented the foundations of Western spirituality, and the third principle expressed the foundation of Eastern spirituality. By combining these three principles the New Jerusalem Community was expressing a synthesis of the East and

West. The Western spiritual impulse was the means for transformation, and the Eastern spiritual impulse was the goal of spiritual transformation. Thus these two spiritual impulses were complementary to each other and together created a wholeness that either one separately would not have.

Robert was recognized as the *focalizer* of our community and offered his writing of these three principles to the community as a proposal for our community statement. I agreed with Robert's proposal, but I would have expressed these principles in a slightly different way. In my opinion, the East and West should receive equal weight, yet this was not representative of the community as a whole, which leaned toward the Western approach to spirituality. I would join the first community principle, God's Will, with the second principle, loving relationships. This combination would be one Western principle of loving relationships as an expression of God's Will. I would identify this Western principle simply as the *Relationship Impulse*.

This Western principle is based on what is called "dualism" or "duality," which is the idea that God and man are separate and in the process of uniting. Loving relationships are an expression of this duality, in which apparently separate people are joining in love. Dualism makes perfect sense as long as we believe the ego is real and the three dimensional world is real. Since the West accepts the world at face value, dualism is the basis of all Western religions. Nevertheless, from an Eastern perspective the idea of dualism is ultimately illusory. The Relationship Impulse is vital because the world does have a "relative reality"—meaning it appears very real in relation to our egos, our bodies, and the world around us. Because this relative reality is so undeniably convincing, it is difficult for Westerners to understand that this is only a "dream reality" and is not the "absolute reality" or "ultimate reality." As an analogy, imagine you are looking at a painting of people and objects in the world. Your eyes can see only the paint on the surface of the picture. What you see symbolizes accepting the relative reality of the dualistic world, in which objects and forms appear to be separate. If the painting is beautiful, it will depict different colors and forms working together in a harmonious and unified way. By analogy, this unity represents the loving relationships of the Relationship Impulse.

Continuing with the analogy, your mind tells you that below the surface of the paint there is a white linen canvas, which is the foundation of this painting of forms. In this analogy the white linen represents the Ground of Being, the absolute reality. To balance out the Western principle, the Relationship Impulse, there is the Eastern principle, which maintains that there is a universal Ground of Being, upon which the forms of our world are painted. It is what I call the *Unitive Impulse*, based upon the reality of the already existing unity with God, which is always present, though hidden from our everyday awareness. Eastern philosophy provides the term "nondualism" to describe this pre-existing divine union, which we can never lose in spite of the appearances of separation.

Returning to the painting analogy, imagine you turn the picture around and look at the back of the painting. In this case, instead of mentally assuming there is a white linen canvas, you can actually *directly see* the white linen. By analogy, this turning of the mind around is enlightenment, in which you directly experience the Ground of Being, instead of just assuming that it is there below the surface of the illusory world of form. This direct experience of awakening, if it is deep enough, shatters the worldly dream of separation and brings a strong conviction in the validity of the Unitive Impulse, which the Western mind finds so difficult to accept.

Both the Relationship Impulse and the Unitive Impulse involve love. The application of the Relationship Impulse encourages us to be involved with developing loving relationships, which imply joining with others to overcome separation. The awareness of the Unitive Impulse allows us to affirm that transcending outer forms there is a deeper level of existence, in which we abide in the eternal ocean of God's Love. Although we may appear to be in the process of joining with others, actually we are already in reality united in loving relationship with all our brothers and sisters in God. The Relationship Impulse and the Unitive Impulse stand for different aspects of God's Will. The Relationship Impulse would be God's Will manifested in the *expression* of love, which is a male expressive principle. The Unitive Impulse would be God's Will manifested in the *beingness* of love, which is a female receptive principle.

There is a tendency to think that the West is all about dualism and the East is all about nondualism, but this is actually an oversimplification. The East inspired the Unitive Impulse, as exemplified by yoga nondualism and Zen enlightenment. However, evolving right alongside the expression of nondualism has been the worship of thousands of Hindu gods and goddesses, involving dualism. In the West there was a long history of the struggle between the expression of gross dualism and the seeking of something higher, closer to oneness, yet still dualistic. An individual example of this struggle was Abraham, who worshipped many gods and then was called to follow one God. Another example was the worship of many dualistic Egyptian gods and Akhenaten's worship of the one God, Aten, symbolized by the sun. Then 150 years after Akhenaten there were the same many dualistic Egyptian gods versus Moses and one God. Later there were the numerous Roman gods verses God, the Father of Christ.

These were movements from more dualistic elements to less dualistic elements. But over the past two thousand years many Christian mystics have gone even further away from dualism and experienced the kind of unitive awareness that is characteristic of the heights of Eastern spirituality.

Of course, these mystics are in the minority. However, they symbolize the ever-evolving direction of Western spirituality, which is growing beyond duality toward its inevitable marriage with Eastern spirituality based on oneness. This movement from duality toward oneness represents growth in the direction of the Biblical heavenly "New Jerusalem"—so lofty a state of oneness that it transcends the physical world of dualism.

My influence in the community was to frequently draw attention to the importance of integrating meditation into our lives. We can learn to deepen our loving relationships of the Relationship Impulse by the meditative practice of seeing the divine presence in our brothers and sisters and seeing the divine reflections even in the world of form, although these are ultimately illusory. We can learn to deepen our receptivity and meditative practice of the Unitive Impulse by being aware that meditation is not an isolating practice just between God and the individual. Our meditation is an opportunity to uncover both our pre-existing relationship of union with God and our pre-existing relationship of union with our brothers and sisters. Consequently, meditation truly understood is never a solitary practice. However, my emphasis on meditation was considered by the community as a whole to be of only secondary importance and did not become one of the major guiding principles of the community.

Just as I wanted to make adjustments in the three principles submitted by Robert to the community, the other community members likewise submitted their varied opinions on what to include or exclude from the community statement. Eventually all three of the principles that Robert identified were accepted by the community. There was a fourth community principle that was also adopted, which was:

Fourth principle: We recognize Jesus as our guide and master.

Adopting these four general principles—God's Will, loving relationships, union with God, and Jesus as guide and master—required the consensus of all community members, and it was always a major accomplishment for all of us to come to agreement on anything. Although these principles did make their way into a written statement by the community, it did not mean that every community member had to adopt a certain dogma. Community members were free to believe whatever spiritual ideas would be most helpful for their own growth as determined by themselves.

In general, each of our community members fiercely guarded their individual freedom of choice. This proved to be both a liability and an asset. The liability was that the emphasis on individual freedom limited us in truly joining at a deep level. For example, our focus on individuality stifled attempts at leadership designed to facilitate group worship. On the other hand, our emphasis on individual freedom provided a positive influence by highlighting the uniqueness and equality of each member. Consequently, our community never came anywhere close to becoming a cult, which is typically characterized by isolation of members from the larger community and by everyone conforming unquestioningly to a single rigid dogma established by one charismatic and dominating leader. All of us had jobs and relationships in the general community of Sedona and any New Jerusalem Community initiative was able to proceed only after passing through painstaking scrutiny by each member.

You may be wondering why I have gone into so much detail in an autobiography about our community principles. It's because these same principles are incorporated within my own personal path of Christian yoga. A significant addition to the four principles already described is that my personal path includes a commitment to yoga disciplines, especially meditation. This is an emphasis on inner development to balance an equally important emphasis on the outer spiritual practice of manifesting loving relationships. This combination of inner and outer spiritual growth is my means of inviting the Holy Spirit to penetrate into all aspects of my life in order to follow the example of Jesus. A more detailed description of my Christian yoga path is provided in a later chapter.

I do not expect you to necessarily agree with any of the four community principles or with my own personal ideals, or for that matter with other spiritual ideas mentioned in this book. However, perhaps by being exposed to these spiritual concepts, you will be inspired to ask yourself, "What are my own spiritual principles?" Even if you belong to a church or spiritual organization that has a particular dogma, I encourage you to write down your personal list of guiding principles. I believe that putting your spiritual principles down on paper in your own words will help you to gain clarity in your own unique spiritual journey.

---

1. Many years ago I came across three stories of monks: One was about a Christian monk who raised a child that was not his own. Another was about a monk who had his Bible stolen. And a third was about a Zen monk who had all his belongings stolen. Because I could not remember the details or even the sources of these three stories, I decided to bring together elements from each of them to create the new tale of Brother Bernard, which also includes aspects from outside these stories.

2. Brahma, the Creator, is not to be confused with "Brahman" the Supreme Cosmic Spirit in Hindu Vedanta philosophy. In the West, God is generally thought of as both the Father (equivalent to Brahma as the Creator) and the ultimate Reality, the Ground of Being (equivalent to Brahman as the universal Spirit).

45

EAST HALF
AND
WEST HALF

≈ • ≈

Prior to deciding upon the New Jerusalem Community principles, there were many letters sent back and forth between Anaheim and Sedona regarding the synthesis of the East and West being manifested in the world and in our community. In response to a letter from Robert, I decided to offer my own additional thoughts of how this synthesis was being played out in the two halves of our newly named New Jerusalem Community. Below are excerpts from my letter, which like all of our letters became part of our community journal:

> The basic idea is that a lot of our conflicts have arisen because of a lack of recognition and therefore lack of respect for each other's roles. Also, if we as a group are to truly be an embodiment of a synthesis of the East and the West, then how is this joining of two apparently contradictory philosophies manifested in our community? The conclusion I have come to is that the Anaheim Half represents the West and the Sedona Half represents the East.
>
> Incidentally, the Anaheim Half is a "West Coast" group originally that went east to join with its other half, at least initially. Likewise, the Sedona Half (Virginia Beach Half) was originally an "East Coast" group that traveled west to join with its other half.

In this letter I provided an extensive list of ways that the Anaheim Half represented the Western community principles of doing God's will and expressing loving relationships and service in the world. Sarah was a Moses-like visionary and served as a heart-centered relationship hub extending to all other community members. Robert had his visions of God's activity being played out in the drama of our lives as an unfolding of His Plan in human history. Wendy's strength was manifesting God's work of service in the world, and she planned to assume the role of a minister in the future. All the members of the Anaheim Half lived, worked, and expressed a traditional Western lifestyle.

I likewise listed how the Sedona Half, which was focused on receptivity and meditation, manifested the Eastern community principle of seeking union with God. In contrast to the masculine emphasis on expressive qualities of outer manifestation in the world found in the West, the East prizes the female emphasis on receptive attributes, including intuition. In our group Pamela symbolized this feminine influence, providing grounding with her love of mother earth. David and I symbolized another kind of receptivity—the direct inner receptivity to God's Spirit in meditation. Our receptivity was based on our trust in His abiding Love and Presence, and we had a strong desire for ultimate divine union. I was the most purely Eastern member of our group both in strengths (daily practice of yoga disciplines) and lacks (need to improve manifesting in the world and be more relationship-oriented). The East has a long-standing tradition of spiritual seekers being totally committed to God, living in wilderness places, and relying on divine providence for nourishment, instead of the usual route of finding employment in the world. David had a previous history of trail-blazing this path, and in this regard Pamela and I followed in his footsteps in our Sedona experience. The fact that we lived as nomads in tents in the Arizona desert was an example of the Eastern kind of stripping to the core associated with practicing nonattachment and awakening to the divine presence.

After identifying the Anaheim Half with the West and the Sedona Half with the East, I elaborated in my letter on how each half was positively influencing the other half to create a balance of the East and West, as follows:

> In order to truly embody the East/West principles into a synthesis, we have been in the process of joining together and learning from each other. The Western-oriented Anaheim Half is learning to be more Eastern in these ways:
>
> 1. Setting aside attachments to physical things.
> 2. Practicing meditation more.
> 3. Seeing God, rather than self-effort alone, as the direct author of supply.
> 4. Integrating Tom's Eastern interests, including the nondualism of Hindu Vedanta. [Tom was living in Anaheim at this time.]

The Eastern-oriented Sedona Half is learning to be more Western through these means:

1. Being guided to get jobs God would have us manifest.
2. Being open to new relationships and extending outwardly.
3. Improving relationships to become more of a family unit.
4. Moving into a home with physical conveniences.

All this is good, but we need to also face the fact that because we have had different values, we have tended to polarize at times rather than see what we could learn from each other. Sarah's recent letter addressed this idea of each of us coming from the perspective of our own worlds. She referred to Robert's vision and her vision, versus David's visionary ability. I think we tend to view the other person's liabilities rather than their strengths, so we see them as the enemy rather than as a helper.

Let me make this more personal, and I hope I don't make myself out to be too much of a victim in my description. I would like to start by saying that at the beginning of my relationship with David, he really didn't value me, because he was viewing me from my outer manifestation. It has only been in time that he has come to see me at a much deeper level and value me more. In fact, our latest growth in this direction is that he and I are again working together on my meditation book.

The same pattern is true of my relationship with Pamela. Recently when Pamela and David were in a discord situation, my relationship with Pamela improved because she found she could rely upon my help and concern for her. Also, I have grown in Western ways of being more grounded to balance out the East in me.

I think the same pattern of initial rejection, which over time will change to appreciation, is occurring in my relationship with the Anaheim Half members. Right now I believe we are in between rejection and appreciation. I think the initial rejection I felt was based upon your lack of valuing for the Eastern qualities that I embody. In my opinion, you have not cultivated those Eastern qualities within yourselves and distrusted that I really did and do embody those qualities. At the same time, there was a magnification of my liabilities in the Western areas that are your strengths—being grounded, outward appearance, appropriate social actions, etc. Of course, these Western liabilities encouraged the Anaheim Half to also call into question my inner essence.

Generally Barry [Sarah's fiancé] is an exception to judging my outer masks, and Sarah could glimpse my inner essence, but was thrown off by my outer masks. I never did feel Robert or Wendy could see through my masks; however, I do feel they tried. I know you all tried and are still open to seeing God in me, just as I am doing likewise.

P.S. I have one more thought about an East/West synthesis. If the West represents God at work in history and the East represents divine union seeking, then what is the culmination of these two?

It's the Second Coming. It is the historical event which we in the West are anticipating and preparing for. And it also simultaneously represents the fulfillment of the ultimate Eastern ideal of direct union with God. The result will be both transcendence and transformation of the physical into a new creation—NEW JERUSALEM.

A few years before writing this letter, I made the statement for the first time that this community was an "arranged marriage" by God. At that time I had no idea that He would arrange this union as a marriage of the East and the West. Although I wrote the above letter to acknowledge the tension and learning opportunities in our community regarding East/West issues, I did not realize the full ramifications of this issue. For example, I was in the process of writing my Christian meditation manual, and I had long ago decided to include Eastern influences, but without identifying them as such. It did not occur to me until many years later to come out of the closet and rewrite my meditation manual as an outward expression of a true synthesis of the East and West.

I did incorporate the advisory feedback of David, Sarah, and Robert in the process of writing the manual, which helped to expand my perspective. As mentioned in the above letter, I often made the plea of asking other community members to see beyond my masks and see the divine within me. My plea was, in a sense, asking members to set aside the Western focus on outer forms and rely instead on the Eastern emphasis on the divine within. It would take a long time in the community for me to finally switch that frame of reference around and focus mostly on my own need to consistently look past the masks of my brothers and sisters and to see the divine in them. When I was able to deepen my ability to see the divine in others, I still wanted others to see through masks and see the divine, but my motivation was more for their benefit than for my sake.

Nevertheless, at a personal level I appreciated those times when others did actually reach a deeper level of perception beyond outer appearances.

Sarah and I had many talks about this idea of seeing beyond the mask of appearances, and she wrote a letter to me about wanting to heal our relationship:

> I know I have wronged you in our relationship, Don, and I want to take responsibility for that. I put a lot of petty things in front of my eyes to obscure me from seeing the you that I love. I am very sorry for that. I really treasure you and what you stand for.

Both Sarah and Robert, among others, helped me in the process of writing my meditation manual, and I think this experience helped them to see a deeper level within me. Although my book did not describe my own inner spiritual life, the manuscript indirectly served as a window providing a view past my masks. Below is an excerpt from a letter Robert wrote to me providing his intuitions and feedback about my manuscript:

> Also, in writing you about these [intuitions], I feel myself opening up to your purpose as I haven't before. The part of you that is close to God has always felt veiled to me. I recall having a conversation with you on the couch out here, where I told you that, and you couldn't believe that I couldn't see through your mask. I'm sure you remember that conversation. Well, I have never been good at seeing below the surface, and I seem better at putting together the evidence presented on the surface.
>
> Anyway, I feel as though I am starting to see beneath your mask. Remember we talked about there being three *you's*. One was the outer "clown," as you put it. The second was the heart person, who just wanted love. And the third was the monk of God. I guess we all related to you on different levels, some of us only on the first. I think I have mostly seen you on the first and second levels, as have most of us in the community.
>
> About the *third you*, I have found you either persistently silent or, as with your book or your monkhood, seemingly very attracted to particular forms that you feel express this you. Now I see that both of those are your reactions to this you not being seen or acknowledged. I feel similar reactions about parts of me. If no one out there gets what is inside of me, that thing starts feeling very vulnerable. But I am starting, I think, to get a picture of this third you. I am getting this image, sparked by reading the [meditation] book, of you conversing with the outside world and being a certain person, and then going off to be with God and becoming a completely different person in a completely different world.

The world I picture is one of spiritual depths of consciousness, and the person I picture is strong and sure in this world and totally absorbed in, dependent on and sustained by love for and from God, wanting and needing nothing else, caught up just in that. I don't know how accurate this is, but it is just the sense I am getting of there being a totally "other" you from the one that has been presented to me.

Anyway, I think that I am getting to know you in a way that I have not before. This feels really important to me. While I am writing this, my chest is feeling freed up. I think I am "getting" you in a whole new way. I don't know quite what to say about this. I know I am making it sound dramatic, but it does seem really important to me, like a veil is being drawn aside—about you, about the book, about your relationship with me and with the community.

I don't know quite what to do with this, but maybe hearing back from you about your reactions to what I am saying will help me. I think I will talk to Sarah, too. What I am thinking is that I need to learn a new way to relate to you. And I guess that will take some time and some thought. And especially it will take seeing that third you with increasing clarity.

All of this feels really good to me, but it also is a little disorienting. Because I see you are relating to the world and the world (including myself) is relating to you through this particular image of you, but this image is totally a disguise. It is kind of disorienting to see that this is so. Do you know what I mean? It is like waking up to the fact that you have been living with your spouse for twenty years but have never really known her.

During a previous visit in Anaheim, Robert and I had taken a long walk together so we could talk. I had a long-standing habit of wearing very loose-fitting clothes so my natural abdominal breathing would not be restricted. Walking required a periodic tug upward to keep my beltless pants from falling perilously low. Since I was well aware that my baggy pants gave me a clownish look, I described my outer mask to Robert as my "clown" mask, which is why Robert used that term in his letter. In my conversation with Robert I told him that I felt we all have clown masks, although we can paint different faces on ourselves to make happy-face clowns or sad-face ones. Using Course terminology, Robert agreed, saying happy-face clowns put on "the face of innocence" and give a happy smile to cover over what they are really feeling inside. The sad-face clown masks are the "victimizer" or "victim" roles we assign to ourselves.

A lot of my particular clown mask had to do with my outer appearance. I drew the notice of others not only from my unflattering clothes, but also from walking with an odd-looking long stride and by clumsily dropping glass objects. Even when I was not moving, I still managed to call attention to myself just by sitting. That was because I would always sit ramrod straight for mental clarity, rather than using the customary relaxed slouch on the couch that prevents energy from rising up the spine. External forms seemed superficial to me, especially after my past work with mentally retarded clients, who often presented an awkward outer appearance. Since I wouldn't use externals as a basis for evaluating another person, I couldn't see why they were so important to others evaluating me. I also described myself to Robert as "someone who just wants to be loved," because of feelings of being a victim of others' judgments of me. More important than my outer appearance, my inner pattern of seeing myself as victim gave me a sad-face mask that was understandably more troublesome to others and to me.

In my inner world I felt God looked past all my masks, and I opened up to His unconditional love for me. However, when I functioned in the world, I wondered why my community members did not greet me with that same nonjudgment and love that I received inwardly. The mask of identifying myself as a monk was also a concern for others because of me having a sense of specialness about that role, which reflected my pride rather than the humility that might be expected from a monk. I too was concerned about my spiritual pride, but saw no reason to beat myself over the head about it. I knew there was much more depth to my monk role than this pride. A lot about that role has to do with intimacy with God. This inner intimacy is difficult to relate to another person and often not appropriate to share, so, as Robert noted in his letter, I was silent about that part of my spiritual life. In my conversation with Robert I specifically asked him to look deeper within me to see beyond my obvious off-putting masks.

Robert's letter showed that he had taken my request seriously. He concluded his letter saying he really wanted to develop our relationship, which I also wanted. This was an example of the kind of breakthrough that I believe God had intended through our community's arranged marriage. In addition, it was correspondingly a growth movement in the direction of synthesizing the East and West in us. For Robert, this growth was an outreach from his comfortable Western perspective to adding the Eastern orientation of seeing the divine in another. What I would want to add to Robert's insights in his letter is that seeing that third me, the monk in God, is also a role. But it is a role that better reflects the divine in me than the more superficial masks. You might say that there is a fourth me, deeper than the monk, that is the Self in Christ. Robert through his study of the

Course was certainly intellectually well aware of this Self, who is the true me and not a role. The Course maintains that this Self is my true nature as the Son of God, part of the One Christ that we all share. The objective of my monk role was and is to be a reflection of this Self in me, which I really wanted Robert to see, because his doing so would help him to affirm his own Self in Christ. I was certainly greatly satisfied with Robert seeing the monk in God in me, and in my response to him I let him know my gratitude for his recognition.

Later, after pondering both Sarah's acknowledgment and Robert's letter, I felt that I had missed something. When I was in Anaheim I had asked community members to see through my masks, and I realized that both Sarah and Robert had come a long way in doing as I had asked. I appreciated their extending love to me in that way. However, I still had a problem. Here's a story that explains what my predicament was:

Wylie walked into a psychiatrist's office. The psychiatrist asked, "What's your problem?"

"I keep hearing a clucking sound. My problem is I can't figure out where the clucking is coming from."

The psychiatrist said, "You have a chicken on top of your head."

"That's funny. I've read about healing through humor. Proverbs say, 'A cheerful heart is good medicine....'[1] But this is no laughing matter. I have to find out where this clucking is coming from. I saw my medical doctor, and he told me that there's nothing wrong with my ears. He said that it's not a physical problem and I should come to you because the problem's in my head."

"The problem is actually *on top of your head*," the psychiatrist said. "I wasn't making a joke when I said there's a chicken on your head. If you don't believe me, go ahead and reach up with your hands and see for yourself."

So Wylie reached up and exclaimed, "Oh! Wow! That does feel like a real live chicken is up there after all. I feel so relieved to know where that clucking is coming from. You've solved my problem. Send me your bill. Thank you very much." Wylie got up to leave.

With Wylie about to exit through the doorway the psychiatrist said, "Haven't you forgotten something?" expecting him to remove the chicken from his head.

"No, I have everything," Wylie said as he walked away with the chicken still on his head.

Later at the local food store the psychiatrist happened to run into Wylie, who was easy to spot because of the chicken on his head. The psychiatrist walked up to Wylie as he was putting a large bag of bird food in his cart and asked, "I noticed you haven't come back. Are you sure there isn't anything I can still do for you?"

"Can you teach my chicken to sing my favorite song, *Let It Be?*"

"No, that's out of my range of expertise."

"Doc, that was a joke! Of course I know chickens only cluck. Speaking of clucking, I want to thank you again for solving my problem."

"But I don't understand. Don't you still have the problem of the clucking sound?" the perplexed psychiatrist asked.

"When I came to your office I told you my problem was that I heard clucking and didn't know where it was coming from. You helped me find out where it came from so, as far as I am concerned, you solved the problem. I never asked you to get rid of the clucking. It's so familiar to me now that I don't know what I would do without it. Like I said, my favorite song is *Let It Be*.""

Just as Wyle was in denial about the chicken on his head, I was at one time in denial about my masks, which were as obvious to others as a chicken on my head would have been. Similar to Wyle coming out of denial with the help of a psychiatrist, I had learned to come out of denial about my masks by accepting that I had defense mechanisms of denial, judgment, and projection. Just as Wylie was satisfied with discovering where the clucking was coming from, I was satisfied with this psychological understanding that I thought thoroughly explained where my masks were coming from. Wylie wouldn't think of actually taking the chicken off of his head because he had become so accustomed to it, and he even nourished it with bird seed. In the same way, my masks had become so familiar to me that I wanted to nourish them by justifying them. Having learned all about my masks, I wasn't ready to apply that knowledge to the next step of taking off my façade. If other people, like Sarah and Robert, had a problem with my masks, it was *their* problem. I asked them to see through the image I presented and overcome their problem. But when they actually did see beyond my masks, I realized that I had unfairly placed the burden on them and others to see through my masks. Instead I needed to take responsibility myself for the inappropriateness of my outer "clown" and the other masks I had been presenting.

In my letter at the beginning of this chapter I wrote, "I hope I don't make myself out to be too much of a victim in my description." This showed I had only a partial intellectual awareness of my problem, but not enough to rid myself of it at the practical level. Thus I was following the pattern of Wylie who had just enough awareness to bring him out of denial, yet not enough to produce a change in his everyday life. Generally speaking, in spiritual growth matters, my intellectual understanding was far ahead of my ability to apply that awareness. As a result, I found myself doing a lot of self-justifying to avoid the other extreme of self-condemnation. Sarah's and Robert's new insights, showing they were seeing through my masks, helped me to perceive more clearly that the problem wasn't out there with them, as a victim would assume. I had to somehow learn to see through my own masks at a much deeper level.

I took a much closer look at the pieces of my shadow puzzle locked in the back of my mind. I had to admit to myself that I had been collecting "psychological trading stamps," a term used in Eric Berne's book, *What Do You Say After You Say Hello?* These stamps are the accumulation of all the little hurts and bits of anger that happen over time. When I visited in Anaheim, I had to stay outside in a tent when everyone else could sleep inside. I couldn't complain because I was glad to have a respite from the Sedona desert. The Anaheim Half treated the Sunfellow family to a trip to Disneyland, as was appropriate for the children's sake. The fact that I was left out wasn't a big deal because I didn't have my heart set on going. Nevertheless, I just wanted to be invited. David and Pamela at various times were invited to go to the movies by individual Anaheim members, and I was not. Each time a minor hurt had happened, I said to myself that it didn't really matter, yet I still stored it away as a trading stamp. The psychological idea was to collect enough stamps to make a stamp book, and then I could trade the book in as a justification for a big emotional outburst. My emotional displays were typically private affairs along the weeping lines, rather than angry tantrums expressed to others. But even such outbursts didn't really free my mind of the trading stamps. In fact, my emotional displays only made those trading stamps seem much more real and important than they really were. It was clear that this trading stamp mentality was an overall pattern I had exhibited in all my relationships, most notably with David. I could see this meant that I knew very little about how to manifest forgiveness. I could also see that I was so focused, as I had told Robert, on just wanting to be loved that I did very little myself about giving love to others. This was a sobering realization considering that, as a monk, I wanted to be an example of love as Jesus was.

My strength was letting God's abiding love well up from within and nourish me in my inner world. But that was not enough. I needed to let His love flow through me to others. Then I would really be following Jesus, who always made others his top priority. I needed to let more of the light in my inner world come out and be reflected in the image and the activity I put forth in the outer world of form. In general, I felt I needed to be more aware of how I could become more loving and how I could see through the masks of others to see Christ within them. But how was I going to do that? When I had thought of myself as a victim and privately wallowed in tears so many times in the past, the immediate distressing event was a concern. However, the greater overall concern was that I had many lofty spiritual aspirations, and yet I felt so stuck within my ego. At some point along the way it dawned on me that my whole thought system, like Wylie's limited thought system, didn't have the depth necessary to release me from the box in which I seemed to have placed myself. Eventually I became open to a way out of my box that I had for a long time nibbled at and chewed, but had decided not to swallow and digest.

The "marriage" of our community members with each other was very challenging. As with any marriage, the partners were different from each other, which was disconcerting at times. Nevertheless, these differences also provided great opportunities of learning from each other. Often our relationships were a matter of one step forward and then two steps back, yet some breakthroughs lasted. Perhaps the most significant breakthrough on my end was that eventually I would accept *A Course in Miracles*, which brought me much closer to Robert. I had acknowledged that there were valuable ideas in the Course, yet for years had staunchly resisted the idea of becoming an actual Course student. But finally when the time was right, I did become a Course student and adopted the Course as my new thought system—a change that would mark a turning point in my life.

The Course encouraged me to place greater emphasis on inviting the Holy Spirit into my mind to bring healing. I focused on asking the Holy Spirit to help me uncover the hidden pieces of my shadow puzzle so I could let go of fear and accept divine love instead. The Course gave me a greater depth of understanding of my subconscious mind that is the source of my shadow puzzle and the source of my ego masks. Much of my personal growth has been about changing unhealthy ego masks into healthy ego masks, and that has been very necessary to do. However, the Course went a step further to also remind me that regardless of the state of my ego, I am not the ego at all. It helped me identify with my Source instead of my ego. Besides deepening my understanding, the Course also helped me to apply that understanding toward increasingly taking off my masks by letting the divine light shine through me into the lives of others. Just as my personal path and the New Jerusalem Community as a whole were a blending of the East and the West, the Course was likewise a synthesis of Eastern philosophy and Western Christianity. In addition to incorporating the four community principles described in the previous chapter into my own personal practice of Christian yoga, I discovered that the Course philosophy was entirely compatible with my practice of yoga disciplines as a means of following in the footsteps of Jesus.

---

1. Proverbs 17:22, RSV.

46

ON THE MOVE

≈ ◦ ≈

Camping in Sedona had been a continuous time of being faced with many needs and trusting in God to provide for those needs. Indeed our trust was well founded and our needs met, but just barely. With moving into a trailer and both David and I having jobs outside our home, we found that our needs were being met more gracefully. We were grateful for our reversal of fortune and relieved to let go of the tension of wondering when the next forest ranger was going to tell us to move. Pamela and a neighborhood friend collaborated on starting a mini-school, so the children would have more educational opportunities. We met some fellow seekers and became more integrated into everyday life in Sedona.

David suggested we sell the newer model van that Sarah had recently bought for us with money she had received from an inheritance. David and I felt it was a good idea because we could split the money and buy two cars so we could both have our own rides to work. Pamela felt we would be wiser to keep the van. Interestingly, David's initial strong feeling melted away with time and prayer, and we acknowledged that Pamela's intuition had been correct. This was a sign of how far Pamela had come in learning to trust in her intuition and to speak up about her inner feelings.

We had always held our money in common, but after a while in our new situation, we decided to split up our finances and costs. This enabled me to purchase a VW rabbit after obtaining a car loan from the bank. The new car put me in a position to do something that I had wanted to do for a while, which was to make a trip back to the East Coast to visit family and friends after the school year was over. However, the real reason for the trip was that my heart had been closing down because of all that I had been through. I had begun to feel like an "appendage" to the Sunfellow family—not quite a full family member, yet not a stranger either. We talked a lot about different ways all of us could come together and become more of a harmonious family. We had gotten away from meditating together, and so we reestablished times for joint meditation. We had social activities designed to help us come together as a family unit. Nevertheless, there was a sense that each of us was walling ourselves off from one another.

We could go just so far in loving and accepting each other, and no further, because of our various limitations and judgments.

Part of me had become somehow dependent on David and Pamela, and I needed to rediscover who I was apart from anyone else's influence. Consequently, when I left for an open-ended vacation in June of 1988, I felt I was going to "find my heart." As an afterthought in packing, I took a paperback of *A Course in Miracles* that Robert had given me. It even had a signature from Bill Thetford, who assisted Helen Schucman in her scribing of the Course. I had taken the book with me as a reference book, not for reading cover to cover.

Previously I had resisted the Course because I had carefully nurtured my own thought system, which was like one of my paintings—something I had created and loved because I had created it. Also, I hadn't gone to Course study groups like many people who've come to the Course, although I had obtained a lot of Course information from friends like Stuart Dean, Allan Greene, and Robert. However, the idea of adopting an extensive set of specific spiritual principles didn't appeal to me, and I found the sheer size of the Course, 1249 pages, to be daunting. Thus I had read only selected parts of the Text, Workbook, Manual, and Clarification of Terms. What led to changing my mind about the Course was that I now started to read it from the beginning. I liked the thought-provoking and inspiring ideas I encountered, so I just kept on reading all the way through my cross-country trip. At some point I realized that my own thought system was accurate as far as it went, yet it was not comprehensive. It was like I had been playing a harmonica all my life, and I thought it was wonderful music. Then I heard a classical symphony for the first time, and I understood that there was so much more to music than I had realized.

I had also come to realize that my own thought system was unable to help with my long-standing pattern of collecting minor hurts as if they were trading stamps and cashing them in periodically with a session of weeping, in which I would see myself as a victim of what someone else had said or done. On a rare occasion this weeping display would be done in public with my tears pointing an accusing finger at another person, but usually this occasional crying was a private affair. However, the accumulation of past minor resentments was not enough in itself to bring on a weeping episode. There was also the self-condemning awareness that by clinging to perceived injustices I was failing to live up to my goal as a monk of following the loving example of Jesus. This failure on my part gnawed at me most deeply and was the trigger for the occasional solitary tearful outbursts of self-pity mixed with self-condemnation. The Course would explain to me exactly why I was collecting these grievances and playing the role of a victim, as well as indulging in self-condemnation. Its spiritual principles would show me how to see the truth instead, though I didn't yet know this. What I *did know* was that the emotional turmoil that went along with this pattern seemed to be the main reason my heart was closing down. Living with a roof over my head had brought more peace into my life, but the emotional flare-ups that had mostly occurred during the stressful times of camping had already taken their toll on me. I knew I needed to do something on this trip to find my heart again. I was ripe for something new, so as I read the Course in more depth and with more openness than in the past, my former resistance melted away. In time the inspiring words of the Course would show me the way back to an open heart.

I first visited my sister Lillian in Texas and then went to Missouri to visit Tom, and together we celebrated my acceptance of the Course. Tom had left the community after attempting to live both in Anaheim and in Sedona but found that job opportunities didn't open up for him. He felt even more disillusioned by the feeling of not being fully accepted by the other community members, though he would return to the Sedona community at a later date.

Next I visited my brother Rick and his family in Chicago. I spent time with my nephews Dave, Matt, and Jimmy, the oldest, who was my godson. Jimmy, now 19 years old, had a broken right leg in a cast, but he didn't let that stop him from doing anything. He still lifted weights and even made a point of taking me to see my favorite baseball team, the Red Sox, while they were playing the White Sox in Chicago.

After that I went back to Connecticut to see my parents, and then made my way south to renew friendships in Virginia. Naturally I wanted to visit Allan Greene in his new home and was ushered to his bedside. He smiled broadly as he introduced me to a lady friend and gave me the good news that this woman was his new wife. Allan, who liked to talk to me about the Course, was delighted when I gave him my own good news about becoming a Course student. He said, "For a long time I was the Course student, and you were the Jesus student. However, now we are sharing with each other because just as you are becoming a Course student, I am becoming a Jesus student. Whenever I see you, Jesus seems to become more important to me—like right now in my life. When you and I last talked in New Market, you told me about going off to study Zen, but how did you get from Zen to Jesus?"

"I am surprised you remember exactly where I left off in my story," I said.

"Of course I remember, because I enjoyed hearing about your past adventures. You live out there in Sedona, and I am here in Virginia Beach, so we may never see each other again. Before you go I would like to hear how things turned out for you back then."

With this invitation from Allan, I picked up narrating the story where I had left off:

Before breaking up with my girl friend, Marie, I first went to Rochester in upstate New York to scout out the Zen center and see if I really wanted to relocate to there. I went to the center and was allowed to talk to Philip Kapleau, an American roshi who had studied Zen Buddhism from many years in Japan. It was a given that he, being a roshi, had been to a spiritual destination where he could lead others like me, just as he had been led by his own roshi.

I've told you about my college years and how upset I was at some of my teachers, who seemed to me to be so petty and judgmental. But this man was a teacher who had captured my imagination—an authentic teacher, one who could help me answer that troubling question, "Who am I?" He was not physically imposing. In fact, he was ordinary looking and short, and his manner was businesslike, yet he spoke with obvious conviction. I was allowed to talk with him shortly after I arrived, and I told him of my hope to relocate to the area. He told me quite a few people had been arriving recently, and I was welcome as well. He invited me to help with work on the large house that served as the Zen center, and I readily accepted. There had been an extensive fire a few months earlier, and I helped peel the old charred paint away so the wood could be repainted. Zen is associated with meditation, but it is actually about living one's whole life with *mindfulness*. This means *being one with every activity* as it is occurring—including, for example, being one with the mundane activity of peeling charred paint off of wood.

The next day I was able to attend a workshop led by the roshi. First he gave a talk about Zen Buddhism. At one point he said that when the Buddha experienced enlightenment, he realized, "I am the One." I myself interpreted that to mean, "I am God" or "I am one with God," but as the roshi pointed out, in Zen Buddhism there is no word for God. There is only *Buddha nature*, which everyone has equally, although it goes unrecognized until it is experienced. He then asked if there were any questions, and one man asked, "How was all this world created?"

The roshi gently replied that Zen Buddhism isn't interested in addressing how the world was created in the past. He explained that Zen is about *experience*, and experience always occurs in the present moment. Filling the rational mind with intellectual conjecture separates you from applying mindfulness focused on your experience now. Zen Buddhism is concerned with discarding the past and future in order to give your full attention to the present moment.

To illustrate his point the roshi concluded with this story:

There were two monks who met a woman at a river bank. The woman asked the monk to carry her across the river. One of the two monks carried the woman across, and then the woman went away. The other monk was scandalized by the fact that his fellow monk had touched a woman. An hour later the monk confronted his companion, saying, "You know that, being a monk, you are not supposed to touch any woman. Why did you carry her?"

The monk responded, "I put the woman down a long time ago. You are still carrying her now."

After his talk the roshi led us to the *zendo*, the meditation room, to further emphasize that *zazen*, the practice of Zen meditation, is something to be practiced, rather than discussed intellectually. He talked about the importance of holding the awareness in the *hara*, the area just below the navel. Then he gave specific instructions regarding how to practice counting meditation, in which the counting is done in coordination with observing the natural breathing. He explained that in this kind of breathing, the lower abdomen expands with each inhalation and contracts with each exhalation, so the chest and stomach are not involved.

The roshi demonstrated sitting postures. He recommended bowing the upper torso forward and then slowly raising the spine to the erect position in order to find the proper body balance. He then recommended rocking the torso from side to side. This sideways movement starts with a large arc and then moves to successively smaller ones. When the sideways arc becomes very small, the spine is then gently brought to a centered and motionless position, as a final preparation for beginning meditation. Following the roshi's presentation we had a twenty-minute meditation together.

To complete the workshop, the roshi answered personal questions privately. I was the last person in the long line of those to see him. When it was my turn, I sat down and began to talk, while suppressing my all-too-persistent need to urinate. But he said he wanted to go to the bathroom before we continued our conversation. I told him I needed to go to the bathroom also, so I followed him to the upstairs bathroom. It occurred to me that he had picked up my thought that I needed to urinate and that he had only said he wanted to go for my benefit, yet there was no way to tell for sure. When we returned, I asked, "How can I become egoless? I have a lot of pride, and my meditation practice only makes me more proud."

He answered, "You can use your pride to eliminate your pride. It is all right for you to be proud of meditating—as long as it helps you to continue meditating. You sit steadfastly, and you tell yourself you are doing a good job. Sure, that is pride and ego. However, it encourages you to sit better and to continue your practice. Then the sitting itself will have the effect of stilling the mind and leading it toward egolessness. So you use the ego to eliminate the ego. You use your pride to eliminate your pride."

After that visit, I knew that I had found a teacher whom I could trust. I went back to New York to finalize my separation from Marie and then returned to Rochester in April of 1969. The first day there, I met Joel, who invited me to move into a house near the center, where he and five other members lived. Joel told me that one day while traveling in Mexico, he was meditating facing a wall with his eyes partially opened (one of the ways to practice Zen meditation). "Suddenly," he said, "a large swirling mass of light appeared in front of me and moved toward me. I was thrown into a state of panic, and the light disappeared. For a while I was afraid to meditate again. That's why I came here. I decided that I needed to find a qualified roshi, instead of trying to do it all on my own." In spite of his momentary fear, I got the impression that Joel was a very strong person in every respect—physically, emotionally, and spiritually—and I admired him.

Joel had a younger brother, Jack, who also lived in our house. Jack told me, "I used to think I was possessed by the devil. I would go up to strangers and scream at them and do other strange things. I felt like there was this weird force compelling me to do these things, so that's why I thought it was the devil possessing me. However, I told the roshi about this, and he told me that I was mistaken. He told me not to believe in such things as devils, so I don't anymore."

Jack was always intellectualizing about something. But Zen Buddhism consists of practicing sitting meditation and then practicing mindfulness while participating in the activities of daily living, without getting involved with intellectual theories. Jack would even go overboard sometimes by directing his ideas of proper spiritual conduct toward other household members. One time when Jack was getting carried away with expressing himself, another household member, Noble, reminded him in a gentle manner, "There is only *one* teacher here," referring, of course, to the roshi. This quickly brought Jack to silence.

Noble was a very responsible person and dedicated student. He had a deformed foot, which I believe added to his stature because it gave him a certain conviction about the futility of this world of appearances and a seriousness about seeking enlightenment. I felt his outward disability was possibly a blessing in terms of sparking the kind of motivation that none of the rest of us had. I felt a kinship with him, and this may have been because in a past life I too had a disabled foot, though at the time I wasn't yet consciously aware of that life [as the Spider Boy]. Noble paid a reduced rent and lived in the lowliest place in the house, the drab cellar. He seldom spoke, refraining from the mindless chatter of the rest of us, but when he did speak he expressed himself in a way that showed good judgment and commanded respect. He had experimented with drugs as most of us had, but when drugs proved to be a dead end, he felt there was nowhere to go other than investing in meditation practice.

Another housemate was Pasqual, who was emotional and sympathetic. He had experiences with expressive group psychotherapy similar to my own. The youngest housemate was Richard Chamberlain, who took a ribbing because he had the same name as the famous actor. He was the quietest and gentlest of the group.

Then there was Howard, who became my best friend. I still smile when I think about him. He looked like one of those statues of a chubby laughing Buddha. Howard told me, "I was living in a 'free expression' community in California. One day some members of the community decided that I had done something terribly wrong that I had not actually done. They beat me up with a stick and kicked me out of the community. That's when I decide to come here. Here they hit me with a stick too, but it's for my own good— for my enlightenment."

In the practice of meditation at a Zen center, you can put your hands together in prayer position and raise them to request being hit. Because of your request the roshi or one of his monks will come and hit you with a stick on the fleshy part of the shoulder that leads to the neck. This involves two quick whacks on the right side and two on the left, to stimulate and deepen meditation. I weighed about 135 pounds, twenty pounds less than when I was in high school, so I didn't have much flesh on me to cushion the blows. Sometimes I would have red marks afterwards. The hitting became a distraction for me, so I stopped requesting it.

There were other Zen customs that I needed to adjust to. One day Noble invited me to go with him to the early morning meditation from five to six o'clock. As we walked the short distance to the center, he said, "I heard that one of the testimonials in the roshi's book is about his own experience of enlightenment."

"Do you know which one?" I asked.

"It's the testimonial of the 'American Ex-businessman.' It took him five years of living in strict Japanese monasteries before he had his *kensho*, his first enlightenment experience. But I am sure he has had deeper and deeper levels of enlightenment after that first one. The training to become a roshi is very rigorous, and a lot of spiritual depth is required to be able to be a spiritual leader for others. I heard from one of the monks that kensho isn't always a big dramatic event. The first experience of enlightenment can be just an experience of oneness. For example, you can be just looking at an object in nature like a tree. You can feel complete oneness with the tree and that feeling of oneness can possibly be your experience of kensho."

While I was telling this story to Allan, I wished that I had had a copy of *The Three Pillars of Zen* so I could show him roshi Philip Kapleau's description of his kensho:

> "The universe is One," [my roshi] began, each word tearing into my mind like a bullet. "The moon of Truth—" All at once the roshi, the room, every single thing disappeared in a dazzling stream of illumination and I felt myself bathed in a delicious, unspeakable delight ... For a fleeting eternity I was alone—I alone was ... Then the roshi swam into view. Our eyes met and flowed into each other, and we burst out laughing....[1]

After the morning meditation, Noble said that he had been invited to go to a private breakfast with the roshi and to bring one other person. He asked me to accompany him, and I agreed. But he cautioned me, saying, "This is an honor, so make sure you are on your best behavior." I nodded but thought, "What a strange thing to say—of course, I'll be on my best behavior." We went behind the center to the back building, which housed the office and living quarters of the roshi and his two monks, Pierce and Howell. Pierce was all business, as serious and disciplined as they come. By way of contrast, Howell spoke with a gentle voice that expressed his warm heart. Pierce bent down and reached into the bottom of the refrigerator to pull out a few grapefruits, and he asked in a friendly way, "Do you like grapefruit, Don?"

Thinking he was giving me a choice, I said that I would rather have an orange.

His tone changed abruptly as he asserted, "We will all have grapefruits." I was beginning to realize that being on my "best behavior" meant being on my best *Zen Buddhist* behavior. But I didn't yet know the traditional customs, including the emphasis on doing everything together in a uniform manner, without any individual sticking out from the group. I figured if I didn't say anything else, I wouldn't get into any more trouble during this breakfast.

We all sat down at the table in the small kitchen. The roshi banged the wooden clappers together to signal the start of the meal. As I sat there, I thought I was safely protected by my silence. Pierce started to fill up my bowl with oatmeal, which I didn't really like very much. He kept putting more and more in my bowl, and his face looked displeased as he was doing it. I didn't want to seem rude by stopping him, so I continued to say nothing. Biblically, my "cup runneth over" is supposed to be a good thing, but seeing my *bowl* "runneth over" was embarrassing. Noble mercifully came to my rescue. He whispered for me to rub my hands together in prayer position as the customary signal to stop the oatmeal avalanche, and I immediately followed his advice.

So there in front of me was more oatmeal than I wanted to eat, and yet I assumed it was probably the custom to eat everything in my bowl. In order to be on my best behavior, I consciously ate very slowly, contrary to my usual tendency of eating too quickly. But as I was slowly stuffing down this oatmeal, which I didn't even want, there in front of me was a bowl of very tempting muffins. I thought that one muffin would be my reward for downing all the oatmeal. However, I ate so slowly that everyone else had already finished as the roshi rang the clappers together again to signal the end of the meal. My eyes still on my reward—I reached my hand out for the muffin. Alas, you guessed it—the roshi looked at me angrily and said, "You have a lot to learn!" Needless to say, that muffin suddenly became like a red-hot rock as it dropped from my hand back into the bowl. I would have liked another kind of rock—one I could crawl under, but there was nowhere to hide. I did do one thing right—I said nothing. I thought Zen masters never got upset, yet I was mistaken, though I would have preferred having this assumption corrected in some other way. That was my last morning meal with the roshi, and he was right—I did have a lot to learn, and in spite of my embarrassment I still felt he was the one who could help me to learn.

---

1. *The Three Pillars of Zen*, compiled and edited with translations, introductions, and notes by Philip Kapleau. (Garden City, NY: Anchor Books, 1980), p. 239.

47

PLEASURE AND PAIN

≈ • ≈

"Are you getting tired of listening to me, Allan?" I asked.

"When I have had enough and I want you to stop, I will just rub my hands together!" Allan said with a smile. Unable to use his hands and typically making fun of his disability, Allan gave me the green light to go ahead, and so I did:

Of all my house mates, I think you would have liked Howard the most because he had a good sense of humor like you. We were all too serious. However, Howard brought out the little child in me. When I was with him, I could see that if this world really is an illusion, I might as well have fun with it. One day we redesigned the kitchen walls with a whole roll of aluminum foil to make it look ridiculous. Another day, I bought a watermelon for Howard and me and placed it on our kitchen table—a wooden door held up by two cardboard boxes. We cut it in half and placed each half in front of us. But just before we dug in with our spoons, Howard looked at me with his impish smile and asked, "Do you know what I always wanted to do?"

"No, Howard, but I have a feeling it has something to do with this watermelon."

"You must be psychic. I always wanted to put my face in one of these!"

I said, "Well, that wouldn't exactly be my heart's desire. On the other hand, it sounds like fun. Let's do it together."

"OK, I guess we won't need these spoons. But let's not 'jump into this head first,' and risk injuring ourselves! I am first going to eat out the best part, the center, to create a hole big enough for my whole face."

"Let's do it," I agreed, and so we began eating out the center of the watermelon by sticking our faces in the middle of it. After a bit of earnest eating we were both sticking our whole faces in the watermelon and laughing hysterically.

Jack came into the kitchen and asked, "What are you guys doing? Is this any way for Zen students to act?"

"Oh, look, Howard. Mother Superior is here to tell us we have been bad boys. We need to repent." As I made the sign of the cross, I said, "Dominus

Nabisco Shredded Wheat. Forgive me, Mother Superior, for my numerous watermelon transgressions! And, Howard, what do you have to say for yourself?"

Howard, his face still dripping with watermelon juice, just as mine was, began singing joyfully, "Amazing grace! How sweet the watermelon that saved a wretch like me! I once was lost, but now Mother Superior has found me—was blind but now I see—yes, I see watermelon seeds everywhere!"

Jack stood there disapprovingly and then realizing it was useless to admonish us said, "You guys are too much," and he walked out of the kitchen unsuccessful in his attempt to make us feel guilty about enjoying ourselves.

Of course, these diversions revealing the absurdity of this illusory world were intermittent and overshadowed by daily spiritual disciplines. Joel lent me *The Complete Illustrated Book of Yoga* by Swami Vishnudevananda. The roshi had recommended that students who wanted to do yoga should limit their yoga practice to one hour per day. I had never been to an actual yoga class, so I just assumed the various postures that were pictured in the book. One series of postures I especially liked was the Sun Salutation, which is sometimes called the Sun Exercise. It is a sequence of twelve postures, which gives the body alternate backward and forward stretches. In the beginning portion of the practice it felt invigorating to lift my arms overhead and lift my head upwards. When I finished all twelve body positions, I invariably felt a tingling sensation in my spine, and my whole body felt revitalized. I also enjoyed the breathing practices, which I felt had the effect of clearing my mind.

A few weeks after moving in, I was in my room relaxing, when the words came to me, "Pleasure and pain are the same." I had no clue what this meant. A short while later I went to a group meditation at the center. While I was concentrating on counting my breaths, my mind wandered, and I could feel pain in my legs. Mentally I thought, "Why should this pain bother me? The pain is in the body. Ah! This is how pleasure and pain are the same. Both depend on attachment to the body. But I am not a body. So both pleasure and pain are really meaningless because I am not a body. Then what am I? Oh, I have stopped counting. Stop intellectualizing right now, and start counting again."

I was able to forget the pain and set aside the intellectualizing through focusing wholeheartedly on counting the breath. When the bell rang to end the sitting period, the sound of the bell pierced deep into my head, and that sound kept ringing long after it normally would have ended. I was struck by the beauty of the continuously reverberating sound, which I assumed was a one-time experience. However, I found out subsequently that this hearing breakthrough would recur every time the bell would ring at the end of any meditation.

This particular session of meditation was on Wednesday evening, which was the day for *dokusan*, personal interview time with the roshi. It was my first time at dokusan, and I followed the directions that I had been given. When the roshi rang the bell in his private interview room, the door opened as the previous student left, and I entered the room. While bowing forward, I placed my palms together at the chest in prayer position, called *gassho*, which is a greeting, a thank you, a sign of respect, or an expression of reverence. After closing the door I walked over to the roshi, who was sitting cross-legged at the other end of the room. I sat in a cross-legged position and lowered my forehead to the floor in front of him and extended by hands on the floor with the palms turned downward. The roshi turned my hands over to place them in the correct position, facing upward. Having the palms turned upward indicates that the student comes empty handed to the Zen master and is ready to receive.

For the interview I sat erect and stated the type of meditation I was practicing, which was counting the breath. The roshi asked if I had any questions. I told him about the bell ringing beyond the way it normally would. I also told him about hearing the words, "Pleasure and pain are the same," and he nodded his head in agreement. Next I said, "Yesterday while I was outside peeling paint from the building, I mentally visualized Howell hugging me. Then an instant later Howell came over to me and talked to me."

The roshi replied, "You are probably developing some psychic ability. Don't bother with that. It is just a by-product of meditation. It is not the goal of meditation. Just continue your practice." I asked for and was given permission to attend the upcoming *sesshin*, which is the term for a spiritual retreat. The purpose of the sesshin is to experience enlightenment. It is a very intensive practice of meditation—over eight hours per day.

Just before the retreat I was looking for a job in the area, and I felt guided to a big grey building with an unusual architectural style. When I entered the building, I was pleasantly surprised to find out that it was a planetarium. I was able to speak with the person in charge, who told me that one of his staff was leaving in two months. He told me to come back in six weeks to confirm that I still wanted the job and said he would definitely hire me then. It was a general handyman job, and on the weekends I would run the projector for the planetarium shows. He introduced me to the staff, and since a planetarium show was just beginning, he invited me to sit down and enjoy the show in the domed auditorium. When I left, I was filled with gratitude. Life seemed to have a natural flow, and I was just going with that flow so that everything was unfolding gracefully.

At one of the last lectures that the roshi gave before the retreat, he talked about a very old woman who sat with a bent back and stooped shoulders during a sesshin. To the other retreatants, who could sit perfectly erect, she seemed like the most unlikely candidate for enlightenment. However, on the sesshin, due to her single-minded determination, she was the only one who was awakened. The roshi gave many other examples of seekers who went to great lengths to experience the awakening of their true nature, and he encouraged us to follow their example. He said that Jesus was a *Bodhisattva*, a great teacher, who delayed his own enlightenment to serve others and that he was an example of compassion and love. But the roshi cautioned us, "You must give up everything for enlightenment. You must even give up attachment to love if you want enlightenment. You must become completely desireless. You cannot be attached to anything to reach enlightenment."

The sesshin was for six days in May, ending with a full moon. We went to a house in the country that was big enough for fifty or sixty participants. The meditation room called the *zendo* had pillows lined up along all four walls. In addition, there was a partition placed lengthwise in the center of the room, with pillows on both sides. When I entered the zendo for the first time, I sat down on a pillow next to Joe, facing the partition in the center of the room. For a reason unknown to me, the roshi called me aside and told me to sit at the end of the room on one of the pillows placed on a platform raised a few feet above the floor.

When I went to the place chosen for me, I sat down in the full lotus, and the thought came to me, "I am a Buddha," but I did not think I was any more of a Buddha than anyone else. Zen Buddhism maintains that everyone is already living in the state of enlightenment, meaning everyone is the Buddha but unaware of the condition because of illusion. By thinking that I was a Buddha I was claiming my pre-existing true nature, which each person possesses.

Our challenging daily schedule began with a two-hour meditation in the early morning. There were four sitting meditations, which each lasted about half an hour. After each half hour meditation period, we had a five-minute walking meditation called *kinhin*, which helped to loosen up the legs. There were three similar two-hour stretches for meditation in the late morning, afternoon, and evening. In addition, there was a one-hour lecture by the roshi and another time set aside for chanting.

Right in the beginning of the sesshin, I made a decision that I had not planned to make. I decided to sit in the full lotus for every meditation, no matter how painful. There was a certain amount of pride involved in making that decision, but I was using my pride to motivate me, as the roshi had said I could. Also, my reasoning was that sitting in any position would be painful, so I might as well accept the pain and sit in the posture that would be most beneficial.

Sitting in the full lotus with the left leg crossed over the right leg places most of the pressure of the posture on the right ankle. As I focused on counting my breath for one meditation after another, my right ankle was consistently causing me very acute pain. At other times, the pain was more generalized, covering both legs or even the entire body. Two ways were suggested by the roshi to deal with pain. The first was to concentrate more firmly on my practice and ignore the pain. I quickly learned to concentrate wholeheartedly, because I knew that failure to do so would increase my awareness of the pain. Nevertheless, with the number of hours we meditated each day, there was no way to avoid it entirely.

When I became distracted by pain that I couldn't ignore, I employed the second method, becoming one with it. Instead of trying to avoid the pain, I would temporarily let go of focusing on counting the breath, and I would concentrate on feeling the pain totally. This was a direct confrontation with not only the pain, but with the fear of it. I fully joined with it. I became the pain and reminded myself that it was only pain. After my cowardice at the draft physical and being told at group therapy that I could not take the discipline, I set my mind on never allowing myself to give in to the fear of pain or to the pain itself. There were times when it became extremely intense, and I felt strengthened to discover that I could actually become one with it. However, I was tempted to become fearful and to give in when I was pushed to the limit. The pain was always most intense just before the bell rang to begin the kinhin, the walking meditation. The saying "saved by a bell" took on new meaning for me. When the bell rang, no matter how sore or numb my legs were, I stood up on my feet as quickly as possible.

The beginning of the retreat was difficult for everyone. There was a day when we had a tremendous storm, with dramatic thunder and lightning. It felt as if what was happening outside was a reflection of the inner storms we were all facing in each of our psyches. One time as kinhin started, I stood up and was shocked to see Joel sobbing uncontrollably. He was a strong meditator whom I looked up to. Later in the retreat I saw Pierce sobbing, too. If these strong meditators were losing it, how could I possibly continue to face my pain and overcome it? Whenever these comparison thoughts entered my mind, I refocused on my meditation practice.

I told you about students being hit to stimulate meditation, but on the sesshin, participants would be hit even if they didn't request it. However, participants could ask the roshi to exclude them from being hit. This was because Americans have difficulty with accepting this Zen practice and therefore would find it a distraction rather than a positive stimulation. I was already experiencing more pain than I had dreamed possible for me to endure, and I did not need any more, so I asked the roshi to exempt me, and he agreed.

More than half way through the six-days, I was able to go deeper in my meditation than ever before. As I was meditating and had successfully penetrated past my pain, I suddenly had a strong impression of being stalked. I had just heard the sound of the roshi's stick hitting students on the other side of the room. Nevertheless, instinctively I felt as if the roshi was tip toeing toward me all the way from the other side of the room just to hit me with the stick. It was a strong feeling that I couldn't shake by concentrating more deeply on my meditation practice. My conscious mind told me this intuitive feeling must be wrong because the roshi had promised me that I would not be hit. And just then there came two swift whacks on each side from the roshi's stick.

I was entirely filled with absolute rage and actually felt a pure red energy well up from the base of my spine and envelop my whole body. It took every ounce of my self-control to place my hands together and to bow forward in the gassho position, as the customary signal of appreciation. The roshi had indeed stalked me in particular because he came all the way from the other side of the room and hadn't hit anyone else along the way, as he normally would. As overpowering as my anger was, I couldn't afford to cling to any such emotion or else the pain in my legs would consume me. So I just continued to meditate.

Allan interrupted my account to ask, "After your roshi hit you when he said he wouldn't, what did you say to him about it during your next interview?"

"Nothing," I responded and continued:

I didn't bring up the incident and neither did he. I knew he would say that he did it to help me become enlightened. If I told him he should not have hit me, I would have been claiming to be a victim. I understood that I wasn't a victim, and I knew he really was trying to help me. In Zen practice sometimes a surprise can trigger enlightenment. So the roshi intended for the hitting to be a surprise that would shock me into the experience of enlightenment. It shocked me into a state of anger instead, but maybe that was not so bad. I had already been facing pain and fear, so maybe it was good to confront anger as well.

I could always manage to cope with any emotions that came up in meditation and would feel jolts of energy suddenly jumping through my body. In the middle of the retreat, sometimes when I stood up for kinhin my whole body would shake involuntarily. As I attempted to walk meditatively with my hands clasped at my chest in the proper position, my body would tremble with wave-like currents of energy welling up from my gut. This experience of the body shaking felt like deep fears were being released.

In contrast to the trembling that occasionally occurred during kinhin, the sitting meditation became very intense and focused, so the body sat as solidly as a rock. I was drawing on an inner strength I did not know I had. However, I was well aware I was walking a razor's edge. At any moment I could just fall apart emotionally and give in to pain if I allowed myself to do so. Nevertheless, I was steadfastly determined that I would not surrender to it.

I was able to maintain my composure through focusing continuously on the hara below the navel, where my hands were held. At one time of crystal-clear focusing on the navel region, I felt a very intense light and energy concentrated in that area. The light was just a single point of energy, but the experience felt very concrete because the point radiated outward and rotated slowly on a horizontal axis, sending light up in the back and down in the front as it rotated and radiated. It felt to me as though this point of light might be the "seed of enlightenment," which would bear the fruit of enlightenment at a later date, or at least that is what my ego told me. I had never heard of such a thing as a seed of enlightenment, but I did know from testimonials that enlightenment often came at a later and unexpected date after putting forth great effort to meditate.

As we had been instructed, I maintained my meditation focus on the hara. Sometimes after initially concentrating at the navel, I could feel a strong flow of energy rising up the torso from below. Although I continued to be centered on the navel area, sometimes the energy would shift all by itself to the center of the chest or to the heart. Never one to follow the rules blindly, I decided to throw caution to the winds and go with the flow. Consequently, when the energy spontaneously went up to the chest area, I abandoned my focus on the navel and allowed my attention to become fully centered in the chest. Then the energy might move to the forehead, so I would shift my focus to there. Next I might feel a band of energy around the crown of my head, and if that happened, I would bring my awareness to the top of the head.

Occasionally, we practiced some group exercises to loosen up the body. To complete the exercise period we were instructed to find a partner. Following Pierce's directions, who led the group, we took turns giving each other a brief back rub. Every time I gave a back rub, I felt drained of energy, but I did not mind because as soon as I meditated the energy came right back.

I was saying how earlier in the retreat, the pain was localized mostly on my right ankle, and that I could just divert my attention away from the pain by focusing deeper and deeper. However, as the retreat went on sometimes the localized pain spread to my whole body, so I felt like one big acute sore. When my whole body experienced pain, I couldn't meditate normally, so I focused on the pain itself, producing a feeling of oneness with the pain. Through this oneness with the pain, I could overcome it. I could *become* the pain. I think I was able to do this because, being a beginner—youthful, naive, and proud—I did not know what I could not do. But a few days later, at the peak of this pain, something totally unexpected happened. I switched spontaneously from being one with the pain itself to being one with each person around me, who was also in pain. I felt a deep sense of compassion for everyone in the room. Allan, it was what you know through the Course as the "holy instant" in which everything of the past disappears in an instant of communion. This communion is not only an opening to the divine itself, but a joining with the divine in others. In that instant I wasn't concerned with my pain. Instead I empathized with the suffering of everyone in the room, and indeed of everyone in the world. It was as if all the people in the world entered my heart and said, "We are your brothers and sisters and your children. Your suffering is for us, and our suffering is for you, because we are one." With this connection with all seekers, I understood we were all in this together. We were all in prison together—and we had to get out together. For the first time I realized seeking spiritual growth was not about me; it was about *us*.

This holy instant itself was a joining with my brothers for an instant of spontaneous union. Nevertheless, as an aftereffect of this experience, something felt terribly wrong, and it was not my pain or the pain of others. What felt wrong was the way we, this specific group of fifty or sixty individuals, were each trying to get out of prison, which felt like hell. Each of us was trying to be the Buddha, sitting here to achieve a meditative state like the Buddha and as individuals trying to escape this prison by becoming enlightened. It felt like we were spiritual Olympic athletes competing to win the gold medal. It felt wrong that only the strongest spiritual athletes should be able to transcend this world.

I thought, "Why shouldn't we all be enlightened, not by effort, but by free gift?" I reached out to God in my mind and prayed that the doors would be opened for everyone to transcend this world, not just the strongest spiritual athletes. This moment stands out in my mind because it was such a pure moment of compassion, in stark contrast to how selfish I had been all my life.

Shortly after this unexpected experience of connection with my brothers and compassion for the human condition, something surprising occurred. My heart had opened, and I was able to sometimes perceive my brothers differently. This change in inner perception of my brothers was reflected in a change in my outer visual perception of them. Zen meditation is practiced facing a wall or partition. However, when the roshi gave his daily lecture, we turned our seating position around to face the center of the room. We were not formally meditating, just listening attentively. Rather than sitting in my usual full lotus, I sat in a relaxed cross-legged position, and my line of vision fell directly on the bodies of other participants. Following the experience of expressing compassion and prayer toward others, I looked at another brother's body and discovered colors receding and solid shapes disappearing. To my amazement, the body of a brother became entirely filled with glowing light, with some parts of the body brighter than others. At the time I was not aware that a person could see the divine in another person, which is what the Course calls "Christ vision." But the experience felt like I was making some kind of significant connection with the divine in my brother, and when I had this experience of seeing light in others, it felt strengthening for me.

From these experiences of the holy instant, compassion, and Christ vision, I was first exposed to the lesson that meditation is not the solitary practice that it appears to be and the goal of meditation is not an individual goal. Nevertheless, I was not able to fully appreciate the significance of this awareness at the time, so I returned to focusing on my individual quest for enlightenment.

In addition to meditation, during a portion of the day I did work chores at the same time as the other retreatants. However, the roshi changed my assignment to washing dishes, so I worked when others did not. When others had work assignments, I had free time and lay down on the floor with my blanket over me. I didn't sleep, but rather concentrated on relaxing and drawing energy to my right ankle, which was under such strain from sitting.

Pierce saw me lying down while others were working and, although it was supposed to be a silent retreat, he asked me to explain why. I told him my unusual work assignment was scheduled for a different time. However, he told me I shouldn't lie around while others were working. As a result I decided to go outside. After walking at a distance from the house, I sat on the ground briefly and noticed moisture from the ground soaking into the seat of my pants. Then I got up with the feeling that I should search for something, but I didn't know what—except it was something related to enlightenment. Letting my intuition guide me, I closed my eyes and started running fast. Suddenly I felt a strong impression to stop, and when I did, I opened my eyes and saw a large wooden log. It was elevated above the ground so that if I had kept on running I would have broken my leg. I decided it would be safer to walk with my eyes closed, instead of running, and I walked into an ant hill.

Next I noticed an old wooden shack and was drawn to it. I walked around it to discover that there were only three sides to the small wooden building, and the back side was completely open. I walked inside and then saw what I felt I had been looking for. It was a door lying down flat on the center of the dirt floor. When I first saw it, I thought, "Ah! This is the *farthest door of dharma*." As a part of the daily activities we always recited four vows, and one of these vows was, "I will open the farthest door of dharma." Dharma is the universal law of cause and effect. To open this door means to go beyond all suffering and beyond illusory forms to experience perfect enlightenment.

[The painting on the opposite page titled *The Farthest Door of Dharma* displays the opening of a door in the upper right portion of the picture. This abstract expressionistic door has a rounded top, and its doorknob is represented by a single tiny dot, a bright white one. Some yoga forms of meditation involve focusing on a very small dot as a means of bringing about the ultimate spiritual awakening, which opening the farthest door of dharma symbolizes.]

It was as if I had stumbled onto St. Peter's pearly gates, and all I had to do was open them in order to enter heaven. Of course, I knew I was just acting out a fantasy. Obviously this was only a physical door. Nevertheless, for me it symbolized discovering the goal of enlightenment. I felt happy to find this symbol, and happiness was a rare and precious commodity on this retreat that had thus far been an all-too-serious confrontation with pain. I smiled as I stepped onto the horizontal door and placed myself in the center of it. Feeling like a playful little child, I jumped up and down three times on the door. I felt I was symbolically acting out knocking on the farthest door of dharma in order to gain access to a world beyond this one. As I came down on the door each time, I could hear the sharp sound of my leather shoes banging against the wooden surface of the door.

As I was jumping on the door for the third time, a strong and sudden thought came very clearly to my mind, "There is a snake underneath this door." My playful attitude changed to seriousness. I thought with my rational mind that this must be just my imagination. I walked off the door, bent over, and lifted the door up high so I could see everything underneath it. There in the exact spot over which I had been jumping was a coiled snake. When I saw it, I was completely overcome by fear. I stood frozen in horror for a second and then lowered the door to the ground. I had faced every emotion during meditation on the retreat without losing control of my emotions. But here I staggered away in total panic as tears streamed down my face. The fear had nothing to do with being bitten or physically harmed,

THE FARTHEST DOOR OF DHARMA

which didn't even enter my mind. Rather, it was some kind of primordial fear I couldn't explain.

Standing outside of the shack, I focused on regaining my composure and on no longer giving in to the fear that had overcome me. When I regained control of my emotions, I felt I had to go back. I had to face my fears. I had to go back and look again to make sure that I hadn't imagined this. I went back in and carefully lifted the door. Holding it high, I stood there and this time looked without any emotional reaction. Now I could see clearly it was a dark red snake, still coiled as before.

I had seen other snakes before, but this one was distinctly different. In my experience a snake will normally run or at least move, if it is exposed. Yet this snake remained coiled in a circle at least a foot in diameter. It remained motionless, and I got the odd impression that I was interrupting the snake's meditation. Most animals in this situation would project fear. However, I got the impression that this snake was projecting anger toward me. Having overcome my fear, I looked at it now with caution and fascination. The snake was looking directly at me. After staring into its eyes, I turned my glance away and felt certain that this was no ordinary snake. Then I looked back again at its eyes. I felt a strange power emanating from it and decided not to keep my eyes on it any longer. The impression I got was that this snake was a powerful spiritual entity of some kind.

By coming back to the door, my mind was reassured that I had not imagined the snake. More importantly, my return allowed me to overcome my initial fear of this creature. I slowly lowered the door. I noticed an old rusty hatchet nearby, but didn't consider any aggression toward the snake. I walked away calmly with a feeling that something of deep significance had just happened. I wondered if I had in some way touched upon the farthest door of dharma, which involves facing death. What kind of fruit this experience would bear, I did not know.

When I saw the roshi at dokusan, I told him about the snake. Nothing I had ever told the roshi during interview time had produced the slightest reaction from him. However, he had a look of concern about the snake and asked me a lot of questions about it. A short time later the roshi addressed all the students and announced that he did not want anyone to wander away from the house. He did not say why, but I knew the reason.

In spite of the roshi's instructions, my intuition told me I had to go back the next day and lift that door a third time. This time there was no snake. I thought that if this was the farthest door of dharma, it was fitting that behind the door there was nothing. As I left the shack, I noticed a molted snake skin. It was a dark reddish color. I wondered if the snake had molted overnight. From this whole experience with the snake I felt a deeper sense of seriousness and determination.

48

A MEMORY WALK

~ • ~

"You said you thought the snake you saw was some kind of 'spiritual entity.' What did you mean by that?" Allan asked. I answered by continuing my narrative:

I don't know for sure, but I think it was some form of negative spirit. The roshi said there are no devils. But I had read a story about the Buddha that just before his enlightenment he was tempted by the illusions of Mara, the Buddhist name for Satan. According to the Bible, Jesus was tempted by Satan, too. So it seems that Satan gets most involved with those individuals that have a chance of overcoming the illusions of this world, like the people on a sesshin. I did get the feeling I mentioned earlier, that the snake was meditating—of all things. Maybe Satan was there at the retreat like a gatekeeper to make sure nobody got through the "farthest door of dharma." Actually something did happen at a later date, after the sesshin was over, that made me think the snake may have been a devil or even Satan. I'll tell you about that later, but I've seen other snakes both before and after seeing that red one, and all of those snakes seemed like ordinary animals. All I know for sure was that the one I saw on the retreat was no ordinary snake.

In any event, the experience encouraged me to go deeper within during meditation. The next time I went to dokusan, I asked for a *koan*. Allan, you probably already know that a koan is a question that the roshi gives to the student to focus on, instead of counting the breaths. There is no answer in the usual sense to the question posed by the koan. The only real answer is the experience of enlightenment itself. For example, one famous koan is, "What is the sound of one hand clapping?" There is no satisfactory intellectual answer to such a question. In fact, the koan is designed to thwart the rational mind and thus to exhaust the ego. When I was a kid, I played pinball machines, and I would shake the machine to make the pinball move faster. But if I shook the machine too hard, the pinball machine "tilted" and the game was over. The koan shakes the ego until the exhausted ego "tilts," resulting in the sudden experience of enlightenment.

The koan that the roshi gave me was "Mu," which is pronounced like the sound of a cow, "moo." Earlier in the sesshin the roshi told the following story to explain Mu:

The Zen master Joshu was asked, "Does a dog have Buddha nature?"
Joshu answered, "Mu!" This answer literally means "no." But if you are given this koan, you do not need to become concerned with the literal meaning. Your answer to the question "What is Mu?" cannot be an intellectual response. Your task will be to *experience* Mu. That experience will be your answer to the koan.

The roshi told me to simply repeat Mu and become one with Mu. Thereafter, my every thought converged on this one thought of Mu. Every emotion of fear, anger, or pain became focused on Mu. Like all koans, it started as a question, "What is Mu?" But eventually it became both a question and a statement, "Mu, Mu, Mu, Mu, Mu, Mu...."

It wasn't enough to do sitting meditation on Mu. Zen is sometimes mistakenly thought of as only a way to meditate. In Zen practice, though, all activity needs to be done with mindfulness and mindlessness. The mindfulness consists of placing all of your attention on what is being done in order to be one with the activity. The mindlessness consists of letting go of mental preoccupations, such as dwelling on the past and anticipating the future, in order to be in the present moment. This mindfulness and mindlessness allows the student to do all activities wholeheartedly.

This single-mindedness can, of course, be practiced without a koan. But if a koan is used, it can be kept constantly in the mind during every activity of daily living. I found I could hold Mu firmly in mind throughout the day, but the most difficult time was during eating and the work assignments. I ate sparingly and worked in the kitchen washing dishes. During the work assignments we were allowed to talk if the work required it. Jim, a black student who worked with me in the kitchen, said with some irritation, "Why don't you stop that humming?"

"Oh," I replied, "I'm sorry. I didn't realize I was doing that." Mu had become so much a part of my consciousness that I was audibly humming it, or rather "Mu-ing" (moo-ing) it, without even realizing it.

At one point during the retreat the roshi spoke while we were practicing sitting meditation, and this is what he said:

I will tell you a story to indicate how you should hold on to your koan. A Zen master received his student for dokusan. The student asked, "How can I hold on to the koan? It keeps slipping away."

The Zen master asked, "What did Jesus Christ say to express his pain on the cross?"

"My God, my God, why have you forsaken me?" the student replied.

The master said, "No, he did not say, 'My God, my God, why have you forsaken me?'"

The student was puzzled and so inquired, "Then what did he say?"

The roshi paused at this point and then bellowed as loud as he could, "MY GOD, MY GOD, WHY HAVE YOU FORSAKEN ME?" After another brief pause, he added, "It is with this same power and determination that you must hold on to your koan."

During the sesshin we waited our turn for dokusan in chairs outside the meditation room. As I sat waiting, I was looking at the person sitting in front of me when his head just simply disappeared so I could see right through it. When it was my turn for the interview, I told the roshi about the man whose head had just disappeared. The roshi responded emphatically, "So what?"

"I didn't think of it that way," I said. I got the message—I was here to eliminate my ego, not to inflate it. After that I didn't think it was necessary to tell him about unusual occurrences. For example, I didn't tell him about seeing other students filled with bright shining light during his lectures.

During a break in the schedule, one student was shocked to hear the silence of the house broken by a blood-curdling shriek coming from the upstairs bathroom. He rushed to the bathroom door, flung it open, and asked very excitedly, "What happened?"

"I was stung by a bee," I confessed, standing there rather sheepishly. He looked at me incredulously, perhaps even mockingly, wondering how a simple bee sting could produce a loud piercing scream like the one he had just heard. The bee had been flying at the screen on the bathroom window, trying to get outside. To help him out, I had pried the screen open slightly, but he was reluctant to go through this small opening. Consequently, I gave him a little nudge with my index finger, and that was when he stung me. It actually hadn't occurred to me that he would sting me, and so I screamed more out of surprise than physical pain. But behind that scream was the force of all the other emotions I'd been containing during meditation, so it was a good cathartic release. If I had been holding my koan firmly at the time, perhaps it could have brought on the experience of enlightenment because of the element of surprise. For example, I had heard the story about the monk who fell over backwards, breaking his arm, and in the process of falling he received enlightenment. Another monk dropped a dish, and as it broke on the floor, he was enlightened.

By the last night of the sesshin, I had held Mu as well as I could, but had no enlightenment. There was a full moon that night, which is considered ideal for a sesshin. The roshi told us it is traditional to stay up all night on the last evening of the retreat in order to put forth one final push for enlightenment. I felt my tank was running on empty as I had already given all I could give, so I went to my room to sleep on the floor. After lying down for a few minutes, I felt guilty and then went outside to meditate. The moon was beautiful. It seemed more beautiful to me than usual, because I had never before stopped to appreciate it. I sat on the ground meditating for about a half hour. My heart was not really in to staying up all night. I had already given more than I thought possible. I felt a last ditch effort would be halfhearted and foolhardy, so I went back to the house and went to sleep.

The next morning I went to my last dokusan. The roshi said, "You were very courageous during the retreat. You faced a lot of things. My first sesshin was like that. You are to be commended for your effort and strength." I couldn't believe what he was saying because I was feeling very cowardly. I thought he was reading my mind and just said I was courageous because he was trying to make me feel better about myself. Later, after the final meditation time, I walked into the zendo and looked at the only person in the room, Steve, who was a very strong meditator. He was weeping. When he heard me in the room, he jumped up quickly and turned facing me. Our eyes met, and I could see that he didn't want to be seen crying. He walked out as I went to my place and sat. It was my turn to cry. I still felt very cowardly and inept. I was an unenlightened failure.

The retreat was finished with the last meal. I had eaten very little during the retreat, to help deepen meditation, but during this meal I could eat until I was full. The koan is only given for the time of the sesshin, so I naturally dropped holding onto it. After the meal I stood in the hallway and observed the people. I felt strange without Mu. I felt I didn't know who I was anymore. I didn't seem to be anybody. In a short while this feeling passed.

I went outside and sat next to a student named Ron. He told me, "You were really a strong sitter!" I was surprised at his words, but for the first time I thought, "Maybe I am not a failure after all." Looking back on the retreat now, I am amazed I could have sat in the full lotus all that time. But at the time I was so disappointed I had not been enlightened that all I could see were my shortcomings. I felt my fear, even my fear of enlightenment itself, had prevented enlightenment. I felt this was cowardly of me. It was hard for me to accept any congratulations for what I felt was a failure on my part. Yet before I knew it, I was hugging friends. I gave a friend named Jamie a big hug. As I walked away from him in order to lie down on the lawn, I was wearing no shoes, so Jamie said, "Hey, you have your socks on."

I affirmed joyfully, "We have survived a sesshin! What difference does it make?" We smiled at each other as my socks got dirty in the earth I was walking on.

A short while later, I was in a car with my friends driving back to our house. We stopped, and everyone got out to buy ice cream, in order to indulge in a pleasure that the retreat would not allow. I was, of course, invited to participate in the ice cream indulgence, but right then I realized I wasn't interested in going back to business as usual in my life. It occurred to me that the retreat did not have to end. I decided to pick up Mu again and hold on to it. I held Mu for many days, but in order to do that I found it necessary to maintain silence. I felt I had to pursue Mu on my own and so did not go to the Zen center. I held on to Mu for two weeks after the retreat was over. I had held it very strongly and continuously, but found myself forgetting Mu for as long as five minutes at a time. Finally I conceded to myself that I was losing my intensity of holding Mu, and so I gave it up. Because I had given up my Mu quest, I was extremely disappointed and discouraged, again feeling like a failure.

Right after making this decision and in this state of depression, I walked down to the end of the street right to where the Zen center was located. With the sun shining I sat down on the ground in front of a stone pillar on the corner of the street. My head and gaze were held down, expressing the dejection I felt inside.

I heard footsteps coming from the right. Then the footsteps stopped in front of me. I looked up, and there standing in front of me was a man with an ordinary looking face. He was a stocky man with a ruddy complexion. Because I was wearing an old faded shirt and pants cut off above the knees, I wondered why this neatly and conservatively dressed man had even bothered to stop and look at me. He smiled and asked in a friendly tone, "Would you like to join me on a *memory walk?*"

Although I heard exactly what he said, I inquired, "What did you say?" I asked him this because I had never before heard the term "memory walk," and I wanted him to repeat those words.

He said, "I'm taking a memory walk. Would you like to come with me?"

I didn't say anything. I just smiled as my way of saying, "Yes." I stood up, and my depressed feelings vanished entirely. In fact, I felt remarkably happy. Nevertheless, I was still wondering why this well dressed man in his fifties would come over to a shabbily dressed complete stranger like me and ask me to take a walk with him. He led the way as we walked across the street away from the Zen center. Then he spoke again in his gentle and pleasant voice, "I used to live in this area, and I have come back for a visit. I am going to stop at this church. Would you like to come with me?"

I said, "Sure." I had never really even noticed that there was a church there at the corner, right across the street from the Zen center, but I did remember having heard the church bell and having enjoyed its sound. The man led the way as we went into the church through a side door and into a small room. Next we went through another door and into the main area of the church. We were at the front of the church, over to one side. We didn't speak. I followed the man as he walked to the center. We stood together in the middle aisle facing the altar, although I had not looked at it yet.

Instead, I was looking to my left at the peaceful face of the man who had brought me here. He raised his arm, and I followed his gesture with my eyes. I saw that he was pointing to the large white marble cross over the altar. Just as my eyes fell upon the cross, I fell over backwards onto the floor. I had been standing solidly with both feet on the floor when I felt some unseen force come over me and drop me to the floor. However, the unexpected fall was neither frightening nor traumatic. In fact, it was not even an ordinary fall under the law of gravity because the body quite literally *floated* down in slow motion. It felt strange to feel my body slowly descend backwards and land on the floor like a feather gently coming to rest. Consequently, there was no need to break my fall with my hands, and I was not hurt in the slightest way but was thoroughly surprised.

While still lying on the floor, I turned away from the cross and looked back at the man, who remained standing with his arm still pointed to the cross. Although I had fallen backwards right in front of him, he had not the slightest expression of surprise on his face. He lowered his arm, and his face remained perfectly at peace. After looking up at the cross one more time, I stood up. The man walked back the way we had come, and I followed him. When we returned to the small room that led outside, he turned around to face me before leaving the church. He said calmly, "I must go now."

I knew that if he had wanted me to go with him, he wouldn't have turned around and made this statement, letting me know that I had to stay and that he had to go. "Can I ask you something?" I inquired.

"Go right ahead," he said reassuringly.

"Can I hug you?"

He smiled and said lovingly, "That won't be necessary. We can shake hands." Perhaps he understood that my request was made out of a combination of my love on the one hand and my inappropriate attachment on the other hand, so shaking hands would be more appropriate than a hug. I extended my hand to him. He shook my hand and placed his left hand on top of my right hand for emphasis. Then he went out the door, and I returned to the sanctuary.

I walked around the church looking at the lovely stained glass windows. Finding a spot way in the back, I knelt on the floor. Unexpectedly I was overcome with tears, but didn't know why I was crying. With my legs tucked underneath my body, I rolled up into a ball on the floor and placed my hands over my face. I felt a sudden wave of energy jolt through my body. I lost control of my bladder function, causing me to urinate in my pants.

After a while I got up and walked around the church again and felt filled with an overpowering feeling of love. Also I felt I had some kind of connection to Jesus in a past life. Everything looked exceedingly beautiful, and my heart was filled with joy. I walked out of the church and sat on the green grass right outside. As I gazed peacefully at everything around me, the intense feelings of love and joy continued undiminished. Well, Allan, there it is. That's my story of how I went from Zen to Jesus.

"I have just one question," Allan said. "Who do you think that man was who asked you to take a memory walk?"

"Just like I told you that the snake I saw was no ordinary snake, that man was no ordinary man. When I was lying on my back on the floor of the church after falling and when I looked up and saw his serene face, I knew he was not of this world. Was he an angel? Yes, I believe he was. Certainly he was a messenger of love because that was the effect of his visit on me. There is an epilogue to this story, and if we meet again, I will tell it to you. We haven't seen each other for a long time so I wanted to get an update from you on that past life I think we had together. Have you had any new insights about a possible past life we had together?"

"No change in status. I won't say we weren't together in a past life, but I can't confirm it either. If I learn something new, I'll let you know," Allan said without any defensiveness.

"You said Jesus is becoming more important to you. How so?" I asked.

Allan said, "As I have been studying the Course, I am realizing that this is really Jesus speaking to me through the pages of this book. As a result I am thinking of Him more as my personal teacher."

"I guess, as you said, we are becoming more like each other, with me accepting the Course and you accepting Jesus." When I said goodbye, I figured we might not see each other again, but perhaps it didn't matter. Maybe there were no more past life issues to resolve between Allan and me. After all, we were friends now.

A beneficial aftermath of my talk with Allan was that it brought my awareness back to my shadow puzzle, which I had put on the back burner of my mind. I realized that the experience of my memory walk with the stranger was especially important in relation to the hidden parts of my mind. The obvious connection with my subconscious mind was that back then was the first time I understood that I had some significant relationship with Jesus. However, the new element that I uncovered was that the incident of safely falling in the church now seemed like a symbolic healing of the traumatic experiences of falling in my past lives as the Pole Man and Spider Boy.

49

BACK TO SEDONA

~ ○ ~

While I was in Virginia Beach, I was able to visit with Chester, Stuart, and Dylan, who was now separated from Rose. Most of all I appreciated spending time with Rose, who had been a source of encouragement and support through telephone contact even while I was living in the desert. On my return trip to Sedona I stopped to see David's brother, Walter, and his family in North Carolina. What stands out about that visit was talking with their young daughter, Rosaline, who said she had been visited several times by a "light being" who came to her in her room and was her friend. Her descriptions were so vivid that her parents and I felt that she had really been visited by a guardian angel.

I stopped again to visit my sister Lillian in Texas, and she showed me an article about a miracle that had occurred the year before in Lubbock, in the northern part of that state. I stopped there on August 15, 1989, the first anniversary of the miracle and saw a large gathering of people at St. John Neumann Church. I was particularly interested in the miraculous events of August 15, 1988, which occurred after the 6 PM start of an outdoor mass— the exact same time and date of our community meeting in which we adopted the name of the New Jerusalem Community.

The church pastor, John James, had visited Medjugorje, where visions of Mother Mary had been experienced regularly since 1981. I have heard about a husband and wife, Susan and Milt Sanderford, who visited Medjugorje and cried out in prayer, "But Mary, we're not even Catholic!" Mother Mary responded, "So? Neither am I!" Having been inspired by Her universal message of love and peace, John James in the early part of 1988 set aside special time for prayer and fasting in Her honor. Then he started a small prayer group of six members devoted to God through prayer to Mother Mary. In this prayer group, Mary Constancio, then later Mike Slate and Teresa Warner, heard Her speak to them with an inner voice. A beautiful fragrance of roses could be smelled in the chapel where their prayer group prayed, even when there were no flowers present. Through these visionaries the word spread that a special blessing would occur on

August 15, the feast of the Assumption. Between 13 and 15 thousand people showed up for the outdoor mass held on that day.

The night before, on August 14, the vigil of the Assumption, thirty people were present and saw a formation they called a "dove of light." This flying formation of lights flew once across the sky and then changed direction and flew straight up, disappearing into the sky. Reportedly this same phenomenon had occurred in Medjugorje. On the day of the Assumption it rained in the afternoon, but cleared up by 6 PM, the starting time of the outdoor mass. Shortly thereafter the sun broke through the clouds, and many people saw spiritual images, yet not everyone saw the same images. One person said he saw Jesus with a crown as King of the universe, while another saw Him with a crown of thorns and closing His eyes as He died. Others saw Mother Mary in the clouds holding baby Jesus in Her arms or saw Her face in the center of the sun. One lady brought a silver crucifix on a rosary, and the figure of Jesus on the cross changed to gold.

On that day these believers universally agreed that the sun was acting oddly. Many saw it spinning in a circle and sending out many colors. Some even said they saw the sun "dancing," moving in the sky. A wave of golden color covered the whole crowd at one time, and later a wave of blue covered everyone. When I visited, I asked many people to tell me their stories of what they had experienced the year before, and they each had a different experience. Many just felt a deep inner peace. The profound and dramatic experiences of the year before didn't happen again during my visit. Nevertheless, when I looked at the sun, it appeared to be spinning clockwise, and others there with me saw this too. I have tried to look at the sun since then and have not been able to duplicate what I saw that day.

After leaving Texas I went to a hot springs north of Santa Fe, New Mexico in the town of Ojo Caliente and then visited a very small church in Chimayo. The church was very modestly decorated. A caretaker there let me know why this church was so remarkable. He showed me a very large storage area full of crutches. He said these were left behind by people who had come to this place for healing and discovered they no longer needed them.

I also visited a church in Santa Fe, New Mexico, the Loretto Chapel. Originally called the Our Lady of Light Church, the chapel was built in 1878, but the designers neglected to include a means of ascending the twenty-two feet leading to the choir loft. Seeking a heavenly remedy to their earthly problem, the Sisters of Loretto decided to make a nine-day prayer, called a novena, and dedicated it to the patron saint of carpenters, St. Joseph. On the last day of their novena a gray-haired man on a donkey

"MIRACULOUS STAIRCASE" AT THE LORETTO CHAPEL

showed up and offered to build them a staircase. He built the spiral staircase with two 360 degree turns, and he used only wooden pegs instead of nails. His tools were just a hammer, a T-square, and a saw. The carpenter was observed placing pieces of wood in large tubs of hot water, presumably used to curve the wood, yet the type of wood used is mysterious in that it cannot be definitively identified. As I looked at this feat of carpentry excellence, I could see why it's sometimes called the "miraculous staircase." I wondered how it could have been made, marveling at the fact that it has *no visible means of structural support.* When the carpenter had completed his project, he disappeared before he could be paid or even receive thanks. To this day, many, including myself, believe the extraordinary carpenter was an angel or perhaps even St. Joseph himself.

When I arrived back at the trailer in Sedona, it was nighttime. The Sunfellow girls were fast asleep in the room that had been mine. When I had left Sedona for my trip, David and Pamela had cautioned me that there might not be a place for me when I returned, and on my first day back we sat down together to discuss the living situation. Pamela began the meeting by saying, "That room that was yours, Don, is now the girl's room, period! As far as I am concerned there is nothing more to discuss!" David agreed that it probably would be best for the girls to have my room, but he didn't agree with the way Pamela had expressed herself. He regretted her lack of flexibility and unwillingness to participate in a discussion in which we could make a group decision, as we had done throughout the past two years together.

I realized that Pamela was acting like a mother bear protecting the needs of her cubs. However, I would have appreciated a meeting in which I could have the opportunity to hear David and Pamela's concerns. Then we could have prayed together to ask for divine guidance. I am sure I would have moved out anyway, but it would have been done much more gracefully as an affirmation of our love for each other. I was allowed to pitch a tent outside and after several months moved into a one-room garage apartment in the western part of Sedona.

A lot of changes were happening in our community. The long awaited move of the Anaheim Half began with Sarah and Barry relocating to Sedona. We also had "associate" members—people interested in the community but not yet members. One associate member was Ken, who had lived with the Anaheim Half. He moved to Sedona and later became a community member. Another associate member was Mark, who had made the cross country bike ride with Barry, and he too moved to Sedona.

Later when Robert, Wendy, and Tom finally moved to Sedona, they rented a large house together, and both Ken and I accepted their invitation to live with them. Fortunately, Sarah, Barry, and Mark lived right next door in another large house, and David and Pamela were only a five-minute walk away. In this country setting near the state park at Red Rock Crossing, we were all finally together as planned, five years after we first got together in Anaheim. You might think that we would be one big happy family, but the following community meeting entry from September of 1990 tells a different story:

> We decided to admit that our lives and our community as a whole are unmanageable; that we want to let go of the destructive patterns that are causing this condition and surrender our lives and our community to God and Jesus, Who alone have the power to restore us to sanity. This means a suspension of all community business (except, of course, the absolutely necessary business of the "wifey" coop committee, without which we would all be sunk); this means a period of emptiness in which we reflect on our blocks and call on God and Jesus to deliver us from ourselves....

We kept the name of the New Jerusalem Community, but everything else was thrown out. Our weekly business meetings had become rather contentious rehashings of old unresolved issues that were sucking the vitality out of the community. With these meetings discarded, we could focus on learning the most important lesson before us, which was how to lovingly relate to each other as friends. Robert and David, who had taken opposite positions on many topics, became much closer friends. Overall, a deeper appreciation of acceptance and love began to manifest throughout the community, and by October of 1991 we had come together again enough to resume community meetings. We were even able to actually put out our first newsletter, *New Jerusalem News*, which contained our ideals and history, as well as individual statements from community members.

In this initial newsletter we each had an opportunity to put down in writing our individual thoughts on the community and our roles in it. In the past I had felt that the community had not been accepting of my role as a monk since most members were married, so I decided to write about my experiences related to being called to be a monk in the world. I visited David when he happened to be alone at his house and showed him my first draft. He said, "This is supposed to be about the community, but you are making this about yourself."

There was truth in what he said since the pride of my ego was evident both in my writing and in my view of my role as a monk. However, there was also a pure desire for God that was present in me and in my role as a monk. My experience of David was that he was very quick to notice and point out the ego portions in me while overlooking the good. I said, "It is my understanding that our individual statements are supposed to be about our perceptions of the community, and this writing of mine does relate to my role in the community."

David said again, "It's supposed to be about the community, not about your experiences."

Feeling judged again, as I had so many times in the past, I confronted David. "Maybe this has too much of my ego in it, but the impression I get of you is that you are sitting in judgment of me and my ego. I just want to be accepted. I just want to be loved." I had made this plea many times to David and to other community members. I felt there had to be a way for us to learn to accept each other without making the other person's ego become the most important thing about them.

David responded by saying, "You have to *earn* my love first."

"FUCK YOU!" I became completely overcome with rage and shouted with all my might, "FUCK YOU! I HAVE TO EARN YOUR LOVE? FUCK YOU!" After all the years we had been together, including the two years in the desert, David was telling me I had to *earn* his love. "FUCK YOU! FUCK YOU! FUCK YOU!"

I was standing in the doorway to his room, and he was sitting with a look of shocked disbelief. We had in the past had countless disputes, which at times ended with me in tears, but we had always managed to speak in a civilized manner to each other. I had never heard a curse coming from him, and likewise he had never heard me curse either. Of course, a physical confrontation was out of the question. I am sure David had no idea that what he had said would trigger this kind of intensely angry response from me. After a few more curses, I stormed off, leaving him to ponder the situation. My response was about me for years wanting him to accept and love me and always being disappointed. His comment made me feel that he would never love me, because he didn't know what love was if he thought that love needed to be earned. Earned love is not love; it is a bargain between egos.

After I got back to my house, I calmed down, and a short while later David knocked at my door. I was no longer caught up in my anger, and we talked. David said, "I apologize. I should not have said that you have to 'earn' my love." I thought it was very gracious of David to extend himself to me in this way. After all, I was the aggressor in our dispute. But looking at him I could see from his face and expression that he had come because he had never seen such extreme emotions expressed through me. Thus he wanted to make sure I had not gone completely off the deep end. I reassured him that it was nothing more than a temporary emotional storm, which had now calmed down. I told him, "I apologize for the degree of anger I expressed. In the time we spent camping there were a lot of pent up emotions that never got expressed. So my outburst was a backlog from the past. I also apologize for swearing. I feel embarrassed about cursing because that is not an acceptable way for me to express myself."

This experience caused me to reevaluate myself. I realized that I still had my dysfunctional trading stamp mentality. The Greek word *logizesthai* is an accountant's term for recording an item in a ledger, but it also means the keeping of an account of the slights and offenses of others. In regard to David I had been keeping an account of trading stamps for a long time, always cashing in my stamp books as a justification for a rare public or occasional private weeping display. This was the first time I cashed in a stamp book for an angry public tantrum. In the instant of my outburst, I felt fully justified. A part of me felt it was good for David to see that I could actually get angry, since he had never seen me lose my temper before. However, I quickly realized that my anger only gave me a temporary illusion of power, and left the guilt of attacking a brother in its wake.

I had not yet learned how to apply my understanding of the Course to prevent collecting and cashing in trading stamps, but I was able to recover speedily and reestablish a loving state of mind, focused not only on forgiveness of David, but forgiveness of myself. I had to admit to myself, and later to David as well, that he was actually right after all about needing to make my statement in the newsletter more about the community and less about me. I wrote a new newsletter statement in which I described the community as my "spiritual family." As with any family we have fights (like the one with David), but then we learn how to forgive each other and thus manifest love. In this family I saw Jesus and Mary as our parents leading us to an awareness of how to forgive and find oneness with God.

In addition, I reexamined my neediness in regard to desiring others to accept and love me. I realized I had not been following the example of Jesus in this regard. Jesus focused on accepting and loving others, regardless of whether he was accepted and loved in return. I understood I was mistakenly thinking of love as a bargain and my angry display expressed that I felt David was not living up to his end. In my outburst I had projected onto him my own fault of making love a bargain. This was an emotional turning point for me in which I learned to focus more on giving acceptance and love than getting it. Ironically, as I switched to this giving perspective, I automatically felt inwardly more accepted and loved. The biggest positive outcome of this whole experience was that I finally felt freed from the inappropriate need for approval from David. In all of my ongoing relationships I still had to deal with issues of rejection, judgment by others, and wanting acceptance and love from others. However, I felt I was making noticeable progress in these areas, especially with the help of insights provided by the Course.

On the job front I mailed in an application for a position at a local home for disturbed boys. I asked in prayer to be guided by the Holy Spirit, and specifically to be shown if this new job was right for me. Guidance comes in many forms, sometimes in ways least expected. Immediately after my job interview, I walked to my car and discovered the answer to my prayer in the form of two car tires that had been slashed. This rude awakening redirected me to return to work at the Montessori school. This time I worked with a different teacher and in a class with only one hyperactive student, making my job much less challenging.

Next I got a job in Cottonwood as a case aid at a private agency that was contracted to provide social services through state and federal funds. In this job I met with needy people and was able to provide short-term assistance. One client that stands out in my mind was a man who had a serious stomach problem because a malicious person he knew had given him a drink with sulfuric acid in it. The limited assistance I could provide included gasoline vouchers, rental assistance, and utility assistance. I could inwardly empathize with my clients because of having been in such a needy position myself living in the Sedona desert, but I didn't tell anyone about my recent past.

My supervisor, Florence, was upset about our office director, Ted. She said he at times had alcohol on his breath and exhibited poor judgment. She expressed her concerns to Ted's supervisor, Jerome, stationed at the Prescott office. However, her complaints fell on deaf ears because Ted and Jerome were best of friends. Finally in protest Florence resigned, and I took over her duties until a new person could be hired. Ted invited me into his office and asked, "Would you like to be hired for the case manager position that we have open now?"

I responded, "Yes, I am already doing the job now and would like to continue."

"I am going to hire you. Congratulations, I am sure you will do a good job," Ted said as we shook hands.

Two days later Ted invited me into his office and inquired, "Do you have any interest in applying for the case manager opening?"

I answered, "Two days ago we talked about this. You said you were going to hire me for the case manager position. Has something changed since we talked then?"

Ted said, "You are mistaken. This is the first time we have talked about the case manager opening."

"You are joking, aren't you? You invited me into your office two days ago. You offered me this job, and I accepted. We even shook hands when you congratulated me on having the job," I asserted.

"I do not know what you are talking about. I never offered you the position, but you can put in an application for the position if you want to apply," Ted said in an unemotional monotone.

I stared at him in stunned disbelief. I could hardly believe that he could look me in the eye and speak with so little regard for the truth. I was more confused than angry. With all the self-control I could muster, I withstood the temptation to call him a liar. Without saying another word I turned around and walked out of his office. Later I called Florence at her home and asked her why Ted hired me and then disavowed having hired me. She explained, "Ted probably called his boss, Jerome, in Prescott and told him that he had hired you. Then Jerome told Ted that since I had trained you, I probably had also told you all my complaints about Ted. Consequently, Jerome told Ted not to hire you since he considered you to be 'tainted' by your association with me."

Prior to this event I had not had any problems with Ted. I was well aware of Florence's concerns about him, but had decided to reserve judgment. However, after my own firsthand interaction in which he showed no integrity, I resigned, giving two weeks' notice. I was able to successfully overcome my tendency to think of myself as a victim and instead felt that this vocational door was closing because a new, as yet unseen door was about to open. While waiting for that employment door to open, I maintained a positive attitude. Through prayer I was able to come to a place of forgiveness for Ted. This forgiveness was not as much for Ted's benefit as it was for my own well-being. Forgiveness kept my mind open to the divine influence, and I realized that being at peace about my former job would help to prepare me to be receptive to future opportunities.

50

FAILURE AND SUCCESS
IN SOCIAL WORK

≈ ○ ≈

During the mornings I did my daily meditation, yoga postures, a deep relaxation, and breathing practices, as I had for years. Whenever possible, I would lie down next to a window in a sunny area for the practice of deep relaxation. I felt a very short time in the sun was important for good health. (Recent research has confirmed that vitamin D, which can be derived from sunlight, is much more important for health than previously thought.)

While practicing these morning disciplines one day, I received a phone call from someone I had never met. Her name was Rhonda, and she was a case manager for the state of Arizona in the Division of Developmental Disabilities. She explained that she had received my application, which I had submitted for a state job as a social worker. One of her questions was, "Where are you coming from?"

"From Virginia Beach, Virginia," I answered.

"Wow, that's going to be a long commute for you!" she responded lightheartedly, which was refreshing, coming from a professional person. When I later went in for a job interview, I wore a suit and tie but took off the coat when I saw everyone casually dressed. After the interview, I said, "Let me see if I can remember everyone's name," and then proceeded to name each of the seven interviewers. I was told later that one of the reasons I was hired was that the interviewers were impressed by my memory. In my new state job I served developmentally disabled clients diagnosed with cerebral palsy, epilepsy, mental retardation, or autism. I also served children under the age of six at risk of developmental delay.

Being grateful for this opportunity, I made every effort to be a perfect case manager and was once recognized with an award for being the "Case Manager of the Year" for all of Arizona. But perfection at the form level isn't possible, and the pursuit of perfection is not desirable if it means becoming burned out. After several years I learned to tone down my intensity and striving for perfection, which allowed me to feel more at ease in my job.

During the first few years, there was one major problem that was a concern for everyone in our office. Morris, our Area Program Manager and my supervisor's supervisor, was very critical and demanding. For example, he once wrote up a complaint report on my supervisor, Charlie, for having twenty-five cents extra postage on an item he was mailing out. Thus Charlie was afraid of Morris, and everyone in our office had experienced an unpleasant run in with him, except me, the new guy.

Morris's function was to be a financial gatekeeper, but at times he seemed to be more concerned about pinching pennies than providing needed services for our clients. Without consulting our Cottonwood office, Morris unilaterally decided for financial reasons to eliminate the Growth Group Program that had been serving our youngest children. I was asked to be the sacrificial lamb to bring our discontent with the decision to Morris' attention. At our next large office meeting, Charlie, our supervisor, was supposed to attend, but he intentionally did not even show up because he didn't want to be there when the fireworks went off. I sat next to my coworker, Bennett, who was writing "blah, blah, blah" to jokingly record the words of Morris as he talked on endlessly. He was speaking in a condescending tone that didn't invite input from us. Then Morris finally said the magic words, "Growth Group Program." I spoke up, "Morris, I have been asked by my coworkers to tell you that we collectively are upset that you made the decision to terminate the Growth Group."

"It's my call to make these decisions, as the Area Program Manager," Morris replied. Having a cerebral approach to discussions, he never showed any emotion and took obvious pride in being unflappable in any situation.

I said, "We understand that you have the right to make the decision. But we would like you to seek our input and suggestions as part of your decision-making process. We feel you take an authoritarian approach...."

Morris interrupted me, "I had the right to make this decision the way that I made it, and you will just have to live with it."

"As I was saying, we don't appreciate your authoritarian approach," I said with a mildly angry tone. I was very careful to express my anger in a controlled way, without raising my voice. I continued in a low, angry tone, "The Growth Group was helping a lot of our children and their families. There are two kinds of systems. There is the closed system that makes all the decisions from the top down. There is the open system that draws upon the input of all the workers in the decision-making process." As I was talking with my controlled anger, Morris's normally expressionless face for the first time was actually turning redder and redder. "You are running a closed system, and we don't like it. We don't think your decision about the Growth Group is in the best interests of our clients. We...."

I was interrupted as Morris's red face finally exploded, "YOU AND ME, OUTSIDE!" This was the first time I had even heard Morris raise his voice at all, but he was bellowing extremely loudly and had completely lost his composure. As he stood up, he swung his arm and knocked a stack of books from the table onto the lap of our family support provider, Emily. He was so angry and animated that everyone in the room got up and practically ran out of the room. Most people thought that when he had screamed "You and me, outside!" he was challenging me to a fist fight outside. However, he was really only wanting to talk to me alone. By the time I stood up, relatively calmly, the stampede to get out of the room was over. All the people who had encouraged me to speak up for them were gone. Morris and I walked to my office.

As I looked at Morris in my office, I could see that he had regained his composure. Nevertheless, he was embarrassed that he had so completely lost control of his emotions and created a spectacle of himself in front of the group. We calmly discussed the Growth Group decision, and I expressed a laundry list of concerns that the other staff members had expressed to me and that I thought he should have been aware of before he made his decision. I apologized to him for having presented the matter in such a confrontational manner. He said that he had heard our concerns now and that he could write up a complaint report about my challenging him. However, he decided to forgive and forget—saying that he would never mention this event again. But the real reason why he didn't want to write up a complaint report was that it would highlight his own shortcomings, revealing that in front of the whole staff his unflappable mask had fallen off in a whirlwind of uncontrollable anger.

He promised that he would not bring this issue up to his boss, our District Program Manager. I found out later that he went back on his word and did give his version of the story to his boss, probably exaggerating my emotions and downplaying his own. Although I had not lost control of my anger as Morris had, I had expressed a controlled anger and did not feel justified in doing so. I realized that I had butted heads with Morris because we both had a prideful streak, but it was just that his arrogance was more outwardly evident than my own. I felt I had a lot to learn about how to love others, especially those who displayed unpleasant masks. I did at least theoretically believe in the spiritual principles of the Course, but was having a difficult time putting them into practice in the everyday events of life.

After the altercation, Morris put his unflappable mask back on, but we perceived him as weaker and less intimidating than before. I made a point of praying for him and reminding myself to see him as a child of God, rather than getting caught up in the mask that he presented. For Morris, the long-term upshot of the altercation was that within a year he decided he was not really suited for his supervisory position. He quit his state job and went back to college to become an accountant, which meant he could focus on predictable numbers rather than unpredictable people.

From the incident with Morris I learned that those who stand up to be counted in a large organization are the first to be cut down to size. In my teenage years my brother Paul told me his means of functioning in the large organization of the army. When the sergeant wanted a hard job to be done, he would always choose someone whose name he knew. Paul's strategy was therefore to be anonymous—to fade into the background as much as possible. This was no lofty philosophy, but it sounded reasonably practical. I would try to take a back seat in relation to my supervisors, while still serving my clients to the best of my ability. My supervisor, Charlie, was stationed in our Prescott office and only came to our Cottonwood office once a week. Consequently, we had the freedom to run our office as we saw fit without someone constantly looking over our shoulders, and Charlie liked our self-sufficiency because it meant much less work for him.

When Morris left, Charlie was promoted to become the Area Program Manager. At a much later date we were at a staff training one day when Charlie said, "I have been holding something against you for the past few years, and I want to get it off my chest. Remember that conversation we had two years ago when we were driving to Phoenix together? You told me about *A Course in Miracles*. Do you remember?"

"Sure, I remember." He and I were driving a teenage female client to a new group home in Phoenix. This developmentally disabled client had sexually abused two children and was so emotionally unstable that I didn't want to make this trip without assistance. Charlie had kindly volunteered to go with me. After we had helped the client get settled into her new home, Charlie had told me on the return trip that he was a Christian. He asked me about my religious beliefs, so I told him about the Course. "What was it about our conversation that bothered you?" I asked him.

"You said that this world is a dream. I was really angry at you about that, and I have held that against you all this time. So I apologize for that."

"I had no idea that you were upset with me," I said with a surprised expression. I liked Charlie and thought the feeling was mutual. Charlie gave everyone at our office the impression that he was a free spirit. It would not be unusual for him to show up at our office wearing a colorful Hawaiian shirt and sandals. He made no secret of the fact that he was a product of the pot smoking and free love hippie movement of the 60s. Also he was an accomplished musician with a local band. His nontraditional demeanor made me feel he would be open-minded, so I had felt comfortable talking to him about some of the unusual ideas expressed in the Course. I told him, "I certainly accept your apology, but I don't understand why my thought that the world is a dream would make you upset. Of course, people have different philosophies. I wouldn't be upset about any philosophy that you or anyone else might have. Wait a minute, that's not quite true. Once I worked as a recreation therapist in a psychiatric facility and had a talk with a teenage patient there. He told me that he admired Hitler's philosophy because he took what he wanted, proving that will power is the only important thing in life. I took exception to this philosophy, but since he was a mental patient I felt compassion for him rather than being angry. I don't understand why you would be angry at me because I believe the world is a dream, since most of the Eastern philosophies believe the world is a dream. It's just a philosophy. Why would you take it so personally?"

"By saying the world is a dream, I felt you were saying that my life is meaningless since I think of dreams as being meaningless," Charlie replied.

"I apologize to you for leaving that impression with you. If you had challenged me about this, I could have told you that I was not saying that your life is meaningless. Nevertheless, I can tell you now that I absolutely believe you are meaningful and your life is meaningful. Do you mind if I talk to you about the Course now to explain why I feel that way?"

"Go right ahead," he said.

"I still believe the world is a dream, but you are meaningful because God created you as part of Himself and so God has given you your meaning that can never be taken away. The dream nature of the world doesn't take away your meaning that God gave you, and it cannot take away your reality. Plus, what you have done with your life in this dream is meaningful because you have devoted your life to serving developmentally disabled clients. Service is an expression of love. God is also Love. There is a Course quote that says only our '...loving thoughts ... are the world's reality.'[1] Whenever we express love in the world, we give this world all the reality that it has. The Course also says that '...everything that comes from love is a miracle.'[2] Our interactions in our work with our clients and families are 'expressions of love'[3] that the Course calls miracles. These miracles bring reality to our dream world. It's OK with me if you think my belief that the world is a dream is a ridiculous idea. But I want you to be reassured that I certainly respect you and feel your life is very meaningful."

"Thanks for clarifying that," Charlie said. "So you think the world is a dream, and I think it's real. That's no reason for me to be upset with you. I felt I needed to talk to you about this because I have been unfair to you to hold my feelings against you. Now I think I can let go of my hard feelings."

I said, "Well, good! I'm glad you got that off your chest." There was more to our conversation, though, than was actually said. Prior to our trip to Phoenix, Charlie had given me the very clear impression that he would hire me as the new supervisor if he ever got promoted. Without saying so aloud, he was also asking me to forgive him for not promoting me. If he had offered me the vacant position, I would have accepted it. But in the intervening two years the supervisor job had gotten so much harder to perform that I was actually glad that I hadn't been promoted. I just didn't want the headaches that would have come with the position. I realized that I was ideally suited for my own job and was not well suited to the office politics that were required of a supervisor.

The other thing that was not talked about directly was that Charlie's objection was not just about the dream nature of the world. His problem was really about his ego being threatened. It's the same reason why most people have difficulty with the Course since it is not just a philosophy but also a form of psychotherapy that directly confronts the ego by saying that it is unreal. It shouldn't be surprising then that individual egos encountering the Course feel threatened because the very existence of the ego is called to question. I could truly tell Charlie that he is meaningful, but I thought it would be inflammatory rather than helpful to tell him that *his ego is meaningless*, even though his reality in God is not.

From Charlie's admission I learned to be careful about who I shared the Course with and how I expressed myself. This was necessary because the Course's bluntness about the ego can be threatening to anyone who believes he *is* an ego, meaning that he believes he is a separate body and a separate mind, unconnected with others and unconnected with God. Since God is unlimited, accepting the reality of our oneness with God means expanding our awareness beyond the littleness offered by the ego. However, Charlie was invested in his ego and that is an investment in the littleness of this dream world. Right after my revealing conversation with Charlie, I happened to come across the Course description below, which explains why it's important to question the belief in littleness and why the ego's thoughts are unreal and meaningless. This quotation says that we cannot effectively question or evaluate our own ego's thought system because we perceive ourselves to be inside that thought system. However, we can call upon the judgment of the Holy Spirit to help us with a perspective that is outside of the ego's influence:

> Lack of knowledge of any kind is always associated with unwill-ingness to know, and this produces a total lack of knowledge simply because knowledge is total. Not to question your littleness therefore is to deny all knowledge, and keep the ego's whole thought system intact. You cannot retain part of a thought system, because it can be questioned only at its foundation. [The ego itself is this foundation.] And this must be questioned from beyond it, because within it its foundation does stand. The Holy Spirit judges against the reality of

the ego's thought system merely because He knows its foundation is not true. Therefore, nothing that arises from it means anything. He judges every belief you hold in terms of where it comes from. If it comes from God, He knows it be true. If it does not, He knows that it is meaningless.

Whenever you question your value, say:

"God Himself is incomplete without me."[4]

In the above quotation the Course uses the term *knowledge* to mean the full awareness of our oneness with God, which we will regain when we wake up to our true spiritual nature. This "knowledge is total,"[5] meaning it is complete awareness of reality, in contrast to the partial awareness of perception that we have now in our ego condition. But even in the partial awareness of our ego condition in this dream world, we can still have our perceptions come from God or come from the ego. I told Charlie that our loving thoughts are meaningful and real because these thoughts come from God and are called *true perceptions*. Unloving thoughts come from the ego and are called *false perceptions*. These false thoughts that come from the ego speak of our littleness, telling us that we are separate from God.

Attachment to the littleness of the ego is a stumbling block to accepting your true oneness with God. If you live a full lifetime, I believe you will be touched by the Spirit at least one time so that you will experience to a lesser or greater degree your true oneness with God in you. Having been touched by the Spirit, it is easy for the ego to later reassert its influence to tell you that the sense of freedom and expansiveness you experienced was a mirage. The ego will tell you that you are arrogant to accept your oneness with God and your safety is in the familiarity of littleness. Nevertheless, the experience of oneness cannot be easily or entirely erased from the mind. If you have already experienced oneness, no further explanation is needed. If you have not yet experienced oneness and if you can keep an open mind, you can look forward to your future appointment with destiny. Like so many other seekers, I too had experienced oneness with God in me. However, I was also not immune to the familiarity of littleness. Holding on to the belief in littleness was the underlying cause of my struggles with victim consciousness, although the Course would remind me that my attachment to littleness was an illusion that I could learn to set aside.

As a social worker there were times when I found it very difficult to not be taken in by the illusions of littleness that were presented to me. In fact, some situations were so filled with the illusions of darkness that it was hard to see the slightest glimmer of light. But even in these situations I sought to find a silver lining to give meaning to what appeared meaningless. In my state job there was one case that stands out as the most challenging and disappointing because of its apparent meaninglessness. Nelly Aikens was a two-year-old child who had undergone surgery for a heart defect, and she was at risk of developmental delay. Her parents, Rachel and Buck, were only eighteen years old, and they had two other children in addition to Nelly, both of them healthy. We had arranged for therapy and assigned our community nurse, Cynthia, to monitor Nelly's health. The physician had ordered regular formula feeding designed for nourishment and for her to gain weight, yet she wasn't gaining weight. Nelly could potentially die from being unable to receive the nourishment she needed.[6] The parents had been given a set number of feeding bottles and specific instructions on when to feed her. When Cynthia counted the bottles, however, she was able to easily see that the parents were not in fact giving Nelly the bottles according to her scheduled feedings. There were also concerns about possible drug use by the parents. After the parents had received repeated warnings regarding their feeding responsibilities, I reported the case to Child Protective Services and requested an investigation.

I wanted the children to be taken out of the home by Child Protective Services, but they didn't want to rely on Cynthia's word and insisted on Nelly being examined by a doctor. On Friday, Owen, the Child Protective Services worker, and I went to the home. We took Nelly with her mother, Rachel, to the doctor for a physical examination. The doctor told us that the child wasn't being fed by the parents as directed, and he wrote a statement that Nelly was in danger of dying due to parental neglect in feeding.

After this meeting, Child Protective Services insisted that the doctor write that Nelly was in "imminent" danger. I contacted the doctor again, and he refused to write the word "imminent." His reason was that the danger involved is really a slow starvation, which could result in death after one day, one week, or one month. I had scheduled a meeting with Owen and his supervisor, Sharon. She, however, took off, leaving a message that Child Protective Services refused to take custody because the doctor didn't use the word "imminent." Sitting in Owen's office, I was fuming mad, barely resisting the temptation to act unprofessionally by erupting into a verbal tirade. Instead, I asked as calmly as I could, "How much does this decision have to do with the fact that it is 4:30 on a Friday afternoon, and you don't have a provider readily available to take the child?"

"You are right. We don't have a provider, but that had nothing to do with the decision," Owen said unconvincingly. "All I can do is what my supervisor Sharon told me. If you have a beef with this, you can take it up with her on Monday."

"You mean the supervisor scheduled to meet with me now but who abandoned ship to get a head start on the weekend?" I asked rhetorically. I walked out without waiting for an answer that I knew could not justify what I considered gross incompetence.

Another reason I had reported the case to the Child Protective Services was that Rachel had repeatedly failed to take Nelly to her medical appointments. But because of our investigation on Friday, Rachel took Nelly to her appointment on Saturday in Flagstaff with her cardiologist. Rachel gave the social worker and doctor in Flagstaff a sob story about how she was being unfairly investigated by the state. She succeeded in getting the cardiologist to write a letter saying that Nelly's problems were not due to the parents neglecting to feed her, which that doctor was in no position to determine. When I contacted Owen on Monday, he told me they now had two different doctors with two conflicting opinions, so Child Protective Services would definitely not do anything to take custody of the child.

Exactly two weeks later our physical therapist arrived at Nelly's home at 11 AM and discovered that both parents were still asleep. They perhaps had been using drugs the night before, sleeping it off into the late morning. The therapist went to Nelly's room and was horrified to discover that she had turned blue and wasn't breathing. An emergency 911 call was made. Nonetheless, Nelly could not be revived. The parents obviously had not even checked on her until our therapist arrived, which also meant they could not have been giving her the scheduled morning feedings.

So what was the point of Nelly's short life and death here on earth? Other very responsible parents of developmentally disabled children had told me how blessed they were to have their son or daughter in their lives, even if that child lived only a short time. They felt that their children, often needing constant medical care, had been their teachers. Some parents who were metaphysically oriented said they thought that their children had intentionally chosen to come into the earth precisely because their dependency would draw out the best in those around them, inspiring them to manifest love and service. But if that was true, what was I to make of this situation which seemed to bring out the worst in others? At first I could see only darkness and meaninglessness.

I was disgusted at how Owen and his supervisor Sharon immediately washed their hands of any responsibility for the situation and were both subsequently moved up the Child Protective Services promotional ladder. I went to the funeral and saw the tears of the teenage mother and father. Rachel and Buck gave no outward expression of having made a mistake, yet it seemed apparent that they were finally and genuinely shocked into reality, devastated by the terrible consequences of neglecting their daughter. Maybe Nelly's death would serve the useful purpose of helping them to take stock of their lives and more conscientiously accept the responsibility for raising their other two children.

As for me, what could I learn that would give Nelly's life and death meaning? I felt I was on the battlefield of spiritual growth, standing between being tempted by the ego's desire to judge and allowing judgment to be rightly placed in the hands of the Holy Spirit. I had learned from the Course that I could not condemn any one of my brothers or sisters without simultaneously and unwittingly condemning myself. A month after Nelly's funeral I made a point of visiting Rachel, and my hard feelings toward her negligence softened after hearing her talk longingly about her daughter. To come to a place of forgiveness, I prayed for Rachel, Buck, Owen, and Sharon on a daily basis. I lost track of Owen, but worked cooperatively with Sharon on many other occasions that involved Child Protective Services. I found her to be very conscientious and competent in her work, especially with one very difficult case in which she very strongly and successfully advocated for the best interests of one of my clients. She even showed up for one of my yoga classes years later. I pray for my students during yoga classes, and I found myself to be filled with love for Sharon, and she was bubbling over with enthusiasm after the class was over.

Eventually I freed myself of my judgments of the people involved in this tragedy, but Nelly's life and death was much more than just an opportunity to learn how to forgive others. Her life had an ongoing impact on my future work so others benefitted by my experience with her. That silver lining giving meaning to Nelly's life and death would soon become apparent.

My job was not just to be a bureaucrat pushing papers with a constantly changing case load. Rather as a case manager, I built long-standing relationships with many families and became a part of their lives. This was the first child I had lost. I was devastated. Yes, I did a lot of finger pointing to find someone to blame, but in the end my finger pointed directly to myself. Yes, I had objectively done everything seemingly possible to avert this disaster. Yet I was left endlessly questioning every little thing I did and did not do in the situation. I felt that somehow I had failed this vulnerable little girl. But wallowing in self-pity and self-condemnation would serve no useful purpose and would not dignify her death or give it meaning. I looked again at my advocacy for Nelly and instead of justifying myself, I concluded that I could have advocated more strongly than I did. I could have gone to the Child Protective Services office and insisted until I was blue in the face that they simply had to take Nelly into their custody. I could have impressed upon them the sense of urgency I felt personally about her life hanging in the balance, needing only their nod to assure her survival. It may have made no difference on the form level, but at least I would know that I had done absolutely everything in my power to advocate for my client.

This realization that I could have advocated more strongly would be fruitless if that is all there was to it. "If only" serves no useful purpose, but "next time" does serve the very useful purpose of learning from the mistakes of the past rather then repeating them. I decided that Nelly's legacy for me would be that her death would be my constant reminder to leave no stone unturned in my advocacy for my future clients. Whenever I had a difficult case in which I had to do advocacy either with my own division's supervisors or with other agencies or providers, the memory of Nelly was clearly etched in my mind, urging me on to be persistent and firmly insistent if needed. I would honor her memory by my unwavering advocacy. From my altercation with Morris I had temporarily learned not to make waves, but I abandoned that strategy since it would hamper my advocacy. This new bulldog attitude toward advocacy stood me in good stead for all my future years of work for the state. If I fought hard for every little thing, I would soon lose my credibility, so I made sure to choose my battles carefully and only then proceeded full steam ahead with my tenacious advocacy, regardless of the consequences to me. My steadfast advocacy was never more needed than with a very difficult case that fell into my lap not too long after Nelly's passing. The success of that case, which will be described next, can be attributed to Nelly. I couldn't help her directly to stay alive, yet I could keep her memory alive in my heart and in my mind and let that memory inspire me to help others. Nelly's heritage to me was that I would never again fail to give my vulnerable clients the relentless advocacy that they needed and deserved.

Fortunately the successes of our developmental disabilities office were more numerous than the failures. Dominic Rodriguez was a client of mine who had epilepsy and mild mental retardation due to brain damage. He took medication to prevent seizures. The medication accelerated the negative effects of his unfortunate drinking of alcohol, making him emotionally explosive. Dominic in a drunken super stabbed another person and was brought to trial for the felony of aggravated assault. I advocated for him to go to a twenty-four-hour supervised residential placement instead of jail, where he would most likely be victimized, especially because of his developmental disabilities. The first obstacle was that his court-appointed lawyer refused to return my calls, as I was insisting that Dominic be ruled incompetent to stand trial. Finally, I wrote a letter to the judge, and the judge reprimanded the lawyer, who then was very cooperative with me.

I had the court appoint a public guardian due to Dominic's mental incompetence, but the judge was still going to sentence him to eight years in prison if I could not arrange for a supervised residential placement. Then one of my supervisors tried to undercut everything I was doing by submitting Dominic's name for reevaluation of his eligibility status. This was a particularly heartless move to circumvent the state from having to pay for the residential placement that Dominic desperately needed. I vigorously fought this reevaluation by writing a ten-page letter giving reason after reason why Dominic's eligibility should not be questioned.

In response to my letter, I received a phone call from the state medical director, our doctor in Phoenix, who tried to tell me why Dominic did not qualify. I confronted the doctor, citing specific state policies and procedures that showed his conclusions were based on inaccurate information. When he realized that he could not refute these state policies and procedures, he removed himself from the decision-making process. The doctor assigned a state nurse to determine Dominic's eligibility status. I sent a stack of medical records six inches thick to this nurse. She concluded that Dominic did indeed qualify in both the categories of epilepsy and mental retardation due to brain injury. All this determination process took more than nine months, which forced Dominic to be in jail unnecessarily for all that time.

Dominic didn't like going to court month after month and hearing me tell the judge to be patient and give me more time. When I went to visit Dominic at the jail, he said he was going to tell the judge that he wanted to stay in jail because he was tired of this dragging on so long. I had to plead with him to not give up and not resign himself to staying in jail.

Then it took even more time to arrange for a residential placement in Phoenix. My higher-ups did not want to pay for the placement and instead wanted Dominic to go to jail as a natural consequence to his criminal behavior. However, they agreed to the placement when I convinced them the behavior was caused indirectly by his disability. I was able to show them through medical documentation that the drinking fit that caused the assault was greatly amplified by the mixture of the alcohol with the medication he was taking for his epilepsy. Finally, when everything had been arranged, the judge put him on eight years' probation, contingent on his residential placement and him not touching alcohol ever again. If he broke probation, he would automatically go back to jail, but he never did have a misstep. Eventually he even graduated from requiring twenty-four-hour supervision. Dominic got his own apartment and his own job and is now living independently and happily. He even visited my office ten years later to thank me for giving him the opportunity to succeed.

---

1. T-12.III.7:1, p. 222 (p. 206).
2. T-1.I.3:3, p. 3 (p. 1).
3. T-1.I.3:1, p. 3 (p. 1).
4. T-9.VII.7:2-10, 8:1-2, p. 177 (p. 165).
5. T-9.VII.7:2, p. 177 (p. 165).
6. The technical term for poor weight gain and physical growth failure in infants and toddlers is "failure to thrive" (FTT), sometimes called "faltering growth." True malnutrition is generally considered a weight less then 80% of the ideal weight for that age. A lack of age appropriate height and head circumference are also indications of growth deficiencies.

51

LIGHTER MOMENTS

~ • ~

I worked as a case manager for sixteen years until I finally retired. I considered this work to be my *Christian karma yoga*, and this service form of yoga was just as important as my daily postures, breathing practices, and meditation. My coworkers were an extraordinary group of free-thinking people, who truly functioned as a team celebrating the uniqueness of our clients and ourselves. In many ways my work in the world at this job was a more successful attempt at unity than my spiritual community because of our joint single-minded purpose of serving our clients.

When Rhonda or I would get too serious at work, we would remind each other, "It's all a joke." The meaning was that this is an illusion, and so we could lighten up and enjoy the ride. We began every day on a light note by sitting together and reading our daily horoscope predictions in the newspaper, although no one took the astrology seriously. Sometimes we shared stories from our past. For example, Rhonda told us a funny story about when she was a case manager for a Mennonite group home for developmentally disabled adults. Her story may be called "the mystery of the disappearing cheese." Rhonda and the group home manager were certain that one slightly overweight resident, Beverly, was the source of the problem, but they had no evidence. All of the home's American cheese, in individually wrapped slices, was missing, and they could only find the empty plastic wrappings. It didn't seem possible that Beverly could have eaten all of it, but a thorough search didn't turn up even a single slice.

Rhonda explained, "Beverly firmly denied that she had anything to do with it, and the group home manager and I were just about ready to give up on our search. The expression on Beverly's face, however, showed that she felt proud for putting one over on us. Looking at her intently, I wondered what she could possibly have done with it all. Just then a light went off in my mind, and I said confidently, 'I know Beverly's secret!' Beverly lowered her gaze down to the floor, because she knew she had been caught. I slowly put my hand over her head and lifted up her wig. There was the cheese! Not only that, but it was a very hot day, and it had melted right onto her scalp. I blurted out, 'Oh, look! A melted cheese head.'

Everyone started laughing hysterically, even Beverly, and we couldn't stop laughing. The moral to this story is that if you are going to steal cheese, don't put it on your head on a hot day. So that's my 'cheese head' story, and Beverly didn't take any more after that."

Rhonda also told us the story about her client Ralph, who was taken to Las Vegas years ago by his mother, Violet. They went to a show headlined by a famous country singer. She thought it might have been Reba McEntire, so I will use her name here. As Reba was singing, Ralph started to rock back and forth more and more, and Violet was concerned that he might become disruptive from being over stimulated. Suddenly Ralph got up and walked up front and right onto the stage, while Reba kept on singing. No one made any move to stop him, and he walked right up to her. Standing beside her, he leaned his head over on her shoulder. Then because he knew the song, he lifted his head, and he began singing right along with Reba and even held the microphone along with her. The remarkable thing is that she took all this graciously in stride. When the song was over, everyone was clapping, and Ralph bowed forward, repeatedly accepting the applause. I couldn't imagine this happening today in our security-conscious society, but even back then the whole thing was amazing.

One day when we came to work, we discovered that our laptop had been stolen from the office by someone who had removed the air conditioner to gain access to the building. The police found a footprint that they thought belonged to the thief and showed it to Rhonda and me. When a young man, the son of one of our providers, came into the office, Rhonda thought his shoes might match the footprint. He left the building, and Rhonda followed him out. She told him that she was taking a survey of the most common shoe sizes of people who come into the office. She asked him to step on a white piece of paper for his sample, and he agreed. Rhonda brought the print to the police, but the shoe size didn't match the person who stole the laptop. Ironically, however, the print was an exact match for footprint evidence found at a series of local jewelry store robberies. The young man was arrested, convicted, and sent to jail.

Although during the day our staff focused on our work, we also took advantage of opportunities to celebrate life. One time our top boss, the District Program Manager, called, and she wondered what the commotion was that she heard in the background. Rhonda, always speaking her truth, said rather happily, "That's just us dancing and singing joyously because our mission has been accomplished." We were actually doing a silly dance around the office in celebration because we had just finished moving five clients and all their belongings out of a potentially dangerous abusive situation and had done so on a moment's notice, out of necessity.

On another occasion Rhonda and I had to move two other clients out of an abusive situation with the help of a police officer escorting us. Adding to the drama and difficulty of the situation was that during this move there was the worst thunder and lightning storm that I had ever seen in Arizona. When Rhonda and I had accomplished the move, we were exhausted and soaked to the bone. But instead of letting the weather get us down we were hugging, dancing, and laughing in the rain. Then Rhonda looked up and pointed to the cloud formations in the sky and said, "Look! There's Charlie looking down on us from heaven and laughing." The clouds resembled a smiling bald man, reminding us of Charlie's appearance and good humor. Charlie had been a well-liked supervisor and later Area Program Manager until he was taken from us by a brain tumor.

Justin, the supervisor replacing Charlie, worked only a few memorable years in our office before retiring. Similar to Charlie, Justin had a good sense of humor, and many years later Rhonda and I called him spontaneously. We left a singing message on his telephone that went like this:

> Good morning to you.
> Good morning to you.
> We know you're retired.
> Too bad you've *expired*.
> Many blessings to you.
> Many blessings to you.

Then we burst out into silly laughter. Of course, Justin was certainly not "expired" and enjoyed our message. The lyrics and melody, as well as the good singing voice, were provided by Rhonda, as I tagged along with my willing, yet off-pitch vocalization.

Another coworker was Rhonda's husband, Colin, who was a family support provider and good friend. I spent free time with him talking about spiritual matters, meditating together, and praying for our clients. Colin told me he had a shoulder stiffness problem so I showed him how to do the five exercises that I found effective in my work environment. These were very simple and easy to do in a controlled and unhurried manner, yet it would take me only five minutes to do them while sitting right at my desk. I started doing them on a daily basis as I turned fifty when some tendonitis surfaced in my right elbow. As it turned out, my "tennis elbow," as it was called, would completely disappear without returning. As a supplement to my yoga disciplines, I still do these five exercises every morning and afternoon and would suggest them to anyone. If you are interested, they are described and illustrated in Appendix D, "Exercises," for your consideration. These exercises are for the upper body and can be done while sitting or standing.

Although Colin was not a Native American himself, he had integrated that culture and form of spirituality into his life. He had a traditional house with Rhonda, yet he also owned his own teepee. Once he took me to a group sweat lodge ceremony. At this ceremony one of Colin's friends played the *didgeridoo*. It's a wind instrument three to ten feet long used by the Aborigines of northern Australia. This one was a cylinder four feet long. I was amazed that the musician made an uninterrupted tone both on the inhalation and the exhalation. His lips vibrated continuously while he used what's called *circular breathing*. He inhaled through the nose while he simultaneously exhaled out of the mouth using the tongue and cheeks. The combination of the heated stones and music made the purifying sweat lodge ceremony much more intense than the mild saunas I was used to.

I introduced Colin to James, my old friend from Virginia Beach. James had been working for many years as the coordinator for an outreach program serving the poor in his native Canada. He came to our New Jerusalem Community for a visit and several years later would become a community member himself. Colin and James became fast friends, sharing their common interest in hiking and outdoor survival skills. He invited James and me to meditate with him in his teepee. After our meditation together, Colin led us to an out-of-the-way local hot springs. As we walked on the path toward the hot springs, we came across a man coming away from it. He was wearing only his "birthday suit" and sandals. Colin explained that sometimes people at the hot springs didn't wear clothes. Sure enough, when we arrived, we discovered that no one was wearing clothes, so we took ours off too. This was a small hot springs, about the size of a hot tub. We sat in the water facing a beautiful young lady, Marcia, who said she worked at the New Frontier's Food Store in Sedona. Similar to so many young seekers who come to Sedona, Marcia was an open, friendly, and enthusiastic person, and we had a lively conversation with her.

After this experience, it crossed my mind that this might be just what our New Jerusalem Community needed—to sit around naked with each other to overcome our inhibitions and help us communicate better. I quickly dismissed this possibility, knowing the personalities of the community members, and didn't feel any impulse to tell community members about this adventure. However, James had no such reservations. He shared with the community his humorous slant on our conversation with Marcia. He joked about our efforts to avoid staring, as we kept our vision at eye level, rather than lowering our gaze. Pamela said that she wasn't "taken in" by James's story, and I didn't comment. A few days later Pamela came back to me and told me with a smile, "I thought that the hot springs story was a joke. But then I met Marcia at New Frontiers, and she confirmed the story."

JAMES GREGORY IN FRONT OF COLIN'S TEEPEE

AT THE EDGE OF THE GRAND CANYON RIM

Then I had to deal with being kidded about being a monk spending my time with naked ladies.

Although I lived in the tourist town of Sedona, I was not very interested in sightseeing myself. But James encouraged me to go with him to spend a day at Arizona's biggest tourist attraction—the Grand Canyon. We had a wonderful time seeing the majesty of nature. You might think that with my history as the Pole Man, I would have been afraid of heights. Yet I very much enjoyed standing and sitting at the edge of the Grand Canyon rim, although James kept telling me he was nervous about my tendency to place myself in such a precarious position, so close to disaster. Subsequently I had a dream of falling off the edge of a cliff, but instead of falling to my death, I simply and happily floated down slowly with full control and landed softly on the ground below. Then a dark witch came over to me as I was holding a lighted candle, and she blew it out. However, the flame came right back all by itself. The witch blew out the flame two more times and each time the flame returned. I interpreted this dream to mean that my Pole Man past life was being healed. Yes, the great fall of the Pole Man blew out my light in that past life, but the relighting of the candle in the dream showed that through reincarnation my life cannot really be blown out. More important than my life returning was that the Pole Man's bitterness was being replaced by a loving heart. I believe that part of the healing of my heart came from doing the kind of work that was bringing love and healing into the lives of my clients, helping them reach their highest potential.

Our secretary at work, Tina, asked me if I would perform the marriage ceremony for her wedding, if she got one of those mail order reverend certificates for me, and I agreed. The only stipulation I made was that the couple would have to come up with their own vows, and they were happy to do so. Tina's husband, Dawson, was a case manager in the Prescott office, and all my coworkers attended. On a beautiful sunny day the wedding was held outdoors on the historic grounds of Douglas Mansion in the nearby city of Jerome. The reception was held indoors where we had a chance to celebrate with music and dancing. It was not only a wonderful wedding, but also a great bonding experience for our office.

As it turned out, Dawson eventually came to our Cottonwood office and became our supervisor. He also became the beloved Santa Claus for the annual Christmas Party for our clients and their families—the highlight of every year. One time Dawson ordered a fancy ergonomic chair, and when he opened the box, he found a flimsy plastic shower chair inside. Dawson irritably exclaimed, "What the hell is this?" We broke out into laugher, and Dawson joined us as it dawned on him that we had made the switch.

At one of our joint staff trainings, which combined the Cottonwood and Prescott offices, I was surprised to be asked to give a yoga class. This invitation felt really good because usually I had to hide my interest in practicing spiritual disciplines due to being a state employee. Seven of the yoga postures I taught in this class are described in Appendix E, "Yoga Postures." Before teaching this yoga class, I gave the following introduction:

This will be a class in classical yoga, also called "raja yoga." There are eight steps involved in classical yoga. However, today I will talk about only four of these steps. The third step is the *asanas*, which are the postures. But the literal translation is "steady pose." Unlike exercises, the steady holding of the postures in yoga gives a good stretch to the body without straining. This stretch releases toxins into the blood stream where they can be removed by the body. The breathing practices of yoga help to remove these toxins from the blood stream. These breathing practices are the fourth step of yoga, which is called *pranayama*. Learning to hold the body in a steady pose and to do the breathing practices that calm the mind are preparations for being able to sit in a comfortable cross-legged position for meditation.

The seventh step of yoga is meditation, called *dhyana*, which is the holding of one thought in the mind continuously. The fifth step of yoga is *pratyahara*, which is the withdrawal of the senses from the sense objects. This is an aspect of yoga that is not well understood. We live in a society in which we see advertising on television that tells us to buy this or that object. Our senses through our eyes go out to see the object being advertised to entice us into wanting that object. The message of this advertising and of our culture in general is that something out there will satisfy us and bring us peace.

Pratyahara is based on the opposite premise. Pratyahara is a way of affirming that peace is not outside of you in the world of the senses. Peace is within you. In the practice of pratyahara the senses are withdrawn from the outside world so you can focus your full attention on the peace that is within you. What this means at a practical level is that you will be asked to keep the eyes closed during most of this yoga class. I will provide very specific directions so you can do the postures without having to open your eyes. In between postures you will be in a relaxing pose so you can focus on the peace within. In fact, the whole class can be one continuous meditation on the goal of yoga, which is peace of mind. Also to hold the awareness within while practicing pratyahara, it is important to refrain from talking out loud. If you have any questions during the class, raise your hand, and I will come over to you. You can whisper your question to me. I can whisper my response quietly without disturbing the other participants in the class, who are practicing pratyahara. We will start the class by closing the eyes now to begin your practice of pratyahara so you can focus your awareness on the peace within.

One participant, Gary, who worked out of the Prescott office, arrived twenty-five minutes late after we were already doing the postures. Naturally he missed the introductory instructions to avoid talking aloud or looking around during the yoga class. Of course, Gary kept his eyes wide open and was even talking out loud, making comments about the postures. Not wanting the other participants in the class to be distracted by his comments, I said, "During this class we are attempting to be silent to keep the focus on the peace within."

Gary was offended by my comment and immediately walked out of the class. Later I made a point of seeking him out and talking with him. In the past I would have made an issue out of the fact that he arrived so late and would have pointed out that his tardiness was why the uncomfortable situation had occurred. But I had learned a lot about avoiding blaming, about not requiring another person to accept their responsibility, and about not attempting to justify myself. I simply said to Gary, "I am sorry if what I said offended you in any way."

He said, "OK," although he was obviously still a little upset. However, the next time I saw him at another joint staff training, he had let go of his upset feelings. Sometimes issues do need to be addressed directly and pointedly in regard to others accepting responsibility. Yet, if I had done so in this particular case, it would have been counterproductive, making it more difficult for my coworker to let go of his upset feelings.

This was such a minor incident that it may seem unworthy to even be mentioned, but I have included it here to point out that I am learning that every moment in our lives is an opportunity to express love. According to the Bible, Peter denied Jesus three times, as Jesus had predicted, and then Peter repented with many tears. Just as Jesus's prediction was fulfilled, Peter saw Jesus looking at him, which triggered his repentance.[1] The Bible doesn't describe the expression on the face of Jesus. Nevertheless, I believe a hypothetical version of the story that Jesus smiled at Peter. We know Jesus for the great things that He did in His life. However, I believe He set an important example for His disciples by not missing the very small opportunities in His life to express love—through overlooking mistakes and through a kind word, a wink, or a smile. The poet William Wordsworth believed, "The best portion of a good man's life is the little, nameless, unremembered acts of kindness and love."

---

1. Luke 22:61, RSV.

52

A COURSE HOUSEHOLD

~ • ~

Looking back now I can see that at various times in my life my ego has assigned to another person the temporary role of being an authority figure from whom I sought approval. Dylan had served that ego purpose when I lived with him, and David served that purpose certainly in our adventures living together in the desert. In the wake of my altercation with David about "earning love," I withdrew my ego need for approval from him. I then just shifted the assignment of authority figure to Robert, since we were now living in the same house.

The distancing between David and me had been in the works ever since my decision to make the Course my thought system. I have often wondered how things might have been different if David had also made the leap to accepting the Course, but, of course, I will never know what would have happened. What did happen is that eventually David announced he no longer felt comfortable with being an active member of the New Jerusalem Community, so he became an inactive member. The power struggle that had been going on between David and Robert for a long time had created distance in their relationship. Consequently, Sarah assumed more of a leadership role in the community. David felt he had lost his central role and just didn't feel as much a part of things as he had in the past, so he was losing interest. He didn't have it in him to do anything half-heartedly.

In addition, there was distancing in the relationship between David and Pamela. They felt they needed to separate to find their own way, but this separation didn't involve any third-party relationships. They still maintained a very close relationship, and together they continued to raise their children and built a strong foundation for Tory, Jeremia, Shawna, and Rayel to all become productive adults. David, without participating in the official community meetings, did continue meaningful friendships with all community members. In fact, his relationship with Robert improved. Since I had withdrawn my projection of the authority figure role on him, David and I enjoyed each other's company, too. The memory of him appearing judgmental faded away like a mirage as a new, more mature David emerged—a much more open-minded, loving, and accepting person.

In addition, I had learned from the Course that my former judgments of David, which had seemed justified, were merely illusions. They were projections of guilt, laid upon him to hide from recognizing the guilt I felt within myself. But I was not yet able to put that intellectual understanding into practical application by seeing all situations and all people with the eyes of forgiveness. I was hoping that living with other Course students would help me let go of judging others and instead look for the divine in everyone.

Living with Robert, Wendy, Tom, and Ken provided a unique learning opportunity for us, both as community members and as Course students. We could bond together to become better community friends, but also could rally around a common spiritual belief system and practice. We collectively seized this opportunity and began the yearly cycle of Workbook Lessons together on the first day of January and after completing the first year started over again each year. In addition, Robert was becoming a more acknowledged Course authority, author, and lecturer. His very first Course writing was, "An Introduction to *A Course in Miracles*," a booklet that was a huge success.[1]

Each week Robert gave a lecture to our small household group, and we would ask questions. These sessions were taped and sent to others for inspiration. During these lectures I would listen silently and feel my mind and heart opening up as I looked at Robert, and every time I could see a bright white or at times golden light around him. The light would become very bright, sometimes filling his head as I gazed steadily at him in a meditative frame of mind. I felt I was practicing seeing Christ in him.

During one of these taped lectures, I became extremely absorbed into a very deep meditative state, even though I had my eyes open, as I saw Robert and indeed everyone in the light. The experience was so deep I felt myself elevating everyone into a higher consciousness with me. Finally one person said, "Did you feel that? It feels like the Spirit is overshadowing all of us." Every single person in the room said they felt the same thing. Even Robert, who was admittedly unaware of mystical sensations, acknowledged this palpable feeling of the divine presence in the room. My experience in the past with Robert had been that if I talked with him about what was happening within me, he would perceive this as an ego expression on my part. Consequently, I didn't tell anyone what I had experienced.

I thought that these lectures helped to draw us closer together as a spiritual household, but unfortunately Robert decided to discontinue them. After two full years of doing the Workbook Lessons, I decided to stop doing them as a daily practice and focus instead on repeating the Jesus Prayer. Robert heard about my decision and asked me, "I wonder if you would reconsider your decision to stop doing the Workbook?"

"Robert, it says right in the Course itself that the Workbook is only a one-year study course. At the end of one year you are told to simply allow yourself to be guided by the Holy Spirit in your next step spiritually. I have already done two years—one more year of Workbook Lessons than is required."

Robert challenged my statement by saying, "But *how well* did you do the Workbook Lessons?"

"Come on, Robert. The Course does not say that you have to do the Workbook Lessons perfectly before you can complete the one-year course. Besides, my natural inclination was to do the Jesus Prayer, and I set that inclination aside for the sake of us joining to do the Workbook together. However, now I have more than fulfilled the Workbook requirement. I need to be true to what works best for me, and that happens to be the Jesus Prayer."

Robert persisted, "Let me tell you why I am asking you to continue. Because we have all been doing the Course Workbook collectively, it helps us all to be of one mind."

"I can still be of one mind with everyone here," I said. "The Course says that if you can do any one lesson perfectly, you can accomplish everything that the Course has to teach. The one lesson I want to do is Workbook Lesson 183, the repeating of the Name of God. The Course specifically addresses the Name of Jesus. It says, 'So has his name become the Name of God....'[2] So as far as I am concerned, the Course is giving its permission and even recommendation to use the Jesus Prayer."

Robert continued, "But the Course Workbook is more intense because it lets us get to the point of remembering God consistently. For example, toward the end of the lessons I can set my watch to ring every half hour or every fifteen minutes or shorter periods to remind me to refocus on God."

"Robert, I have experienced holding a divine word, not every fifteen minutes, not every five minutes, but every single second!" I said this vehemently because I felt Robert was speaking to me in a patronizing manner. "I feel you have a 'father knows best attitude.' You are trying to talk to me about an intensity of divine focusing that I was practicing when you were less than ten years old. I believe you have a fundamentalist view of the Course by thinking people have to repeat the Workbook Lessons year after year in the search for perfection. I think the Course allows for freedom of individual expression, and the Jesus Prayer certainly falls within that Course framework."

That was the end of the conversation. Robert continued to do the daily Workbook Lessons and to teach others the value of starting a new cycle every year. Years later I found out that Robert had at some point stopped doing the daily lessons. I was surprised to also discover that he had adopted Workbook Lesson 183, repeating the Name of God, as his specialized form of meditation. Although Robert used the word "God" rather than the word "Jesus" to represent the Name of God, I couldn't help but notice the very slight reversal in roles. Over the previous several years I had gradually made a great turnabout in my whole thought system in which I systematically adopted most of the thoughts that Robert held dear, and he helped me greatly in that process. It was nice to see him adopt the thought of repeating the Divine Name that I held so dear, although I could take no credit for his change in perspective since his motivation came entirely from the Course itself.

When our household first got together, Robert felt guided to start a center based on the principles of *A Course in Miracles*. He enlisted our help in coming up with a name. To do this, we played the "Guidance Game," created by our community to help us become aware of the promptings of the Holy Spirit.[3] David had hand painted the game board, and there were twelve decks of cards, which came from various sources, and I had made two of the decks by laminating thought-provoking headings with unusual photographs clipped from magazines. Our previous experience in playing the Guidance Game underscored the fact that the Holy Spirit could circumvent our egos if we would give our "little willingness"[4]—sometimes "very little willingness"—to be guided.

Nevertheless, I came to this particular game with a hidden agenda that limited my openness to being guided. Previously I had a dream in which I saw the letters "CEE," which I assumed were the initials for the name of the new center. From that I determined that the name was "Course Educational Extension." Kaye, who had recently joined our household, replacing Ken, had independently felt the name was "Miracles Extension," which I felt confirmed the importance of the word "extension." Consequently when the game began I was puffed up with the expectation that the game would confirm my choice of a name. It wasn't long before my balloon was popped.

Robert took the first turn and drew several cards that didn't provide clarity, and then it was my turn. I explained my proposed name and asked to receive guidance on it. Before I chose the first card, I asked for God's Will to be done. This was my little willingness, but I was still very aware of my ego's investment in my preconceived name. The card I picked up showed a picture of pollution. I asked to try again and got another pollution-related picture. However, I didn't want to admit how ego-invested I was, so I pretended not to know why the cards were so negative. I chose again and got another negative card. The Holy Spirit was taking me up on my little willingness, in spite of my resistance.

Robert, who was good at seeing repeated patterns, noticed something about my three cards and the ones he had chosen for his turn also. All these cards suggested that a pure impulse had become distorted or polluted by humans. Robert suggested, "Maybe the name is trying to come through to us as a pure impulse, but we are perhaps distorting it with negative thoughts. I don't think we will get very far unless we talk about our fears and attachments that may be blocking the process."

"OK, I confess," I said. I described my hidden agenda. Then I was surprised to hear others, one by one, describe their fears and preconceived ideas that had also been blocking us. The specifics aren't that important. The point was that after we cleared the air by expressing our hidden concerns, we had a joint prayer, and this time we really did join together in willingness to be guided. I gave up being stuck on my chosen name and the other players gave up their attachments as well, so we were all more open.

This marked a turning point in the game, and our joining in silent prayer was perhaps a subtle version of what the Course calls a "holy instant," in which we join with others and experience the divine presence. We didn't have any flashes of transcendental light, but we could all sense an entirely different feeling in our group. Indeed in hindsight, after the name had been revealed, we could look back to this time and acknowledge that as soon as we had cleared our minds, the very next card revealed the divine impulse that had been trying to get through to us.

After our joining together, it was Wendy's turn that did the trick. Before she began, Tom helped to focus us by saying, "Really, the name has already been chosen. Jesus named it. It's just up to us to recognize what has already been given." When Wendy began her turn, she asked the Holy Spirit to guide us to the name Jesus had already chosen for us.

She chose an absolutely remarkable card. It was a picture of four people lying down to form the shape of a cross, with their heads meeting in the center and their bodies radiating outward. They were lying inside of a circle drawn on a floor and inscribed with sacred names in many languages. We took turns brainstorming on thoughts provoked by this image, but none of our ideas led to the name that we sensed was right there, ready to be uncovered. We all agreed that the image was indeed fascinating, and much of our conjecture focused upon the enticing names inscribed on the circle's perimeter and what these words might mean.

During our prolonged discussion, Robert happened to say, "People appear to be enclosed in a circle of protection." When I heard these words, the word "circle" literally jumped out at me. It was more than just an idea that happened to pop into my mind. It felt like the Holy Spirit was tapping me on the shoulder and saying to me mentally, "That's it! The word 'circle' is part of the name."

There is a certain kind of energy and feeling that comes with this kind of spiritual prompting that I cannot describe, yet which is quite distinct. I've had inspirations in the past that have been more complete and intense, such as information that aided Robert. For example, I was inspired to come up with the Course quotation of "A Better Way" to use as the name for our Course newsletter. When inspirations such as this occurred, I would normally share them immediately. But in this case I held back, because my ego wasn't satisfied with just *one* word. My ego wanted to come up with the whole name.

I noticed there were candles in the picture around the circle, so I thought the name might be "Circle of Light." Then I thought that was the kind of name *I* would choose, but it was too generic. I felt it had to be more Course-related. I remembered there was a specific "circle of something" in the Course's Text. I felt that this "circle of something" was the name we were seeking.

Some background information would be helpful here. A week prior to the game, Robert told me that the name that he was considering was the *Atonement Learning Foundation*. I told him, "I know that 'the Atonement' in the Course refers to God's Plan to bring us back to heaven, but I don't like the word 'Atonement' for the name of our Course center. Many people associate the word 'atonement' with the idea of making up for sins, which is not the meaning used in the Course. Plus the word 'atonement' sounds too intellectual." Naturally Robert smiled from ear to ear, and I said, "Oh, I get it. You like it precisely for the reason I dislike it."

"Of course," Robert replied. "Why should I object to the word being too intellectual? If Jesus doesn't have a problem with the word 'Atonement,' why should I? Besides, I think it's a great word to summarize the teachings of the Course." Needless to say, I was not convinced and retained an aversion to intellectual words like "atonement."

So here I was in the game with an inner conviction that there is a "circle of something" in the Text that would be the name of the center. But Robert had left the room to attend to his children. I was certain he would know the exact "circle of something" quotation in the Text. My ego planned on asking Robert the right question, and then I would say dramatically, "That is the name of the center." The suspense built within me as I awaited Robert's return. Finally when he returned, I turned to him and asked with great anticipation, "Isn't there a quote in the Course where the word 'circle of something' is used?"

I was poised and ready for what was about to be my ego's moment of triumph. Robert responded in a matter-of-fact manner, "Well, of course, there is the 'circle of Atonement.'"

I was completely dumbfounded. I knew the "Circle of Atonement" was the name. Yet even though I had come up with it, I didn't like it one bit. My mind went on tilt. I didn't say, "That's the name of the center," as I had planned. In fact, I was too shocked to say anything. Before I could recover from my initial shock at hearing Robert's words, I was immediately stunned again, but this time by Wendy. The idea that I had planned on expressing leaped from Wendy's mouth as she exclaimed, "Maybe the 'Circle of Atonement' is the name!" That thought, once expressed, was like a chain reaction. Everybody was tuned into that name. We read the section of the Text that describes the circle of Atonement.[5] Robert, who is artistically gifted, showed us a drawing he had previously made to illustrate this section. His drawing depicted Jesus along with other people within a circle and in a state of divine communion, and this drawing looked much like the image in the game card we had chosen. All of this convinced me to give up my aversion to the word "atonement" and accept the name that we had been guided to.

In spite of my initial reluctance, I was genuinely happy that we had come up with the name that Jesus had chosen for the center, yet I was upset that no one knew I had had an inspiration about the name. I was unable to let go of this ego attachment to recognition. When it was all over and everyone agreed on the name, Tom said, "Well, Wendy, I guess you said the name first."

Wendy replied graciously, "No, actually Robert said the name first."

Then Robert acknowledged, "Yes, I said the name first. But it was in response to Don's question about the use of the word 'circle of something' in the Course."

I was upset because I wanted them to know that it was not an accidental question, but rather came from a real inner inspiration. My ego wanted the credit for the inspiration. So I attempted to recount to them what had been going on in my mind. I tried to veil my desire for credit, yet I felt so transparent and ego-based that I stumbled around verbally and didn't sound very convincing at all. I was embarrassed by my ego-attachment to recognition.

The day after we chose the name, I was able to talk with Robert. He helped me to accept that it's OK to want recognition as part of my human nature that unavoidably includes having an ego. Of course, ideally we don't really need recognition or approval when we identify with our true Christ Self, but we have to accept our present limitations that hinder us from accepting our true Identity.

I generally tend to be overly serious about evaluating my actions. But a few weeks after my talk with Robert I was able to look differently at this whole naming experience with the help of Tom's friend, Suzanne, who would later become a community member. I was able then to see how the Holy Spirit appears to have a sense of humor. When Robert said, "circle of Atonement," my ego was ready to jump right on whatever name he would say in order to get credit for it. Instead, my ego was totally surprised and frustrated. I couldn't take credit for anything, because the Holy Spirit chose a name that I didn't like and didn't want. Then the Holy Spirit had everybody else jump on the name so my ego got no credit at all. My ego was left to sheepishly squeak, "I really did have an inspiration—honest." It's almost like the ego was the butt of a cruel, ironic joke by the Holy Spirit; or at least that's how it appeared to my ego at the time.

In a conversation with Suzanne, I explained my original inspiration of "circle of something" and what my ego did with it. Then I said, "Now you know why they call it the 'holy instant.' That's all the time the ego will allow for the divine inspiration. As soon as an instant of inspiration occurs, the ego sneaks right in and takes credit for it." We both started laughing.

Next Suzanne said, "Every time I think of a holy instant, it will have a whole new meaning for me." In Course terminology the "holy instant" refers to an experience in which the seeker lets go of the past and future and enters the present moment. It is an experience of the divine presence beyond the normal limitations of time and space. The holy instant can be experienced by joining with others who recognize the divine in each other.

I replied, "We should call it the 'holy hundredth of an instant,' because the ego sneaks right in there so quickly to cut off that inspiration and take credit for it." By this time we were both literally rolling on the floor with laughter. We were really laughing at our egos, agreeing that we both do this all of the time even though we could see the inherent contradiction and absurdity of our egos taking credit for the Holy Spirit's inspiration.

Speaking of humor, when our household group picked the center's name, we completed the Guidance Game with a chuckle. After we came up with the name the "Circle of Atonement," we were about to end the game when someone said maybe we should continue playing. The concern raised was that maybe we needed to choose a specific name for the teaching function of the center. Most of us, though, were thinking along the lines of the quote attributed to the philosopher Alan Watts, "When you get the message, hang up the phone."[6] Robert even asked skeptically, "Do we really need to do this?" Then reluctantly he said, "Oh, all right, I'll take a turn." Robert picked a card that depicted the face of Jesus being persecuted and a large hand, presumably of Judas, holding pieces of silver. Robert read the quotation on the picture, "What do you *really need?*" We laughed, remembering the exact words Robert had just spoken to express his reluctance to take another turn.

Robert was very pleased with the name, the Circle of Atonement, since he was convinced it was the name Jesus had chosen. He summarized the heady enthusiasm that we were all feeling in a paragraph he wrote for our Course newsletter:

> That image of the circle of Atonement in the Course says just about everything I would ever want to say about doing a *Course in Miracles* center. It implies that we would be a miniature example of the global circle of Atonement, a place within which reigned the experience of joyous, guiltless communion with each other and with God. It says that Jesus would be there in our midst and that we would be both his students and his fellow teachers; that our purpose would be to extend to the world his true message, freed of traditional distortions. It says that our single purpose would be to release the world from guilt and that our single message would be forgiveness, based on the truth that we, being God's Son, are guiltless. It says that we would be a community of people joined together in common purpose, in holy relationship, yet that within this unity there would be a multitude of special functions. Each one of us would teach and learn and join in his or her own special way. It says that we would not be an elite group, but that our whole purpose would be to extend outward to others and help draw them into the larger circle of divine communion, for only in doing so would we believe in our own inclusion in that circle. And it says that through us the power of God would flow out to all the world, to gather all of His children back into the holy temple of His presence.

Robert later brought to my attention one last aspect of the naming process for the new Course center. He felt that the image of the circle of Atonement, in which everyone is being invited by Jesus into a circle of divine union, is the Course's version of the biblical New Jerusalem. He pointed out that our playing of the Guidance Game and naming decision just happened to occur on August 15, 1992, exactly four years to the day after we had similarly been guided to come up with the name for the New Jerusalem Community. This gave Robert, and me as well, the impression that the Course center and our community were being inspired by the same divine Source and were linked together. Also, I wondered if there was a connection to Mother Mary, since August 15 is the date of Her Assumption. It seemed that both groups possessed the ultimate goal of leading souls toward being taken up into heaven, into the New Jerusalem, just as Mary in Her Assumption was taken up to Her divine destination.

So that's the story of naming the center, but this raises a question I am still asking myself—"Why am I sharing this writing with you now?" Is it for the pure intention of hopefully inspiring others spiritually? Or is it for ego recognition? Both—and, of course, that's OK. Ideally I would like to say that my motivation is entirely pure, but lessons of the naming experience have shown me otherwise. Unfortunately my pure inspiration still lasts only for a "holy hundredth of an instant" before my ego sneaks in there, seeking recognition. The ego is strengthened by too little self-awareness, which is denial, and equally strengthened by too much self-awareness, which can become self-consciousness and even self-condemnation. Although I cannot eliminate the maneuvering of the ego, I am still learning to not take my ego activities too seriously and to instead identify with my true nature in Christ and to invite the Holy Spirit to help me find the right balance in all areas of my life.

The Course talks about our "special function," which is the task that the Holy Spirit is guiding us to accomplish. It is a task that no one else can complete, and it is essential to the accomplishing of God's overall Plan, which is the Atonement. Robert wrote the following excerpt for the Circle of Atonement newsletter:

> Then, in January, at our weekly study group here in Sedona, I did a talk on all the things that the Course says the Holy Spirit will do for us. I had talked about guidance, the fact that He will make every decision for us. And I had just finished talking about how He will design our special function for us, choosing a form of forgiveness and healing that will fit our strengths and abilities perfectly.
>
> Then my housemate, Don Giacobbe, spoke up. It turns out that he had just experienced a very powerful inspiration, which he felt strongly was from the Holy Spirit. It was a message for me and my work. He then described a full-blown idea for a booklet series and newsletter. It combined all three of the things I had been thinking about—newsletter, booklet, and dictionary. (The dictionary, he said, seemed to be my misinterpretation of the same basic impulse.) And what's more, the idea seemed to fit me—what I love to do and what I have to offer—perfectly.
>
> So the idea felt very inspired and appropriate. Its appearance seemed like a concrete demonstration of what I had been talking about—how the Holy Spirit will guide you and choose your special function for you. The idea also was complete. I didn't need to add anything to it. I felt the deepest gratitude toward Don. And from that point on I began expecting this would be much of my function with the Course for some time.

I very much appreciated Robert's special function of serving as an interpreter and writer of the Course principles and practices. I have been given a similar special function to write about the Course, but from the unique perspective of my own personal experiences, which has been a blending of the East and West. You will notice that in later chapters of this manuscript there are an increasing number of Course quotations and principles that have been interwoven into the story of my life. A life story is more than a series of events. It is an invitation to come into another person's world, including his world of thoughts, and to see the unfolding of his life through his eyes. Many of the ideas in the Course are unusual and very challenging, so you may not agree with all of them. In fact, you may be strongly opposed to some of the concepts. My brother, Rick, for example, strongly objected to the Course and so, respecting his choice, I refrained from talking to him about its principles. Unfortunately, that means I also had to refrain from sharing with him about areas of my life and understanding that are the most meaningful to me.

The Course has become the ocean of thoughts in which I swim, so I am asking you merely to come into the water for a swim with me. You don't have to take this ocean home with you if you don't want to. Perhaps all that you will learn from reading this material is that someone is swimming in an ocean that is very different from your own, or perhaps very similar. Here I am mentioning only the oceans of different thought systems. Of course, in actuality we are all swimming in the same Ocean of God's Love.

---

1. "An Introduction to *A Course in Miracles*" can be purchased inexpensively from the Miracle Distribution Center, 3947 East La Palma Avenue, Anaheim, CA 92807, www.miraclecenter.org, 800-359-2246 (phone), or 714-632-9115 (fax).

2. M-23.2:8, p. 58 (p. 55).

3. www.nhne.org is David Sunfellow's *New Heaven New Earth* website where he offers an updated version of the Guidance Game that he calls *The NHNE VisionQuest Game*. He also has a complete history of how the original Guidance Game and his own updated version came about and a description of how to play the game with enough information to perhaps make your own very similar game. To reach the information about the games click on "NHNE's Pre-2006 Database" on the home page of www.nhne.org. Next scroll down to "NHNE VisionQuest Game," which then leads to "A Brief History" describing the origins of the Guidance Game. David also has a website for his wedding photography business, www.sunfellow.com. David Sunfellow can be emailed at integral@nhne.org or mail can go to P.O. Box 2242, Sedona, AZ 86339, Telephone 928-282-3200 or 928-282-6120.

4. T-18.IV, pp. 380-382 (pp. 354-356).

5. T-14.V, pp. 282-284 (pp. 262-264).

6. Alan Watts, *The Joyous Cosmology: Adventures in the Chemistry of Consciousness* (New York: Vintage Books, 1965, 1970), p. 26. This quote is not contained in the original 1962 edition of the book, but can be found in the later editions.

53

ANOTHER SURPRISE
MEETING

≈ • ≈

I got an unexpected call from Allan Greene a few days before Christmas in 1993. Although he had just had another of his many surgeries, he was in good spirits. Allan let me know that he felt very inspired by Robert's writings on the Course and that he had attended a Course seminar that Robert conducted in New Hampshire. But the big surprise was that Allan had contacted Robert about the possibility of moving to Sedona to live. Allan explained that he was no longer married and felt it was time to make a change in his life.

After relocating to Sedona, Allan would tell Robert, "When we met in New Hampshire, I felt that studying here with your perspective on the Course was important enough to make the effort to get here. I came to do more of what I've been trying to do alone. I came here to reinforce what I know and make it workable." Allan wanted to become actively involved with the Circle of Atonement and have interaction with like-minded seekers.

After their initial meeting in New Hampshire, Robert communicated with Allan on the phone on a regular basis for many months. During this time Allan had been hospitalized repeatedly. Overall, he had undergone a series of nine operations. One of his legs was amputated due to poor circulation, and Allan over this whole period would lose 50 pints of blood. It was highly unlikely that he would survive, let alone be able to move to Sedona.

Nevertheless, he asked Robert to be on the lookout for a house in Sedona that would meet his needs. Because of his limited mobility, he would only be able to actively participate in the Circle of Atonement activities if he could live near our Course household. Then unexpectedly the house right next door became available because Sarah, Barry, and Mark, who lived there, decided to move to a less expensive house in Sedona. Robert convinced the property managers to rent to Allan, in spite of the fact that he did not meet their income requirements and that he was still in New Hampshire.

Many of Allan's friends, family, and doctors expressed very serious reservations about Allan proceeding with his plan to relocate, and in particular they questioned the wisdom of taking the cross country trip from New Hampshire to Sedona. Allan did have some minor health problems along the way. Nevertheless, he arrived in Sedona at sunrise on Easter morning of 1994. A letter from one of his doctors said:

> Congratulations. I actually would have thought that the Second Coming was somewhat more likely than your successful arrival at Sedona. You obviously have sought the Kingdom well, as your accomplishment was hardly a result of a few hours in the operating room and some outstanding nursing care. There obviously is something you know that the rest of us haven't yet figured out.

Since I didn't arrange this unexpected turn of events ending with Allan's arrival in Sedona, I took it as a sign that it must be God's Will for Allan and me to be together again, just as it was arranged for Allan and me to meet in New Market, Virginia, exactly ten years earlier. Because of Allan's difficulty with mobility, he couldn't come to our Course household, even though it was next door. However, that problem was easily solved when we made Allan's house the new meeting place for the Circle of Atonement.

Since Allan now lived right next door, I saw him quite a bit. We decided to join for a common purpose and thus reestablish the holy relationship that we had initiated when we were last together. Our common purpose was to manifest forgiveness and to see Christ in each other, so we meditated together to help us do that. We would visit every Saturday afternoon for a conversation and a twenty-minute silent meditation.

Allan had made the cross country trip driving in his van with Debra, his niece, and an emergency medical technician, Julius, who was also a friend. At a later date, Martin, Allan's long time friend and caretaker, also came. One day Martin was driving to Flagstaff in Allan's van and got in a terrible accident, which killed the other driver and almost killed himself. It appeared to the police that Martin had driven over the divide and so was on the wrong side of the road, but the investigation was inconclusive. Martin could not recall anything that happened. I visited him in the Flagstaff hospital while he was in intensive care, and he could barely speak. Later I learned that Martin had taken the van without Allan's permission. Allan assumed that Martin was probably drunk, but since this was only conjecture on his part, he hadn't shared his suspicion with the investigating officer. After Martin recovered enough to come back to Sedona, I spent time doing prayer healing with him on Saturdays, after seeing Allan.

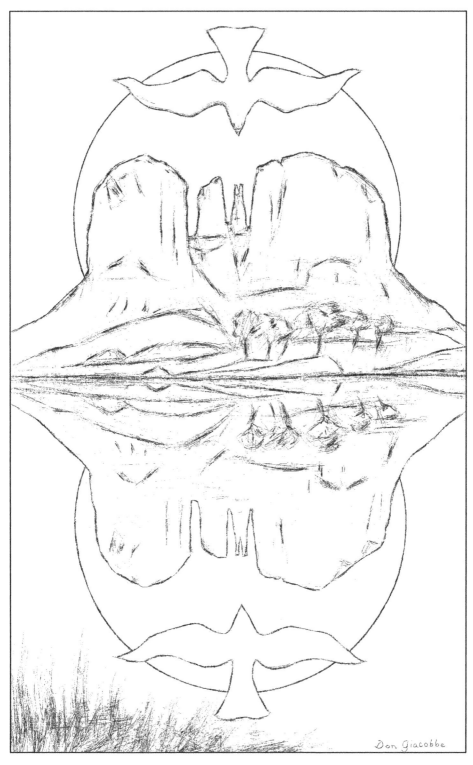

SUNRISE IN SEDONA

JESUS AND THE HOLY SPIRIT

Then another long-standing friend of Allan's showed up as a house mate. It was Flora, who like Martin needed healing. She had recently been in a love relationship for the first time in her life. While she was with her new found love, Darren, he had stepped right in front of a car and was killed. This happened just ten days before Allan arrived in Sedona and none of Flora's family could console her. But she was comforted by Allan's invitation to join him, and she came to Sedona within two weeks of Darren's death. Like so many others in our group, I spent time with Flora to help her talk out her emotional anguish. Since she was an artist, we had a lot to talk about on that level also.

I had already forgiven Allan for our past life together, but it then became apparent that Martin and Flora had also been involved in my past life as the Pole Man. I felt that the difficulties that both of them had encountered were somehow a working out of events set in motion in that previous life. I didn't feel drawn to express this to them as I had with Allan, but I did feel strongly that I was called to be a healing influence in their lives.

My friend Bruce Shelton arrived for a visit in Sedona, bringing with him a painting I had made of Jesus. The picture is shown on the opposite page, and the color version is on the back cover. I had left this painting behind when I had lived in an apartment with Bruce in Virginia Beach. But when the painting arrived, I discovered it had a horizontal slash underneath the left eye of Jesus. It seemed like more than a coincidence that when I woke up the morning before the painting arrived, I had a horizontal gash under my left eye. I had no idea how that wound could have occurred in my sleep. I painted over the mark in the painting, and naturally my wound healed. My best guess on the meaning of this dual marking was that I needed more healing to be a better reflection of the Christ in me. I also had a dream in which I saw my painting of Jesus, but in that dream the eyes were blue although I had painted them as brown. I promptly repainted the eyes making them blue to conform with my dream version of the picture.

On weekends I took leisurely walks to the nearby Red Rock Crossing and enjoyed nature in a way that had eluded me in the past while I had been doing nomadic camping. Cathedral Rock in the background was magnificent in itself, but its beauty was amplified by the reflection of it in the water of the Verde River. I bought a camera costing all of $2.50 at a thrift store, but it took surprisingly good pictures of this exquisite scene. I felt this area not only had a natural beauty, but it also felt like a very spiritually blessed place. I hoped to capture that sense of holiness when I made the drawing "Sunrise in Sedona" (shown on page 547). In this sketch the stylized dove is, of course, a symbol of the Holy Spirit. My art work was now miles apart from my former paintings done in New York, but in one way they were both the same: They were both attempts to depict what was deepest with me. In the past I felt the darkness went the deepest within. There was always some light in those old paintings, but it was surrounded by much darkness. In my new art work the reverse was true because I realized that the light is deepest within me. Consequently, the sun took a larger-than-life role. The exaggerated sun in this drawing of Red Rock Crossing represents the divine presence, just as it did in ancient times.

I had also made some drawings of Mother Mary and baby Jesus, and even these displayed a gigantic sun in the background. (One of these drawings is shown on the opposite page and was inspired by Raphael, the Renaissance painter.) Bruce Shelton bringing the painting of Jesus back to me had the effect of inspiring me to start painting again. For example, I painted *Madonna and Child in the Light* (shown on the page 552) with the enlarged sun blazing in the background. My new paintings were aimed at making visible, finite images of the Invisible Infinite. Thus they were similar to stylized Byzantine icons, which were made primarily as devotional offerings that acknowledged the divine presence and only secondarily as works of art expressing technical skill. Also I enjoyed making bright-colored magic marker drawings since they were so simple and easy to do quickly.

One day at a thrift store I bought a very large, excellent painting for $25. Possibly painted in the 1800's, it depicted a swan on a lake. The only problem with the painting was that it was damaged. There was a one-inch cut right through the canvas next to the swan. I put a backing on the canvas where the cut was and then repainted that area. In the repainted area right next to the original swan, I inserted a companion white swan. The repair and repainting successfully removed any trace of the original cut. The next time I saw Allan I gave him the painting as a gift and told him, "These two swans are symbolic of you and me and how our relationship is healed."

Allan said, "I guess this is the right time to tell you something that I have come to realize. I had a reading before I came to Sedona in which I was told that in a past life long ago I had gone 'far beyond any reasonable bounds in the abuse of power.' So I believe you were right all along about our past life experience together."

"Thanks for telling me that," I said. "But I gave you my forgiveness a long time ago, so I don't think your realization is for my benefit. However, I think it is for *your* benefit. Your current physical limitations could be due to not forgiving yourself for the past. Perhaps you have been given this realization, not to dwell on it, but to simply give it to the Holy Spirit in order to heal any old guilt from the past. How about if we both offer up any past emotions or guilt we may have to the Holy Spirit for healing?"

Allan agreed and after our meeting on that day we never specifically discussed my past life as the Pole Man again, except for one occasion when

MOTHER MARY AND JESUS IN THE LIGHT

MADONNA AND CHILD IN THE LIGHT

Allan asked me, "When you told me about your past life, you said that in a dream you were given the names of the two major figures that you had a conflict with. One was my name, but what was the other one?"

"The other name was Benedict."

"Did you ever find this Benedict person?" Allan asked.

"No, I never did meet anyone named Benedict. Maybe in the future I will. But after all that I have learned in the Course, meeting this person is not as important to me as it once was. Now it doesn't matter what he did or did not do in my past. Whether I meet him or not, I still have to find healing in the present moment by forgiving everyone, including myself."

Although I had forgiven Allan for whatever role he had played in my past life as the Pole Man, there were fragments of my shadow puzzle still affecting me. I felt it was mostly the Pole Man experience that was influencing me to perpetuate a victim pattern, which I no longer wanted. The idea of being a victim is supported by the belief that something bad has happened to me that is caused by someone else, a victimizer, and that I am not responsible for what has happened. But I had been studying Course quotations, like the one below, that challenge the whole self-deceptive notion of being a victim:

> Deceive yourself no longer that you are helpless in the face of what is done to you. Acknowledge but that you have been mistaken, and all effects of your mistakes will disappear.
>
> It is impossible the Son of God be merely driven by events outside of him. It is impossible that happenings that come to him were not his choice. His power of decision is the determiner of every situation in which he seems to find himself by chance or accident. No accident nor chance is possible within the universe as God created it, outside of which is nothing.[1]

Over the previous four years I had been internalizing the lessons of the Course on how to accept responsibility for my experiences. I had learned from the Course that everything that happens to me occurs because I have invited or allowed that experience. Since my own choices bring my experiences, I could take responsibility for my choices. Taking responsibility doesn't mean feeling guilty about my choices. It means making different and better choices to bring different and better results into my life.

Many years earlier when I lived in Virginia Beach with Dylan, he had actually told me about my victim pattern. He said I *wanted* to be a victim, so I would attract situations that would make me feel like a victim, but I didn't believe him. However, after studying the Course, I discovered that I had at various times managed to place myself in the position of being a victim in relation to community members. I thought of specific examples to help me see this victim pattern, and one of these was a Thanksgiving Day incident. Our household had decided by vote that a certain living room area of the house would be used for prayer and meditation, so there was a prohibition against eating any food or drink in this area, to acknowledge it as a "sacred place." But on Thanksgiving Day, with many visitors joining us, people were indiscriminately eating and drinking in the sacred area. No one in the household except me seemed to care about maintaining the sacredness of the area by enforcing the rule we had all agreed upon. I decided to be a victim of the situation and stayed in my room, refusing to participate in the celebration. Looking back on this now, I can see how I made a form-related issue more important than expressing love, making a big deal out of nothing just so I could play out my victim pattern.

After remembering this and a whole series of other self-imposed victim situations, I could see that others didn't really make me into a victim. Instead, I victimized myself each time by deciding that I was a victim because of some inconsequential matter. I could have just as easily decided not to be affected by situations that gave the outward appearance of unfairness. What was really surprising about this was that I sensed that in a strange way I was subconsciously attracted to being a victim, as Dylan had originally told me. I could see I had unwittingly sought out "opportunities" to become a victim. Apparently, at some unconscious level I wanted to perceive myself as a martyr at the hands of others so I could get sympathy and have others feel guilty about hurting me.

When I saw this pattern with crystal clarity for the first time, it seemed silly to me that I could be acting so foolishly, especially about such insignificant matters. I think that what I was doing subconsciously was replaying the Pole Man experience over and over by making myself into a victim. But after discovering the full extent of this pattern, I still sometimes found ways to take on the victim role. Nevertheless, I discovered I could also accept responsibility for choosing to do this to myself. Since it was my choice to perceive myself as a victim, I could make a new choice to let go of that victim role. In addition, because of my heightened awareness of the problem, I actually began to catch myself in the process of being attracted to the victim role. On those occasions when I felt like a moth being attracted to a flame, I found I could take measures to prevent myself from reproducing my former self-defeating victim pattern. This new perspective was helping me to heal the original Pole Man experience that had set the victim pattern in motion and helped me to let go of any last bits of subconscious unforgiveness that I may have still unknowingly been harboring toward Allan.

At the time I was coming to grips with this victim pattern, I received a letter from my friend Patience, who had formerly worked with me at Volunteers of America in Virginia Beach. Earlier, I had sent her a letter telling her about my use of the Jesus Prayer, and now she wrote back about her experience of using that method of prayer:

> My experience with the Jesus Prayer started when I was in high school twenty years ago and read Salinger's *Franny and Zoey*. In the book, Franny repeats the Jesus Prayer over and over again like a mantra, and I liked that. When I was in college, a friend gave me *The Way of a Pilgrim*, which explains the Jesus Prayer and tells the story of a seeker who used it faithfully. I was very inspired and began repeating it silently during my daily activities whenever I remembered. It did feel like it became a part of me, running quietly with or without my conscious awareness of it.
>
> Almost ten years later I was living with my two-year-old daughter and very briefly with a violent man. One night he awakened me out of a sound sleep and began beating me. He sat on me, pinned my arms with his knees, and battered my head repeatedly. I was sick and feverish, and felt my consciousness slipping away. It felt to me at the time that I was going to die, and I feared that my daughter would be left alone. At that moment I found myself silently repeating the beautiful little Jesus Prayer. The Jesus Prayer came from my heart, accompanied by a blue light, which came out of my heart and surrounded my attacker. He stopped beating me. Isn't it amazing how the worst of things really can be opportunities for good?

Patience gave no hint in her letter of the slightest inclination to perceive herself as victim or to project that idea to me. She vividly demonstrated to me that the perception of being a victim is really an inner choice, not something determined by the inappropriate actions of others. Her example was a sobering reminder that I too could resist the temptation to indulge in thinking of myself as a victim. After all, I was not faced with the very difficult challenge of being physically assaulted, as Patience had been. To follow her example, all I had to do was to accomplish a simple task—to stop mentally beating myself up with victim consciousness in the much less dramatic and even petty occurrences of my life. My victim pattern would persist for a time, but I felt I had gained enough insight into my problem to be able to eventually overcome it by applying what I had learned.

The Course affirms, "Remember that no one is where he is by accident, and chance plays no part in God's plan."[2] Other people play a crucial part in our process of following God's plan and learning how to love and find healing. I felt this was true for me. I was glad to be living in a household with others who supported my belief in the Course principles that were assisting in my healing. Also in my work I often encountered clients who were feeling victimized. By helping them deal with issues related to victimization, I felt I was indirectly healing my own victimization issue.

One aspect of my job that I didn't like was our frequent and typically boring staff trainings. On the other hand, some staff trainings were designed for personal enrichment and were enjoyable. At one of these I received a healing of my Pole Man lifetime. It occurred at a staff training at the Northern Arizona University campus in Flagstaff, where we had a "Ropes and Initiative Challenge." I was in a randomly selected grouping of ten state workers from various cities. We were presented with challenges to work as a team to come up with creative solutions to problems. We started with a "trust circle" in which we were able to take turns being supported and lifted by the team. For one challenge there were three tires stacked one on top of the other, and rising out of the center of them was a wide and very tall pole. The goal was to raise the three tires off the pole. I was able to come up a strategy for our group to lift the tires and remove them from the pole. Being tall and thin, I volunteered to be lifted up by the group as I simultaneously lifted the tires one at a time. After being physically held up by the group for the third time and lifting the last tire off the pole, I allowed myself to fall backwards intentionally and have the team catch me. For me, it was an instance of trusting others beyond what I would normally have allowed.

The biggest challenge for me involved another pole in the ground that was as high and as wide as a telephone pole. Small wooden steps along the pole enabled me to climb up and reach the top. Then accomplishing a more difficult task, I was able to raise myself so I was standing on the very top of it. I had a rig around my body with ropes held by four spotters, just in case I fell. For the last part of this challenge I jumped far off the top of the pole and rang a distant bell, which was the goal. When I jumped, I trusted that the four spotters would be able to pull on their ropes to prevent me from being hurt and, of course, they did their job and slowly lowered my body back to the ground. I felt this whole scenario was a set-up by divine arrangement to help me heal my Pole Man lifetime, in which I hated everyone around me as I clung desperately to a pole before plunging to my death. In this present-day correction and healing, I was able to be high up on a pole in a dangerous situation and yet be supported by others whom I trusted with my safety and my life. This experience felt strengthening on all levels. According to the Course, if we are open to divine assistance, the Holy Spirit will arrange our lives to help us find healing. It seemed that this whole experience had been perfectly orchestrated to facilitate my healing.

---

1. T-21.II.2:6-7, 3:1-4, p. 448 (p. 418).
2. M-9.1:3, p. 26 (p. 25).

54

A FATEFUL CHOICE

~ • ~

During my Saturday meetings with Allan we sometimes talked about Course ideas since we held these in common, or sometimes we just talked about how the past week went, before having our prayer and meditation time. Eventually he asked, "When you last told me about your time in Rochester years ago, you said that there was more to the story. Would this be a good time to tell the rest of it?"

"Sure," I said. And so I began . . .

Where I left off was that I had just met the man who took me to the church. Afterwards, I was sitting outside on the grass with a profound feeling of love filling me. A man and a woman came over from the Zen center and sat down with me. I loved them, too, just as I loved everything in my vision. They said they were going back to the center, and I went with them. Along the way I picked a purple flower and, when we arrived at the center, I walked into the back office and left the flower on the roshi's desk. Then I went to the front of the main building and sat on the steps, still feeling just as loving and happy as before.

Then the thought came to my mind that the roshi had said, "You must even give up attachment to love if you want enlightenment." Since I was filled with love, I decided to consciously renounce this love I was feeling. I didn't want to be attached to anything—so I could become enlightened. I told myself resolutely, "I don't want this love any more, because I want enlightenment." Having made the decision, I walked down the street headed for my house when a black dog started barking vehemently at me. This was the first time I had seen him on this well-traveled path. I actually wondered if the barking dog was an omen of having made a bad decision, but I dismissed this interpretation at the time.

Looking back with the 20/20 vision of hindsight, I feel now that I was being guided to give up my search for enlightenment. It was only because I had stopped trying to become enlightened that the divine grace of the experience in the church had happened. I didn't understand the full significance of being led to the church to follow the loving example of Jesus or that I was being guided to let go of the search for enlightenment through Zen practice. It never even occurred to me that this experience of loving everyone and everything was in itself an experience of enlightenment—certainly not the deepest kind, but perhaps a lesser experience. Now I do believe it was indeed a form of the mild *kensho* that some seekers experience as their first enlightenment, in which they feel oneness with an object in nature. However, at the time I disregarded the value of a lesser awakening because somehow I got it in my mind that enlightenment had to be a cosmic oneness that entirely transcended this world of appearances. That cosmic oneness was the only goal I cared about.

With this ultimate goal in mind, I continued with daily spiritual practices. I no longer focused on one thought as I had with the koan during the sesshin. Instead I adopted an attitude of keeping a meditative state of mind all the time. I still did some sitting meditation, but most of my formal meditative practice consisted of two-hour periods lying down. Sometimes when I placed my awareness in the hara I felt an unusual expansion of energy in the navel area and felt strangely like I was "pregnant with enlightenment." During the sesshin I had experienced a radiating point of light in my navel that I thought was perhaps the "seed of enlightenment" that would produce a spiritual awakening at a later date. Now I felt as if this seed of light was growing like a child that is conceived and grows until it is born. Usually I did a two-hour meditation in the morning and another one in the afternoon. In the afternoons I liked to meditate lying down in the grass with bugs crawling all over my body. I didn't go to the Zen center, but mostly stayed home and made bread or yogurt for the household and also did house cleaning regularly.

Howard and I went into business together—if you could call it that. We made hand-crafted candles in the cellar. We melted wax in several tin cans on a hot plate and then added a crayon to each can to get different colors. A one-inch or two-inch layer of colored, hot wax was poured into a quart size milk carton that was already fitted with a wick secured at the top and bottom. After that layer cooled, another layer of a different color was added, and the process was repeated until the milk carton was filled to create a candle with many horizontal layers of colors. Finally I would convert the candles into works of art by using a paring knife to carve them into colorful pagoda-shaped sculptures. We sold them in the neighborhood, although to my dismay Howard sometimes gave the candles away.

One day I walked to the busiest street in town and sat down on the sidewalk. Although I wasn't doing a lot of sitting meditation, I had gotten into the habit of sitting in the full lotus wherever I was, whether eating, reading, or just sitting and relaxing. I didn't bother to take my sneaks off, as I normally would have at home. While I sat there with two candles in front of me, a lady with a child surprised me by dropping a quarter in my lap. Only then did I realize she must have thought that I was a disabled person because of the way my legs were crossed. I quickly said, "I'm not really begging. Here you can have your money back." But my speaking only frightened the poor lady, so she rushed off, protectively grabbing her child's hand to get away as quickly as possible.

Another woman came along and admired one of the candles. She said she couldn't afford to buy it, so I gave it to her. Right after that a little boy and his mother came by and liked the other candle, so I gave that one away, too. When I got up to walk back to the house, I felt a wonderfully exhilarating joy. It was only then that I realized why Howard gave candles away.

About the third week in June, as an expression of my desire to learn detachment, I decided to shave my head. Actually, Howard shaved my head, and I shaved off my moustache as well. Shaving my head was a symbol of starting my life over again. Then I in turn shaved Howard's head, which left Noble as the only one in our house still with hair on his head. The same day we shaved our heads, Howard and I took a walk and boys in the neighborhood started hollering and laughing at us. One youngster ran up behind me and stuck his ice cream cone in my back. I told Howard casually to just keep walking and let them laugh at us.

Another time, Howard and I were in the basement making some candles when a curious little boy from next door came to see what we were doing. He looked at me and said, "What would you do if I spit in your face?"

I said pleasantly, "Nothing," so the boy spit in my face—a juicy one right on my nose. The boy quickly ran away, thinking there would be some sort of retribution. However, I wasn't disturbed in the least. In fact, I was mildly amused, so I didn't even wipe the spit off, but just continued with the candle making. Howard had heard us talking, but hadn't seen what happened. Then he turned and saw me. He smiled and said, "Ooh, Don!" He took a rag and cleaned my face.

On Thursday, soon after Howard and I had shaved our heads, we went to the park to sell candles. As we were walking home in the late afternoon, a young man unexpectedly stopped us to tell us he really liked the candle that I was holding—the only one we hadn't sold or given away that day. I handed him the candle that he admired, and he handed me a capsule of LSD. I thought this must be divine providence and so decided I would take it. When we reached the house, I took the pill and asked Howard to keep an eye on me just in case. I went to my room and started a meditation lying down. About twenty minutes later, I felt a flow of energy in the navel area, but nowhere else. I sat up and meditated for a short while, until I heard a knock on the door. It was Howard, who asked if everything was all right. I nodded. I stood up and felt wonderful. My mind was extremely clear and alert, and there was no visual distortion, as might be expected with LSD. The only physical anomaly was that the energy in the navel increased so it felt like a river of energy flowing from that area outward and upward.

With a strong feeling of confidence, I decided to go outside and Howard came with me. I hadn't been talking, but when a next-door neighbor came toward us and greeted us, I responded by saying, "Hi." The sound of my voice surprised me. The sound came from the deepest part of my gut, and when it came out, it sounded almost as though I hadn't even said it. As I walked, I felt as though I didn't even have a body. My legs were moving, but I just seemed to be floating along. We reached the very large parking lot area in front of the planetarium where I had been assured a job. The planetarium employees inside, some of whom I had met when I was there for the job interview, were staring at us and some were pointing and laughing. In contrast to the long black hair and the conservative clothing of my previous visit, I must have looked funny with my bald head, old shirt, and cut-off pants. Though they laughed at our appearance, I felt happy that they were happy, even though the job was most likely now lost.

I looked up at the sky and saw the clouds jumping around very quickly and almost dancing. It was absolutely beautiful, with a kaleidoscope of all colors—pastel colors—constantly changing. I never saw anything like it before or since. The clouds were so exquisite and unexpected that my rational mind told me that this must be a hallucination caused by my taking LSD. I pointed to the sky and asked Howard, "What do you see?"

Howard answered, "The clouds are doing tricks in color." Only then did I know that I was not imagining this color show being put on by the clouds, since Howard had not taken any drugs. We stood there looking up at the dynamically moving clouds. By this time the energy that had originated in the navel area had expanded to fill my whole body with energy. My body didn't seem solid at all. It just felt like something through which the energy flowed. My consciousness was located where the top of the head was. But the top of the head didn't appear to be there. Instead it felt like there was just an open space where the top of the head had been. From the whole body and especially the head, it felt like energy was radiating outwardly and especially upwardly. It felt so powerful that I thought the clouds were jumping in the sky because of the energy emanating from my body. This conclusion was supported by the fact that only the clouds directly above us were acting in this strange manner.

I felt I should do something constructive with all this energy, and the best idea I could think of was to share it. Consequently, I said to Howard, "I want to give you a blessing. Would you mind kneeling?" Howard smiled and knelt down. I placed my hands on his head and focused on giving him this energy that was so abundantly flowing through me.

Afterwards we walked back toward the house. I closed my eyes to see what it would be like to walk in the dark. I walked forward quickly and a sudden fear came over me, so I opened my eyes. My earlier confidence had disappeared in a flash with that single fear. I looked up toward the sky and spoke inwardly—to whom, I did not know, "Show me what to do." When we reached the house, I went upstairs to my room to be alone. The energy flow had lessened considerably, although I could still feel a lot of it flowing from the navel area. I went down to the kitchen, where Howard was seated on the floor and Richard was heating tea in front of the stove. I stood in the doorway and Richard took one look at me and said, "You look like you're on acid." He wasn't serious, but I didn't know that at the time.

I turned to Howard, sitting at our table, an old wooden door, and asked, "Did you tell him?"

"No, I didn't tell him," he answered.

We both looked back at Richard, and smiled. Richard said, "Come on, you guys, stop kidding me."

I decided to go to the center, where the evening meditation had already started. As I opened the main door, the roshi was coming out of the meditation room. I bowed in gassho to him and he bowed in return. A person cannot enter the zendo during sitting meditation, so I waited until kinhin and then went to the end of the walking line of students and sat for the last meditation. Afterwards, the roshi came over to me and asked me to give a message to Noble when I went back to the house. I asked the roshi if I could talk to him privately. He agreed and we went to a side room. As I was about to tell him that I was on an acid trip, I felt that I shouldn't tell him. I told him that what seemed so important a minute ago now seemed not important. I excused myself and went outside. Instead of walking, I skipped happily down the street like a little child. I looked over my shoulder and noticed the roshi standing outside the doorway and observing me as I skipped away joyfully.

As I came back to the house, it was getting dark outside and many small children were holding large candles. I immediately realized that Howard was up to his old tricks again. When I saw him in the kitchen, he said, "I hope you don't mind me giving away all the candles."

I smiled broadly, "Of course not, Howard."

"I guess we aren't very good businessmen, but we make people happy," he concluded.

The energy continued flowing in my body while several house mates, returning from the evening meditation, came into the kitchen. One of these was Jack, who said to me in a reprimanding tone of voice, "You and

Howard have been acting like the Oriental fools in those old Zen stories, the way you have been carrying on."

It was true we were being rather unorthodox, but I was irritated at Jack because I felt this was none of his business. In particular I didn't want him to manipulate Howard into feeling guilty just because he was being his child-like and to my mind loveable self. I said sternly, "What gives you the right to make this judgment?"

He replied, "I'm not the only one to think this way. Tonight after meditation the roshi asked me how long you've been like this, and I told him you've been acting strangely for some time."

I didn't feel it would be wise to continue the conversation any longer, so I went back to my room and lay down on my mattress on the floor. The momentary anger toward Jack had upset my frame of mind, so all my good feelings disappeared. The flowing navel energy remained, but instead of creating a good feeling, it felt like nervous energy. I was very nervous all night and couldn't sleep at all. I thought back on how wonderful I had felt earlier, and associated this with the confidence I had. A better word for this confidence might be *faith*. In this nervous condition and sleepless state I could see that my faith was a false faith, since it didn't last. I didn't hallucinate or freak out from the LSD, as sometimes happens, but just felt this unending nervousness.

I had the presence of mind to use this occasion to pray, even though I was unsure exactly who I was praying to. Feeling that what I lacked most was faith, I prayed very fervently that some day in the future I would have "a faith that could never be taken from me." I didn't want a false faith that would take me up and then drop me down, like a drug that wears off. I wanted a faith that once it was given would never cease to be with me. I prayed with my whole heart and felt certain that one day my prayer would be answered. Allan, I think I will stop here and continue another time.

Allan said, "My guess is that you got the faith you asked for, but I'll be happy to wait for the next installment to find out. I have a joke that you might like to hear. It's about where different people place their faith. There were three spiritual seekers who found themselves in hell. One was a Jew, another was a Catholic, and the third was a Power of Mind practitioner. The Jew and the Catholic were sweating and complaining about how hot it was. The Catholic asked the Jew, 'Why do you think you ended up here in this hot place?'

"The Jew answered, 'I think I ended up here because I lost my faith. I stopped going to temple and I ate pork.'

"The Catholic explained, 'I believe I ended up here because I also lost my faith. I stopped going to church and I ate meat on Fridays.' The Power of Mind seeker was ignoring the Jew and the Catholic, but the Catholic turned to him and asked, 'Why do you think you ended up here in this hot place?'

"The Power of Mind seeker angrily exclaimed, 'I'm not here and it's not hot!'"

I laughed and said, "That's pretty funny, Allan. I won't take this joke as an indication of your theology, since I know you don't believe in hell."

"It's true I don't believe in fire and brimstone, but actually I do believe in hell. Any one of us can make a living hell out of our lives in this world by our attitude. I told you the joke the way I heard it, but I have my own epilogue to the joke. In my epilogue the Jew and the Catholic forgive themselves by seeing the divine in each other. They decide to join together for the common purpose of asking for divine assistance. They hold hands in prayer and they both wake up in heaven."

I inquired, "What happens to the Power of Mind seeker?"

"The Power of Mind seeker stays where he is. He is perceptually correct when he says, 'I'm not here,' because he really is in heaven. But he doesn't really believe his own philosophy. Even though he denies that he is in hell, his anger betrays him. No one can wake up in heaven while still holding on to anger. He thinks he can reach heaven as a solitary goal attained through holding on to a mental belief maintained by the forceful power of his individual will. But the real way to heaven is by having a loving mind, free of fear and anger. We learn how to love by joining with others in holy relationships and seeing the divine in our brothers, like the Jew and the Catholic seekers in my epilogue were able to do," Allan declared.

I offered, "Since we both want to wake up in heaven, this would be a good time for us to invest in our holy relationship and have our attunement now." So that's what we did.

55

WHO WAS THAT?

~ • ~

For a few months I delayed the telling of the next installment of my story because I found it difficult to talk about some of the events. Finally, when I was ready, I began again one Saturday morning.

I couldn't sleep during the night after taking the LSD, but I did sleep a few hours in the early morning. When I awoke, I was terribly depressed, more than I had ever experienced. Although the navel area had returned to normal, the entire body felt as if the life force had been sucked out of it. The physical and mental exhaustion and emptiness lasted most of the day. As evening approached, I felt better and asked Howard to take a walk with me.

We went to the nearby woods and then to the top of a large hill. We practiced sitting meditation, and I felt very good afterwards. Then we walked through the woods. Pointing at a squirrel scampering at a distance ahead us, Howard said, "Too bad we can't walk around naked like the animals."

"Howard, there's nothing stopping us from doing that now!"

"Actually I always thought it would be fun to run naked, so let's try it," he said, so we took off our clothes and ran through the woods naked. It did feel freeing, and we were giggling like little children. After a brief but exhilarating run, we meditated again as it was starting to get dark. Afterwards, we got dressed and walked back toward the house. As we were walking, Howard said, "I hope you don't think I'm crazy, but I saw something odd when we were back there. I don't know if I imagined it or if I really saw it."

"What was it?" I asked.

"When you were meditating I opened my eyes and looked at you. Your whole body was glowing with a white light, and the light was around you, too."

I said, "You didn't imagine it, Howard. If you see light in me, it must be because you are becoming aware of the light in yourself. But when unusual experiences like this happen, it's probably best not to talk about them to others, although I appreciate you telling me."

When we returned to the house, I went to my room and felt drawn to the words, "Oneness manifesting Oneness." I decided to hold onto these words and repeat them like I would a koan. But these words were really more of a statement affirming the perfect oneness I wanted, rather than a question like a koan to puzzle my mind. I stayed up the entire night with this one thought effortlessly rolling over in my mind. The time passed very quickly.

In the very early morning while everyone in the house was still sleeping, I made some chamomile tea and sat at the kitchen table to drink it. As was my habit, I was taking the tea from the cup with the spoon and lifting the spoon to my mouth. While I observed the spoon in my hand, my mind seemed to stop thinking. The thought of "Oneness manifesting Oneness" was not there either. The mind was completely empty. This state of true emptiness lasted only an instant. Then the mind had a monitoring thought of acknowledging this emptiness, and with this monitoring thought the mind returned to a lesser but still very clear state. As I watched my body movements with the spoon, I felt like an observer of the body motion, rather than the mover of the body.

I then noticed a book within easy reach on the table. I took it in my hands and saw that it was just an ordinary small book, not particularly spiritual. For some reason I decided to pretend that it was the Bible or some similar spiritual book. Carrying it with me, I stood up and walked into the next room, where there was an elevated platform in the back. I stood up on that platform and faced the center of the room. I felt I was in the process of giving myself some sort of message, and I wondered, "What am I trying to tell myself? Does this mean I will be a preacher, carrying a Bible or other spiritual book and speaking from a platform?"

As I was entertaining this thought, I heard the screen door on the porch bang shut, and then I heard the front door open and close. Everyone was still asleep, and I had been up all night, so I knew that no one had left or would be returning. Obviously someone had just come in from outside, but who could it be? I stepped down from the platform and went to the front area and saw Jack wearing a long black coat I hadn't seen before.

"Now, Allan, this is the part I didn't want to tell you about and why I delayed in talking to you about my story."

"You don't have to tell me if you don't want to," Allan offered.

"Just let me preface this by saying that you may have to stretch your imagination to believe what I am about to say. Although the person I was looking at had the body of Jack, he appeared to be *Satan*," I said in a serious tone.

"Did he have horns and a tail?" Allan said with a big smile, kidding me to make light of my seriousness, which I knew was his way of helping me to relax. So I continued.

I said that you might have to stretch your imagination to believe me, but you won't have to stretch your imagination quite that far. No, he didn't have horns or a tail. It was definitely Jack's body, but looking at him, my intuition saw the devil, especially in his eyes. It wasn't a mild intuition but a strong one, like the intuition of the snake under the door at the sesshin. In fact, it felt like I was looking at the snake again in looking at this devil. Maybe the snake and this devil were different forms of the same entity. At least when I first saw this devil, I didn't panic and run away like I had done when I first saw the snake. Although I had an immediate fearful reaction, I was able to maintain my composure.

The devil in the form of Jack sat down at one end of the front area of the house, and neither he nor I spoke a word. I went into the kitchen and heated some water for more tea. As I sat waiting for it to boil, my thoughts went like this: "I am just imagining this because Jack told me he had once been possessed by a devil. Two days ago I was angry at Jack for his comments about Howard and me. I must be projecting my negative feelings onto Jack by imagining I see a devil in him."

After the water had boiled, I made my cup of tea and returned to the front room. The body of Jack was still sitting silently as before. I had cast enough doubt on my intuition to consider that I might be wrong about him being a devil, although it was certainly unusual for Jack, who was always intellectualizing, to be so quiet. I sat at a right angle to him about ten feet away so he could see me looking straight ahead from the end of the room. I could not see him looking at me, and I wasn't going to turn my head to the right to see him. I used my spoon and carefully sipped the very hot tea, just as I always did. Then the thought came to my mind to swallow the whole cup of tea all at once. Immediately I gulped the whole cup down, even though I knew it was very hot. It scalded my throat.

I felt that this thought to swallow the tea had somehow come from the mind of the devil and that he had influenced me to do that self-injuring act of burning my throat. My throat was not seriously damaged, but I was stunned. I stood up and walked as calmly as I could through the kitchen and opened the door to the cellar. I took one step down the stairs and turned around and closed the door behind me. I held onto the knob with both my hands in order to make sure that the devil didn't follow me.

Here is what I was mentally telling myself: "OK, I'm afraid. But isn't this ridiculous? I am holding the door shut to keep out the devil. Forget about getting a grip on the doorknob. I have to get a grip on myself. I am only imagining that this is the devil. Just because I had a thought to swallow the cup of tea doesn't mean the idea came from the devil's mind. It's just my own mind playing tricks on me. Remember, the roshi said that there are no such things as devils in reality."

After all that reasonable self-talk I convinced myself to go back and not let my inappropriate fears get the best of me. When I returned, there was Jack's motionless and silent body as before. This time I sat on the floor in the center of the room and turned my back to him. After a moment, Jack got up from where he was sitting and walked over to me. I turned my head to the left side as he approached me. Standing behind me and bending over on my left side, he spoke for the first time, saying, "I know you love me, don't you?" He smiled. Seeing Jack's face close up, I felt even more strongly that I was looking at the devil.

His words struck fear into me like a dagger. To me it felt as if he was saying, "I know you love sin and evil, don't you?" His smiling face was less than a foot away from mine, and I could see for the first time that his pupils were completely dilated. He had the look of a walking corpse. There was obvious terror on my face, more fearful even than the panic I felt when I first saw the snake. He could see my overwhelming fear, and yet he continued to smile with an unchanging expression that seemed pasted on his face. There was no uncertainty in my mind. I was convinced that this was the devil asking me to love him.

I quickly got up and left the house in a state of hysteria. I was running and crying as I ran all the way to the Zen center. I pulled at the locked door of the back building where the roshi was and pounded on the door, making a racket. No one came right away, so I went to the back of the main building. Finding an open door, I ran inside and upstairs to the bathroom. I turned on the faucet and washed my hands and face. Then the roshi appeared, and he asked me to come to his office in the back.

I sat down and said, "If it's all right with you, I would like to close my eyes and meditate for a few minutes before we talk." The roshi nodded his approval, and we meditated. After a couple of minutes, I opened my eyes. Then he opened his eyes and immediately said, "Acid!" He obviously must have read my mind, because Howard was the only one who knew, and he hadn't told anyone. He added, "You know you shouldn't take that stuff."

"Yes, I know it's not good. I was going to tell you about it on Thursday when I took it, but something stopped me. Anyway, that day I entered the 'gateless gate.'" By using that term, I was claiming to be enlightened, but it was actually my unsettled state of mind that was expressing itself. I could have told him instead about the profound feeling of love and oneness that I experienced at the church after the man took me on the memory walk, citing that as a lower level experience of enlightenment, but the memory of the event didn't enter my mind at the time. Even if it had come to mind, I would still not have talked about it to the roshi, because it seemed that the experience was due to some kind of relationship with Jesus, with the church, and with the man who took me there.

The roshi then said, "I will test you. Is this all right with you?" He asked this because the deepest states of enlightenment convey a certainty. This certainty can be so profound that the recipient may refuse to be tested, on the grounds that there is no need for someone else's, even a roshi's, approval and confirmation. So the fact that I would accept being tested showed the roshi that I did not have this kind of profound certainty.

"Yes, you can test me," I said.

The roshi spread his arms fully apart horizontally and asked, "How far apart are my hands?"

"I don't know," I answered honestly. "I don't have any answers. But I did see amazingly colored clouds dancing in the sky, and I felt I was glowing with light."

"When did this happen?"

"Thursday while the acid was still affecting me, I felt a tremendous energy coming through my body. It felt like this energy was radiating in all directions, maybe even up into the clouds. When I looked up, I saw the clouds above my head dance with many beautiful colors. Howard was there with me, and he saw it, too, so it wasn't a hallucination from the acid. Then last night at dusk when it was getting dark outside, Howard and I were meditating together. Howard said he saw me glowing with a white light in and around my body."

The roshi was unimpressed, saying, "This may mean something, but this is not enlightenment."

"I WANT PERFECT ENLIGHTENMENT!" I screamed at the very top of my lungs.

The roshi remained perfectly calm when these words leaped out of my mouth, and he said in a very even and composed tone, "That is a good goal to have." I was shaking all over and tried to say something, but I just stammered. The roshi commanded in a very firm voice, "Get yourself together!" Immediately I sat up straight in the chair and felt a surge of energy come up my spine and into my head. He then said, "As you know, we are having a sesshin starting today. I know you have not signed up for this sesshin, but for this week you can have a retreat of your own at your house. Concentrate on your meditation and put aside everything else. Don't get sidetracked by any psychic experiences."

I thanked him and got up to leave. When I reached the door, I turned and prostrated myself like I would during dokusan and then left. As I walked back to the house, I suddenly realized that I had told the roshi nothing about my experience of seeing the devil in the form of Jack. I wasn't trying to hide it from him, but it just never came to my mind while I was talking with him. It was strange that I forgot this incident, because that was the reason why I had run to the center in such a panic. But it was just as well, because he probably wouldn't have believed me anyway.

By the time I arrived back at the house, it was still early in the morning. As I walked upstairs to my bedroom, Joel was coming out of the room he shared with his brother Jack. With the door open, I could see Jack lying there in his bed. As I stood there looking, Jack sat up and turned his body toward the doorway. I asked, "Are you just getting up now?"

"Yes, I am getting up. Why do you ask?" Jack inquired groggily with his sleepy, but quite normal (not dilated) eyes.

"I thought that maybe I saw you earlier this morning downstairs. So that wasn't you that I saw?"

"It wasn't me, unless I was walking in my sleep. It must have been someone else that you saw."

"Yeah, it must have been someone else."

A short while later, the monk Pierce showed up at our house and asked Howard to come to the center. When Howard came back to the house, he said, "I talked with the roshi, and he gave me a message for you. He said you shouldn't have a retreat. Instead you should relax, take it easy, and not meditate."

"Did the roshi ask you any questions about me?" I asked.

"He asked me if I noticed any strange things that happened concerning you."

"What did you say?"

"I told him that you seemed normal to me and that I didn't see anything strange happening in relation to you," Howard told me confidently.

"It's good you told him I looked normal to you. But did you tell him about seeing the clouds do tricks on Thursday or about seeing the white light on my body yesterday?"

"No, I didn't tell him about that stuff. Remember when we were in the woods, you told me that you felt it was best not to tell other people about having unusual experiences."

"You're right. I did say that, and silence is the best policy in most cases. However, I talked with the roshi before you saw him, and I told him about the colorful clouds dancing and the white light incident, and I told him that you were with me. He wanted to see if you would confirm what I had told him. Because you didn't, he thinks I was lying or that my imagination was getting the best of me. He may even think that I was having hallucinations or delusions since I admitted to taking LSD. That must be why he gave you the message for me to take it easy and not to meditate."

Howard looked concerned and asked, "Do you want me to go back and tell him about the dancing colored clouds and seeing your body light up?"

"No, Howard, that's all right. Maybe it happened this way for a reason. Let's just leave it the way it is. Let's just keep everything that has happened between you and me." Howard then nodded his agreement.

"Allan, I think that's enough for now. These old events are hard for me to talk about, so maybe in a month or so we can go to the next installment. How does that sound to you?"

"That's fine with me," he said. "However, I do have a question. You were describing how you felt and reacted to this devil twenty-five years ago, but how has your thinking changed about this experience?"

"I still think I saw a devil or the devil, but I believe the devil is an entity that is also part of God, just like you and me. However, he is committed to manufacturing illusions. So I have asked myself, how would I respond to the devil now if he said, 'I know that you love me, don't you?' Ideally I would say, 'I love you because you are part of God, part of the reality that I share with you. But I do not love your illusions that you are attached to.' Of course, I don't know if I would have the composure to say or think that, but the major thing I would like to do is to not give in to fear as I did then. I do not know if I will ever see the devil again, but I do know I will have to stare death in the face one day, and I think it will be the same kind of challenge. The idea will be to let go of fear by seeing illusions as meaningless and to trust in God as the only reality, in which you and I truly live and have our being. So does that answer your question about the devil?"

"Mostly, but I have had a lot of perceptions that I believed, and then later found out that I was mistaken. Do you think your seeing of the devil could be just a misperception or maybe even a hallucination?"

"I was actually reluctant to tell you about seeing the devil. It's just too incredible to believe and so I understand why you might be skeptical. I have had a lot of misperceptions in the past, and in fact there were times in my life when I was thinking very irrationally, and I will tell you about those times in the future. I don't mind admitting those mistaken perceptions and times of irrational thinking, yet this isn't one of them, and there is no possibility of a hallucination. I have never had any visual hallucinations, even when I took LSD. The only time I ever even considered I might be hallucinating was when I saw the colorful clouds jumping around in the sky, but fortunately Howard was there to confirm what I was seeing. No one was with me when I saw the devil, but I will never forget those eyes. His pupils were so dilated that I couldn't see the brown iris at all. Drugs can dilate the eyes, but I have never seen eyes quite that dilated, with the exception of an open-eyed corpse I once saw in a hospital where I worked. I know it sounds farfetched to say that I saw the devil, but that is what I believe happened."

"Well, just one more quick question. If Jack was still in bed, where did the devil's body come from?"

"Angels are able to present themselves in human form. According to Christian tradition, the devil is a fallen angel, and he has the ability to present himself in any form he chooses. For example, he can show himself in the form of a snake or in a human form. The body I saw wasn't Jack being possessed by the devil; it was the devil presenting himself in a manufactured duplicate of Jack's body. But it seems that the devil couldn't duplicate the eyes very well, because there was no life in them."

"That answers my question," Allan acknowledged.

"Do you believe I really saw a devil?" I asked.

"You were certainly right when you said that it requires a stretch of the imagination to believe that you saw a devil. On the other hand I believed you when you told me in the past about encountering angels. Since I believe you saw angels, it's not really that much more of a stretch of my imagination to believe that you saw a devil. So, yes, I do believe you saw a devil or the devil."

"Thanks, it's nice to be believed. Do you want to meditate now?"

"Sure," Allan agreed, and so we meditated together as usual.

56

LAST DAYS IN ROCHESTER

~ • ~

Allan, I'm sure you recall those old television episodes of *Twilight Zone* that Rod Serling would begin by saying something like, "You're traveling through another dimension—a dimension not only of sight and sound, but of mind." Well, that's where I was going in June of 1969 at the point in my story where I left off last time. My mind was in a very strange place. For several days whatever I desired would come to me. For example, if the thought came to my mind that I would like an orange, someone would come up to me and ask me if I wanted an orange. Another simple example: I was in my room, and the thought came that I wanted to go to the park. Just then someone knocked on the door to my room and asked if I wanted to go on a ride to the park.

You could say this is coincidence, because these kinds of experiences happen to everyone occasionally. What made them unusual in my case for these few days was that they occurred continuously. In Buddhist philosophy everything is interconnected, and nothing exists by itself or for itself. It seemed to me that I was continually experiencing this interconnectedness—normally overlooked in everyday mundane living—in which we mistakenly take for granted that objects and events are isolated from each other.

On the one hand, it appeared that if I wanted something, it manifested. On the other hand, I considered it equally possible that I was psychically picking up what was going to happen just before it happened, and then my mind simply chose to want whatever was about to happen. In either case, I decided that perhaps I was imagining this getting of whatever I wanted, so I consciously decided to set up a test. I lay down on my bed with my eyes closed and said to myself, "I want to eat something, but I will not get up or do anything myself to make this happen." A few minutes later someone came to my door and knocked. I had just said to myself, "I will not get up or do anything," so true to my word I didn't even respond to the knock.

It was Howard, and he opened the door and came in anyway, even though he had never done that before. Still with my eyes closed, I heard him ask, "I've got a cookie for you. Do you want it?" I didn't answer because I had already told myself that I wouldn't do anything myself to make it happen. I thought he would logically just walk away, but instead he sat down on the bed next to me. Then he opened my mouth and put the cookie half in, half out of my mouth. But again I had said that I wouldn't do anything, so I didn't even chew it. Seeing that I wasn't moving my jaws, Howard put his hands on my face and repeatedly opened and closed my mouth. He continued in this manner until the cookie was completely chewed, and only then did he leave the room.

So, you see, my every form-related desire was being fulfilled effortlessly. However, even that did not satisfy me because I still wanted enlightenment, which was not form-related. In order to have enlightenment I felt I needed to let go of all my form- related desires. I thought desirelessness would lead to enlightenment. Then I remembered that common herb that Adam, my friend from Westbrook, had told me about that took away all of his preferences so that he became completely desireless. I obtained the herb and ate it. It was distasteful, so I only ate as much as I could stomach at one time.

It did everything Adam said it would and more. I became completely desireless. My former state of having all my desires fulfilled disappeared because I no longer had desires for anything. Taking the herb also took away my emotions and my personality, so I had no preferences. Essentially I became a non-person. I had become like some hospital patients I would meet years later in my work as a recreation therapist. My job was to interest patients in enjoying life because it would motivate them for recovery. However, the older ones who were ready to pass on to the next world would lose all interest in anything this world had to offer. I had become like them.

Under normal circumstances, preferences come from thinking of past choices and wanting to repeat the familiar and pleasant ones. But in my unusual condition my past had no influence whatsoever on me. In fact, it was as if I had no past at all. I certainly didn't have amnesia, and an occasional past memory would pop into my mind, triggered by something happening in the present moment. Nevertheless, generally my thoughts were simply not directed toward anything in the past, and, for that matter, not toward the future either. My mind was in such a dark place that I had even forgotten that I had taken the herb. Consequently, I did not have the consolation of anticipating that its effect would probably wear off after several months, as it had for Adam. In addition, I had a reaction to the herb that Adam hadn't described to me—I started sometimes to have unusual impulses. Because I had no preferences, and no discrimination to decide whether to act on these impulses, I would just act on them whenever they arose, no matter how irrational they might have seemed to me in my normal state.

Prior to this time I had experienced many unusual states of mind. These included psychic experiences, but not what I would consider to be irrational behavior. The most bizarre experience I'd had was when I saw the devil in Jack's body. However, even though that experience may sound irrational, I can't attribute that experience to an irrational mental perception on my part. To this day I am convinced that I really did encounter the devil, but I am just as certain that at a later date, immediately after taking the herb, my mental condition dramatically deteriorated into an irrational state.

For example, one day I went to the church opposite the Zen center and stood looking at the altar. I had an impulse to scream, so I screamed loudly, but without any particular emotion. Another time I decided to go to the church and bring a large candle, which was inside a glass jar. Standing at the top of the stairs leading out of the house, I had an impulse to throw the candle down on the ground, so I did, breaking both the candle and the glass jar. I also did a lot of walking. Sometimes I would go to a lake near the house, and I once acted on the impulse to jump into it.

Because I had no emotions, my face was expressionless. Once I was walking downtown, and I stopped at the side of the road to look down a drain at the light reflecting on the water. A man driving by stopped his car, came over to see me, and asked if he could help me. I said I was all right, and he left. Another friend from the center came to my house to see how I was, and he asked me to make a drawing. It was his way of testing my mental state, but I drew a good drawing of his head, so he was reassured. I had not lost my fine motor coordination skills, but at times I would lose control of my bladder. At those times I would feel a flash of energy come over my whole body, and I would urinate in my pants and think nothing of it. In addition to visiting the church across from the center, I went to other churches, and losing bladder control happened on three of those occasions.

I had some money, but remembered the roshi talking about financial concerns being a stumbling block for seekers. I went outside and gave away part of my money to strangers, who were first surprised and then pleased. The money wasn't important to me, and it made others happy. A man was selling roses so I bought a bouquet and brought it to the Zen center. There was no one there because they were at a sesshin, so I put the flowers on the roshi's desk. I took the last twenty-five dollars I had and went with Howard to the store, where we bought food for the household. We didn't need the food, but I just wanted to spend all the money so that I wouldn't have any.

It was almost the end of June, and everyone in our household was moving out because the landlord had complained that there were too many people living there. I didn't know where I would go, but wasn't concerned.

Howard had gone to New York and said he would be coming back in a few days, but he didn't. By the last day of the month, I was the only one left.

That last evening I was sitting on the couch in the living room and a white dog appeared at the front door, which I had left open. I don't know how the dog managed to open the outer screen door on the porch that led to the front door. The dog looked at me and trotted over to the couch. He lie down and put his head in my lap as though we were familiar old friends. I put my hand on him and felt I was blessing him. The dog was very old, and his white hair was probably the grey hair of old age. It looked like he didn't have much longer to live. I felt he had come to me for a blessing as a preparation for his passing away. Since the dog appeared to be approaching death, I wondered if the dog was an *omen of death* for me as well, though this was of no concern to me because I had no preferences. After about an hour the dog got up and walked slowly to the door. He looked back at me as if to say, "Thank you and good-bye," and he left.

That night I prepared for leaving the house the next day by gathering together a few items I would be taking with me. I stuffed all the rest of my belongings in a duffle bag and put it in the cellar. The next morning, on the first day of July when the new tenants arrived, I received their permission to leave behind my duffle bag. I walked out the front door, and lying on the ground was an old knapsack, which happened to have a slash of wet paint on it. I picked it up and stuffed my few things into it. I tied the knapsack to a walking stick and put it over my shoulder. I surely must have looked the way the Fool is depicted in the Tarot cards. I wandered off with no particular destination in mind.

As I walked along something odd happened. I felt as though I stepped into a very different state of mind, but I cannot even begin to adequately describe it. At the time, it felt to me as though I had walked into another dimension. Imagine that you are watching a story on television and the picture blanks out for a second or two, and then it suddenly returns about where it left off. My experience was sort of like that; only in my case, the three-dimensional world entirely disappeared, bringing me into some altered consciousness, and then the world reappeared. My mind didn't blank out like someone fainting. If anything, my mind was somehow energized, and my awareness was heightened rather than dulled. However, it happened so suddenly and was over immediately, so I had no time at all to figure out exactly what had happened. But in that instant of this strange state, there was one thing that was tangible that did happen, even though it is hard to believe.

After coming back from that instant of stepping into the altered state of consciousness, my right hand was still in the exact same position it had been in previously, holding the stick in place over my right shoulder.

However, I noticed right away that the weight of the stick was greatly reduced, so I turned around to see why the stick was so light and saw that the knapsack had fallen to the ground. Except for the instant of altered consciousness, I was certain I had continuously held the stick at an angle so the knapsack could not have fallen off the end of the stick. Besides, I had tied two knots so securely that they would not have allowed the knapsack to slide off the stick even if it was tilted downward. I assumed that the knots must have unraveled to allow the knapsack to fall, so I examined them. However, they were not untied, and the only conclusion I could come to was that the knapsack had fallen *through* the stick. I don't know how that is possible. What I do know for sure is that the knapsack must have fallen at precisely the same instant I had stepped into that altered state.

As I continued walking, I came upon a cherry tree on someone's lawn. I ate some cherries as my meal for the day. When I resumed walking, I came upon a large cement bridge with cars going underneath it and over it. At the top of one of the slanted cement walls that supported the bridge, I found a ledge hidden from view. I decided to stay there for the night. It was cold, and I couldn't sleep with the noise of the cars going overhead all night.

In the morning I stood at the edge of the cement ledge on which I was perched and urinated from there. I looked up and saw a man staring at me from a distance. I couldn't see his face, but my impression was that he didn't approve of me. Normally I was emotionless, but this man's looking at me made me feel disgusted with myself for the first time. I asked myself, "What am I doing here urinating off a bridge? Where am I going?" I decided then that I would go back to my parents in Connecticut and get myself back together again. It did not occur to me until years later that perhaps I came to my senses at that time because of the strange experience I had the day before in which I thought I had stepped into another dimension. Maybe I had received some sort of unsolicited divine blessing that I was oblivious to when it happened, but there's no way for me to know for sure.

Having decided to leave Rochester, I remembered that the day before when I was packing my things away, I had found a check for $16 that I didn't even realize that I had with me. I went to the Zen center to see if I could find someone to cash this check. I was told to go into the roshi's office and ask him if he would cash it. I asked him if I could talk with him.

"Yes, come in. We can only talk for a few minutes because I am very busy."

I told him, "I've decided to leave here, and I was hoping that you might be able to cash a check for me so I can pay for the bus fare."

He was pleased and said, "I think you've made the right decision. Sometimes after meditating a long time, it's good to take a nice rest." He gave me the $16 in cash, and then he handed the check toward me, saying, "Here, why don't you take this too?"

"No, I can't do that," I insisted. "You keep the check. I don't need it."

"Do you have friends to stay with?" he asked.

"Yes, I do. I want to thank you for something. I want to thank you for teaching me humility. What I mean is, I feel humbled by everything that has happened, and I feel grateful for that," I said without any expression.

The roshi said, "One day a while ago I saw you, and you looked like Jesus Christ, because you were so filled with love on that day."

"What day was that?" I asked, still without expression, but wondering if he was reading my mind in regard to Jesus and my visits to churches. I hadn't told anyone about the man taking me on a memory walk to the church, but I wondered if he was psychically picking up on that specific experience.

His face showed obvious disappointment at my question. He replied, "I don't remember what day exactly."

"I have found myself wandering around from church to church. Would you suggest any church that I might visit in the future?"

"The churches around here are rather sterile. You would probably like to go to Mexico, not to the big churches, but to the small ones. They have an intimacy about them that I think you would like." Then he changed the subject. "Where have you been sleeping?"

"I found a place under a bridge nearby."

He made a joke about sleeping under a bridge. I don't remember the joke, but I do remember he smiled at the punch line. I wasn't trying to be rude, but I didn't smile in response to his attempt to make a joke. In a strange way we had switched places in one respect. During my dokusan experiences in the past he was invariably expressionless, and I was animated, but this time I was expressionless, and he was animated. Perhaps this was because he was trying to reach out to me, seeing that I was in need. He cleared his throat after seeing my lack of response to his joke, and asked, "Would you like something to eat?"

"No, thank you," I responded, although I hadn't eaten except for the cherries I had the day before. I asked in my monotone voice, "Did you like the roses?"

"Oh, you were the one who left those roses! That was very kind of you. Thank you. Please let me give you a present in return," he said and pulled open a drawer and handed me a package of incense. I accepted his gift, and he asked, "Would you like to stay over for one more day? You can sleep in this back room tonight, and then go on your way tomorrow in the morning."

I agreed. He shook my hand and wished me well, but I had an unusual feeling. I felt intuitively that if I slept over, he would somehow during my sleep affect me with his psychic force. I thought he would probably do this for a good purpose to help me, but I did not like the idea. As soon as I stepped outside the door, I knew I wouldn't come back to the Zen center. Right away I saw a friend and asked her if she would give me a ride to my old house to pick up my duffle bag in the basement and then a ride to the bus station. She did this kindness for me, and I asked her to tell the roshi that I had changed my mind about staying overnight. I had just enough money for the bus ride to New York City, with two quarters left over.

I used one quarter for the subway to go to Janet's apartment at 13 St. Mark's Place, where I had last seen Marie. I didn't expect it, but she and Janet were both still there, and they let me sleep over. However, Marie was frankly shocked at my bald head and expressionless face, and I could see the fear on her face. I didn't know if she was afraid *of* me or afraid *for* me, but with my monotone voice and expressionless face and shaved head, I was not the same person she had known. I slept over just that one night and left early the next morning, leaving behind the concerned faces of both Marie and Janet. With the one quarter I had left, I took the subway to a bank in Astoria, Queens, where I still had fifteen dollars left in a bank account. I closed out the account and had just enough money to take the train from New York to Connecticut.

When I had left Marie and Janet, I thought those were the last two friends I would see in New York City, but something quite unexpected happened. As I was walking on the street headed toward Grand Central Station, I saw a friend named John Nuzzo coming toward me. He had worked with me as a guard at the Whitney Museum, and at that time he also worked as a free-lance illustrator. I was a little jealous of the fact he was making money from his artistic skill while I was not. One morning at work as I was getting ready to go home after my night shift, my supervisor told me he was considering firing John for coming in late. I said, "John has other interests, so I don't think it would bother him too much to give up this job." Shortly after that John was fired. My conscience pointed a finger at my jealousy, as well as my hypocrisy—after all, I had almost been fired myself for being late to work. Fortunately, I saw John before he left and told him about my totally inappropriate comment to the supervisor. Explaining how terrible I felt for probably contributing to his firing, I apologized and asked him to forgive me. John graciously forgave me, but I could see by the expression on his face that I had disappointed him, so I still felt guilty about what I had done.

When I greeted him by name on the street, he didn't even recognize me at first, because my appearance had changed so much. So I said, "I'm Don from the Whitney Museum."

John's whole face brightened up with joy, and he gave me a big hug. In that instant I knew that he really had forgiven me, and I even smiled. As you know, Allan, the Course tells us that when forgiveness happens, it's a miracle of love for both the giver and the receiver. That smile in response to being forgiven was certainly a miracle for me. It was the first sign of an expression on my face since I had taken the herb. John had long black hair and a moustache, just like I had when we had worked together as museum guards. Seeing my shaved head, he said enthusiastically, "I bet you aren't working at the Whitney any more!" He added jokingly, "Did you become a Hari Krishna devotee, and are you going to sell me some candy or flowers?"

I said in my monotone voice, "I went to a Zen center in Rochester, and now I am on my way to catch a train back to my parents' home in Connecticut. It was really nice to see you here. You look good."

"Life has been good to me," he said in an upbeat manner. We wished each other well and soon parted. The smile I displayed in response to John's forgiveness turned out to be only a temporary interruption in my state of mind and didn't really break the spell hanging over me like a dark cloud blotting out the sun. Nevertheless, in my somewhat trance-like condition, I wasn't out of place in my final walk through the streets of New York, where the first thing you learn is to be entirely expressionless and uninterested in anything around you.

"Let's stop here, Allan. How about if we continue in a month or so?"

That was fine with Allan, who was flexible about how we spent our time together. Sometimes we just hung out together watching television, before having our twenty minute silent meditation.

57

BACK TO CONNECTICUT

~ • ~

A month or so later, during one of my weekly visits with Allan, I picked up the story where I had left off. The pieces of my shadow puzzle I called "Spider Boy" and "Pole Man" are bracketed in the text of this chapter because I didn't use these specific terms while talking to Allan. Because I had forgiven him, I only talked about my past lives occasionally. Since I did not want Allan to get the mistaken impression I was blaming him for the past, I especially avoided references to the Pole Man lifetime.

I knew my parents were at the summer cottage at 41 Dolphin Avenue in Westbrook, which was about a three-minute walk to the ocean, so I went there. It was Thursday, the day before the July 4th holiday weekend. [The cottage looked the same as it did fifteen years earlier when the picture shown below of my mother, my brother Rick, and me was taken.]

CHILDHOOD PICTURE SHOWING WESTBOOK COTTAGE

When I arrived unannounced, my parents were surprised at my coming, but even more surprised by my shaved head and zombie-like manner. Mom gave me a big hug. "I like you better with hair," she said. "You'll have to just grow it back. Look, here are two of your watercolors that I just put in frames today." She enthusiastically showed me the two boating pictures. "I was just going to put them both up on this wall, but now that you're here, you can help me."

After we put up the pictures, Mom asked, "Did they beat you there?"

Not mentioning anything about the stick used for hitting during Zen meditation, I asked instead, "Why would you ask something like that?"

"I had a dream a while back that they were hitting you at that Zen place. I guess it was just my imagination getting the best of me." I found out later that Mom had just gone through a very stressful emotional period in which she had the strange feeling of not knowing who she was. Mom told me she kept asking herself, "Who am I?" It appears that she was psychically picking up on and internalizing my identity struggles. It was not long before Mom and Dad sat me down, and Dad said, "You know you will have to pay rent if you stay here. What kind of job are you planning on looking for?"

I really hadn't thought about getting a job. "Maybe I can find a job at a hospital as an aide."

"You're a college graduate," Dad said, "and you want to be an aide in a hospital? I don't get it. Why would you want to do that?"

"I would like to help people who are sick." Actually I was the one who was sick and needed help, but there was very little self-reflective thinking going on in my mind.

They both made a face of dissatisfaction with my vocational choice, and Dad said, "I don't understand it, but it's your life. Just remember you will have to start paying rent. You can stay here and rest for a couple of weeks. But if you want to work in a hospital, you will have to go back to Meriden to apply for a job there." By the far out look in my tired eyes they could see that I wasn't myself, but they were in too much denial about my condition to see that I would need more than a couple of weeks to rest and recover. It didn't occur to them that not only did I need rest, but that no one would hire me the way I looked and expressed myself.

I was able to relax lying in the sun on the beach and to swim in the ocean. I went to church with my parents on two consecutive Sundays and received communion, but didn't go to confession. I spoke very seldom and generally only when someone asked me something. One day when it was very cloudy and no one else was on the beach, I was walking with my longtime childhood beach friend, Freddy Balducci. I looked up toward the sky and hollered as loud as I could, "SUN, SUN, SUN, SUN, SUN, SUN!"

"What are you doing?" Freddy asked.

"I want the sun. I am a sun worshipper."

"I'm a sun worshipper too, but why are you hollering?"

It had become normal for me to want nothing. Wanting something—even wanting the sun in this odd manner of yelling it out was a welcome departure from my perpetual desirelessness. The hollering actually felt good, because it was the first bit of emotion that I had experienced in a long time. It was also the first spontaneous thing I had done in a while. I responded to Freddy's question, "I'm calling the sun—telling it to come out." Perhaps in calling out to the sun, I was really calling out for God's Light to dawn in the cloudy mindlessness of my mind. However, a plea for divine help was certainly not in my conscious awareness at the time.

Freddy made a questioning face, but then he smiled. I knew he thought I was acting strangely, but I felt he was spending time with me *because* I was acting strangely, to hopefully help me to snap out of my robot-like state. In my childhood I had spent many happy summer days involving beach activities, touch football, or playing cards with Freddy, his older brother Bobby, and his younger brother Joey. Remembering how we had often gone fishing together in the past, Freddy invited me to go on a fishing outing the next day. I agreed to go, but I said I was a vegetarian and was not interested in doing any fishing myself. Joey came with us, and Bobby would have come too, but he wasn't in Westbrook at the time. We went in the Balducci's boat, an ordinary old rowboat with a small outboard motor on it. We dropped anchor a long way off shore near a large rock formation that formed a small island.

As Freddy and Joey were fishing, I bent my head over and stared into the water. My prescription sunglasses slipped off and fell in. Without giving it a second thought, I stood up and dove in after the fast disappearing glasses. As my body knifed into the water, I immediately opened my eyes to look for the glasses. But instead of seeing them, all I saw was a large rock as my diving body slid past it, barely missing it by a few inches. Then, surprisingly, my hand hit the still sinking glasses, and I closed my fingers around my retrieved prize.

When my head popped up to the surface, Freddy was hollering loudly and excitedly for me to come back to the boat. I swam around the big rock I had almost hit. I hadn't seen the rock from the boat before diving in because it rose up from the bottom like a giant pillar with its top a foot below the surface, making it hard to see. I handed my glasses to Freddy and pulled myself back into the boat. "I saw you dive in. Did you know that you just missed that rock there?" Freddy asked as he pointed to the rock hiding just below the surface. "You could have killed yourself! You must have a guardian angel watching over you. Why did you dive off the boat?"

I seldom talked unless asked a direct question. "My sunglasses fell in, and I went after them," I replied in my unvarying monotone, without expressing or feeling the slightest bit of regret.

"Well, it's a miracle that you're alive, and it's another miracle that you could find your glasses in that water. But you have got to make me a promise. Promise me you won't jump in the water again," he said firmly and seriously.

"I promise," I said. In all the events that had happened to me recently it had seemed like I was living in a world in which everything was going in slow motion, including me. However, this incident seemed different because it happened so quickly, and I responded so immediately. In that respect the incident was invigorating, but my feelings were so numb that it didn't really dawn on me at the time that I should feel grateful about avoiding what could easily have been a disastrous injury or even death, smashing into the rock. [I was not yet aware that I had narrowly missed ending my life like the Pole Man falling from the pole and having his body hit the rocks below. Another parallel was that just as I had intentionally leaped from the boat, Spider Boy had committed suicide by jumping off a pier and drowning in the ocean.]

The rest of the outing was uneventful except for the many fish that Freddy and Joey caught, which wasn't all that unusual. When we got back, Freddy gave my parents some fish for dinner and as many additional fish as could fit into the tiny freezer in their undersized refrigerator. He humorously joked about my diving into the water and miraculously recovering my lost sunglasses. He did not want to unnecessarily alarm my parents, so he diplomatically didn't say a word about my dangerous near-miss of the submerged rock, correctly assessing I would not mention it either.

On another day Freddy took me for a long walk, as usual in our bare feet. We walked along the beach toward the long peninsula that had at its end the cement wall remnants of a building that had burnt down. Years before I had walked out there to the ruins of that building, even though my parents had warned me not to go there because of the broken glass in that area. On my way back I had stepped on a piece of glass hidden in the sand and cut the big toe on my right foot. I had to hobble all the way home and confess to my parents that I should have listened to them. [Without realizing it, I was playing out the pattern of the past life as the Spider Boy in which I went to a dangerous, forbidden old building as a child and came back with an injured right foot.] But on this walk with Freddy it was high tide, and the path to the end of the peninsula was covered over with water, making it into a temporary island. Consequently, we turned around and went back a different way, going through nearby Pilot's Point. There was a boat marina there and also a pier extending into the very deep water. For one summer before the security tightened at the marina, I used to like diving off of that pier, especially at low tide. [With no conscious awareness of my past lives, perhaps I was unknowingly attracted to the pier because Spider Boy had ended his life by jumping off of one.]

When we got back to my parents' cottage, Freddy launched into telling my parents about the time years before when he said I had cured him of a lifetime of cigarette smoking. He explained:

One night at the beach I was in a car with my brothers, and Don was smoking a cigarette, which he did only occasionally. I told Don, "I'd like to have a cigarette to see what it's like."

"OK," Don said, "but I don't think you can handle it."

I said, "What do you mean? I can handle anything you can!" So Don gave me a light, and I had my first cigarette. But I started choking from the smoke, and Bobby, Joey, and Don started to laugh at me. And the more I choked, the more they roared with laughter. Finally I couldn't take it anymore, so I opened the door and got out for some fresh air. I stomped my foot on the cigarette and angrily proclaimed, "I'm never going to smoke again in my life," and I never did. At the time I was real angry with my brothers and Don because I didn't like them laughing at me. But Don calmed me down by saying, "We were just kidding. We didn't want to hurt your feelings. It's not a good thing to start smoking, so you're better off without it."

However, that's not the end of the story. Years later I found out why they were really laughing so hysterically. While I was smoking my first cigarette, I was sitting in the passenger seat, looking straight ahead, and Don was sitting directly behind me in the back seat where I couldn't see him. From behind me he started to blow smoke all around me—from my left and right and even over the top of my head. I was surrounded by a whole dense cloud of his smoke, but because I hadn't smoked before, I thought all that smoke was coming from my own cigarette. My brothers could see what Don was doing, and all three of them broke out in laughter because I had no idea what was going on. My brothers and Don didn't tell me the joke right away because they really didn't want me to start smoking. They finally told me about it years later because by then I hadn't smoked for so long that I wasn't going to start up. So that's how Don tricked me into having a healthier life without cigarettes.

I think Freddy graciously told this story to my parents in order to bring back a familiar memory to my mind and hopefully restore in me some sense of normalcy. It seemed obvious that everyone around me probably believed that the Zen Buddhists I had been with must have brainwashed me because all they could see in me was a shell of my former self. Freddy's well-intentioned story didn't even bring a smile to my face as I listened unresponsively.

Two weeks passed by, and I knew my parents wanted me to be looking for work. When I heard that Alvin, another beach buddy, was driving north through my hometown of Meriden on Thursday, July 17th, I asked him for a ride. Alvin and his wife drove me to my family's home in Meriden, and I invited them inside to each pick one of my works of art to keep. Alvin's wife chose an outdoor watercolor scene while he chose a semi-abstract acrylic painting. I asked him, "Do you know what that is a picture of?"

Alvin was a jovial person who normally would make me laugh without even trying, and in his characteristically joyful manner he said, "I don't know what it is, and I don't care. I just know what I like."

"Well then, it's yours." Under the circumstances I didn't tell him that the picture was a close up and rather obvious representation of an erect penis in red on a blue background, and then right beside it was a vagina in blue on a red background. Afterwards I wondered if he or anyone else would ever notice the subject matter of this picture, but I was sure Alvin would laugh out loud if he ever made that discovery.

My brother Rick and sisters Lillian and Joanna were married and had moved away from Meriden. My oldest brother Paul was at our parents' home on one of his intermittent stays, so he and I watched television that night. Paul called to me as I was going to bed, so I went into his bedroom to see what he wanted. He said, "I read the book you sent to me about Zen." Although Paul was not motivated to do well academically in public school, a thirst for knowledge awakened in him once he got on his own, and he became an avid reader. Consequently, on the previous Christmas I had given him a copy of Kapleau's *The Three Pillars of Zen*. "Your seeking enlightenment is foolishness. It doesn't make sense to seek to eliminate your ego. When you get to where you are going, there won't be any *you* there to enjoy it," he said and paused for me to respond. But I just looked at him with my blank expression, so he continued in a quiet yet disdainful tone, "And look at what you are doing to yourself. You look lifeless and awful. You don't care about anything. You don't care about Mom or Dad or me. You don't even care about yourself."

Then something snapped deep within me, like a volcano unexpectedly erupting, as I screamed, "I LOVE YOU!" I had always felt distant from my brother Paul, and yet knew I cared about him. My words conveyed this ambivalence since they expressed the idea of love, but the overpowering forcefulness could hardly be called loving. However, the emotional force couldn't be called fear, anger, or pain either, so I don't know how to identify it. It just felt like I was a witness to a primal energy that exploded through

THE ALTAR OF MOUNT CARMEL CHURCH

me and then was gone as suddenly as it had come. I waited for Paul to say something, but he looked stunned, as though he couldn't speak, so I turned around and walked away.

Many months later Paul would remind me of this incident, saying, "I have been in bar fights and lots of other dangerous situations. But I was never as afraid in those situations as I was when you shouted at me. I don't know what came over you at that time, but whatever it was, it scared the hell out of me." My emotional outburst was an anomaly, inconsistent with my dull, passionless manner and usual monotone.

On the following day I had forgotten all about my encounter with Paul. After walking about a mile to the Meriden Hospital to apply for a job, I was interviewed by a woman who told me there were no openings. Her glance upward toward my shaved head gave me the impression she wouldn't be calling me back any time soon—remember this is conservative New England in the last year of the sixties.

I spent the rest of the day wandering around visiting various churches. By the time I reached Mount Carmel Church, it was dark outside. I had spent the Sunday mornings of my childhood admiring the beauty of the stained glass windows and the majestic strength of the giant marble pillars imported from Italy. However, here surrounded entirely by darkness, all I could see clearly was the altar illuminated by a single light. There was the large black marble cross in contrast to a bright golden background, but most striking of all was the figure of Jesus Himself with His arms stretched out on the cross—an appropriately pure white marble form that gave the illusion of almost glowing from within. Although I had seen it many times in the light of day, even in my current apathetic state of mind I could see for the first time how exquisitely beautiful it was, shining in the darkness. I sat there looking up at His form for a long time—yet impassively, without any inclination to pray. Of course, I knew the marble sculpture was only a representation of Jesus, yet high up on the cross He seemed so distant and inaccessible. There was no thought of His all-pervading presence that could have been found within my own heart, if only I had looked for it there.

Next I made my way to Saint Joseph's Church. Here I went up past the altar rail, where normally only the priests go. Perhaps in the back of my mind there was a reminder of the unwavering love my own human mother had for me as I stood there before a life-size statue of Mother Mary. She seemed more approachable to me than Jesus had, so I prostrated myself before Her. With my head to the floor I could see, under one of Mary's feet, the head of a snake, symbolizing the devil. Lying on the floor was my way of entrusting myself to my heavenly Mother's loving care. I was planning to stay right there for a good long time, but someone came in and started locking the doors. It was dark, and he couldn't see me. However, I was startled by his presence and stood up and walked out. I wish I had stayed. Leaving the church, I thought I was alone. Nevertheless, I had given Mother Mary an invitation to pray for me. Now with the benefit of hindsight, I believe She silently walked with me into the darkness of the night and would stay with me as my companion in the dark days that would follow, though I was totally oblivious to Her presence.

I started walking and arrived at South View Street, where my house was, but I decided I would just keep walking. I didn't know where I was going but decided to go wherever my feet seemed to be leading me. I walked down a street that ended in a cliff-like drop-off of solid rock, [perhaps similar to the one I had fallen down as the Pole Man when he let go of the pole.] I had sat right at the edge many times as a child, but now for the first time I carefully climbed down to the bottom of it and kept walking. A dog looked at me from a distance and barked. I remembered the last time a dog barked at me, in Rochester, and how I had wondered if it was an omen. I wondered again if it was an omen of making a bad choice, but I kept going and right before me was a cemetery, which I entered. I walked from grave to grave because I felt I was looking for something. There was a large mausoleum, and I knocked on its front door several times. I went around to the back of it and lifted a horizontal door or hatch which led underground. I then walked down a flight of stairs to a second door, which I tried to open, but it was locked. I went back up to the outside door and closed it over me, so I was on the underground steps in complete darkness between the two closed doors. I felt I was somehow confronting death or the fear of death. After about ten minutes, I opened the outer door and went outside again. I reclined on top of that horizontal door for a while.

After that I wandered throughout the cemetery in an all-night vigil. The sun rose and I saw a flock of birds fly overhead. I came upon a beehive, which I observed for some time. Below the beehive I noticed a grave marked "Lord." Then I looked over my shoulder in back of me and noticed some other graves. I walked over to them and saw a grave marked "Stringer." I thought of a spider and also thought of the three sisters who decide human fate in Greek mythology. One sister spins the thread of life, another measures the length, and the third sister cuts it.[10] I felt as though I came here to choose between these two graves—*Lord* or *Stringer*. I looked back and forth between the two. Finally I made my choice and prostrated myself before the grave marked *Stringer*. I felt Stringer represented death and the spider, and somehow that seemed to be what I was looking for. I remembered how a woman in my group therapy marathon had told me she could see me standing in fear at the edge of a bottomless abyss. Here in this bowing before the grave I was agreeing to jump into this dark pit, rejecting life and choosing death. One thing is for sure—if not for divine grace, my wish for death would have been granted, and I would not be alive today to tell this story.

Feeling I had found what I was looking for, I walked to a nearby fence and climbed over. While walking home, I picked a Black-eyed Susan. As I looked at the flower, a white spider hidden underneath the petals crawled around and revealed itself. I put the spider on the ground and took the flower with me. Not having slept all night, I went to bed, but only slept a few hours. After awakening, I ate the Black-eyed Susan and walked outside to the back yard. Parked there was a blue 1961 Chevy that my brother Rick had told me previously I could have. It had not been started for over a year, which meant the battery was undoubtedly dead. Nevertheless, I turned the key several times trying to start the car, and, of course, nothing happened— not even the slightest sound.

Although these attempts confirmed that the battery was dead, I raised the hood and placed my hands on the battery. I concentrated fully on passing energy from my body and hands into the battery, and I could feel powerful energy in my hands. It didn't enter my mind that this might be a ridiculous waste of time. In fact, I was certain I was actually charging the battery. I got back inside the car and when I turned the key, the engine started right up. My Uncle Jim, who lived next door, came over and asked me, "How did you start this thing?"

"I turned the key and it started," I said, without mentioning placing my hands on the battery.

He looked perplexed. "That's strange. After all this time you would think the battery would be dead."

"I guess it will have to be a mystery," I said, and he went back to his house. As I sat there with the car running in the back yard, I decided to just lie down on the seat and go to sleep and let the carbon monoxide bring my life to an end. It didn't occur to me that suicide with a running car must be done in an enclosed space. I thought I was actually facing imminent death. However, I couldn't go to sleep. All I could do was sweat.

As I lay there, I thought of the stories the roshi had told us at various times about Buddhist monks willing to face great pain or even death in order to achieve enlightenment. There was the striking story of the monk who held burning incense in one hand and a sword in the other. He vowed that he would be enlightened before the incense burned away completely or else he would commit suicide. He became enlightened. The goal of enlightenment had long since been absent from my mind, having been replaced by desirelessness. Yet in this moment in which I was giving up my desire for life and desiring death instead, it occurred to me that I could make another choice. I thought, if I am ready to die, I might as well try to be enlightened in the process.

PINE TREE WITH AN UNUSUAL SHAPE

I turned off the car engine, got out of the car, and walked to the front of the house. There were three very tall pine trees standing like sentinels in a row hugging the front of the house. Off to one side there was another pine tree. It was my favorite childhood tree, in spite of the fact that I had fallen out of it as a child, hurting my right foot [like Spider Boy]. Compared to the large size and Christmas-tree shape of the other three pine trees, it was small, with an unusual 'S' shaped trunk, giving it the distinctive oriental look of a bonsai tree. Perhaps I was attracted to it at this time because the Buddha had received his enlightenment under a tree—the Bodhi Tree. If I had really wanted to closely follow the example of the Buddha, I would have sat down in the shelter of my own tree and meditated to seek enlightenment, but that's not what happened. I decided to *stand* next to my favorite tree to receive enlightenment (without having any awareness at the time of the story in Buddhist texts saying that after his enlightenment the Buddha stood for a whole week with unblinking eyes in front of his Bodhi Tree, gazing at it in gratitude).

Standing right next to the unusually shaped tree, I leaned forward, placing both my hands on the trunk. I then put my weight on my left foot and bent my right leg at the knee and crossed the lower half of the right leg over the left leg, resting it just above the left kneecap. I was making a cross out of my legs, similar to the Hanging Man card in the Tarot deck. However, at the time I didn't consciously know why I was choosing this leg position. I had a past life [as the Spider Boy] in which I committed suicide because of an amputated right leg, and that was the unconscious reason for standing only on the left leg, but I was unaware of that past life at the time. While I was in this one-legged position, I closed my eyes and vowed not to move or do anything until I became enlightened.

A little girl who lived in the neighborhood came over and asked me if I wanted an apple. It reminded me of Eve being offered an apple in the Garden of Eden, although this was a pine tree, not an apple tree. I ignored her, and two of my older cousins, Jimmy and Bobbie, who lived in nearby houses, came over and asked if I was all right. I didn't answer, and I figured they would go away. Instead they picked me up and carried me into the house. I decided that because I had made a vow not to do anything until I became enlightened, I would not respond to anything or anyone. They phoned my father. He arrived, and I didn't respond, so he called an ambulance that took me to Memorial Hospital, where my father was a trustee. The doctors examined me, but couldn't find anything physically wrong. However, probably because my father was a trustee, they kept me in intensive care anyway, just in case. I was fed intravenously.

At some point my mother showed up with my father. She was pleading for me to recover, crying loudly and becoming hysterical. I almost opened my eyes then to tell her I was all right, but Dad with the help of the nurses encouraged her to leave because she was getting so upset.

This weekend was a fateful time for America—an odd mixture of the extremes of disaster and celebration. On the Friday night and Saturday morning that I was wandering in the cemetery, Mary Jo Kopechne lost her life by drowning in a car driven off the bridge at Chappaquiddick. Senator Ted Kennedy, who had driven the car, left the scene of the accident and had a sleepless night of his own as the Kennedy myth of Camelot was extinguished, changing the course of American politics.

This was also the time of celebrating the Apollo 11 mission to the moon, set in motion by John F. Kennedy, who correctly predicted a man on the moon before the end of the decade. I was admitted to the hospital on Saturday and on the next day, Sunday, July 20, 1969, a little after 4 PM, the lunar module, the Eagle, would land on the surface of the moon. In the intensive care unit I listened to the radio that the nurses were playing. The commentator said that the Eagle was about to descend to the lunar surface. He explained that this landing would be the trickiest and most hazardous part of the first attempt to place a man on the moon.

Right then I opened my eyes for the first time. Lying in bed, I placed both my hands facing each other above my navel area and felt energy in them just as powerful as when I had charged the car battery. With my hands facing each other there was a tremendous buildup of energy, creating a vibrant ball of energy between my hands. I was doing this at the exact time when the Eagle was making its critical descent, and the world was literally holding its breath to see if the mission would succeed or not. Just then one nurse said, "What's he doing? I'm going to stop him."

But the other nurse spoke up, "No! Leave him alone. He's all right." In the very last seconds of the landing I lowered the dynamic ball of energy directly into my navel area. In Rochester I had felt at one point like I was pregnant with the seed of enlightenment in my navel area. Here I felt I was recharging myself just as I had recharged the car battery. Afterwards I closed my eyes again as before, and I felt a sense of completion about everything that had happened.

A priest came in and gave me the last rites. Right after he left, I decided that I couldn't continue as I had been and that I would start talking. I opened my eyes and asked a nurse if I could have ice cream, and she brought some. I stayed in intensive care one more day and then was moved to another room.

"Allan, I think I will end it here. Let's resume in a month or so. Is that OK with you?"

"That sounds fine. But I want to ask you a question about the moon landing. I always thought that the landing had some kind of important spiritual significance. What do you think about that now?"

"I agree. It's almost as if the moon was like a spiritual female egg and the astronaut, Neil Armstrong, was the male sperm. When he walked on the moon, it was this sperm and egg being united to bring about some kind of evolutionary spiritual conception. So I think Neil Armstrong's statement, 'One small step for man; one giant leap for mankind,' was talking about a spiritual leap for mankind. But there is a gap between conception and birth, so this is the gestation period, and maybe the Second Coming will be the eventual birth.

"Allan, since you brought up the moon landing issue, most people don't know that the landing of the Eagle didn't go as planned. The computer that was supposed to handle the landing failed, so Neil Armstrong had to rely entirely on manual controls. Where the landing was supposed to take place, there were unexpected rocks and boulders that could have been extremely dangerous. Consequently, Armstrong had to burn up valuable fuel while hovering over the surface trying to find a level place to put down. When he finally landed, there were only twenty seconds of fuel left.[11] A future astronaut, Charles Duke, who was in the command post in Houston, said that during the last seconds of the landing, the Eagle was running on fumes. Duke walked on the moon in a later Apollo mission, and I actually got a chance to meet him in person at the Virginia Beach Convention Center. He was a speaker at a Christian convention, and I was there promoting my Bible game, the *Good News Game*. I had a private conversation with him that lasted about half an hour. I got the impression he was a very humble man and that his experience in space had made him a more spiritual man.

"Another astronaut, Edgar Mitchell, had a spiritual realization on his journey back to Earth after walking on the moon in the Apollo 14 mission. As he gazed upon the marvel of the universe, he suddenly and for the first time experienced an inner awareness of his connectedness with all that exists. If I remember right, he said, 'I was not separate from the universe. It's part of me.'[12] Are you ready for our own twenty-minute mystical meditation journey?"

"Let's do it," Allan said, and so we did.

---

1. The three sisters of Greek mythology are Clotho, who spins; Lachesis, who measures; and Atropos, who cuts.

2. William J. Cook with Gareth G. Cook, "When America Went to the Moon," *U. S. News and World Report*, July 11, 1994, p. 58.

3. Ibid., p. 57. Also in Edgar Mitchell and Dwight Williams, *The Way of the Explorer*, (New York: G. P. Putnam's Sons, 1996), pp. 57-59.

58

UNDERCLIFF

~ o ~

When we last talked, I had been given the last rites at Memorial Hospital and then decided to start talking again. All this time I thought I was faking, without realizing that for me to do all this was in itself proof that I needed help. Some people believe Judas thought he was doing something good, until after the fact he suddenly realized he was doing evil. Like Judas, in an instant I realized the full impact of how low I had sunk and all the grief I had caused everyone, especially my family. That was the only time it occurred to me that I was possessed by an evil force, like the evil that I had seen in the devil and in the snake in Rochester. I felt I had somehow unknowingly invited the consciousness of a negative spirit within my mind to make it the home of evil. Perhaps I had even welcomed in *that devil, that snake*, whom I may not have left behind in Rochester after all. In my bed I raised the covers over my head as if to hide from the evil that I felt I had brought into my mind. But, of course, there was no use hiding. I was disgusted with myself and struck with horror at the thought of being possessed. I screamed as loud as I could and grabbed a glass and threw it—not at anyone, but at a wall. This kind of introspective evaluation of myself and resulting outburst was uncharacteristic of my generally unreflective and unemotional condition.

Within a few minutes of my outburst I was being forcibly restrained. I offered no resistance at all as I was placed in a straight jacket and whisked away in an ambulance to Undercliff Mental Hospital. Upon my arrival there, I was asked to commit myself to a ten-day voluntary stay, so my parents wouldn't be required to pay, and I complied. Oddly enough, the thought of being possessed had entirely disappeared from my mind and didn't return to my conscious awareness during my entire stay at Undercliff. Looking back on this now, it is astonishing that something that was so strongly impressed upon my mind at Memorial Hospital could have so suddenly evaporated. Perhaps because I had been so terribly distressed by the idea of being possessed, my mind suppressed this traumatic thought altogether. On the other hand, people who are taken over by a negative spirit invariably do not consciously recognize the presence of the outside force affecting them, so perhaps the most remarkable thing of all is that I had even one breakthrough realization of being possessed.

At Undercliff I met some very unusual patients, as you might expect. One patient, Louise, kept telling me she wanted me to go to Europe with her, but I got the impression she was not leaving any time soon herself. There was also Claudia, who insisted on giving me cigarettes, which I accepted from her just so I could give them to Maureen, who kept asking me for them.

I was twenty-four years old, and there was a patient there about my age who showed me that mantras aren't just for those consciously on the spiritual path. His name was Joey, and he walked around all the time endlessly repeating "kitty shoes, kitty shoes, kitty shoes...." In fact, those were literally the only words he ever spoke. He did a lot of pacing back and forth in the one giant, windowless room where all our beds were lined up one after the other like an impersonal army barracks. When Joey stood in one place, he displayed repetitive hand movements and continually rocked his whole body from side to side. Based on my later experience as a social worker for developmentally disabled clients, I believe that he was not actually mentally ill. I think he was autistic, because he had so many repetitive behavior patterns similar to some of my autistic clients. Joey's odd behaviors annoyed some of the other patients, but I accepted him as he was, just as I accepted all of the other patients.

Another patient, Sally, gave me a small ceramic frog, which I didn't particularly want, but took to please her. Then she convinced me to go with her to an area where she could give me something without the attendants seeing. When we had privacy, she squeezed out some cream from a tube and rubbed it on my forehead and announced, "This is happy cream just for you."

I asked, "Will it make me happy?"

"Yes, yes, of course. That's what happy cream is *for*," Sally responded emphatically, while nodding her head and smiling broadly. Then she abruptly walked away. Putting the cream on me did seem to make *her* happy, but it didn't have the desired effect on me, nor did I expect it to.

Although I was generally devoid of desires, there was one thing I did want. I wanted my freedom. I had never been confined before, and I wanted to leave this place. Even in my limited awareness I could see that there wasn't anything therapeutic going on here since this was just a warehouse for people with mental problems. In an unusual moment of reflection I wondered how many of these patients would be stuck here for the rest of their lives. I didn't want to be in *that* number. I realized that just because I had signed in for a ten-day stay, that didn't mean I would actually be allowed to leave after ten days. Even though I wanted my freedom, I wasn't overly concerned about it because my mind was in such a fog that nothing seemed to bother me too much.

One day I was sitting in the small television room with Jeff, one of the younger attendants, who looked bored as usual. As far as I could see, the attendants were actually guards, without any therapeutic function. They just sat around like firemen, waiting for an alarm to come in the form of a patient acting up and needing their intervention. The idea of actually ringing the fire alarm occurred to me. After all these years, I don't recall if it was an impulse similar to the ones I had received in the past or if it was just an idle thought that happened to pass through my mind out of boredom. Perhaps to express my discontent with being at the mental hospital, I said impishly to Jeff, "What would you do if I walked down the hall and pulled the fire alarm?"

"You don't want to do that, do you, Don?"

Without answering him, I got out of my seat and left the room to walk down the hall. Jeff stayed behind but then followed me at a distance and hollered very loudly down the hall to the other attendants, "He's going to ring the fire alarm." I hadn't yet decided to ring the alarm, but when he said that, I figured I might as well do it since I was being blamed for it anyway. As I ran toward the alarm, several attendants converged on me and carried me to my bed, where I was given a needle in the rear end—probably a tranquilizer. This sounds like a dramatic and emotional event, but actually I experienced only mild amusement and there was no emotional reaction within me. When I woke up the next day, I found that I was strapped into my bed by what was called a 'posey.' After talking to some of the staff and promising to behave myself, they released me from this restraint.

That is when it fully dawned on me that I had to be more careful about my behavior. In Rochester I could easily get away with exhibiting silly, off-the-wall antics like hanging aluminum foil on the wall, sticking my face in a watermelon, or running naked through the woods, as I had done with Howard. Here a repeat of similar harmless, but out of the ordinary behavior would have been disastrous. Although the verbal threat of the fire alarm started out as only a bit of mischief, the actual attempt to ring the alarm was a much more serious matter, showing my mental instability and requiring an appropriate response. Nevertheless, I was still surprised to discover first hand that these people really did have the power to lock me up and throw away the key. From this point onward my clear goal was to get out of this place as soon as possible, but how? Running away was out of the question. Although I knew I was in a mental hospital because I was acting somewhat abnormally, there was a cloud over my awareness that didn't allow me to think of myself as being mentally ill. In spite of greatly minimizing the seriousness of my condition, the one thing I could assess correctly about my health was that I felt worn out and needed rest. But I considered the chances of getting that rest in this place were between slim and none. The obvious solution was to simply *appear* to be healthy by conforming to the rules and by not making any waves, in order to secure my release—hopefully at the end of the ten-day stay.

A ray of sunshine entered my bleak situation in the form of unexpected visitors. There wasn't any therapeutic recreation program at Undercliff, yet one day a group of sixteen female square dancers showed up to provide entertainment. Their leader spoke through a microphone and asked for volunteers to come forward to participate in the square dancing. I stepped forward to volunteer, in spite of the fact that I was a terrible dancer even under normal circumstances. I asked the leader if I could speak into the microphone, and without hesitation she handed it to me. Surprisingly I broke out of my long-standing monotone and raised my voice to proclaim loudly, "Come forward and join the dance!" However, no other patients stepped forward.

The leader then led me to one dancer in particular and said, "This is your partner." All of the dancers were young women. Fifteen of them were remarkably beautiful without the aid of any cosmetics. All were dressed in very vibrantly colored outfits. My partner stood in extremely stark contrast to the other dancers. She was the only one with black hair, and it was pulled up in an unflattering bun making her look prudishly older than she was. Instead of a colorful outfit, she wore a solid black dress with two wide black straps positioned like suspenders over a white blouse. She had a very thin body, but the strongest contrast with the other performers was that her face was very homely.

My partner and the other square dancers were simply a troop of service-oriented entertainers, similar to the kinds I would invite to come to the hospitals where I would be working as a therapeutic recreation specialist. Yet a memory persists of what my irrational mind thought at that time. When I was first introduced to my dance partner, I looked at her and thought to myself that she was symbolically an *omen of death*, in the same way I had perceived the old white dog coming to me in Rochester as a sign of my impending death. My mind was thinking in a distorted way and focused on death, and so I misinterpreted this situation in line with my irrational thinking.

Having seen my partner in this way, I immediately accepted her because at this point I had no reason to be afraid of death. Without any preferences or desires, I had no motivation for living and thought of dying as a relief. I would do nothing to bring it upon myself, but would welcome it to come to me. My partner and I didn't speak to each other, but when I looked at her, I noticed that her face and eyes in particular showed not the slightest bit of anxiety or uncertainty. In fact, she looked quite peaceful and self-assured. I interpreted this to mean that death would be coming to me in the near future as a peaceful blessing. Indeed during the square dances I felt that I was being blessed by my partner and the other dancers.

The leader called out the square dancing moves as the music played, and I followed along as best as I could, mimicking the other dancers. Some square dances involved leaving my partner to dance with other partners and then returning to my original partner. In the final dance there was a sequence in which half of the dancers moved around in a clockwise circle and the other half moved around in the opposite direction. I had to extend my left hand to receive the hand of a dancer who was coming toward me and passing me on the left side. Next I had to extend my right hand to receive the hand of a dancer who was coming toward me and then passing me on the right.

Halfway around the circle I made a mistake and broke the continuity of the dance. The music abruptly stopped, and the leader came over to me. She spoke lovingly and helped me to retrace my steps to where I had made my mistake. Then from that exact point we continued and completed the dance without any additional mistakes. In spite of my mistake, I felt that I had indeed received a blessing from these dancers. Since nothing happens by chance, even now as I look back I feel that God had a definite hand in bringing these dancers to me at this precise moment in time. They had not come to me as an omen of death, as I had thought then. Rather they had come as an omen of life. Could they have been a troop of angels coming to help me break out of my spell? The idea seems grandiose, but whoever they were they had a very positive influence on me in an otherwise bleak circumstance. They certainly acted like loving and healing angels to me, even if they weren't. I was momentarily somewhat uplifted by this dance experience. Although I was not significantly brought out of my persistently unemotional state of mind, there was one very important change that would soon manifest, perhaps related to my social interaction with these dancers. The change was that for the first time I felt some genuine compassion for others and expressed it. My concern for the welfare and freedom of others would soon prove to be my own ticket to freedom.

Shortly after my arrival at Undercliff, I was weighed in at 132 pounds, considerably less than the 155 and 165 pound weight classes that I had wrestled at in high school. My lack of preferences extended to choices of food and the desire for eating itself, so I had little appetite. As a routine matter, almost all of the patients at Undercliff were being given drugs so that they wouldn't create problems. I was now receiving a drug that gave me a very big appetite and was very soon eating everything they put in front of me. Although I had been a vegetarian for a long time, I even ate meat without having any reservations about it.

However, the drug was blurring my mind. Since I was already a zombie, I didn't need something to make me even more of one. After several days I learned to put the pill under my tongue, and then later I would spit it out. Also at this time I was attending a group therapy session with a social worker named Steve. It was nothing like the emotionally expressive kind of therapy that I had undergone in New York. Here, we just sat together and talked, although most patients in our small group wouldn't say anything. Some of them sat with a sleepy, glazed-over look in their eyes, while others slumped over like they were in a stupor because they were so obviously over-medicated. I spoke up, "I don't think it is very helpful that everyone here is so drugged. What kind of therapy is this? Do you think this is right?"

I had addressed my comments to Steve, but instead of answering my question, he asked the other patients how they felt about what I had just said. Nobody answered, probably because of being drugged. After the meeting, Steve said to me privately, "You made a good point in the meeting about the medications. I have a concern about that too." He asked me about my background, and I told him about my recent experiences. "You look like you've been through a lot," he said. I agreed because I felt like a tired old man.

I asked if I could see the psychiatrist and was allowed to do so. After I sat down, the psychiatrist said, "Steve told me that you were concerned about the welfare of the other patients, and he thought that was very kind of you to be so concerned." I gathered that patients having compassion for other patients wasn't something that the psychiatrist had seen very often, which isn't surprising, considering the self-absorption of the mentally ill and the effect of the drugs being pumped into them.

"It was kind of him to say that," I replied. "I asked to see you because I signed up for a ten-day voluntary day stay here, and the ten days have passed. I was told that my parents are going to visit here tomorrow, and I wanted to ask you if I could go home with them tomorrow."

"Before we decide that, maybe you can tell me why you think you are here?"

I explained, "I was on a six-day Zen retreat, and we meditated for more than eight hours a day. It was my first time meditating that long. It strained my mind and so I needed a time to rest. My parents wanted me to get a job after two weeks, but I guess I wasn't quite ready to go back to work yet. I need some more time to rest, although I don't think this is the best place for that. I feel I will get a better rest at the beach than I will here." I didn't mention taking the herb because that thought never came to my mind.

STAINED GLASS WINDOW DEPICTING THE ANNUNCIATION

The psychiatrist said, "I will let you go with your parents on a trial basis for a week. If it doesn't work out then you will have to come back. But you will have to continue to take your medication, so you won't have a relapse. Is that acceptable to you?"

"That sounds fine to me. Thank you for letting me go," I responded in my usual monotone. I offered no verbal objection to taking medication, because I planned on continuing to only pretend to take it. In a weather anomaly for the two weeks that I was at Undercliff it rained every day, and on the very brief intervals when it was not actually raining, the sky was still overcast. But when my parents arrived for their visit on the day after I saw the psychiatrist, the sun was shining for the first time. I told my parents that I could go with them, but they didn't believe me. They checked with the psychiatrist and found out that I was telling the truth. He must have told them I needed a long time to recover, because they told me later that I didn't need to get a job and that I could rest as long as I wanted.

As we drove away from the hospital, I asked my parents to buy me some buttermilk. They were surprised and asked me why. I told them I just felt my body needed it, but the odd thing about that was that in my entire life I had never even tasted it. After we stopped to get a quart, I asked them if they would drive to Mount Carmel Church so I could be alone there for a few minutes. They agreed without asking me why because they figured I wanted to pray. I remembered my attraction to churches in Rochester, but other than that I actually didn't know why I made the request. I went into the church alone and walked around looking at the stained glass windows. I was especially attracted to the colorful depiction of the Annunciation in which the angel Gabriel told Mary that She would be the mother of Jesus. At that time I didn't recall having prostrated myself before Her statue a few weeks earlier at Saint Joseph's Church, yet here I was again being drawn to Mother Mary. After looking at the window displaying the Annunciation, I chose a pew and just sat there without praying. After being continuously surrounded by unstable people and mostly disinterested hospital staff, it just felt safe and peaceful to be able to sit alone in our family church. Although I wasn't consciously asking for God's help, maybe just coming to the church was itself a request for divine assistance.

Right after leaving the church we drove from Meriden to the beach, where I was able to swim and lie in the sun every day. But I was not well. It is hard to describe my state of mind. When I broke the glass at Memorial Hospital and was taken to Undercliff, I thought for the first time that I was possessed. But that kind of introspection and self-evaluation of my mental state rarely occurred. Generally speaking, I had no self-conscious, reflective mind. It was as if I was watching a movie of my life one frame at a time, with no concern at all for the past or the future. Consequently, there were no pangs of guilt and no worries about what might come my way down the road. Such freedom from self-questioning would have seemed wonderful if there had been someone home in my mind to ponder such benefits. I just experienced things as they happened without evaluating them, although at times I irrationally misperceived situations, as I had with the square dancers.

I always had the same unwavering, dull expression on my face. When I went to the bathroom and happened to look in the mirror, even I could see in the vacant gaze of my eyes that there was no one home. Of course, this should have been disturbing to me, as it would have been for any reasonable person. Yet my blankness had no impact on me, although it obviously bothered others, which didn't concern me either. In fact, I had no emotional reactions to anything or anyone. There was no anger, no fear, and no pain. That sounds pretty good, until you consider there was no enjoyment or happiness either. I remember getting into the shower, and I wouldn't even bother to adjust the water temperature, because if it was very hot or very cold, it didn't matter to me. I felt the same empty feeling about every daily activity, and I had the same lack of responsiveness to everyone, whether I was relating to a child or an adult.

For example, I remember at the beach playing with children, not those at the boisterous age, but the very young ones. We played with sand, making drawings or castles, and used rocks or shells for decoration. The playing was what was important, not the finished product. Once I heard my mother expressing her concerns to my father. "He's just like a child. After all these years, he's a child again. What are we going to do?"

"He just needs time. He'll be OK in time," my father said to reassure her.

Would time have been enough to cure me? Adam, who gave me the idea of taking the herb, had gotten into a state of mind like mine. He didn't know who he was, and he didn't care if he lived or died. He recovered after many months when the herb wore off, so I suppose I could have recovered in time just like he did. Recently, I wanted to understand why the herb affected me the way it did, so I did some research. I believe this herb had an adverse affect on the proper functioning of dopamine, producing symptoms similar to schizophrenia. Dopamine is one of over a hundred neurotransmitters that carry signals from one brain cell to another, and it specializes in producing the feeling of pleasure. A malfunctioning of dopamine in the brain is associated with the symptoms of apathy and social withdrawal. In addition, it can adversely affect the normal experience of pleasure. There are two aspects involved in the experience of pleasure: One is the desire and motivation involved in anticipating pleasure.[1] This is commonly called "wanting." The other aspect is the direct experience of pleasure called "liking." Abnormal functioning of dopamine primarily inhibits wanting.[2] If prolonged it can result in a hypnotic-like state devoid of normal feelings or interests and can lead to the condition called *anhedonia*, the inability to experience pleasure.

The herb had given me the desirelessness that I had originally sought in taking it, but it was more than I bargained for, robbing me of my entire motivation for living. Theoretically at least, when the effect of the herb had worn off, I would have recovered. However, now I do not know for sure if time would have been enough to restore me to normal. If my only problem had been a lack of desires, emotions, and preferences, then the herb that had triggered this state would have eventually lost its ability to interfere with normal dopamine activity, bringing back my motivation for living and a recovery. But with hindsight I now believe there was another, deeper problem. That deeper problem was that I was possessed by a negative spirit of some sort, although at that time I was totally oblivious to any idea of being possessed (with the exception of the single insight at Memorial Hospital). In this state of possession, there were absolutely no visual hallucinations, but there was impulsive and irrational behavior.

Occasionally, irrational impulses would arrive in my mind, not through hearing inner voices, but as "thought messages." They would suddenly be "impressed" on my mind as though they had come out of left field, without any thought process leading up to them. These messages just appeared in my mind as forceful directives to perform unusual or irrational actions. There was a sense that I was somehow being told nonverbally what to do and that I had to comply. But since these directives were in my mind, it did not occur to me that they could be coming from an outside source. Consequently, I would immediately carry out these impulsive actions without considering any alternatives. These impulses started in Rochester with the examples I gave earlier of screaming in front of a church altar, throwing a candle on the ground, and jumping into a lake. I believe receiving these initial "messages" was the first stage of being influenced by a negative spirit because my mind was in a weakened condition allowing this to happen. It didn't dawn on me consciously that I was being influenced by a negative spirit until I was at Memorial Hospital. When I screamed and threw a glass against the wall, those weren't impulses coming from mental messages being impressed on my mind. Throwing the glass demonstrated my own disgust with myself, but it also expressed my anger at the negative spirit influencing me. The scream contained an inarticulate groan coming from the deepest part of my psyche calling out to be rescued. I didn't consciously think of God, because I was like a drowning man calling out for help from wherever it might come. But God hears our calls for help even when we don't use His Name. As I said at the beginning of this chapter, after I was carried off to Undercliff, I completely forgot about my realization that I was being possessed and subsequently no awareness at all that I was still being influenced by a negative spirit.

Although I was never told my clinical diagnosis, I do not think any typical clinical diagnosis could have been accurate. If I had to guess what label the psychiatrist gave to my condition, it was most likely schizophrenia. Social withdrawal, apathy, and anhedonia are all common symptoms of schizophrenia, which is widely thought to be related to improper dopamine functioning in certain parts of the brain.[3] However, I did not have any visual hallucinations and did not hear inner voices, which are also symptoms of schizophrenia. Any traditional clinical diagnosis of my condition would not have taken into account the drug-like effect of the herb I had taken to produce some of the same symptoms that are found in schizophrenia.[4] Also a clinical diagnosis would not have recognized the possibility of possession. Another thing to consider is that I believe the susceptibility to possession was due at least in part to the effect of the herb. Perhaps when the effect of the herb wore off, the susceptibility to possession would have gone away too.

Being possessed didn't mean I was being controlled by a negative spirit all the time. Apparently there was a struggle going on within me, yet I was not consciously aware of it. An expression of the positive side of that struggle was that I started reading the New Testament for the first time. Starting at the beginning, I read some of it every day. Another symbol of the positive side of my inner struggle was my fascination with flowers. Whenever I came across a flower, I would stop to look at it with undivided attention. Because of familiarity, we normally overlook objects as they actually appear in our vision and see only our concepts of these objects. In my blank state of mind, however, I was totally absorbed by the flower itself, in the present moment, without consideration of the past or future. Perhaps it was the beauty of the flower that attracted me, but there was no need at the time to analyze or label the flower when the experience itself was more than enough to focus my attention.

Although my mental state was devoid of preferences in the usual sense, it may be more accurate to say my preferences had boiled down to only two choices—life or death. The struggle that was happening within me was really a struggle between the attraction for life and the attraction for death. Earlier, this struggle played out on the form level when I had locked myself in my car with the engine running. Before that the struggle was a concrete choice in the cemetery between the gravestones labeled "Lord" and "Stringer." In the cemetery I had also found the flower with the spider on it. Looking back now I can say that my fascination with flowers represented my attraction to life. But there was an equally strong attraction to spiders, representing my attraction to death. I would seek out hidden places to find spiders and observe them with the same fascination I had when observing flowers. They were easy to find underneath the cottage, which was held up three or four feet off the ground by poles. Usually my mind was blank when looking at spiders, but also there was a recurring thought of death.

My attraction to flowers and spiders could also have been influenced by abnormal dopamine functioning caused by the herb that I had taken. Imbalances of dopamine can transform perception through affecting the *salience*, meaning the *noticeability* of certain objects or events, giving them exaggerated significance. Consequently, one thing comes into awareness and simultaneously everything else goes out of awareness in a process similar to the way a camera lens allows a picture to be taken showing a central object in very clear focus and leaving the background out of focus. Both the noticeability and desirability of some things can be greatly amplified and very strongly linked when dopamine is not working properly. This combination is called *incentive salience*, which is a psychological process that makes some particular stimuli appear much more attractive and desirable than normal.[5] This could explain why I would focus on flowers, magnifying their importance and why I found them so desirable that I would often even eat them. The best tasting ones were Tiger Lily flowers that were abundant in the area. The symptom of abnormal eating is called *pica behavior* and is treated with medication intended to regulate dopamine activity. In my case management work I have a developmentally disabled client who also has schizophrenia along with pica behavior. Of course, he takes medication, but he still has to be closely monitored at his group home and day program to ensure that he does not eat small stones, pennies, and other small objects. Dopamine irregularities can make some pleasant stimuli appear more pleasant than normal, but can also make some unpleasant stimuli seem more unpleasant than normal. This could explain my focusing on spiders and assigning them the added importance of being a reminder of death. My time with each spider ended with its death, quite literally at my hands—a dispassionate execution and fitting ending, I thought, for a symbol of death.

Although I remained desireless and disinterested in life in a general sense, incentive salience could account for my unusual preoccupation with flowers and spiders. But in the case of the spiders, at least, there was another basis for my obsessive attraction to them. Normally, there is a partition in the mind between the conscious mind and the subconscious mind, but for me at that time, the partition was not there. I believe subconscious past-life impressions were influencing me. Years later I discovered that I had one past life in particular in which I was hurt and in danger from spiders [as the Spider Boy], and I believe that may have been why spiders were so much in my awareness. It is probably why I had prostrated myself before the cemetery gravestone that said, "Stringer." But the most pressing reason for my fascination was that in looking at a spider I felt I was at least symbolically looking at death. I was attracted to death, and the alternative of enlightenment had long since left my mind entirely. In spite of my attraction to death, at this time I was not considering doing anything to bring it about by my own hand.

Even though I do believe I was possessed, I don't think that possession is an excuse that absolves me of accepting responsibility for my condition. I do not believe it is possible to be a victim of outside forces. For my mentally unbalanced state of mind and for my possession to take place required my invitation. I believe the Course philosophy that says we can only victimize ourselves by our own choices. Consequently, I was responsible for bringing this mentally unbalanced condition upon myself by extreme willfulness on my part and by my choice to take the herb, which in turn made me vulnerable to outside negative influences.

After I had invited this unnatural condition by my own choices, it would be reasonable to expect that either one of two things would have happened as a result of the possession. One is that after a short while I would have ended up dead, perhaps even by suicide. The other is that I would have been labeled with a diagnosis of serious mental illness for the rest of my life and would be taking medication to regulate my brain chemistry as a way of controlling my mental condition.

As a social worker today, I work with clients who are developmentally disabled, and some of them have an additional diagnosis of schizophrenia. They take various forms of *psychotropic* medication, which are mind-altering drugs. I can guarantee you that none of my schizophrenic clients will ever become cured of their serious mental illness by these medicines, nor will they ever be taken off medication. To be insane means to be out of touch with reality. As you and I both know, Allan, the Course considers all of us to be "insane"—not because we are out of touch with the reality of this world, but because we are out of touch with the reality of God. According to the Course we are insane because we have egos that make us think we are bodies and limit our awareness of our true spiritual nature in oneness with God. However, here I am talking about the more pathological clinical insanity that I have encountered in my social work. So what I am saying is that my life was headed down the drain, and at the time I was not aware of how lost I really was. I certainly was in no condition to be able to bring myself out of my state of mind, and to be honest, no one else could cure me, including the psychiatrist. I can identify with the nursery rhyme that ends, "All the king's horses and all the king's men couldn't put Humpty Dumpty back together again."

After I had been out of Undercliff for a little over a week, I walked down to the end of Dolphin Avenue where our house was located. It was the end of the street away from the ocean, where there was a little wooden pier and a small waterway or creek that filled up at high tide and was empty at low tide. I did a headstand right at the end of the pier. I had an impulse to fall over backwards off of the pier, even though it was low tide and there was no water in the creek. I probably would have acted on this impulse, as I had invariably done in the past, but immediately I heard the loud voice of my father calling me. He had come out looking for me and saw me doing the headstand. He hollered forcefully from a distance, "Donald! Donald! What are you trying to do?"

I slowly came down from the headstand and said, "I was getting some exercise."

"You might fall off that pier and hurt yourself. Look at that." My father pointed to the creek bed below and said, "There's no water in the creek. Promise me that you won't do any more exercising here at this pier."

"Sure, I promise," I said in my usual monotone. If indeed I was struggling with a negative spirit, it seemed I was losing the battle. What if I had another impulse to engage in some other life-threatening act? Would I hear another outer voice calling me back to life again as I had on the pier? Or would I welcome the beckoning of the abyss [as the Spider Boy had so willingly done by jumping off the pier to end it all]?

As I walked mindlessly away from the pier back to the cottage with my father, I didn't ponder any of this at all because I didn't realize just how desperate my situation really was. My father had called me to safety, but considering his timing he must have been guided by my heavenly Father, Who had not abandoned me. Yet in the barren desert that my mind had become, I had received nothing more than a sip of water—a temporary delay of the inevitable—a reprieve from self-execution. In my parents' cottage there was a tacky knickknack on the wall, left behind by the former owner. It showed a man with his body inside a toilet and his hand reaching up to flush it, with the words written above him, "Good-bye cruel world!" It was supposed to be funny, but instead was morbidly pessimistic. I never liked it very much seeing it as a child, but now it appeared I was also about to say "good-bye" to the world by flushing myself down the toilet. After all, with my life hanging by nothing more than a spider's thread, I didn't care one way or the other whether that thread was broken. With no preferences I had no reason to live, and it could not be long before I was entirely swallowed up by darkness. My mind had already jumped off the deep end, and it was only a matter of time before my body followed.

The next day was Tuesday, August 12. Lying in my bed in the morning, I had the strangest feeling that I had two pairs of arms and two pairs of legs, and these arms and legs were fighting each other for possession of my body. Then clearly and dramatically one pair of arms and legs suddenly departed. This all happened very quickly, making a very deep impression on me. It was definitely not a dream. Then I recalled the incident at Memorial Hospital that I had totally forgotten—the great distress of feeling possessed by an evil force. With the return of this memory came the thought that I indeed had been possessed—and, more importantly, there was the certainty that this possessing negative spirit had now been extracted from me.

After this experience, I had no more occurrences of bizarre behavior. My unbalanced mental condition improved and I felt a new mental clarity, yet I cannot say that my mind was entirely cured of irrational thinking. Also, I was still without emotions and expressionless in my demeanor as a left-over effect of the herb I had taken. However, my fascination with flowers had disappeared, and my attraction to spiders had also vanished. I no longer had any impulsive behavior triggered by mental messages, which I now believe had been prompted by the negative spirit. With the noticeable improvement in my mental condition serving as a confirmation of my initial assessment, I was reassured in my conviction that the negative spirit possessing me had been cast out. I knew also that *I* did not cast it out. There were no "calling cards" left behind to let me know how this healing could have possibly happened.

On the evening of the same Tuesday that the negative spirit was cast out there was a tremendous lightning storm—more dramatic than any storm I had ever seen before or since. The next day I read my Bible as usual. It was a typical sunny day at the beach, and I had no irrational thoughts or behavior. That night there was no outer lightning storm, but I had the strangest dreams I had ever experienced—if indeed they could be called dreams. They were actually impressive flashings of brilliant light, repeated over and over again—what might be called an "inner lightning storm."

"This is probably a good time to stop, and we can resume about a month from now," I said.

"I'm ready to meditate," Allan said. Before meditating I silently thanked God again for the many divine blessings that I had been given—both those that I was aware of and those that I was not.

---

1. Ruden, Ronald A., M.D., Ph.D., with Marcia Byalick, *The Craving Brain*, (New York: Harper Collins Publishers, 1997), p. 18.

2. Berridge, K.C., "The Debate over Dopamine's Role in Reward: The Case for Incentive Salience," *Psychopharmacology (Berlin)*, April 2007, 191(3), pp. 391-431. "CONCLUSION: In short, dopamine's contribution appears to be chiefly to cause 'wanting' of hedonic rewards, more than 'liking' or learning for those rewards." (p. 391)

It is commonly assumed that "liking" and "wanting" automatically go together, but research seems to indicate that they are regulated separately in the brain and that dopamine primarily affects "wanting." Abnormal dopamine functioning can *directly* inhibit the "wanting" of pleasure. However, this inhibition can in turn *indirectly* prevent "liking" from occurring through the lack of motivation, which would not allow the enjoyment experience of pleasure to take place.

3. *Magill's Medical Guide*, Fourth Revised Edition, Editor in Chief, Dawn P. Dawson, (Pasadena, California and Hackensack, New Jersey: Salem Press, 2008), Volume IV, p. 2401, "Schizophrenia operates by disrupting the way in which brain cells communicate with each other. The neurotransmitters that carry signals from one brain cell to another might be abnormal. Malfunction in one of the transmitters, dopamine, seems to be the source of the problem."

4. Ruden, Ronald A., M.D., Ph.D., with Marcia Byalick, *The Craving Brain*, (New York: Harper Collins Publishers, 1997), p. 19. More research is needed to determine what other neurotransmitters besides dopamine, such as serotonin, glutamate, and GABA, may be involved with schizophrenia. Perhaps the herb that I had taken mimicked schizophrenia by adversely affecting neurotransmitters other than dopamine. For example, serotonin inhibits the anticipatory effect of desire and motivation produced by dopamine. Consequently, consistently high levels of serotonin (without equally high levels of dopamine) could potentially short circuit the normal "wanting" effect of dopamine, producing a state of perpetual desirelessness. In the healthy person a combination of high levels of both dopamine and serotonin is the key to maintaining mental harmony, called a "biobalanced" state: "If dopamine is the 'gotta have it,' serotonin is the 'got it.' It is the rising dopamine that motivates us to action, and it is the attainment, the full belly, the safe place, the completed sexual act that raises serotonin. The brain is in a high dopamine and high serotonin state. Contentment floods our being. We feel safe, satisfied, and secure." (p. 19) When there are consistently low levels of dopamine or low levels of serotonin or low levels of both, mental disharmony results.

5. Ibid., p. 55.

59

THE OPEN DOOR

≈ • ≈

Today I brought my Bible with me, Allan. As I told you last time, I started reading the Bible in that August of 1969, and this is the exact same New Testament that I was reading then. After reading for a little less than two weeks, I reached the end, the Book of Revelation. On the morning of Thursday, August 14, I woke up and remembered the dreams I told you about last time, of seeing light—flashing light in various degrees of brilliance. Later that same morning about one or two hours before noon I was reading Revelation. I was reading the letters to the churches and had reached the sixth letter, which I am going to read to you now:

DOOR WITHOUT WALLS

And to the angel of the church at Philadelphia write: Thus says the holy one, the true one, he who has the key of David, he who opens and no one shuts, and who shuts and no one opens: I know thy works. Behold, I have caused a door to be opened before thee which no one can shut, for thou hast scanty strength, and thou hast kept my word and hast not disowned my name. Behold, I will bring part of the synagogue of Satan who say they are Jews, and are not, but are lying—behold, I will make them come and worship before thy feet. And they will know that I have loved thee. Because thou hast kept the word of my patience, I too will keep thee from the hour of trial, which is about to come upon the whole world to try those who dwell upon the earth.[1]

The key words that strike me now are the words "door" and "Satan." The word "door" reminds me of the "farthest door of dharma," sometimes called the "gateless gate." [The idea of enlightenment is expressed as a door and as the gateless gate in my abstract painting, "Door without Walls," shown on the opposite page.] The word "Satan" brings to mind the door that I had opened with the snake underneath it in Rochester, although my mind was actually blank at the time I was reading this section in 1969. However, there is more to this quotation:

I come quickly; hold fast what thou hast, that no one receive thy crown. He who overcomes, I will make him a pillar in the temple of my God, and never more shall he go outside. And I will write upon him the name of my God, and the name of the city of my God—the New Jerusalem, which comes down out of heaven from my God—and my new name.

He who has an ear, let him hear what the Spirit says to the churches.[2]

Right after reading these words, I broke into tears. Other than the outburst toward my brother Paul and the anger expressed at Memorial Hospital with the temporary realization of being possessed, this was the first real emotion I had felt since taking the herb in Rochester. This emotion actually felt good, but I had no idea at all why I was crying. I had been reading on my bed, and after crying I continued to lie on my bed to relax for a while.

Then I got up hurriedly and walked as fast as I could toward the front doorway, but without going so fast as to draw attention to myself. I didn't know where I was going or why I was in such a hurry. I quickly pulled open the screen door and sped down the steps of the front porch. At the bottom of the steps I moved forward and turned my body toward the left and looked directly up at the sun. As I looked upward, I spontaneously threw both arms over my head. In yoga this body position is the first part of what is called the Sun Salutation. As soon as I threw my arms overhead and saw the sun, I was instantly and completely overcome by a brilliant, blazing white Light. I must have literally jumped out of my body, because I no longer had any awareness of it.

There was no up and no down, no right and no left, no front and no back, and no inside and no outside. I was nowhere and everywhere. I was in state of awe and amazement at the Light, which had struck me with full overwhelming force. The Light was all-powerful, without limit or form. The Light had a center and simultaneously was expanding in all directions at once. I was that Light. Since I had no body awareness, in a sense the Light itself was my "formless body." By a crude analogy it was as though I was in the center of the sun itself and my arms and legs were the rays of the sun expanding infinitely. But the Light was not a physical light like the light of the sun. It was the Light of pure consciousness, and *I was that pure consciousness—that Light*. It was a state of indescribable ecstasy and freedom.

Somehow at the beginning of this experience I clearly heard my mother's voice saying the words, "The lights went out!" At the time I was not able to analyze what these words meant or to see the irony in them, because the Light had gathered all of my attention, and indeed my entire being was absorbed into the Light. This Light was not something that I could simply observe as a spectator apart from what is observed. The Light and I were one. My whole being and consciousness were totally immersed in this white Light, which was overpowering. My mind was in a state of total, all-consuming wonderment, unable to comprehend fully what was happening in a conceptual sense. Even now, Allan, I cannot describe it to you and do justice to what this Light was like.

I was in complete fascination with the Light for an indeterminate amount of time. Then the thought came to me, *Where is my body?* I had no answer to this question and felt fear at the idea of not having a body. This tiny thought and the emotion of fear attending it were enough to bring about a change in the experience. My sense of ecstasy and expansive freedom evaporated. Within the infinitely expanding Light, I suddenly felt it contracting. Since I identified with the Light, I felt I was contracting along with it, and with this contraction the full steady force changed to pulsations.

Next I heard an explosion that replaced the Light in my consciousness, just as thunder follows lightning. The sound was louder than any earthly thunder and it, too, began to pulsate. It was like a gigantic drum booming continuously. The pulsating sounds were powerful waves that forcefully overlapped one another in very rapid succession, creating a continuous bombardment. More than being just a barrage of exceedingly loud sound, it contained an enormously dynamic energy which gave it a great power.

As the pulsating sound and energy reverberated, I distinctly felt my consciousness contracting and being projected back into the body. I was totally absorbed by the dynamic sound and energy, which was extremely frightening and produced excruciating pain. In fact, it was more painful than anything I had ever experienced, and I cannot imagine anything that could possibly be more painful. There had been no pain when I didn't have body awareness, so the pain I was experiencing was from being projected back into the body. As body awareness returned, I first became aware of my head. With the awareness focused there, each pulsation of sound and energy brought more body consciousness and at the same time a frightful, all-consuming pain.

As the sound and energy continued to pulsate, I could feel the hands, which I discovered were positioned over the ears. As the deafening loud and painful sound continued, I found the body was rolled up in a ball on the cement patio with both legs side by side, tucked underneath. It was the most compact fetal position the body could be in with the face turned down and the forehead touching the cement patio. The whole body was racked with pain from the pulsating sound and energy. Each pulsation of energy produced a wave of body consciousness that brought pain, followed by an instant in which body awareness would disappear altogether. This pattern kept being repeated in very rapid succession.

The combination of both the loud sound and pain continued, but then lessened in intensity. After a while the sound disappeared, but the powerful waves of energy continued. With the sound gone, the pain disappeared. However, the waves of energy continued to alternately bring the body into conscious awareness and then release it from conscious awareness. At this point the experience of the body appearing and disappearing in awareness wasn't painful but was disorienting. Eventually the body awareness became continuous, but the waves of energy continued pulsating through it, though not as forcefully as before.

During this entire time I remained in the fetal position and could not possibly move at all. My body was now located several yards away from where I had originally been standing, and I had no awareness of moving to this new location. The energy waves that continued to pulsate were no longer causing pain, but I still could not move. My rolled-up body was near one of the metal chairs on the patio. Eventually the energy waves lessened enough for me to begin to move, so I reached out and grabbed part of the chair. My hand on the metal chair must have grounded the energy, because the energy waves disappeared. I was able to very slowly pull myself up and sit in the chair, even though I was still extremely disoriented by the whole experience.

I wanted to be in the chair because if I was found rolled up in a ball on the patio, my parents would be concerned and might think I needed to go back to the mental hospital. I had no residual pain and no bruises or cuts. I focused on regaining my composure because I was still in a state of shock. As my father came from inside the house and walked down the steps, I tried to look as normal as possible. He walked over and stood in front of me. He didn't seem to notice anything unusual about my appearance, but he had gotten used to me looking strange. He asked, "Donald, would you mind going to the store and ask Baxter if he is having trouble with his electricity? Our electricity has blacked out in the house, and I want to see if it's just our house or if it's a general power failure."

I agreed and walked to the store, located at the beginning of our dead end street. As I walked, I still felt disoriented, as if I was moving in slow motion. I then remembered having earlier heard my mother's voice coming from inside the house saying, "The lights went out!" However, it seemed odd that the lights would go out in the house precisely when the Light was overpowering me. When I reached the store, Baxter, the store owner, said that the store had lost all its electrical power. Other people had come in and said that their cottages were also blacked out.

As I was walking back to the house and reaching the patio, it occurred to me for the first time that I had actually received enlightenment. It might sound strange that it took me so long to come to this conclusion, but that is how disorienting the experience was. There was also a second, very important, simultaneous realization. I understood that everyone already exists in this Light that I experienced, so everyone is perfectly equal in the Light. In other words, I had experienced what already was there before I found it. The Light is where we all really live and have our being eternally, whether we are consciously aware of that Light or not.

I went inside and told my parents about the general power failure and went to my room to rest. I realized that what had happened was more than a subjective internal experience because the power of the Light had affected the objective external world by blowing out the electricity in the area. This is surprising if you believe the external world is the foundation of reality. But as you know from the Course, Allan, the external world is an illusion, which only appears to be real because of the ego. The Light that I saw is the real underlying Reality. This Light is the ground of Being, like an artist's white canvas which is then overlaid with layers of colored shapes that prevent the canvas itself from being seen. Just as there can be no painting without a canvas, there is no world without the canvas of Light that supports its appearance.

You might think I would be pleased to have experienced enlightenment, but I wasn't. The foundations of my being had been shaken to the core, and I was still recovering. I had always imagined that enlightenment would be entirely joyful. It certainly was incredibly ecstatic when I first saw the awesome Light and felt that I was one with it. But then the rest of the experience and the intense pain was not what I expected. I felt I had died and come back to life. Since death is the withdrawal of the spirit from the body, saying that I died is an accurate way of describing the experience.

Allan interjected, "That's ironic. Don't you think so?"

"What's ironic?"

"You said that you had been focused on death and wanted death, and then you went ahead and did experience death. Isn't that ironic?"

"Yes, it is ironic, but I didn't appreciate the irony at the time. It shows that we really do get what we want. So I guess we have to be careful about what we ask for. Originally, in my right mind, I wanted enlightenment and then, being out of my mind, I wanted death. I got what I wanted on both counts, but it was much more than I bargained for. What I experienced was much more powerful than I could possibly have imagined, both in its initial positive nature and then in its negative aftereffects. It seems significant to me that the excruciating pain was not due to the spirit being freed from the body, but from the spirit being contracted back into the limited body because fear had entered my mind.

"Anyway, about ten minutes after returning to the house, the electrical power came back on. Although initially I felt resentful about the negative aspects of the experience, I was able to get a better perspective after a short period of relaxing and reflection. Then I walked outside again, and looked up at the sun, and threw up my arms over my head, but without the spontaneity expressed earlier. I knew that this wouldn't make the experience happen again, though I faintly hoped that it would. However, I felt that this gesture was necessary as a way of expressing that in spite of the tremendous shaking up and the fear and the pain of it, I was willing to experience it again. At the time it was also my way of asking the question, 'Why couldn't I stay in the Light and why did I have to come back to the body at all?' I wondered what would have happened if I hadn't asked the fear-producing question, 'Where is my body?' which triggered the return to body awareness.

"If I had the understanding of Course principles way back then, it would have been very helpful for me. For example, I could have remembered one of your favorite Course quotations. Do you know the one I am thinking of?"

"That's easy," Allan said. "It must be, 'I am not a body. I am free. For I am still as God created me.'"[3]

"Exactly right. Also there are numerous statements in the Course about our true nature being light. One of these is, 'Ask for light and learn that you *are* light.'[4] Another passage describes each of us as aspects of '...the Son of God, who was created *of* light and *in* light.'[5] During my experience I did realize that I was the Light when I felt as if my arms and legs were the rays of this all-powerful Light expanding infinitely. What was conveyed in Course terminology was 'knowledge,' which is the awareness of Reality as an experience of divine union.

"But *knowledge*, which is the experiential awareness of Oneness, is not the same as the partial awareness offered by perception, which is based upon the separateness of the ego. Although I had knowledge imparted in the experience of Reality, I didn't have a firmly rooted and truthful perception at the mental level of what was happening. If my perception of being the Light had been solidly established, I would have seen that the question, 'Where is my body?' was meaningless and not worthy of fear. Although knowledge transcends perception, loving perceptions can lead to the knowledge of Reality, but *fearful* perceptions cannot. Now I understand that the real reason I couldn't stay in the Light is that I didn't have the right thought system to fully accept enlightenment. What I needed to have was a solid mental foundation that was anchored in love rather than in fear.

"I've been attracted to the Course because it's a thought system that teaches me how to let go of identifying with my ego and how to instead identify with the Light. I think everything in the Course boils down to learning correct identification. Before I read the Course myself, I remember having a conversation with Tom in which he read me the quotation that said, '...like your Father, *you* are an idea.'"[6] Tom explained to me that according to the Course we are *Thoughts* in the Mind of God. He believed it was true, but it didn't sound very comforting to him. I told him that I was aware that the Catholic theologian, St. Thomas Aquinas, taught the notion that each of us exists in the Mind of God as an idea. Since this idea is in the Mind of God, it is not a mere passing thought. This divine idea has permanent reality because it exists in God. So, Allan, what do you think about being an Idea in the Mind of God? Does that sound appealing to you?"

"When you have a body like mine, trading it in to become a Thought within the Mind of God sounds pretty good," Allan said good-naturedly.

"Well, you have a more open-minded view than most people, who would be threatened by the idea of being without a body. I know Tom wasn't very enthusiastic about being an idea. I can't say that at first I liked the concept either, but in time I have come to believe that this concept is why I have needed the Course. I could believe that I am not a body and not an ego as the Course teaches, but I needed to fully understand that if I am not concrete, I must be abstract. I warmed up to the concept by realizing that heaven is an abstract state of consciousness and I couldn't wake up to that awareness unless I accepted my abstract nature. When you share an idea with someone else, you don't lose the idea yourself. You keep the idea in your mind, and so does the person with whom you shared your idea. The fact that you are an Idea in the Mind of God enables you to give all of yourself to every other being in heaven, and all other beings in heaven can give all of themselves to you. This celebration of total sharing is the joy of heaven.

"From the Course I learned that God's ideas are expressions of light. The quotation that comes to mind is, 'The cornerstone of God's creation is you, for His thought system is light.'[7] As ideas in the Mind of God we are expressions of light, as well as of love. I appreciated the Course emphasis on each of us being Light, because it confirmed what my personal experience had already revealed to me. What I am getting at is that I needed to fully accept these abstract concepts about my true nature, such as being the Light, so that when I experience the Light again during this lifetime or at the end of it, I will be able to let go of the body and embrace the Light as my true Self instead of becoming afraid of my true nature. That means I have to learn how to accept love and let go of fear even now in my everyday life. Consequently, I have to learn the lessons of forgiveness."

Allan said, "As you were saying, we are ideas in the Mind of God. That means we are part of God and we cannot be separate from Him or from our brothers and sisters. But we can fill our perceptual minds with illusions and so imagine that we are separate. Forgiveness replaces the illusions of separation with the truth of our oneness with God and our oneness with our brothers and sisters. One of the ways the Course defines forgiveness is to say it is the '...healing of the perception of separation.'"[8]

"That's a good definition," I said, feeling no separation between us.

For the meaning of forgiveness I had to look no further than the child of God sitting in front of me. If I had perceived Allan as an ego with a limited mind, locked into a limited body, it would have created a sense of separation between us. It would also make me think that I, too, am an ego. Forgiveness allowed me to look past the form of his body, and instead see Christ in him. Seeing the divine in Allan allowed me to accept myself as also being an aspect of the Son of God, part of the one Christ that we all share. My past-life, hated enemy had become my cherished friend, seen through forgiveness in the light of his true nature. Nevertheless, I had not yet learned to generalize that forgiveness to everyone and every situation.

I continued, "Through forgiveness I am learning to let go of fearful perceptions of separation and replace them with loving perceptions of oneness. The lessons I am learning about forgiveness are helping me to form a more loving mental foundation. This foundation is necessary as a preparation for awakening to the direct experience of eternal oneness—of my true nature as being the Light, which is what enlightenment is.

"The ideal way enlightenment happens is similar to the way fruit slowly ripens on a tree until the time comes when it is finally ripe and then falls from the tree naturally. I was like a green fruit that jumped off the tree before it was ripe. Having the wrong idea about enlightenment, I naively thought I could possess it like a trophy. I was foolishly seeking to exalt my ego by obtaining a state of consciousness beyond the ego exclusively through my own self-effort. Yet how could I possibly find success and satisfaction for the ego by transcending the ego? My pride blinded me to the obvious problematic contradiction between the holding on to the ego inherent in my selfish motivation and the letting go of my ego required to attain my lofty goal. Because I lacked humility, I did not understand that enlightenment is a gift from God, regardless of how much effort is involved. It is a gift because it is a return to the recognition of our existence, which has always been, is now, and will always be, a gift from God. But this gift is not something that I could have and hold in my hands like other gifts I was used to. It was a gift of God giving Himself—a gift that held me at the very source of my existence. However, I was not ready to receive this gift. I was still too attached to the ego, which is the idea of existing as a separate body. Because I could not let go of the ego-based idea of body awareness, I could not more fully identify with my true nature in oneness with the Light.

"There is a specific reason why I am telling you this, Allan," I said and then hesitated.

"What is it?" Allan inquired.

"We will all have to face death sooner or later. So I am telling you about this event that happened to me because I think that my experience was similar to death itself. The Course doesn't specifically spell out exactly what happens after death, but in general I believe the Tibetan Buddhist version of passing over to the other side. There is a distinction between the 'afterlife' and 'heaven.' The afterlife is where we temporarily stay in consciousness after the loss of three-dimensional physical consciousness, typically called 'death.' Death is, of course, not the end of life itself, but is the end of a particular ego mask we have been wearing for one lifetime. The afterlife is a place or places where we wait for a time before we are reincarnated through picking up a new ego mask. Jesus alluded to our various afterlife options by saying that in His 'Father's house there are many mansions.'[9] On the other hand, heaven is not literally a place with a location. It is figuratively a 'place' of consciousness—a state of awareness—that is everywhere and always with us, yet we have to awaken to this ultimate divine Reality that is our true nature in God.

"Normally the ego mask in the world prevents us from waking up, but with the giving up of the ego mask at death we have the best opportunity to awaken to Reality. Along with the Tibetan Buddhists, I believe that when we die, we have the greatest potential to see the Light that I just described, and this opportunity becomes a moment of truth for us. Seeing this Light presents us with two alternatives: One alternative is that we can accept the Light and become one with it. The other alternative is that we can revert to our familiar ego identification and become fearful, as I did by asking the question, 'Where is my body?' I am explaining this to you because, if you are aware of it in advance, you can be prepared to choose to accept the Light instead of choosing fear and attachment to body awareness. If you become fearful deciding to invest in the ego and in body awareness, you will become reincarnated. But if you really want to be free, you will choose to identify with the Light. However, if you want to identify with the Light in the afterlife, you have to start identifying with the Light in this lifetime *now*. You have a real advantage that most of us don't. Because the body has been such a limiting factor in your life, you have more motivation than most of us to let go of body awareness."

Allan acknowledged, "My body is a prison. I am looking forward to escaping. I want freedom. Workbook Lesson 199 is entitled, 'I am not a body. I am free.' The first two lines of that lesson are, 'Freedom must be impossible as long as you perceive a body as yourself. The body is a limit.'[10] I am tired of being limited. I am ready to be unlimited. I am looking forward to letting go of the body. With all the operations I have had, I thought I would have checked out already, but I guess I will have to wait a little longer for my moment of truth. And I don't want to come back to another body, so hopefully I will choose the Light."

I said, "I want to let you know about something that I think is very exciting. To describe the Divine Light that opens the door to heaven, the Course uses the term 'blazing light' to distinguish it from the lesser lights we may experience. I did some research and discovered the words 'blazing light' are used four times in the Course. I brought my book with me to show you these quotations if you would like to hear them."

"Let's hear them," Allan said.

"OK, one of the most significant things I found out is the relationship between the blazing light and the *face of Christ*. The Course often talks about seeing the face of Christ in the faces of our brothers and sisters, but the deepest level of seeing the face of Christ is the seeing of the blazing light. This first of the four quotations says this light is being hidden by the fear of God, which is called the "fourth obstacle" to finding peace:

> The fourth obstacle to be surmounted hangs like a heavy veil before the face of Christ. Yet as His face rises beyond it, shining with joy because He is in His Father's Love, peace will lightly brush the veil aside and run to meet Him, and to join with Him at last. For this dark veil, which seems to make the face of Christ Himself like to a leper's, and the bright Rays of His Father's Love that light His face with glory appear as streams of blood, fades in the blazing light beyond it when the fear of death is gone.[11]

"When we can finally let go of our fear of God, we can look upon the face of Christ and accept the Light and Love of God. I suppose the face of Christ can also be called the 'face of the Son of God.' I know you like to remind yourself that you are the Son of God. So this blazing light is what the Son of God looks like," I added.

Allan brightened up. "So since I am the Son of God, this must be what *I* look like."

"Absolutely. It's the vision of what you look like, and what I look like, and what we all look like. When you see it, you are seeing your own face."

"You're not saying this is Christ Himself, because Christ is in heaven beyond form and beyond visions. This is His face, meaning an image of Him. Is that right?"

"Yes, that's right, but it's not just any vision or any image. It's the highest vision that can possibly be seen. It's the highest 'true perception' that we can have here on this side of heaven. It is a vision of divine Light, like the Light I described to you in my experience of awakening. The purpose of all Christian seeking is to lead to eventually seeing the face of Christ. Similarly, the goal of all Buddhist seeking directed toward enlightenment is to ultimately see the transcendental Light of this face. There are many levels of experiencing enlightenment, but each one is a deeper layer of indirectly, and hopefully directly, encountering this same luminous face. Likewise yoga is directed towards embracing this face. It is called the face of Christ, but it is truly the universal aim of all spiritual seeking of all religions because, as we just said, it is the face of every seeker. Here is where we can awaken to our true identity in Christ as the one Son of God.

"It is possible to see this face, this all-encompassing Light, while here in this world. However, I think every one of us has a much greater chance to see this expanding Light when we pass over to the other side. As you pointed out, the face of Christ is an image, and therefore it is within form, but more importantly it is the part of the afterlife that leads directly to the imagelessness of heaven itself. However, that doesn't mean we will in fact see His Face in the afterlife, because we may not be *ready* to see it."

"Are we ready to see the face of Christ in the afterlife just by knowing that this blazing Light is there waiting for us to see it?" Allan asked.

"It is important to anticipate seeing the Light when we die, especially at the instant of death itself, and that's why I am telling you about it. But that anticipation, in itself, does not really prepare us to encounter the Light. It is not enough to just see the Light. We also have to embrace the Light by responding to it with love rather than fear. That quote I just read said we must learn to let go of the fear of God, which hides the face of Christ. The second quote about the blazing light explains what happens if we can embrace the light. It says that uncertainty is replaced by certainty—the discursive mind's use of perception is replaced by the knowledge of heaven. Here's the quote:

> And now God's *knowledge*, changeless, certain, pure and wholly understandable, enters its kingdom. Gone is perception, false and true alike. Gone is forgiveness, for its task is done. And gone are bodies in the blazing light upon the altar to the Son of God. God knows it is His Own, as it is his. And here they join, for here the face of Christ has shone away time's final instant, and now is the last perception of the world without a purpose and without a cause. For where God's memory has come at last there is no journey, no belief in sin, no walls, no bodies, and the grim appeal of guilt and death is there snuffed out forever.[12]

"This quotation associates the seeing of the blazing light with the return of the memory of God. With this memory being awakened there is also a realization of one's own true nature as God's Son. That's probably why the term 'blazing light of truth,' is used in the third quotation. It's in the form of a prayer that goes like this:

> *I thank You, Father, for Your plan to save me from the hell I made. It is not real. And You have given me the means to prove its unreality to me. The key is in my hand, and I have reached the door beyond which lies the end of dreams. I stand before the gate of Heaven, wondering if I should enter in and be at home. Let me not wait again today. Let me forgive all things, and let creation be as You would have it be and as it is. Let me remember that I am Your Son, and opening the door at last, forget illusions in the blazing light of truth, as memory of You returns to me.[13]*

The Light represents divine Love and so the way to prepare to see and accept it is to learn the lessons of forgiveness and love presented to us every day in our lives. The Light is everywhere so the glimmerings of the face of Christ can be seen shining through every one of our brothers and sisters. Consequently, the best way to become ready to see the blazing Light is to open our hearts to loving all of our brothers and sisters and seeing the divine in them."

Allan agreed. "That makes sense because the Course does say that manifesting forgiveness and love is our true function here in the world. The Course also has the comforting idea that sooner or later everyone will wake up, but it's up to each of us to decide how much time we want to delay before finally making that decisive choice to fully open up to divine grace."

I said, "Since everyone will wake up eventually, it couldn't possibly require us to be supreme spiritual athletes to succeed. All we need to do is to learn how to forgive and open up to love. But I also think we have to want waking up more than we want anything the material world has to offer. Then we can surrender to God's eternal gift of Himself to us. If we can be open to seeing this vision of the Son of God in the afterlife, I believe we will be able to see this blazing Light and fully wake up to our true nature in heaven. Then we won't have to come back here and try again. So what do you think? Will you be ready to see your true face before you were born?"

"Oh, yeah. I'll be ready, willing, and able, because I certainly don't want to come back here again. After all, what have I got to lose?"

"That's just it. We have nothing to lose, and everything to gain," I said. "I really like the idea that the blazing light is what each of us is eventually destined to see. I think of this blazing light as the *doorway* to heaven, and it is the true 'gateless gate' that the Zen Buddhists talk about to describe enlightenment. Christian mystics report seeing a luminous white light, and likewise yoga mystics describe seeing a dazzling light in their profound experiences of *samadhi*. Yoga philosophy maintains that the life force enters the body through the top of the head and descends to the base of the spine where it is stored as the kundalini. The kundalini can rise up through the seven spiritual centers, called the *chakras,* and out of the top of the head, producing a spiritual experience of a radiant light. Then it returns to the base of the spine after the experience is over. Similarly the kundalini rises up when death occurs, although in this case it does not return. It exits the seventh chakra at the top of the head, leaving behind a lifeless corpse. Just as the kundalini can uncover a brilliant light in a temporary spiritual experience, it can reveal the same blazing light in the experience of death. Although the light is there for us to see at the time of death, we must be open to fully accepting it.

"The Course says, '*The face of Christ* has to be seen before the memory of God can return.'[14] When it says in this quote that the face of Christ *must* be seen before we can go back to heaven, it's talking about seeing the blazing light. That Light is what I have already seen, but I couldn't fully accept it at that time. I look forward to seeing it again so I can have another opportunity to respond with love instead of fear and to let go of everything in the world. Just like you, I hope to embrace the Light in that moment of truth in the afterlife so I won't have to come back here and try all over again to find the Light."

Allan commented, "I never noticed these quotations before, but I'm glad you brought them to my attention."

"I have one more quotation. The fourth and final use of the words 'blazing light' in the Course can be found in Workbook Lesson 67. This lesson recommends a form of meditation to let go of all thoughts. If there are distracting thoughts, it is recommended to repeat the words, 'Love created me like Itself.'[15] The point of the lesson is that the mind guided by the ego is 'preoccupied with false self-images'[16] and other mistaken ideas that limit our awareness. This lesson explains, 'We are trying today to undo your definition of God and replace it with His Own. We are also trying to emphasize that you are part of His definition of Himself.'[17] If we can get past the fluctuating thoughts of the discursive mind, there is the possibility of seeing the dazzling light that would reveal our true nature. This is the quote:

> Yet perhaps you will succeed in going past that, and through the interval of thoughtlessness to the awareness of a blazing light in which you recognize yourself as love created you. Be confident that you will do much today to bring that awareness nearer, whether you feel you have succeeded or not.[18]

"It is unlikely that the blazing light will be seen during meditation. But the last line above points out that even if we do not succeed in seeing the Light through this process, we will still gain the benefit of increasing the awareness of the inner light. Seeking the blazing light reminds me of what Michelangelo meant when he said, 'The greatest danger for most of us is not that our aim is too high and we miss it, but that it is too low and we reach it.' I can't think of any higher aspiration than seeking to find our true nature in the Light. In addition, this Workbook lesson focuses in particular on finding our true Identity in the fact that God, Who is Love, has created us as an extension of Himself and therefore we are made of Love as He is.

"In a way, Allan, our meditation time is a mini-version of the moment of truth when we will see the face of Christ and allow the memory of God to return. Each meditation is an opportunity to let go of body awareness and choose the Light. The more we can let go of the ego that is attached to body awareness, the more we can experience the Light."

"Before we meditate to enter the Light, I have just one question," Allan said. "I noticed that the quotation that seemed to trigger your experience contained the words 'New Jerusalem,' and you are in the New Jerusalem Community, so what is the importance of that?"

"It does seem significant that those words triggered the experience and that I am now in the New Jerusalem Community," I replied. "The New Jerusalem is used in the Bible to symbolize the transcendent experience of oneness with God, so it is appropriate that those words played a part in my own transcendent experience. Of course, at the time I had a limited biblical background with the Bible and didn't intellectually comprehend the meaning of the words. You and I and everyone are seeking the New Jerusalem as our ultimate Home in heaven and that is why the community chose that name. There is still a little more to my story, which I'd like to save for another time. Are you ready to meditate and open up to the Light and to the New Jerusalem now?"

"As ready as I will ever be," Allan responded, and so we focused on letting go of body awareness and choosing the Light.

---

1. Revelation, 3:7-10, CCD.
2. Revelation, 3:11-13, CCD.
3. W-pI.r.VI.201-220, p. 386-397 (p. 376-387) For those not familiar with the Course, W-pI refers to part one of the Workbook. Most Workbook references are for single lessons, but in this particular notation r.VI stands for review number six, comprising Workbook lessons 201 to 220. All twenty of these Workbook lessons use the three-line quotation cited here in this reference. Most Workbook lessons are not reviews and therefore the "r" is not used with them.
4. T-8.III.1:3, p. 141 (p. 131).
5. T-11.III.4:6, p. 199 (p. 185).
6. T-15.VI.4:5, p. 315 (p. 293).
7. T-11.In.3:2, p. 193 (p. 179).
8. T-3.V.9:1, p. 46 (p. 41).
9. John 14:2, CCD.
10. W-pI.199.1:1-2, p. 382 (p. 372).
11. T-19.IV.D.2:1-3, p. 420 (p. 391).
12. C-4.7:1-7, p. 86 (p. 82).
13. W-342.pII.1:1-8, p. 474 (p. 464).
14. C-3.4:1, p. 83 (p. 79).
15. W-67.pI, p. 113 (p. 112).
16. W-67.pI.5:2, p. 114 (p. 112-113).
17. W-67.pI.2:8-9, p. 113 (p. 112).
18. W-67.pI.4:3-4, p. 113 (p. 112).

60

DIVINE GRACE

~ o ~

When we last talked, I was describing my recovery from the aftermath of seeing the Light. Recently I looked up some quotes that seem pertinent. I went to the library and found a quote from Philip Kapleau's book, *The Three Pillars of Zen*. It's attributed to a famous enlightened teacher, Bassui, who described the direct experience of what he called *Mind* or *Essence*, which can be interpreted as being Buddha nature. Here's the quote:

> If you push forward with your last ounce of strength at the very point where the path of your thinking has been blocked, and then, completely stymied, leap with hands high in the air into the tremendous abyss of fire consuming you—into the ever-burning flame of your own primordial nature—all ego consciousness, all delusive feelings and thoughts and perceptions will perish with your ego-root and the true source of your Self-nature will appear.[1]

What strikes me about this Zen Buddhist description of enlightenment is the idea of leaping with hands high in the air into the fire of the "primordial nature." This fiery revealing of the true Self-nature describes specifically what I had experienced in my leap toward the sun. However, in the case of my leap, my ego consciousness was only temporarily set aside and was not extinguished. There is a Course quotation that uses this same idea of leaping to higher awareness:

> When the light has come and you have said, "God's Will is mine," you will see such beauty that you will know it is not of you … The bleak little world will vanish into nothingness, and your heart will be so filled with joy that it will leap into Heaven, and into the Presence of God. I cannot tell you what this will be like, for your heart is not ready. Yet I can tell you, and remind you often, that what God wills for Himself He wills for you, and what He wills for you is yours.[2]

THE LEAP TO SATORI

Thus the Course describes the enlightenment experience here as a leaping into heaven. [This jump to enlightenment is visually expressed in my painting *The Leap to Satori*, shown on the opposite page and in color on the back cover.] However, the direct experience of God, which the Course calls *revelation*, induces the response of awe,[3] which is what I first experienced. It is the appropriate response of the creature to the Creator. But the Course also says that being in the presence of God can be fearful if the proper preparations are not made. If these preparations have not been made, then, the Course states, "...awe will be confused with fear, and the experience will be more traumatic than beatific."[4] Then it goes on to say in the same section, "Revelation may occasionally reveal the end to you, but to reach it the means are needed."[5] The point I am making is that the end of the road was suddenly shown to me, but I now have to follow the road before me to be able to return to the divine Presence without the fear that changed it from an awesome experience into a traumatic one.

When the Course says "the means are needed" to reach the direct experience of divine Presence, it is referring to following the teachings of right thinking and right living that are described in the Course itself. One of these basic teachings is that you cannot go from seeing the world as a place of fear, danger, and evil and then enter into God's presence without being traumatized. The Course teaches that you first have to change your view of the world so you perceive the world as a *happy dream*,[6] which is a reflection of heaven. This preparation for heaven is brought about by practicing forgiveness. The Course idea of forgiveness is healing your perceptions of separation and affirming your oneness with everyone and everything. In practicing forgiveness you are really practicing seeing the divine reflection here as a preparation for accepting your own divine nature in God. This involves letting go of illusions based on anger, fear, and guilt. I am studying the Course to learn how to do that now.

Getting back to the story I've been telling you, I didn't have the Course principles to rely on at that time. Even then I realized I needed to correct my thinking, but I had to do so within the framework of the Catholic faith, since that was the only Christian option with which I was familiar. The following morning, I read the very next section of Revelation in the Bible, which is the letter to the seventh church. Part of that section reads:

> As for me, those whom I love I rebuke and chastise. Be earnest therefore and repent. Behold, I stand at the door and knock. If any man listens to my voice and opens the door to me, I will come in to him and will sup with him, and he with me. He who overcomes, I will permit him to sit with me upon my throne, as I overcame and have sat with my Father on his throne.[7]

This quotation refers to the image of a door, but the key idea is that the responsibility rests with the seeker to open the door to Christ. At the time of reading this quotation, it seemed to be speaking to me of repentance. I learned much later in a Bible study class that the word for repentance is *metanoia*, which literally means having a change of heart. However, just reading these words didn't really sink in until I went to church that day. Normally we wouldn't be going to church on Friday, but it was a "holy day of obligation." It was August 15, the Assumption of Mother Mary, in which church tradition says She left the earth and was taken up into heaven. The Assumption may be considered Mother Mary's entrance into the New Jerusalem. Also, our community chose to name itself after the New Jerusalem in 1988 on August 15, and therefore Mother Mary may be a behind-the-scenes spiritual influence in our community, just as I believe She was and is in my personal life.

August 14 is another important day for the New Jerusalem Community because David and Pamela first arrived in Sedona to plant the seeds of our community here on August 14, 1983 and, of course, August 15 was their first full day. August 14 is the "vigil of the Assumption," and it is recognized, especially in the Eastern Orthodox Churches, as a day when healings and other blessings come to seekers through divine grace. I remembered prostrating myself in St. Joseph's Church before the statue of Mother Mary about a month earlier, and now, during the Mass for the Assumption, I wondered how much her intercession may have helped me in my ordeal, since I had been healed the day before.

On previous occasions I had received communion in church without going to confession. On this Friday church service I was intending to receive communion again. Just before the communion started, the priest held up the host, which is a thin wafer of bread, and he addressed the congregation with the words, "Behold the Lamb of God, who takes away the sins of the world. Happy are they who are called to His supper."

The whole congregation responded by saying, "Lord, I am not worthy to receive you, but only say the word, and I shall be healed." As I was kneeling beside my father and mother, I started to say these words, "Lord, I am not worthy....," but I couldn't finish. I burst into tears. I had already been healed the day before, but I felt I was not worthy to have been healed. I did not feel worthy of receiving communion. I couldn't stop crying. After a while my father touched me and said tenderly, "Yes, it is a very moving ceremony." My father's kindness only made me cry more as I thought of all the pain that I had caused both him and my mother.

I didn't receive communion that day. I needed and wanted to make a good confession first. The next day my parents drove me to the church so I could go to confession. During the confession I started crying again, and the priest was patient with me. I was relieved afterwards. I knew it was necessary for me to return to my roots in Christ. Looking back on how the man in Rochester had taken me on a "memory walk" and led me to the church, I could see with the clarity of hindsight that I was being guided to follow Christ rather than the teachings of the roshi. Nevertheless, I remembered that the roshi had said some things that might be helpful in my return to Christ. For one thing, he had said that sometimes after a man has his first enlightenment, called *kensho*, he can make the mistake of having pride in his experience. This is considered the *awful smell* of enlightenment. The seeker can make the error of becoming more egotistical than before and think he is better than his brothers and sisters. If this happens, he does not realize his perfect equality with everyone in the Light.

I realized that I had nothing to brag about. After all, I had driven my mind into an unbalanced condition. In spite of all the irrational behavior I exhibited, I never considered at the time that I was out of my mind. Only as an aftereffect of seeing the Light did I realize that I had been mentally unbalanced and that this Light had cured me. Actually I was healed by divine grace in two events. The first was the healing of my possession by the casting out of the negative spirit, and the second was the healing of my mind by seeing the Light.

After my confession I was able to take responsibility for weakening myself at all levels by my spiritual pride, lack of moderation, and poor discretion. I was able to accept that I had been possessed, but without using this as an excuse for my condition. If I had been less egotistical and if I had a pure heart, I would not have been so easily influenced by a negative spirit. Once I had weakened myself through presumption and spiritual gluttony, I became powerless to bring myself out of my condition and even incapable of knowing how much I needed help. Now, after having taken responsibility for reaching the bottom of the pit by my own efforts, I was able to see clearly see that I had been saved entirely by God's grace.

In no way did I attribute the experience of the Light to my repetition of the *Mu* koan during the sesshin, although it is true that enlightenment sometimes comes at some time after a sesshin. I remembered that it was immediately after dropping the Mu koan that the man had brought me to the church to show me the cross of Christ. Remembering falling down before the white cross reminded me of the divine grace that comes through Jesus Christ. I felt strongly that Jesus and indeed Mother Mary had interceded on my behalf to bring God's grace to me when my life was hanging in the balance. After my confession and reflection on divine grace, I felt filled with gratitude, and I still feel grateful.

Years later I would read *The Seven Storey Mountain*, the autobiography of Thomas Merton. He was a Trappist monk, but I learned in his life story that he was actually converted to being a Catholic as an adult. When I read the description of his baptism, I was reminded that the priest actually performs an exorcism on the adult convert as part of the ceremony.

[I didn't have the book with me to show the exact quote to Allan, but the quote from the book is below. Breathing into Merton's face, the priest said:

"Depart from him, thou impure spirit, and give place to the Holy Spirit, the Paraclete."

It was the exorcism. I did not see them leaving, but there must have been more than seven of them. I had never been able to count them. Would they ever come back? Would that terrible threat of Christ be fulfilled, that threat about the man whose house was clean and garnished, only to be reoccupied by the first devil and many others worse than himself?

The priest, and Christ in him—for it was Christ that was doing these things through his invisible ministry, in the Sacrament of my purification—breathed again into my face.

"Thomas, receive the good Spirit through this breathing, and receive the Blessing of God. Peace be with thee."[8]]

Merton wrote about Christ through the agent of the priest casting out negative spirits in his baptism, but it reminded me that I had undergone an adult baptism of my own, only without the priest being involved. It was Christ Himself Who must have breathed on me and relieved me of my negative spirit, and then followed that up with an even more dramatic directed experience of baptism in His Light. After his adult conversion, Merton felt very grateful that he was starting his life all over again after being cleansed by Christ, and this was also how I felt back then after my own adult healing and conversion back to Christ. Merton had wondered about Jesus warning of the possibility of the negatives spirit returning, but I had no such concern. After all, Jesus had also said that those who are forgiven little will love little, and those who are forgiven much will love much. I felt I had been forgiven much, and after my long drought of emotion I began to feel the stirrings of love welling up within me. I had been lost at sea with no hope of survival, yet instead of being swallowed up by the ocean of my own willfulness, I was engulfed by the Light and transported to the safe harbor of Christ. Having received such a great healing, I would do nothing to dishonor that gift of divine grace by ever abandoning my Savior again.

The day after my confession, on Sunday, I went to church. When I received communion, tears streamed down my face, but this time they were tears of gratitude. However, when I came home after Mass, I was in my room crying again because of thoughts of unworthiness. My parents heard me and came into my room. My mother asked, 'What's the matter?' I apologized to them for all the grief that I had caused them. While crying I said, "When I was at Memorial Hospital, I wasn't physically sick. I was faking. I'm sorry."

"But even if you were faking, as you said, that in itself meant that you needed help," my mother said. "We don't care about what happened in the past. We don't want you to worry about what happened. We just want you to rest and get better now." Both my parents were very loving toward me. My mother was this way naturally. I especially appreciated the effort that my father made to open his heart to me by showing me signs of affection that he had not exhibited toward me in the past.

My healing on August 14 was the time when four hundred thousand people began their trip from long distances to the small town of Woodstock in New York to participate in the defining event of my generation. The 1969 Woodstock Festival itself ran from August 15 to 17 as a celebration of music, peace, life, and love. All the alienating barriers of race, sex, social status, and sectarian religion came tumbling down in a spontaneous act of joining in which everyone was welcome. In spite of the drugs, I felt these pilgrims were really coming together to seek God just as I was.

I relaxed at the beach until the end of the summer, and my personality and emotions gradually returned to normal. With the Vietnam War still raging in September, I received another notice for an army draft physical in New Haven. I could have asked the psychiatrist at Undercliff for an exemption due to mental illness. He would have given me this if I had asked, but I knew I was no longer mentally unbalanced, and I never did go back to Undercliff. I could have faked the physical exam again as I had done twice before, but I wouldn't consider doing that this time. I still did not want to be controlled by outside forces that would overrule my own choices. Most importantly, I did not believe that Jesus or God would give me permission to kill another person, even though the government would give me its full blessing to do so. Nevertheless, I firmly decided that I would put my trust in God's Will, and therefore I would make no attempt to fail the physical. I was embarrassed about how I had acted in the past in my efforts to avoid being drafted and was committed to not making this same mistake again, even if it meant going into the army.

When the blood pressure test was given, I passed it, just as I had fully expected to do. Next the examiner took my pulse reading, and it was abnormally high, which I certainly didn't expect. I came back later that day, and it was still high. I had to stay in New Haven for two more days to be retested twice more each day. All the pulse readings were high, so I failed the physical without even trying. Maybe this happened because of being nervous about returning to this place, but since this happened naturally, I accepted it as God's Will for me. Since this was the third time I had failed the physical, the exemption became permanent. Whenever I had regular physical examinations by a doctor in the future, my pulse was never high.

After it became clear I would not be drafted, my brother Paul kindly bought me an expensive new suit, a dark blue one, which would be useful in future job interviews. I had always been a very selfish person, but after my experiences that summer, I began to work consistently in various social service jobs, which are mentioned in Chapter 3 and Chapter 5. I felt it was my way of giving back to God for the divine grace I had received. I had a new goal in life—to do God's Will and live a life of service to others.

"There's only a little more to my story. Let's save it for next time," I said.

Allan responded, "I could tell from your voice tone that it was difficult for you to talk about this. Since you are living a life of service, I'll tell you a joke about three men who were living a life of service. They were each describing how they make sure to donate a portion of their earnings to God. The first man said, 'I don't do tithing. I have my own method of giving back to God. I draw a circle on the floor, and then I throw all of my earnings up into the air. All the money that falls outside the circle I give to God. All of the money that falls inside the circle I keep.'

"Then the second man offered his method. 'I have a similar method. I draw a circle on the floor, and I also throw all of my earnings into the air. All of the money that falls inside the circle I give to God. All of the money that falls outside the circle I keep.'

"Finally the third man spoke up. 'I throw all of my money up into the air and let God take whatever He wants. Whatever falls on the floor I keep.'"

I laughed, "I'll have to remember that one."

"I'm ready to meditate, if you are," Allan said.

"I'm ready. Let's go. Or rather, let's *let go.*"

---

1. Philip Kapleau, compiled and edited with translations, introductions, and notes, *The Three Pillars of Zen*, (Garden City, New York: Anchor Books, Anchor Press/Doubleday, 1980), p. 186.
2. T-11.III.3:5, p. 199 (pp. 184-185).
3. T-1.II.3:1, p. 7 (p. 5).
4. T-1.VII.5:8, p. 16 (p. 13).
5. T-1.VII.5:11, p. 16 (p. 13).
6. T-18.V, pp. 382-384 (pp. 357-358).
7. Revelation 3:19-21, CCD.
8. Thomas Merton, *The Seven Storey Mountain*, (New York: A Harvest Book, [first published in 1948] 1999), pp. 244-245.

61

AN EXTRA BLESSING

≈ ⚬ ≈

From where we were last time we talked, let's skip ahead a year to the summer of 1970. I was staying with my parents at the beach cottage in Westbrook. While there, I enjoyed taking long walks in the water at low tide and had developed a knack of finding buried clams by stepping on them. About a third of a mile offshore from the sandy beach was a rock the size of a small house. At low tide one sunny day, I went out and meditated on that rock for a short while. Coming back, I was repeating "Jesus" as I often would while walking, saying "Je" with every step of the right foot and "sus" with every step of the left foot. As I stepped with my right foot, my heel did not sink into the sand as usual, but felt something hard. Knowing it was a clam, I gave thanks to God with unusual gratitude. For some reason, I felt especially happy for having found this particular good-sized clam.

Later that afternoon, my father came home from work with groceries in the car. To help out I carried a gallon of wine into the house, but dropped it. The jar broke and wine covered the linoleum floor. In the past Dad might have said, "God damn it, can't you do anything right?" However, for the past year he had learned to control his anger and had become especially kind to me, so he just made a face. As I was cleaning the floor, I felt intuitively that I had done this to give myself a message. Since I couldn't figure out the content of the message, I made a quick prayer, asking God to reveal to me the meaning of my breaking the bottle of wine.

I soon forgot all about this prayer, as I prepared for dinner by making a tomato clam sauce, using the big clam I had just found. Since my father liked clams, I gave him half of the tomato clam sauce to have with his macaroni dinner. While Dad was chewing a mouthful, his teeth struck something hard. Pulling the object out, he held a beautiful shiny pearl between his fingers. We were all surprised, because we had never even heard of a pearl being found in our area of the beach. Also, although we knew oysters could produce pearls, we did not know they could be found in clams. I thought it was odd that I hadn't seen the pearl when I had opened the clams and cut them up to make the sauce. I told my parents we should keep this a secret to avoid questions and prevent people from digging up the beach unnecessarily.

We weren't sure who should have the pearl, since I found it in the ocean and Dad found it in his mouth, but Dad told me he wanted me to have it. I said, "I guess I'll have to find another pearl so we can both have one."

Dad, ever the realist, responded, "You could never find another pearl in a million years at our beach." However, I felt it was only a matter of faith, so I prayed to find another pearl before the end of the summer. A month later, in the final few days of August, I was walking in the ocean at low tide and went out very far. I happened upon a friendly, stocky stranger. Next to him was a boat, and he had a clamming rake he was using as he stood in water up to his knees. I asked, "Are you looking for clams?"

"No, actually I am looking for hermit crabs to use for fishing bait." He smiled and said, "Do you like clams?"

"My father and I like to eat clams," I told him.

"I caught these clams here, and you can have them if you want them," the stranger said as he held out five clams.

"Are you sure? Don't you like clams?" I asked.

He smiled and said, "I think these are for you. All I want is hermit crabs."

"That's kind of you. Thanks," I said as he put the five clams in my hands. I wished him well and turned around to walk back to the shore. I felt intuitively that there was a pearl in one of these clams. It occurred to me that, if I was right about finding a pearl, I would feel uncomfortable if I did not do something to compensate the stranger and express my appreciation for his kindness. I had already walked maybe two hundred feet away from him, but stopped there and spent time looking around for hermit crabs. After finding a bunch, I walked back to the stranger, who was still there by his boat in the water. "I was walking back and saw these hermit crabs, so I picked them up for you," I said happily.

"You are very thoughtful to do that. Thank you," he said as I handed him the hermit crabs.

"I hope you catch a lot of fish with these hermit crabs. Bye for now."

"I hope you and your father enjoy those clams. Good-bye," he said. I turned around and took maybe twenty steps, before the thought entered my mind that I had met this man before—but where? I glanced back, but was astounded to find that he was gone. His boat was gone too. But how? There was no time for him to have gotten out of view and there was no one out there as far as the eye could see. Then I remembered where I had seen him before. It was in Rochester. He was the stranger who asked me to take a "memory walk" and took me to the church to fall down before the cross of Christ. After realizing this, I knew there must be a pearl in one of the clams he had given me. When I came home, I eagerly opened the clams with a knife, but I had to work deliberately in order to avoid cutting myself. While opening one clam, I was delighted to see the pearl I had fully expected. This pearl was smaller than the previous one and not as well formed, yet it was the answer to my prayer to find another. I gave thanks to God for His extra blessing.

It was not until after I had received the gift of the second pearl that I could clearly see God's purpose in giving these gifts. I recalled having dropped and broken the bottle of wine and seeing the wine all over the floor. Since this happened just before the pearl was discovered at dinner time, I felt the two incidents were related and had definite spiritual significance. In the breaking of the wine bottle, I could see a sign of the suffering I had inflicted upon my parents as a result of extremes I had gone to the previous summer. In the finding of the pearls, I could see a sign of an opportunity to compensate my parents in a minor way for the anguish I had caused them. I went to a jeweler and had both pearls mounted on crosses. I placed the crosses on gold chains and gave them to my parents, who wore them around their necks.

Shortly after that, I decided I wanted to be a Trappist monk in order to dedicate my life to God alone. I felt there were too many distractions in the everyday world and was concerned that, in time, I might forget about God. I went to St. Joseph's Abbey in Spencer, Massachusetts and was allowed to talk to the abbot, Thomas Keating. In later years, he would become known as one of the foremost teachers of Centering Prayer, perhaps the most popular form of contemplative prayer. At the time, however, I did not know anything about Christian contemplation. When the abbot asked me about my prayer life, I said, "I am repeating the Name of Jesus and coordinating this with my breathing."

"So you are saying the Prayer of the Heart," the abbot said in a casual manner, as if I should know exactly what he was talking about.

"What's the Prayer of the Heart?" I asked.

"It's a form of prayer associated with the Eastern Orthodox Churches, such as the Russian and the Greek," the abbot explained. "But anyone can use the prayer. The full form of the prayer is 'Lord Jesus Christ, Son of God, have mercy on me, a sinner.' Most often it is used in a shortened form such as, 'Lord Jesus Christ, have mercy on me,' or even simply 'Jesus' as you are using. It's also called the Jesus Prayer."

I thanked him for his explanation and told him why I had come to the abbey, saying, "I asked to talk with you because I want to be a Trappist monk."

"Why do you want to be a monk?" he inquired.

I told the abbot what happened the previous year in Rochester and in Connecticut. I explained that I was in a mental hospital. Then I told him how I had looked into the sun and was taken up into the Light. He was the first person I told about this experience. As I told him how I had been saved by divine grace, I became overcome by tears of gratitude to God. Thomas Keating, a tall, gentle man, was very kind to me as I spoke. He suggested I go to church every day and give myself more time to consider the monastic vocation. He asked me to continue with my spiritual practices and, after a year, return to discuss my aspirations. He also asked me to have my records at the mental hospital sent to him for evaluation in regard to my monastic potential. At the end of our conversation, he asked if I wanted a blessing, and I said I did. I didn't even think to kneel, and in his humility he didn't ask me to, so he simply blessed me while I stood.

Throughout the year, I went to Mass at 6:30 AM every day. At the end of the year, following his advice, I returned. In fall 1971, I sat before a monastic official who had conferred with the abbot. He said, "Our Cistercian Order is very demanding. Not everyone who applies is accepted, and some who are accepted do not last very long. There are a lot of Catholic orders, so why do you want to be a monk at a Trappist monastery in particular?"

I replied, "I'm naturally drawn to the practice of meditation, and I'm attracted to the silence and contemplative lifestyle of the Trappists."

Then he told me that he appreciated my interest, but I would not be accepted as a monastic candidate. I asked for the reason and he said, "I have your records from Undercliff. Do you know what your diagnosis was?" The tone of his voice indicated he was attempting to be sensitive, yet his face looked like he had just smelled something unpleasant.

"No, I was not told my diagnosis," I said. When he put his head down to stare at the paperwork he held in his hands, I assumed he was looking at the word "schizophrenia." That seemed like the most likely diagnosis the psychiatrist would have chosen based on the symptoms I had exhibited. My symptoms were somewhat similar to the behavior of some of my dually diagnosed clients who have both a developmental disability and have the diagnosis of schizophrenia. However, I don't believe I ever really had schizophrenia. The psychiatrist hadn't been given enough information to make an accurate diagnosis. For example, I did not tell him I had taken an herb that duplicates some of the symptoms of schizophrenia. In addition, the psychiatrist was not aware of the fact that I had not seen visual hallucinations and had not heard inner voices, both of which are common symptoms of schizophrenia.

There was a lot more information the psychiatrist didn't know. As a matter of fact, there was much more that I didn't know, but would learn later. I had assumed my experience was unique. Because I hadn't yet studied yoga philosophy in depth, I didn't know what I had experienced was an all-too-common "kundalini crisis" brought about by imbalances in the upward flow of energy through the chakras. I had not yet heard of Edgar Cayce, so I was unaware that, before I was born, his readings had documented many spiritual anomalies similar to my own, including the influences of negative spirits.

[When I had worked in Virginia Beach as a counselor for Interact, the after-hours social service hotline, my supervisor was Henry Reed. As it turned out, he later became an author who wrote the following description of Edgar Cayce's readings regarding unusual spiritual openings:

A number of people sought readings from Edgar Cayce because they were having strange experiences: headaches with visions, energy sensations in the body, flashes of past-life recollections at odd moments, tremblings, bizarre and uncontrollable psychic experiences. He often described these events as the result of imbalances in the body corresponding to disturbances in the chakra system....He noted also, in cases of "possession" or involuntary contact with entities, that when chakras are prodded open, they allow the energies from other subconscious minds to filter into a person's own energy system in a manner that would not otherwise occur. As the transducers of psychic energy, properly functioning chakras operate not only as psychic communicators, but also as a shield against unwanted communication. Cayce, and others since, have noted that the use of drugs and alcohol can produce "holes in the aura" that correspond to vulnerabilities in the etheric body due to improperly functioning chakras. These invite invasion from outside influences.[1]

Edgar Cayce encouraged those who had unusual spiritual experiences to embrace these as important opportunities for growth. Such experiences involving the kundalini and chakras have happened so frequently that within clinical spiritual psychology there is a subspecialty for dealing with these psychospiritual openings. A pioneer researcher in this field has been Dr. Stanislav Grof, along with his wife Christina. They coined the term "spiritual emergency." In 1980 they founded the Spiritual Emergency Network. Henry Reed described this network, writing, "In their work, they have found that kundalini crises can mimic any of the known psychiatric disorders. Traditional psychiatry tends to use medication for the treatment of these crises, but the practitioners in this new network have evolved an alternative system of treatment aimed at helping the person integrate the energies that have been released, while also attempting to stabilize the chakra system."[2] Stanislav and Christina Grof wrote books and articles, maintaining that psychospiritual crises can be an opportunity for reaching a new level of awareness. Consequently, a spiritual emergency can become a "spiritual emergence," summarized in this way:

> One of the most important implications of the research of holotropic states is the realization that many of the conditions, which are currently diagnosed as psychotic and indiscriminately treated by suppressive medication, are actually difficult stages of a radical personality transformation and of spiritual opening. If they are correctly understood and supported, these psychospiritual crises can result in emotional and psychosomatic healing, remarkable psychological transformation, and consciousness evolution.[3]]

If the information that I learned later had been available to me in the early 70s, it would have been helpful for my own understanding. However, I doubt that it would have changed the psychiatrist's mind regarding my diagnosis. It certainly would not have had any impact on the opinion of the monastic official who now sat in front of me. It was abundantly clear to me that the diagnosis on the hospital report was already indelibly etched in his mind. "This is a very hard life," he said. "We are concerned that your history at the mental hospital is an indication that this monastic lifestyle may not be the best for you." He spoke with a graveness and sense of finality that convinced me there was no use in me trying to change his mind. He concluded by saying, "Since you are interested in meditation, I would like you to talk to Brother Basil. He has a strong background in meditation, so I think it would be helpful for you to talk to him."

Later, I did speak with Basil Pennington, who also eventually became known as an advocate of Centering Prayer. He told me, "Being in a monastery is not the only way to serve God. God must have a reason for you to be in the world."

I was unconvinced by what they told me. I still felt certain God had called me to be a monk. But I understood it did not matter what I said at this point, because I was not going to be accepted into the monastery due to my records at the mental hospital. I couldn't deny I had been mentally unstable, regardless of the specific diagnosis. There was no use claiming I had taken an herb that mimics the symptoms of schizophrenia. Saying that the herb had made me susceptible to the influence of negative spirits or that I had been possessed would do no good at all. I couldn't prove I did not have schizophrenia. Since I didn't know about kundalini crises [or spiritual emergencies] at that time, I was aware of only three possibilities—schizophrenia, the drug-like herb, and possession. But as far as I was concerned, all three of these were really beside the point. The only consideration I found relevant was the fact that God had suddenly and dramatically healed me. That's why I thought at the time, "Don't these monks believe in healing and in miracles? I was healed by God! Isn't that good enough?"

I had told Thomas Keating I had been healed by a profound experience of God's Light. But in relation to my specific diagnosis, I could see that such a statement must have been viewed as a grandiose claim put forth by a mentally ill person. The tears of gratitude that overcame me when I originally told my story to the abbot had already spoken more eloquently of my divine healing than any words could. Yet again, the diagnosis must have convinced the abbot that my tears were only a confirmation of my mental instability. Having been labeled by my diagnosis, I didn't have any credibility. I could not very well go back and insist I had been healed by God with any expectation of being believed.

There was nothing more I could say to Basil Pennington, who was only attempting to help me come to grips with the fact that I would never be a Trappist monk. Yes, I could apply somewhere else. But it dawned on me that my diagnosis would follow me wherever I went, so I could not reasonably expect to be accepted as a Catholic monk anywhere else. I dejectedly walked back to my retreat room at St. Joseph's Abbey, and did the only thing I could—I cried bitterly to God. Then a solution occurred to me: I did not need an organization to determine whether or not I could be a monk. The monastic vocation is primarily a commitment between God and His monk. Right then, with my tears as my witness, I made my vow directly to God, affirming, "God, I vow to You to be a monk in the world." From that moment onward, my life was dedicated to Him and included a commitment to celibacy. I kept my vow, remaining celibate for ten years. Then I broke my vow and had several years of not being a monk, before returning to being a celibate monk, as I am now. With hindsight, I can see that Basil Pennington was right when he said, "God must have a reason for you to be in the world."

That's the end of my story, except for one more thing. I never told you about how I came to meet you in New Market at Christ Land. I was driving from Celo, North Carolina to Virginia Beach, and I stopped at a rest area along the way. As I was showing a map to a man at the rest stop, he put his finger right on New Market, and I felt he was guiding me there. Then I walked away from him and looked back after several steps, and he had disappeared. After he disappeared into thin air, I realized he was the same stranger who took me to the church in Rochester, and the same one who gave me the clams at the beach in Connecticut. Without his intervention in North Carolina I never would have gone to Christ Land and discovered that you were there.

"Why didn't you tell me back then?" Allan inquired.

"I didn't know you well enough then. I didn't know if you would believe I really saw a stranger who disappeared and that I thought he was an angel. A while back you said you believed me when I told you about my experiences of seeing a devil and seeing angels. Now that I have told you about my history of mental illness, does that change your belief that I really did see a devil and angels?"

"If you were still taking psychotropic medication today, twenty-five years later, I might revise my thinking. However, your history of mental instability is obviously very ancient history. Also, you had a miraculous recovery back then, so, yes, I still believe you," Allan affirmed, reassuring me that I had not lost my credibility with him by revealing too many skeletons in my closet.

"Thanks. The angel visiting me to guide me to go to New Market would not have happened unless it was really important for you and me to be together. I want you to know how much I appreciate the time we have had together. I especially appreciate you being so receptive and letting me do all this talking about my life. It has helped me to relive the past and get a perspective on a lot of things that have happened to me. So that is the last thing that I wanted to say. Do you have any questions?" I inquired.

"I do have a question, but let's save that for next time. Are you ready for some *meditation medication?*" Allan asked with a smile.

"Sure," I said, "That's the only kind of medication I take."

---

1. Henry Reed, *Awakening Your Psychic Powers*, (New York, St. Martin's Paperbacks, 1996) pp. 183-184.

2. Ibid., 184.

3. Stanislav Grof and Christina Grof, "Spiritual Emergencies: Understanding the Treatment of Psychospiritual Crises," 1989, 1990, p. 1, which can be found on the internet at www.realitysandwich.com/spiritualemergencies. Recommended books: Stanislav Grof, *The Adventure of Self-Discovery*. (Albany, NY: State University of New York Press, 1988) and Stanislav and Christian Grof (Editors), *Spiritual Emergency: When Personal Transformation Becomes a Crisis*. (Los Angeles, CA: J.P. Tarcher, 1989).

62

SORTING PERCEPTIONS

≈ ○ ≈

Allan said, "When we last talked I said I had a couple of questions. When you were in Rochester you prayed and asked for a faith that could never be taken from you. Do you think that prayer was answered?"

"Yes," I said. "After seeing the Light I have certainty about God being reality. We are all part of that reality. I don't know how long I saw the Light, but it seemed like I was outside of time and space. Faith normally means believing without seeing. Because I saw the Light, I know it is there and that there is nothing more powerful than that Light. My prayer was answered, so I will never question that God exists or that God loves me.

"Instead of the Buddhist word satori or enlightenment, the Course uses the word *revelation* to describe this kind of direct encounter with God, [depicted in my painting *The Gift of Revelation*, shown on the following page and in color on the back cover]. The word revelation is probably used because God, Who has always been there, is suddenly revealed as a divine gift to the individual. In this experience, total awareness of God is given, along with certainty about that awareness of divine oneness. However, the total awareness imparted cannot really be adequately conveyed to others with words. The Course uses the word *knowledge* to represent the total awareness that is imparted during the direct experience of God. In this direct experience the individual is joined in oneness with God, so there is no sense of separation. Since the ego is the idea of separation, it is completely set aside during the direct experience of oneness with God. After the experience is over, the ego sense of separation is reestablished in the mind. When that happens, knowledge itself is lost, leaving behind only a memory of oneness. The total awareness of knowledge is replaced by the partial awareness of perception, which relies on dualism based on experiencing a sense of separation. Dualism requires a subject and object that appear to be separate. The subject is the perceiver who thinks he is separate. The object is that which he perceives apart from himself. Perceptions, relying on dualism, cannot fully explain the oneness that occurs in revelation. Also when the ego sense returns, the mind will be filled with true perceptions that do reflect the divine Truth, but there will also be

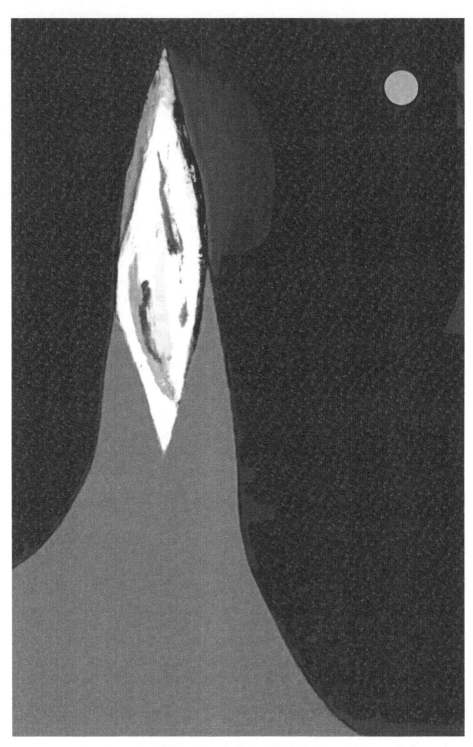

THE GIFT OF REVELATION

false perceptions that do not reflect the divine Truth. So after being given knowledge, I had to go back to body consciousness and reevaluate all my perceptions to sort out my true perceptions from my false perceptions. I did not have the Course to help me do this then, so my starting point was my Catholic religious thought system.

"I found that although I had certainty about God, I was not so settled about my perceptions of myself—unsure of what were true perceptions of myself and what were false perceptions of myself. I was especially uncertain about my perceptions related to worthiness. I knew God loved me, but I questioned whether I was worthy of His love. First let me affirm something positive about my Catholic faith that helped me back then. At that time I needed to acknowledge the guilt I felt inside and being a Catholic helped me do that.

"I feel like during my life I have been putting together a jigsaw puzzle that I call my 'shadow puzzle' because the puzzle pieces are hiding in the shadows of my mind. My Catholic faith helped to solve some of the mystery of exactly what lies beneath my conscious awareness, but left many unanswered questions. In recent years I found a more complete and accurate picture of my subconscious mind in the Course."

"I came across the term 'shadow figures' when reading the Course, but I am not sure exactly what that those words mean. What are shadow figures, and do they have anything to do with your shadow puzzle?" Allan inquired.[1]

"I came up with the term 'shadow puzzle' before I had learned about 'shadow figures' in the Course. Nevertheless, understanding shadow figures is needed in order to solve the puzzle of the subconscious mind. According to the Course, we manufacture shadow figures by taking old images from our past and bringing them into our daily life. My father was a strong authority figure and, as a child, I was sometimes angry with or afraid of him. When I grew up and met an authority type person, I did not really relate directly with that person. Instead, I superimposed the image of my father onto that person. When I was apparently relating to that person in front of me with fear or anger, I was actually relating to my father, who was a shadow figure in my mind. Because I was relating to someone who is not there, I was obviously just investing in my private world of illusions. In addition to shadow figures from this lifetime, I have related to shadow figures from past lives. To overcome these shadow figures, I practice seeing Christ in everyone instead of perceiving my manufactured illusions."

"So does your shadow puzzle consist of all your past life and present life shadow figures?" Allan asked.

"The shadow puzzle is all of those shadow figures, but also includes all the other aspects of the subconscious mind that are influencing me without my awareness. The Course has given me a road map of the subconscious mind that will help me to solve the shadow puzzle by bringing all the dark shadows of my mind into the light," I stated. The reason the Course has to be studied is that it contains a very wide range of interconnected ideas. Allan was focused mostly on his identity as the Son of God, but I wasn't sure if he was aware of all layers of the mind the Course describes, so I explained to him, "The Course says we hide behind many masks in the subconscious mind. The top mask is the face of innocence that pretends everything is all right. Below that mask is the victim that is angry for being abused by others and by the world. Beneath that mask is the ego that is the victimizer, who attacks others and the world. Below that mask is our guilt. This may be called the 'mask of guilt,' but on the positive side, this mask can be called the 'call for love,' which is likewise the call for God's help. When I was in church in 1969, I said, 'Lord, I am not worthy to receive you.' I needed to do this to realize I had a tremendous amount of guilt within my mind. It was also a call for love, which was expressed in the second part of the statement I made in church, 'But only say the word, and I shall be healed.'

"The Catholic faith, like many traditional Christian denominations, helps us to face and to come to grips with this deep level of guilt within our psyche. The other more superficial masks normally hide this deep level of guilt, but here is where we are in great anguish about living in a world of sin, guilt, and attack. At this level it appears to us that we have made sinners of ourselves, who are at war with our brothers, the world, and God. Here we are obsessed with our sins, which we feel have caused real damage. We feel we are terribly guilty and deserve to be punished, which makes us afraid even to look deeply at this inner mask. Facing all of this, we call out to God for help, even though we do not feel worthy of receiving that help. I am grateful for my Catholic upbringing for helping me to call for love and receive healing by doing so.

"But the strength of the Catholic faith is also its weakness. Yes, there is a positive side to the mask of guilt, because it encourages us to call for love. I think of this mask of guilt, as the 'sinner mask,' because it's the source of my sinner identity. The weakness of the Catholic faith is that it keeps me at the level of this fourth mask and prevents me from proceeding to a deeper and better reflection of my true nature. Allan, you're probably already aware of these four masks from your study of the Course."

Allan responded, "I am aware of the face of innocence, the victim, the victimizer, and what you call the 'sinner mask,' but I was not aware of the order that you laid out. I thought that the sinner mask was more of a surface thing because a Christian will say, 'I am a sinner because we are all sinners.' But it sounds like you are talking about a deeper level of emotion in which a person might pray to God with tears saying, 'I am a sinner. Lord, help me.'"

"Yes, I am talking about that deeper hidden level of guilt. It's the guilt that can sometimes be felt in prayer. It's good to uncover that guilt and call for God's Love and healing. However, the reason why the Catholic faith is no longer good for me is that it teaches me that I am inherently a sinner and therefore guilty and not worthy. Being raised as a Catholic, I learned that sin is real and has real effects causing real damage and resulting in real guilt. In my Sunday school catechism class, I was taught that a serious sin would put a mark on my soul. This grievous sin was called a 'mortal sin' or, in other words, a 'deadly sin.' If I died without confessing it, the grave nature of that sin would be so offensive to God that I would have to go to hell. I was told God is all Love and all Justice. His Justice demands that I go to hell for committing a mortal sin and His Love encourages me to not sin and to go to heaven. As a child it did not occur to me that the Catholic version of God's Love sounded very much like human love that fluctuates on and off depending on outer circumstances. I never asked, 'How could a loving God allow me to go the hell and still be considered a God of Love?' It never occurred to me that my soul is in fact my spirit, and spirit being formless cannot be marked. Marking my spirit would be like trying to plant a flag on the surface of the sun as the United States has done on the moon. Also, as a child I never questioned the idea that sin was real and caused real damage. One of my childhood chants was, 'Row, row, row your boat gently down the stream. Merrily, merrily, merrily, merrily, *life is but a dream*.' It just seemed like a silly song, but now I have come to see the truth in it, because life really is a dream. And if life is a dream, then what do you think that means in regard to sin?" I asked.

"It means sin must be a dream, too," Allan said confidently.

"Exactly! What we have here in the world is dream sin causing dream damage resulting in dream pain and dream guilt. Yes, evil, sin, and guilt do seem real enough in the dream, because our dream bodies can hurt other dream bodies. But this harm can only happen within the dream, not in the reality of the spirit world. Imagine that a child has a nightmare and screams in his sleep. His father comes to him and the child awakens and says, 'Dad, I had a terrible dream and I committed terrible sins. I feel awful about what I did. And you were in the dream too. You were very angry with me and told me to go away.'

"The father isn't going to say, 'You really are a terrible child because you did bad things in your dream and so I don't love you anymore.' Instead the father will say, 'That was just a nightmare and nightmares aren't real. You're safe now in your own home and I love you as always.' I use this example, because when we come back to our heavenly Father as prodigal sons and daughters He will say, 'That was just a dream world of form and your mistakes weren't real. You're safe now in your true Home and I love you as always.' Of course, I'm preaching to the choir here because you already know this from the Course."

"Yes, I do. There is a Course quote that I like that talks about our dream nightmare. It's right at the beginning of the Course." Turning his head slightly and using his mouth, Allan picked up his wooden utility stick. The rubber cushioned end of the stick had been stationed within a few inches of his mouth, where it was always located for easy access. Without the use of arms or legs, this stick was Allan's sole 'appendage.' He used the stick as his navigating tool to turn pages of a book, to talk on his telephone, or to change TV channels. To find the quote Allan was talking about, he used the stick to turn the pages of the Course book that was always on a little desk right next to his bedside. Turning his head to the side, Allan placed the stick back in its normal resting place. "Here's the quote: '*You* are a miracle, capable of creating in the likeness of your Creator. Everything else is your own nightmare, and does not exist. Only the creations of light are real.'[2]

"Our nightmares in our dream world don't exist in God's reality. With no real damage, except for dream damage, there can be no evil, sin, or guilt. That doesn't mean we are justified in making sins, or what the Course calls 'mistakes.' Dream sins still cause dream pain, and out of compassion we don't want to have anyone experience even dream pain. For the sake of love we want to correct all our mistakes as much as possible. But the point you were making earlier is that our sins don't make a mark on our souls, since our true spiritual nature cannot be defiled by the dream world of form. Unlike the traditional interpretation that makes God into someone requiring retribution, the Course makes God into the God of Love and only Love. The message of the Course then is that we are not bodies, which can indeed be harmed. Instead we are spiritual beings, and our eternal and true spiritual nature cannot be harmed. As spiritual beings we are each part of God, who is reality. God is holy and all of us, who are part of God in reality, are holy. The appearances of the world, including our perceptions of evil, sin, and guilt, are illusions. So we are always choosing between believing in the reality of God, which is our true nature, and the unreality of illusions, which our egos are attracted to. However, it is easy to see why so many people believe in the reality of sin, since the world appears so real to our physical eyes and we can't see God with our physical eyes."

I said, "It's true we can't see God, but we can feel His Love. If I still believed in the reality of sin, I would also have to believe that God's Love is conditional, depending on my behavior in the dream world. But I have come to believe that God loves me always, under all circumstances, no matter what mistakes I make at the form level. In short, as the prodigal son,

I can never be seen in the eyes of my Father as being unworthy of love or unworthy of heaven."

Allan offered, "I also like the Course's emphasis on God's unconditional Love. It's good that the Course has come along to help remind you of that."

"It certainly is. The Course is teaching me that I am worthy. It shows me that below the sinner mask of guilt and the call for love is the *right mind*. It is the healed mind that loves everyone and loves God without any ego attachment. The right mind is not our true identity, but it is an accurate reflection of our true nature. It is a mind that forgives not by seeing sin as real, but rather by seeing in the very beginning that sin is not real. Allan, as you said, sins are really only mistakes, which can be corrected. The right mind can see perceptions of separation as merely illusions that produce no real damage and are not sinful or deserving of guilt and punishment. The right mind can allow mistakes to be corrected without labeling these mistakes as sins. The right mind sees the actions of others only as various expressions of love or calls for love. The right mind perceives that everyone is worthy of love, regardless of outer appearances.

"The Course also shows us that below the right mind is the Christ Mind, which is our true Self, beyond the three dimensional world of form, space, and time. We are in the Christ Mind right now in reality because God created us as part of Himself. We are holy because God, who is holy, created us holy. We are loveable because God, who is Love, created us as an extension of His love. We are light because the Course says we were '...created *of* light and *in* light.'[3]

"A specific reason why the Catholic faith does not work for me now is that it talks about me being a body and simultaneously being a spirit and does not account for the inherent contradiction in those beliefs. The body is concrete and physical. However, the spirit is abstract and transcends the physical world. I made the mistake of asking, 'Where is my body?' when I saw the Light, and that question ended the direct experience of the Light. Consequently, I needed a spiritual philosophy that teaches me that the body is an illusion that hides my true reality. The Course teaches that I cannot be a body. I cannot be concrete and physical because my Father, who is not concrete and not physical, did not make me concrete and physical. It is fair to say that I have a body that I can use, but I cannot say that I am a body.

"I have talked with you in the past about the surprising Course concept that each of us is an *Idea* in the Mind of God—a *Thought* in the Mind of God. That sounds like a strange idea. But it seems strange to us only because we are so used to thinking of ourselves as bodies. We spend most of our time and effort in eating, cleaning, moving, sexing, and sleeping.

These activities of the body make it seem odd to consider that we are abstract beings. It feels more comfortable to believe the ego is real. The ego is the idea I am separate, and the body is the proof I am separate. Along with the idea I am an ego and a body comes the idea I can sin and produce real damage. This causes guilt and guilt causes fear of punishment. Through our belief in guilt we attract ways of hurting ourselves, like sickness, to bring about the punishment that we feel we deserve. So the idea of being concrete and physical may be familiar, but it has a lot of negative ramifications.

"At first it may not seem appealing to just be an abstract idea that has no real home in the physical world. But think of the advantage of being abstract. If you give a physical thing away, you seem to lose it, and someone else gains it. It appears that giving is a way of losing. The Course points out that if you share an idea with someone else you get to keep the idea, even when you give it away. Thus giving is a way of keeping, not losing. Since we are Ideas in heaven, we can have the unimaginable joy of lovingly sharing all of ourselves with everyone and only gaining and never losing. When God created us, He did not create a body apart from Himself. Instead God created us as a perfect Thought that He kept in His own Mind even as He created us. We have never left our Home in the Mind of God, which we call heaven. If we close our eyes in a lighted room, that room will appear dark to us, even though light is surrounding us. We have closed our eyes in heaven, so we are dreaming of illusions in this three dimensional world. When we meditate, we are attempting to wake up at least a little bit to remember that we are right now at Home in heaven and surrounded and filled with light that is our own true nature.

"Allan, I guess I got carried away there for a few minutes talking about all of these Course principles that you already know about, but it's just my enthusiasm bubbling up. Did you want to comment on any of this or are you ready to remember the light in meditation now?" I asked.

"It's nice to get reminders about the Course ideas. It's interesting how we have switched roles. I used to tell you about the Course and now you tell me about the Course. You must have learned a lot from living with Robert," Allan said.

"Robert has been my teacher of the Course, and it's been a blessing. He is like a Jewish rabbi, who knows the Torah backwards and forwards. I can ask him any question about the Course and he can come up with a quote and where to find it. I think his best skill is condensing the Course into simple concepts that are easy to understand. If it was not for Robert, I probably would never have been willing to take a closer look at the Course and finally accept its principles. When you first introduced the Course to me, I thought I already knew the important spiritual principles. I was too prideful to admit that some of my perceptions were wrong, and I was not open to other spiritual principles that I had not even considered. But Robert helped me to see that there was a lot more to the Course than I originally realized, and that it requires studying to really understand it. When we last talked, I told you about how I was not allowed to become a Trappist monk and was upset about it at the time. But if I had become a Trappist monk, I probably would never have allowed myself to step outside the theology of the Catholic faith. Consequently, I would have never been able to learn the Course principles, which have been so important to me in the past five years. Do you have any final questions?" I inquired.

"I have one more question, but let's save that for next time. Let's have our meditation," Allan said. While we meditated, Allan's friendly parrot, Poncho, landed on my shoulder. I paid no attention to it and it flew away, like stray thoughts in meditation that are ignored and fall away. Allan's other pet, Dave, an iguana, was less friendly, and so slow moving that it gave the impression that it must be meditating all the time.

After the meditation, Allan put his wooden pointer stick in his mouth and touched the end of it on a newspaper ad. After placing the stick in its resting place, Allan said, "That ad I just pointed to shows that ribs are on sale at Safeway, but the shopping has already been done here at our house. Would you mind buying nine pounds of ribs for me? I'll pay you, of course?"

"I'll be happy to do it. This will be like a new experience for me. Being a vegetarian, I haven't thought about meat in years. I'll buy that meat for you, but nine pounds of ribs sounds to me like an awfully hefty meal," I said.

"I told you I wanted you to get me some ribs. I wasn't asking you to give me a *ribbing* about my appetite, when you know full well that I am going to put most of those ribs in the freezer," Allan said with that big grin he had whenever he made a pun, which was often.

"OK, I promise to give you the ribs without the ribbing," I said with my own smile.

"This has been a spiritual test to see if you can see things differently, as the Course asks us to do. I am impressed because you have passed the test. I guess you are ready to transition to a new level of awareness—'meat consciousness,'" Allan said jokingly. "And since Christ opened his mind to meat, too, the next step for you is Christ consciousness."

I said, "Well, I'll have to visit the Safeway meat department more often, now that I know it can lead to Christ consciousness."

---

1. T-13.V.3:1-8, p. 248 (p. 231).
2. T-1.I.24:2-4, p. 4 (p. 2).
3. T-11.III.4:6, p. 199 (p. 185).

63

JACOB'S LADDER

~ • ~

"How's your Course prayer and meditation group going?" Allan asked.

"We usually have a small group and it has been working out very well," I responded. For about a year, I had been leading a monthly group that was open to the public, but it eventually petered out due to lack of attendance.

"When we last talked, I told you I had one final question. 'What kind of meditation do you practice?' Allan asked.

"Since you were brought up Jewish, I am sure you are familiar with the Old Testament story of Jacob's ladder. Jacob rested and had a dream in which he saw angels ascending and descending on a ladder that stretched from earth to heaven. This is a symbol of various levels of consciousness. Jacob's ladder also symbolizes the spine and the seven spiritual centers, or yoga chakras, in the body. For me meditation is a way of climbing up Jacob's ladder from lower levels of awareness in the body to higher levels.

"Even though there are seven rungs on Jacob's ladder corresponding to the seven spiritual centers of awareness, only four of these rungs are important focusing points for meditation. These four rungs or focusing points follow a sequence in meditation from the bottom up. I meditate first by focusing my awareness at the area just below the navel. This is similar to Zen meditation, which focuses on the hara in the navel area. I invite the Holy Spirit into this area and feel this area being filled with light, love, and energy. Then I repeat the process in each subsequent focusing area.

"With intuitive timing, I next focus in the area of the heart center. Then I concentrate on the brow area at the center of the forehead. Finally I bring my awareness to the crown of the head. You can think of my body in this meditation process as a Christmas tree with seven circular rows of lights. When I focus on the second row up from the bottom, the two bottom rows light up. When I turn my attention to the fourth row, all four bottom rows are illuminated. When I raise my awareness to the sixth row, all six rows light up. Then I concentrate on the seventh row, which is a small circular area of light. That would be the top of the Christmas tree, which would correspond in my body to the crown toward the back and top of my head.

"That's four steps, but there are two more. In the fourth step I hold the awareness only in the crown of the head, but in the fifth I expand my awareness so I feel oneness in the whole body all at once. In other words, I feel the whole Christmas tree light up as a unit, not as separate parts. The sixth step is less form related and more abstract. This final step is the letting go of body awareness altogether and being open to the divine presence without words. For each of these six steps, I begin by repeating a Divine Name mentally, then let go of the words to experience the divine presence, which for me feels like the presence of energy, light, and love all in one."

Allan said, "You have four focusing points, but there are seven spiritual centers. Why don't you meditate on each of the seven chakras?"

I explained, "Maybe it would be easier to understand this if we relate the chakras to the endocrine glands, which is what Edgar Cayce did in his readings. Let's talk about the three centers not used for meditation. The first chakra is related to the gonads, the sexual organs. You don't want to stimulate the secretion of sexual hormones from the gonads, so that's why you don't meditate there for obvious reasons. The third chakra is related to the adrenal glands near the solar plexus. That center is about power as it relates to fear and anger involved in the flight or fight syndrome. You don't want to meditate there because you don't want to stimulate the secretion of the adrenal hormones needed for strong emotional expression. The fifth chakra is related to the thyroid gland in the throat. The thyroid regulates the body metabolism. You don't want to meditate on the throat and stimulate the secretion of thyroid hormones affecting the metabolism because digestion is a different process than meditation. That's why it's not a good idea to meditate until a long while after eating. Does that explain why we don't meditate on three of the seven chakras?"

"I gather you are saying those three chakras aren't involved in the meditation process at all," Allan summarized.

"They are not directly involved as focusing points, but they are involved. In the book of Revelation it talks about opening seven seals. This refers to the opening of all seven chakras in a comprehensive meditation practice."

"How does your combination of techniques open all seven seals or chakras?" Allan asked.

"I'm sure you remember me telling you that during a profound spiritual experience, or at the time of death, the kundalini rises full-force through all the chakras to reveal a blazing light. That's when all the seals and chakras open fully. But this sudden raising of energy is only a rare and extreme release of the kundalini. Much more commonly, the kundalini rises in a gradual and mild manner that opens the chakras in a gentle way. The techniques I am describing are designed to encourage the natural rising of the kundalini through all of the chakras in a step-by-step manner. To ensure

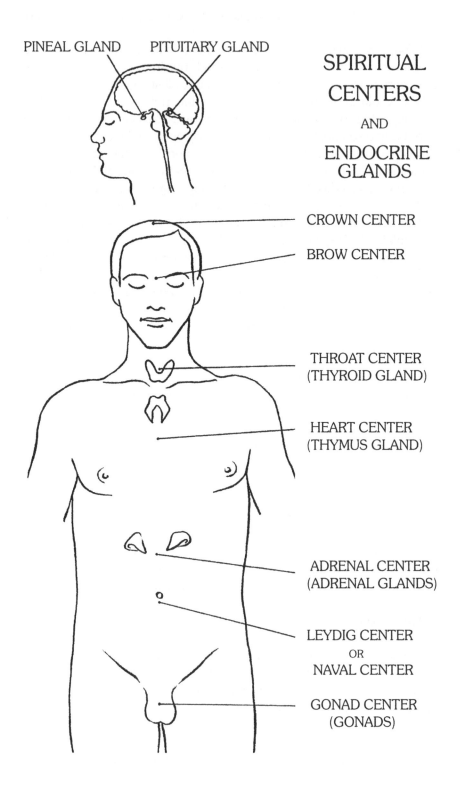

PINEAL GLAND   PITUITARY GLAND

SPIRITUAL
CENTERS
AND
ENDOCRINE
GLANDS

CROWN CENTER

BROW CENTER

THROAT CENTER
(THYROID GLAND)

HEART CENTER
(THYMUS GLAND)

ADRENAL CENTER
(ADRENAL GLANDS)

LEYDIG CENTER
OR
NAVAL CENTER

GONAD CENTER
(GONADS)

that this balanced raising of the kundalini energy takes place in the ideal way, it is very important to surrender the whole process to the Holy Spirit. With each of the six different techniques, I feel I am inviting the Holy Spirit to participate in the raising of the energy and the opening of the chakras. When I experience being filled with light during meditation, I feel this is the effect of the kundalini raising and the chakras opening in accordance with the action of the Holy Spirit.

"The first method, which focuses on the navel, is crucial to getting the energy to move upward. Cayce called the navel area the Leydig center, which is not medically recognized as an endocrine gland that secretes hormones, but is related to temptations involving the imagination and sexual urges. Cayce maintained there is something that functions like a door at the navel area in the Leydig center. By focusing the mind at the navel area this door opens and affects the flow of energy in the gonads below. The gonad energy itself is neutral, but when that energy moves downward it can become sexual energy used for sexual purposes. When the door in the navel area is opened through meditation, the downward moving gonad energy moves upward and can then be used for spiritual purposes. In terms of the seven seals of Revelation, focusing at the navel area opens both the first and second seals or chakras."

"That must be why the Zen Buddhists focus so much at the navel," Allan concluded.

"Exactly. They must know that getting the energy to flow upward is crucial to the effectiveness of meditation practice. On the other hand, yoga encourages meditating at the higher centers."

"What happens when you change your focus to the heart center?"

"Just as meditating at the navel area draws energy upward from below, meditating at the heart level draws energy upward from the navel area and the adrenal area. This opens both the third chakra at the adrenal area and the fourth chakra at the heart area. Cayce associated the heart center with the thymus gland, which is located in the center of the chest. He said that at the physical level it is part of the immune system and spiritually it had to do with opening to devotion."

Allan wondered, "When you meditate at the heart center, does that mean you focus on the center of the chest or on the heart area itself on the left side?"

"You can meditate on the location of the physical heart or you can meditate on the center of the chest. Years ago I used to focus a lot on the physical heart as a personal devotion to Jesus. Sometimes I felt what might be called a 'flame' or 'spark of light' when I focused on love in the heart area. In more recent years I focus on the center of the chest because the energy that rises up from below just naturally goes there when I meditate. I think focusing on the center of the chest accelerates the raising of energy in the body in my practice a little more than meditating on the heart itself. But either focusing point will be effective in raising energy. The most important thing at this level is being open to the inner feeling of love. Consequently, the neutral energy rising all the way upward from the gonads is dedicated to the purpose of expressing or opening to divine love."

"Are there endocrine glands associated with the brow area and the crown of the head too?"

"Yes, the brow area is linked with the pineal gland, which is related to the rational mind and using the mind as a tool of the Spirit. It is also associated with light, and because of that it helps regulate our sleep cycle that is attuned to sunrise and sunset. Focusing at the brow area draws energy upward from the heart through the throat and into the head. When the loving energy from the heart goes into the brow center, the mind can be fully dedicated to the spiritual purpose of manifesting the energies of love. So you can see meditating at the brow opens the fifth and sixth chakras. Then finally focusing at the crown area draws all the energy that been raised into the seventh chakra. The crown of the head is associated with the pituitary gland. Thus opening this final chakra affects the secretions of the pituitary gland, which is called the master gland because it can regulate the functioning of all the other glands. The seventh chakra is related to the highest vibrations of light, love, and oneness. It can integrate all the energies and raise and coordinate them into a harmonious wholeness. It has to do with spiritual transformation and transcendence. So that explains how these techniques open all the seven chakras and the seven seals of Revelation."

Allan looked puzzled and said, "I know you are a Course student, and this seems light years away from what the Course says about the body. The Course doesn't speak very highly of the body. The Course doesn't place any emphasis on body awareness, does it?"

I responded, "Actually the Course maintains that the body is neutral. It's like what Cayce says about the gonad energy. It is really neutral energy so it becomes sexual energy if used for sexual purposes and it becomes spiritual energy if used to manifest the spiritual purpose of expressing love. The true value of the body according to the Course is dependent upon the purpose you assign to it. If the body is used lovelessly, it becomes a tool of the ego that reinforces the idea of separation and is not helpful for our growth. On the other hand, if the body is used only for communication, it becomes an instrument of the Holy Spirit. Using the body awareness in meditation does not have the body as an end in itself, which is how the ego uses the body. Using the body in meditation is intended to make the body into a means for communication with our inner spiritual nature. This whole process of focusing on various points in the body is intended to invite the Holy Spirit into all the seven levels of your consciousness. What better purpose can the body be used for than to communicate with Spirit and help us open to divine love. One of the specific meditation methods the Course does advocate is repeating Divine Names of God to help us wake up."

Allan asked, "Can you give me some examples of the types of Divine Names that might be used?"

"You can use any name that reminds you of God. I know Robert has used the word 'God,' and more recently he has switched to the word 'Father.' A person who has a personal devotion to Jesus can use the Divine Name of 'Jesus.' If someone wants to focus on the universal Christ presence, he can use the Divine Name of 'Christ.' You can repeat a quality as an affirmation, such as 'love,' 'light,' or 'peace.' Also you can combine a Divine Name with a spiritual quality. For example, you can use 'Jesus Love' or 'Christ Light."

"Could I use a short Course quotation?" Allan inquired.

"Absolutely, whatever words inspire you can be used. Do you have any other questions about the six steps of this meditation practice?"

"I think you have explained it very well, but it still seems different from what the Course recommends," Allan said.

"A lot of it is different, but in addition to repeating the Divine Name there is another aspect that is the same. The Course does not provide instruction on focusing on part of the body or spiritual centers. However, the omission of mentioning spiritual centers in the body in the Course does not mean there are no spiritual centers. The major purpose of the Course is to teach forgiveness and talking about spiritual centers is not necessary to that teaching, so it is omitted. No, I take that back. Do you remember the Course section called 'The Holy Meeting Place'?" I asked.

Allan nodded, "Sure."

"I believe 'the holy meeting place' is actually a reference to the seventh chakra. Let me read from your book what it says." Allan gave a nod toward his paperback edition of the Course, so I picked it up and said, "This section talks about a holy altar and says that you cannot offer a gift to God at this altar without offering it to His Son because the Father and Son are both together in this altar. Then it describes the altar as the holy meeting place in this way:

All this is safe within you, where the Holy Spirit shines. He shines not in division, but in the meeting place where God, united with His Son, speaks to His Son through Him. Communication between what cannot be divided cannot cease. The holy meeting place of the unseparated Father and His Son lies in the Holy Spirit and in you.

All interference in the communication that God Himself wills with His Son is quite impossible here. Unbroken and uninterrupted love flows constantly between the Father and the Son, as Both would have it be. And so it is.

Let your mind wander not through darkened corridors, away from light's center.[1]

"That last sentence indicates that this altar, this meeting place, is light's center. I think this meeting place where God and His Son, the Christ, reside is the seventh chakra. It's kind of like the inner version of the Holy of Holies. You must know about the Holy of Holies."

Allan responded, "Of course, that was the holiest altar in Solomon's temple in Jerusalem. It was such a holy place that the Jewish head priest could only go in one time per year on the Day of Atonement. He had to purify himself before going to that altar. Some unworthy priests went into the Holy of Holies and were consumed by the fire of God. They would tie a rope around the head priest's leg before he went in so that if he was burnt up by the fire of God, they could pull his body out without having to go in themselves. So you think the Holy of Holies within the physical body is at the top of the head in the seventh chakra."

"Yes, and just as the priest had to be purified before going into the Holy of Holies, we must purify our minds if we want to enter light's center in the seventh chakra, where God and His Son, the Christ are located. Meditation is the purifying of the mind that is needed."

"Aren't we already pure, being the Son of God?" Allan asked.

"Yes, we are pure in the sense of being guiltless and holy as the Son of God. But the Course also says we have placed other gods on the altar and need to follow the guidance of the Holy Spirit to accept the Atonement. Of course, this is a different kind of Atonement than the Jewish Day of Atonement. The Atonement is on the altar ready for you to receive it and is the gift that opens you to God. Here's what the very next section says:

> The Atonement is so gentle you need but whisper to it, and all power will rush to your assistance and support. You are not frail with God beside you. Yet without Him you are nothing. The Atonement offers you God. The gift that you refused is held by Him in you. The Holy Spirit holds it there for you. God has not left His altar, though His worshippers placed other gods upon it. The temple is still holy, for the Presence that dwells within it *is* holiness.
>
> In the temple, holiness waits quietly for the return of them that love it. The Presence knows they will return to purity and to grace.[2]

"Although we are sinless, we still have to remove these other gods that we have placed on the altar and worshipped instead of God. The images of these gods block our awareness of God's presence, and purification is needed to remove them."

"So is there something in that section describing how to remove those images of gods?" Allan asked.

"Yes, there is. Right on the same page there's an analogy to describe this purification process:

> In this world you can become a spotless mirror, in which the holiness of your Creator shines forth from you to all around you. You can reflect Heaven here. Yet no reflections of the images of other gods must dim the mirror that would hold God's reflection in it. Earth can reflect Heaven or hell; God or the ego. You need but leave the mirror clean and clear of all the images of hidden darkness you have drawn upon it. God will shine upon it of Himself. Only the clear reflection of Himself can be perceived upon it.
>
> Reflections are seen in the light. In darkness they are obscure, and their meaning seems to lie only in shifting interpretations, rather than in themselves. The reflection of God needs no interpretation. It is clear. Clean but the mirror, and the message that shines forth from what the mirror holds out for everyone to see, no one can fail to understand.[3]

"This section goes on to say that the mirror analogy is talking about the *mirror of your mind*, which is the reflection of God:

> Could you but realize for a single instant the power of healing that the reflection of God, shining in you, can bring to all the world, you could not wait to make the mirror of your mind clean to receive the image of the holiness that heals the world.[4]

"What the Course is talking about is that we have filled the mind with all sorts of images. If we can let go of all those images, God would cast His reflection of light into the world. In Eastern philosophy it is very common to hear this exact same analogy of a mirror to describe the cleaning of the mind that occurs in meditation. From an Eastern perspective, any thoughts are blemishes on the mind. The goal is to clean the mind so much that you can let go of all thoughts. When you can let go of all thoughts, what is left is the direct experience of God Himself. A partial cleaning of the mind will not produce the direct experience of God, but it will still be very beneficial. Cleaning most of the thoughts from the mind can make the mind so clear that it can produce an indirect experience of God. This section of the Course that I just read, called 'The Reflection of Holiness,' describes this indirect experience as a 'reflection of God,' caused by cleaning the mirror of the mind. It is true the Course is not using the word meditation in its mirror analogy. Nevertheless, I believe that is what it is referring to. The Course does give instructions about taking time for attunement every day and opening to the divine presence. The Workbook does not give just one method and say this is how to meditate, but rather presents many different practices that can be used to deepen your attunement with Spirit. For example, the Course often recommends repeating inspirational words to calm the mind and then letting go of those words to experience the divine presence. This experience of wordless attunement is a description of what Christians generally call *contemplation*, although the Course doesn't specifically use that word in the Workbook lessons. The book of Revelation says that when the seventh seal was opened, '...there was silence in heaven....'[5] This silence is contemplation in which you rest in the divine presence, which is what the Course advocates.

"The first five steps of the techniques I use are examples of *meditation*, which is the continuous holding of one thought in the mind. The sixth step is an example of contemplation, which is the letting go of all thoughts. This sixth step is almost identical to the technique called *Centering Prayer* taught by Thomas Keating and Basil Pennington, the monks I met at St. Joseph's Abbey. It is also the basic teaching of the Course on inner attunement. However, I believe the five preliminary steps of meditation are very important for making the sixth step of contemplation more effective. This is just a sketchy way of describing my attunement practice. Actually, sometimes the Spirit just comes over me during an attunement, and when that happens, these steps are unnecessary. Perhaps advanced meditators would not benefit by the first five techniques, if they can calm the mind easily and are already experiencing contemplation. But most people cannot do that. For them, the first five methods can help calm the mind and prepare it for contemplation. I don't usually like to talk about my practice, because I like to keep that between God and myself. It is my form of intimacy with my Beloved. But since I have told you everything else, I figured I might as well tell you about this too."

"So do you call your series of techniques *Jacob's Ladder Meditation?*" Allan asked.

"That would be a good name to describe the step-by-step process. But if that were the name, some people might think it is specifically a Jewish method of meditation. Actually, a Jewish person can employ this method and use a Jewish Divine Name for God. However, this combination of techniques was designed primarily as a means of focusing on Christ. I originally called it *Christ Centered Meditation*, but recently have been calling it *Christian Yoga Meditation* because it includes focusing on the yoga chakras. Directing the attention to the spiritual centers in the body helps us to gain control over the mind and open up to the Spirit."

Allan said, "Thanks for sharing that. I find it hard to control my mind in meditation, but I still feel making the attempt is helpful. Actually, my favorite Course section is, 'I Need Do Nothing,' because it affirms that I don't have to do anything to become the Son of God. I am already the Son of God. It says we shouldn't meditate with the idea of looking to the future for freeing ourselves from a present state of unworthiness and inadequacy. In other words, we can find our oneness now by realizing, 'I need do nothing.' Doesn't that invalidate any need to meditate or contemplate?"

I responded, "I know that section is used by some Course students to invalidate the need for meditation or contemplation. That section does emphasize the holy relationship as a means of joining with others to find peace outwardly and inwardly. Years of preparation are not needed because this joining can be accomplished now. However, there is no doubt that the Workbook provides numerous examples of applying techniques of meditation and contemplation, which are likewise recommended in the *Manual for Teachers*. What's forgotten about the idea of 'I need do nothing' is the question of 'What does it mean to do nothing?' The answer is given in the last two paragraphs of that section, which I will read now:

> To do nothing is to rest, and make a place within you where the activity of the body ceases to demand attention. Into this place the Holy Spirit comes, and there abides. He will remain when you forget, and the body's activities return to occupy your conscious mind.
>
> Yet there will always be this place of rest to which you can return. And you will be more aware of this quiet center of the storm than all its raging activity. This quiet center, in which you do nothing, will remain with you, giving you rest in the midst of every busy doing on which you are sent. For from this center will you be directed how to use the body sinlessly. It is this center, from which the body is absent, that will keep it so in your awareness of it.[6]

"So to do nothing is to 'rest.' There is a 'place of rest within you.' In this place of rest the Holy Spirit resides. You have to let go of body awareness to find this place of rest. This place of rest is called here the 'quiet center, in which you do nothing.' I draw two conclusions from this passage. The first conclusion is that this 'quiet center' is another way of describing the holy meeting place, which we have already talked about. It is the inner altar and inner Holy of Holies. This passage says this is the 'center from which the body is absent.' This center is the seventh chakra. I have associated the seventh center with the focusing area of the crown of the head, but some Eastern philosophies say this transcendental center is actually located not in the head, but outside the body just above the top of head. If this is true, the focusing area of the top of the head is the doorway to this center, which requires a letting go of body awareness to experience it. The passage says that although this center is beyond body awareness, the body itself can be directed through this center by following the guidance of the Holy Spirit residing in this center.

"The second conclusion I have reached about this passage is that this rest beyond body awareness is how I describe successful contemplation, in which the thoughts of the mind become silent. Contemplation is a way of being in a state of mind manifesting, 'I need do nothing.' The Course does not recommend spending years of long meditation for some future reward of salvation to overcome present unworthiness, when in fact you can have this direct experience of rest right *now*. I agree that this experience is available now for everyone. Joining in holy relationships is one means of finding inner peace now, but so is contemplation. I recommend the first five steps of meditation as a preparation for the sixth step of contemplation because it is hard to immediately do nothing when our whole lives have been spent in incessant doing, doing, doing."

Allan said, "I gather what you are saying is that contemplation is the art of doing nothing."

"Yes, although I prefer to think of it as the art of resting in the divine presence," I said. "In addition to the analogy of a mirror showing the reflection of God, Eastern philosophy has another very similar analogy. It is the analogy of a clear and calm lake at night that is so still it perfectly reflects the image of a full moon. The crystal clear lake without a ripple symbolizes the mind without thoughts and thus represents the letting go of thoughts that happens in contemplation. If a body goes into a lake, what happens? The body stirs up the lake bottom so it becomes muddy, losing its clarity. Also the body puts ripples in the lake so it cannot reflect the image of the full moon. If the body is removed from the lake, what happens? The lake naturally becomes clear again as the mud settles to the bottom and the ripples disappear. Nothing has to be done to make the lake become clear and calm, other than to remove the body. In the same way, the mind becomes clear in contemplation by simply letting go of body awareness and letting go of thoughts that would otherwise stir up the lake of the mind. So you see, having a calm mind and finding the inner place of rest in contemplation is a matter of doing nothing with the body or mind."

Allan commented, "I like that quote you read about the inner place of rest being the 'quiet center of the storm,' where you can return even when you are in midst of outer activities. It's like the eye of a hurricane, where you can find peace as an aftereffect of meditation. It reminds me of Brother Lawrence, who held onto the presence of God even in the midst of all his outer activities. To him there was no difference in his awareness of the divine presence, whether he was in silent prayer and meditation or doing his work duties in the kitchen."

I responded, "Brother Lawrence is a good example of the kind of person who wouldn't need to use something like the methods of meditation that I recommend. Certainly meditation and contemplation aren't the only way to climb up Jacob's ladder and find rest at the rooftop of your awareness, where you can do nothing. My recommended combination of techniques may be too structured for you or other seekers. You need to find a way of calming your mind and finding rest that works for you."

Allan said, "I would really like to meditate better so I can find the inner resting place. You talked about doing nothing with my body and mind. I don't have a problem with doing nothing with my body, but I do have a problem doing nothing with my mind. I don't know how to make my mind like a calm lake with no ripples. How do I make my mind so still that it is doing nothing?" Allan asked.

"OK, the Course says specifically 'to sink into your mind'[7] past your superficial thoughts to find the place of peace within. I'll read you a passage from Workbook Lesson 41, which is the first introduction to contemplation. This same basic idea is repeated in different ways in other lessons:

At the beginning of the practice period, repeat today's idea very slowly. Then make no effort to think of anything. Try, instead, to get a sense of turning inward, past all the idle thoughts of the world. Try to enter very deeply into your own mind, keeping it clear of any thoughts that might divert your attention.[8]

"You start by mentally repeating an affirmation. The next step is to let go of repeating the affirmation, but return to repeating the affirmation if the mind becomes distracted. Then you sink below the surface thoughts of the mind and into the deeper part of the mind. The basic idea is to allow yourself to be drawn to that deepest part of the mind. That deepest part of the mind is described differently in each Workbook lesson. Some examples of the goal you are reaching toward are 'the light,'[9] 'deep peace,'[10] 'reality,'[11] 'the Kingdom of Heaven,'[12] 'the holy place,'[13] and 'God.'[14] Although all these words describe the same goal of the "resting place"[15] of the mind, it helps to choose one of these descriptions to enable you to zero in on your spiritual destination for your attunement. It is essential to set your goal and allow your mind to be naturally attracted to it by your wanting of it. You don't have to necessarily repeat the words describing your goal, unless you are distracted. The Course is encouraging you to let go of all words, even the words describing your goal. Then you can experience the reality of your goal directly, beyond words. Through slipping past distracting thoughts, your mind will be drawn to its natural resting place. You can observe passing thoughts, but then you let yourself gently move past them to the deepest part of your mind that is your goal, referred to as 'the eternal calm of the Son of God.'[16] This whole process of finding the resting place of the mind is contemplation, and no different than the sixth technique of my combination of methods."

I have already written, but not yet published, a meditation book called *Meditation Inspired by Christ and Yoga*. It's an expanded version of my first book *His World: A Christian Meditation Manual*. My new book explains in detail how to practice the six techniques of Christian Yoga Meditation, which lead to the experience of contemplation.

Allan said, "When I try to become quiet within, my mind jumps all over the place. Meditation for me is like trying to tame a wild horse."

"We have a meditation period every time we get together, but we can skip that if you don't find it helpful. There are a lot of other ways of contacting Spirit besides sitting in silent meditation," I said.

"I do have a problem calming my mind, but I still think the attempt is helpful. Actually I do better with it when you and I meditate together, so I would like to continue to do that. Since our minds are joined, maybe your peaceful mind is helping me calm my mind. But really my best way of contacting Spirit is to simply affirm my worthiness as the holy Son of God. I try to do this all the time by following Brother Lawrence's advice in his book, *Practicing the Presence of God*."

I offered, "The best spiritual practice is the one you *use*. So if practicing the presence of God works, that's terrific. Since we will be having a meditation shortly, there is one more very important thing I want to say about that, but it also applies to your practice of the presence of God. The Course does give some examples of different specific techniques, but what techniques you choose to use are not the most significant aspect of the attempt to contact Spirit. The primary emphasis in the Course is on the importance of the mental attitude you hold in approaching your spiritual ideal. For example, here I'll read from Workbook Lesson 44, which says:

Then try to sink into your mind, letting go every kind of interference and intrusion by quietly sinking past them. Your mind cannot be stopped in this unless you choose to stop it. It is merely taking its natural course. Try to observe your passing thoughts without involvement, and slip quietly by them.

While no particular approach is advocated for this form of exercise, what is needful is a sense of the importance of what you are doing; its inestimable value to you, and an awareness that you are attempting something very holy.[17]

Then in Workbook Lesson 45 it says:

For this kind of practice only one thing is necessary; approach it as you would an altar dedicated in Heaven to God the Father and to God the Son. For such is the place you are trying to reach. You will probably be unable as yet to realize how high you are trying to go. Yet even with the little understanding you have already gained, you should be able to remind yourself that this is no idle game, but an exercise in holiness and an attempt to reach the Kingdom of Heaven.[18]

"I mention this idea because I want to reinforce something you are already doing, since you are so focused on your single-minded intention of affirming your nature as the holy Son of God. Silently meditating inwardly on your intention is nice if you want to do that sometimes, but from what I can see you are carrying that awareness with you in your daily life experiences and that is wonderful. So I can see how you are following the example of Brother Lawrence in his daily practice of the presence of God. Also I know you do the Course Workbook lessons daily, and that is a very good spiritual practice because many of those lessons focus on forgiveness as a means of transforming the mind."

"How do you feel forgiveness fits in with calming the mind and finding that resting place you described?" Allan asked.

"I should say more about forgiveness, because it is vitally important to calming the mind. Even before accepting the Course principles, I learned from practical experience that whenever I was holding onto any feelings of unforgiveness, I had trouble meditating and contemplating, so I could not access the inner resting place. I felt this was what Jesus was describing when he said to not bring your gift to God's altar when you are holding hard feelings against anyone. He said to first go to be reconciled with your brother and only then come to that altar and offer your gift."

Allan said, "That makes sense. I think of that resting place you are talking about as also being our 'final resting place' of heaven, where God, Christ, and the Holy Spirit are. To get to that final resting place, the Course says we need forgiveness more than anything else. How about if I read to you a part of the Course I really like that describes this?"

"Sure, I've done a lot of reading, so I'd like to hear you read," I said.

"Find the section called 'The Lifting of the Veil,'" Allan directed me. I placed the book open to that section on his table by his bed. He used his wooden pointer stick to turn one page and then read three paragraphs:

> Free your brother here, as I freed you. Give him the selfsame gift, nor look upon him with condemnation of any kind. See him as guiltless as I look on you, and overlook the sins he thinks he sees within himself. Offer your brother freedom and complete release from sin, here in the garden of seeming agony and death. So will we prepare together the way unto the resurrection of God's Son, and let him rise again to glad remembrance of his Father, Who knows no sin, no death, but only life eternal.
>
> Together we will disappear into the Presence beyond the veil, not to be lost but found; not to be seen but known. And knowing, nothing in the plan God has established for salvation will be left undone. This is the journey's purpose, without which is the journey meaningless. Here is the peace of God, given to you eternally by Him. Here is the rest and quiet that you seek, the reason for the journey from its beginning. Heaven is the gift you owe your brother, the debt of gratitude you offer to the Son of God in thanks for what he is, and what his Father created him to be.
>
> Think carefully how you would look upon the giver of this gift, for as you look on him so will the gift itself appear to be. As he is seen as either the giver of guilt or of salvation, so will his offering be seen and so received. The crucified give pain because they are in pain. But the redeemed give joy because they have been healed of pain. Everyone gives as he receives, but he must choose what it will *be* that he receives. And he will recognize his choice by what he gives, and what is given him.[19]

"I notice there is even a line in here that says, 'Here is the rest and quiet you seek...,' which reminds me of the resting place you talked about. So what do you think about forgiveness as the means to find this resting place?" Allan asked.

"Well, Allan, you are my brother and you stand beside me at the door to this final resting place of heaven. I see you as the guiltless Son of God, and I give you the gift of salvation, knowing that as I have given I will receive," I said.

Allan smiled and said, "Well, Don, you are my brother and you stand beside me at the door to this final resting place of heaven. I see you as the guiltless Son of God, and I give you the gift of salvation, knowing that as I have given I will receive."

"So be it."

"So be it."

"That was fun. Something we can do, if you want to, is if you or I come across a Course passage we find particularly inspirational, we can share it when we get together."

"I like that idea, so let's do it next time," Allan agreed.

From studying the Course at that time, I felt I understood the meaning of forgiveness. Because Allan and I had become friends, it was easy for me to remove the perception that we were separate from each other. The door to salvation is always open, but I could perceive the door to be barred and through that perception make it so for me. Since everyone is my brother, I could not bar the door to salvation to anyone without imagining the door is barred to me. Although I could parrot this concept, my awareness of it was clouded over, probably because I wanted it to be. I was simply not ready to see guiltlessness in everyone and offer salvation to everyone, so I did not really know the meaning of forgiveness. We normally think understanding must come first and then the application of forgiveness would naturally follow. But the Course reverses this assumption by stating, "And it is recognized that all things must be first forgiven, and *then* understood."[20]

1. T-14.VIII.2:10-16, 3:1, pp. 289-290 (p. 269).
2. T-14.IX.3:2-9, 4:1, p. 291 (p. 271).
3. T-14.IX.5:1-7, 6:1-5, p. 292 (p. 271).
4. T-14.IX.7:1, p. 292 (p. 271).
5. Revelation 8:1, RSV.
6. T-18.VII.7:7-9, 8:1-5, p. 390 (pp. 363-364).
7. W-pI.44.7:2, p. 72 (p. 70).
8. W-pI.41.6:3-6, p. 63 (p. 63).
9. W-pI.44.10:1-2, p. 70 (p. 70).
10. W-pI.47.7:2, p. 76 (p. 76).
11. W-pI.41.7:4, p. 64 (p. 64).
12. W-pI.47.7:3, p. 76 (p. 76).
13. W-pI.131.11:7, p. 241 (p. 234).
14. W-pI.49.4:8, p. 78 (p. 78).
15. W-50.pI.5:5, p. 79 (p. 79).
16. W-50.pI.3:3, p. 79, (p. 79).
17. W-pI.44.7:2-5, 8:1, p. 70 (p. 70).
18. W-pI.45.8:4-7, p. 72 (p. 72).
19. T-19.IV.D.i.18:1-5, 19:1-6, 20:1-6, p. 424 (p. 395).
20. T-30.V.1:6, p. 635 (p. 591).

64

RESTING PLACE

~ o ~

I began, "When we last met, we talked about sharing inspirational passages, so I have one I want to share. Remember we talked about the 'resting place,' which I feel is located in the seventh chakra. I found another Course passage that uses the same words 'resting place.' I'll be reading from the section called 'The Changeless Dwelling Place':

> There is a place in you where this whole world has been forgotten; where no memory of sin and of illusion lingers still. There is a place in you which time has left, and echoes of eternity are heard. There is a resting place so still no sound except a hymn to Heaven rises up to gladden God the Father and the Son. Where Both abide are They remembered, Both. And where They are is Heaven and is peace.
>
> Think not that you can change Their dwelling place. For your Identity abides in Them, and where They are, forever must you be. The changelessness of Heaven is in you, so deep within that nothing in this world but passes by, unnoticed and unseen. The still infinity of endless peace surrounds you gently in its soft embrace, so strong and quiet, tranquil in the might of its Creator, nothing can intrude upon the sacred Son of God within.
>
> Here is the role the Holy Spirit gives to you who wait upon the Son of God, and would behold him waken and be glad. He is a part of you and you of him, because he is his Father's Son, and not for any purpose you may see in him. Nothing is asked of you but to accept the changeless and eternal that abide in him, for your Identity is there. The peace in you can but be found in him. And every thought of love you offer him but brings you nearer to your wakening to peace eternal and to endless joy.[1]

Allan commented, "I enjoyed that last sentence that 'every thought of love you offer' to your brother brings you closer to 'awakening to peace eternal and to endless joy.'"

"I like that too, because it shows that loving relationships can be the way to find the resting place within. I also like that it is saying this resting place is actually heaven, where God and the Son of God are located, just like you had pointed out when we last met. So we are carrying around heaven inside our consciousness even now, and our job assigned by the Holy Spirit is to wake up to that awareness. Did you come up with an inspirational passage you would like to share?" I asked.

"Yes, I have three paragraphs I want to read. Here's the first paragraph:

You are the means for God; not separate, nor with a life apart from His. His Life is manifest in you who are His Son. Each aspect of Himself is framed in holiness and perfect purity, in love celestial and so complete it wishes only that it may release all that it looks upon unto itself. Its radiance shines through each body that it looks upon, and brushes all its darkness into light merely by looking past it *to* the light. The veil is lifted through its gentleness, and nothing hides the face of Christ from its beholders. You and your brother stand before Him now, to let Him draw aside the veil that seems to keep you separate and apart.[2]

"Isn't that beautiful how it describes each of us being aspects of God's Son?" Allan asked.

"Yes, and I like the way it talks about brushing aside darkness to look 'past it *to* the light' in each other." Allan was always coming up with new ways of reminding himself of his true Self, where he had placed his treasure. Whenever I would do most of the talking, my perception of Allan was limited. But at times like this, when I could just listen, I would see white light surrounding Allan. And sometimes, like on this occasion, I could see the light filling him, reflecting the Son of God in him, as the passage he read described.

"This section I am reading from is called 'The Link to Truth.' The next two paragraphs describe how the Holy Spirit is the link to truth and keeps us connected to God and Christ. Here is what it says:

Since you believe that you are separate, Heaven presents itself to you as separate, too. Not that it is in truth, but that the link that has been given you to join the truth may reach to you through what you understand. Father and Son and Holy Spirit are as One, as all your brothers join as one in truth. Christ and His Father never have been separate, and Christ abides within your understanding, in the part of you that shares His Father's Will. The Holy Spirit links the other part—the tiny, mad desire to be separate, different and special—to the Christ, to make the oneness clear to what is really one. In this world this is not understood, but can be taught.

The Holy Spirit serves Christ's purpose in your mind, so that the aim of specialness can be corrected where the error lies. Because His purpose still is one with both the Father and the Son, He knows the Will of God and what you really will. But this is understood by mind perceived as one, aware that it is one, and so experienced. It is the Holy Spirit's function to teach you how this oneness is experienced, what you must do that it can be experienced, and where you should go to do it.[3]

I said, "That last sentence is reassuring. We can rely on the Holy Spirit to constantly come to our rescue by teaching us oneness when our egos can see only separation."

Allan offered, "This passage doesn't use the words 'resting place,' but it is describing that same place, because it talks about the place in our minds where the Father, Son, and Holy Spirit are joined in oneness. It's also the part of our minds where we share God's Will. It's hard for us to understand that God's Will is our own true will. But it is the job of the Holy Spirit to remind us that we really do only want God's Will, and nothing else will satisfy us. It is God's Will for us to experience the oneness that is already within our minds, but from which we think we are separate."

"That's really a nice passage. The Course has a way of saying a great deal in just a few paragraphs. I have a question I want to ask you. In the past I have monopolized most of our conversations, and you have been a gracious listener, but now it's your turn. I'll go into 'listening mode,' and you can go into 'monologue mode.' What would you like to tell me about your past?" I asked.

"It's not there anymore!" Allan said with obvious glee.

"My past isn't there anymore either, but that doesn't stop me from talking about it," I said.

Allan explained, "I told you previously that I wanted to perform the service of being a good listener for you and welcomed your marathon monologues. I still feel that way. But what I haven't told you is that actually sometimes it's an effort for me to talk for extended periods of time, so it's a blessing for me to listen rather than talk. However, I can tell you a very condensed story. I had a normal childhood in Brooklyn until age 12. At that age I was playing baseball and was hit in the back with a baseball. I was hit so hard I was knocked unconscious. After that I wasn't quite right physically and sometimes I had problems with my balance. When I was 21, I was in my sister Linda's house and I was at the top of the stairs when I lost my balance and started to fall. The strangest part of this is that for an instant I felt like I was allowing myself to fall, although I don't know why. Anyway, I fell backwards and that is when I really messed up my health. After that my health steadily declined over the years." Allan paused to rest.

I was shocked by Allan's description of falling down the stairs marking the turning point of his physical decline. What surprised me in particular was when he said, "...for an instant I felt like I was allowing myself to fall..." The Course teaches that we assign guilt to ourselves because of past negative deeds. Subconsciously motivated by this stored guilt, we attract to ourselves various forms of sickness, injury, and mishaps as self-inflicted punishment for our past transgressions. Immediately I wondered if Allan had assigned this fall as his punishment for bringing about the fall of the Pole Man, who finally let go of the pole and had his body destroyed by falling and rolling down a rock cliff. However, I did not share this, not wanting to draw attention to the obvious parallel between Allan's fall and my past life fall as the Pole Man, because I felt the issue of our past adversarial relationship had long since been fully resolved. There was no need to bring up the issue again in light of the Christ I now saw sitting before me in the form of Allan. Just like when I listened to Robert and saw the glow of light in and around him, so too I saw the light in Allan.

Allan continued, "I went to City College and majored in psychology. After graduating with a master's degree, I was able to work with kids in school as a counselor. By the time I met you I could walk with a cane, but with surgery after surgery, here I am in my present condition. As you know, the Catholics believe in the Assumption—Mary's body being taken up into heaven. I am being taken up bodily too—only I am making the transition *one piece at a time.*" Allan said this with a broad, mischievous smile. "Only one of my surgeries was botched. It was my first surgery to amputate my hand. I almost sued them, but instead ended up saying, 'Look, I gave you a hand, can't you give me a hand?' But I decided to let go of my discontent, just like everything else. At times I've been tempted to think my life has been ruined, but fortunately those are not my sentiments now. Because Flora lost her lover, Darren, she told me the other day, 'My life is ruined.' What do you think I told her?" Allan asked.

"I couldn't begin to guess," I said.

"I told her, 'It's good your life is ruined!' and she said to me, 'You are the only person I know who could say that to me.' Of course, she knew that having her life in this world be ruined could motivate her to see that this life is an illusion and heaven is her real home and Darren's real home. I guess I have been hard on her, just because I have been telling her the truth. I would say to her, 'You have to decide if Darren is dead or not. If you believe he is dead, there is nothing to do. If you believe that losing the body

is not the end of life and therefore he is alive, what are you fretting about?'
But she would tell me, 'I'm not ready to hear the truth.'

"The other day a couple of buttons fell off her shirt, and I told her, 'I
guess I've been pressing your buttons so hard they are falling off.' She
thought that was funny, but then we got into an argument that was mostly
my fault. Flora sometimes tells me I talk like a 'king barking orders to his
slaves,' so maybe I came off a bit too authoritarian. She and I set up a
schedule for us to get together and she wanted to change it. I gave her a
hard time about making changes. The next day I could see my ego had
gotten the best of me, so I told her, 'All I know is that wasn't me.' She knew
that was my way of saying I am the Son of God, not the ego mask. I
showed Flora a chocolate heart with raspberry filling and asked her to
break it in half. We each had half to finalize the resolution of our temporary
ego altercation. So now whenever I am confronted with a potentially
distressing situation, I ask myself in the very beginning, 'Is it ego or
eternity?' I have been choosing 'eternity' and have been finding peace
that way."

Allan concluded, "I don't seem to be able to talk much more. I have
been having trouble breathing lately."

Allan had been having blood circulation problems. Fortunately he was
sitting on a technologically advanced bed designed to reduce the likelihood
of the dreaded bed sores that are caused by remaining in bed continuously.
These bed sores can become infected, causing serious complications, and
in rare cases can lead to death. To prevent bed sores there was a powerful
air blower that constantly sent air into and out of his bed, making it a
sophisticated air mattress. This high-tech bed helped a great deal because
Allan was literally floating on air. However, he had for years had circulation
problems in his extremities, and in the first part of 1995 had surgery to
remove his left hand. In March he had another surgery to remove his gal
bladder, so he was in a weakened condition when I made this visit on April
22. We meditated together, and afterward I gave Allan a photograph of him
I had taken the week before because I did not have a picture of him. [This
is the photograph of Allan in Chapter 29.]

On the following Tuesday I got a call from Allan, asking me to come
over to his house. When I showed up, Allan said, "I called you...," and he
paused to take a breath before continuing, "because I am having trouble
breathing." After catching his breath he stated seriously, "I feel this could
be the last roundup for me." He paused again and asked, "Can we pray
together now?"

"Absolutely. We can meditate for as long as you want. When you feel we
are done, just make a sound to let me know," I said and we meditated.

The next day Allan was still having difficulty breathing. Consequently, he was taken to the Cottonwood hospital, but they were not sure what was causing the respiratory problems. On that Wednesday, I had to go to court to testify on behalf of Dominic Rodriguez, the client mentioned previously in Chapter 51. I had already ensured that he would not loose his eligibility for state services, but at this time he still had an eight-year jail sentence hanging over his head. He would definitely go to jail for his assault charge unless I could manage to secure a twenty-four-hour supervised placement for him. I told Judge Anders that I requested a residential placement, but I was not sure if it would be approved. Judge Anders reluctantly granted another continuance in a long line of such delays. Right after this, I made my way to the Cottonwood hospital to visit Allan, who said, "I am ready to go Home, but I just don't want to slowly suffocate."

When I first came into Allan's room there was a man dressed in green hospital clothes, and he was asking Allan, "Can I get anything for you? Do you need anything special to eat?"

"Thanks for asking," Allan said, "I don't really need anything." The man excused himself and left.

The man was so accommodating and friendly that I said, "It looks like you have made friends with the orderlies."

Allan smiled, "That's my doctor! He's the one who did my surgeries. As you can see, he is very kind. But they still don't know what's causing my breathing problems."

On Thursday I learned that Dominic's residential placement had finally been approved after nine months of advocating and job-related political maneuvering. It was a day of celebrating the fact that my client would finally be released from jail and would go into his new placement in Phoenix. When I went to visit Allan in the hospital this same day, he told me, "I am going to the Phoenix hospital." It was easy to see the connection between both my client and Allan going to Phoenix to be in a better place. "I am leaving in just a short while." Allan paused and said, "The hospital in Phoenix has more experienced doctors." Pausing again he added, "I hope they can figure out what is going on."

"Do you want me to go with you?" I asked.

"My sister Linda is visiting, and she's going with me...." Allan stopped to take a breath and then concluded, "I'll be OK."

On Friday when I came to work, I found out that Bruno, the dog owned by my married coworkers, Tina and Dawson, had died the night before. This was a great loss for my coworkers, who thought of Bruno as a family member, and so they did not come to work. In the afternoon, I went to their house to offer my condolences. Also on Friday, I visited my client Dominic's family and discussed his new placement in Phoenix. In addition, I called

Allan in Phoenix. He told me he was glad that he came to the Phoenix hospital for a more thorough diagnosis.

Although Allan wasn't available for our usual Saturday get-together, I prayed and meditated at our regular 1 PM meeting time. At 8 PM I watched a movie called *Escape to Witch Mountain*. It was a about people who came from the "light" to earth and then joined in pairs with others in order to leave this world and escape back to the light. They viewed the world as a jail and wanted to be released to freedom. In the end, many people joined and went back into the light. There was also a transition figure that helped others to make the transition.

Immediately after this movie there was an episode of the TV series *Sisters*, in which all of the sisters and their families went on a 3,000-mile trip to a resort called "Villa Esperanza." The meaning of "esperanza" is hope, so I felt the sisters were going to the place of hope, just like the people in the movie who were going to their place of hope in the light, symbolic of transitioning to heaven. Similar to the movie, the people in the TV show joined in pairs after first having disagreements that they overcame through forgiveness. Also like the movie, there was a transition figure, in this case a female ghost, who could not move to the higher world until she had helped these people to overcome their differences and join with each other. This pairing up reminded me of the importance of holy relationships described in the Course.

I was struck by the word "esperanza" because in two days I planned to go to Phoenix to see Maria Esperanza. She is acknowledged as a living saint and healer in her native country of Brazil and by many believers around the world. I was looking forward to seeing my best friend, Rose, who was flying in from Virginia Beach to visit on Monday so we could both see Maria Esperanza at the Gammage Auditorium in Phoenix. I knew Allan had been instrumental in convincing Rose to come to Sedona because of their friendship, but Allan had not told me he gave Rose a substantial amount of money to finance the flight.

After watching these shows, I wrote down the parallels I had observed between the two shows. This is something I had learned from Robert, who found that these kinds of outer events that seem coincidental may actually be foreshadowing future events. The shows were over at 10 PM. Shortly thereafter, Wendy knocked on my door and told me that Allan had passed away in the hospital in Phoenix. Our household gathered together for a time of prayer offered to Allan's transition to his new Home. Only then did I realize how the earlier movie and TV show were foreshadowing Allan's transition. Allan was in the prison of his limited body, and, like the movie characters, he was escaping into the light. Like the TV characters, Allan was making his trip to a place of peace that was his *esperanza*—his hope. Allan had found his unique way to climb Jacob's ladder and enter the resting place by finally awakening to his true nature—the holy Son of God that he steadfastly affirmed in spite of his outward appearance. Yet just as the movie and TV show implied, no one enters the final resting place of heaven alone. Consequently Allan's openness to forgiveness and holy relationships with others was his means of opening to the divine Light.

At times in the past, Allan had felt isolated from others. So when he came to Sedona, he let it be known that the door to his home was open to all. Robert recorded in the Circle of Atonement newsletter the wide variety of activities that Allan graciously welcomed to his home:

> Since his arrival the house has been used for our regular classes and our support meetings, for Course-based counseling, meditation meetings, a potluck for local Course students and a personal retreat. Also, many visitors to the Circle have stayed with Allan, for anywhere from a few days to two months.[4]

Allan relished the whirlwind of activity around him and was delighted to perform the service of making his home into an outer holy meeting place and a symbolic reminder of the inner holy meeting place open to all. The key to Allan's personal awakening and final entrance into the inner meeting place of heaven was not only in seeing himself as the guiltless Son of God, but in his seeing of everyone he met as likewise the holy Son of God. Having in this way given salvation to each brother and sister who entered his home, Allan received salvation as he had given it. Thus each brother became for him his savior, giving him the key to the changeless dwelling place. Since Allan kept the door to his home—and, likewise, the door to his consciousness—wide open, it was only fitting that he would walk through the open door of heaven and into the Light.

---

1. T-29.V.1:1-5, 2:1-4, 3:1-5, p. 614 (p. 570).
2. T-25.I.4:1-6, p. 519 (p. 483).
3. T-25.I.5:1-6, 6:1-4, pp. 519-520 (pp. 483-484).
4. Robert Perry, "Allan Greene and the house next door," *A Better Way*, Vol. 4, No. 3, September 1994, p. 3.

65

MEMORIES OF ALLAN

~ ● ~

It was obvious that Allan had come to Sedona for his transition. Many people played a part in this transition, but I was mostly aware of just my part in what was clearly a divine Plan. At least consciously, Allan had come to Sedona to be closer to Robert and his knowledgeable interpretation and teaching of the Course. Robert provided his own viewpoint on Allan's transition and his impact on the lives of others by putting his thoughts into the following memorial writing, titled "In Memory of Allan Greene":

Over the year that Allan was living here in Sedona I experienced several "signs" about his eventual death. Most of us have had some experience with meaningful coincidences. One of my personal preoccupations had been reading these events, interpreting them as one would the symbols in a dream, and then using the interpretation as higher guidance which helps me make decisions and look at situations from a truer perspective. When accurately interpreted, I find that these meaningful coincidences or signs communicate a wisdom that definitely exceeds our own.

The first such sign about Alan occurred the morning he arrived. It was Easter morning, April 3, 1994. We had expected him to be here a few days later, but his trip across the country with Debra, his niece, and John, a friend who was also an EMT, went more quickly than expected. Allan seemed to place great significance on the fact that he entered the canyon in which Sedona lies on Easter sunrise. Several times he told the story of how he had almost landed in the hospital in Albuquerque the night before, but had decided, after a brief, "inhospitable" stop there, to drive all night through to Sedona.

The fact that he arrived not only on Easter, but at sunrise, struck me also as possibly meaningful. I then realized a definite coincidence in the events of that morning. The moment that Allan's van had pulled up, my children were being "babysat" by the video, *E.T.* As many people have noted, *E.T.* is a science fiction Christ story. It seemed to me more than chance that Allan had arrived at Easter sunrise and during the watching of a sci-fi Christ story.

So I looked at the parallels between the Easter story and *E.T.* There were three obvious ones:

1. Both stories were about a being from above, from the heavens.
2. In both, this being came to this world for a time, but simply did not belong here. He was not at home here. He was out of his natural environment.
3. In both, this being eventually got to leave this world and go back home to where he belonged. This was not a sad thing but a cause for celebration.

The symbology was not hard to figure out. Allan was clearly the being from above, as evidenced in his long-term, consuming dedication to the life of the spirit. And he just as clearly was out of place here (I thought of E.T., with his obvious physical differences from normal humans and of the scene in which he is surrounded by doctors and hooked up to machines). Life in this world was just too confining for him. Thus, he was only here for a season. He was a blessing to us while he was here. But eventually he would have to leave this prison and return home. And this would be a wonderful thing, a cause for celebration.

I also saw this as a sign about Allan's time here in Sedona. Since he arrived here on Easter morning that meant to me that it would probably be here that he would experience *his* Easter morning. I assumed that it would be from Sedona that he would leave this world and go home.

Many months passed and his health seemed to become stronger and more stable. Then in October I was in St. Louis and went to see the movie, *The Shawshank Redemption*, with some friends out there. As the movie ended, the first words to appear on the screen— while the final scene was still playing and before the final credits started rolling—were these:

IN MEMORY OF ALLEN GREENE

I was taken totally off guard and had a very emotional reaction. It took me some time to recover. As with his arrival on Easter morning, I wondered if this uncanny coincidence was a sign. Not only was the name only one letter shy of being a perfect match for Allan's, but, like the earlier sign, it seemed to refer to his death. I then thought about the plot of the movie and realized that it too fit the earlier sign completely.

The movie was about a man who was sent to prison for life. He truly did not belong there. He not only did not commit the crime of which he was accused, but he was on a different level from the rest of the prisoners. You could say that he was from a higher plane. This resulted in the paradoxical situation of him feeling drastically out of place and of him being a true upliftment to the entire prison. Eventually, however, he escaped. He got to be free from prison. It was this freedom that was pictured in that last scene over which were superimposed the words: "IN MEMORY OF ALLEN GREENE."

I mentioned these occurrences to Allan along the way. His usual response was just to chuckle and crack a joke. Having his death predicted was quite commonplace for him.

Then *The Shawshank Redemption* came back into my life one day late in March. I had just returned from California and went over to spend some time with Allan. He was going into the hospital in Cottonwood to have his gall bladder removed (he had just had his left hand removed while I was away). My wife was planning on seeing *The Shawshank Redemption* at the local theater, and, since she couldn't find anyone to go with, and since I hadn't seen her for days, I decided to go along. As I was about to leave Allan to rush off and see the movie, I realized that this was the last time I would see him before he went into the hospital and I was going off to a movie which I felt predicted his death. This seemed like an ominous sign. I wondered if he might not survive this hospital stay and so I told him this. He joked that I might want to kiss his feet before leaving.

I felt intuitively that he would not die on this trip to the hospital, and, of course, he didn't. But I still felt this event meant something, especially since he arrived back from the hospital on April 3— one year to the day from his Easter morning arrival of last year. I concluded—and voiced to others—that this sign was probably a foreshadowing of a time when he would leave for the hospital and would not come back.

That time, it turned out, was his very next trip. I had a sinking feeling when he called me last Wednesday to help him get into his van so that he could go to the hospital. The combination of him knowing that he was "a very sick puppy" and his lack of any clear idea of what it could be was disturbing. This sinking feeling increased when he had to move from Cottonwood hospital to a superior facility in Phoenix. I thought it quite possible (though frankly not probable) that he would not be coming back. However, my concerns were largely allayed when he told me over the phone not to arrange a trip down to the hospital yet, as he might be back here by Saturday night. Thus, it was a shock when I got home Saturday night and heard the news. It seemed like it just came too soon.

Yet I am absolutely sure it was in perfect timing. Not only had Debra just been out here for a visit a week before, but his old friend, Martin, had at that same time just come back to the house. And sure enough, the very night of his death another in this string of signs occurred.

I was out that night, but for some odd reason Wendy, Don, and our two children were watching the old Disney movie called *Escape to Witch Mountain*. As it turned out, this movie was an uncanny repeat of the exact same themes from the earlier signs. It was about children who came to the earth from the light, from another dimension. They did not really belong here; this was not their home. Additionally, the two protagonist children were actually being imprisoned by a man who wanted to exploit their otherworldly gifts. They finally escaped, however, and made it to a place where people of their kind were able to leave this world and return to the light from which they came. And this, of course, is what they did.

I also felt it was significant that over the days of Allan's final hospitalization, Don, our housemate and an old friend of Allan's, finished a nine month long process of advocating for a handicapped client of his. The result was that this client was released from a prison sentence and able to instead go into a home designed for his rehabilitation.

These coincidences gave me not only a framework for looking at Allan's death, but also at his life and at what he came to Sedona to accomplish. Quite simply, they depict him as a heavenly being. And that, it seems to me, is the very idea that he was trying to learn. He had been trying to learn that idea for years, and it seemed to me that hearing me teach it was part of what drew him out here to Sedona. Much of Allan's spiritual progress consisted of frequent and pivotal realizations that he had. When one of these realizations came to him he would reflect on it, share it with others, and use it as a powerful tool in healing his daily upsets. Almost every realization he shared with me was a different slant on the fact that he was not this body, not this personality, that he was a transcendental being who was merely dreaming that he was human. His favorite section from *A Course in Miracles* is entitled, "I Need Do Nothing." What he got from this section is the understanding that holiness didn't need to be earned by anything he did (which, of course, was a great relief for a quadriplegic). It merely needed to be uncovered as one's natural state—part of one's true identity as a spiritual being. As he liked to put it, he was not a human being having a spiritual experience, but *a spiritual being having a human experience.* Over and over, this was the content of the realizations that lifted him above his frustrating outer affairs, his interpersonal conflicts, the pettiness of his own ego, and the pains and limitations of his imprisoning body.

As his time here neared its end, he seemed to get more and more focused on this single fact—his true identity as a spiritual being. A couple months ago he came by a small Eastern scripture that developed this idea in great detail. It had a profound effect on Allan, drawing together and strengthening what he had already come to. By the time I had my last conversation with him, he remarked to me that he felt resolved about his time here—if indeed it was time to go—because he had gained such strong conviction about his heavenly nature.

Of course, these signs have also given me a very positive perspective for viewing Allan's death, in bright contrast to the natural pull of my emotions. We may weep when a man like Jesus has to leave us and return to his Father. We may cry when E.T. takes off in his spaceship. But we have no illusions about whom we are crying for. It is not for them, for we know that they are being freed from prison. We know that they are going home. All of this—our feelings and his departure—seemed to me to be perfectly captured in some lines from *The Shawshank Redemption*:

> Those of us who knew him best talk about him often. I swear, the stuff he pulled. Sometimes it makes me sad, though, Andy being gone. I have to remind myself that some birds aren't meant to be caged. Their feathers are just too bright. And when they fly away, the part of you that knows it was a sin to lock them up does rejoice. But still, the place you live in is that much more drab and empty that they are gone. I guess I just miss my friend.

One important aspect not mentioned by Robert above is that the movie *The Shawshank Redemption* actually focused on not only the main character, Andy, but also his close friend, Red. Andy was the first to find redemption, meaning escape from prison. However, then Red was also freed and they were reunited joyously in the end. This pairing to eventually find peace and joy after enduring much struggle was the repeated theme found in *Escape to Witch Mountain* and *Villa Esperanza*. This illustrates the importance of two people joining for a common purpose in a holy relationship as a means of spiritual fulfillment.

I would like to think that my holy relationship with Allan assisted him in his transition, as indeed I know his impact on my life will help me make that same transition someday. Of course, there were many other significant holy relationships that Allan had, such as with Robert and with Rose. The following is Rose's description of some of her memories of Allan at the time of his transition:

> In the many years that I knew Allan, going back to when we were baptized in the Jordan River together, he came close to death a number of times. He seemed quite accepting of this, and he even joked about it on occasion. One time I suggested that his death might be an opportunity to do a life-after-death experiment. I asked him to let me know if he was all right after he passes away. I also requested him to do it in a way that wouldn't "spook" me and he agreed.
>
> When I went to bed on Saturday, April 29, I had some difficulty sleeping, but didn't mind too much because I was in a wonderful uplifted state of eager anticipation. I was happily looking forward to my trip to Arizona on Monday that had been made possible by Allan's gift to pay for part of the plane ticket. As I lay awake in the hours of the night, I heard the words "Allan Greene is now Rabbi Greene," and these words were clearly repeated several times. I felt joyful, almost like laughing, and decided that when I first saw Allan a few days later, I would greet him as "Rabbi Greene" and we would have a good laugh together. I didn't find out that he had died until Don called me on Sunday to let me know. So the statement that I had heard on Saturday, the day he died, was Allan's way of letting me know that he was OK. His words were very characteristic of his sense of humor. True to our agreement, he did not "spook" me. The word "rabbi" is usually translated as "master" or "teacher." Allan was letting me know that he had graduated to another higher state of being, and a different role.

When Rose arrived in Phoenix from her airplane flight, I picked her up in my car. We made our way toward the Gammage Auditorium to rest before seeing Maria Esperanza later that evening. I told Rose about seeing *Escape to Witch Mountain* and *Villa Esperanza*, and the significance in relation to Allan's passing that night. Since the unusual word "esperanza" was in both *Villa Esperanza* and Maria Esperanza, we both wondered if something significant would happen when we saw Maria Esperanza. At the Gammage Auditorium we read the handouts we were given, which included a description of Maria Esperanza as follows:

Maria Esperanza de Bianchini was born in 1928 in Venezuela. A happily married mother of six daughters and a son, and wife of Geo Bianchini for thirty-eight years, Maria Esperanza has received personal apparitions since childhood from Our Lady and Saint Teresa. Since March 25, 1976, it is reported that Our Lady has been appearing to Maria as "Mary, Virgin and Mother of Reconciliation of all People," promulgating loyalty to God and His teachings of unconditional love, humility, repentance, and forgiveness.

Some of Maria Esperanza's extraordinary gifts include: reading souls, healing, levitation, bilocation, the stigmata on Good Friday, the fragrance of roses, the eruption of a rose bud from her chest on fourteen occasions, and the Host miraculously appearing on her tongue. She is considered one of the major mystics of the 20th century, being equated with Padre Pio, whose spiritual daughter she was.

Rose and I going to see Maria Esperanza meant seeing her from a distance—we were seated in a high balcony looking down on the stage in the large jam packed auditorium. I didn't have any memorable response to the events of the evening, but the following is Rose's description:

The program included some conventional Catholic events, which became tedious and boring as the evening wore on. This may have been partly because my inner clock was three hours ahead of Phoenix time due to my flight here from the East Coast.

Finally, after a few hours when it was fairly late, Maria Esperanza came out onto the front of the stage and began to speak. I could not understand her words, but when she spoke I had a profound experience of something piercing my heart. I remember that I nearly fell off of my seat as I put my hand over my heart. To this day, I don't know exactly what happened. Perhaps it was a blessing.

The next day, Tuesday, May 2, Rose and I attended Allan's funeral, which was delayed one day by Linda, Allan's sister, so Rose could attend. Rose and Linda had gone to Israel together on the trip Allan paid for in 1977. The funeral was at Allan's house, where everyone who knew Allan shared their stories, remembered his jokes, and sang his favorite song, "Amazing Grace." One of the handouts at the funeral was written by Allan himself. It was a sign that he prominently displayed wherever he lived to let visitors know what to expect.

NOTICE TO VISITORS

I have already repented, been saved and born again, had a bar mitzvah, been baptized in the Jordan River and in the Holy Spirit with fire, seen the Light and have washed in the waters of forgiveness.

I have also been prayed for sufficiently to believe that if God wasn't aware of my needs before, He certainly is now.

Therefore I would just like to quietly and peacefully watch television while waiting for the Second Coming.

Sincerely, Allan Israel Greene

When Allan passed away in April of 1995, I had just turned fifty that same month. Because Allan was so much a part of my life and part of revealing my shadow puzzle, it seems appropriate here to make a shift in the direction of this book. I have written a lot about my shadow puzzle, but what would a solution to this puzzle look like? When we complete a jigsaw puzzle, it means we have put all of the pieces together. But the fact is, I could not possibly uncover *all* the pieces of my subconscious mind and put them together to finally solve the shadow puzzle. However, let's consider this question: "What was my original goal in wanting to reveal the various puzzle pieces and put them together?" When I was in college at Central Connecticut and hung from the theater balcony, I was feeling the meaninglessness of my life, and so I wanted to find the meaning that was missing. Several years later, while standing on the top of Castle Craig, I had already returned to Christ at age twenty-four, but I still wanted to find a deeper understanding of the meaning of my life. By age fifty I had been able to reveal and put together enough of my shadow puzzle to find at least some of that deeper meaning, and since then I have continued to make progress. Now I would like to shift the emphasis of this autobiography away from describing the specific events of my life and toward sharing with you what I have discovered about the meaning of my life. The upcoming final five chapters address issues that are at the core of my spiritual life, since that is where I have found the most meaning in my life.

66

OPENING TO THE LIGHT

~ • ~

Not long after Allan's passing in April 1995, I formed a close friendship with a dedicated Course student named Jeannie Cashin. She invited me to her home in Prescott, where she introduced me to Bob Eddins, her partner at that time. While I was there, Bob told me his favorite story, "Plato's cave." Here's my memory of what he told me:

Plato's cave is an allegory of our experience of life on this planet. Plato gives Socrates the credit for describing a world in which people live in a cave. There is a shaft leading out of the cave to the daylight, but the people can't see it. They are chained permanently to the ground so they cannot turn around and see the way out. They can only look at a wall right in front of them. Behind them is a fire burning, which casts shadows on the wall in front of them. Between the fire and the chained prisoners is a path along which figures walk and run carrying all sorts of objects. Prisoners cannot turn around to see these figures, but they can see the shadows of them cast on the wall. The prisoners do not know these are only shadows, and so they think the illusory forms they see are real themselves. If they hear the figures behind them talking, the prisoners will think the forms made by the shadows are doing the talking. The objects being carried by the figures behind the prisoners would appear as only two-dimensional forms and so would not be perceived as three-dimensional objects that they really are. The shadow consciousness of the prisoners represents the consciousness of our egos, which can perceive only from a limited viewpoint that is really a misinterpretation of the truth.

According to Plato we are like these prisoners who can see only the shadows in front of them and not the light behind them that casts the shadows. The question this allegory raises is, "If one of the prisoners could turn his vision around, what would be the result?" He would see the bright glare of the fire, but at first the light would be so bright it would blind him. He would be confused. With his eyes hurting, he would turn away from the light. Since he is so familiar with the shadows, he would conclude that the shadows are clearer and make more sense to him than what he saw when he turned around.

However, let's imagine that someone could turn around and become gradually acclimated over time to seeing the light of the fire. Then the question would be, "What if this one prisoner could break his chains and make his way through the rugged passageway that leads from the darkness of the cave to the light of the sun?" Just as he was blinded by seeing the fire for the first time, he would be traumatized to suddenly see the sunlight after being in the dark cave for so long. In fact, he would be so blinded by the brilliance of the light that he would be unable to see anything at all. He would be even more confused than when he first saw the fire in the cave. But Plato believes this blindness to the light is only temporary, and he could eventually become accustomed to the brightness of the sunlight. The escaped prisoner would at first learn to come out of the cave only at night, when he could see the objects of the earth dimly illuminated by the lesser light of the moon, which is after all only a reflection of the light of the sun. Eventually he could walk around in the daylight and see everything clearly. He could even glance at the sun itself for an instant, instead of just seeing its light reflected off of the objects on the earth.

Now let's imagine that this brave prisoner leaves the sunlight and returns to the cave. The question is, "What would happen if the escaped prisoner told the cave dwellers that the forms seen on the wall are only unreal shadows and that there is a bright and beautiful light right outside their cave?" Well, those prisoners of darkness wouldn't have any way of comprehending what he would tell them. Actually, they would think the escaped prisoner is quite mad. They might simply make fun of his wild ideas. But if they are strongly attached to their own ideas of darkness, they could say, "He's a heretic disturbing the natural order! Everyone knows the forms we see on the wall are real, and not illusions, as he says. There is no great light outside the cave. He's teaching lies to our children!" If they could free themselves from being tied up, some offended prisoners might even kill the bold escapee rather than believe him.

That's the allegory of Plato's cave. Plato uses this story to illustrate his belief that when we experience reality, it is not something we can grasp immediately and is actually quite confusing, especially initially. We cannot handle the truth because we are so used to and comfortable with our limited daily experience of life here on earth. However, Plato maintains that we can learn to handle reality and truth if we are willing and determined to undergo a radical transformation. But he cautions that this path is a very long and difficult process, similar to the way the escaped prisoner slowly gets used to the fire in the cave, the moonlight, the sunlight reflected in objects, and finally the sun itself. It has to be a radical transformation since it must change the fundamental nature of how we perceive our identity.

The word Plato uses to describe this transformation is *paideia*. It is often translated as meaning "education." But the true meaning is much closer to the Greek word *metanoia*, used by Christians to mean a dramatic change of heart. This change is not just having a new intellectual idea. Paideia, as Plato meant it, is a 180-degree turn of the whole person toward his or her core. This redirection toward one's inner essence brings a realization of the reality of one's being based on personal experience rather than intellectual conjecture. From the ancient Greek perspective this reorientation was the fundamental purpose of education, but today the term education is related only to the kind of intellectual learning we receive in school and college. To Plato, becoming educated meant a journey of transformation leading inward toward one's inherent essence. This march to the center is a discovery of inner being. And once this discovery is made, we can eventually become acclimated to it. Acting out of that inner core, we can determine what outer actions to take that are in accord with our essence.

Hearing the story of Plato's cave reminded me of my own experience of the Light. I would like to share with you some of my reflections on why the experience of inner Light is meaningful for me. When I had my psychic reading with Jim Branch in Virginia Beach, the first question I submitted to him in his trance state was, "What is the nature of my soul purposes and my specific mission for Christ in this life?" The validity of his source was confirmed for me by the reading's reference to my awakening experience of divine Light, of which Jim Branch had no conscious awareness, as follows:

> Now this one has been a part of those experiences in times past, which did reveal in part, in portion, the vision of the Universal Christ. And these impelling forces have made a permanent imprint upon this individuality. Indeed, the upwellings of these through the subconscious forces had guided, directed, this one toward those similar patterns in the sojourn. As this one perceived, these forces had poured suddenly into the experience into the conscious mind, causing the illumination [Christian word for enlightenment] and the keen yearning for final union with the Universal Christ Forces.

When I first heard this reading, these words describing my awakening reminded me of God's blessing and His Love for me, and I shed tears of gratitude. The reading answered the question about my spiritual mission by stating that my purpose is to help others so that they "might gain greater understanding of the balance of Light and darkness." I told the story of Plato's cave in this chapter because I identify with the escaped prisoner who returned to the cave to explain to others what he had seen. When my awakening happened in 1969, I could not very well tell those around me what had happened. What if I had said, "I escaped from the cave of this world and have seen the Light of Eternity. We live in the Light I saw, although we appear to live in this world of darkness and light"? No one would have understood what I was talking about. Actually I didn't have the perceptual awareness to understand or articulate the experience with my rational mind in any way that would be helpful to others. Even now it's still difficult to describe what I saw outside the cave and make it understandable and practical to others, yet I feel that task is my mission for Christ.

The reading stated, "There is of great necessity that this understanding innate, which this one does bear, be transferred." It also refers to the "direct transference of same unto those whom this one would contact" and then refers to transferring this understanding in writing. Yet my purpose is not to just say or write, "There's a Light outside the cave!" That proclamation by itself is not enough. My mission is to convey practical ways of bringing about the long-term process of transformation that Plato talked about to make the slow transition from the darkness to the Light. The reading identified that my book of meditation techniques would be published first, as it has been, although a new, very much expanded book is now written, but not yet published. The reading also indicated that in my latter years the life experiences would be shared, as indeed it is being shared in these very pages. I have also written another book about Christian yoga that I hope to also publish soon. Through this Christian yoga book, as well as the meditation book and life story, I hope to fully articulate a complete path for transformation as a life journey. It's most certainly not the only path to escaping the cave and finding the Light. But it is the one I have been given, and the one I have to share with others who might be interested in the benefits it offers. The next chapter describes in detail my vision for the path of Christian yoga, which I specifically call *Miracle Yoga*. The chapter after that, "A Monk in the World," relates my understanding of what it means to be a monk who practices inner attunement and outer extension, while remaining quietly woven into the fabric of normal everyday living.

One reason I have shared my experiences is to encourage you, the reader, to be open to having your own spiritual experiences. With that in mind, I would like to ask you to consider conducting an attunement experiment. For this experiment you will be using your imagination, but not to imagine a fabrication of the mind as you usually would. Instead I will be asking you to imagine something that is real, but normally hidden from your conscious awareness. I will ask you to imagine the reality of the divine light that is indeed within you. If you decide to conduct this experiment, follow these directions:

Sit in a comfortable position in which you can relax your body. Then bring your awareness to the heart area, either in the center of the chest or in the location of the physical heart. Now use your imagination to envision an inner light that starts as a point of light. In your imagination, let that point then grow into a flame of light. Let the flame expand and fill the heart area with light. Allow that light to carry with it a loving feeling. Then let the light and love radiate outward and fill the whole body. After the body fills with light and love, allow it to expand a foot in all directions surrounding the entire body. Let the light form a sphere encompassing the whole body. Allow the light and love of the sphere to expand to encompass the city in which you live, sending light and love to all other beings in that area. Next expand the light and love to encompass all of your country, and then all of the world, including all living beings. Then expand to encompass the solar system and, later, all of the universe. Lastly, let your light and love extend to all life, even life beyond the world of form, so your light and love reach all of God's Creation. Now, very importantly, feel that you are sharing all of yourself— giving all of your light and love to every living being created by God. Extending your imagination even further, sense that all other living beings are giving all of their light and love to you. Rest in the peace of this celebration of light and love. After resting in this peace, you proceed to reverse the process. Allow your light and love to come back step by step. Bring your awareness from this transcendental sharing back to form, back to the universe, the solar system, the world, your country, your city. And finally, return the light and love to your heart area to conclude this exploration of your divine nature.

As a result of my experience of Light, the most important thing I want to share with you is this: You live in the Divine Light *now*, as do I, along with all our brothers and sisters. The Divine Light is inseparable from Divine Love. Consequently, you live in Divine Love *now*, as do I, along with all our brothers and sisters. You live in Light because you are eternally part of God, Who is Light. Your loving Father gave you Light as your true nature. You can hide from your true nature as Light, as a prisoner in Plato's cave, but God's eternal gift to you can never be taken away from you. You don't need a dramatic direct experience of the Light to realize your true nature. As Plato maintained, spiritual growth is not a one shot experience of the Light, which in itself can be confusing. It is a long process of transformation in which we can learn to become more and more familiar with the Light.

There are two primary ways of becoming increasingly accustomed to the Light: One is meditation and the other is forgiveness. The practice of meditation on a daily basis is the *direct* means of transformation, because it is the inward journey of opening to the Light Itself. Each meditation helps you to familiarize yourself with the inner Light and brings you one small step closer to the time when you will fully accept the Light. The application of forgiveness is the *indirect* means of transformation. It's like the indirect process used by the escaped prisoner, who gradually became acclimated to the sun by first seeing sunlight only as a reflection of the moon at nighttime and later as a reflection off of objects during the day. Similarly, forgiveness allows you to see the Divine Light indirectly as a reflection in the faces of your brothers and sisters. Seeing that outer reflection of light in others draws forth in you an awareness of that same light within you.

According to the Course, this is not just a perceiving of light intellectually in others and yourself. It's really an exchange in which light is given and received. In this exchange the giver and the receiver of forgiveness both gain light and love simultaneously. This exchange in which both gain is called a *miracle*. This miracle of forgiveness is your means of looking past outer appearances presented by the ego and body and allowing the light and love that is hidden within you to come out, be seen, and be expressed in your relationships. Your practice of forgiveness, in which you exchange light and love with your brothers and sisters, will help you believe in and identify with your own true nature as Light and Love. How you see your brothers and sisters is how you will see yourself. Thus forgiveness affirms the divine presence not only in others, but also in yourself. God can be experienced within through meditation, but in your daily life you can find God most easily by seeing Him in others. Forgiveness leads eventually to realizing that, "God is not in you in a literal sense; you are a part of Him."[1]

Coincidentally, not long after hearing the story of Plato's cave, I began to increasingly see light in the faces of people and even in objects. This was reminiscent of the visual experience I had when I took one puff of marijuana and walked through the park in Virginia Beach. Yet in the past I had other experiences of seeing light visually that were not drug induced. When I had studied Zen in Rochester, I had seen light in others at times. While I was camping in the Sedona forest, there was Tom's visit when I could continuously see him filled with light. On several other occasions when I had been in various churches, I had seen the heads of everyone visibly glowing with white light. Most recently I had seen light in Robert when he gave talks on the Course. I could also see light in Allan during some of our conversations. But the difference now was that I could see light in others whenever I wanted to. All I needed to do was look with my heart. The love I felt within enabled me to visually see light wherever I placed my gaze with the full attention of my mind. I could even see the whole panorama of my vision filled with light. This ability reminded me of Plato's escaped prisoner, who could not look at the sun directly, but had to acclimate himself to the light. He did this first by going out at nighttime to see by the reflected light of the moon. Similarly, I wasn't seeing the blazing Divine Light as it really is. I was seeing a shining reflected light that was only symbolic of that Divine Light. Nevertheless, seeing this reflected light displayed everywhere was quite fulfilling. Seeing a world filled with light required only that I focus my mind on opening my heart to love.

I wondered if others had similar experiences of seeing light visually, and while reading *A Book of Angels*, I came across the experience of Sophy Burnham. When she was a hospital patient, her mind became so unified that she could perceive everything with crystal clarity. Immediately afterward, she discovered she possessed a surprising ability to see the world around her filled with light. Here is her description:

> I saw with extraordinary clarity. I marveled at it: *This is the way artists see*, I thought, humbled by the miracle of a towel rack, the fold of a sheet. A tree outside the window, the children playing football on the grass reduced me to tears.... One day standing at the window, looking at the sky and clouds, I was smitten by the order of the universe.... I understood ... everything—things that today I don't even have the language to pose questions about, and the beauty of this order was so sharp that tears coursed down my cheeks. And more extraordinary, when I looked out the window, the leaves and trees and grass were flashing with an inner light. I saw light shining from the skin of people, pouring off the hands and faces both of nurses and of fellow patients.... Back in Washington in my own garden, I bent in worship at this radiance pouring from the leaves and grass, from every living thing. "Look. Look at the light," I would say. And then realize that other people didn't see it flaming off the vines "like shining from shook foil." For two weeks I could see the earth flaring with this living light, and then it began to fade away.[2]

Similar to Sophy Burnham's experience, I noticed that whenever I saw light visually, my mind was very clear and perceptive. Whenever I wanted to see light visually I would have to consciously focus my mind. But for me mental clarity alone was not enough. I also had to open my heart so my mind was focused on love, and only then could I see light externally. My ability to do this consistently was an outgrowth of my study and application of the Course, which advocated the development of *Christ vision*.[3] This type of vision is not in itself an outer visual experience. Christ vision is the ability to perceive with the "eyes of love," or what might be called the "eyes of Christ." It is the loving activity of the Holy Spirit that enables us to manifest *true forgiveness*, which is the seeing of the divine presence of perfection and holiness in others, as will be described in Chapter 69. Consequently, Christ vision can also be called seeing with the "eyes of forgiveness." This is a state of perception in which the mind is unified and centered on love. Naturally, through Christ vision, the mind can be focused on love without seeing light visually.

Although Christ vision is not a visual experience all by itself, the ability to see light visually is a *by-product* of Christ vision. I have coined the term *Light vision* to describe the experience of seeing light visually in the world and to distinguish it from Christ vision. There is an inner light, not an outer visual light, which is the source of both Christ vision and its by-product Light vision. This is called *true light* in the Course. Here is a Course description of this inner light and how it relates directly with having a unified mind:

> True light that makes true vision possible is not the light the body's eyes behold. It is a state of mind that has become so unified that darkness cannot be perceived at all.[4]

Many have reported the experience of this true light that is a high state of awareness in which the mind becomes totally unified, but without the visual component of Light vision. The Trappist monk Thomas Merton had a startling experience of Christ vision, although he would certainly not have used that term to describe it. He was a young man, not yet a monk, who was at a Mass at the Church of Saint Francis in Havana. A bell rang three times, and he heard the voices of school children singing, which he described in this way:

> [They sang] … with such loud and strong and clear voices, and such unanimity and such meaning and such fervor that something went off inside me like a thunderclap and without seeing anything or apprehending anything extraordinary through any of my senses (my eyes were open on only precisely what was there, the church). I knew with the most absolute and unquestionable certainty that before me, between me and the altar, somewhere in the center of the church, up in the air (or any other place because in no place), but directly before my eyes, or directly present to some apprehension or other of mine which was above that of the senses, was at the same time God in all His essence, all His power, all His glory, and God in Himself and God surrounded by the radiant faces of the uncountable thousands upon thousands of saints…. And so the unshakable certainty, the clear and immediate knowledge that

Heaven was right in front of me like a thunderbolt and went through me like a flash of lightning and seemed to lift me clean off the earth.[5]

In his life story *The Seven Storey Mountain*, Merton elaborated on his encounter with the divine, describing how it was an experience of light, though not visible light:

It was a light that was so bright that it had no relation to any visible light and so profound and so intimate that it seemed like a neutralization of every lesser experience.

And yet the thing that struck me most of all was that this light was in a certain sense "ordinary"—it was a light (and this most of all was what took my breath away) that was offered to all, to everybody, and there was nothing fancy or strange about it.... It disarmed all images, all metaphors.... It ignored all sense experiences in order to strike directly at the heart of truth, as if a sudden and immediate contact had been established between my intellect and the Truth Who was now physically really and substantially before me.... But this contact was not something speculative and abstract: it was concrete and experiential and belonged to the order of knowledge, yes, but more still to the order of love....

Another thing about it was that this light was something far above and beyond the level of any desire or appetite.... It was love as clean and direct as vision: and it flew straight to the possession of the Truth it loved.[6]

Merton described his experience as momentary, but leaving him with a sense of joy, peace, and happiness that lasted for hours and became indelibly marked in his memory. He said above that during his experience nothing extraordinary was happening at the sensory level, yet I wondered if there might have been a subtle movement of energy within his body that went unnoticed. In my own experience, when Christ vision and the attending Light vision occurred together, I realized that my mind was unified by focusing on love, yet I felt something else as well. I noticed energy rising upward in the body, especially along the spine, and from the upper torso into the head. Because of this rising energy, I felt that the occurrence of seeing light as a by-product of Christ vision was also due, at least in part, to the rising of the *kundalini*. According to Eastern philosophy, the kundalini is the energy stored at the base of the spine that rises up during spiritual experiences. This energy can rise up full force during an overwhelming enlightenment experience, but also could rise up gently during meditation. Normal yoga practices help to make the physical body a fit vehicle for the raising of the kundalini. In addition, some specific extreme yoga practices are designed to accelerate the raising of the kundalini, but I did not pursue the use of any of these. Instead, I took a Christian yoga approach by asking the Holy Spirit to be in charge of raising the kundalini in a moderate and safe manner in accordance with God's Will for me. This approach is in accordance with the Course recommendation to ask the Holy Spirit to "...decide for God for me."[7]

On a regular basis I began to feel the mild raising of the kundalini energy during daily meditation periods and felt my whole body being filled with radiating light. When I wanted to see light externally, I would make sure to sit or stand with the spine erect and would focus the mind just as I did for my attunements. Although my eyes were open, I could still feel the rising kundalini energy and light within radiating outward. It occurred to me that I could see light outwardly because the same light I felt within was being extended to the outer world in my vision.

However, I could not find in yoga literature a specific verification of the connection between Light vision and the kundalini until I came across *Kundalini: The Evolutionary Energy in Man*, the revealing autobiography of Gopi Krishna. As an aftereffect of raising the kundalini, Gopi Krishna saw a silver luster wherever he looked. This experience became part of his daily life, which he explained as follows:

> A surge of emotion too deep for words filled my whole being, and tears gathered in my eyes in spite of myself at the significance of the new development in me. But even in that condition, looking through tears, I could perceive trembling beams of silvery light dancing before my vision, enhancing the radiant beauty of the scene. It was not difficult to understand that, without being aware of it, an extraordinary change had taken place in the now luminous cognitive center in my brain and that the fascinating luster, which I perceived around every object, was not a figment of my fancy nor was it possessed by the objects, but a projection of my own internal radiance.
>
> Days and weeks passed without alteration in the lustrous form of sight. A bright silvery sheen around every object, across the entire field of vision, became a permanent feature of my being.[8]

Gopi Krishna noted correctly that his seeing of light outwardly was a projection of the inner light in his own mind. As the years went by I regularly went on intensive meditation retreats, which helped to facilitate experiencing Light vision. These retreats reawakened my awareness of the inner light through the natural raising of the kundalini guided by the

Holy Spirit. The benefits I received in these intensive retreats encouraged me to eventually increase the frequency of my twenty-five-minute sitting periods of meditation from twice daily to first three and now four times daily. Typically when it is late at night and I'm tired, I will shorten the last meditation to fifteen minutes. Meditating one or perhaps two times per day is quite sufficient for most people, but I felt I wanted more, especially after retiring from my state job.

Retirement was a time for reevaluating my life, so I asked myself, "What is the most meaningful thing in my life?" The answer was obvious—it's my relationship with God. Food nourishes me and breath nourishes me, but that nourishment is time limited. When I take my last bite of food, and when I take my very last breath, there will only be my relationship with God to rely on. I figured I might as well learn to rely on Him now. Meditating more was my way of investing in eternity right away instead of waiting until there is no other option. However, the increased time for attunement was not something I was imposing on myself out of a sense of obligation that I owed to God from being a monk. Rather it was simply an outgrowth of tasting God's Love and naturally wanting more of that nourishment. As a result, my attunements improved, and I felt inner energy obstructions being removed. Inner blocks stemming from past lives can obstruct the raising of the kundalini. I found that, as I let go of past life blocks, there was a natural rising of the kundalini and an increase of the likelihood of becoming aware of the inner light and seeing light outwardly.

Today, after becoming very familiar over the years with experiencing Light vision, I can still focus my mind on people and objects to visually see light externally, yet I find myself doing it less and less. In the past the visual experience of Light vision has been a healthy reminder of the divine presence pervading all of life and an encouragement for me to practice my spiritual disciplines. Nonetheless, this optional by-product of perceiving holiness is no longer important to me. What remains important to me is to continue to be firmly rooted in the content of holiness. Since seeing light visually is only a symbol of the content of holiness in the mind, I find myself being increasingly drawn toward this content itself. Although I have a strong conviction that the divine presence and inherent attending holiness is within everyone, including me, that's not enough. The application of daily spiritual disciples is necessary to solidly reinforce that conviction. Spiritual disciplines counteract the cares of the world that can bring distractions and illusions into the mind to cloud my thinking. My two main spiritual disciplines are setting aside times for inner attunement and relying on Christ vision to perceive the world without needing a visual experience to confirm the holiness in others. Inwardly opening to the Holy Spirit and outwardly seeing with the eyes of forgiveness and the eyes of love is all that's required.

Along the way I have noticed some encouraging steps forward in my awareness and attunement. In the past, whenever I relaxed my body completely, there was still an area in the right foot, mainly around the big toe, that was not fully energized due to past life blocks. A reassuring confirmation of making peace with the Pole Man and subsequent Spider Boy past life issues was that finally the entire right foot was fully energized whenever I completely relaxed. In addition to my sitting meditation periods, I had incorporated a midday relaxation period into my daily schedule in the form of a lying down attunement. After removing the block in my right foot, I found that the lying down relaxation periods were often as spiritually uplifting as my regular sitting meditation periods. Because these lying down relaxation times were so effortless, they provided opportunities to surrender more completely to the Holy Spirit, and I felt I was being filled with love, light, and energy from head to toe. Overall there was a deep feeling of inner peace and a sense of being embraced by the divine presence.

On a daily basis, the sitting meditations and the lying down attunements included various degrees of being filled with light. The inner experience of opening to light was primarily a gift of grace and secondarily an aftereffect of more than thirty years of practicing daily spiritual disciplines. In addition, this experience of being filled with light was consistently attended by feelings of love and energy. There was also joyfulness, which occurred intermittently. The occurrence of these inner feelings was due in part to both retaining sexual fluids and maintaining sexual purity. In the daily sitting meditations, the light and energy rose in the body from the bottom upward and produced an uplifting feeling that increased in intensity slowly and steadily. This would often build to a sustained elevated state of keen heightened awareness, sometimes producing a jolt of energy jumping upward through the body. Ideally the attunement would culminate in a letting go of body awareness in the experience of contemplation.

Even though the positive inner feelings experienced in the energy of the body can encourage our practice, these are not the most highly prized aspects of the attunement experience. Many seekers do not have these inner feelings, and their practice is still very spiritually nourishing because it is rooted solidly in their faith. The real goal of meditation, which is the holding of a single loving thought in the mind, is actually to lead to the letting go of body awareness in contemplation. In contemplation there is a letting go of all thoughts while also letting go of body awareness, and this helps to open and unify the mind. As contemplation deepens over time, it produces peace of mind and a deeper faithful trust in God and in His love than any body awareness experience can provide.

The midday lying down attunements were consistently relaxing and revitalizing, but did not produce the same elevation of consciousness in the head as experienced in sitting meditations. However, these lying down attunements produced an intense feeling of light and energy mostly in the heart center in the middle of the chest. Usually this energy moved upward in the body, but at times a sweet touch of bliss would well up in the heart center and expand outwardly in all directions to fill the rest of the body. A lying down attunement in the morning or evening had no such effect, since perhaps the body was too sluggish after awakening in the morning and too tired at the end of the day. Attunements in general, and especially in the morning and evening, are more effective in the sitting position than the lying down position because the erect spine brings about a greater degree of mental alertness, preventing the tendency toward drowsiness.

The most important issue in regard to past lives is how they produce an effect *now*. I hadn't fully solved the shadow puzzle by age fifty, because there were still fragments hidden in my subconscious mind that would need to be revealed in the upcoming years. However, I had revealed enough of the darkest aspects of the subconscious mind so that my traumatic past lives no longer had a strong impact on this lifetime. Therefore, my awareness expanded and my attunement improved. The victim pattern that had been perpetuated in past lives and repeated in my current life was not entirely gone, but it was being healed and would eventually be eliminated.

I have talked about the shadow mostly in negative terms because that is the most obvious way we are limited by the dark side of the psyche. However, the shadow is really all of what we consider unacceptable and therefore push out of our awareness. How many of us fully bring forth all of our hidden talents and abilities? Just as we can find negative qualities unacceptable, we can think our positive qualities are unacceptable and relegate them to subconscious status. Here is a question I would like you to ask yourself right now: "What is the most significant positive aspect of myself that is hidden in the shadow of my subconscious mind?" I'll give you my own answer shortly. Some of us have difficulty seeing, acknowledging, and bringing forth the positive aspects of ourselves that remain latent in the shadow side of the mind. Yet we can learn to be open to these positive sides of ourselves and integrate them.

My answer to the question regarding the most significant hidden positive quality is *love*. I believe love is the most hidden aspect of ourselves because our true potential for love goes much deeper than we can possibly imagine. My former psychotherapy group in New York had the right idea about getting pent up emotions of fear, anger, and pain out in the open and released. After these dark shadows were released, the goal in that therapy was to reveal the inner love. But the psychotherapy goal provided a limited vision of what love is that omitted the love of God. There are three kinds of love mentioned in the Greek versions of the New Testament—*phileo, eros,* and *agape.* The emphasis on psychotherapy was on *phileo,* which is love between friends. Sometimes I experienced this friendly love after my psychotherapy sessions, but that opening to love did not carry over significantly to apply to my relationship with Marie. However, when I began to meditate for the first time, some other darker parts of my psyche were released. As a result, I was more open to revealing the love that was also hidden in my subconscious mind. It was then that I experienced *eros,* romantic love, in my relationship with Marie. But hidden in the darkest corner of the shadow is the deepest kind of love, called *agape.* This is the love of God that is hidden within every child of God because God Himself put His eternal Love in us when He created us. This is the most fulfilling form of love hidden behind the shadow that is increasingly revealed as we remove each subconscious fragment of darkness. Opening to agape love is the fruit of walking the long path of spiritual transformation. This revealing of agape allows us to navigate through the world gracefully, touching the hearts of others and giving us the power to transcend our human limitations. It is also fuel for inner attunement that opens us to intimacy with God, Who Loves us from within.

But can we accept agape? Can we accept this deepest and most hidden form of love, so it can come out from behind the shadow? This requires bringing the shadow into our conscious awareness. Revealing the shadow involves three qualities—*open-mindedness, watchfulness,* and *acceptance.* The shadow is caused by denial that closes the mind. To overcome denial, we need to have *open-mindedness* that expresses our desire to know what is hidden by denial. We also need to ask the Holy Spirit to help us open our minds to see beyond what we can normally see. Secondly, we need *watchfulness* to be mentally alert to hints or symbols presented to us of what is hidden. Watchfulness helps us to recognize that something is being revealed to us from our subconscious minds because we are ready for this learning. Some of our best symbols come to us through dreams, and others come to us by events of life or the words of other people. If we have cultivated both open-mindedness and watchfulness, we can feel the Holy Spirit telling us to pay attention to theses symbols and hear their messages. The third quality needed to reveal the shadow is *acceptance.* An attitude of acceptance is especially important because the shadow itself consists of our hidden and unacceptable parts. As these unacceptable parts of the shadow are brought out of hiding and consciously accepted, agape will also be revealed and accepted so we can increasingly open our hearts to God.

I have talked a lot about my past lives such as the Pole Man and the Spider Boy. I have done that because these former lifetimes were so emotionally charged they were infringing on my current life. Consequently, it was out of necessity that I had to come to grips with these past lives to release their emotional impact that was still affecting me negatively. Nevertheless, I do not think everyone has to have an inner recognition of past lives or even a philosophical belief in them. Each of us has our own unique journey, and for most seekers it is not necessary to be aware of specific past lives. The important thing is how we live our current lives.

After completing this chapter, I felt that I needed to include an additional general comment here for the sake of clarity. The uncomfortable feeling for me in writing this book is that I am recording in words for all to see the very things that I would normally consider too personal to talk about. Describing my spiritual experiences falls into this category. Just as a married couple would not talk about their sexual intimacy, there would usually be no reason for me to talk about my inner intimacy with God. Nevertheless, my written disclosures here seem appropriate as a means of letting others know what's possible in the spiritual life and as a way to encourage the seeking and finding of the divine presence.

Self-revealing nakedness is necessary to maintain the integrity of writing an autobiography, yet I am somewhat embarrassed by my pride and ego that are all-too-prevalent in describing my spiritual disciplines in these pages. With that in mind, I would like to correct a possible misimpression I may have given implying that my meditation practice is more advanced than it really is. I have described the highlights and blessings of my interior spiritual life in this book, but inner attunements are like popcorn kernels— no two are alike. There will always be peaks and valleys. No one, including myself, has a spiritual path that is straight and smooth. There will always be challenges to overcome, dry periods, and unexpected events on the path. For example, when there are temporary emotional concerns or physical ailments, these can adversely affect opening to spirit. However, even these setbacks can serve as opportunities to turn to God in the darkness of faith.

---

1. T-5.II.5:5, p. 76 (p. 70).

2. Sophy Burnham, *A Book of Angels* (New York: Ballantine Books, 1990), p. 216.

3. What I call "Christ vision" is written in the Course as "Christ's vision" to indicate that it is the vision possessed by Christ. Consequently, when we see with this vision we are seeing with the eyes of Christ. Christ vision is also called the "Holy Spirit's vision" in the Course to express the idea that we are perceiving with the help of the Holy Spirit seeing through us.

4. W-pI.108.2:1-2, p. 195 (p. 191).

5. Thomas Merton, *The Secular Journal of Thomas Merton*, (New York: Farrar Straus and Cudahy, 1958), pp. 75-78.

6. Thomas Merton, *The Seven Storey Mountain*, (New York: A Harvest Book, [first published in 1948] 1999), pp. 311-312.

7. T-5.VII.6:11, p. 90 (p. 83).

8. Gopi Krishna, *Kundalini: The Evolutionary Energy in Man* (Boulder, CO, and London, England: Shambhala, 1971), introduction by Frederic Spiegelberg, psychological commentary by James Hillman (pp. 144-145).

67

CHRISTIAN YOGA
AND MIRACLE YOGA

≈ ◦ ≈

As was mentioned previously, I had a past life in India as a spiritual teacher, which has encouraged me to practice and teach Christian yoga and be an embodiment of the marriage of the East and West. Since the New Jerusalem Community itself was divided into a Western camp, the Anaheim Half, and an Eastern camp, the Sedona Half, there were a lot of opportunities for me to see firsthand how to synthesize the East and West. When merging two different religious perspectives into one thought system, it is very difficult to come up with a combination that truly carries the divine influence inherent in each perspective. Fortunately that difficulty has already been successfully handled by *A Course in Miracles*, which I have adopted as my theological foundation for blending the East and West. Obviously Christian yoga, which uses yoga practices as a means of growing toward the goal of Christ, can be a spiritual path in itself without having the theological underpinning of the Course. Similarly the Course can be a spiritual path all by itself without the addition of yoga practices. However, I believe the combination of the two potentially distinct paths into one path of Christian yoga based on the Course provides a dynamic opportunity for growth that could not be provided by either one of these paths separately.

It might be helpful here to describe how Christian yoga by itself is a synthesis of the East and West. Yoga in the Hindu tradition, and especially in the Tantric tradition, can be considered "systematic internalization." In yoga everything is internalized, specifically meaning brought into the body. The entire universe, the macrocosm, is interiorized, including all of the dimensions of existence beyond time and the three physical dimensions of the universe. So a smaller version of the macrocosm is symbolically represented within the body as the microcosm. The spine represents the axis of the universe around which all else spins and along that axis are the seven spiritual centers called *chakras*. The systematic internalization produced by yoga practices penetrates not only into the body, but more importantly into the spiritual centers themselves. Everything in the universe that spins around the central axis of the spine is brought into the chakras, especially into the heart center and the crown center, where all opposing forces come together in oneness. Yoga attainment is often thought of as the union of divergent forces to realize the oneness of God.

Just as yoga in general is an internalization, Christian yoga is likewise a systematic internalization, but with an emphasis upon Christ. As a Christian yogi, the body is perceived as a member of the body of Christ. Christ's body encompasses the universe. His body encompasses and transcends form, space, and time. There is nothing that exists outside of Christ, just as there is nothing that exists outside of God, the only difference being God is the First Cause, who created the Christ. The Christian yogi then has a single task—to internalize Christ Himself, who is the One in the All.

Within the Christian yogi then is the cross of Christ in which his ego dies daily. His breath inhales the love of Christ for him personally and for all of mankind. In this inhalation he takes in the words of Christ on the cross, "Father, forgive them; for they know not what they do."[1] He knows these words are for himself and all his brothers, and he knows a deeper meaning not expressed, "Father, forgive them for they do not yet know who they *are*, as your holy children." His breath exhales the last expiration of the cross, "Father, into your hands I commit my spirit."[2]

When the yogi meditates, he sees himself as one of the disciples waiting in the upper room for the Holy Spirit to descend unto his crown in parted tongues of fire to purify and cleanse him of all that would separate him from oneness. Christ rose from the dead indeed in a moment of time for all mankind once and for all, but the Christian yogi is not content with an intellectual assent to this event in history. His mission is to immerse himself in the fire of God so the ego may be burnt to ashes, and he may rise from the dead also. However, it will not be the former yogi rising from the dead; the Christian yogi's realization is that it will be the Christ that is resurrecting again within him in the eternal present moment. The Christian yogi experiences Christ within as a "felt" experience of inner communion with the divine presence.

This important emphasis on inner communion with Christ is what distinguishes Christian yoga from traditional Christianity, as was first mentioned in Chapter 8. Thomas Keating in his book on contemplation, entitled *Open Mind, Open Heart*,[3] discussed the value of mystical graces, which he described as, "the inflowing of God's presence into our faculties or the radiance of His presence when it spontaneously overtakes us." Regarding contemplative or mystical graces, which may be considered "felt" experiences of divine communion, Thomas Keating pondered the following question:

Is it possible to be a contemplative and attain the transforming union without going through the experience of the mystical graces just described?

This is a question that has puzzled me over the years because contemplation as the experience of the inflow of God's grace has generally been considered a necessary sign of the gift of contemplative prayer. However, I continue to meet people are very advanced in the spiritual journey who insist that they have never had the grace of contemplative prayer as a felt experience of God. Having spent thirty or forty years in a monastery or convent in order to be contemplatives, some of these people are tempted at times to feel that their lives have been a gigantic failure. They wind up in their sixties or seventies believing that since they never had such an experience, they must have done something wrong. Here are people who have given their whole lives to the service of Christ and yet have not internal assurance of having had even the least mystical grace.[4]

Thomas Keating concluded that contemplative prayer is still valuable in itself without having an experiencing of the radiance of God's presence. He made reference to the *Guidelines to Mystical Prayer*. The author, Ruth Burroughs, a Carmelite nun, offered her proposal that there is a difference between *lights on* mysticism and *light off* mysticism. She sited examples of one "lights on mystic" who experienced mystical graces in contemplative prayer and one "lights off mystic" who practiced contemplative prayer without any confirming felt experience. Both experienced transforming union, the marriage of the soul and God that is considered the summit of contemplative life. Her premise was that a contemplative seeker can be having a mystical infusion of faith through contemplative prayer without a confirming conscious experience, since there is no faculty that can perceive faith. Thus Thomas Keating stated that the essence of contemplative prayer is, "The way of faith. Nothing else. You do not have to feel it, but you have to practice it."[5]

I agree that faith is of primary importance and is indispensable to Christian contemplative spiritual seeking. Faith alone can elevate the seeker to transforming union, but I wonder how often Christian seekers give up contemplative prayer because they do not have a felt experience to confirm their faith. Traditional Christianity maintains that the receiving of mystical graces is a gift from God. However, I believe God does not play favorites, and He would generously give this gift to many more seekers if they would take measures to predispose themselves to receive it. According to Thomas Keating's quote above, even living in a monastery or convent does not guarantee that a seeker will receive mystical graces. There is something missing from traditional Christianity in the area of preparing the seeker to receive mystical graces. Even Thomas Keating writes, "Is there something that we can do to prepare ourselves for the gift of contemplation instead of waiting for God to do everything? My acquaintance with Eastern methods of meditation has convinced me that there is."[6]

One way Christian yoga can lay the foundation for the contemplative experience is the practice of hatha yoga postures to elevate physical vitality and keep the spine flexible and ready for sitting meditation. Another factor is practicing breathing techniques to enable the body to be a suitable vehicle for receiving the higher vibration of mystical graces. Christian yoga offers meditation techniques, such as Christian Yoga Meditation, for opening the spiritual centers within the body in contrast to traditional Christianity that does not even acknowledge the presence of spiritual centers within the body. There are also subtle energy currents running through the entire the body recognized by Eastern philosophies, but overlooked in the West. The Christian yoga postures, breathing practices, and meditation techniques increase the flow of these subtle energy currents. Through daily practice the energy currents can become so revitalized that they can be consciously experienced by the Christian yogi. In addition, the enhanced and free-flowing energy currents can be used by the Holy Spirit as avenues through which mystical graces can be consciously felt as inner feelings. The inner feelings of the divine presence, light, love, joy, and peace that were described at the beginning of this chapter are examples of these mystical graces. The overall point here is that the general orientation of Christian yoga is geared toward making the body a fit instrument for inner communion with Christ.

In the awakening of Christ within comes the awareness of one's own Self as the Christ Self. But equally important is that expanded awareness of oneness brings with it the realization that other seekers are participating in the one Christ. Consequently the seeker can see his true Self in all his brothers and sisters. Along with any true realization comes compassion and gratitude. Out of this gratitude comes a dedication to helping to bring about the liberation and happiness of all conscious beings. A Christian yogi can become a teacher of this goal of extending to others, just as Buddhists become teachers who embrace a similar ideal. Thus what begins as a Christian yoga internalization ends as a Christian yoga externalization. Being a teacher does not necessarily mean calling oneself a teacher. Teaching can be done simply by example, and sometimes more effectively than through calling oneself a teacher.

The goal of traditional Hindu yoga is to attain the highest level of samadhi, producing God realization, which corresponds to Zen Buddhist enlightenment, culminating in the awakening of Buddha nature. In the

Course this direct uncovering of union with God is called revelation. Of course, permanent union with God is the ultimate aim of all spiritual seeking. However, the temporary experience of direct union with God in revelation is not the primary goal of the Course or of Christian yoga based on the Course, although spiritual growth practices can lay the groundwork for such a direct experience of the divine to occur. Obviously a one time peak experience can accelerate one's spiritual growth, but the focus in Christian yoga and the Course is on the practical side of seeing spiritual growth as a lifetime marathon rather than a slice-of-life sprint.

The term *Christian yoga* has been used extensively to describe any combination of yoga with following Christ. In order to specifically identify the type of Christian yoga that is based on the Course, I use the term *Miracle Yoga* to distinguish it from Christian yoga in general. The objective of Miracle Yoga is to live in Christ each and every day and allow His Spirit to be expressed through you bringing blessings into the lives of others. Sometimes the Course is mistakenly thought of as merely a set of lofty metaphysical concepts. However, its spiritual principles are meant to be consistently applied to everyday life. The Course is invariably silent about the various self-help forms of the world, such as diet, exercise, health, and breathing practices. This omission is intentional in order to highlight the Course's central message about content taking precedence over form— meaning specifically that there is a divine presence and spiritual purpose beyond the illusions of form presented by the world.

One of the main goals of the Miracle Yoga, is to live a life based on *forgiveness*, which allows you to see past the illusions of form and to recognize the reality of the divine presence in everyone and everything. Seeing the world through the eyes of forgiveness can potentially enable you to have Christ vision and see a world filled with love. The goal of obtaining Christ vision is to learn how to open your heart to the divine love all around you and in you as your source and substance. It may take your whole lifetime to fully learn this single lesson that love is your true nature. Forgiveness is your practical means of learning this lesson because it removes the inner obstacles to the awareness of love's abiding presence.

Unlike revelation that can possibly be a one time experience of the divine, if it occurs at all, forgiveness is available to everyone all of the time. Hopefully the proper application of forgiveness can be learned and become your way of approaching everyday life on an ongoing basis. Forgiveness helps you to not only see the divine in others, but also to trust in that same divine presence within yourself as your true Christ Self, because how you see your brother will inevitably be how you see yourself. Since forgiveness in the Course requires discrimination between the real and the unreal, it corresponds to the type of Hindu yoga called *jnana yoga*, which is the seeking of God through mental understanding and discrimination. In the blending of East and West, the practice of *Miracle Jnana Yoga* is based entirely on the Course and the application of forgiveness, which affirms the divine reality in everyone and overlooks the unreal illusions of the ego.

Although the thought system of the Course is the basis for Miracle Jnana Yoga, you may prefer practicing your own unique form of Christian yoga with another thought system. You could potentially choose a dualistic Western thought system that maintains that the seeker and God are separate and in the process of joining. In my opinion this is a diluted form of Christian yoga that leaves out the gift that the East has to offer the West. This gift is the perception that the seeker and God are already united and the seeker is simply waking up to this already existing union. If the Course is not your cup of tea, I recommend the perennial philosophy, advocated by Huston Smith and Aldous Huxley, as a nondualistic thought system to facilitate the practice of your own form of Christian jnana yoga.

Since the Course does not specify what forms can assist in spiritual growth, this is left up to the individual's guidance received through calling upon the Holy Spirit. Miracle Yoga is for those Course students who are guided by the Holy Spirit to use the forms of yoga that help them make spiritual progress. In addition to applying Miracle Jnana Yoga, the path of Miracle Yoga includes *Miracle Raja Yoga*, involving meditation practices, *Miracle Bhakti Yoga*, expressing love, and *Miracle Karma Yoga*, based on service to others. The Course philosophy has a unique affect on how each of these forms of Miracle Yoga is expressed. For instance, Miracle Karma Yoga in the form of selfless service is similar to both traditional Hindu karma yoga and Christian karma yoga, as is described in Chapter 5, but with one distinct difference. Other forms of karma yoga are based on the idea that there is a law of karmic retribution—a divine accounting system, saying we must face the good and bad fruits of our actions. Miracle Karma Yoga affirms the idea of cause and effect, yet is based on the unusual Course idea that God does not believe in karmic retribution. According to the Course, karmic retribution is entirely self-imposed, and not determined by God, Who only forgives. This different outlook on karma is described in Chapter 70 and elaborated upon in Appendix G, "A New Look at Karma."

Unlike the four forms of Miracle Yoga already mentioned, there is a fifth category that does not correspond to any type of traditional Hindu yoga. This distinctive form of Miracle Yoga is called *Miracle Relationship Yoga*, which includes the expression of holy relationships, described in the Course as the joining of two people in a common purpose. Miracle Relationship Yoga also emphasizes that all of our relationships, whether casual or long term, are opportunities to recognize that we are already joined with all of our brothers and sisters in Christ and in God right now and forever.

Naturally Miracle Yoga would include all of the basic hatha yoga body postures and breathing practices, which are actually part of Miracle Raja Yoga as a preparation for being able to sit still for meditation. The ideal for a balanced approach would be to practice a combination of all the various forms of Miracle Yoga mentioned above, although one or more of these may receive greater emphasis depending upon the natural inclinations of the seeker. I have already written but not yet published a book called, *Miracle Yoga for Living in Christ*, which will provide instruction in how to practice hatha yoga and the various forms of Miracle Yoga.

I have established *Miracle Yoga Services* to provide an educational and spiritual foundation for advocating the practices of yoga and the Course as a means of following Christ. To start any new organization requires three things—a good idea, initiative, and friends. Miracle Yoga based on the Course is a good idea. My initiative has been writing my books, but some form of initiative will have to come from friends. The involvement of friends is especially important for this organization so its foundation can rest on holy relationships of people with common interests and a common purpose of combining yoga, Christ, and the Course.

Miracle Yoga Services will have at least potentially four phases, which could overlap. The first of these emphasizes publishing. Right now I am called to be a teacher functioning as a writer, and I am content with that because it gives me time for solitude. I have written four new books, but only this autobiography is published. I am not what might be called a "natural writer"—in other words, I am not technically skilled in the art of putting words together. I certainly have benefited by the help of others in making my writing more concise and presentable. In fact, I am seeking a new editor, especially a copy editor. I am not expecting to find an entirely voluntary editor, but am hoping to find one who is open to the Course philosophy. I am also looking for volunteers to catch obvious errors through doing proof reading, which does not require professional experience. My only writing virtues are clarity and the message itself that I have to share. For years I thought of myself as an artist because visual expression was where I had the most natural talent, so it still seems a bit strange for me to think of myself as a writer. Fortunately I had an English teacher in high school who told me many years ago that a writer is simply someone who has something worthwhile to say and an inner impulse to communicate that message to others. On that count I can accept my role as a writer.

My picture of the world is that there are many people who want to be kind and express love and find happiness through serving God, but are confused about how to do that. This confusion comes from all the seeming contradicts presented in life. There is a bombardment of information coming at us from all directions—the television, newspapers, movies, and the ever-consuming internet. It is a bewildering mixed message pulling us in a thousand different directions seeking our attention and allegiance. In this context everything in our lives becomes reduced to an eclectic collection of sound bites—with God becoming just one of these sound bites. My mission as a writer is to cut through all the chatter of frenetic information and to communicate as clearly as I can what people want to know and indeed need to know to make sense out of the world. It is simply the message of God's Love for us. If we can accept His Love on a daily basis, then everything else in our lives will fall into place. Although there are certainly numerous ways to open up to God's Love, as a writer, I can only speak with conviction about what has worked for me. That's why I offer the practice of Miracle Yoga as an option for those who are drawn to this way of making God's Presence and Love the central focus of life.

Because Miracle Yoga is an internalization of Christ, it involves a turning inward to find the divine within, which is very personal and often private. However, since Miracle Yoga is also an externalization of Christ there is a need for communion in which like-minded parts of Christ come together. The second phase of the Miracle Yoga Services will emphasize internet communication. I currently take messages at miracleyoga@gmail.com, and I have the domain name *miracleyoga.org* set aside for a future website. At this future website, with the help of others, I hope to establish a social network to provide a meeting place for joining in consciously living in Christ. A Miracle Yoga social network could provide a useful service for those who want to study the Course, extend love, provide selfless service to others, turn within for meditation, practice yoga postures and breathing practices, and join in holy relationships for a common purpose. The internet has the great advantage of being able to contact seekers all over the world and to link them up in consciousness to overcome the illusion of separation that the three dimensional world perpetuates.

I feel certain the publishing phase and the internet phase are part of God's Plan for Miracle Yoga Services. I am hopeful there will be two more phases, but that possibility will depend on the interest of others and, of course, God's Will. Potentially the third phase would be the formation of a *Miracle Yoga House of Prayer*, which would be a small household of dedicated people living together to practice Miracle Yoga. The focus would be on bonding together through meditation and extending to others through prayer. In addition to being the scribe for the Course, Helen Schucman brought forth *The Song of Prayer*. This short pamphlet explains that prayer can be more than making specific requests of God. The term *true prayer* is used to describe this higher level of prayer that allows us to open up to Christ within ourselves and to Christ within others.

Prayer is a stepping aside; a letting go, a quiet time of listening and loving. It should not be confused with supplication of any kind, because it is a way of remembering your holiness. Why should holiness entreat, being fully entitled to everything Love has to offer? And it is to Love you go in prayer. Prayer is an offering; a giving up of yourself to be at one with Love. There is nothing to ask because there is nothing left to want.[7]

After this prayer group bonds together in a holy relationship in this third phase, the fourth phase of Miracle Yoga Services would be for this core group to provide direct instruction—person to person, face to face, heart to heart. This phase would involve establishing a physical location, a *Miracle Yoga Center*, where yoga practices based on the spiritual principles of the Course could be taught. Similar to the Course itself, Miracle Yoga does not require joining any organization to practice it, because it is a philosophy and way of life open to anyone. Nevertheless, some sort of physical location would be helpful in providing learning aids and encouragement for practicing Miracle Yoga. It could serve as a meeting place for classes, workshops, and lectures. Because of my past life in India, I still feel a kinship with the homeland of yoga, even though I have never been there in this lifetime. One day I hope to see a *Miracle Yoga Ashram* become established in India. After all, since Miracle Yoga is an offspring of the marriage of the Eastern and Western spiritual traditions, it is only right for it to be represented in both the East and West.

At some point hopefully Miracle Yoga meditation retreats could be held in which small groups of people could devote themselves to practicing forms of inner attunement for five or six days and then return to their regular everyday lives after having been spiritually revitalized. If I am in the role of a teacher on such retreats, I would be willing to accept students just for those brief time periods. Very temporary student and teacher relationships are ideal in my opinion because short-term arrangements avoid the possibility of attachments by either the teacher or student. Long term teacher and student relationships would have to be limited in number because I don't think I could be an effective teacher if I have too many students. Besides, from the Course's perspective the goal of the student and teacher relationship is to facilitate temporary learning opportunities so the student can become a teacher of God himself. Thomas Merton felt that the sacred role of the spiritual teacher was to help others to open themselves to God's Love and reach divine union with Him. According to Merton, this direct sharing of spiritual teachings is a function that will and must persist. Describing this sacred function, he wrote, "It is imperishable. It represents an instinct of the human heart, and it represents a charism [meaning grace] given by God to man. It cannot be rooted out, because it does not depend on man. It does not depend on cultural factors, and it does not depend on sociological or psychological factors. It is something much deeper."[8]

If I do become a teacher with students, I don't want to fall into the trap that I have seen so many gurus fall into of creating an idealized self-image that would be impossible to live up to. Along these lines I have no interest in pretending to be a spiritual master or even a perfect example of spiritual living. After all, Christian seekers already have a spiritual master in the person and presence of Jesus, and He provided a perfect example of spiritual living. I rely on Jesus as my own personal teacher and likewise on the Holy Spirit as the Teacher of Teachers. My role as an advocate of Miracle Yoga is to encourage others to similarly rely on these same teachers. Unlike the guru role of being the authority figure, my role in Miracle Yoga is to share with others what I have learned from a position of equality. My purpose is to see Christ in everyone and to let my students, as my equals in Christ, teach me to appreciate God's presence in everyone. I will teach love, because love is what I need to learn, and my students will be my teachers in learning how to love.

The student and teacher relationship is a holy relationship with the common goal of learning for both. We will probably have only a few lifelong holy relationships and I believe these are rejoinings of souls who have had previous lives together. The idea of reincarnation is controversial, especially for Christians. Although the Course does not recommend teaching reincarnation, it does not totally discount the belief in past lives either, because both students who believe and students who do not believe in reincarnation can benefit by applying the principles of the Course. This seemingly contradictory approach to reincarnation is addressed in Appendix F, "Reincarnation," for your consideration.

---

1. Luke 23:34, RSV.

2. Luke 23:46, RSV.

3. Thomas Keating, *Open Mind, Open Heart: The Contemplative Dimension of the Gospel* (New York: The Continuum International Publishing Group, 2001), Copyright 1986, 1992 by St. Benedict's Monastery, p. 10.

4. Ibid, p. 10.

5. Ibid, p. 11.

6. Ibid, p. 29.

7. Helen Schucman as scribe, *The Song of Prayer: Prayer, Forgiveness, Healing—An Extension of the Principles of "A Course in Miracles,"* Published by the Foundation for Inner Peace, P. O. Box 598, Mill Valley, CA 94942, © 1978, 1992 by the Foundation of Inner Peace, S-1.I.5:1-6, p. 17.

8. Thomas Merton, *Asian Journal,* (New York: New Directions, 1973), "Marxism and Monastic Perspectives," pp. 326-343.

THOMAS MERTON IN 1949 AT AGE 34

68

A MONK IN THE WORLD

≈ • ≈

According to the yoga tradition of Hinduism the student's role is one of four stages in life. The four stages are the student, householder (married life), retired person, and ascetic. The first three are chronological steps that affirm the natural cycle of life. The ascetic life may be entered upon at any time, but often occurs later in life. It is a leaving of the responsibilities of life to become a monk or *sannyasin*, often a wandering hermit. The goal of the ascetic is to let go of attachment to the world in order to prepare for *moksha*, freedom from this world.

This concept of giving up of the world is not my idea of what it means to be a monk. One of my goals in writing this book is to share that any man or woman involved in the world can remain in the world and still become a monk. In particular, I want to show that being a monk is not necessarily limited to living in a monastery or living in seclusion as a hermit or even being part of an organization that authorizes the monastic vocation. That's not to say that I don't honor and respect those many sincere monks who have committed their lives to an established religious order. I have already described the encounters I have had in my young adult life with the Benedictine monk Brother David Steindl-Rast. My personal contact with him, though very limited, has been an ongoing encouragement and inspiration for me throughout the years. I found reading Brother David's book *Gratefulness, the Heart of Prayer* to be especially uplifting.[1] Likewise I have been inspired by the example and writings of the Trappist monk Thomas Merton. Part of my attraction to these two monks is that they have both sought to bridge the gap between the East and West. Brother David is now in his eighties and is still dividing his time between being a hermit and traveling around the world linking up with seekers from other Christian and non-Christian traditions and sharing his message of universal love.

Since I have already elaborated on my contacts with Brother David, I would now like to share more fully why Thomas Merton's life and teachings have been so meaningful for me. Although I no longer identify with Catholic dogma, I can still appreciate Merton's approach to spirituality, which remains truly universal (the literal meaning of the word "catholic").

I was impressed with the simplicity and the clarity that I found in Merton's writing, and which can even be seen in the appearance of his face, especially in his eyes, in the photograph of him on page 708. This photograph was taken around the time that *The Seven Storey Mountain*, Merton's autobiography, was first published in 1949 after he had been at Gethsemani for seven years.[2] The only time he took an overseas trip away from his monastery was a journey to Asia to connect with other seekers. In anticipation of his trip, Merton had written in his journal that he hoped the visit to the East might nurture his own spiritual seeking. He participated in the "Spiritual Summit Conference" in Calcutta, India. At the conference fostering religious unity through open dialogue, Merton spoke of the kind of oneness that could not be obtained merely at the level of verbal exchanges.

> The deepest level of communication is not communication, but communion. It is wordless. It is beyond words, and it is beyond speech, and it is beyond concept. Not that we discover a new unity. We discover an older unity. My dear brothers, we are already one. But we imagine that we are not. What we have to recover is our original unity. What we have to be is what we are.[3]

After the conference he was invited to New Delhi to visit with the Dali Lama. On his journey Merton was shown the Tibetan use of the *mandala* as a means of meditation and received an explanation of the Dzogenchen (the Great Way of All-Inclusiveness). He also was pleased to discover that the Tibetan word for monk was *Trapas*, which just coincidentally happened to sound similar to Trappist. On the second of his three meetings with the Dali Lama, they discussed meditation. Merton stressed the importance of monks being "living examples of the freedom and transformation of consciousness which meditation can give."[4] From the lamas he met he learned that they favored solitude but not absolute solitude. Their primary concern was developing compassion, and they saw solitude as a healthy foundation for then reaching out to others. Merton wrote that the Dali Lama "insists on detachment, on an 'unworldly life,' yet sees it as a way to complete understanding of, and participation in, the problems of life and the world."[5] Well aware of the balance between solitude and social extension, Merton was impressed with the Dali Lama and felt that in him he had met a kindred spirit.

While visiting in Darjeeling, India, Merton expressed reservations about the current direction of Western spirituality, stating, "We need the religious genius of Asia and Asian culture to inject a fresh dimension of depth into our aimless thrashing about. I would almost say an element of heart, of *bhakti*, of love."[6]

After making numerous stops along the way, Merton finally arrived in Bangkok, Thailand to attend the conference that had prompted the trip in the first place. Earlier in his journey Merton had met an exiled Tibetan lama, Chogyam Trungpa Rimpoche, who had told him stories about fleeing from the Chinese Communist troops. Remembering these stories while giving a lecture at the conference, Merton told one about a Buddhist abbot escaping from the Chinese Red Army. While on his way to the border, the abbot came across another monk. But this monk was being slowed down because he traveled with twenty-five yaks carrying what he considered "necessary" provisions along with the "all-important" treasures of the monastery. Leaving the monk with his treasures, the abbot pressed on ahead with the advantage of traveling lightly. He finally reached the safety of India without any treasure except for the preservation of his life. The slow-moving monk was still clinging to his yaks and the treasure when he was captured. He learned his lesson of what's truly important in a monk's life the hard way, and it was the last lesson he would learn.

Merton challenged his listeners to learn the lesson of the story by saying, "We can ask ourselves if we are planning for the next twenty years to be travelling with a train of yaks." He concluded that monasticism is "total inner transformation. Let the yaks take care of themselves."[7]

In Merton's story he was articulating what has been for me personally the most significant theme of his teachings, which is summarized in his frequent references in prior years to the prophet Jonas and the whale. Because of my background working in the field of developmentally disabilities, I was pleased to hear that Merton had received drawings by developmentally disabled children, and some of them displayed Jonas inside the whale. Merton felt these drawings were the only authentic works of art he had encountered since coming to Gethsemani. From Merton's perspective Jonas, emerging from the whale was the symbolic uncovering of the true self. This idea that there is a real self or, more accurately, a real *Self* within us waiting for our recognition of the Truth is a distinctively Eastern concept. Yet for Merton, being a Christian, the true self is found in Christ, the ideal of the West. Jonas represents the true self. The whale has swallowed up Jonas and so he is immersed in the ocean. Consequently, for Merton the whale stands for our jobs, our successes, our failures, our illusions, and whatever we associate with our outer identities. Thus the whale is all that is keeping us from revealing the true self. "Many … baptized in Christ have risen from the depths without troubling to find out the difference between Jonas and the whale. It is the whale we cherish. Jonas swims abandoned in the heart of the sea …. We must get Jonas out of the whale."[8] Obviously the yak-herding monk was one of those seekers who was clinging to the whale, while failing to pay attention to Jonas.

In his lecture Merton said that the function of the monk is to be one "who seeks full realization ... [of his true self and] has come to experience the ground of his own being in such a way that he knows the secret of liberation and can somehow or other communicate it to others."[9] Although Merton sought his true self in Christ, he felt a respect and certainly a fellowship with other seekers who were likewise seeking their realization of the true self in their own distinctive traditions.

At the time of his Asian journey, Merton had felt that his days of living exclusively at Gethsemani were coming to an end. Three years before he had been given permission to have his own hermitage on the grounds of the monastery. Nonetheless, he pondered options for finding a new place to live in order to fully express his spiritual destiny. A new abbot had been installed at Gethsemani, and he was more open than the previous one to Merton pursuing his spiritual yearning. Merton's desire was to manifest a paradox. I would use the term "travelling hermit" to describe this paradox of going inward to find the true self and extending outward into the world as well. While on this trip, he wrote to the new abbot, "The important thing for me is not acquiring land or finding an ideal solitude but opening up the depths of my own heart. The rest is secondary."[10]

As it turned out, Merton was right about his intuitive feeling that he would no longer be limited to the confines of Gethsemani and also right about finding a new place that would help him to let Jonas emerge from the limitations of being inside the whale. However, his longing to find a new place of transformation was finally satisfied by quite an unexpected, even astounding, turn of events.

Merton ended his conference lecture by saying, "So I will disappear." The lecture was given in the morning of December 10, 1968, and there was a follow-up evening session that was also scheduled. On that same day in the middle of the afternoon, his lifeless body was found in his room lying on the floor. The room had the smell of burnt flesh. A five-foot standing fan had fallen and was lying diagonally across his body. One of the people who had come into the room attempted to lift the fan and received an electric shock so he could not let go of the metal shaft of the fan. He might have ended up like Merton if it had not been for another person in the room pulling the plug. A police test determined that there was a faulty electric cord inside the stand of the fan that caused Merton to pass away with his body being burnt due to electrical shock. His autobiography referred to men being drawn closer to Christ after first being *burnt* by the world. The prophetic last words of Merton's life story were, "That you may become the brother of God and learn to know the Christ of the burnt men."[11]

Learning about the death of Merton by electrocution when he was 53 years old reminded me of the unusual experience I had of feeling as though

I was being electrocuted, which was described in Chapter 6. It was a bizarre kundalini experience in which I felt electric-like energy flash through my body. After that experience I felt that there is some sort of connection between electricity and the kundalini rising. Also I believe that when a person dies, the life-force of the kundalini locked into the base of the spine rises up fully and ideally leaves the body through the top of the head. This final and full rising of the kundalini is the seeker's best opportunity to become fully enlightened and wake up in the Arms of God. Electrocution from our worldly perspective may seem like a terrible way to exit the world, but I believe there may have been a grace in it that helped facilitate the rising of the kundalini. Of course, this is only conjecture on my part. Nevertheless, I believe Merton fully awakened to his true self in Christ. Merton took the traveling hermit's ultimate solitary journey leading to the celebration of joining with others in the divine communion of heaven.

At the time of his passing, Merton had with him a card inserted in his breviary[12] showing an icon of Mother Mary and the child Jesus. On the back of the card Merton had written a quotation by an early Christian ascetic, John Carpathios. The words were meaningful to Merton because they served as a reminder of how to approach God. Thus these words prepared him for his last journey, in which, in my opinion, he fully revealed Jonas and finally let go of the whale forever:

> If we wish to please the true God and to be friends with the most blessed of friendships, let us present our spirit naked to God. Let us not draw into it anything of this present world—no art, no thought, no reasoning, no-self justification—even though we should possess all the wisdom of this world.[13]

Since Merton's death happened on his Asian journey, it could be said that he quite literally gave his life in the effort to build a spiritual bridge of understanding between the East and West. His interest in extending his friendship, teachings, and life beyond the limits of Gethsemani was something that Merton had not anticipated when he initially considered becoming a monk. For the first seventeen years of living in the monastery, Merton was under the assumption that living a life of sanctity required a radical separation from the world. But then something happened to alter Merton's thinking, opening his mind to a truly universal outlook.

First he had a dream in 1958 about a young Jewish girl who embraced him with pure affection, which in turn greatly moved Merton to the depths of his soul. He discovered that her name was "Proverb," but she seemed to be ashamed of her name because she was mocked by others. Merton told her that her name was beautiful, and then the dream ended. Several weeks later, he had an experience that he felt was connected to the dream of Proverb. He was required to leave his monastery for an editorial errand in Louisville, Kentucky, and he recorded his experience in his journal:

> [I was] walking alone in the crowded street and suddenly saw that everybody was Proverb and that in all of them shone her extraordinary beauty and purity and shyness, even though they did not know who they were and were perhaps ashamed of their names because they were mocked on account of them. And they did not know their real identity as the Child so dear to God who, from before the beginning, was playing in His sight all days, playing in the world.[14]

Later, while writing his book *Conjectures of a Guilty Bystander*, Merton used his experience on the streets of Louisville as a basis for the following excerpt:

> In Louisville ... I was suddenly overwhelmed with the realization that I loved all those people, that they were mine and I theirs, that we could not be alien to one another even though we were total strangers. It was like waking from a dream of separateness, of spurious self-isolation in a special world, the world of renunciation and supposed holiness. The whole illusion of a separate holy existence is a dream.... This sense of liberation from an illusory difference was such a relief and such a joy to me that I almost laughed out loud.... It is a glorious destiny to be a member of the human race.... To think that such a commonplace realization should suddenly seem like news that one holds the winning ticket in a cosmic sweepstakes.... There is no way of telling people that they are all walking around shining like the sun....There are no strangers! ... If only we could see each other [as we really are] all the time. There would be no more war, no more hatred, no more cruelty, no more greed.... I suppose the big problem would be that we would fall down and worship each other.... The gate of heaven is everywhere.[15]

Merton acknowledged above that living in self-imposed isolation by being immersed in "the world of renunciation and supposed holiness" was not the only way to live a life of holiness. Holiness is not something that can be purchased at the price of choosing to live in a special and separate place apart from others. Rather holiness is innately within the true nature of everyone all the time. A typical Catholic believes the wisdom of the world that maintains there are guilty sinners who do not repent, there are guilty sinners who repent, and there are those few who can be called "holy," because through God's grace they have limited their guilt and sin to a minimum level. Nonetheless, Merton was not a typical Catholic and that is why he is so appealing to me. He pushed the envelope in his search for the truth, and he was surprised by what he discovered about holiness. He realized that holiness was in everyone everywhere in the world, ready to be seen by anyone who has eyes to see it. Merton's comment in the previous quote that if we saw our brothers' true holiness "we would fall down and worship each other" reminds me of the Course perspective on seeing the reality of holiness in others. The following Course quotation describes how we can potentially use the vision that comes from Christ to see with the eyes of love:

> This do the body's eyes behold in one whom Heaven cherishes, the angels love and God created perfect. This is his reality. And in Christ's vision is his loveliness reflected in a form so holy and so beautiful that you could scarce refrain from kneeling at his feet. Yet you will take his hand instead, for you are like him in the sight that sees him thus.[16]

In 1965 when Merton was giving his final talk as the Master of Novices, he encouraged the novices to see the divine presence in others and everywhere in the world:

> Life is simple. We are living in a world that is absolutely transparent and God is shining through it all the time. This is not just a fable or a nice story. It is true. If we abandon ourselves to God and forget ourselves, we see it sometimes, and we see it maybe frequently. God manifests Himself everywhere, in everything—in people and in things and in nature and in events. It becomes very obvious that He is everywhere and in everything and we cannot be without Him. You cannot be without God. It's impossible.[17]

Merton could speak with conviction because of his own experience of the divine presence, but his challenge was to continue to recognize on a daily basis the inherent holiness in others that he had first seen on the streets of Louisville. With his initial recognition in 1958 that holiness can be found everywhere, he might have asked himself the question, "Why stay in a monastery?" Nevertheless, Merton's realization of holiness being everywhere and in everyone did not encourage him to give up his monastic vocation or his growing interest in becoming a hermit. However, his new understanding did transform his inner sense of what it meant to be a monk. His biographer, Jim Forest, summarized Merton's new awareness in this way: "...authentic solitude must be a place both of nonpresence and attendance, nonparticipation and engagement, hiddenness and hospitality, disappearance and arrival."[18] The monk must learn to live with these opposites and integrate them within himself, or more correctly, within himself in Christ. After this opening of understanding Merton significantly expanded his interests and contacts with others outside the monastery.

When Merton first considered his spiritual vocation, he felt he had only two options. One was to live in the world and not be a monk. The other option was to become a monk by choosing to join an officially recognized monastic order. Merton did not consider a third option—the alternative of becoming a monk in the world. I would like others to know that this third option is available. I believe my life has followed a pattern that others could possibly follow in this regard. Of course, there are many ways to dedicate your life to God without specifically taking on the role of a monk. However, if you feel you are being guided to become a Christian monk in the world, you may want to consider these potential guidelines:

GUIDELINES FOR BEING A MONK IN THE WORLD

1. Vow directly to God to become His monk.
2. Dedicate yourself to expressing God's Will.
3. Open your mind to the influence and guidance of the Holy Spirit.
4. Open your heart to the love and help of Jesus.
5. Set aside at least one time each day for devotion and meditation.
6. Make a commitment to celibacy, involving retaining sexual fluids.
7. Practice some way of serving your brothers and sisters.

You can be a monk and practice Christian yoga or Miracle Yoga, but that is not a requirement for being a monk. The seven recommendations noted above for being a monk in the world can be practiced by anyone belonging to any Christian church or no Christian denomination. Being a celibate monk does not mean giving up loving relationships or even setting aside marriage. The monk is married to God. And since he is in a love relationship with God, he is in a love relationship with all of God's creations—including all of his brothers and sisters in whom he sees the face of Christ. In this sense, he is not doing something new or unique. He is merely recognizing and accepting again what has always been eternally true and what will be forever his rightful place in the kingdom of God.

I have made it clear that a monk in the world can have any church or other religious affiliation or can have no such affiliation. But if you want to be a Christian monk, it is important to have a Christian philosophy that will help you to function in that role. In this regard I believe practicing Christian yoga can be very helpful in providing structure for your spiritual practices. Yoga disciplines help to raise energy in the body for spiritual purposes, which in turn help the monk to see celibacy as a blessing and not a sacrifice. In addition, I encourage the monk in the world who is open to the Course to practice Miracle Yoga, because this way of life provides a balance of meditation, understanding, love, service, and holy relationships. The Course philosophy helps the monk to look past the appearances of guilt everywhere in the world, and instead enables the monk to see the world through the eyes of forgiveness perceiving holiness in everyone. The next chapter, "True Forgiveness," will elaborate upon the ability to focus on the presence of holiness in the world.

Since the monk in the world makes a "vow" to God, this concept needs clarification. A vow means a commitment, but it is contingent entirely on God's Will for him. He makes such a vow only because he feels God is leading him in this direction. Nevertheless, if at some future date God should guide him in another direction, then he would need to make changes accordingly. For example, he may be called to be a monk for only a certain amount of time. Hypothetically God may unexpectedly (without his conscious seeking) bring into his life another person as his marriage partner. The point is that the vow is always a commitment to doing God's Will wherever that leads. And that is always a dedication to opening the heart to divine love since God's Will is always the will of His Love. Merton expressed this well in saying, "The life of the soul is not knowledge, it is love, since love is the act of the supreme faculty, the will, by which man is formally united to the final end of all his striving—by which man becomes one with God."[19] This love is not only the monk's goal. It is ultimately the goal of every seeker from every creed.

Because monks set aside the sexual impulse, they are sometimes looked upon as being passionless people. Nothing could be further from the truth. There is no deeper or more compelling passion than God's Love for His children and His children's love for Him. This intoxicating love is the secret delight of a monk who through inner communion has learned to channel his life force upward to its divine Source. Not every monk will reach the heights of divine love, but it is the vocation of every monk to know at least by faith that he lives in the ocean of God's Love. Thus he is challenged to live accordingly. Hopefully he will become an increasingly clear mirror, reflecting his divine Source. Even the monk who is not a clear reflection can still fulfill his function by dedicating his life in the everyday world to doing God's Will of Love to the best of his ability. We can, of course, do God's Will without necessarily being a monk. So why does a man become a monk? Because giving his life to God as a monk makes his heart sing like no other vocation.

The monk in the world, who may be a man or woman, lives a simple, humble, and ordinary life—inwardly pervaded by dedication and devotion to God and outwardly committed to loving his brothers and sisters in Christ. He does not offer unsolicited preaching of peace to others, but just focuses on remaining at peace himself. He still makes mistakes when he loses his peace, yet corrects himself by forgiving others and himself through opening up to the Love of God. Such a monk can blend into everyday life without even being noticed by others. In the monk's very ordinariness he becomes extraordinary in our Western society obsessed with striving for specialness.

---

1. More about Brother David can be found on his website gratefulness.org. His photograph in Chapter 7 was made available through the courtesy of this website.

2. Merton's photograph displayed through the permission of the Abbey of Gethsemani.

3. Ibid., pp. 307-308, also see pp. 315-317.

4. Ibid., p 112.

5. Ibid., p. 113.

6. From a tape transcribed by Brother Patrick Hart.

7. Thomas Merton, *Asian Journal*, (New York: New Directions, 1973), "Marxism and Monastic Perspectives," pp. 561-568.

8. Ibid., pp. 326-343.

9. Ibid., pp. 326-343.

10. Thomas Merton's letter to Dom Flavian Burns, October 9, 1968; included in *The School of Charity: The Letters of Thomas Merton on Religious Renewal and Spiritual Direction*, edited by Brother Patrick Hart, (New York: Farrar Straus and Giroux, 1990), p. 402.

11. Thomas Merton, *The Seven Storey Mountain*, (New York: A Harvest Book, [first published in 1948] 1999), p. 462.

12. A breviary is a book containing the prayers for the canonical hours.

13. E. Kadloubovsky and G. E. H. Palmer, translators, *Writings from the Philokalia on Prayer of the Heart*, translated from the Russian text, 'Dobrotolubiye,' (London: Faber and Faber Ltd., [1951]1971, 1975) (also reprinted in 1992). This is one of three volumes of the Philokalia printed in English by Faber and Faber Ltd. This quotation was hand written in Greek by Merton and had apparently been copied from the original Greek version of the Philokalia.

14. Thomas Merton and Boris Pasternak, *Six Letters*, intro. Lydia Pasternak Slater, (Lexington Kentucky: The King Library Press, 1973), letter dated October 23, 1960.

15. Thomas Merton, *Conjectures of a Guilty Bystander*, (New York: Doubleday and Co., 1966), pp. 140-142.

16. W-161, 9:1-4, p. 305, (p. 298).

17. Thomas Merton, cassette tape, *Life and Solitude*, side B, "Hermit's Legacy: Life Without Care" (Electric Paperbacks).

18. Jim Forest, *Living with Wisdom: A Life of Thomas Merton*, (New York: Orbis Books, 1991), p. 123.

19. Thomas Merton, *The Seven Storey Mountain*, (New York: A Harvest Book, [first published in 1948] 1999), p. 209.

69

TRUE FORGIVENESS

~ ◦ ~

I would like to begin this chapter with one more conversation I had with Allan Greene. I told Allan, "I heard a great story called, 'The King's Gem.' It's about a king who had a very large and beautiful gem, but he discovered upon close inspection that there was a straight line flaw right on the flat part of the gem. The king asked his advisors if anything could be done to correct the problem, yet they could give no answer. However, a wise man stepped forward and said he could provide a solution if the king gave him the gem for a day. The king agreed, and the next day the wise man returned and handed the gem to the king. When the king examined the gem, he saw two leaves etched on the sides of the flaw and at the end of the flaw there was a beautiful rose inscribed. The king was pleased with the solution. Isn't that a wonderful story of how to change errors into blessings?"

Allan responded, "That's a nice story. I can think of another way of telling the story. Would you like to hear my version?"

"Sure, let's hear it."

"The story is exactly the same except the wise man is a *holy* man, and he also took the gem and returned the next day. When the holy man returned, he said to the king, "Before I give you the gem, I would like you and I to pray together and thank God for the healing that has been given." The king agreed. After their prayer time, the holy man gave the gem to the king, who exclaimed, 'There is no flaw in the gem! How did you take the flaw out of the gem?'

"The holy man said, 'I didn't take the flaw out of the gem. You and I just gave thanks for a divine healing. It was for your healing, since *the flaw was in your mind*. You see, the gem was always perfect,'" Allan said. "That's my version. Do you see the moral to my story?"

I answered, "You are saying that when we see flaws in other people, the flaw is within our own minds. The flaw in ourselves is to project guilt by seeing flaws in others, while being in denial of that projection. Thus the way to let go of seeing flaws in others is through forgiveness. Forgiveness allows us to withdraw our projections, so we do not perceive others as being flawed. Forgiveness enables us to see the flawless Christ in our brothers and sisters, by letting go of our illusions about them."

"Congratulations! I see your Course studies have paid off in helping you understand forgiveness," Allan said.

I had learned the Course principles relate to forgiveness, but my more important goal was to apply that intellectual understanding in a practical way in my relationships, and it is still my goal. I learned from the Course that it is a contradiction to think you can give forgiveness to someone and still hold resentment in your own mind. This contradiction says, "You are guilty of wronging me and not worthy of love, but I will forgive you anyway." Yet God sees all of His beloved children as being equally worthy of love, and therefore worthy of forgiveness. Traditional forgiveness holds no gift for you—only a gift for the one you are forgiving—a gift given condescendingly to one who is still seen as guilty of being the transgressor.

However, real forgiveness offers you the gift of healing your own mind along with the mind of your brother. How you see others is a mirror for how you will see yourself. You can choose to see guilt or holiness in everyone you meet. If you choose to see others flawed with guilt, you will yourself feel you are indelibly stained with guilt. If you choose to apply forgiveness and see others as flawless and holy children of God, you will yourself feel you are flawless and holy as a child of God. So applying forgiveness frees others from your limiting perceptions and frees your own mind from the same limiting perceptions. Forgiveness allows you to see the one you forgive, no longer as a lowly transgressor, but as your equal in the perfection of Christ. This heals your mind and your brother's mind in what is called a *miracle*. That's why *A Course in Miracles* is actually a *course in forgiveness*.

True forgiveness advocated by the Course is the letting go of the perception of separation, which produces healing, allowing you to see your equality with your brothers in Christ.[1] When I first tried to forgive Allan, I was feeling he was not worthy of love because he had caused my torture and death in my past life as Pole Man. At that time I felt separate from Allan because I was looking upon him in a condescending way, and so I couldn't release my resentment toward him. But studying the Course helped me to accept my equality with Allan in Christ. I realized all my perceptions of separation were only illusions in my mind. Consequently, I was finally able through the Course to forgive Allan, which was really a letting go of my illusions about him that said he was not worthy of love. What I was really doing was withdrawing all the guilt I had formerly projected onto him in order to recognize the divine in him. Through my forgiveness I was giving him the gift of seeing him as the Christ that he truly is, and I was giving myself the same gift of accepting my own nature in Christ. This was produced by healing my mind through letting go of my perception of separation from him, since he and I are joined in Christ where we are one.

Just because I had forgiven Allan did not mean I had learned everything there was to learn about forgiveness—far from it. I would still have to discover how to see errors of others or even my own errors as blocks to the awareness of love's presence. I would have to learn how to look past these blocks right in the beginning to prevent them from getting a foothold in my mind. I would still have to grow in the direction of seeing every person in every situation through the eyes of forgiveness. That would take me a very long time and I am still working on that one.

As this book nears its conclusion, I want to emphasize the culmination of my experience of forgiveness with Allan Greene because it is such a good example of learning how to apply Course principles. Subsequently I would have many opportunities to learn the lessons of forgiveness in my ongoing and future new relationships. These are recorded in a sequel, providing a continuation of this autobiography. The rest of my life from my experience with Allan onward would be increasingly focused on Course principles, including the practical application of forgiveness. My future learning would focus on learning how to deepen my understanding of forgiveness so I could see every relationship as a means of letting go of the perception of separation. I studied the Course and internalized its lessons, so I was focused on oneness with by brother and oneness with Christ.

Instead of sharing my life in one book as would usually be the case, I have written two separate books to present different orientations and, therefore, two different options for the reader. This book you are reading now includes mostly concrete events and introduces some basic spiritual principles. It also focuses on my purpose of being an example and teacher of Christian yoga, and specifically Miracle Yoga, as was summarized in the Chapter 67. The second book, already written, but not yet published, will be titled, *My Miracle Yoga Life in Christ*. I have decided to use the words "Miracle Yoga" in the title instead of "Christian Yoga" to alert potential readers in advance that the Course principles, especially forgiveness, will be emphasized. My life experiences have provided a personalized course in miracles for me, showing me God's immanent presence within the world and God's transcendent reality beyond the world. This continuation of my autobiography is presented as a way for the reader to learn much more about the principles of *A Course in Miracles* in the framework of my attempts to live out these principles in my response to the events of my everyday life.

As a continuation of *Memory Walk in the Light*, my next book will begin where this first autobiographical book leaves off, in 1995, when I had lived fifty years. This sequel will still be a narration of very important concrete events. New pieces of my shadow puzzle, as well as more of the identity puzzle of my life as a whole, would be uncovered and bring new insights. For example, more about Pole Man would be surprisingly revealed. I would make some extremely poor and embarrassing choices. Nevertheless, these mistakes would become steppingstones to learning important lessons. I would make progress in letting go of my victim consciousness. I would resign from the board of the Circle of Atonement and by mutual agreement the New Jerusalem community would run its course to an unexpected disbanding, but the loving relationships that had been built would remain intact. I would continue to see light visually in people and in objects, and surprisingly would be able to help some friends discover that they have the ability to see light visually as well. Yet all these concrete experiences have been written as they were perceived by me through the lens of the Course.

Whereas the first book introduces some Course principles, the sequel will provide an opportunity for the open-minded seeker to take a much deeper look at these spiritual principles and their application to daily life experiences. I recommend this continuation of my autobiography for the reader who would like to read more about my life in the context of Course principles, such as forgiveness. Forgiveness, the central teaching of the Course, is the means of letting go of fear:

> Forgiveness is the means by which the fear of death is overcome, because it holds no fierce attraction now and guilt is gone. Forgiveness lets the body be perceived as what it is; a simple teaching aid, to be laid by when learning is complete, but hardly changing him who learns at all.[2]

Forgiveness is needed to accept the divine within, because it enables us to see through the illusion of a concrete body to perceive the light of our true nature in Christ shining through. But it would take me a long time to eventually understand forgiveness and learn to apply it consistently. My peak experience of Light described in this book was the seminal moment of my life. This experience of spirit was overpowering and compelling, but did not fit into any perceptual framework that would enable me to explain it to anyone. In fact, I could not adequately understand it perceptually myself at the time that it happened. The experience of Light showed me the final destination, which I am going to one day reach again, but did not show me how to get there. I would have to learn that forgiveness is my means of navigating in the concrete world of form in order to one day walk without fear into the Light permanently. We will not be able to let go of fear and accept the Light unless we can learn to understand and apply forgiveness.

Only forgiveness can relieve the mind of thinking that the body is its home. Only forgiveness can restore the peace that God intended for His holy Son. Only forgiveness can persuade the Son to look again upon his holiness.[3]

The Course refers to God as "Divine Abstraction."[4] However, He is a divine abstraction that loves you very personally with His whole Being, and you likewise love Him with your whole being. Here is one of the quotations in the Course that is the most meaningful for me: "For still deeper than the ego's foundation, and much stronger than it will ever be, is your intense and burning love of God, and His for you."[5] You live in Love whether you are consciously aware of it or not. Spirituality is the process of letting go of the blocks to love that the ego presents and uncovering the all-consuming love that is hidden within and allowing it to overflow into your daily life.

If it is true that all of spirituality goes back to Divine Love, why isn't the inner seeking for God the primary teaching of the Course? The reason goes back to the fact we have identified with the ego. The ego, although an illusion, is an attack on everything that exists. It attacks the reality of God, others, and even our own reality. Since the ego is the idea of separation, it must function by always attacking. Yet we cannot overcome the ego by attacking it. We must not make the mistake of thinking the ego is our "enemy," because doing so would give the ego a reality it does not have. The ego is not good or bad. According to the Course, the ego is merely meaningless. If I said, "Two and two is seven," it would be recognized as just a meaningless idea. This specific false idea can be corrected simply by acknowledging the truth that two and two indeed equal four and not seven. Similarly, we must undo the ego by seeing that it is a meaningless idea. We must replace the false idea of the ego with the truth. Since the ego is the false idea of separation, we can undo the ego by healing this sense of separation through accepting love instead as our own true nature in God.

Love is joining ourselves with God. But since we appear to be in bodies, and God is Spirit, it is hard for us to relate to His transcendent nature. The easiest way for us to learn about love is to join with others who are each representatives of God, since every person exists in God just as we do. Because God is so very abstract and all-embracing, the idea of loving and joining with Him may be too overwhelming for us. Just as I could not fully accept the Divine Light in my experience at age twenty-four, it could be intimidating to be fully embraced by God, Who is all-powerful, as well as all-loving. We have to start to learn how to love God, Who is beyond our normal awareness, by first loving others. It was for this reason that St. John said, "...for he who does not love his brother whom he has seen, cannot love God whom he has not seen."[6] Overcoming the ego idea of separation and joining with our brothers is our means of preparing to overcome our sense of separation from the all-encompassing reality of God and His Love. Buried deep within every mind is a great fear of God. And deeper still is the transcendent love of God that we all yearn for. But first we must get by our fear of our brothers and accept our love of our brothers, who live in God along with us. Of course, we need to have love for ourselves, but if we do not have love for others, we will close our awareness to the love that is always within us.

Thus our brothers and sisters are our best and most tangible representatives of the reality in God that our egos have separated from. As we work out our relationships with our brothers and sisters, we heal our severed relationship with reality. This is necessary because the ego maintains its sense of illusory reality through attacks in the form of denial, projection of guilt, anger, resentment, fear, and judgment. But what if we can reach past the barriers of illusions maintained by the ego? What if we can melt away the false boundaries that pretend to separate us? What if we can join in love with others manifesting true giving, not the "giving to get" of bargaining? Then we would not be limited by the illusion of separation and we could set ourselves outside the ego's influence, undoing its ability to attack. This letting go of illusions of separation is forgiveness. Overcoming our sense of separation is why forgiveness is your great need and my great need.

The ego and everything in the world teaches us to view God and others from our perspective of separation. This leads us to the conclusion that separation from God and from our brothers is a fact of life. Consequently, we feel unworthy and we must do something to make ourselves worthy of correcting our imperfections. Forgiveness offers another choice—to view others and ourselves from God's perspective. What is God's perspective? God does not have an ego so He does not see us as separate from Himself. God sees us as part of Himself so He sees us in our inherent true nature—in our holiness, light, love, and perfection. "Impossible! Nonsense!" the ego protests. But God answers, "I created you eternally perfect and changeless so nothing can change your divine perfection in eternity."

Nevertheless, isn't this totally impractical? How can the perspective of God—the viewpoint that right now we are perfect in Him—be applied to our living here in the world of form where everything appears so imperfect? The answer is true forgiveness. We do not have to correct the flaw in the king's gem—meaning we do not have to correct our apparent outer imperfections to acquire perfection. We are only required to accept the inner perfection that has already been given—to accept that the king's gem has always been flawless. It is called *true* forgiveness because it enables us to see what is forever true about our brothers and sisters—namely their perfection, which reminds us of our own perfect divine nature. Forgiveness only requires us to let go of all our illusions about our brothers and sisters that limit them, making them less than what God created. Allan Greene saw perfection in others and believed he too was perfect as God created him, in spite of a quadriplegic body that told him otherwise. We are only as limited as we allow our minds to maintain a vision of littleness that contradicts the vastness of God's eternal knowing of us as we truly are in Him. All of spiritual growth is merely a matter of coming into alignment with what God already knows about us until we reach the point where we can fully accept our perfection in Him.

Today as I think of Allan's version the story of the king's gem, I can recall the countless times I have looked upon my brothers and sisters as flawed gems, only to realize now that the flaw in each case was actually within my own mind. I will use the example of my relationship with David Sunfellow to symbolize my repeated failures to see the truth. Previously in this book I described David as being "judgmental" because that is a correct historical record of what I felt in the past. With the help of hindsight and true forgiveness, I have come to perceive things quite differently. The opinion I once held of David was a disservice to him in two distinct ways. First, I mistakenly perceived his ego, and second, I neglected to see his true nature beyond the ego. At the level of the ego, I was wrong because I was seeing through the eyes of my own ego, hypocritically projecting my own judgmental nature onto him along with guilt. I fortified my false witnessing by noticing others who also saw David as judgmental, but failed to take into account that they possessed my same ego pattern of playing the role of a victim by projecting judgment and guilt. David was an easy target for projection, not because of his weaknesses, but because of his strength in being a strong independent person with excellent leadership qualities. He seemed aloof at times, but for all I knew he was merely withdrawing to avoid joining with me in playing my game of judgment and projection. I am not saying David's ego was not capable of judgment and projection. I am only asserting now that my ego is not capable of evaluating another ego without gross distortion occurring. The Course quotation below describes the price I was paying for looking for errors in David's ego:

> To the ego it is kind and right and good to point out errors and "correct" them. This makes perfect sense to the ego, which is unaware of what errors are and what correction is. Errors are of the ego, and correction of errors lies in the relinquishment of the ego. When you correct a brother, you are telling him that he is wrong. He may be making no sense at the time, and it is certain that, if he is speaking from the ego, he will not be making sense. But your task is still to tell him he is right. You do not tell him this verbally, if he is

speaking foolishly. He needs correction at another level, because his error is at another level. He is still right, because he is a Son of God. His ego is always wrong, no matter what it says or does.

If you point out the errors of your brother's ego you must be seeing through yours, because the Holy Spirit does not perceive his errors. This *must* be true, since there is no communication between the ego and the Holy Spirit. The ego makes no sense, and the Holy Spirit does not attempt to understand anything that arises from it. Since He does not understand it, He does not judge it, knowing that nothing the ego makes means anything.

When you react at all to errors, you are not listening to the Holy Spirit. He has merely disregarded them, and if you attend to them you are not hearing Him. If you do not hear Him, you are listening to your ego and making as little sense as the brother whose errors you perceive. This cannot be correction. Yet it is more than merely a lack of correction for him. It is the giving up of correction in yourself.[7]

My false perception of David was preventing me from listening to the Holy Spirit and allowing correction to take place within my own mind. By perceiving only a distorted picture of him, I failed to see his true perfection and holiness in Christ. Now that I have let go of my false perception of David, I can affirm that he is a flawless gem made in the image and likeness of God, as are all my brothers and sisters. For me, Allan's version of the story of the king's gem is a reminder to allow the Holy Spirit to correct the flaws in my own mind so that I can truly see the flawlessness of all that God created as part of Himself. All that is required of me is to disregard what is not true about my brother and to accept what is true. This is the essence of true forgiveness in that it declares my brother's reality while setting aside what can never be his reality. My brother lives in Christ, but he is not alone. I am right there with Him in Christ because our Identity is shared. When I allow the Holy Spirit to let me see my brother as he is in Christ, my mind is healed of false perception. Only then can I accept myself as I am in Christ. Thus my brother becomes my savior as I see him as God's Son and simultaneously confirm my own place in the Sonship.

It is so easy to fall into the habit of making judgments by the standards of the world that it takes a redirecting of the mind to establish a new way of perceiving. This will not happen by itself. First, there must be a desire to change. Then there must be a concerted effort to bring about that change. The Course provides a means of transitioning the mind from making judgments of others to applying true forgiveness. However, there are other voices speaking in behalf of seeing the divine perfection in our brothers and sisters. For example, one such advocate is Jerry Paul, the author of the inspirational messages of *Dwell in Love*. He wanted to find a practical way to commune with the Spirit of God in other people. Here is the technique he came up with as an expression of true forgiveness:

> It consisted of first imagining the person for whom I was praying as standing in front of me and then releasing the image while imaging pure and holy Light in his or her heart. In other words, I was substituting in my imagination a holy and perfect image—holy Light in the heart—for the unholy and imperfect image of the person who needed healing, which was my interpretation of what the person was, based on impressions I had received through the bodily senses and the judgments of my discriminating mind. Once I had imagined perfection—this is the true meaning of forgiveness—the door was open for communion on the level of spirit between that person and myself to take place. Imagining perfection and holy Light in the place of imperfection, *and actually believing it is there*, allows us to experience the Presence of God in another person. It is then that we realize there is nothing except God, and that perceptions of anything other than this are like a mirage that dissolves. When we really believe we are in the presence of holiness, all criticisms and grievances have been released and we have accepted that God's Love is unconditional. In the presence of unconditional Love there is no fear.[8]

This seeing of perfection in true forgiveness is the same as seeing Christ in others, which I have identified in a previous chapter as Christ vision. I have also described forgiveness as the process of *looking and overlooking*. The "overlooking" consists of seeing past the ego blocks that would distort our awareness. This overlooking is a withdrawal of the ego's normal practice of denial and projection of guilt. The "looking" consists of directing the mind toward perceiving the true nature of Christ in others. This forgiveness process of seeing Christ in others brings healing to the mind. The Holy Spirit participates in this process by healing the mind that is no longer sending out a projection of guilt. Similarly the one who is forgiven will receive healing of his mind. According to the Course, it is possible that the one who is forgiven would not receive healing immediately if he is not receptive at that time. Nevertheless, more light has come his way and the Holy Spirit will hold his healing for him, waiting for him to one day open his mind to receive it. This healing that occurs in both the one who forgives and the one forgiven is an exchange of light and love, which is a miracle in which both gain equally.

Jesus is our best reminder of how to walk the spiritual path, but there are others who serve as examples of manifesting forgiveness. One such example is Corrie Ten Boom, the author of *The Hiding Place*. Out of compassion she and her sister hid Jews in their home to protect them from the Nazis. But they were both arrested and sent to a concentration camp. Corrie survived, although her sister did not. After World War II, Corrie returned to her home in Holland and cared for others who were victims of the Nazis. She discovered that survivors who were able to forgive their former enemies were also able to return to society and rebuild their lives, regardless of their physical limitations. On the other hand, the victims who wallowed in their bitterness stayed as invalids.

Corrie had learned in her own suffering to call upon God's help. As a result, her faith was greatly strengthened. She was guided to return to Germany to share with others her inspirational message of forgiveness. One of her postwar lectures was held in the basement of a church in Munich. She saw in her audience a man who had been a guard at Ravensbruck, the concentration camp where she and her sister had suffered for several years. After her talk, he came up to her. He said he had become a Christian and appreciated her willingness to forgive the German people. However, he asked Corrie for her personal forgiveness and extended his hand to her. She froze. She was aware that she needed to forgive him, but momentarily she couldn't rise to the occasion. There was no love in her heart, so she prayed to Jesus for help. Here is how she described her struggle:

> I tried to smile, I struggled to raise my hand. I could not. I felt nothing, not the slightest spark of warmth or charity. And so again I breathed a silent prayer. Jesus, I cannot forgive him. Give me Your forgiveness.
>
> As I took his hand the most incredible thing happened. From my shoulder along my arm and through my hand a current seemed to pass from me to him, while into my heart sprang a love for this stranger that almost overwhelmed me.[9]

Corrie Ten Boom took no credit for this miracle of forgiveness, since by herself she could not overlook all the pain she had endured at the hands of her Nazi captors—symbolized by the one who stood before her. She fully acknowledged that Christ had accomplished the forgiveness because only His unconditional love could overcome her resistance. Yet she set an example for all of us. She knew she wanted to change her perception, and she was willing to ask for divine help to manifest forgiveness. Such a request will never be turned down. Spirit will always provide a divine solution to a human misperception. Because of our human nature, we can become deceived by outer appearances and decide that someone does not deserve love, which is the justification for withholding forgiveness. However, Spirit knows that everyone deserves love and therefore deserves forgiveness, because everyone has been created by God and remains part of God forever.

I gave the first draft of this autobiography to my sister Lillian. Before her retirement she had been a teacher and school counselor. I welcomed her advice since I wanted input from someone who was reading about Course principles for the first time. In our conversation after reading this chapter on forgiveness, she asked, "Why do you apply forgiveness to everyone, even to the world?"

I replied, "You and I were brought up Catholic so we learned that we forgive others for what they have done to us. It's hard to understand the Course perspective because it teaches that you never forgive others for what they did to you. You forgive others for what you have done to your own mind to close off your awareness of love. You really love everyone because you are joined with them in God. Imagine that you are a branch on a tree, but you can only look outward, and you cannot see the trunk. From your viewpoint as a branch with limited vision, you think that you are floating in the air. You can see other branches beside you that seem to also be floating in the air. Since you cannot see the trunk, you cannot see how you are connected to all the other branches that share the same nourishing sap that flows through you. Of course, you can't really believe that you are a branch, but you do believe you are a body. When you see other people in this world, they appear to be separate from you because they have bodies that are separate from your body. But here is the key idea: In reality you are not a body. You are joined in the Mind of God that is like the trunk of the tree. You and everyone else are extensions of the Mind of God. In my analogy a branch can imagine that it is separate and floating in the air, yet the imaginings of the branch do not change its connection to the tree. Likewise your imaginings of separation do not change your fundamental nature as part of God and joined with your brothers and sisters."

Lillian asked, "How does that explain why we need to forgive the world?"

"You see the world as a place where everything is separate. When you forgive the world, you let go of your idea that everything is separate. You appear to be in the world, but as strange as it may seem, the world is actually inside your mind, which is inside the Mind of God. When you forgive the world, you are healing your own mind."

"Why do you have to forgive everyone? Can't you perhaps make some exceptions of people you don't forgive?" Lillian inquired.

"When you don't forgive a person, you are saying that this particular person is unworthy of love. The truth is that everyone is worthy of love."

Lillian asked, "Don't you think some people do things that are so wrong that they are not worthy of love?"

I replied, "A person may do an extremely unloving act, but that person in his true nature is still worthy of love. Think of God's Mind as an infinite circle of Love. You and everyone else are always inside this circle. If you decide that someone is unworthy of love, you mentally manufacture an illusion of casting out this person from the circle. By doing this you have abandoned the true all-inclusive and infinite nature of the circle and replaced it with a finite and illusory circle. When you perceive that this person is outside of the circle, the price you pay for this is that you will unknowingly cast yourself outside of the circle alongside your brother. When you reject a brother for his unloving act, you have committed an unloving act yourself by rejecting him. Even if you only have one person that you believe is unworthy of love, you will inevitably likewise believe subconsciously that you are also unworthy of love. With your conscious mind you will think that you are punishing him by withholding your love from him, but, without knowing it, you will be punishing yourself by closing off your awareness of the divine love that is within you. Remember that the divine love within you excludes no one from its embrace."

Lillian said, "I am asking you about this because there is one person that I just cannot forgive. He has passed away, but I still can't forgive him."

"If you can forgive him, it will not be for his benefit. It will be for your benefit because it will heal your mind, restoring its natural state of love. Think of a child who does some terrible thing because he does not have the understanding of an adult. Would you be willing to forgive a child who did something hurtful because of his lack of understanding?"

"Yes, I could forgive a child. However, this person that I cannot forgive was not a child. He was an adult and should have known better."

I said, "But actually he is a child of God. As a child of God, he did not have a good understanding of what he was doing. Out of his ignorance he did very terrible things. Now that he has passed away, he will have a lot of lessons to learn to correct his ignorance. I believe in reincarnation so I expect he will get another lifetime to learn the lessons he needs to grow up and become aware of God's Love within him. If the situation was reversed, do you think he would forgive you?"

"If I had done to him what he did to me, there's no way he would have forgiven me," Lillian replied.

"That's right. He would not forgive you because he is ignorant of God's Love within him and within you. However, you are aware of God's Love, so it is only right for you to forgive him, even though he would not forgive you. You don't want to express ignorance yourself because that would only make the same mistake he has made. When we were growing up together, Dad used to tell us, 'Two wrongs don't make a right.' If you are able to forgive this person, it will be what the Course calls a miracle. Through this miracle you will send a blessing to him even though he is not alive in this world. But that blessing will come back to you, keeping your mind open to God's unconditional Love for you that also extends to him. You don't want to reproduce his ignorance, when you could be extending God's Love instead."

"But if I forgive him, won't I be condoning his behavior."

"You won't be condoning his behavior. You will just be distinguishing between what he did, which was unloving, and who he is as a child of God lost in his own ignorance of his true nature. His unloving acts were actually his distorted way of calling for love. He wouldn't have called for love in distorted ways if he was aware of God's Love that is always within him. With your greater awareness of God's Love, you can forgive him by giving him the love that he was calling for without condoning his behavior."

Lillian said, "I've just found it really hard to forgive him because he has hurt other people besides just me. Don, I hear what you are saying, and it sounds right. Nevertheless, it's still hard for me to forgive him, but I know it's important to try since the idea of forgiveness keeps coming back to me so I can't ignore it. I advised someone else whom he hurt to forgive him. That person followed my advice and was finally able to forgive him. Yet I haven't been able to take my own advice—at least not yet."

I suggested, "What you can do is ask for help. It's the Holy Spirit's job to assist us in opening up to God's Love. But the Holy Spirit cannot help you without your invitation. You have to ask in prayer for the Holy Spirit's help. If you do that, you will find your heart opening little by little until you can find forgiveness for him. You will feel relieved when you are finally able to let go of your hurt feelings and send love to him."

Lillian said, "I'm open to what you are saying. I'll have to give it some time to sink in because this has been so difficult for me."

Understanding true forgiveness is helpful, but taking the next step of practicing it is healing. With that in mind, now I will conclude this chapter by suggesting that you conduct a ten-minute experiment in practicing true forgiveness. If you are not already a Course student, this experiment will give you an idea of what a Workbook lesson is like. Below is an excerpt from Workbook Lesson 121, "Forgiveness is the key to happiness." If you would like to take advantage of this opportunity to experience the miracle of forgiveness, you can start by following Corrie Ten Boom's example and ask Jesus, the Holy Spirit, or God to help you open your heart and to correct any misperceptions you may be holding in your mind. Then after your invitation to Spirit, read and follow these Course instructions:

The unforgiving mind does not believe that giving and receiving are the same. Yet we will try to learn today that they are one through practicing forgiveness toward one whom you think of as an enemy, and one whom you consider as a friend. And as you learn to see them both as one, we will extend the lesson to yourself, and see that their escape included yours.

Begin ... by thinking of someone you do not like, who seems to irritate you, or to cause regret in you if you should meet him; one you actively despise, or merely try to overlook. It does not matter what the form your anger takes. You probably have chosen him already. He will do.

Now close your eyes and see him in your mind, and look at him a while. Try to perceive some light in him somewhere; a little gleam which you had never noticed. Try to find some little spark of brightness shining through the ugly picture that you hold of him. Look at this picture till you see a light somewhere within it, and then try to let this light extend until it covers him, and makes the picture beautiful and good.

Look at this changed perception for a while, and turn your mind to one you call a friend. Try to transfer the light you learned to see around your former "enemy" to him. Perceive him now as more than friend to you, for in that light his holiness shows you your savior, saved and saving, healed and whole.

Then let him offer you the light you see in him, and let your "enemy" and friend unite in blessing you with what you gave. Now are you one with them, and they with you. Now have you been forgiven by yourself. Do not forget, throughout the day, the role forgiveness plays in bringing happiness to every unforgiving mind, with yours among them.[10]

---

1. T-3.V.9:1, p. 169 (p. 157).

2. W-pI.192.4:2-3, p. 365 (p. 355).

3. W-pI.192.5:5-7, p. 365 (p. 355).

4. T-4.VII.5:4, p. 70 (p. 64).

5. T-13.III.2:8, p. 242 (p. 226).

6. First letter of John 4:20 RSV.

7. T-9.III.2:1-10, 3:1-4, 4:1-6, pp. 166-167 (p. 155).

8. Jerry Paul, *Dwell in Love* (Pine Level, AL: Isaiah Publications, 2008), pp. 3-4.

9. Corrie Ten Boom with John and Elizabeth Sherrill, *The Hiding Place* (New York: Bantam Books, 1974), p. 238.

10. W-121.pI.9:1-3, 10:1-4, 11:1-4, 12:1-3, 13:1-4, pp. 215-216 (pp. 211-212).

70

GOD'S LAST JUDGMENT

≈ ○ ≈

I have come a long way from the time when I was hanging from the balcony in college to alert myself to the fact that there was something wrong with my life. Much of my early undisciplined life was pervaded by an uneasy feeling—an undercurrent of mild but consistent anxiety. At that time I couldn't figure out the source of that feeling. However, I would later discover it was a deep-rooted sense of guilt. Although some of that guilt came from past lives, my current life was steeped in this generalized guilt, and it could only be healed in the here and now. Whenever I have experienced a contact with Spirit—whether ordinary or dramatic—it has been accompanied by a natural outpouring of gratitude that washed away any sense of guilt. Perhaps this is why I perceive spiritual disciplines as a welcome blessing for me rather than a chore. Over the years I have developed a daily *attitude of gratitude* with which I greet every day in the morning and take to sleep with me each night. This has not just happened automatically. I have had to consciously nourish this attitude by repeatedly directing my mind and actions to make every day into a Thanksgiving Day.

Gaining a sense of thankfulness involves positive thinking, but it is even more important to ask in prayer for God's help in opening up to Him—meaning being receptive to the divine within as well as recognizing His Presence manifested outwardly in other people and in the world. In establishing an outlook of gratitude, one idea has been the foundation for my life and happiness. It is the idea that God loves me personally. This is, of course, part of a larger overall idea expressed in possibly the most popular quote from the Bible—"God is love."[1] But I prefer to give the quote a capital "L" because His Love is greater than our human love that is so conditional, therefore fluctuating and limited.

Parts of the Old Testament depict God as being righteously wrathful, which contradicts the idea that God is all-loving. Similarly, even the New Testament provides an image of God offering righteous justice that would send some of His children to hell to be punished forever. This belief in divine justice provides an illusory picture of God made in the image and likeness of *man*, not the other way around. In my study of the Course, I discovered that God's idea of justice is that everyone deserves heaven, and I found nothing that contradicts that God is Love.

The Course offers spiritual principles that are different than some ideas in the Bible and also different from some commonly held ideas in Eastern philosophy. For example, the Course takes the position that evil, sin, and guilt are illusory. In order for me to accept this viewpoint, I had to reconcile this understanding with my former study of karma. The idea of hell is that we have to pay for our grave mistakes, and this is very similar to the concept in yoga philosophy of paying for our karma. However, the Course maintains that, as far as God is concerned, there is no such thing as karmic retribution. The belief in karma means our sins have real effects that cause real damage, and we will have to pay for that damage. In the past I would keep an account of the offenses of others the way some people collect stamps. Occasionally I would cash in the accumulated stamps by releasing my pent-up grievances in a display of private or even on rare occasions public emotion. But then, with the help of the Course and the application of forgiveness, I was able to discard this foolish and unloving practice. Similarly, those who believe in hell also think of karma as God's collecting of stamps—His accounting system, which He uses as a means of judging our worthiness for heaven or hell. The Course would say that those who see God as a judge with a karmic accounting system are just projecting their own judgments onto God, making Him into an ego image of themselves.

The belief in karma is the idea that our past actions determine what we deserve and produce our present positive or negative circumstances. We appear to live our lives under the effects of karma, but this appearance is due entirely to our own belief in karma. God has nothing to do with this cherished, self-imposed belief in assigning rewards and punishments based on past actions. According to the Course, karma does not exist because the past does not exist and has no real power to determine our conditions. Nevertheless, the past can affect us if we allow it to do so by believing in it and by specifically believing in guilt, which in turn requires self-assigned punishment. The Course does affirm cause and effect, but it maintains that the past cannot be the cause of anything. Cause and effect occurs through our *present choices* that are the cause of our current circumstances.

We are accustomed to believing the past can affect us, so it is hard to accept the Course saying, "…the past is gone, and what has truly gone has no effects."[2] Let's use a simple illustration to explain this difficult idea. Imagine a ship, which was loaded with cargo in New York, is currently at sea headed toward London. In this analogy, New York represents the past, and London represents the future. The ship stands for the present and for the individual mind, which only functions in the present. If I said that the ship is carrying New York, no one would believe such an impossible idea.

Yet many people do believe the mind carries the past, even though this is quite impossible. New York is gone and has no effect on the ship, just as the past is gone and has no effect on the mind. It is true that the cargo was loaded in the past in New York, but only the cargo that is on the ship *now* can have any effect. Similarly, only the thoughts we have in our mind now can have any effect on us. The cargo can be dumped off of the ship at any present moment, and likewise we can let go of any thoughts presently in the mind, including any memories or thoughts related to the past. Cause and effect do take place, but only in the present where we can decide what to keep in the mind and what to discard. This puts us in control of what we experience. Discarding unhealthy thoughts and keeping healthy thoughts will be calming to the mind. Similarly, discarding healthy thoughts and holding onto unhealthy thoughts will be disturbing to the mind. The only cause of our current condition is a present decision in the mind.

My former understanding of karma, explained in Chapter 5, represents the traditional Eastern philosophy that there are three kinds of karma: The first is accumulated karma, which is the total of all past experiences. The second is fruit-producing karma, which is experienced now and must be experienced. And the third is new karma that will produce fruit in the future. In my mind I thought of the accumulated karma as *past karma*, the fruit-producing karma as *present karma*, and the new karma as *future karma*. Now I realized there is no such thing as past or future karma. There is only *present karma*, which I prefer to call *present cause and effect*. It is the cause and effect occurring in the mind in each present moment. Decisions may have been made in the past, but these would have evaporated if the mind is not holding these decisions currently. We could have loaded our minds with mental cargo at any time in the past, even in past lives. Past lives can affect us now only because of the thoughts we currently hold in the conscious or subconscious mind about them. That is why it was so important for me to bring my traumatic experiences as the Spider Boy and Pole Man to my conscious awareness so I could become fully aware of this unhealthy mental cargo stored away in back of my mind. Then I could make a current decision to throw that emotional turmoil overboard. This is why I have been and continue to be motivated to bring the hidden pieces of my shadow puzzle out of the darkness and to release them into the light through forgiveness.

The stored thoughts in the mind are constantly renewed, and it is this keeping of them in our present consciousness that makes them affect us. In this sense the mind is like a computer that stores information and will hold it until we decide to delete it. If no new decisions are made, former decisions automatically remain in effect and are currently active in the mind. That is why miracles of forgiveness involve changing our minds to remove decisions currently in the mind, which could have been decided long ago, but remained in effect in each present moment since then. Old decisions that currently continue to remain in the mind involve holding on to illusions, such as illusions of the past. Consequently, miracles replace our illusions about the past and reveal the reality of divine truth that is always within us now.

Our present choices and actions can affect our navigating through the world of form, but can have no effect on *who we are in reality*. By forgiving ourselves and others, we can let go of our false beliefs in the past. Also, forgiveness helps us to let go of the negative effects of our present choices by showing us that our own mind is investing in ego-based illusions that do not have the power to produce effects. Forgiveness heals our minds by replacing these illusions with the truth of our reality—the truth that God is our only Cause. Since God is our Cause, we are His Effect, His holy Son. Our purity may appear to be lost in the illusions of this world, but when God created us in eternity, the holiness He gave us must be forever ours.

The idea that God does not believe in karma is elaborated upon in Appendix F, "A New Look at Karma." Instead of requiring retribution for our mistakes, God only forgives by overlooking all errors and seeing the truth of our holiness and oneness with Him. Although we may think our actions deserve rewards or punishments, God always knows we deserve only love at all times. In God's loving awareness, all of our errors in thought or behavior evaporate altogether into nothingness. Unfortunately, we have the tendency to hold on to the memory of these unloving acts and to blame ourselves for them. In contrast to the accusations we make against ourselves, God sees only our innocence so we remain holy in His eyes. Nevertheless, believing in guilt, we would make the mistake of punishing ourselves with karmic retribution. We would hold ourselves accountable for the past mistakes God has already forgiven. We may even believe we have done something that is unforgiveable. Yet there is nothing that cannot be forgiven because everything has already been forgiven. This must be so because of the unwavering Love of our Father. No matter what sins we think we have committed or what punishment we think we deserve, God still sees us as being just as sinless as when he created us in His own image of holiness with no stain of guilt and fully deserving of heaven at all times. The only question we need to ask ourselves is this: "Can we learn to see ourselves with the eyes of love as God sees us in our true holiness?"

Jesus offered very challenging ideas to the Pharisees of His time, and they hated Him for it. But Jesus was only trying to offer a new vision of God that showed He is a God of Love, not a God of man-made rules and not even a God of man-made love. Even Saul as a Pharisee hated what he considered the heretical ideas of Jesus and wanted to persecute Christians.

He changed his mind when he had a personal transforming vision of Light in which he directly encountered Jesus, and subsequently he became the Apostle Paul. I too had a vision of divine Light that showed me a world that transcends the world of form. I learned that this transcendental world of Light is the doorway to my true Home. Although I resisted the Course at first, I finally realized that it was describing more clearly than the Bible this transcendental Home and telling me how to get there.

I learned from the Course that there are two primary factors in finding our way back Home. One aspect is to take advantage of the opportunity to see the face of Christ as the Light that I have already described to Allan in Chapter 59. This Light can be seen even in this lifetime, but everyone will have a chance to see this vision of the Son of God at the moment of death. I am not talking about the lesser light that is often reported by those who have near death experiences and see people or objects illuminated. I am referring to the overpowering and blazing Light, which obliterates all forms in its splendor. It will be every soul's opportunity to accept this Light as the doorway to eternal joy in heaven—the opportunity to hear our Father say, "Thou art my beloved Son; with thee I am well pleased."[3] I am speaking figuratively here, not literally, for no words can express this divine union. Yes, these are the words spoken to Jesus by the Father in the Bible, but from the Course's perspective we are all part of the one Christ and each of us is His beloved Son.

This first factor of seeing the Light is absolutely necessary for us to find our way Home because, "*The face of Christ* has to be seen before the memory of God can return."[4] But even if the Light is seen, will it be accepted? Whether we will be able to accept the Light will depend entirely on the second factor in finding our way Home, which is our *preparation* for seeing the light. In Chapter 59 I have highlighted the limited times in which the Course discusses the important event of seeing the Light. But instead of focusing on this event itself, the whole emphasis of the Course is on this second factor of being prepared to see the Light.

This preparation has to do with having a mind that is open to receive the divine embrace. The Course is designed to help us open our minds, which means not only accepting new ideas, but also letting go of old ideas that close off the mind. For example, the traditional belief in karmic retribution nurtures the idea of guilt in the mind and raises the question of whether heaven is deserved or not. Discarding the idea of karma has been addressed above and in Appendix F to help open the mind to the idea that God's Love could not possibly support the idea of karmic retribution. The central message of the Course is that we can prepare ourselves to go Home by learning how to forgive. Through the lessons of forgiveness we learn to see the divine presence hidden in the world and in everyone around us.

Seeing the divine presence indirectly in our brothers and sisters prepares us to one day directly encounter and embrace God Himself in the Light. The Course also recommends various methods of inner attunement to experience the divine presence within, which is in turn a preparation for accepting the Light as the face of Christ and doorway to heaven.

Although both the Bible and the Course say that God is Love, there are differences in how each book draws a picture of what that means. I was disturbed by these differences between the Bible and the Course because I could not accept both interpretations. I accepted the alternate thought system of the Course when I could see clearly the impact of the differences. The parts of the Course that depart from traditional Biblical thinking were necessary in order to hold firmly to the truth that *God's Love is totally unconditional*. For instance, the Course maintains there is no hell because a God of Love would never allow any of His children to be punished in hell.

In the Bible, Jesus tells us of the wonderful story of the Good Shepherd, who leaves the ninety-nine sheep in his flock, and searches for the one lost sheep until he rescues it. Of course, Jesus Himself is the Good Shepherd. In the Course vision of salvation, Jesus will go after, find, and rescue His lost sheep, so not even one will be lost forever in a place called hell. This image of God extending through Jesus to every soul is such a lofty and inspiring vision of perfect Love that right now it brings tears to my eyes as I write about it. I know I was one of those lost sheep who has been found and will wake up in heaven one day, just as all my brothers and sisters will come back Home for a transcendental celebration.

Why is this idea that God is Love so important to me? First, let me clarify that it is an idea about God, but not a definition of God. A definition of a refrigerator is needed to make sure it is not confused with a chair. A definition of a chair is needed to distinguish it from a refrigerator. Thus definitions of refrigerators, chairs, and other objects limit and circumscribe them so we will know they are one thing and not another. We can have ideas about God as everyone does, but these ideas cannot define God since His Limitlessness cannot be limited and circumscribed with concepts.

If none of our ideas can encompass God as a definition, what use are our ideas of Him? My idea that God is Love is meaningful and valuable to me, not as a definition, but as a means of *allowing God to define and encompass me*. God gave me His Love when He created me, and He never took it back, because unlike human love that runs hot and cold, His Love is changeless and eternal. Perceiving God as everlasting Love means His Love encompasses me and fills me and tells me that my own true nature in Him is love. I can learn to let His Love flow through me to forgive everyone I meet by seeing His Love encompass and fill them as their true nature. I can sit in prayer and meditation and allow His Love to encompass me and fill me so I can rest in His Arms. I can know that I deserve heaven for no other reason than the fact that God loves me. If I deserve heaven because God loves me, then everyone deserves heaven, because God loves all of His children equally. Since God is Love, we must be living even now in the timeless ocean of His Love, and no one could possibly be excluded.

Our ideas about God, whether correct or incorrect, will not change Him in the slightest degree and will not change our reality in Him. But our ideas about ourselves will change our *awareness* of ourselves. If our ideas about ourselves are true, they will open us up to the awareness of the truth within ourselves. If our ideas are not true, they will perpetuate illusions about ourselves. God Who is Love never sees us as unworthy sinners. However, when I was a practicing Catholic, there was no way to get around the universally accepted Christian premise that sinfulness is unquestionably a fundamental and inescapable fact of life. As a Catholic, I found that the belief in my sinfulness was a serious stumbling block to fully opening up to God's Love for me because I mistakenly did not feel I deserved His Love. As a traditional Christian, I focused on the forgiveness of God and of Jesus to help me deal with my sinner mentality. I could also go to confession and receive forgiveness through my priest. In this way I could feel God's Love to a certain degree while still perceiving myself to be a sinner, who was receiving forgiveness. Besides the forgiveness coming from God, Jesus, and my priest, I still needed someone else's forgiveness. I needed to forgive myself, and found that forgiveness harder to come by. Along with the idea of being a sinner came the thought of being unworthy and guilty, which made me feel undeserving of forgiveness. Thus, while thinking of myself as a sinner, I could not open up to God's Love as much as I would have liked.

The option of releasing the idea of being a sinner first presented itself through studying Eastern philosophy that maintained I had a true divine nature that was my reality. Naturally I could make mistakes at the form level, and I would want to correct these as much as possible. However, such mistakes did not define my identity because they did not alter my true nature in reality. Sinfulness, unworthiness, and guilt only make sense within the context of the ego, which is the idea that I am a limited body and a limited rational mind. Yet the ego itself is unreal and not my true identity. Since the ego is a false frame of reference, the ideas that I am a sinner, unworthy, and guilty are merely false ego concepts. But even false concepts are very powerful if the mind believes them, and my mind had been steeped in the belief of my sinfulness. I felt I needed to let go of perceiving myself as a sinner, otherwise I would remain blocked in my ability to receive God's Love. Nevertheless, I found it very difficult to break away from my sinner mentality because of the conditioning I received as a

Catholic. Even after I was no longer a practicing Catholic, the habitual thought patterns remained because they were so deeply engrained into my mind from childhood.

The belief in Eastern philosophy was helpful, but it did not address how to forgive myself in a way that would enable me to truly let go of my ego attachments. When the Course came along, it taught me over time how to forgive myself by forgiving others. It showed me a type of forgiveness that allowed me to see the divine nature and holiness of others. Through this forgiveness of others, I began to forgive myself by perceiving my own divine nature and holiness.

Studying the Course finally helped me to overcome the barrier of a sinner identity. But it would take me time to make the transition from my former thought system to my new one. I would have to practice the Workbook lessons and study the Text and Manual to make that transition. The basic idea of the Course that I am not a sinner—I am holy because God created me that way—is easy to understand intellectually, but hard to really believe. After all, whether I call them sins or more appropriately call them mistakes, I had still fallen short of being loving so many, many times. I had struggled with guilt for such a long time, it was hard at first to accept the possibility that I am in reality eternally holy. The Course gently reminded me that all evil things that seem to happen in this world, including all my own foolish and willful mistakes, are pure illusions having no effect at all on my reality or on the reality of anyone else. I remembered when I worked as a youthful recreation therapist and met so many older patients who were dying and filled with guilt and regrets. I had resolved at that young age to live a life free of guilt and regrets, but had failed to do so in spite of my lofty ideals and my vocation as a monk. The Course offered me true freedom from my guilt and regrets by showing there was no basis for such beliefs. My choice boiled down to accepting my own judgment of myself as being guilty or accepting from the Course God's judgment of me as holy. Becoming immersed in the Course finally convinced me that I was wrong about myself and God was right. It is generally believed in many different spiritual traditions that when we die, we will face a final judgment. Here is the Course presentation of that final judgment:

> You who believed that God's Last Judgment would condemn the world to hell along with you, accept this holy truth: God's Judgment is the gift of the Correction He bestowed on all your errors, freeing you from them, and all effects they ever seemed to have. To fear God's saving grace is but to fear complete release from suffering, return to peace, security and happiness, and union with your own Identity.

God's Final Judgment is as merciful as every step in His appointed plan to bless His Son, and call him to return to the eternal peace He shares with him. Be not afraid of love. For it alone can heal all sorrow, wipe away all tears, and gently waken from his dream of pain the Son whom God acknowledges as His. Be not afraid of this. Salvation asks you give it welcome. And the world awaits your glad acceptance, which will set it free.

This is God's Final Judgment: "You are still My holy Son, forever innocent, forever loving and forever loved, as limitless as your Creator, and completely changeless and forever pure. Therefore awaken and return to Me. I am your Father and you are My Son."[5]

It is hard for anyone who considers himself a sinner to read this description for the first time and immediately believe this is in fact God's Last Judgment. I certainly didn't. But I *wanted* to believe what I now call God's "Eternal Emancipation Proclamation"—a declaration of our everlasting holiness in Him, granting freedom from our chains by correcting all the apparent effects of our self-imposed sins (errors or mistakes). I started by believing it was possible. After thoughtful consideration, it seemed plausible and later probable. Eventually by the time I finally decided to accept the Course as my new thought system, I had come to believe it was indeed true. I realized that I am worthy of God's Love because He made me in His image and likeness, which was hidden, but which He never took away. I am holy because I am part of God and therefore part of His Holiness. My former sinner mentality enabled me to say "Yes" to Christ outside of myself, and that was a good thing as far as it went. My new awareness of holiness taught me to say "Yes" to Christ within. However, I don't think I will *completely accept and internalize— meaning truly realize experientially*—the transcendental reality of God's Last Judgment until I fully wake up in my Father's Embrace in heaven. Yet it would be a mistake to think God is delaying His proclamation of His Love until some future date. God never tires of telling us in countless ways how much He loves us. He waits undisturbed in perfect peace for us to take our fingers out of our ears.

A close friend of mine confided in me that she had been experiencing a recurring fear of death, and she asked me for my advice. She had been brought up as a Catholic, as I had, and so she had been indoctrinated to believe that she was a sinner. I wanted to convey to her that God sees us as His holy children and does not pay attention to what we call our sins. Although the Course had helped me to understand that God loves us so much that He would bless us in our transition to the afterlife, I did not think that studying the Course philosophy would be her cup of tea. Thus, instead of recommending the Course, I gave her the names of several books that provided testimonials of near-death experiences. I told her that reading these would give her a better idea of what to expect in the afterlife. She read the books I suggested and told me that her fear of death had subsided. In fact, she felt very inspired to read the stories of people who temporarily transcended the normal consciousness of this world. These people had discovered that there is no need to fear death. One testimonial stated:

> Life is like imprisonment. In this state, we just can't understand what prisons these bodies are. Death is such a release—like an escape from prison. That's the best thing I can think of to compare it to.[6]

One of the consistent themes found in almost all near-death experiences is the presence of an indescribably wonderful divine love and light. One example is the story of Joe Geraci. In 1977 he was declared clinically dead for two or three minutes by his hospital doctors. During this temporary loss of normal worldly awareness, Joe was experiencing a very different world that he described in this way:

> It was a total immersion in light, brightness, warmth, peace, security. I did not have an out-of-body experience. I did not see my body or anybody about me. I just immediately went into this beautiful bright light. It's difficult to describe; as a matter of fact, it's impossible to describe. Verbally, it cannot be expressed. It's something which becomes you and you become it. I could say, "I was peace; I was love." I was the brightness; it was part of me ... You just know. You're all-knowing—and everything is a part of you—it's—it's just so beautiful. It was eternity. It's like I was always there and I will always be there, and that my existence on earth was just a brief instant.[7]

In 1952 Jayne Smith had a near-death experience when she was in danger of dying as she was giving birth to her second daughter. During this experience she was aware that she had died but she was still alive, and she felt filled with overwhelming gratitude. Losing body consciousness, Jayne felt she was "an infinite being in perfection." She saw a bright light that was brighter than any earthly light. She described her experience of the light:

> And this enormously bright light seemed almost to cradle me. I just seemed to exist in it and be part of it and be nurtured by it and the feeling just became more and more ecstatic and glorious and perfect.[8]

Jayne had a mental telepathy conversation with a "being" of light:

"I know what's happened; I know that I've died." And he said, "Yes, but you aren't going to be staying because it isn't time for you yet." And I said to him, "This is all so beautiful; this is all so perfect; what about my sins?"

And he said to me, "There are no sins. Not in the way you think about them on earth. The only thing that matters here is how you think."

"What is in your heart?" he asked me.

And somehow I immediately was able to look into my heart, and I saw that there was nothing in my heart except love. And I understood exactly what he meant. And I said to him, "Of course."[9]

She felt this awareness of inner love is something she had always known but had forgotten. Similarly God has placed His Love in each of our hearts that we have forgotten, and we need to awaken that love. She asked this being if she could take back all of her new awareness to earth to tell others. He told her, "You can take the answer to your first question—which was about sin..." He said she would forget other parts of her new awareness.

Along with remembering that there are no sins, Jayne also remembered that in her near-death experience she understood that all the apparently terrible things that happen here on the earth are part of God's perfection. Yes, that means all the wars, death, and destruction are part of a plan God has for our lives. Everything is perfect, and we do not have to be worried about anything. Every single person is safe and protected by God forever. I was inspired by reading about Jayne's experience because it was a helpful reminder for me that God sees only holiness in all His children. Invariably such near-death glimpses of the spiritual world provide a confirmation of the Course's picture of God and His unconditional Love.

At an emotional level the reason why I have been attracted to the Course is that passages like the one above about God's Last Judgment have helped to remind me of the love God has placed in my heart. Before being exposed to the Course, I had already spent many years believing in the philosophy of yoga that has the goal of achieving peace of mind. From yoga I learned that peace could be found primarily by using various disciplines, such as meditation, to go within and experience the divine presence. The Course presented me with a different premise to consider. It advocated setting aside times for inner attunement, but it maintained that peace cannot be found only by looking within. The Course said that if I wanted to find peace of mind, I must look beyond myself and find the divine within my brothers and sisters. Seeing the divine within others would convince me that the divine presence must be within me as well. Also from the Course I learned that I am responsible for the decisions that bring the perceptions of either peace or discord to my mind. The Course emphasizes miracles since these are changes in perception that manifest love instead of fear. In spite of the demanding occurrences of life, I discovered that I could change my thinking from perceptions of fear to perceptions of love and forgiveness. Overall, the Course has met my needs since it has helped me express a balance between the Eastern approach of seeking the divine within and the Western approach of seeking the divine by developing love relationships with my brothers and sisters. Although the Course has become my means of opening to divine love inwardly and outwardly, it presents challenging ideas that are not suitable to meeting the needs of everyone.

We each need to learn individual lessons to find our way back Home. The Course sees itself as one optional path among many others that can assist us in our spiritual growth process. What if you are a traditional Christian who believes in a hell where evil sinners are punished forever? And what if you want to hold firmly to this belief and other similar Biblical beliefs because such concepts are the foundation of your faith? If you are happy with your current religious beliefs, I have no need to convert you to my way of thinking based on the Course. Far be it from me to interfere with your faith. Obviously not every faith can have all correct beliefs, because various faiths have conflicting ideas. Nevertheless, your faith, whatever it is, does not have to be based on all correct ideas about God in order to bring you to heaven. Surely the God of Love will find a way to bring you Home, even if your perceptions are not entirely accurate. You are given the path to your Father that will be most helpful for your individual growth, whether it is a traditional religion or a less traditional path. If you are not open to an alternative Christian thought system, then thank you for coming this far with me on my memory walk in the light. I hope the journey we have just taken together will perhaps be helpful to you in some way as you continue to walk the individual path you have been given by Spirit. As you travel with love in your heart, whatever road you take will be the right one.

---

1. First Letter of John 4:16, RSV.
2. T-28.I.1:8, p. 589 (p. 547).
3. Luke 3:22, RSV.
4. C-3.4:1, p. 83 (p. 79).
5. W-pII.10.3:1-2, 4:1-6, 5:1-3, p. 455 (p. 445).
6. Raymond Moody, Jr., *Life After Life*, (New York: Bantam Books, Inc. published by arrangement with Mockingbird Books, 1979), p. 97.
7. Kenneth Ring, *Heading Toward Omega*, (New York: Quill, William Morrow, 1985), pp. 53-54.
8. Ibid., p. 62.
9. Ibid., p. 62-63.

APPENDIX A

~ • ~

HOW TO MEDITATE USING THE JESUS PRAYER OF THE HEART

It is fitting that if someone has extra food, he should share from his abundance. However, food is more than just physical. Although the physical needs must be met, it is spiritual food for which most people are hungry, whether they are aware of this need or have suppressed it. If a person has found a source of spiritual food that could feed those who are hungry, he is obligated to reveal such a source. Here, I would like to reveal a source of spiritual food that is not well known, but which is abundantly able to feed all those who partake of it. This spiritual food is referred to in the following quotation:

> But little by little, after a fairly short time I was able to picture my heart and to note its movement, and further with the help of my breathing I could put into it and draw from it the Prayer of Jesus in the manner taught by the saints Gregory of Sinai, Callistus, and Ignatius. When drawing the air in I looked in spirit into my heart and said, "Lord Jesus Christ," and when breathing out again, I said, "Have mercy on me." I did this at first for an hour at a time, then for two hours, then for as long as I could, and in the end almost all day long….
>
> When about three weeks had passed I felt a pain in my heart, and then a most delightful warmth, as well as consolation and peace. This aroused me still more and spurred me on more and more to give great care to the saying of the Prayer so that all my thoughts were taken up with it and I felt a very great joy. From this time I began to have, from time to time, a number of different feelings in my heart and mind. Sometimes my heart would feel as though it was bubbling with joy—such lightness, freedom and consolation was in it. Sometimes I felt a burning love for Jesus Christ and for all

God's creatures. Sometimes my eyes brimmed over with tears of thankfulness to God...[1]

This quotation comes from a book written many years ago by an unknown Christian author. Entitled *The Way of a Pilgrim*, it is a wonderfully simple and beautiful story of the adventures of a man who wandered through Russia in the nineteenth century. At a time when everything seemed to be going wrong for him in his life, he decided to become a spiritual seeker. He didn't know how to pray effectively, so he went to an old monk and asked him. The wise monk gave him the Prayer of the Heart to repeat as his spiritual food. The long form of the prayer is, "Lord Jesus Christ, Son of God, have mercy on me, a sinner." *The Jesus Prayer*, as it is called, can be employed in any one of several shorter forms, such as:

> Lord Jesus Christ, have mercy on me.
> Lord, have mercy.
> Christ, have mercy.
> Jesus, mercy.
> Jesus Christ
> Jesus

I describe the Jesus Prayer as spiritual food because I was experiencing its nourishment within myself due to my own practice. I wanted to teach others how to open themselves up to this same divine blessing. There was a good turnout for these Jesus Prayer classes when I taught them at the Yoga Center. Many participants were more interested in yoga than Christianity and came out of curiosity more than anything else. Some had been turned off by traditional Christianity, but remained open to experiencing the Universal Christ that is not limited to any one religion. One time a student asked me, "Why do you personally use the Jesus Prayer?"

I answered with a question of my own, "If you were to go on a safari in Africa would you go alone?"

"No, I'd take a guide."

"There's your answer!" I said. "Yoga philosophy says that we can take four kinds of safaris into four states of consciousness. You and I are now on the safari into the conscious state in the world of form. Tonight when we go to bed, we will enter the second safari, which is dream state of sleep, and also the third safari, which is deep dreamless sleep. And finally there is the safari into superconsciousness. We call upon the Name of Jesus Christ in our conscious waking state, but in doing so we are inviting Him to come with us into all of our states of consciousness. Not only that, but with inviting Him we are also welcoming the Holy Spirit to be another safari guide, along with Jesus. However, you do not have to be convinced of the benefits of the Jesus Prayer before practicing it. You can simply repeat the Divine Name with an inner feeling of openness. The true value of the Jesus Prayer will be revealed to you as you use it."

For inspirational purposes, I liked to quote passages from the *Writings from the Philokalia on Prayer of the Heart*, as for example this one:

> And so every hour and every moment let us zealously guard our heart from thoughts obscuring the mirror of the soul, which should contain, drawn and imprinted on it, only the radiant image of Jesus Christ, Who is the wisdom and the power of God the Father. Let us constantly seek the kingdom of heaven in the heart, and we are sure mysteriously to find within ourselves the seed, the pearl, the drink and all else, if we cleanse the eye of the mind. This is why our Lord Jesus Christ said: "The kingdom of God is within you,"[2] meaning by this the Deity dwelling in the heart.[3]

Although at the Yoga Center I was practicing the Jesus Prayer in the form of an unceasing prayer as much as possible throughout the day—as is advised in the quote above—in my teaching I advocated a more moderate approach to repeating the Divine Name because this is more appropriate for most seekers. Instead of constant prayer I suggested calling upon the Name of Jesus Christ as part of your daily routine or whenever you're inspired to do so. For example, you can repeat the Jesus Prayer especially upon waking in the morning and just before going to sleep at night, or simply during mundane activities such as riding in a car, brushing your teeth, or even sitting on the toilet. It is especially suited to doing repetitive exercises or doing yoga postures and breathing practices. But to instill the Jesus Prayer within your mind at a deep level I recommended to my students the setting aside of regular meditation times every day.

Eastern methods of attunement include body awareness as a means of making meditation methods more effective. However, Western forms of attunement do not usually include focusing on body awareness, so today the West has made the Jesus Prayer into an entirely mental practice, eliminating the holding of the awareness in the heart. But it is the focusing on the heart that gives this method its ability to penetrate deep within and enkindle devotion. It has far less effect if performed only in the mind.

Focusing the mind is important, but meditation is not just a mental technique. It's really about developing and deepening your relationship with God by opening to His presence within. During your conversations in close relationships, perhaps you have noticed that when you *spoke from your heart*, you were able to really connect with others in a more deep and meaningful way than if you had spoken just with your head. Similarly when you have communion with the divine within in meditation, you can connect best by including your heart in the process. Many spiritual traditions consider the heart to be the midpoint between heaven and earth where we in the human condition can most easily find a balance of body, mind, and spirit, bringing wholeness and healing. So in my teaching at the Yoga Center I explained the key factor of holding the awareness in the heart, thus returning to the version of the Prayer of the Heart that flourished in the Eastern Orthodox Churches of Greece and Russia.

St John Chrysostom described how a Christian should practice the Prayer of the Heart by saying: "He should always live with the name of the Lord Jesus, so that the heart absorbs the Lord and the Lord the heart, and the two become one."[4] He also said, "Do not estrange your heart from God, but abide in Him and always guard your heart by remembering our Lord Jesus Christ, until the name of the Lord becomes rooted in the heart and it ceases to think of anything else. May Christ be glorified in you."[5]

Following the advice of the early Fathers of the Church, I provided instructions on how to hold the attention of the mind in the heart. Through yoga I was well aware of the benefits of learning to calm the breathing in order to calm the mind, which was well known by the early Christian monks. For example, St. John of the Ladder said, "May the memory of Jesus combine with your breathing; then will you understand the use of silence."[6] Hesychius said, "…let the Jesus prayer cleave to your breath— and in a few days you will see it in practice."[7] Monks Callistus and Ignatius together wrote instructions for monks on how to practice the Prayer of the Heart: "You know, brother, how we breathe: we breathe the air in and out. On this is based the life of the body and on this depends its warmth. So, sitting down in your cell, collect your mind, lead it into the path of the breath along which the air enters in, constrain it to enter the heart together with the inhaled air, and keep it there."[8] I recommended repeating the first half of the Jesus Prayer on the inhalation and the second half on the exhalation, while simply observing the breathing without manipulating it in any way. This will calm the breathing and result in calming the mind.

Of course, this would require an affirmation of at least two syllables. In terms of choosing the word or words to use, I recommended using a very short version of the Jesus Prayer because this helps to focus the mind. The most essential element is including the Divine Name of Jesus Christ in some form, and it is this that makes it the Jesus Prayer. Any of the examples of the wording of the Jesus Prayer mentioned above could be used, but I usually recommended repeating the Name of "Jesus" or "Jesus Christ" or "Christ" perhaps with another word, such as "love," "light," or "peace." I did not recommend using the longest form of the Jesus Prayer, "Lord

Jesus Christ, Son of God, have mercy on me, a sinner." I did not want to emphasize the idea of the seeker being an unworthy sinner. For this reason I did not encourage the repeating of the word "mercy," unless there was an understanding that asking for mercy is just an invitation for becoming aware of God's ever-abiding Love. However, instead of using the word "mercy," I felt combining the Divine Name with the word "love" was a better way to open the heart to God's Embrace.

In addition to focusing on the words in coordination with the breathing, it is recommended to maintain the awareness in the heart area. For most people the best way to do this is to just hold the attention of the mind in the location of the physical heart or in the middle of the chest, considered in yoga philosophy to be the heart center. Sometimes a meditator may feel a sensation of energy or a slight pressure without pain in the heart area, which is quite normal. However, in rare instances, when focusing on the physical heart, a meditator may experience a noticeable pain in the heart or the heart may beat faster than normal, and if this happens, discontinue your meditation session. As an alternative, you can meditate holding the awareness in the center of the chest, but if this problem recurs, discontinue focusing in the chest area altogether. Even without holding the attention in the heart area, just coordinating the Jesus Prayer with the natural breathing can be a very effective means of using body awareness to calm the mind for meditation.

Although I wanted to teach the techniques advocated by the early Christian monks, my primary purpose was to impart their overall attitude. Consequently, I emphasized that focusing on spiritual intent in the practice of the Jesus Prayer was much more important than mastering the correct techniques. Naturally a certain amount of effort would be required to make the Prayer of the Heart effective, but I taught that the real secret of this method is in opening up to receive the love and divine grace that God would so willingly give every seeker.

Perhaps you are an experienced meditator, but what if you haven't meditated before and would like to give the Prayer of the Heart a try? Or what if you have already tried to meditate and didn't feel you were well suited to this practice? Let's compare learning how to meditate with learning how to swim in the ocean. The first time you try to swim you will splash around and struggle just to keep your head above water. You could give up right then, convinced that swimming is too difficult for you. However, if you persist with many more days of applying yourself, you will eventually find that you can swim. Then when you gain confidence in your ability to swim, you can even learn to let go and relax, becoming so calm in the water that you can float and become aware that the whole ocean is surrounding you, lifting you up, and sustaining you with its buoyancy.

Similarly after your initial attempt at meditation you will probably discover just how unruly the mind is. When you try to focus on the one thought of the Jesus Prayer in meditation, you will undoubtedly find that your peace of mind is drowned out by waves of distracting thoughts. You could give up after this first attempt, convinced that you don't have the ability to meditate. But if you want to succeed, you will have to be persistent in your practice. The mind is accustomed to multiplying its thoughts, and it takes time to reorient the mind toward limiting thoughts in the direction of simplicity. It requires repeatedly redirecting the mind in daily meditation to achieve this simplicity of mind. If you are determined and consistent in your practice, you will learn how to calm the mind and open yourself to inner peace. With further practice eventually you can learn how to relax and to "float" in a spiritual sense—meaning rest in the Eternal Ocean of the divine presence that is always gracefully surrounding you, lifting you up, and sustaining you with light and love.

If you are serious about learning how to meditate, I recommend that you conduct a twenty-eight day demonstration of your willingness to increase your awareness of the divine presence within. Outlined below are a set of procedures for your consideration. I recommend meditating for twenty-eight consecutive days because it takes that long to break the habit patterns of the mind. These procedures are not rigid rules, but only optional guidelines so feel free to make any adjustments in them that would be appropriate to your needs.

GUIDELINES FOR MEDITATION USING THE PRAYER OF THE HEART

1. THE DEDICATION — Before starting your meditation, dedicate your attunement by stating to yourself what you consider to be your ideal, your highest spiritual aspiration. Then as part of this dedication you also mentally review your purpose, the mental attitude you choose to help you grow toward your ideal. For example, for most Christians the highest ideal would be "Christ" or "Jesus" and an example of a possible mental purpose might be, "Thy Will be done."

2. THE PLACE — Choose a quiet place to meditate and use the same place every day.

3. TIMING — Meditate at the same time each day ideally for a twenty-five minute period, although you may choose a shorter time period that will better meet your needs. Use a digital timer so you will not have to be concerned about monitoring the time.

4. THE POSTURE — Sit on a chair with the spine straight but not tense. Or if you are limber, you can sit on a folded blanket or pillow in a comfortable cross-legged position on the floor. Although having the spine erect is recommended, you may choose to practice meditation while lying down.

5. RELAXATION — Choose a method of relaxing the body. For example, take a few deep breaths or imagine a white light of blessing filling and surrounding the entire body. I highly recommend doing the Edgar Cayce head and neck exercise slowly: "...bend the head forward three times, to the back three times, to the right side three times [bringing the right ear toward the right shoulder], to the left side three times [bringing the left ear toward the left shoulder], and then circle the head each way three times."[9]

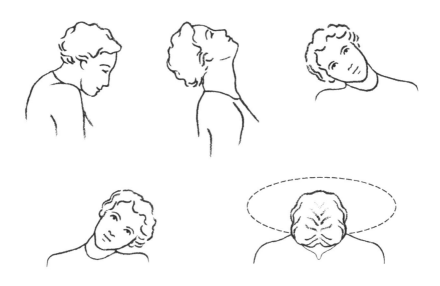

6. MEDITATION PRACTICE — To practice the Prayer of the Heart, decide upon a word or a few words that would include "Jesus" or "Christ." Bring the awareness to the heart area in the center of the chest or to the location of the heart itself. Then incorporate the breathing by repeating the first half of your affirmation on the inhalation and the second half on the exhalation. Ignore stray thoughts, neither being attracted to them nor trying to push them away. Stray thoughts will pass away as you simply maintain your awareness on the word or words chosen for meditation. Each time your affirmation slips away from your awareness, gently return to it while maintaining an attitude

of nonjudgment and self-acceptance toward yourself. Understand that you are engaging a sacred process in which you are opening yourself to the awareness of the divine presence that is always within you.

7. COMPLETION OF MEDITATON — If desired, you can restate your spiritual ideal and your mental purpose at the end of meditation and/or give thanks for your attunement experience. Remain seated momentarily and then slowly get up without disturbing your peace.

8. ATTITUDE — Do not judge the depth of your meditation with your rational mind. Be patient and persistent in your practice. Set aside any expectation of specific results you want to see happen. Be willing to wait the full twenty-eight days before evaluating the demonstration of your willingness to become aware of the inner divine presence. Keep your heart open and remember to be receptive to the guidance of the Holy Spirit, Who is the real teacher of meditation.

The Prayer of the Heart is one of the best methods for a beginner to learn how to practice Christian meditation, but it is just one way of using the Jesus Prayer for attunement. In addition to focusing on the heart, there are many other intermediate and advanced meditation techniques that incorporate repeating the Divine Name of Jesus Christ. These various techniques that use the words of the Jesus Prayer lead toward the silence of wordless contemplation. More detailed information about how to practice the Prayer of the Heart and descriptions of other forms of meditation and contemplation can be found in *Meditation Inspired by Christ and Yoga*, my meditation manual, which will be published after this autobiography is completed.

---

1. *The Way of a Pilgrim and The Pilgrim Continues his Way*, translated from the Russian by R.M. French, (New York: Seabury Press, 1972), pp. 40-41. Originally published by the Seabury Press; rights owned by Winston Press, Inc., Minneapolis, MN.
2. Luke 17:21, CCD.
3. E. Kadloubovsky and G. E. H. Palmer, translators, *Writings from the Philokalia on Prayer of the Heart*, translated from the Russian text, "Dobrotolubiye," (London: Faber and Faber Ltd., [1951]1971, 1975) p. 333 (also reprinted in 1992).
4. Ibid, p. 194.
5. Ibid.
6. Ibid.
7. Ibid.
8. Ibid, p. 192.
9. Reading #3549-1, Edgar Cayce Readings © 1971, 1993-2005 by the Edgar Cayce Foundation. Used by Permission, All Rights Reserved.

APPENDIX B

~ • ~

AN ORDINARY PLAY

It's good to set the goal of excellence in whatever we do. But it's better to seek excellence for its own sake, as an expression of the divine life within rather than as a means of competing to gain "specialness" at the expense of others who are imagined to be less special. Even so, oftentimes the result of seeking excellence is ordinariness. One of the facts I've been faced with in writing this autobiography is my ordinary writing ability. In particular I have been unable to create a truly vivid picture in words that would do justice to the beauty and uniqueness of the many people I have encountered in my life. Nevertheless I have spent so much of my life in a misguided and vain attempt to find "specialness" that it has been comforting to learn over the years that it is just fine to be ordinary. The acceptance of my ordinariness helps me to appreciate my equality with all my brothers and sisters.

The script for "Learning How to Be Ordinary" has been included here not because of its literary merit, which is very limited, but simply because of the moral of the story. It is my hope that there may be some who'd like to put on this simple and brief play to help spread the word that we uncover our true worth not in competition but in finding our equality with others.

The play can be put on with or without audience participation. If there is no audience participation, the script can be used exactly as it is presented below. However, to implement audience participation, the conversations that Big Lion has with Elephant, Mouse, and Monkey can be omitted and replaced by Big Lion talking to individuals in the audience. In this case, the following announcement would be made before the play:

We invite you to be actors in this play through audience participation. At one point in the play the main character, Big Lion, will ask some of you, "What animal are you and are you ordinary or special?" If you are one of those asked, please respond by saying what animal you are and why you are special. Here are some examples: You could say, "I'm an elephant, and I'm special because I am big," or "I'm a giraffe, and I'm special because I am tall." I am telling you in advance so you will be ready to tell Big Lion what animal you are and why you are special.

"LEARNING HOW TO BE ORDINARY"

Little Lion: We've decided you have the biggest roar and the loudest laugh of all the lions in the jungle. So we are going to make you the King of the jungle. Here is your crown.

Big Lion: But I don't want to be the King of the jungle.

Little Lion: This is a very special honor. Don't you want to be special?

Big Lion: No, I just want to be ordinary.

Little Lion: Well, even if you don't take the crown, you are still a very special lion. You can't be ordinary. Not with your roar and your laugh.

Big Lion: Rrrrrroooorh! There! That's my last roar, and I'm not going to laugh anymore either. Now I won't be special anymore.

Little Lion: You're still not ordinary. A lion who doesn't roar and a lion who doesn't laugh—that's very special!

Big Lion: I can learn how to be ordinary. I'll ask someone who is ordinary how he does it, and then I will do what he does.

Little Lion: Everyone else wants to be special. Why do you want to be ordinary anyway?

Big Lion: That's just it. Everyone else is trying to be special, so they just don't have time to just be themselves. I don't want to be like everyone else.

Little Lion: Oh! If you don't want to be like everyone else, then you must want to be special. Is that right?

Big Lion: Yes. I mean, NO! I'm getting confused. All I really want to be is just ordinary.

Little Lion: The very fact that you want to be ordinary—that makes you very, very, very, special! I've never met anyone as special as you are!

Big Lion: I'm getting more and more confused as I am talking with you. I'm going to find someone who can teach me how to be ordinary.

Little Lion: Wait! Don't go! You just can't give up being King of the jungle. No one who is ordinary could do that. Why don't you just stay here and admit that you're special and nothing can change that?

Big Lion: I'm sorry. But I just have to go. Goodbye.

Big Lion: Hi, Elephant. I'm looking for someone who is ordinary. Are you ordinary?

Elephant: No, I'm special. I'm the biggest elephant around, and that makes me special.

Big Lion: Hi, Mouse. Are you ordinary?

Mouse: No, I'm special. I have the squeakiest voice around, and that makes me special.

Big Lion: Hi, Monkey. Are you ordinary?

Monkey: Of course not. I'm too clever to be ordinary.

Big Lion: Who are you?

Owl: WHO!

Big Lion: That's what *I* said. *Who* are you?

Owl: WHO!

Big Lion: Stop repeating me and tell me who you are!

Owl: Haven't you ever heard an owl before? WHO is what I do!

Big Lion: Well, instead of doing *WHOing*, maybe you can do something else for me. I've spent all day looking for someone who is ordinary, but can't find anyone. Are you ordinary?

Owl: Yes.

Big Lion: YES?

Owl: I mean—yes and no.

Big Lion: Are you trying to tell me that you are ordinary and not ordinary at the same time?

Owl: No, the truth is that I'm ordinary, and I don't want to admit it.

Big Lion: Why don't you want to admit it?

Owl: I'm afraid you won't like me if I admit I'm ordinary.

Big Lion: Oh, you don't have to be worried about that. I like you just fine. I fact I have been looking for someone like you to show me how to be ordinary.

Owl: Really?

Big Lion: Yes, really. How can I learn to be ordinary?

Owl: Are you sure you want to be ordinary?

Big Lion: Oh, yes! I do, without a doubt.

Owl: It's actually very easy to be ordinary. All you have to do is admit it.

Big Lion: What do you mean?

Owl: Just what I said. Admit it.

Big Lion: I don't get it.

Owl: Let me spell it out for you. You just say the words, "I am ordinary," and then you are ordinary.

Big Lion: You mean that's all there is to it?

Owl: Yes.

Big Lion: That's amazing!

Owl: Go ahead and try it.

Big Lion: All right. "I am ordinary."

Owl: There you are. Now you are officially ordinary.

Big Lion: But I don't feel any different.

Owl: You aren't.

Big Lion: Then how come I'm ordinary now, and a minute ago I wasn't?

Owl: Because you just admitted it.

Big Lion: I don't understand.

Owl: You've always been ordinary. But because you thought of yourself as special, you couldn't see that you were actually ordinary.

Big Lion: You mean all those other animals are really ordinary, but they don't want to admit it?

Owl: Now you are catching on. Everyone is going around pretending to be special.

Big Lion: Why? Why don't they just admit that they are ordinary?

Owl: Because they don't like themselves just as they are. That's why they try to be special—so they can like themselves for being better than someone else.

Big Lion: You mean if they liked themselves just as they are, they wouldn't have to try to be special and better than someone else.

Owl: Yes.

Big Lion: Then I'm going to tell them that they are all ordinary, and they don't have to try to be special anymore. But most of all I'll tell them that they can love themselves just as they are, and that they can love each other as equals.

Owl: I wouldn't do that if I were you.

Big Lion: Why? Won't they be happy to know that they can love themselves just as they are?

Owl: They won't listen to you. They don't want to be told that they are ordinary. You would be revealing a secret they do not want to hear.

Big Lion: If it's the truth, somebody has to tell them. It might as well be me. Bye for now.

Owl: OK, but remember I warned you. Good luck. You'll need it.

Little Lion: Hi, Owl. Did you hear what happened to that lion who had the biggest roar and the loudest laugh?

Owl: No, what happened to him?

Little Lion: He called together all the animals of the jungle for a meeting on the top of a large mountain. Then he told them that they were all ordinary, and that they were all equal to each other. He said that because they were all equal they didn't have to try to be better than each other. He said they could love themselves just as they are and love each other as equals.

Owl: So what happened then?

Little Lion: They said he was lying. They said he was saying this just to be more special than anyone else. Everyone got very angry. They rushed upon him and threw him off the top of the mountain.

Owl: I'm sorry to hear that.

Little Lion: Do you know who could have put such foolish ideas into that lion's head?

Owl: Oh—ah—ah. No, I don't.

Little Lion: And to think of it. We were going to make him the King of the jungle and give him a crown! He would have been so special. What an opportunity he missed.

Big Lion: Where am I? What is this door?

Voice: This is the door to heaven.

Big Lion: How come I can't open it?

Voice: You must knock on the door three times and then answer the question correctly.

Big Lion: OK. (knock... knock... knock)

Voice: Who is it?

Big Lion: It's Big Lion. I had the biggest roar and the loudest laugh in the jungle.

Voice: Go away!

Big Lion: (knock... knock... knock)

Voice: Who is it?

Big Lion: It is someone who is just ordinary.

THE DOOR OPENS

APPENDIX C

~ • ~

SOLUTION TO
THE CHINESE PUZZLE

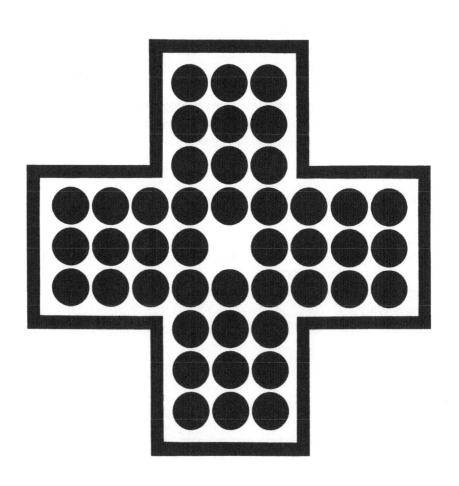

The Chinese puzzle in the shape of a cross is shown in the diagram on the opposite page, and the puzzle pieces are indicated as 44 black circles. If you want to try your hand at it, you can make your own puzzle by cutting up 44 small pieces of paper or you can even use 44 dominoes, checkers, or pennies.

To solve the Chinese puzzle you jump one piece over another and remove the piece that has been jumped over. The object is to keep jumping until there is only one piece left. Of course, the puzzle pieces cannot be moved outside of the cross-shaped border shown in the diagram. To make the puzzle harder you can add the requirement that the last piece must end up in the very center.

If you want to solve the puzzle yourself, don't look at the following three pages that provide the solution. If you do decide to look at the solution, you will find 44 small diagrams of the puzzle. The first diagram in the upper left hand corner of the next page shows the starting picture of the puzzle. To the right of the first diagram is the second one, showing the puzzle after one piece has been removed and another piece has been relocated. By comparing the first and second diagrams you can easily figure out which piece has been removed and which one has been relocated. Each of the successive diagrams must be compared with its predecessor to determine which piece has been removed and which one has been relocated.

In the solution provided here, the final piece comes to rest in the center of the puzzle. I am aware of very slight variations in which the puzzle is solved by ending up with only one puzzle piece. But in these variations, the last piece does not end up in the center. However, I am not aware of all the possible ways in which this puzzle can be solved. You may come up with the same solution provided here or a very slight variation, yet I cannot rule out the possibility of your solving the puzzle in a unique way, different from the solution provided here.

In my original attempt to solve this Chinese puzzle, it took me three days to figure it out, but by the time I wrote this book many years later I had forgotten my original solution, so I had to start all over. I finally did solve it a second time, but it took me three days, just as it had the first time. Consequently I tip my hat to you if you can figure it out in less time.

It does take an element of logic to figure the puzzle out. However, my advice is to ask for divine assistance. I do not think it is necessary to restrict divine help to significant matters. It is appropriate to ask for divine help even for figuring out a puzzle and other unimportant matters, because each time we do so we remind ourselves of what is important—our loving Father's presence that is always with us.

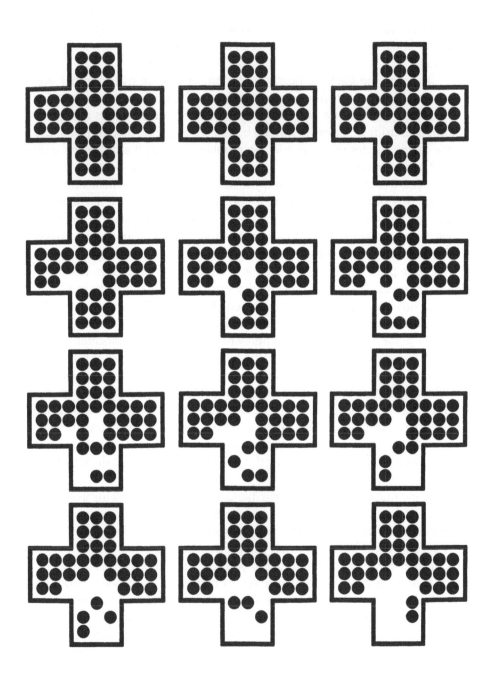

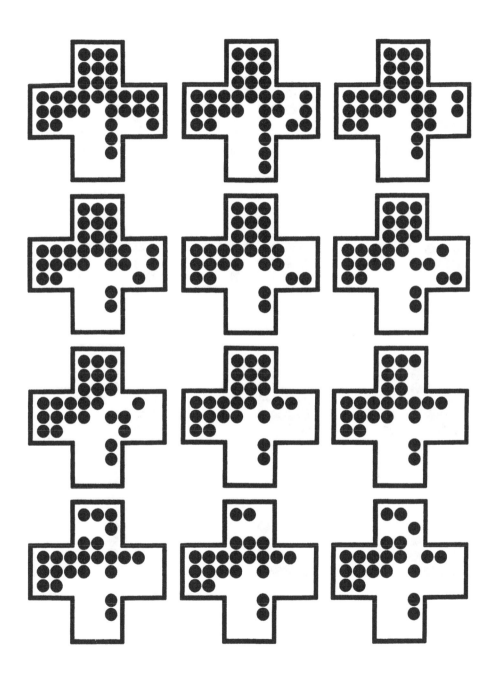

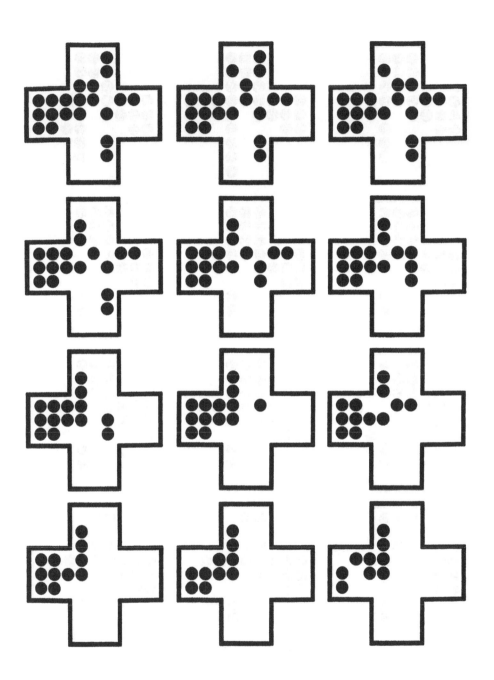

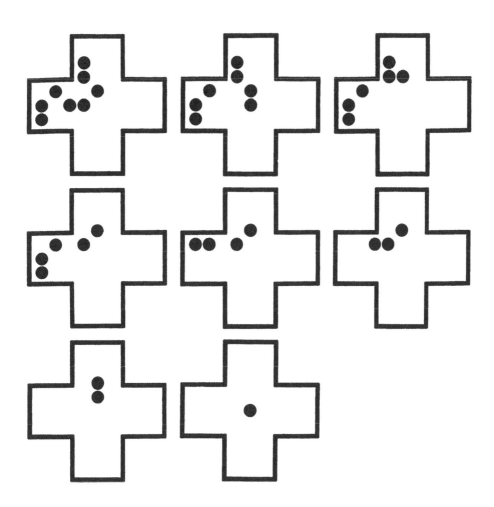

APPENDIX D

~ • ~

EXERCISES

1. UPWARD STRETCH — Inhale deeply while reaching both arms straight up toward the ceiling. The arms can be raised along the sides of the body or in front of the body. Then while exhaling, lower the arms. Repeat twenty times in a deliberate manner with full control.

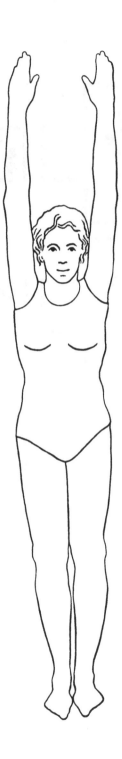

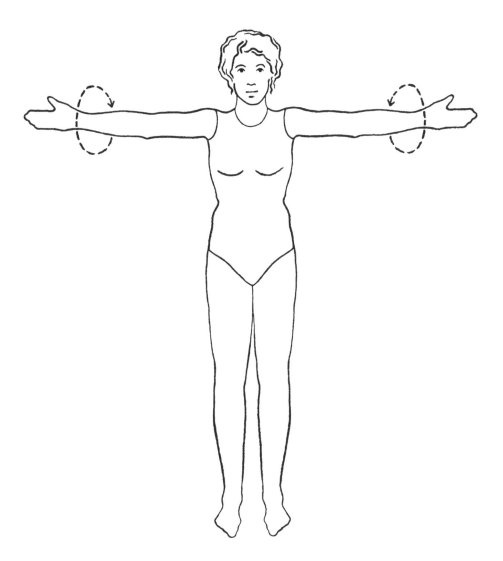

2. ARM ROTATION — Stretch out both arms horizontally to your sides forming a "T" shape with the torso. Then rotate the arms in a circular motion twenty times in one direction and twenty times in the other direction. If you want to coordinate the breathing with this exercise, you can inhale when the rotating arms are moving upward and exhale when the rotating arms are moving downward.

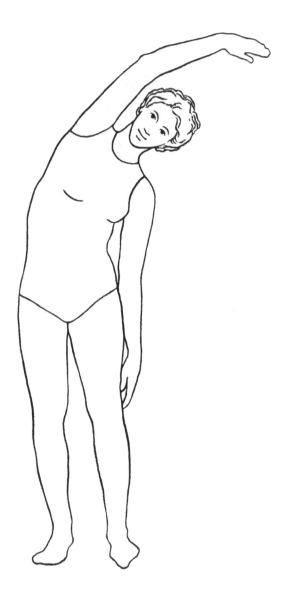

3. SIDE BEND — Raise the right arm straight up and bring the left ear toward the left shoulder. Tilt the whole upper torso sideways to the left as far as is comfortable. Pause to hold this stretch. Then you return the spine to the erect position and lower the right arm. Next raise the left arm straight up and bring the right ear toward the right shoulder. Tilt the whole upper torso sideways to the right. Repeat three times in each direction.

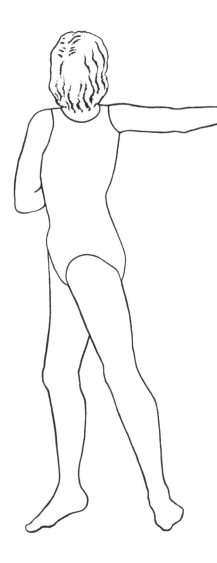

4. SPINAL TURN — Bring the right arm behind the back and twist the whole upper torso to the right with the head looking far to the right. Pause briefly to hold the position. Then bring the left arm behind the back and rotate the torso to the left with head turned to the left. Repeat each twist three times.

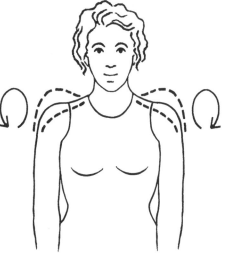

5. SHOULDER ROTATION — With the arms dangling loosely by the sides of the body, rotate the shoulders. Bring the shoulder joints backward, up, forward, and down, creating a circular motion. Repeat twenty times. Next you rotate the shoulder joints forward, up, back, and down. Repeat twenty times.

The five exercises above can be practiced while standing or sitting. For the counting in these exercises, I repeat the word "Christ" along with each number. Some of these exercises were inspired by the readings of Edgar Cayce, who recommended circular rotations of the arms in the morning to increase the circulation in the head and to help wake up the body. He also recommended circular rotations of the legs in the evening to bring the blood flow away from the head, as a preparation for sleep.[1] These circular leg rotations are helpful for anyone who has a tendency toward insomnia.

What I liked about the five upper torso exercises was that they could be done by anyone, even by some of my clients who were confined to wheelchairs or other clients who were too old to do more strenuous exercises. At one time it was thought that exercises were mostly beneficial for us when we are young, but that has been proven to be a fallacy.

> We have already seen that mental and physical neglect (the "disuse syndrome") promotes premature aging. No group is at higher risk for depression, disease, and early death than people who are completely sedentary, and by now the value of regular exercise for all age groups has been well documented. Physiologists used to believe that exercise primarily benefits us at a young age, when muscles are in their prime developmental stage. However, research with the elderly has conclusively demonstrated that someone who takes exercise at any age, including centenarians, will receive the same increase in strength, stamina, and muscle mass.[2]

This quotation shown above comes from *Ageless Body, Timeless Mind* by Deepak Chopra, M.D., who explains not only how to live a longer life, but also how to live a healthier, more productive and fulfilling life. Because exercise is equally helpful for young and old, and for women and men, I recommend setting up a daily schedule for exercising.

Exercises of this type focus mostly on actively and repetitively moving the body muscles, keeping them in tune, while yoga postures place the emphasis on holding the body in specific postures in order to stretch the body and in particular to increase flexibility. I see exercise as an important secondary means of maintaining a healthy body. However, I still primarily recommend the time-honored practices of the yoga postures and breathing practices, which prepare the body as a fit vehicle for practicing meditation. Appendix E describes how to practice seven basic yoga postures.

---

1. Reading #288-11. Edgar Cayce Readings © 1971, 1993-2005 by the Edgar Cayce Foundation. All Rights Reserved.
2. Deepak Chopra, M.D., *Ageless Body, Timeless Mind*, (New York: Harmony Books, 1993), p. 124.

APPENDIX E

~ • ~

YOGA POSTURES

I told my friend Stuart Dean about the five simple exercises described in Appendix D, and he emailed me, saying, "I am considering doing some yoga postures. Starting yoga with a class and a commitment of several weeks to learn 20 or 30 poses seems like a lot, even to me. But if I could try out three to five essential ones on my own for a while, well, I would be very happy to do that. For the same reason, I thought your five easy exercises were great. They are easy to learn, easy to do, and helpful to the body. I would be willing to research how to do each yoga posture, but which ones would you recommend?"

I emailed him back, saying "The most important thing about yoga is to encourage flexibility of the spine. If you want to do four postures, you could choose two forward bending postures and two backward bending postures. It is best to alternate forward and backward bending postures. For example, you could do the *Half Forward Bend* and followed by the *Cobra*. Then next you can do the *Full Forward Bend* and the *Half Locust*. [Illustrations and instructions for doing these postures are presented later in this appendix.]

I recommend these four postures for the beginner. However, for a very physically fit person who has a strong back, I would recommend a minimum of the following five postures in sequence: *Shoulder Stand*, *Fish*, *Full Forward Bend*, *Full Locust*, and *Cobra*. [These postures are illustrated and described later in this appendix]. Doing these five postures every day would be more beneficial than going to hour-long yoga classes once a week. Nevertheless, many people who take yoga classes fail to integrate a minimum number of yoga postures into their daily routine."

I also told Stuart that the exercises, such as the Side Bend and the Spinal Turn, give the spine more flexibility than just forward and backward movements. These are considered exercises if there is a very brief pause holding each stretch. However, they can just as well be called yoga postures if they are done while standing and if the sideways bending and twisting positions are held for a longer period of time to maximize the stretch without straining.

Later Stuart sent an email, informing me, "I went with a friend to an introductory yoga class yesterday. We went through more than a hundred positions in under an hour, something I never want to do again. But I look forward to doing the limited number of postures you recommended."

I responded, "It's good that you got instruction on the Shoulder Stand and other postures so you know how to do them. When teaching classes, I emphasize doing the yoga postures as a meditation. That means even the breaks between postures are part of the process. Consequently, my classes are one long meditation rather than a collection of as many postures as possible. It is best to do a few postures every day and do them well in a meditative frame of mind."

In my own daily practice, after completing my yoga postures, I do the five exercises described in the previous appendix. Then I do several forms of *pranayama*, literally meaning *control of the breath*. If you would like to do a very simple breathing practice, I suggest *Yoga Deep Breathing*, which ideally is done in front of an open window or outdoors. While inhaling slowly and deeply, you first fully expand the abdomen, then expand the lower chest, and finally expand the upper chest, allowing the shoulders to rise slightly. While exhaling slowly, you lower the shoulders and contract first the upper chest. Next you contract the lower chest, and finally the abdomen. Separate stages are described here, but the breathing is actually done in one fluid motion, inhaling from bottom to top and exhaling from top to bottom. You repeat this Yoga Deep Breathing at least ten times and then allow the breathing to return to normal.

But what is *normal* breathing? Unfortunately what often passes for normal breathing in the West is shallow upper-chest breathing. From a yoga perspective "*true* normal breathing" is a more natural and healthy form of breathing than using only the chest. No one has to tell a baby how to breathe normally. If you watch a baby breathing, you will clearly see that its natural rhythm of breathing is to use primarily the abdomen and not the chest. This true normal breathing found in yoga is actually *Abdominal Breathing* in which the abdomen naturally expands with each inhalation and contracts with each exhalation.

The advantage of Yoga Deep Breathing is that it fully expands the entire breathing capacity by using not only the abdomen, but also the lower and upper chest. After establishing a daily habit of Yoga Deep Breathing, you may want to add a mild form of breath retention. For this variation you pause at the end of the inhalation and retain the breath briefly, perhaps a few seconds or longer, as long as there is no discomfort. In addition, you can allow the duration of the exhalation to be longer than the inhalation— as much as twice as long. My recommendations for various other breathing practices and for yoga postures will be presented in detail in my upcoming book, *Miracle Yoga for Living in Christ*.

The most familiar form of yoga is hatha yoga, which is the yoga of the physical body. Your practice of hatha yoga can have one of two distinctly different meanings depending upon what you are seeking. If you are seeking only physical health, then yoga could be a means to that end. On the other hand, you may want to practice yoga to deepen your Christian spiritual life. Progress in yoga can allow your body to be a better vehicle for increasing the depth of your meditation and can improve your chances of spiritual transformation as a follower of Christ. In this case, yoga would be the means and Christ would be the end. This spiritually motivated form of yoga can be called "Christian hatha yoga." But hatha yoga itself is universal and so can be used as a means of growing toward any spiritual ideal.

The physical benefits from the body postures come from holding steady postures in order to stretch the body without straining. The stretching of muscles, ligaments, and tendons helps to increase flexibility and suppleness. Sometimes when doing various postures you may feel one particular area of the body that is being stretched. While holding the posture, you can bring the awareness of your mind to that area that is being stretched. When you have your awareness on the stretch, you do not strain or pull harder, but just *relax into the stretch.* While focusing on the stretching of the body, you also can focus on Christ so your practice is really one long meditation. In order to facilitate your communion with the divine within, I recommend repeating the Name of Jesus or Christ while doing the postures.

The following seven basic postures, including two optional poses, are recommended for those who have a healthy spine and are already in fairly good shape:

1. Shoulder Stand
2. Fish
3. Half Forward Bend (optional)
4. Full Forward Bend
5. Half Locust (optional)
6. Full Locust
7. Cobra

The concluding pages of this appendix describe how to practice all of the seven postures in the sequence mentioned above. Nonetheless, I would still recommend participating in at least one yoga class to receive firsthand instruction. The illustrations that follow show the ideal way of holding each posture. However, beginners are cautioned not to force their bodies to conform to these ideal positions. It is very important to listen to your body and do only what it is easily capable of doing. The goal is to simply stretch the body without any straining while also communing with Christ within.

1. SHOULDER STAND — The starting position is called the *Relaxing Posture*, in which you are lying on the back with the arms along side the body and the palms turned upward. Practicing the *Shoulder Stand* involves three stages. If there is any tension, return to the previous stage or to the starting position of lying on the back. Also, come out of the Shoulder Stand if there is any need to swallow or use the throat in any way. Beginning from the Relaxing Posture, bring the legs together. The arms are straight and along side the body, and you turn the palms *downward*. Press downward on the palms and raise the legs to 90 degrees, perpendicular to the floor. You hold this first stage briefly.

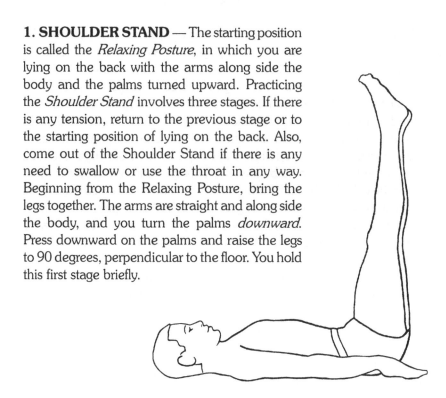

For the second stage, you apply pressure downward with the palms of the hands. Then lift the back, and raise the legs overhead to a position parallel to the floor. You hold this posture briefly. This second stage of the Shoulder Stand is called the *Plough*. Ideally the toes touch the floor, but it is fine for beginners to hold the legs exactly parallel to the floor.

Next bend the arms at the elbows and place the palms of the hands along the spinal column to support the body. Then raise the legs upward into the third stage, which is the Shoulder Stand itself. The torso and legs are ideally held perpendicular to the floor. It is all right if you cannot hold the body in a straight line as shown in the illustration here of an ideal posture. While you maintain the Shoulder Stand, it's important to hold a position that's comfortable and one you can sustain easily with stability. You can hold the position for about a minute, if you can do so comfortably. This yoga posture is also called the *All Members Pose* since it's beneficial to all parts of the body, in particular the thyroid gland, which controls the body's metabolism.

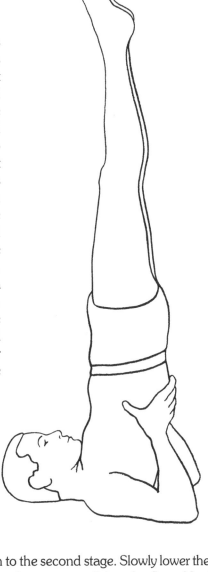

To come out of this posture, return to the second stage. Slowly lower the legs into the Plough, in which the legs become parallel to the floor. Next remove the hands from supporting the spine, and lower the arms to along side the body so the palms of the hands are placed downward on the floor. Then apply downward pressure on the palms and slowly lower the back vertebra by vertebra to the floor bringing the legs to the 90 degree position, perpendicular to the floor. Briefly hold this second stage. Finally, with the palms pressing downward, you keep the legs straight and slowly with full control lower both legs. When the legs are lowered to the floor, you return to the Relaxing Posture lying on your back.

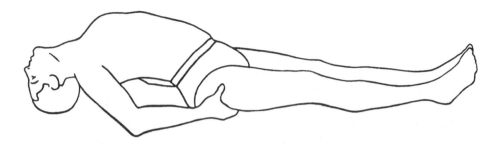

2. FISH — The complimentary pose to the Shoulder Stand is the *Fish*. Place the legs together. Hold onto the thighs with the thumbs on the sides of the thighs and the other fingers tucked under the thighs. Shift the weight of the body to the elbows and raise the body to a half seated position. Arch the back, thrust out the chest, and lower the crown of the head to the floor. You need to remember to breathe slowly and deeply to expand those areas of the lungs not normally expanded. This position is held for about thirty seconds, as long as there is no strain occurring.

To come out of this pose, return the full weight of the body to the elbows. Draw the head in toward the chest and slowly with full control lower the back to the floor. You return to the Relaxing Posture. Slowly move the head from side to side to loosen up the neck, and then return the head to center.

3. FULL FORWARD BEND — To transition from reclining in the Relaxing Posture to the *Full Forward Bend*, you begin by bringing the legs together. While still lying down on the back, the arms are raised above the head while having the elbows straight. Keeping the head between the arms, raise the upper torso of the body up to a seated position or come up in whatever way is most comfortable for you. Then lower the hands to the lap.

To begin the Full Forward Bend, you raise both arms overhead so the head is between the arms and the elbows are straight. Next look and stretch upward as you inhale. Then exhale and bend forward from the base of the spine, while keeping the head between the arms, which remain straight. Hold onto the legs wherever it is comfortable to do so. Point the toes upward and keep the back of each knee flat on the floor, so the proper muscles are being stretched. You can feel the stretch, but it is important to not pull or tug beyond that natural stretch. Allow yourself to relax into the stretch by simply letting gravity exert its force over the body.

After about thirty seconds, exhale and bend forward even further into the posture. Then inhale and raise the body up to a seated position with the head remaining between the arms, which are extended overhead. Keeping the arms overhead, return to the Relaxing Posture by lowering the spine vertebra by vertebra to the floor. When the back reaches the floor, the arms are still raised over the head. Bring the arms to a position along side the body with the palms turned upward.

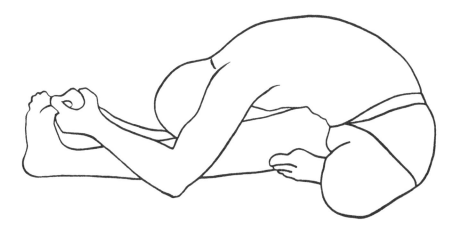

4. HALF FORWARD BEND — The Full Forward Bend has been described first here, but ideally the *Half Forward Bend* is practiced *before* the Full Forward Bend. For this posture extend one leg straight forward and bring the foot of the other leg toward the center of the body, so the sole of that foot is placed against the inside of the thigh of the extended leg. Then bend forward over the extended leg just like you would for the Full Forward Bend. Of course, you would have to first bend forward over one leg and then reverse the leg positions so you can bend forward over the other leg.

5. HALF LOCUST — (above)

6. FULL LOCUST — (below)

After completing the Full Forward Bend and briefly remaining in the Relaxing Posture on the back, you will have to assume the Relaxing Posture on the abdomen to complete the final three postures in this sequence. You turn the body over slowly in whatever way is most comfortable without disturbing your peace. Keep the legs about a foot apart, and allow the arms to be straight and a few inches away from the body with the palms turned upward. The head is turned to one side. The next time you come into this position, remember to turn the head to the other side in order to alternate the way in which the neck is stretched.

For the *Half Locust*, you place the feet together. Straighten the arms at the elbows and place both arms underneath the body with the elbows as close together as possible underneath the body. You either make two fists side by side or open the hands with the palms turned upward and place one hand on top of the other. Then return the head to center, and place the chin on the floor. You will be raising each leg alternately, but remember to keep the hips *level* and pressed downward. Bring the awareness to the right leg and straighten it. Lift the right leg, keeping it straight. Hold for ten seconds without straining, and then slowly lower the right leg. Next bring the awareness to the left leg, straighten it, and lift. Hold for ten seconds and slowly lower. Repeat lifting the right leg one more time, and then repeat lifting the left leg. Finally release the arms from underneath the body and return to the Relaxing Posture with the arms along side the body and the head turned to one side.

After learning to practice the Half Locust without straining, you can practice the *Full Locust*, by using the same process but lifting both legs simultaneously. If you have a lower back problem, you should not practice the Full Locust until you have first strengthened the back by using the other postures over a long period of time.

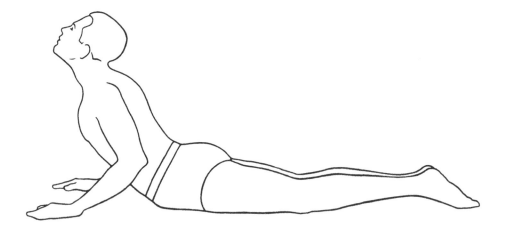

7. COBRA — Starting from the Relaxing Posture on the abdomen, you place the feet together and rest the chin on the floor as a preparation for the *Cobra*. Instead of bringing the chin to the floor, you can rest the forehead on the floor if you are able to do so. You bend the arms at the elbows and place the palms of the hands downward on the floor underneath the corresponding shoulders, placing the fingertips in line with the tops of the shoulders. The bent elbows are close to the body and placed upward.

Raise the head, drawing the chin along the floor. Look upward as you raise the neck and then the upper portion of the back. Slowly roll the spine backwards vertebra by vertebra, lifting only with the back muscles and not with the arms. Raise the hands an inch off the floor to make sure that you are lifting only with the back muscles. After about fifteen seconds of holding the position without straining, return the hands to the floor and slowly lower the back vertebra by vertebra. When the chin (or forehead) returns to the mat, lower the gaze downward. Turn the head to one side and return to the Relaxing Posture with the arms along side the body and the palms turned upward. After resting, repeat the Cobra again. This time after lifting only with the back, you can apply a slight pressure downward on the hands to stretch the back a little further than previously, but still without straining.

Christian hatha yoga provides an opportunity to open up physically, mentally, and spiritually to the influence and action of the Holy Spirit. This inner opening occurs not only while doing the postures themselves, but also during the intervals between postures. After completing each of the seven postures mentioned above, you return to the Relaxing Posture of lying down either on the spine or on the stomach. Throughout these relaxing intervals, it is important to maintain your inner communion with spirit. If you find repeating the Name of Jesus or Christ to be helpful while doing your postures, you can continue to do so during intervals of relaxation. To assist in making your yoga practice into a continuous meditation, you can also coordinate the repeating of the Divine Name with the breathing.

The yoga postures have a beneficial effect on the endocrine glands that regulate the body functions. The body postures also work on the nervous system to calm the nerves leading to a peaceful mind. In fact, seeing hatha yoga as a means of calming the mind is the proper understanding of the true purpose of this discipline. The yoga postures enhance your potential for spiritual transformation by keeping the spine flexible, which ironically enables the back to remain comfortably motionless in meditation. A strong body is also needed to gently and gradually raise the kundalini in a safe and controlled manner with the aid of the Holy Spirit.

After doing the postures for an extended period of time, you may notice that you can stretch further than you could when you first started. However, your progress is not primarily a matter of how well you can perform the postures at the form level. Content is more important than form in the practice of Christian hatha yoga. Consequently, what is happening in your mind takes precedence over how proficient the body is in executing postures. The motivation of your mind, your purpose, is the most important element in your practice of Christian hatha yoga. If you practice Christian hatha yoga with a half-heartedly motivation, you will get half-hearted results. One of the reasons why I emphasize hatha yoga as "Christian hatha yoga" is so you will keep your goal of union with Christ always in mind as your motivation for practicing yoga. By focusing on yoga as the means and union with Christ as the end, your practice of Christian hatha yoga will be as natural and effortless as breathing. Your faith and desire for union with Christ is the key to your success with Christian hatha yoga.

APPENDIX F

~ o ~

REINCARNATION

I believe long-term holy relationships, such as mine with Rose, are nurtured through the process of sharing many past lives together. Because I have mentioned past lives so frequently, it may be helpful to address the perspective of the Course on reincarnation. When the Course is taught as its own self-contained path, reincarnation is not an issue that should be taught by a teacher of God, because it would limit his usefulness. Only students who were willing to believe in reincarnation would be attracted to such a teacher. The Course says that the body you have in this life is an illusion, and so any bodies you may have had in past lives were also illusions. The Course is intended to help you to radically transform your awareness of yourself—to replace your idea of yourself as being a body with the understanding that you are the holy child of God now. From this perspective, reincarnation is meaningless and ultimately impossible, since there is no reality in the body now or in the past.

However, the Course takes no definitive stand on reincarnation and tells the teacher of God to sidestep the issue since the Course can be beneficial for both students who believe in reincarnation and those who do not. The Course addresses reincarnation from the viewpoint of its usefulness:

> Our only question should be, "Is the concept helpful?" And that depends, of course, on what it is used for. If it is used to strengthen the recognition of the eternal nature of life, it is helpful indeed. Is any other question about it really useful in lighting up the way? Like many other beliefs, it can be bitterly misused. At least, such misuse offers preoccupation and perhaps pride in the past. At worst, it induces inertia in the present. In between, many kinds of folly are possible.
>
> Reincarnation would not, under any circumstances, be the problem to be dealt with *now*. If it were responsible for some of the difficulties the individual faces now, his task would still be only to escape them now. If he is laying the groundwork for a future life, he can still work out his salvation only now. To some, there may be comfort in the concept, and if it heartens them its value is self-evident.[1]

Since reincarnation is "is not the problem to be dealt with now," it is not a necessary part of the special curriculum of the Course. But Miracle Yoga is a means of following Christ through the combination of yoga and the Course, and so it is not exclusively a Course path. Thus in advocating Miracle Yoga as a hybrid of yoga and the Course, I feel comfortable with acknowledging and teaching the belief in reincarnation. I don't discount the dangers inherent in the belief in reincarnation, including pride, unnecessary preoccupation with the past, and losing sight of the central focus of seeing the divine in everyone now. In fact, struggling with these dangers has been an inevitable part of my growth experience. I do not hold up focusing on past incarnations as a virtue in itself, but I needed to do this to get to the point where I could let go of the past. Subconscious emotions due to past lives were still active in my present life. Revealing the past traumas that had caused my present condition helped me to come to a place of forgiveness toward others and myself in the present moment. This journey has been my "memory walk from darkness to light," which may also be called my "memory walk to now." It has been a *walk of forgiveness* to realize that all my brothers are worthy of forgiveness, since each one of them is in reality a holy child of God. By forgiving others I have learned to accept that, as a holy child of God, I too am worthy of forgiveness.

I agree with the Course that this worldly life is a dream. Thus the belief in reincarnation must involve manifesting a dream of a dream—the dream of this life looking at the dream of a past life. Although past life memories are *illusions of illusions* not existing in reality, they do have a relative reality within the dream of the world. Without making a definitive statement, the Course implies that reincarnation does have a relative existence.

According to the Course, the roles of the student and teacher form a holy relationship in which partners are joined for the common purpose of learning. The teacher learns to receive by giving and the student learns to give by receiving. Their coming together is not by accident. The Course never specifically calls itself as "self-study" course, but it does talk about "pupils," which gives the clear impression that the ideal way to learn the Course is within the pupil and teacher relationship, described as follows:

> Certain pupils have been assigned to each of God's teachers, and they will begin to look for him as soon as he has answered the Call. They were chosen for him because the form of the universal curriculum that he will teach is best for them in view of their level of understanding. His pupils have been waiting for him, for his coming is certain. Again, it is only a matter of time. Once he has chosen to fulfill his role, they are ready to fulfill theirs. Time waits on his choice, but not on whom he will serve.[2]

This quote implies that the relationship between the teacher and pupil is a recurring karmic interaction that originated in past lives, and that impression seems to be confirmed by the following statement:

> And thus it is that pupil and teacher seem to come together in the present, finding each other as if they had not met before. The pupil comes at the right time to the right place. This is inevitable, because he made the right choice in that ancient instant which he now relives. So has the teacher, too, made an inevitable choice out of an ancient past.[3]

The teacher of God perceives every meeting with anyone as a holy encounter—an opportunity to see the Christ in others to confirm the Christ within. But the goal of the teacher is to eliminate himself as a teacher so that the student eventually becomes a teacher of God himself:

> For the teacher is not really the one who does the teaching. God's Teacher [meaning the Holy Spirit] speaks to any two who join together for learning purposes. The relationship is holy because of the purpose, and God has promised to send His Spirit into any holy relationship. In the teaching-learning situation, each one learns that giving and receiving are the same. The demarcations they have drawn between their roles, their minds, their bodies, their needs, their interests, and all the differences they thought separated them from on another, fade and grow dim and disappear. Those who would learn the same course share one interest and one goal. And thus he who was the learner becomes a teacher of God himself, for he has made the one decision that gave his teacher to him. He has seen in another person the same interests as his own.[4]

Conveying concepts is not the most important aspect of being a teacher of the Course. The teacher is primarily a person who can provide an example of living a life of forgiveness and thereby encourage others to follow that same path. Robert Perry has provided that example for me. I don't see Robert very often these days, but even now I will contact him when I have a question about the Course.

---

1. M-24.1:4-11, 2:1-4, p. 60 (p. 57).
2. M-2.1:1-6, p. 5 (p. 4).
3. M-2.4:3-6, pp. 5-6 (p. 4).
4. M-2.5:2-9, p. 6 (p. 5).

APPENDIX G

~ • ~

A NEW LOOK AT KARMA

Just as the Course makes contradictory references to reincarnation, it appears to be similarly contradictory about karma. As mentioned in Appendix F, "Reincarnation," students tend to be reincarnated with their former teachers because of a karmic relationship, but I could not recall any direct references to the word "karma" in the Course. From my background in yoga I had accepted the basic idea of karma—the concept that actions in past lives determine conditions in this life, or even that actions in this life determine future conditions. Recently I sent an email to Robert Perry stating, "I was wondering how the Course would address the issue of karma. I know, for example, that sickness is guilt made manifest, so guilt plays a unique part in what the East calls karma." I asked for his thoughts, and he sent me a lengthy response.

Robert explained that the published Course does not refer to karma directly, but the original typed dictation of the Course, called the Urtext, does make a reference to "bad karmic choices." This quotation was related to the scribe of the Course, Helen Schucman, and her partner, Bill Thetford. They had both made bad choices in past lives resulting in instability in Helen and weakness in Bill and they were correcting the errors of the past in their current lifetimes. Here's the quotation from the Urtext:

> Your [Helen's] instability and his [Bill's] weakness have resulted from bad choices, and your relationship *now* is crucial for the future.... Both of you are correcting where you have failed before.

In contrast to a few quotes that acknowledged karma, Robert indicated several other passages that cast a negative light on karma. One of these is:

> "Vengeance is Mine sayeth the Lord" is strictly a karmic viewpoint. It is a real misperception of truth, by which man assigns his own evil past to God. The "evil conscience" from the past has nothing to do with God. He did not create it, and He does not maintain it. God does *not* believe in karmic retribution at all.[1]

Robert stated that this quote refutes the notion that God or heavenly beings administer karma as a means of balancing the scales of justice:

> The clear message in this paragraph is that this [meaning karmic retribution] has absolutely nothing to do with God. The implication is that we are trying to pin on Him a process for which we ourselves are responsible. In other words, the "evil conscience" is *ours*. We are unconsciously punishing ourselves for our past mistakes. We are the vengeful conscience of our own personal cosmos, even if consciously we aren't aware of this and try to lay blame at God's doorstep.[2]

Robert went on to elaborate upon how God really thinks. Instead of demanding retribution for all our mistakes, He forgives. As far as God is concerned, all of the unloving acts we carry out disappear altogether into nothingness, in contrast to our own tendency to hold on to the memory of these misdeeds and to chastise ourselves for them. God upholds our innocence so we remain holy in His eyes, but we would require of ourselves karmic retribution for whatever past mistakes God has already forgiven. Consequently, we need to learn how to forgive ourselves by accepting God's love for us that eternally affirms our holiness in Him.

The Course maintains that the past does not exist and has no real power to determine our conditions. However, the past can affect us if we allow it to do so, for example by maintaining our belief in guilt. The Course emphasizes making choices now to determine our present condition. Yet our past actions can have no effect on who we are in reality. Forgiveness of ourselves and others allows us to let go of our false beliefs in the past. Forgiveness reveals God as our true Cause, and ourselves as the Son, His holy Effect. Robert concluded his response, as follows:

> So to summarize what we've seen, I am picturing two lines, one of karma and one of no karma, both running in parallel. On the line of *karma*, I made choices in the past, and those choices did determine my present condition, but only because I held unto them and punished myself for them, only because of my magical belief that they had the power to create me in their image. At the same time, on the line of *no karma*, God has constantly cancelled out those choices, constantly forgiven me, in the knowledge that my choices have literally no power to create me. He knows that *He* created me, and in doing so gave eternal holiness. No matter what I've done, that holiness always remains my true condition. It always remains my present reality. And I can always lay hold of it in that same present—now.[3]

Consequently, karma is a paradox. It exists and does not exist. Blending the East and West requires learning to be at peace with paradoxes. I have included a traditional explanation of karma in Chapter 5, "Service and Karma," because this understanding helps us navigate through this dream world, which the West treats as real. On the other hand, in Chapter 70 and this appendix, I have emphasized the illusory nature of karma because this awareness can assist us in transcending the world of form, which is the primary goal of the East.

The traditional understanding of karma is the basis for the belief in reincarnation in which we encounter the fruits of our karma reaped from past lives. Similar to the paradox of karma, there is reincarnation and there is no reincarnation. We live in a body for a time while taking on an earthly identity, and then we repeat this process in lifetime after lifetime. So in the dream world reincarnation is an important fact of that relative reality. On the other hand, our current body and ego identity is not who we really are in our true nature. In reality we are spiritually parts of Christ in God. Since our bodies are illusory, having one now or having many in past lives makes no difference. Thus reincarnation is just a repeating of illusions, and these illusions prevent us from waking up, as is explained in Appendix F, "Reincarnation." The important thing is that we have to wake up now. That is probably why Jesus did not teach reincarnation two thousand years ago.

Perhaps the most daunting overall paradox presented in the Course is that we are really right now in heaven, only asleep and dreaming of being here in a body and in this world of form. If this is true, why couldn't we just follow the example of Dorothy in the Wizard of Oz? Why couldn't we simply tap our feet together three times, saying, "There is no place like Home," and then wake up in heaven? There is a type of Hindu jnana yoga based on nondualism that directly affirms heaven is here now, and that the world is not real. The chief discipline of this yoga is to deny this world of form to find Reality. This denial is practiced by saying, "neti, neti, neti," meaning "not this, not this, not this." Every form is seen as an illusion and not the divine Truth. Such a seeker may get a headache and say, "I don't have a headache because I don't have a head." Through this type of denial the seeker hopes to wake up to the only true Reality beyond all illusions. However, this extreme spiritual practice is a very difficult path that can even cause the seeker to become mentally unbalanced. Although the Course describes the world as an illusion, it does not advocate a path of denial:

> The body is merely part of your experience in the physical world. Its abilities can be and frequently are overevaluated. However, it is almost impossible to deny its existence in this world. Those who do so are engaging in a particularly unworthy form of denial.[4]

Thus we cannot successfully deny the body and its role in this dream world. Instead of denying the body, we can accept the Holy Spirit's purpose for the body as a tool with which to navigate through this dream world. In this way the body becomes a means for us to wake up if we remain sensitive to the guidance of the Holy Spirit. There is no way for us to force ourselves to wake up. For example, just accepting consciously that we are really sleeping in heaven and then deciding to stop dreaming isn't enough to make us immediately awake up. The fundamental problem is that there is a gap between our conscious mind and the Christ Mind. That gap is the subconscious mind that is filled with a host of illusions. Although a person may consciously reject the idea of karmic retribution and reject the idea of reincarnation, the subconscious mind continues to keep a self-imposed karmic accounting system and holds on to all the accumulated illusions of past lives, especially strong unresolved emotions.

Waking up requires a cleansing of the subconscious mind of its darkest illusions. Even if I say I don't consciously believe in the traditional idea of karma, my subconscious mind is still holding on to karmic ideas and emotions that block the divine light. Part of my process of waking up has been uncovering and putting together the pieces of my shadow puzzle. This has involved learning to let go of the dark corners of my mind where I have been holding on to past life fears and other negative emotions that have prevented me from accepting God's unconditional love. Consequently, it has been helpful for me to bring the emotions accumulated from past lives into the light so they could be released now. Even though reincarnation is only a repeating of illusions of bodily identities, accepting that this illusory belief is part of the subconscious mind can help to facilitate waking up from illusions. Although the belief in reincarnation has been helpful for my growth, I recognize that it is understandably not a necessary or even helpful belief for many Christians, since God has an individualized plan for each of us to return Home.

My path had been a joining of the Western way of seeking God and the Eastern way. The West seeks God by loving and forgiving those who are separate from us. The East seeks God (Reality, Oneness, Buddha nature) by awakening to the awareness that the individual seeker is never separate from his divine Source. My path of Miracle Yoga based on the Course says that Western forgiveness and Eastern awakening can come together in a unique way. In this blending, the Western form of forgiveness based on separation gives way to an enlightened forgiveness that lets go of the perception of separation. The one who forgives sees his forgiven brother as his equal with whom he is joined in Christ. Similarly, the Eastern form of finding God entirely through inward seeking loses its place of prominence in the synthesis of the West and East. The totally solitary approach to God is replaced by finding God through seeing Him in every brother and sister through the eyes of forgiveness. Thus forgiveness and awakening overlap and are no longer separate processes, as when the West and East are separate paths.

In fact, the strongest tool in the process of waking up is forgiveness. True forgiveness allows us to see illusions as illusions and give them up to free the mind from the darkness that blocks the light. Here too there is a paradox. We may initially feel that someone has trespassed against us, but true forgiveness allows us to see that this is an illusion. True forgiveness looks past the dream world where we appear to be harmed, and instead sees the truth. This truth is that no one can hurt us because we are not really separate egos and bodies, which can be hurt. Since we are part of Christ in God, our true nature cannot be hurt. If we identify with our egos, we will think we forgive others for what we believe they did to us—meaning what they did to our egos. Yet if we identify with our true nature in Christ, we can practice true forgiveness by paradoxically forgiving others *for what they never actually did to us*—meaning what they never did to Christ within us. In this sense the idea of forgiveness itself is an illusion because there is nothing that in fact needs to be forgiven.

Forgiveness is an illusion, yet ironically it is the only illusion that helps us overcome illusions, enabling us to move in the direction of waking up to our true nature. Forgiveness allows us to see the world in a different way than we normally would—to look past the illusions and affirm the shining light and truth hidden behind outer forms. It enables us to let go of our fears and guilt and instead see a world of love that is a happy dream. We cannot jump all the way from a world of frightening nightmares to heaven because the distance between the two is too great. But when we apply forgiveness, we can accept the world as a happy dream. When our lives become a happy dream, we are best prepared to make the transition from illusory dreams to awakening in the reality of heaven. The happy dream is so filled with loving sights that it becomes a reflection of heaven. Thus the love experienced in the happy dream enables us to one day fully open up to the all-encompassing Divine Embrace awaiting us in heaven.

Although I understood intellectually these Course ideas of forgiveness, it took me several years before I could consistently apply them. For example, I held on to some grievances toward Robert, as will be explained in the sequel to this book. Eventually, by the time of emailing Robert about the question of karma, I had been able to apply true forgiveness toward him. Through true forgiveness I could see Christ in Robert and realized that previously I had foolishly been holding illusory ideas about him. I emailed Robert thanking him for his response to my question and felt it was appropriate to add the following acknowledgment:

As the years go by I am feeling ever so grateful for having you in my life. Other than our personal growth together, the main thing you have done for me is to be the catalyst for me to learn the Course. Without your presence I never would have been willing to let go of my pride enough to consider that the Course was a much more advanced thought system than the one I had already acquired through my own buffet style of accumulating spiritual insights. In addition to stimulating my interest to accept the Course, you also served as my teacher as well. For this I am also very grateful. Many blessings to you, dear brother—Love, Don.

Many of the ideas in the Course, including the paradoxes described in this appendix, are difficult to grasp at first. Very few beginning students will immediately comprehend and accept the spiritual principles of the Course. After all, the Course quite literally turns our normal perceptual thinking based on the ego upside down, enabling us to perceive the divine in our otherwise apparently mundane world. That's why the Course needs to be studied over an extended period of time. Keeping the mind open and receptive to the loving message of the Course requires both patience and perseverance. Persistent open-mindedness in studying the Course allows us to make a gradual transition in our thinking about the world and about ourselves. This transition is needed not just because a new unconventional perspective is being introduced, but also because familiar old ideas need to be set aside to make way for new ones. To make this transition, the mind needs to be retrained, which explains why the Course describes itself in this way: "This is a course in mind training. All learning involves attention and study at some level."[5] The Text of the Course expresses the spiritual principles such as true forgiveness and Christ vision that remind us of the divine presence within others and within ourselves. In addition, the Workbook with its one full year of daily lessons helps to assist this process of perceiving the divine presence through its application of seeing through the eyes of forgiveness in everyday living.

If you are interested in learning more about the Course, you can naturally purchase the book and simply study directly from it. However, it can be helpful to also have a teacher. The goal of the teacher is to help you learn enough about the Course so that you can one day become a teacher of God yourself. The teacher and student will invariably agree with each other on the generally accepted principles of the Course, but do not necessarily have to agree on every single interpretation. Although Robert and I have slightly different interpretations of some of the finer points of the Course, I greatly appreciate all the insights that he has shared with me to expand my understanding of the Course. However, the most valuable aspect of Robert serving as my teacher was his own enthusiasm and example, which inspired me to both accept and apply the Course on a daily basis as my chosen thought system. It is best to find a teacher in your own vicinity so you can have face-to-face meetings in which you can ask questions and develop a personal relationship. You can seek out local study groups to facilitate your learning. A resource for finding out if there is a study group in your area is the Community Miracles Center[6] and another possibility is the Miracle Distribution Center.[7] If you cannot find a local teacher or study group, you can still learn a great deal through self-study of the Course itself.

In addition to studying the Course itself there are many fine books about the Course written by teachers. One very popular Course teacher is Marianne Williamson. In her book *A Return to Love*, she writes insightfully and convincingly about love and forgiveness. The most famous Course scholar and interpreter is Ken Wapnick, the founder of the Foundation for *A Course in Miracles*.[8] I especially enjoyed reading his book *Forgiveness and Jesus: The Meeting Place of "A Course in Miracles" and Christianity*. Robert Perry at the Circle of Atonement is slightly less well known. In his book *Path of Light: Stepping into Peace with "A Course in Miracles,"* I like Robert's emphasis on the Holy Spirit as the active divine presence, Who with our permission directly intercedes in our daily lives.[9] Both the Foundation for *A Course in Miracles* and the Circle of Atonement can offer helpful information about various ways of studying the Course. This study of the Course is not solely about learning spiritual concepts. The goal is to make the Course concepts come to life in your everyday practical living and learn to extend your awareness of the divine to others.

---

1. Urtext version of the Course passage T- 3.I.3:1-4, pp. 36-37 (p. 32).

2. The entire written response by Robert can be found on the Circle of Atonement website at www.cirlceofa.org by entering the word "karma" in the search function. Among several articles on the subject of karma, Robert's response is the one simply titled "Karma."

3. Ibid.

4. T-2.IV.3:8-11, p. 23 (p. 20).

5. T-1.VII.4:1-2, p. 16 (p. 13).

6. www.miracles-course.org, (click on ACIM Study Group Directory), Community Miracles Center, 2269 Market Street, San Francisco, CA 94114. Tel. 415-621-2556. Fax 415-255-9322.

7. www.miraclecenter.org, Miracle Distribution Center, 3947 East La Palma Avenue, Anaheim, CA 92807. Tel. 1-800-359-2246. Fax 714-632-9115.

8. www.facim.org, Foundation for *A Course in Miracles*, 1275 Tennanah Lake Road, Roscoe, NY 12776-5906. Tel. 951-296-6261. Fax 951-296-9117.

9. www.circleofa.com, The Circle of Atonement, P. O. Box 4238, West Sedona, AZ 86340. Tel. 928-282-0790. Fax 928-282-0523.

ONE SIMPLE TRUTH

Every father wants to leave behind an inheritance for his children that will make their lives better. I am a "monk in the world," not a father with children, yet I also want to leave something behind to make the lives of others better. I have walked a path that others may want to follow, just as I have followed in the footsteps of Jesus, while keeping the door open to helpful Eastern influences. This autobiography is my inheritance, but it is simply a reminder of our Father's inheritance—His gift of Himself—to all of His children. The only gold in this inheritance is the message of love and forgiveness that God wants me to hear, to live, and to share with you.

I hope this inheritance has been entertaining for you to read. However, more than that, I hope it will encourage and inspire you to have your own openings to your true spiritual nature. If you do want to grow spiritually, your progress will depend on two factors that are entirely up to you. Those factors are your level of self-discipline and your degree of self-worth. We learn how to read or write or do math by simply repeatedly putting our learning into practice. Practice takes time and effort. Since practice is not considered a fun activity, it requires a certain amount of self-discipline. I've often heard people say, "I just don't have enough self-discipline to do yoga or to meditate every day," as though this form of self-control is an inherited trait that some have and others don't. Actually we can learn to apply and increase our self-discipline if we are motivated to do so. What do we need to obtain that motivation? When we think we do not possess self-discipline, it means we do not want to pay the price of putting out that effort. But there is a deeper reason: We don't think we are worth that effort. As our self-worth increases we will in turn be more highly motivated to exercise the kind of self-discipline that will help us to grow spiritually. All of the philosophies and techniques of spiritual growth are useless to you unless you are willing to apply them and feel that you are worth that effort.

Jesus told us the story of the prodigal son who squandered all of his inheritance because he lacked both self-discipline and self-worth. But he mustered just enough self-control to make his way back to his father. Yet he still did not have any self-worth, saying to his father that he was not worthy to be called his son. It was not until his father embraced him with his love that the prodigal son realized his true self-worth. You too are the prodigal son. You are responsible for having the self-discipline to put one foot in front of another to walk toward your Father. If there is a single bit of encouragement I could pass along to you as an inheritance, it would be to let your self-worth rest on the firm foundation of one simple truth: *You are right now—and forever will be—in your Father's loving embrace.*

Lightning Source UK Ltd.
Milton Keynes UK
UKOW06n1911140615

253483UK00008B/62/P